Systematic Theology

Biblical, Historical, and Evangelical

Systematic Theology

Biblical, Historical, and Evangelical

by

James Leo Garrett, Jr.

VOLUME 1

WILLIAM B. EERDMANS PUBLISHING COMPANY
GRAND RAPIDS, MICHIGAN

Copyright © 1990 by Wm. B. Eerdmans Publishing Co.
255 Jefferson Ave. S.E., Grand Rapids, Mich. 49503

Printed in the United States of America

Reprinted 1996

Library of Congress Cataloging-in-Publication Data

Garrett, James Leo.
Systematic theology / by James Leo Garrett, Jr.
p.   cm.
Includes bibliographical references and index.
ISBN 0-8028-2425-0 (v. 1)
I. Title.
BT75.2.G   1990
230—dc20   90-3880
CIP

Gratefully dedicated to
my students
in
Southwestern Baptist Theological Seminary
Southern Baptist Theological Seminary
Baylor University
Hong Kong Baptist Theological Seminary

Contents

Preface

Writing a systematic theology is somewhat like building a superhighway. Both involve long-range planning, the computation of probable costs and resources, a decision as to a preferable route among several, obtaining the approval of governing bodies, and the working out of detailed plans. In the case of highway construction land must be purchased, trees removed, hills reduced, valleys filled in, and bridges constructed. Grading must precede the preparation of the foundation and the laying of the concrete, and signs and other markers must be erected before the superhighway can be opened to the public. All these steps are part of the total process.

In the same way this book has been in process, in one sense for forty years and in another sense for five.

This volume and the one that is intended to follow are designed for use by students of systematic theology in theological seminaries and divinity schools, by pastors of churches, in particular those who wish to undertake on their own a fresh study of Christian theology, especially in relation to their exegetical, homiletical, didactic, apologetic, and/or missionary tasks, and by Christian readers who wish to probe more fully into the treasures of Christian doctrine.

I have not written these two volumes of systematic theology on the basis of a prior commitment to or the adoption of any philosophical system or philosophical motif in the light of which the doctrines of Christianity ought to be interpreted. Rather I have proceeded from the premise that good systematic theology ought to be based on the fruitage of biblical theology and the history of Christian doctrine. Hence I have made every effort to locate, interpret, and correlate all the pertinent Old and New Testament texts or passages and the more significant statements from the patristic period to the modern age before undertaking any formulation of my own.

I was granted a full-year sabbatical leave by the faculty, administration, and trustees of Southwestern Baptist Theological Seminary for the preparation of the final typescript for this volume, and for this I am very grateful. Thanks are due to Hong Kong Baptist Theological Seminary, especially its president, George R. Wilson, Jr., and its dean, Jeffrey Sharp, where I was guest professor during the fall semester of 1988, and to Trinity Evangelical Divinity School, especially its academic vice president and dean, Walter C. Kaiser, Jr., where I was in residence during the spring semester of 1989.

I wish to acknowledge a continuing debt to my professor of theology and mentor, the late Walter Thomas Conner, who presented me with the challenge of systematic theology and helped open to me the teaching ministry. I would also express gratitude to my college professor of Christian doctrine, the late Josiah Blake Tidwell, and for my mentors in graduate study: Stewart Albert Newman, the late Georges Augustin Barrois, and George Huntston Williams.

The following persons have meaningfully shared with me the teaching of biblical, historical, and systematic theology: Charles Arthur Trentham, Jesse James Northcutt, William Boyd Hunt, William Lawrence Hendricks, Dale Moody, Wayne Eugene Ward, Eric Charles Rust, David Livingstone Mueller, Jan Johannes Kiwiet, Bert Buckner Dominy, William David Kirkpatrick, Robert Bryan Sloan, and Edward Earle Ellis. I am also indebted to various systematic theologians who have corresponded about and/or offered suggestions pertaining to this volume: Stanley A. Nelson, J. Terry Young, Fisher H. Humphreys, William L. Hendricks, Wayne Ward, Molly Marshall-Green, Robert H. Culpepper, and John W. Eddins.

In addition, I am grateful to the pastors who have read and offered comments and suggestions about portions of this book: William M. Hailey (Kong Kong), Otis Brooks (Birmingham, Ala.), Larry K. Dipboye (Oak Ridge, Tenn.), Charles Wade (Arlington, Tex.), and Thomas K. Ascol (Cape Coral, Fla.). I would also like to thank the professors who have read and commented on portions and offered criticism and advice: Bert Dominy, J. J. Kiwiet, Donald A. Carson, and David Kirkpatrick. None of the deficiencies of this volume is to be attributed to any of these, but their help has been significant.

I would like to express heartfelt gratitude as well to my secretaries, who have labored faithfully and efficiently at various stages and with diverse portions of this book: Judy (Mrs. Max) Ates, Donna (Mrs. Mark) Cook, Mary (Mrs. Richard) Overmier, Suzie (Mrs. Stephen) Sanders, and Cheryl (Mrs. Lannie) Turner.

I have gratefully received encouragement or help concerning this book from Stephen L. Abbott, Sheri (Mrs. Bob) Adams, Lois Armstrong, Timothy and Sharon Beougher, Carl E. Braaten, Thurmon E. Bryant, Mrs. Gladys J. Casimir, Lucien E. and Bobbie Coleman, Stephen Danzey, Russell H. Dilday, Jr., David S. Dockery, William R. Estep, Jr., Steven E. Eubanks, D. David Garland, Timothy George, Finlay M. Graham, Samuel M. James, Jerry Moye, John P. Newport, Linda Oaks, William R. O'Brien, John W. Patterson, Tom E. Prevost, the late Franklin M. Segler, Thomas C. Sherwood, William B. Tolar, Chaiyun and Margaret Ukosakul, E. Jerry Vardaman, John W. Zerdecki, and the Chapel Companion Class of Broadway Baptist Church, Fort Worth, Texas.

I deeply appreciate the preparation of the indexes by a team of busy pastors, all of whom are Ph.D. graduates of Southwestern Baptist Theological Seminary and who serve churches in the Dallas–Fort Worth metroplex: Paul Abbott Basden, Walter D. Draughon, III, Danny Eugene Howe, George A. Mason, Jr., and C. Gene Wilkes. In addition, I acknowledge the helpfulness and competence of Milton Essenburg of the Eerdmans staff.

I hereby express gratitude to the librarians who have helped to make available many of the books and articles used in preparation of this volume: Carl R. Wrotenbery, Robert L. Phillips, and Myrta L. Garrett (Southwestern); Brewster Porcella, Eleanor (Mrs. Timothy) Warner, and Keith P. Wells (Trinity); and Rachel Alice Creecy (Hong Kong).

Finally, I cannot fail to express my abiding and loving thanks to my wife, Myrta Latimer Garrett, and our sons, James Leo Garrett, III, Robert T. Garrett, and Paul L. Garrett.

JAMES LEO GARRETT, JR.

Abbreviations

ACW	Ancient Christian Writers
ANF	Ante-Nicene Fathers
ASV	American Standard Version
CSCO	*Corpus scriptorum christianorum orientalium*
CWS	Classics of Western Spirituality
JB	Jerusalem Bible
KJV	King James Version
LCC	Library of Christian Classics
LPT	Library of Protestant Theology
NASC	New American Standard Version
NEB	New English Bible
NIV	New International Version
NPNF	Nicene and Post-Nicene Fathers
PG	J. P. Migne, ed., *Patrologiae cursus completus. . . Series Graeca*
PL	J. P. Migne, ed., *Patrologiae cursus completus . . . Series Latina*
RSV	Revised Standard Version
TEV	Today's English Version
UBS	United Bible Societies' Greek New Testament

Prolegomena

CHAPTER 1

The Nature, Necessity, and Methods
of Christian Theology

I. THE NATURE OF CHRISTIAN THEOLOGY

At the outset it is essential that we clarify what we mean by the term
"Christian theology." What are the academic and the religious connotations of these words?

First, the word "theology" is derived from two Greek words, *theos*,
"God," and *logos*, "reason," "order," "word," and the like. In modern
English usage such etymology is normally taken to mean that "theology"
is the ordered consideration or study of God.

Second, the term "theology" may be used somewhat broadly and
somewhat narrowly, and such differing usages are quite valid. Three
different usages are especially important for the student of Christian
theology. "Theology," broadly speaking, can mean the entire curriculum
of a theological seminary or divinity school,[1] including everything from
biblical archaeology and Hebrew to Christian education and pastoral care.
In more limited fashion "theology" can refer to all the Christian doctrines
as they are studied individually and in their relation to each other.[2] In a
narrow sense "theology" can be used to refer only to the doctrine of God
the Father, thereby excluding other doctrines such as those of Jesus Christ,
the Holy Spirit, humankind, and the last things.[3]

Third, the use of the term "Christian theology" suggests that there
are indeed other types of theology, even as there are other world religions.
Some of these are Jewish theology, Muslim theology, Hindu theology, and
Baha'i theology.

Fourth, some Christian authors have preferred to use the term

---

1. The reference here is to the smaller or medium-sized seminary rather than to the
larger seminaries that consist of separate schools, namely, schools of theology, Christian
education, church music, Christian psychology, world mission, and/or church social work.

2. This second usage of "theology" approximates the meaning of "systematic theology."

3. See Millard J. Erickson, *Christian Theology*, 3 vols. (Grand Rapids: Baker Book
House, 1983-85), pp. 22-23.

"Christián doctrine" instead of the term "Christian theology." For example, Walter Thomas Conner (1877-1952) defined Christian doctrine as
"that line of theological study that undertakes to set forth the several
doctrines of Christianity in their particular significance and in their relations to one another," and again as "a setting out of the ideas that are
necessary to an understanding of the nature and worth of the Christian
religion."[4] Other theologians have preferred to use the terms "theology"
or "Christian theology." Representative of these is Millard John Erickson
(1932-), for whom Christian theology is "that discipline which strives to
give a coherent statement of the doctrines of the Christian faith, based
primarily upon the Scriptures, placed in the context of culture in general,
worded in a contemporary idiom, and related to issues of life."[5] It is also
possible to understand "Christian theology" as the academic discipline
that studies "Christian doctrine."

With these etymological and definitional matters addressed, we can
now explore in greater detail six basic areas of consideration regarding
the nature of Christian theology.

A. THOUGHT CONCERNING THE DIVINE-HUMAN RELATIONSHIP

Christian theology deals with the "thought side" or the "doctrinal
content" of the Christian religion[6] or is a thoughtful consideration of the
truths of the divine-human relationship. Such a statement, however,
should not imply the utter isolation of the emotional or affectional or of
the moral or ethical aspects of Christianity from the doctrinal.[7] It does give
priority to thought. Moreover, to speak of the truths of the God-man
relationship does imply that Christian ethics can properly be differentiated from Christian theology in that Christian ethics deals essentially
with human relationships. Doctrine and ethics were not separate disciplines for Christians, however, until George Calixtus (1586-1656), a
Lutheran theologian, made the distinction.[8]

Every statement about the doctrines of the Christian religion is in
some sense a theological statement, and every Christian who reflects on
and speaks about his faith is in some sense a theologian. Does the pro-
fessional theologian have any distinctive role from that of every Christian
as theologian? According to Heinrich Emil Brunner (1889-1966), "that
which differentiates the [professional] theologian from the simple old

4. *Revelation and God* (Nashville: Broadman Press, 1936), p. 15.
5. *Christian Theology*, p. 21.
6. Conner, *Revelation and God*, pp. 18-19.
7. In nineteenth-century German Protestant theology Friedrich Daniel Ernst Schleiermacher (1768-1834) attempted to build the doctrinal on the affectional and Albrecht Ritschl
(1822-89) sought to build it on the ethical/social.
8. Jaroslav Pelikan, *The Emergence of the Catholic Tradition (100-600)*, vol. 1 of *The
Christian Tradition: A History of the Development of Doctrine* (Chicago: University of Chicago
Press, 1971), p. 3.

woman who believes in Christ is not his greater faith, but his greater power of thought in the service of faith."[9]

Herschel Harold Hobbs (1907-) has declared that Southern Baptists "have a living faith rather than a creedal one."[10] The present author would contend that that statement poses an improper antithesis. The opposite of a living faith is a dead faith. The opposite of a creedal or confessional faith is a vague or contentless or undefined faith. Admittedly confessions of faith may be differentiated from creeds, and the danger of a decadent faith must be clearly recognized, but our Christian faith should be both living and confessional! One can no more eat choice beef from a boneless cow and one can no more work safely in a skyscraper that has no structural steel than one can practice and communicate the Christian religion without basic Christian affirmations or doctrines.

B. CHRISTIAN INTERPRETATION OF CHRISTIAN DOCTRINES

Christian theology is "such an interpretation of Christianity as a Christian would give."[11] It is a sympathetic, not an alien, interpretation of the Christian gospel. Christian experience is thus a *sine qua non* of Christian theology. Emil Brunner declared: "Dogmatics is believing thinking."[12] John Alexander Mackay (1889-1983) contrasted two distinct approaches to Christian truth, that of the "balcony"—not the balcony of a theater or church building but that which protrudes from the second floor of a Hispanic residence and allows one to view from above the passersby below—and the "road," or the scene of action. Mackay contended that the authentic approach to Christian truth was from the "road," not from the "balcony."[13]

Non-Christians may and do study the Christian religion and write about it. The history of religion or phenomenological approach, now so prevalent in American universities, treats Christianity from an outside perspective, not only sometimes without sympathy with its affirmations but at times with antipathy and hostility toward them.

It would be a mistake, however, to confine Christian theology to the personal or private beliefs of theologians and/or church leaders. Jaroslav Jan Pelikan (1923-) has wisely asserted that Christian doctrine is "what the church of Jesus Christ believes, teaches, and confesses on the basis of the word of God."[14] There should be an essential interrelatedness among these three—believing, teaching, and confessing. But, one should notice, it is the church, and not merely individual Christians, that is involved in the theological task.

9. *Revelation and Reason,* trans. Olive Wyon (Philadelphia: Westminster Press, 1946), p. 16.
10. *The Baptist Faith and Message* (Nashville: Convention Press, 1971), p. 11.
11. Conner, *Revelation and God,* p. 19.
12. *The Christian Doctrine of God,* vol. 1 of *Dogmatics,* trans. Olive Wyon (Philadelphia: Westminster Press, 1950), p. 5.
13. *A Preface to Christian Theology* (London: Nisbet & Company, 1942), ch. 2.
14. *The Emergence of the Catholic Tradition,* p. 1.

In evangelical churches today, especially those which have congregational polity and recognize the preaching-teaching roles of ordained leadership, the pastor and those who minister with him have the heavy but sacred privilege and responsibility to equip the members for living, witnessing, and serving in today's world.[15] A major element in that equipping ministry is Christian doctrine.

C. CHRISTIAN THEOLOGY AND THE SCIENCES

The task and the method of Christian theology are somewhat distinct from the task and the methods of the physical and natural sciences and even of the social sciences.

Before pursuing those distinctions per se, one should raise a prior question: Can Christian theology itself be properly regarded as a "science"? From the medieval era came the idea that theology is "the queen of the sciences." Amid the secularism and scientism of the twentieth century such a statement can easily appear to be anachronistic, for few today see Christian theology as having such an exalted role. Today Christian theology can be called a "science," as some theologians such as Karl Barth (1886-1968)[16] have called it, only, it seems, in the sense that it involves classified or systematized knowledge. But Christian theology is not a "science" in the sense of dealing primarily with realities that are "subject to weight and measurement"—a definition most germane to the physical and natural sciences.

What, then, are the function and the method of the "sciences" today? James Bryant Conant (1893-1978), onetime president of Harvard University, stated: "Science is an interconnected series of concepts and conceptual schemes that have developed as a result of observation and experimentation and are fruitful of further experimentation and observations."[17] The scientific method thus centers in observation and experimentation. Whereas Christian theology does not deny the validity of such scientific method, even when applied to religious experience, it claims another and transcendent source of knowledge, namely, God's self-disclosure, or divine revelation. This claim to divine revelation is rejected by positivists, who see the scientific era as having superseded previous theological and philosophical eras; by logical positivists, who find theological utterances to be meaningless language because they are not scientifically verifiable; and by the devotees of scientism, who wish

---

15. See Findley B. Edge, *A Quest for Vitality in Religion: A Theological Approach to Religious Education* (Nashville: Broadman Press, 1963).

16. *Church Dogmatics,* I/1, trans. G. T. Thomson (Edinburgh: T. and T. Clark, 1936), pp. 1-11. Barth held that Christian theology can be called a "science" in three senses: (1) "it is a human effort after a definite object of knowledge"; (2) "it follows a definite, self-consistent path of knowledge"; and (3) "it is . . . accountable for this path to itself and to everyone." He insisted, however, that theology must not "submit to measurement by the canons valid for other sciences" (pp. 7, 9).

17. *Science and Common Sense* (New Haven: Yale University Press, 1951), p. 25.

to absolutize the scientific method so as to invalidate any other method of apprehending reality.[18]

At the beginning of the twentieth century a leading Baptist theologian, Edgar Young Mullins (1860-1928), sensitive to the current confrontation between the physical and natural sciences and Christian faith, identified both the principal differences in method between the two and areas of agreement as to the tasks and methods of the two. He noted four differences: (1) They deal with different realities (the one primarily material, the other primarily spiritual). (2) Their modes of knowledge differ (sensory experience versus fellowship with God derived from and consistent with a historical revelation of God). (3) They deal with different types of causality (transformation of energy versus interaction of persons). (4) They reach different formulations of their results (laws or mathematical formulas versus unique historical events together with general principles or teachings). According to Mullins, the sciences and Christian theology agree as to task and method in respect to the following: (1) Only facts are taken into account. (2) The realities dealt with are only partially known. Compare further observation and experimentation with 1 Cor. 13:12 and 1 John 3:2. (3) Both seek systematic formulations of what is known.[19]

By such differentiations of task and method one should not imply any necessary contradiction between the conclusions of the sciences and of Christian theology. For several centuries and again early in the present century controversy between the two was quite fierce. Today the situation is somewhat altered. Numerous scientists as individuals recognize the role and validity of the Christian religion, but many operate under naturalistic and nontheistic premises. When, of course, a scientist goes beyond the segment of reality that is his area of specialization and draws conclusions about ultimate reality, he has ceased strictly to speak as a scientist and has become a philosopher or a theologian. This can be illustrated from both Christian and anti-Christian viewpoints.[20]

The Roman Catholic Church took official positions in condemnation of the scientific views of scientists such as Nicolaus Copernicus (1473-1543) and Galileo Galilei (1564-1642), but in the twentieth century it has seemed to regret its former actions. Some Protestant preachers have issued utterances on scientific questions without adequate knowledge or infor-

18. Contrary to the widely prevalent view that modern Western culture is secular and not religious, David S. Pacini, *The Cunning of Modern Religious Thought* (Philadelphia: Fortress Press, 1987), has recently argued, primarily on the basis of the otherness involved in self-preservation, that the modern age is basically religious.

19. *The Christian Religion in Its Doctrinal Expression* (Philadelphia: Judson Press, 1917), p. 83.

20. William Grosvenor Pollard (1911-), nuclear physicist in Oak Ridge, Tennessee, gave the dedicatory address for the Science Building at Texas Christian University in 1952. Speaking on "The Role of Science in a Christian University," he set the function of modern science within the framework of a Christian worldview. In doing so, he assumed the role of a Christian philosopher.

mation. Moreover, much of the present conflict between creationist and evolutionist viewpoints is a conflict between competing worldviews, not, strictly speaking, between the Christian religion and biological science.

D. CHRISTIAN THEOLOGY AND PHILOSOPHY

The task and method of Christian theology, while similar to that of philosophy, are yet distinct from the latter.

Philosophy is humanity's quest for truth. It does not necessarily recognize the validity of truth derived from divine revelation. Philosophy is concerned with values (ethics, aesthetics), with being (ontology), and with how human beings know (epistemology). These are questions that Christian theology cannot and should not avoid.

Both philosophy and Christian theology seek a comprehensive viewpoint from which to draw their conclusions or inferences or make their affirmations. The Christian theologian is distinctive in that he recognizes and works in the light of the self-disclosure of God to humankind, supremely in Jesus Christ. Such revelation becomes normative for Christian theology in a way that it does not for philosophy, even though philosophers themselves may be Christians.

The question as to the impact of various philosophical movements on Christian theology during the course of Christian history will be treated in Chapter 5 under "Natural Theology: Worldviews."

E. CHRISTIAN THEOLOGY A PRACTICAL DISCIPLINE

Christian theology, often construed primarily as a theoretical task, is also concerned with the significance and the application of the gospel's power and its teachings to the lives of human beings, Christians and non-Christians, and to the life and ministry of the churches. The excessively speculative theologies have sometimes failed because of their refusal to recognize this truth.

The relation of Christian theology to practical life and ministry may be a two-way street: theology affects practice, and practice affects theology. On the one hand, Walter T. Conner advised preachers to try out their theology on a sinner or unbeliever.[21] The implication was that a true Christian theology would effectively assist in the communication of the gospel. On the other hand, Wayne Edward Oates (1917-) declared:

> The shepherding ministry . . . is one of the headsprings of the ever-renewing water of life known as Christian theology. This shepherding ministry both vitalizes and purifies our knowledge of God.[22]

As a practical discipline Christian theology has certain significant limitations. First, it is limited in that, although it claims to have received

21. "Theology, a Practical Discipline," *Review and Expositor* 41 (October 1944): 360.
22. *The Revelation of God in Human Suffering* (Philadelphia: Westminster Press, 1959), p. 20.

a *real* knowledge of God, it does not profess to have a *complete* or *perfect* knowledge of God, humankind, and destiny. According to Paul, "our knowledge is imperfect" and "now we see in a mirror dimly" (1 Cor. 13:9a, 12a, RSV). Second, Christian theology is limited in that its aim is practical and functional, not purely speculative. Its task is to help bring human beings into redemptive fellowship with God and to help them grow in Godlikeness. The goal is conformity "to the image of God's Son" (Rom. 8:29). Paul's epistles had ethical or practical sections as well as doctrinal sections, and Jesus' Sermon on the Mount ended with the parable of the two builders (Matt. 7:24-27). Third, Christian theology is, or should be, limited to consistency with the biblical revelation (1 Cor. 4:6). Theologians who work to transform the Christian faith into some contemporary world-view or philosophy contradict this truth.

F. CHRISTIAN THEOLOGY: FIXITY AND CHANGE

Christian theology has an element of finality or fixity and yet at the same time is subject to change.

Christianity affirms that Jesus is the final or ultimate revelation of God (Heb. 1:1-3). Its subject matter is God's supreme and sufficient revelation of himself and the redemption of human beings in Jesus Christ. In this sense it has the element of fixity or finality. The Christian claim is that in the purpose of God Jesus Christ will not be transcended or superseded.

Nevertheless, we as Christians have not fully and completely appropriated God's truth in Christ. God's truth is always greater and more majestic than our apprehension of it. Hence our statements about ultimate truth are not in themselves ultimate. Furthermore, the task of the Holy Spirit as Revealer and Teacher is not to be ignored (see John 14:26; 16:13-15).

Still further, theology is necessary partly because neglected truth needs to be recovered and old truth needs to be restated in the vernacular of the contemporary age. This is why we do not rely solely on theology books written in earlier centuries. Creeds and confessions of faith should be understood in the light of both fixity and change.

Surprisingly, even heresy can have a role in the apprehension of Christian truth. Reinhold Niebuhr (1892-1971) said: "So much truth rides into history on the back of error, and so much 'error' is but a neglected portion of the whole truth, which is an error only in the degree that it has been overemphasized in order to get itself heard and when acknowledged and restored to the whole, ceases to be an error and becomes a part of the truth."[23]

23. "The Commitment of the Self and the Freedom of the Mind," in *Religion and Freedom of Thought*, by Perry Miller, Robert L. Calhoun, Nathan M. Pusey, and Reinhold Niebuhr (Garden City, N.Y.: Doubleday, 1955), p. 59.

In summary, Christian theology, taken to mean the ordered exposition of Christian doctrines, deals with the truths of the divine-human relationship, is such an exposition as would be given by Christians themselves, has tasks and methods that are distinguishable from those of the sciences and of philosophy, is a practical or ministry-oriented discipline, and has aspects both of fixity and of change.

II. THE NECESSITY OF CHRISTIAN THEOLOGY

It is possible, of course, to contend that the academic discipline and ecclesial function known as Christian theology is a highly desirable and eminently useful task within the Christian religion but stops short of being utterly necessary for the well-being of the Christian religion. In the present discussion we will rather advance the view that Christian theology is indeed necessary for the well-being of Christians and of contemporary Christianity.

We will state and answer the objections of those who have denied the need for or the importance of Christian theology before we present the evidences for its necessity.

A. DENIALS OF THE NECESSITY OF CHRISTIAN THEOLOGY

1. The Pietistic Objection or Denial

On the ground that Christianity is essentially personal piety or religious experience and that such piety is obscured or threatened by doctrinal formulations, whether creeds or otherwise, or that such piety gives little significance to such doctrines, pietists have denied or downplayed the need for Christian theological undertakings.[24] Pietists are correct in differentiating second-person religion (prayer and praise) from third-person reflection on religion (theology) but wrong in denigrating the latter. True Christian piety is not a doctrineless faith. The spiritual awakenings of the modern era have usually had theological foundations such as the doctrines of repentance and regeneration. Partly under the impact of Pietism encountered during his youth, F. D. E. Schleiermacher shifted the essence of Christianity from revelation and doctrine to a "feeling of absolute dependence" on God.[25]

2. The Ethical Objection or Denial

On the ground that Christianity is essentially the ethical teachings of Jesus and that doctrinal formulations occupy a secondary or even dispensable role, ethicists have denied the importance of and need for

24. See Philip Jacob Spener, *Pia Desideria*, trans. Theodore G. Tappert (Philadelphia: Fortress Press, 1964), pp. 49, 51. This tract was first published in 1675.
25. *The Christian Faith*, trans. H. R. Mackintosh and James S. Stewart (Edinburgh: T. and T. Clark, 1928), pp. 5-31.

Christian theology. Admittedly "orthodoxy without orthopraxy" can become a defective form of Christianity, but orthodoxy can be coupled with orthopraxy! Leo N. Tolstoy (1828-1910) insisted that the Sermon on the Mount, especially its teaching on nonresistance, is utterly incompatible with the Nicene Creed.[26] Adolf Harnack (1851-1930) thought that the Galilean gospel proclaimed by Jesus consisted of the present kingdom of God, God's fatherhood, the infinite value of the human soul, and the higher righteousness and ethic of love and that this gospel was un-Paulinized and un-Hellenized.[27] Tolstoy and Harnack are examples of the ethical protest against doctrines of any sort as central to the nature of true Christianity.[28]

3. The Nonpolemical Objection or Denial

On the ground that the history of Christian doctrine has often been characterized by controversy, polemic, bitter antagonisms, and divisions, which in turn have separated and alienated Christians from fellow Christians and churches from churches, the nonpolemicists would invalidate or denigrate the entire Christian theological undertaking. This stance is sometimes expressed in terms of the quest for the lowest common doctrinal denominator for Christianity or in forms of a naive ecumenism wherein doctrinal differences are reduced to cultural differences. Others, genuinely motivated by patient, self-giving love, would avoid doctrine because of the excesses of doctrinal polemics. One should never deny that there have been some deplorable chapters in the doctrinal history of Christianity. But there have also been some deplorable chapters in the ethical history and in the missionary history of the Christian religion, and that fact has not invalidated the ethical imperatives or the missionary mandate of the Christian gospel. Moreover, Christian theology is needed for the effective confrontation of non-Christian religions and worldviews quite apart from the history of inter-Christian polemics.

4. The Scientistic or Positivistic Objection or Denial

One may assume that Christian doctrines as the ideational expressions of Christian beliefs or faith-affirmations do not rest on the methods of scientific observation and verification and hence must be regarded as either quite secondary or as belonging to an age that now has passed and thus viewed with suspicion and/or contempt. Accordingly, the positivists of the tradition of Auguste Comte (1798-1857) and those committed

26. *The Kingdom of God Is within You*, trans. Leo Weiner (Boston: L. C. Page & Co., Inc., 1951), p. 87.
27. *What Is Christianity?* trans. Thomas Bailey Saunders (New York: Harper & Brothers Publishers, 1957), p. 51.
28. For further details on the pietistic and ethical objections, see James Leo Garrett, Jr., "The History of Christian Doctrine: Retrospect and Prospect," *Review and Expositor* 68 (Spring 1971): 248-50.

to a scientism that absolutizes the scientific method reject the entire Christian theological undertaking. But positivism, it should be noted, is a philosophy that has merely assumed the existence of three ages or stages of human activity (theological, metaphysical, and positive or scientific).

5. The Linguistic Objection or Denial

Some have contended that religious or theological language is so much in need of analysis and critical recasting that theological formulations should be deferred, if not utterly discarded. The logical positivists earlier in this century in effect denied the validity of the theological enterprise by limiting the scope of meaningful language to "mathematico-logical truths" and "empirical truths." More recently language analysts have provided a less threatening challenge to the task of theology by seeking to clarify language.[29]

6. The Trivialist Objection or Denial

On the ground that Christian theology has in the past dealt with very unimportant and to many persons today irrelevant subjects or topics and that today's world has utterly different concerns and values, some would jettison the entire present theological task. Mention is often made of the supposedly central medieval theological issue as to how many angels can stand on the point of a pin. Theology, however, deals rather with the ultimate and vital issues of human origins, transcendent reality, sin and punishment, evil and suffering, and life after death. These are not trivial in any human epoch or era.

B. AFFIRMATION OF THE NECESSITY OF THE STUDY AND DISCIPLINE OF CHRISTIAN THEOLOGY, WITH NOTABLE HISTORICAL EXAMPLES

One may state the case for the necessity of the study and discipline of Christian theology in a sevenfold manner, and with each of the seven reasons one may cite treatises in systematic Christian theology drawn from the entire course of Christian history that may serve to illustrate the given reason.[30]

1. The Catechetical Reason

Christian theology is necessary as a proper extension of the teaching function of the Christian church or churches. That which is done in catechism classes, Sunday-school classes, and discipleship sessions can be undertaken more extensively and completely through the function of Christian theology. Several major theological systems have been written

---

29. Erickson, *Christian Theology*, pp. 49-50.
30. A more detailed treatment of these reasons and the historical illustrations may be found in the author's "Why Systematic Theology?" *Criswell Theological Review* 3 (Spring 1989): 259-81.

in order expressly to fulfill the teaching or catechetical function that belongs to the Christian churches.

Augustine of Hippo (354-430) wrote *Enchiridion*, or *On Faith, Hope, and Love* (c. 421). Of all Augustine's writings it is the nearest to a treatise on systematic theology. Its structure follows the Apostles' Creed, the Lord's Prayer, and the two great commandments concerning love.[31] *Compendium of Theology* (1272-73), written by Thomas Aquinas (1225-74), deals with faith and hope but does not include love.[32] John Calvin's (1509-64) *Institutes of the Christian Religion* (1536, 1559) follows the basic structure of the Apostles' Creed yet also has many highly polemical antipapal chapters.[33] Emil Brunner's three-volume "Dogmatics" (1946, 1949, 1960)[34] was clearly written to fulfill the catechetical function. Dogmatics, Brunner stated, "is a *function* of the church" and derives "its living basis, its possibility, and . . . its content" from the "teaching function of the Church."[35]

2. The Exegetical Reason

Christian theology is necessary for the integrated formulation of biblical truth. Some theologians have regarded as desirable or useful the systematic, as against the "salvation-history," formulation of the truths of biblical revelation. Some theological systems reflect this primary purpose. Philip Melanchthon (1497-1560) in his *Loci communes rerum theologicarum* ("Basic Conceptions of Theological Matters") (1521, 1555), the first systematic theological treatise by a Protestant, having discovered themes from the Pauline epistles, sought to bring together biblical motifs.[36]

3. The Homiletical Reason

Christian theology is necessary for the accurate clarification, the proper undergirding, and the helpful amplification of the gospel message that ought to be preached by Christian preachers and indeed of the total proclamation of the Word of God by all the people of God. Karl Barth, probably the most influential Christian theologian of the twentieth century, wrote his unfinished, 13-volume *Church Dogmatics* (1936-80)[37] vis-à-vis the role of preaching. This massive work grew out of the author's concern, first as pastor and later as professor, for the authentic undergirding of the

---

31. NPNF, 1st ser., 3:229-76; ACW, vol. 3; LCC, 7:335-412.

32. Trans. Cyril Vollert (St. Louis: B. Herder Book Company, 1947).

33. The principal modern English translations of the 1559 edition have been those by John Allen, by Henry Beveridge, and by Ford Lewis Battles (LCC).

34. Vols. 1-2, trans. Olive Wyon; vol. 3, trans. David Cairns and T. H. L. Parker (London: Lutterworth Press; Philadelphia: Westminster Press).

35. *The Christian Doctrine of God*, pp. 3-5.

36. The 1521 edition: trans. Charles Leander Hill (Boston: Meador, 1944); the 1555 edition: trans. Clyde L. Manschreck (LPT).

37. Eighteen translators contributed to the English edition, Geoffrey W. Bromiley being the major translator; the publisher was T. and T. Clark, Edinburgh.

"event" of preaching and the expectancy of church members to hear the Word of God. Moreover, one of Barth's three forms of the Word of God was that of "the Word of God as preached."[38]

4. The Polemical Reason

Christian theology is necessary for the defense of Christian truth against error within the church or from quasi-Christian movements. At times Christian theological formulation has occurred in response to the challenge of error from quasi-Christian religions and as a clarifying reply to and rejection of such "erroneous beliefs." *Against Heresies* (c. 185) by Irenaeus of Lyons (150?-202?) was a refutation of various Gnostic teachings on the ground that they contradicted the apostolic tradition (Four Gospels and/or the Rule of Faith), together with expositions of various Christian doctrines.[39] Similarly, Ulrich Zwingli's (1484-1531) *Commentary on True and False Religion* (1525) was both a systematic treatise (part I) and an anti-Roman polemic (part II).[40] Today, amid the increasing interaction of Christian deviations and major world religions and the unprecedented pluralism that now characterizes the United States, a major Christian systematic theology could be written for the primary purpose of refuting the truth-claims of religious cults and non-Christian religions now active in North America.

5. The Apologetic Reason

Christian theology is necessary in view of Christianity's cultural context—either in response to the challenge of a leading philosophy in a given era, or in response to the entire cultural situation of the time, including prevailing criticisms of Christianity, or in response to questions about ultimate reality allegedly posed by humankind. Origen (c. 185-253) seemingly wrote his *On First Principles* (c. 229) in response to the Middle Platonism of Atticus and Albinus,[41] and Thomas Aquinas wrote the unfinished *Summa Theologica* (1274) partly in response to the challenge of a rediscovered and resurgent Aristotelianism.[42] F. D. E. Schleiermacher's *The Christian Faith* (1821), written as a sequel to his *Speeches on Religion to Its Cultured Despisers* (1799),[43] was partly a response to the prevailing rejection of the Christian religion by many in German society. He disjoined religious piety from morality and metaphysics in an effort to make such piety acceptable to the "cultured despisers." Paul Johannes Tillich (1886-1965) in his *Systematic Theology* (1951, 1957, 1963) used the "method

---

38. I/1, pp. 98-111.
39. ANF, 1:315-567.
40. Trans. Henry Preble, Charles Tupper Baillie, and Clarence Newin Heller (Durham, N.C.: Labyrinth Press, 1981).
41. ANF, 4:239-382; trans. G. W. Butterworth (1936).
42. Trans. Fathers of the English Dominican Province, 3 vols. (New York: Benziger Brothers, Inc., 1947-48).
43. Trans. John Oman (New York: Harper and Brothers, 1958).

of correlation" by which, he asserted, the questions of contemporary human beings were coupled with answers from revealed truth.[44]

6. The Ethical Reason

Christian theology is necessary as the essential background for the interpretation and application of Christian ethics to personal and social needs and problems. Although Reinhold Niebuhr disclaimed being a systematic theologian and his Gifford Lectures, *The Nature and Destiny of Man* (1941, 1943),[45] did not cover all the major Christian doctrines, he was a major exemplar of the social ethicist who found himself led increasingly to the theological foundations of Christian ethics.

7. The Dialogic and Missionary Reasons

Christian theology is necessary for the proper encounter of Christianity with other major religions and for the more effective propagation of the Christian gospel among all human beings. It is not yet evident that a Christian systematic theology has been written whose primary purpose is either the dialogic or the missionary factor. The books of Hendrik Kraemer (1888-1965),[46] a theologian of missions, illustrate concerns for mission and for dialogue, but in the strictest sense they are not systematic theologies, and one of Emil Brunner's major monographs[47] was marked by the missionary concern. One of the most obvious and important challenges to systematic theology at the end of the twentieth century derives from the dialogic and missionary factors.

In arguing for the necessity of Christian theology we first stated and answered six different types of denials: the pietistic, the ethical, the non-polemical, the scientistic, the linguistic, and the trivialist. Then we explained and illustrated by representative Christian systematic theological treatises seven different reasons for the necessity of the Christian theological task: the catechetical, the exegetical, the homiletical, the polemical, the apologetic, the ethical, and the dialogic and missionary. Now that we have considered both the nature of and need for Christian theology, it is possible to investigate the basic methods used in the Christian theological enterprise.

III. THE METHODS OF CHRISTIAN THEOLOGY

What are the basic methods employed in the study of Christian theology? Are other adjunctive methods used as well? Answers to these questions,

44. (Chicago: University of Chicago Press).
45. 2 vols. (London: Nisbet and Company Ltd.).
46. *The Christian Message in a Non-Christian World* (London: Edinburgh House Press, 1938); *Religion and the Christian Faith* (Philadelphia: Westminster Press, 1956); *Communication of the Christian Faith* (Philadelphia: Westminster Press, 1956); and *Why Christianity of All Religions?* trans. Hubert Hoskins (Philadelphia: Westminster Press, 1962).
47. *Revelation and Reason.*

which are of a procedural nature, will be quite important for a clear understanding of the Christian theological task.

A. BASIC METHODS

1. Biblical Theology

Biblical theology is the exposition on the basis of adequate exegesis and proper collation of all pertinent texts of the theological teachings, or doctrines, of the Old and the New Testaments. Biblical theology has two major divisions: Old Testament theology and New Testament theology. Each of these may be further subdivided according to different types or segments of the biblical writings (e.g., Pentateuch, prophets, and wisdom literature; Synoptics, Paul, Acts, general epistles, and John).

The definition just given is, however, not the only proper or valid definition that can be offered of the term "biblical theology." Millard J. Erickson has noted, in addition, two other such definitions. First, the term can apply to a movement that "arose in the 1940's, flourished in the 1950's, and declined in the 1960's" and that has subsequently been criticized by authors such as James Dick Smart (1906-), James Barr (1924-), and Brevard Springs Childs (1923-). By such usage reference is made to the specific revival or resurgence within the mid-twentieth century of the method first defined above. Second, the term can be used in an evaluative sense to mean any theology that is "based upon and faithful to the teachings of the Bible."[48]

Examples of specific topics within the study of biblical theology include the following: the doctrine of God according to the Psalms, the doctrine of creation according to the Old Testament prophets, the kingdom of God in the Synoptic Gospels, and Paul's doctrine of justification.

2. Historical Theology

Historical theology, known also as the history of Christian doctrine, is the exposition of Christian doctrines according to their formulation and defense during the postbiblical history of Christianity. It can be subdivided according to chronological periods (patristic, medieval, Reformation, post-Reformation, and modern)[49] or according to confessional divisions (patristic, Eastern Orthodox, Roman Catholic, and Protestant).[50] Historical theology deals with the theological decisions of church councils, with creeds and confessions of faith, and with the writings of individual theologians.

Examples of specific topics within the study of historical theology include the following: Athanasius's (c. 295-373) doctrine of the Word of

48. *Christian Theology*, pp. 23-25.
49. This is a Western Christian periodization that does not apply equally well to Eastern Orthodoxy.
50. The Protestant section can be further subdivided according to denominations or confessions.

God, the doctrine of original sin set forth by Augustine of Hippo, John Calvin's doctrine of predestination, and the modern Pentecostal doctrine of the baptism with the Holy Spirit as evidenced by speaking in tongues.

3. Systematic Theology

Systematic theology is the orderly exposition of the doctrines of Christianity as its formulator in the context of his/her confessional tradition understands them, according to an integrated and interrelated method, using the Bible, the Christian tradition, Christian experience, and possibly other sources, and hopefully in the idiom of those to whom it is addressed.[51] Above all, systematic theology should be based on the proper and comprehensive utilization of the materials and results of biblical theology and historical theology.

Examples of specific topics within the study of systematic theology include the following: the revelation of God through nature and conscience, the essential or ontological Trinity, creation out of nothing, Satan, the universality of sin, the virginal conception of Jesus Christ, the Lord's Supper, and bodily resurrection from the dead.

B. ADJUNCTIVE METHODS

Whereas the three most basic methods as previously defined involve the interdependence of biblical studies, church history, and theology, other methods of studying Christian theology involve correlations between systematic theology and other disciplines in the theological curriculum. The latter methods, which are being identified as "adjunctive," do not so much determine the nature or content of systematic theology as they provide the theological foundations for the other disciplines. These adjunctive methods include the following:

1. Philosophical theology, including Christian apologetics
2. Theological ethics
3. Theology of evangelism
4. Theology of mission(s)
5. Theology of preaching
6. Theology of pastoral care
7. Theology of stewardship
8. Theology of Christian education
9. Theology of worship
10. Theology of church music
11. Theology of church social work

---

51. Millard J. Erickson, *Christian Theology*, pp. 66-79, has delineated nine distinct steps one may follow in producing a systematic theology.

CHAPTER 2

The Scope, Sources, and Types
of Systematic Theology

By now it should be evident that systematic theology is both distinguishable from and dependent on biblical theology and historical theology. Other basic questions, however, need to be raised about systematic theology itself. First, what is the scope or extent of the discipline of systematic theology? Second, what sources should and/or do theologians employ in formulating systematic theology? Third, what major types of Christian systematic theology have been published during the twentieth century? Answers to these questions should help to make increasingly clear what systematic theology is and how and why systems of Christian theology differ among themselves.

I. THE SCOPE OF SYSTEMATIC THEOLOGY

The scope of systematic theology may be explored and defined in two parallel ways: (1) by examining the place of systematic theology within the total theological curriculum; and (2) by identifying the subdivisions or chief components of systematic theology itself.

A. SYSTEMATIC THEOLOGY AND THE THEOLOGICAL CURRICULUM

Although there is no universally accepted statement or listing of the components of a well-developed theological curriculum, it is possible to approximate such a well-developed curriculum and by doing so to make more evident the role of systematic theology within that curriculum. Such a curriculum may be identified by the following outline:
1. Biblical Studies
   a. Geography, Archaeology, and History of Bible Lands
   b. Biblical Canon
   c. Biblical Languages (Hebrew, Aramaic, Greek)
   d. Biblical Translations
   e. Biblical Criticism (Textual, Historical, Literary, Form, and Redaction)

18

      f. Biblical Hermeneutics
      g. Biblical Exegesis and Interpretation
  2. Historical-Theological Studies
      a. History of Christianity, or Church History
      b. History of Christian Missions
      c. Biblical Theology
      d. Historical Theology
      e. Systematic Theology
      f. Christian Ethics
      g. Christian Apologetics and Philosophical Theology
      h. World Religions, or History of Religions
      i. Psychology of Religion
  3. Ministry or Practical Studies
      a. Preaching, or Homiletics
      b. Pastoral Care and Counseling, or Poimenics
      c. Evangelism
      d. Practice of Missions, or Missiology
      e. Worship, or Liturgics
      f. Religious Education, or Catechetics
      g. Church Administration and Polity
      h. Church Music, including Hymnology
      i. Church, Community, and Society
         1) Applied social ethics
         2) Church social work
         3) Church and state

Systematic theology builds on the various biblical disciplines, on church history, and on biblical and historical theology. It shares its systematic task with Christian ethics, Christian apologetics and philosophical theology, world religions, and psychology of religion. It furnishes much of the foundation for ministry studies and is in turn acted on by the needs and findings of Christian ministry. Systematic theology occupies a central and strategic place in the theological curriculum.

B. Subdivisions of Systematic Theology

The scope of systematic theology may be perceived not only by seeing its place in the larger theological curriculum but also by identifying its major subdivisions. Again, one finds no universally accepted list of these subdivisions, but treatises on systematic theology generally treat the following topics:

1. Prolegomena (methods, presuppositions, sources, etc.)
2. Revelation, the Bible, and authority (occasionally called bibliology)
3. God: attributes, Father, Trinity (theology)
4. World: creation, providence, supramundane beings (ktisiology, cosmology, angelology, and demonology)

5. Human beings as creatures (anthropology)
6. Human beings as sinners (hamartiology)
7. Jesus Christ: person and work (Christology; sometimes also atonement)
8. Holy Spirit: person and work (pneumatology)
9. Salvation or reconciliation or Christian life (soteriology)
10. Church: nature, membership, polity, baptism, Lord's Supper, worship, mission, ministry, etc. (ecclesiology)
11. Last things: death, after-death, resurrection, kingdom of God, second coming, final judgment, hell, heaven (eschatology)

II. THE SOURCES FOR SYSTEMATIC THEOLOGY

To what sources *do* systematic theologians turn for the content of their systems? To what sources *ought* systematic theologians to turn for the content of their systems? What *rank,* or order of priority, does one find among the sources for books on systematic theology? What rank, or order of priority, *should* there be among the sources for systematic theology? Answers to these questions are important both for the methodology of systematic theology and for the content of specific theological systems.

A. THE BIBLE: THE OLD AND THE NEW TESTAMENTS

Almost all Protestant[1] and certain Roman Catholic[2] theologians name the Bible, or the Holy Scriptures, as the source having the highest rank or priority for systematic theology. For Protestants this is part of the heritage of the Protestant Reformation.

Yet to affirm this priority for the Bible is not necessarily to adhere to it or follow it consistently in practice in writing one's system. For example, Paul Tillich stated[3] that the Bible was the primary source for systematic theology, but one finds that he made only slight use of specific biblical materials throughout the three volumes of his systematic theology.

In specifying the Bible as the primary source for systematic theology, some[4] would place the New Testament above the Old Testament, thus indicating the higher authority of the New Testament.

1. See Karl Barth, *Church Dogmatics,* I/2, ed. G. T. Thomson and Harold Knight (Edinburgh: T. & T. Clark, 1956), pp. 538-660; G. C. Berkouwer, *Holy Scripture,* Studies in Dogmatics, trans. Jack B. Rogers (Grand Rapids: Eerdmans, 1975), ch. 11; Helmut Thielicke, *The Evangelical Faith,* trans. Geoffrey W. Bromiley, 3 vols. (Grand Rapids: Eerdmans, 1982), 3:140-50; Donald G. Bloesch, *Essentials of Evangelical Theology,* 2 vols. (San Francisco: Harper and Row, 1982), 1:51-64.
2. Hans Küng by implication in *The Church,* trans. Ray Ockenden and Rosaleen Ockenden (New York: Sheed and Ward, 1968).
3. *Systematic Theology,* 1:34-40.
4. Henry Cook, *What Baptists Stand For* (London: Carey Kingsgate Press, 1947), pp. 13-15.

B. THE HISTORY OF CHRISTIAN DOCTRINE, OR TRADITION[5]

The Roman Catholic Church, specifically from the Council of Trent onward, has upheld the twofold authority of the canonical Scriptures and unwritten apostolic traditions.[6] At Vatican Council II there was some effort to redefine these two authorities as forming one source, not two.[7] Eastern Orthodoxy continues to hold to the special authority of seven ecumenical councils, extending from Nicaea I (325) through Nicaea II (787).[8]

Especially on the doctrines of the Trinity and the person of Jesus Christ Protestants as well as Roman Catholics and Eastern Orthodox have relied on the formulations of the patristic age, especially the Apostles' Creed, the Nicaeno-Constantinopolitan Creed, and the Symbol of Chalcedon.[9]

Various Protestant confessions, or denominations, especially the Lutheran, the Reformed, and the Anglican, have considered their own particular Reformation confessions of faith as important sources for systematic theology.[10] Even in those denominations which strongly emphasize the primacy of the Bible[11] there is theological indebtedness, whether acknowledged or unacknowledged, to confessions of faith, theological movements, and/or theologians within the postbiblical history of Christianity.

C. CHRISTIAN EXPERIENCE OR PIETY

Some Christian theologians have regarded and utilized Christian experience, whether individual or collective, as a source of systematic

5. Included are creeds, confessions of faith, decisions of church councils and other ecclesial bodies, and the writings of individual theologians.

6. "Decree concerning the Canonical Scriptures," 8 April 1546, in *Canons and Decrees of the Council of Trent*, trans. and ed. H. J. Schroeder (St. Louis: B. Herder, 1941), pp. 17-18.

7. *Dei Verbum* ("Dogmatic Constitution on Divine Revelation") (18 November 1965), 2.10, declared: "Sacred tradition and sacred Scripture form one sacred deposit of the word of God, which is committed to the Church"; *Documents of Vatican II*, ed. Walter M. Abbott, S.J. (New York: American Press et al., 1966), p. 117. Preparatory to the work of Vatican Council II on this issue was Josef Rupert Geiselmann's *Die Heilige Schrift und die Tradition: Zu den neuren Kontroversen über das Verhältnis der Heiligen Schrift zu den nichtgeschriebenen Traditionen*, Quaestiones Disputatae, no. 18 (Freiburg, West Germany: Herder, 1962), chs. 1-3 of which were published as *The Meaning of Tradition*, trans. W. J. O'Hara (New York: Herder and Herder, 1966).

8. See Alexander Schmemann, *Eastern Orthodoxy*, trans. Lydia W. Kesich (London: Harvill Press, 1963), pp. 70-94, 110-11, 118-42, 153-57, 160-68, 172-78, 200-210; George Every, *Misunderstandings between East and West*, Ecumenical Studies in History, no. 4 (Richmond, Va.: John Knox Press, 1966), pp. 55-68.

9. See J. N. D. Kelly, *Early Christian Creeds* (2d ed.; New York: David McKay Company, 1960); R. V. Sellers, *The Council of Chalcedon: A Historical and Doctrinal Survey* (London: S.P.C.K., 1953), esp. p. 350.

10. See Edmund Schlink, *Theology of the Lutheran Confessions*, trans. Paul F. Koehneke and Herbert J. A. Bouman (Philadelphia: Muhlenberg Press, 1961); *Reformed Confessions of the 16th Century*, ed. Arthur C. Cochrane (Philadelphia: Westminster Press, 1966); and E. J. Bicknell, *A Theological Introduction to the Thirty-Nine Articles of the Church of England* (2d ed.; London: Longmans, Green and Company, 1925).

11. Notably those who stand in the believers' church heritage of Protestantism, that is, Mennonites, Baptists, Quakers, Brethren, Disciples of Christ and Churches of Christ, Holiness churches, and Pentecostals.

theology. Especially was this true of F. D. E. Schleiermacher, who defined "piety" or "religion" as "the consciousness of being absolutely dependent, or, which is the same thing, of being in relation to God." Piety is thus not a matter of knowing or doing but of feeling. Furthermore, Christian "doctrines in all their forms have their ultimate ground so exclusively in the emotions of the religious self-consciousness that where these do not exist the doctrines cannot arise."[12]

E. Y. Mullins gave considerable attention to Christian experience in his systematic theology.[13] Was Mullins using "Christian experience" for apologetic reasons at a time when pragmatism and personalism were dominant philosophies in the United States? Or, was Mullins considering "religious experience" as a secondary channel or vehicle for transmitting Christian truth? Or, was "Christian experience" for Mullins an authoritative source of Christian truth? Mullins's lengthy discussion of "Christian experience" in relation to "Christian knowledge" and "Christian certainty" makes it difficult to deny categorically that Christian experience was for Mullins a source of Christian truth.[14]

If indeed Christian experience is rightly to be reckoned as a source for Christian theology, what ought to be its rank? Presumably its authority should be secondary to the supreme authority of the Bible. But is it also less authoritative than postbiblical Christian tradition, and does it therefore have a tertiary position? Many would no doubt concur with this, but liberal Protestants with their emphasis on reason or experience and Pentecostals with their emphasis on religious emotions and charismatic gifts would tend to place experience above tradition.

D. RESOURCES OF CULTURE: PHILOSOPHICAL, PSYCHOLOGICAL, POLITICAL, AND SOCIOETHICAL MOVEMENTS

Christian theologians have often been significantly influenced by movements of thought within their cultures. This has been true even when such movements of thought have not been formally acknowledged as sources for systematic theology. For example, not a few of the Church Fathers were influenced by Neo-Platonism, Thomas Aquinas was influenced by the rediscovered Aristotle, eighteenth-century theologians by the Enlightenment, nineteenth-century Christian theologians by Charles Darwin (1809-82), and late twentieth-century liberation theologians by Marxist-Leninism. Interaction with such movements of thought at times involved drawing concepts, insights, and/or terms from the movements.

Other Christian thinkers have protested against such influence and such borrowing, or at least the excessive employment of such, but even those who have so protested have not escaped the influence of such

---

12. *The Christian Faith*, pp. 12, 5-12, 78.
13. *The Christian Religion in Its Doctrinal Expression*, pp. 12-22, 49-81, 91-107.
14. Ibid., pp. 67-81.

movements. Examples include the influence of Stoicism on Tertullian (c. 155–after 220) and the influence of existentialism on the early career of Karl Barth. The crucial question, therefore, becomes that of the extent and propriety of such influence. Most Christian theologians would place the resources of culture below the Scriptures, tradition, and Christian experience in the list of sources for systematic theology.

E. Non-Christian Religions

The consideration of non-Christian religions, excluding the faith of the Old Testament, as a source for Christian theology is seemingly a modern phenomenon, probably augmented by the interreligious dialogue of the twentieth century. For example, Langdon Brown Gilkey (1919-) has asserted that "clearly there is 'truth' to be found in other traditions" and that "the traditions of other religions can be a creative and authentic resource for Christian theology."[15]

Other Christian theologians, while teaching the revelatory nature of the phenomenon of religions, deny that non-Christian religions per se are a valid source for Christian systematic theology.

The sources that have been used for systematic theology and the ranking of these by various theologians can be readily identified. Questions about the oughtness of the sources are much more complex; variations as to sources may be the key to variations in the content of systematic theologies.

III. SOME TYPES OF SYSTEMATIC THEOLOGIES

The various types of Christian systematic theologies produced during the twentieth century can be classified in at least three ways. One of these methods depends on how the author has utilized and ranked the major sources for systematic theology. A second method is classification according to the denomination or confession with which the author and his book are identified. A third method pertains to the major theological and/or ecclesiastical movements during the twentieth century that the systematic theology reflects or represents.

A. Types in Relation to Sources

Any of the major sources commonly employed by systematic theologians or any combination of these can be so employed as to produce a distinct type of Christian theological system, even to the extent of becoming what some would reckon to be a distorted formulation of Christian truth. Here the examples to be cited will not be drawn solely from the twentieth century; some nineteenth-century titles will be included as well.

---

15. *Message and Existence: An Introduction to Christian Theology* (New York: Seabury Press, 1979), pp. 61-63.

1. Non-Christian Religions

An overemphasis on non-Christian religions as a major source for Christian theology has not yet resulted in a major Christian systematic theology. The approach to non-Christian religions that resulted in the denial of the absoluteness of the Christian revelation was pursued by Ernst Troeltsch (1865-1923),[16] a representative of the history-of-religions school who did not actually write a systematic theology.

2. Culture or Reason

Systematic theology can be written with a heavy dependence on the resources of contemporary culture. This effort is sometimes undertaken with the announced purpose of providing answers to major questions posed in the culture by drawing from the Christian revelation of God. Critics of this method often allege that biblical truth is thus eclipsed by the concerns and concepts germane to a specific culture. Representative of this use of sources was Paul Tillich in his three-volume *Systematic Theology*.[17]

3. Christian Experience

Systematic theology can give major attention to Christian experience either by regarding religion as basically the experience of dependence on God or by reckoning Christian experience as an important channel for, if not source of, Christian doctrine. Illustrative of the former is *The Christian Faith*[18] by F. D. E. Schleiermacher, who sought to shift from religion as thinking or religion as doing to religion as feeling, especially the feeling of dependence on God. Representative of the latter trend was E. Y. Mullins, who in *The Christian Religion in Its Doctrinal Expression* made room for Christian experience but under the authority of the Bible.

4. Church Tradition

Systematic theologies can also be written in such a way as to give priority to the formulations of Christian doctrine that have received ecclesial approval during the course of the history of Christianity. As a result creeds, confessions of faith, and decisions of church councils and of church leaders are seen as establishing the norms or the conclusions for systematic theology. Ludwig Ott (1906-), a Roman Catholic dogmatician, in *Fundamentals of Catholic Dogma*,[19] represented the ecclesial or traditional method. Ott identified the specific level of ecclesiastical authority for each major doctrinal teaching.

16. See especially his *The Absoluteness of Christianity and the History of Religions*, trans. David Reid (Richmond, Va.: John Knox Press, 1971).
17. (Chicago: University of Chicago Press, 1951-63).
18. Trans. H. R. Mackintosh and James S. Stewart (Edinburgh: T. and T. Clark, 1928).
19. Trans. Patrick Lynch and ed. James Bastible, 6th ed. (St. Louis: B. Herder Book Company, 1964).

5. The Bible

Systematic theology can give such attention to biblical materials that other sources for systematic theology are bypassed or deemphasized. Accordingly systematic theology is held to be the compilation of biblical doctrines devoid of other influences, even though the culture and/or the ecclesial tradition may have actually shaped the formulation. Illustrative of this type of systematic theology were Charles Hodge's (1797-1878) *Systematic Theology*[20] and Lewis Sperry Chafer's (1871-1952) *Systematic Theology*.[21]

B. TYPES IN RELATION TO DENOMINATIONS OR CONFESSIONS

Systematic theologies have been written in such a manner as to reflect or represent the theologies of particular Christian denominations or confessions. Not every denomination, to be sure, is well represented among the systematic theologies produced during the twentieth century. The following survey will be confined to books either written in English or translated into English.

1. Roman Catholic

The massive work by Roman Catholic theologians during the twentieth century has often not issued in "systematic theologies" or "dogmatic theologies," as those terms are customarily defined. The most elaborate work that approximates a systematic theology was Karl Rahner's (1904-84) *Theological Investigations*,[22] 17 volumes by a Jesuit theologian that may be described more aptly as a collection of the author's extensive writings than as a systematic or dogmatic theology. Joseph Pohle (1852-1922) produced a 12-volume dogmatic series early in the century,[23] George D. Smith edited an important compendium of Catholic beliefs,[24] and a Dutch theologian, Gerardus Cornelius van Noort (1861-1946), issued a two-volume dogmatics with an emphasis on ecclesiology.[25] Hans Küng (1928-) wrote major monographs on the existence of God, justification, the Christian life, the church, infallibility, and eternal life but not a systematic theology. Reginald Garrigou-Lagrange, O.P. (1877-1964), reinterpreted the theology of Thomas Aquinas, Bernard J. F. Lonergan, S.J. (1904-84), and David W. Tracy (1939-)

20. 3 vols. (New York: Charles Scribner's Sons; London, Edinburgh: T. Nelson and Sons, 1872-73).

21. 8 vols. (Dallas: Dallas Seminary Press, 1947-48).

22. Trans. Cornelius Ernst et al. (Baltimore: Helicon Press and other publishers, 1961-82). Rahner also wrote a single-volume *Foundations of Christian Faith: An Introduction to the Idea of Christianity*, trans. William V. Dych (New York: Seabury Press, 1978).

23. *Dogmatic Theology*, trans. and adapt. Arthur Preuss (St. Louis: B. Herder Book Company, 1929-34).

24. *The Teaching of the Catholic Church: A Summary of Catholic Doctrine* (London: Burns and Oates, 1948).

25. *Dogmatic Theology*, trans. and rev. John J. Castelot, S.S., and William R. Murphy, S.S. (Westminster, Md.: Newman Press, 1955, 1957).

have concentrated on theological method, Avery Robert Dulles, S.J., (1918-), produced monographs on revelation and monographs on the church, and Thomas F. Stransky, C.S.P., has written on the theology of mission. Michael Schmaus (1897-) produced a dogmatic theology,[26] and Frans Jozef van Beeck, S.J. (1930-), the first volume of a "contemporary Catholic systematic theology."[27] Most of the recent catechisms resemble one- volume systematic theologies; of note have been those by Dutch Catholics,[28] by John A. Hardon, S.J. (1914-),[29] by a trilogy of editors,[30] by Andrew M. Greeley (1928-),[31] by Thomas Bokenkotter,[32] and by Alan Schreck.[33]

2. *Anglican-Episcopal*

The production of systematic or dogmatic theologies has not always been as prevalent in the Anglican tradition as in the Roman Catholic, Lutheran, and Reformed, but there have been such treatises during the twentieth century. Handley Carr Glyn Moule (1841-1920) of the Evangelical wing produced a brief volume in 1905,[34] Francis Joseph Hall (1857-1932) of the Anglo-Catholic heritage produced ten large volumes between 1907 and 1922,[35] Darwell Stone[36] and Thomas B. Strong[37] brought out manuals, both in 1913, T. C. Hammond authored a widely circulated one-volume Evangelical treatment,[38] and Oliver Chase Quick (1885-1944) interpreted Christian creedal affirmations in 1938.[39] John Robert Walmsey Stott (1921-) wrote a widely circulated, popular *Basic Christianity*.[40] Frederic Clifton Grant (1891-1974) issued *Basic Christian Beliefs*,[41] and Marianne H. Micks produced *Introduction to Theology*.[42] John Macquarrie

26. *Dogma*, trans. Ann Laeuchli, William McKenna, S.J., T. Patrick Burke, and Mary Ledderer (New York, London, Kansas City: Sheed and Ward, 1968-77). This was a translation of the two-volume *Der Glaube der Kirche*.

27. *God Encountered: A Contemporary Catholic Systematic Theology*: vol. 1, *Understanding the Christian Faith* (San Francisco: Harper and Row, 1989).

28. *A New Catechism: Catholic Faith for Adults*, trans. Kevin Smyth (London: Burns and Oates; New York: Herder and Herder, 1967).

29. *The Catholic Catechism* (Garden City, N.Y.: Doubleday and Company, Inc., 1975).

30. Ronald Lawler, O.F.M. Cap., Donald W. Wuerl, and Thomas Comerford Lawler, eds., *The Teaching of Christ: A Catholic Catechism for Adults* (Huntington, Ind.: Our Sunday Visitor, Inc., 1976).

31. *The Great Mysteries: An Essential Catechism* (New York: Seabury Press, 1976).

32. *Essential Catholicism* (Garden City, N.Y.: Doubleday and Company, Inc., 1986).

33. *Basics of the Faith: A Catholic Catechism* (Ann Arbor, Mich.: Servant Books, 1987).

34. *Outlines of Christian Doctrine* (London: Hodder and Stoughton).

35. *Dogmatic Theology* (New York, London: Longmans, Green and Company).

36. *Outlines of Christian Dogma* (London: Longmans, Green and Company).

37. *A Manual of Theology* (London: Adam and Charles Black).

38. *In Understanding Be Men: An Introductory Handbook on Christian Doctrine* (Chicago: Inter-Varsity Press, 1936).

39. *Doctrines of the Creed: Their Basis in Scripture and Their Meaning To-day* (New York: Charles Scribner's Sons).

40. (Grand Rapids: Eerdmans, 1958). Stott also wrote monographs on the person of Christ, the work of the Holy Spirit, the Bible, confession, and mission.

41. (Edinburgh, London: Oliver and Boyd, 1960).

42. (New York: Seabury Press, 1964; rev. ed. 1983).

(1919-) completed a major one-volume system[43] and a brief theology for laypersons.[44] James Albert Pike (1913-69)[45] and Maurice F. Wiles[46] represented the Broad church perspective. Other recent one-volume expositions include those by Owen C. Thomas[47] and by Anthony Tyrrell Hanson (1916-) and Richard Patrick Crosland Hanson (1916-).[48] In the Broad church tradition John Arthur Thomas Robinson (1919-83) wrote monographs on God, the body, the person of Christ, the Christian life, the Lord's Supper, and the last things. In the evangelical tradition James Innell Packer (1926-) produced several monographs on the Bible and on the Christian life, and Edward Michael Banks Green (1930-) monographs on the resurrection of Jesus, baptism, the Holy Spirit, and the Christian life.

3. Lutheran

Continental Lutheran theologians have produced three major systematic theologies, one in Sweden, one in Denmark, and one in West Germany. Gustaf Emanuel Hildebrand Aulén (1879-1977) wrote *The Faith of the Christian Church*,[49] Regin Prenter was the author of *Creation and Redemption*,[50] and Helmut Thielicke (1908-86) produced a three-volume work, *The Evangelical Faith*.[51] From the American Missouri Synod came Franz August Otto Pieper's (1852-1931) *Christian Dogmatics*, in three volumes,[52] and a one-volume "epitome" of Pieper's dogmatics by John Theodore Mueller (1885-1967).[53] Americans John Alden Singmaster (1852-1926)[54] and Joseph Stump (1866-1935)[55] authored one-volume systems. Edmund Schlink (1903-)[56] and Friedrich Mildenberger (1929-),[57] both Germans, interpreted the Lutheran confessions of faith in volumes that were tantamount to systematic theologies, and George Forell (1919-), an

43. *Principles of Christian Theology* (New York: Charles Scribner's Sons, 1966; 2d rev. ed. 1977).
44. *The Faith of the People of God: A Lay Theology* (New York: Charles Scribner's Sons, 1972).
45. *If This Be Heresy* (New York, Evanston: Harper and Row, 1967).
46. *The Remaking of Christian Doctrine* (Philadelphia: Westminster Press, 1978).
47. *Introduction to Theology* (Cambridge, Mass.: Greeno, Haddon, and Company, Ltd., 1973).
48. *Reasonable Belief: A Survey of the Christian Faith* (Oxford: Oxford University Press, 1980).
49. Trans. Eric H. Wahlstrom (Philadelphia: Muhlenberg Press, 1960).
50. Trans. Theodor I. Jensen (Philadelphia: Fortress Press, 1967).
51. (1974-82).
52. (St. Louis: Concordia Publishing House, 1917-24; 1950-57).
53. *Christian Dogmatics: A Handbook of Doctrinal Theology for Pastors, Teachers, and Laymen* (St. Louis: Concordia Publishing House, 1934).
54. *A Handbook of Christian Theology* (Philadelphia: United Lutheran Publication House, 1927).
55. *The Christian Faith: A System of Christian Dogmatics* (New York: Macmillan, 1932).
56. *Theology of the Lutheran Confessions.*
57. *Theology of the Lutheran Confessions*, trans. Erwin L. Lueker and ed. Robert C. Schultz (Philadelphia: Fortress Press, 1986). Mildenberger treated the Augsburg Confession and the Book of Concord separately.

American, offered his summary.[58] The most recent exposition of Lutheran dogmatics has been a symposium.[59]

4. Reformed and Presbyterian

Authors representing the Reformed and Presbyterian tradition have made major contributions to Christian systematic theology during the twentieth century. Most notable of all these has been Karl Barth's 13-volume, unfinished *Church Dogmatics*,[60] which may be ranked with the systems of Thomas Aquinas and John Calvin. Benjamin Breckinridge Warfield (1851-1921) was the author of *Biblical Doctrines*,[61] Hugh Ross Mackintosh (1870-1936) produced a short volume,[62] and Louis Berkhof (1873-1957) issued an interpretation of Reformed theology that became his systematic theology.[63] John Seldon Whale (1896-?) was the author of a widely utilized text for university students,[64] John A. Mackay wrote an introduction,[65] and James D. Smart issued a popular exposition.[66] Auguste Lecerf (1872-1943) prepared a study of Reformed dogmatics,[67] and Cornelius Van Til (1895-1987) an introduction to systematics.[68] Two major Reformed multivolume systematic theologies from Continental authors began to appear in English during the 1950s: the three-volume "Dogmatics" by Emil Brunner[69] of Switzerland, and the 14-volume "Studies in Dogmatics" by Gerrit Cornelis Berkouwer (1903-)[70] of the Netherlands.

58. *The Protestant Faith* (Englewood Cliffs, N.J.: Prentice-Hall, Inc., 1960).

59. Carl E. Braaten (1929-) and Robert W. Jensen, eds., *Christian Dogmatics*, 2 vols. (Philadelphia: Fortress Press, 1984). Braaten is the author of *Principles of Lutheran Theology* (Philadelphia: Fortress Press, 1983) and of works on the theology of missions and the last things.

60. See above, p. 13, n. 37.

61. (New York: Oxford University Press, 1929). Warfield also produced monographs on the Bible, the person and work of Christ, salvation, miracles, and perfectionism.

62. *Some Aspects of Christian Belief* (New York: George H. Doran, 1923).

63. *Reformed Dogmatics*, 3 vols. (Grand Rapids: Eerdmans, 1932); *Systematic Theology*, 2d rev. ed. (ibid., 1941); *Introductory Volume to Systematic Theology*, rev. ed. (ibid., 1932). Berkhof also wrote the following, which had successive titles: *Manual of Reformed Doctrine* (ibid., 1933); *Manual of Christian Doctrine* (ibid., 1969); condensed as *Summary of Christian Doctrine for Senior Classes* (ibid., 1938). Berkhof also wrote monographs on the atonement, on faith, and on the kingdom of God.

64. *Christian Doctrine* (New York: Macmillan; Cambridge: University Press, 1941).

65. *A Preface to Christian Theology*.

66. *What a Man Can Believe* (Philadelphia: Westminster Press, 1943).

67. *An Introduction to Reformed Dogmatics*, trans. unspecified (London: Lutterworth Press, 1949).

68. *An Introduction to Systematic Theology* (Author, 1947; rev. ed. 1949, 1961; n.p.p.: Presbyterian and Reformed Publishing Company, 1974).

69. *The Christian Doctrine of God; The Christian Doctrine of Creation and Redemption*, trans. Olive Wyon (Philadelphia: Westminster Press, 1952), and *The Christian Doctrine of the Church, Faith and the Consummation*, trans. David Cairns and T. H. L. Parker (ibid., 1962). Brunner also produced monographs on revelation, humankind and sin, the work of Christ, the church, and the last things.

70. *General Revelation* (Grand Rapids: Eerdmans, 1955); *Holy Scripture; Divine Election*, trans. Hugo Bekker (ibid., 1960); *The Providence of God*, trans. Lewis Smedes (ibid., 1952); *Man: The Image of God*, trans. Dirk W. Jellema (ibid., 1962); *Sin*, trans. Philip C. Holtrop (ibid., 1971);

Shorter treatments came from David Haxton Carswell Read,[71] Rachel Henderlite,[72] Addison H. Leitch (1908-),[73] Joseph Haroutunian (1904-68),[74] and John H. Gerstner (1914-).[75] Hermann Diem authored a one-volume *Dogmatics*,[76] Herman Hoeksema (1886-1965), another book about Reformed theology,[77] Hendrikus Berkhof (1914-) a noteworthy one-volume system,[78] and Otto Weber (1902-66) a major two-volume system.[79]

5. Mennonite

Two works that can be called systematic theologies have been produced by Mennonites in the United States, both of these having come out of the Mennonite Church. Daniel Kauffman (1865-1944) edited a more popular book in 1914,[80] and John Christian Wenger (1910-) wrote a more advanced treatise in 1954.[81]

6. Baptist

Baptist[82] contributions to systematic theology during the twentieth century seldom have involved monographs more lengthy than one volume. The final edition of *Systematic Theology*[83] by Augustus Hopkins Strong (1836-1921), a Northern Baptist, was issued in 1907, but this volume, never later revised, has remained in print throughout the twentieth century. E. Y. Mullins's *The Christian Religion in Its Doctrinal Expression* appeared in 1917. W. T. Conner, beginning in 1924, issued volumes that constituted a systematic theology.[84] Thomas Polhill Stafford (1866-

---

The Person of Christ, trans. John Vriend (ibid., 1954); *The Work of Christ*, trans. Cornelius Lambregste (ibid., 1965); *Faith and Justification*, trans. Lewis Smedes (ibid., 1954); *Faith and Perseverance*, trans. Robert D. Knudsen (ibid., 1958); *Faith and Sanctification*, trans. John Vriend (ibid., 1952); *The Church*, trans. James E. Davison (ibid., 1976); *The Sacraments*, trans. Hugo Bekker (ibid., 1969); *The Return of Christ*, trans. James Van Oosterom and ed. Marlin J. Van Elderen (ibid., 1972).

71. *The Christian Faith* (New York: Scribner, 1956).

72. *A Call to Faith* (Richmond, Va.: John Knox Press, 1955). Henderlite also wrote *Forgiveness and Hope: Toward a Theology for Protestant Christian Education* (ibid., 1961).

73. *Interpreting Basic Theology* (New York: Hawthorn, 1961).

74. *God with Us: A Theology of Transpersonal Life* (Philadelphia: Westminster Press, 1965).

75. *Theology for Everyman* (Chicago: Moody, 1965).

76. Trans. Harold Knight (Philadelphia: Westminster Press, 1959).

77. *Reformed Dogmatics* (Grand Rapids: Reformed Free Publishing Association, 1966).

78. *Christian Faith: An Introduction to the Study of the Faith*, trans. Sierd Woudstra (Grand Rapids: Eerdmans, 1979).

79. *Foundations of Dogmatics*, trans. Darreli L. Guder (Grand Rapids: Eerdmans, 1981, 1983).

80. *Bible Doctrine* (Scottdale, Pa.: Mennonite Publishing House); *Doctrines of the Bible: A Brief Discussion of the Teachings of God's Word* (ibid., 1928).

81. *Introduction to Theology: An Interpretation of the Doctrinal Content of Scripture, Written to Strengthen a Childlike Faith in Christ* (Scottdale, Pa.: Herald Press).

82. Unless otherwise identified, these authors were/are Southern Baptists.

83. (Philadelphia: Judson Press).

84. *A System of Christian Doctrine* (Nashville: Sunday School Board of the Southern Baptist Convention, 1924); later revised and issued as two volumes: *Revelation and God: An Introduction to Christian Doctrine* and *The Gospel of Redemption* (ibid., 1945); also condensed as

1942), a Northern Baptist, produced a system,[85] Ralph Edward Knudsen
(1897-?), a Northern Baptist, was the author of *Christian Beliefs*,[86] and John
Alexis Edgren (1838-1908) of the Baptist General Conference wrote *Fundamentals of Faith*.[87] For college textbook usage Josiah Blake Tidwell (1870-1946) produced *Christian Teachings*,[88] William Wilson Stevens (1914-78)
wrote *Doctrines of the Christian Religion*,[89] Dallas M. Roark (1931-) issued
The Christian Faith,[90] and F. Leroy Forlines, a Free Will Baptist, wrote
Systematics.[91] Herschel Hobbs authored *Fundamentals of Our Faith*,[92]
Joseph Franklin Green, Jr. (1924-), wrote a brief introduction,[93] and Curtis Wallace Christian (1927-) provided a guide for formulating one's
personal theology.[94] Eric Charles Rust (1910-) produced a biblical theology[95] and monographs on the doctrine of humankind, the theology of
nature, and the theology of history, and Frank Stagg (1911-) wrote a
theology of the New Testament[96] and monographs on humankind and on
the Holy Spirit. Another major system, written by Dale Moody (1915-),
was entitled *The Word of Truth*.[97] A theology directed to those who minister
to children and a theology addressed to the aging came from the pen of
William Lawrence Hendricks (1929-).[98] Monographs on the saving work
of Christ were issued by James E. Tull (1913-89), by Fisher Henry Humphreys (1939-), and by Bert Buckner Dominy (1938-), and an English
Baptist, Bruce Milne (1927-), wrote *Know the Truth*.[99] Millard Erickson's
Christian Theology first appeared in three volumes and subsequently was
issued in one. The author is affiliated with the Baptist General Conference.
John Paul Newport (1927-) addressed the lay readership,[100] and Morris
Ashcraft (1922-) issued *Christian Faith and Beliefs*.[101] Bruce A. Demarest

Christian Doctrines (ibid., 1937). Conner also wrote monographs on the work of Christ and
the work of the Holy Spirit.
    85. *A Study of Christian Doctrines* (Kansas City, Mo.: Western Baptist Publishing
Company, 1936). Stafford also wrote a monograph on the Holy Spirit.
    86. (Philadelphia: Judson Press, 1947).
    87. Trans. J. O. Backlund (Chicago: Baptist Conference Press, 1948).
    88. (2d ed.; Grand Rapids: Eerdmans, 1942).
    89. (Grand Rapids: Eerdmans, 1967; Nashville: Broadman, 1967).
    90. (Grand Rapids: Baker Book House, 1977).
    91. *A Study of the Christian System of Life and Thought* (Nashville: Randall House
Publications, 1975).
    92. (Nashville: Broadman, 1960).
    93. *The Heart of the Gospel* (Nashville: Broadman, 1968).
    94. *Shaping Your Faith: A Guide to a Personal Theology* (Waco, Tex.: Word Books, 1973).
    95. *Salvation History: A Biblical Interpretation* (Richmond, Va.: John Knox Press, 1962).
    96. *New Testament Theology* (Nashville: Broadman, 1962).
    97. *A Summary of Christian Doctrine Based on Biblical Revelation* (Grand Rapids: Eerdmans,
1981). Moody also wrote monographs on the Holy Spirit, on baptism, and on the last things.
    98. *A Theology for Children* (Nashville: Broadman, 1980); *A Theology for Aging* (ibid.,
1986).
    99. *A Handbook of Christian Belief* (Downers Grove, Ill.: Inter-Varsity Press, 1982).
    100. *What Is Christian Doctrine?* Layman's Library of Christian Doctrine (Nashville:
Broadman, 1984).
    101. (Nashville: Broadman, 1984).

(1935-) and Gordon Russell Lewis (1926-), Conservative Baptists, have completed the first volume of a multivolume set entitled *Integrative Theology*.[102] James William McClendon, Jr. (1924-), has produced the first volume, that concerning ethics, of a projected three-volume work on beliefs common to Christians of the believer's baptism heritage.[103]

7. Brethren

One-volume introductions were written by several Church of the Brethren authors: Daniel Webster Kurtz (1879-1949),[104] John Henry Moore (1846-1935),[105] Otho Winger (1877-1946),[106] Harry L. Smith (1897-),[107] and William McKinley Beahm (1896-1964).[108] James M. Tombaugh's (1857-1932) brief volume[109] and J. Allen Miller's (1866-1935) lectures on systematic theology, published posthumously in 1946,[110] represented the Brethren Church, and Louis Sylvester Bauman's (1875-1950) monograph[111] represented the Grace Brethren.

8. Methodist

Major Methodist systematic theologies were produced at the beginning of the twentieth century, but the flow was diminished during the later decades of the century. Henry Clay Sheldon (1845-1928) wrote *System of Christian Doctrine*,[112] Milton Spenser Terry (1840-1914) wrote *Biblical Dogmatics*,[113] and Albert Cornelius Knudson (1873-1953) authored two volumes[114] that, taken together, constitute a systematic theology. Henry Maldwyn Hughes (1875-1940), an English Methodist, wrote an introduction,[115] and Harris Franklin Rall (1870-1964) a summary.[116] Other general

102. (Grand Rapids: Zondervan, 1987). Demarest has also written monographs on general revelation and on the person of Christ.

103. *Ethics: Systematic Theology*, vol. 1 (Nashville: Abingdon Press, 1986).

104. *An Outline of the Fundamental Doctrines of Faith* (2d ed.; Elgin, Ill.: Brethren Publishing House, 1914).

105. *The New Testament Doctrines* (ibid., 1915).

106. *History and Doctrines of the Church of the Brethren* (ibid., 1919; 2d ed. 1920).

107. *Bible Doctrine* (Upland, Calif.: n.p., 1921).

108. *Studies in Christian Belief* (Elgin, Ill.: Brethren Publishing House, 1958).

109. *Some Fundamental Christian Doctrines* (Ashland, Ohio: Brethren Publishing House, 1919).

110. *Christian Doctrine: Lectures and Sermons* (Ashland, Ohio: Brethren Publishing House).

111. *The Faith Once for All Delivered unto the Saints* (Winona Lake, Ind.: BMH Books, 1947; 9th ed. 1977).

112. (Cincinnati: Jennings and Pye; New York: Eaton and Mains, 1903).

113. *An Exposition of the Principal Doctrines of the Holy Scriptures* (New York: Eaton and Mains; Cincinnati: Jennings and Graham, 1907).

114. *The Doctrine of God* (Cincinnati: Abingdon Press, 1930); *The Doctrine of Redemption* (ibid., 1933).

115. *Christian Foundations: An Introduction to Christian Doctrine* (London: Epworth Press, 1933).

116. *A Faith for Today* (New York, Cincinnati: Abingdon Press, 1936). Rall also authored monographs on God and on salvation.

works were produced by William Atwell Spurrier,[117] by Donald E. Demaray,[118] and by Georgia Elma Harkness (1891-1974).[119] John Lawson (1909-) undertook a restatement of Wesleyan theology,[120] as did a two-volume symposium.[121]

9. Adventist

A recently issued volume by a Seventh-day Adventist theologian, Richard Rice,[122] seems to be the only instance of a systematic theology written within the Seventh-day Adventist heritage. Alva G. Huffer's system[123] reflects the Church of God General Conference (Oregon, Illinois), also called the Church of God of the Abrahamic Faith.

10. Holiness

Bible Theology, written by William B. Godbey (1833-1920),[124] seems to reflect the independent Holiness movement. From the Christian and Missionary Alliance came a monograph by George Palmer Pardington (1866-1915).[125] A Free Methodist author, Harry Edward Jessop (1884-?), wrote a handbook.[126] The Church of God (Anderson, Indiana) has made considerable use of a system by Russell Raymond Byrum (1888-?).[127] From the Church of the Nazarene have come a two-volume system by Aaron Merritt Hills (1848-1935),[128] a major three-volume system by Henry Orton Wiley,[129] a symposium,[130] and a one-volume system by H. Ray Dunning (1926-).[131]

117. *Guide to the Christian Faith: An Introduction* (New York: Scribner, 1952).

118. *Basic Beliefs: An Introductory Guide to Christian Doctrine* (Winona Lake, Ind.: Light and Life Press, 1958).

119. *Beliefs That Count* (New York: Abingdon Press, 1961); *Our Christian Hope* (New York, Nashville: Abingdon Press, 1964).

120. Lawson, *Comprehensive Handbook of Christian Doctrine* (Englewood Cliffs, N.J.: Prentice-Hall, Inc., 1967); reprinted as *Introduction to Christian Doctrine* (Grand Rapids: Francis Asbury Press, 1986).

121. *A Contemporary Wesleyan Theology,* gen. ed. Charles W. Carter, 2 vols. (Grand Rapids: Francis Asbury Press, 1983).

122. *The Reign of God: An Introduction to Christian Theology from a Seventh-day Adventist Perspective* (Berrien Springs, Mich.: Andrews University Press, 1985).

123. *Systematic Theology* (Oregon, Ill.: Restitution Herald, 1960).

124. (Cincinnati: God's Revivalist Office, 1911).

125. *Outline Studies in Christian Doctrine* (n.p.p.: Christian Alliance Publishing Company, 1916; Harrisburg, Pa.: Christian Publications, 1926).

126. *Foundations of Doctrine: In Scripture and Experience; A Students' Handbook on Holiness* (Winona Lake, Ind.: Free Methodist Publishing House, 1938; 4th ed. 1943).

127. *Christian Theology: A Systematic Statement of Christian Doctrine for the Use of Theological Students* (Anderson, Ind.: Gospel Trumpet Company, 1925; rev. ed. by Arlo F. Newell; Anderson, Ind.: Warner Press, 1982).

128. *Fundamental Christian Theology,* 2 vols. (Pasadena, Calif.: C. J. Kinne, 1931; one-vol. abr. ed. 1932).

129. *Christian Theology* (Kansas City, Mo.: Beacon Hill Press, 1940-52).

130. W. T. Purkiser, ed., *Exploring Our Christian Faith* (Kansas City, Mo.: Beacon Hill Press, 1960).

131. *Grace, Faith, and Holiness: A Wesleyan Systematic Theology* (Kansas City, Mo.: Beacon Hill Press, 1988).

11. Pentecostal/Charismatic

An Assemblies of God author, Myer Pearlman (1898-1943), produced a handbook on biblical doctrines,[132] and John Rodman Williams (1918-) has issued two volumes of a three-volume systematic theology.[133]

C. TYPES IN RELATION TO TWENTIETH-CENTURY MOVEMENTS

Systematic theologies have been written not only from presuppositions as to the proper source or sources and from particular denominational or confessional contexts but also as reflective of particular theological movements. The following examples are suggestive, not exhaustive.

1. Ritschlianism

The theology of the German Albrecht Ritschl issued in two groups of followers, a left wing and a right wing. The two-volume dogmatics by Theodor Haering (1848-1928)[134] was representative of the right wing, and the dogmatics by Wilhelm Herrmann (1846-1922)[135] of the left wing.

2. Modernism

Shailer Mathews (1863-1941) in his *The Faith of Modernism*[136] relied on the scientific method for the validation of religious truth.

3. Liberalism

Douglas Clyde Macintosh (1877-1948) was an exponent of experience-based theology.[137] Harry Emerson Fosdick (1878-1969), who wrote monographs on the Bible, on prayer, and on immortality, epitomized theological liberalism as a reconstruction of the old faith, although he did not produce a systematic theology. In later years Lotan Harold DeWolf (1905-), a Methodist,[138] and Langdon B. Gilkey,[139] a Baptist, expounded and/or defended theological liberalism. The writings of John A. T. Robinson and Maurice F. Wiles, previously cited, also belong under this category.

---

132. *Knowing the Doctrines of the Bible* (Springfield, Mo.: Gospel Publishing House, 1937).
133. *Renewal Theology: God, the World and Redemption: Systematic Theology from a Charismatic Perspective* (Grand Rapids: Zondervan, 1988); *Renewal Theology: Salvation, the Holy Spirit, and Christian Living* (ibid., 1990).
134. *The Christian Faith: A System of Dogmatics*, trans. John Dickie and George Ferries, 2 vols. (London, New York: Hodder and Stoughton, 1915).
135. *Systematic Theology*, trans. Nathaniel Micklem and Kenneth A. Saunders (London: G. Allen & Unwin, 1927).
136. (New York: Macmillan, 1924; reprint ed. New York: AMS Press, 1969). Mathews wrote monographs on God and on the work of Christ.
137. *Theology as an Empirical Science* (New York: Macmillan, 1919).
138. *A Theology of the Living Church* (New York: Harper and Brothers, 1953); *The Case for Theology in Liberal Perspective* (Philadelphia: Westminster Press, 1959).
139. *Message and Existence: An Introduction to Christian Theology*. Gilkey has authored monographs on creation, on theological language, and on theology of history.

4. Fundamentalism

Reuben Archer Torrey (1856-1928) wrote on the fundamentals, and B. B. Warfield gave attention to the doctrine of the Scriptures.[140] Although he did not write a systematic theology, John Gresham Machen (1881-1937) embodied the Fundamentalism of the 1920s, although not necessarily that of later decades.[141] The popular books by John Richard Rice (1895-1980)[142] were expressive of Fundamentalism after the midpoint of the century, although he did not write a systematic theology.

5. Neoorthodoxy

The works of Karl Barth, Emil Brunner, and John S. Whale, previously cited, were representative of Neoorthodoxy, as were Reinhold Niebuhr's *The Nature and Destiny of Man*[143] and the writings of William Edward Hordern (1920-).[144]

6. Existentialism

Rudolf Karl Bultmann was most representative of the impact of existentialism on Christian theology, although his contribution was made through a theology of the New Testament[145] rather than through systematic theology. A Dominican theologian, G. M. A. Jansen, clearly espoused an existentialist or "phenomenological" method.[146]

7. Ecumenism

Walter Marshall Horton (1895-1966) attempted to articulate a Christian theology that would serve the cause of ecumenism by giving to universal human questions ecumenical Christian answers.[147] Willem Adolph Visser 't Hooft (1900-1985), a leader in the Ecumenical Movement, produced monographs on the fatherhood of God and the kingship of Christ but not a systematic theology. Thomas Clark Oden (1931-), a

140. Torrey, *The Fundamental Doctrines of the Christian Faith* (New York: George H. Doran Company, 1918); Warfield, *Biblical Doctrines* (New York: Oxford University Press, 1929). Torrey also wrote monographs on the Bible, God, the person of Christ, the Holy Spirit, prayer, and the last things.
141. Machen was the author of monographs on the virgin birth of Jesus and on faith and of *Christianity and Liberalism* (New York: Macmillan, 1923).
142. Rice produced monographs on the Bible, the person and work of Christ, predestination, salvation, the Holy Spirit, prayer, stewardship, the millennium, and heaven.
143. This title was not inclusive enough to be reckoned a systematic theology but included more theological topics than humankind and sin.
144. *The Case for a New Reformation Theology* (Philadelphia: Westminster Press, 1959); *A Layman's Guide to Protestant Theology* (New York: Macmillan, 1955; rev. ed. 1968). Hordern has also written monographs on justification and on theological language.
145. *Theology of the New Testament*, trans. Kendrick Grobel, 2 vols. (New York: Scribner, 1951, 1955).
146. *An Existentialist Approach to Theology* (Milwaukee: Bruce Publishing Company, 1966).
147. *Christian Theology: An Ecumenical Approach* (New York: Harper and Brothers, 1955; rev. ed. 1958). Horton, who wrote a monograph on the doctrine of God, had shifted from liberalism toward Neoorthodoxy.

Methodist, has completed two volumes[148] of a multivolume ecumenical system by utilizing "constructive arguments from two millennia of ecumenical Christian thinking."

8. Historic Premillennialism

Perry Braxton Fitzwater (1871-1957),[149] Harold Lindsell (1913-) and Charles Jahleel Woodbridge (1902-),[150] and James Oliver Buswell, Jr. (1895-1977),[151] wrote systematic theologies that espoused the historic premillennial view of the return of Jesus Christ. The same is true of the more recent systems by Dale Moody and Millard J. Erickson, previously cited. George Eldon Ladd (1911-19?) through a theology of the New Testament[152] and other monographs and George Raymond Beasley-Murray (1916-) through monographs[153] have set forth historic premillennialism.

9. Amillennialism (Augustinian, Kliefothite)

The systems by Louis Berkhof, Milton S. Terry, R. R. Byrum, and T. P. Stafford and the later writing of Walter T. Conner, previously cited, were favorable to amillennialism, as was the system by Albertus Pieters (1869-1955).[154] Monographs pertinent to and supportive of amillennialism were written by Geerhardus Vos (1862-1949), Oswald Thompson Allis (1880-1973), William Hendriksen (1900-?), Floyd Eugene Hamilton (1890-?), George Lewis Murray (1896-?), Russell Bradley Jones (1894-?), Ray Summers (1910-), and Anthony Andrew Hoekema (1913-88).[155]

10. Postmillennialism (Whitbyite)

Augustus H. Strong in his *Systematic Theology*, previously cited, was favorable to postmillennialism, Loraine Boettner (1901-) expounded it in a monograph, and James Henry Snowden (1852-1936) and Roderick Campbell were favorable.

148. *The Living God*, vol. 1, *Systematic Theology* (San Francisco: Harper and Row, 1987), esp. pp. ix-x; *The Word of Life*, vol. 2, *Systematic Theology* (ibid., 1989).
149. *Christian Theology: A Systematic Presentation* (Grand Rapids: Eerdmans, 1948).
150. *A Handbook of Christian Truth* (Westwood, N.J.: Fleming H. Revell Company, 1953).
151. *A Systematic Theology of the Christian Religion*, 2 vols. (Grand Rapids: Zondervan Publishing House, 1962, 1963).
152. *A Theology of the New Testament* (1974). His monographs pertained to the last things and to the resurrection of Jesus.
153. On the kingdom of God; his other monographs have been on baptism and on the resurrection of Jesus.
154. *The Faith and Mysteries of the Christian Faith: A Brief Statement of the Things Christians Believe, and the Reasons Why They Believe Them* (Grand Rapids: Eerdmans, 1926; 2d ed. 1933; reprint 1939).
155. Hoekema authored monographs on the Holy Spirit, humans in the image of God, salvation, and the last things.

11. Dispensational Premillennialism

Lewis Sperry Chafer's *Systematic Theology,* previously cited, was expressive of dispensational premillennialism. Other systems committed to this position include those of William Evans (1870-1950),[156] Emery Herbert Bancroft (1877-1944),[157] Henry Clarence Thiessen (1885-1947),[158] Richard H. Bube (1927-   ),[159] Charles Caldwell Ryrie (1925-   ),[160] and Charles F. Baker.[161] Eschatological monographs by John Flipse Walvoord (1910-   ),[162] Charles Lee Feinberg (1909-   ),[163] and J. Dwight Pentecost (1915-) have reflected dispensationalism.

12. Process Theology

Theologians who have applied the process philosophy of Alfred North Whitehead and Charles F. Hartshorne[164] to Christian doctrines have included William Norman Pittenger (1905-   ),[165] John Boswell Cobb, Jr. (1925-   ),[166] and David Ray Griffin (1939-).[167]

156. *The Great Doctrines of the Bible* (Chicago: Moody, 1912; 1939; rev. ed. 1949). Evans authored monographs on the virgin birth of Jesus, prayer, and the last things.
157. *Christian Theology: Systematic and Biblical* (Bible School Park, N.Y.: Echoes Publishing House, 1925); under the title *Elemental Theology: Doctrinal and Conservative* (Grand Rapids: Zondervan, 1945); rev. ed. under the title *Christian Theology: Systematic and Biblical* (ibid., 1949); 4th ed., rev. Ronald B. Mayers, under the title *Elemental Theology: Doctrinal and Conservative* (ibid., 1977).
158. *An Outline of Lectures in Systematic Theology* (3d ed., rev.; Wheaton, Ill.: Wheaton College, 1942); *Introductory Lectures in Systematic Theology* (Grand Rapids: Eerdmans, 1949); rev. ed. Vernon D. Doerksen (ibid., 1979).
159. *To Every Man an Answer: A Systematic Study of the Scriptural Basis of Christian Doctrine* (Chicago: Moody Press, 1955).
160. *A Survey of Bible Doctrine* (Chicago: Moody Press, 1972); *Biblical Theology of the New Testament* (ibid., 1959). Ryrie has produced monographs on the last things, the Holy Spirit, and the Bible.
161. *A Dispensational Theology* (Grand Rapids: Grace Bible Publications, 1971).
162. Walvoord has written monographs on the Holy Spirit.
163. Especially on millennial views.
164. See below, Ch. 5, III, H.
165. *God in Process* (London: SCM Press, 1967); *Process-Thought and Christian Faith* (Digswell Place, Hertfordshire, U.K.: James Nisbet and Company, 1968); *'The Last Things' in a Process Perspective* (London: Epworth Press, 1970); *Unbounded Love: God and Man in Process* (New York: Seabury Press, 1976); *The Lure of Divine Love: Human Experience and Christian Faith in a Process Perspective* (New York: Pilgrim Press, 1979); *Catholic Faith in a Process Perspective* (Maryknoll, N.Y.: Orbis Books, 1981). Pittenger authored monographs on the person of Christ, the Holy Spirit, the Trinity, providence, humankind, the Christian life, and the sacraments.
166. *A Christian Natural Theology: Based on the Thought of Alfred North Whitehead* (Philadelphia: Westminster Press, 1965); *God and the World* (ibid., 1969); (with David Ray Griffin) *Process Theology: An Introductory Exposition* (ibid., 1976); *Process Theology as Political Theology* (Manchester: Manchester University Press; Philadelphia: Westminster Press, 1982).
167. *A Process Christology* (Philadelphia: Westminster Press, 1973); *God, Power, and Evil: A Process Theodicy* (ibid., 1976).

13. European Eschatological Theologies

Two European Protestant theologians, Jürgen Moltmann (1926-)[168] and Wolfhart Pannenberg (1928-),[169] have given impetus to eschatologically oriented theologies, the former giving attention to contemporary movements for social change and the latter moving Christianity's historical rootage from "holy history" to general or secular history.

14. Liberation Theology

Theologians, especially in Latin America, who have made the theme of economic and political liberation the major or controlling motif in Christian theology have included Rubem A. Alves (1933-)[170] of Brazil, José Míguez-Bonino (1924-)[171] of Argentina, Gustavo Gutiérrez (1928-)[172] of Peru, Paul Juan Luis Segundo, S.J. (1925-),[173] of Uruguay, Hugo Assman of Brazil and Costa Rica,[174] Leonardo Boff, O.F.M. (1938-),[175] of Brazil, and Frederick Herzog (1925-)[176] of the United States.

Black theology in the United States is a specialized form of liberation theology and is exhibited in the writings of James Deotis Roberts (1927-),[177] James H. Cone (1938-),[178] Warren Raymond Traynham

168. Moltmann, in addition to works that reoriented theology to eschatology, has produced monographs that treat the Trinity, creation, the person and work of Christ, humankind, the church, and the kingdom of God.
169. Pannenberg is the author of monographs on theological method, theology and science, humankind, the person and work of Christ, and the kingdom of God.
170. *A Theology of Human Hope* (Washington, D.C.: Corpus Books, 1971; St. Meinrad, Ind.: Abbey Press, 1975).
171. *Doing Theology in a Revolutionary Situation* (Philadelphia: Fortress Press, 1975); published also under the title *Revolutionary Theology Comes of Age* (London: S.P.C.K., 1975).
172. *A Theology of Liberation: History, Politics, and Salvation,* trans. and ed. Sister Caridad Inda and John Eagleson (Maryknoll, N.Y.: Orbis Books, 1973; rev. ed. 1988); (with M. Richard Shaull) *Liberation and Change* (Atlanta: John Knox Press, 1977).
173. *Liberation of Theology,* trans. John Drury (Maryknoll, N.Y.: Orbis Books, 1976); *Theology and the Church: A Response to Cardinal Ratzinger and a Warning to the Whole Church,* trans. John W. Diercksmeier (Minneapolis: Winston Press; London: G. Chapman, 1985).
174. *Theology for a Nomad Church,* trans. Paul Burns (Maryknoll, N.Y.: Orbis Books, 1976).
175. *Jesus Christ Liberator: A Critical Christology for Our Time,* trans. Patrick Hughes (Maryknoll, N.Y.: Orbis Books, 1978); *Liberating Grace,* trans. John Drury (ibid., 1979); *The Lord's Prayer: The Prayer of Integral Liberation,* trans. Theodore Morrow (Melbourne: Dove Communications; Maryknoll, N.Y.: Orbis Books, 1983); (with Clodovis Boff) *Salvation and Liberation,* trans. Robert R. Barr (Maryknoll, N.Y.: Orbis Books, 1984); *Passion of Christ, Passion of the World: The Facts, Their Interpretation, and Their Meaning Yesterday and Today,* trans. Robert R. Barr (ibid., 1987); (with Clodovis Boff) *Introducing Liberation Theology,* trans. Paul Burns (ibid., 1987).
176. *Liberation Theology: Liberation in the Light of the Fourth Gospel* (New York: Seabury Press, 1972); *God-Walk: Liberation Shaping Dogmatics* (Maryknoll, N.Y.: Orbis Books, 1988).
177. *Liberation and Reconciliation: A Black Theology* (Philadelphia: Westminster Press, 1971); *A Black Political Theology* (ibid., 1974); *Black Theology Today: Liberation and Contextualization,* Toronto Studies in Theology, vol. 12 (New York: Edwin Mellen Press, 1983).
178. *Black Theology and Black Power* (New York: Seabury Press, 1969); *A Black Theology of Liberation* (Philadelphia: Lippincott, 1970; 2d ed., Maryknoll, N.Y.: Orbis Books, 1986); *For*

(1936-),[179] and William Ronald Jones.[180] Feminist theology has been represented by the writings of Rosemary Radford Ruether (1936-).[181]

Liberation theology has also been undertaken in Asia by a Jesuit theologian, Aloysius Pieris.[182] The structure of books reflective of liberation theology tends to be quite different from traditional approaches to systematic theology in the Western Christian tradition.

15. Narrative Theology

A recently employed method of approaching systematic theology has been the narrative method, but its precise nature is not altogether clear.[183] One form attempts to set forth Christian doctrines in a narrative framework, which method resembles that of biblical theology with its focus on the mighty acts of God. Another form seeks to utilize the life stories or religious experiences of key Christian leaders as a teaching device to show how beliefs have shaped lives.[184] Still others, notably Gabriel Joseph Fackre (1926-), would seek in some way to utilize narrative as a leading motif in the writing of systematic theology.[185]

16. Conservative Evangelicalism

The systems by G. C. Berkouwer, by Millard J. Erickson, and by Bruce A. Demarest and Gordon R. Lewis, previously cited, are to be reckoned as expressive of the views of conservative evangelicals, although other earlier systems could also be so classified. The same may be said for the monographs by John R. W. Stott, James I. Packer, and Michael Green, also previously cited. Other works representative of this general position include Edward John Carnell's (1919-67) *The Case for Orthodox Theology*,[186] Carl Ferdinand Howard Henry's (1913-) six-volume *God, Revelation, and Authority*,[187] Bernard L. Ramm's (1916-) monographs on

My People: Black Theology and the Black Church (Maryknoll, N.Y.: Orbis Books, 1984); *My Soul Looks Black* (Nashville: Abingdon Press, 1982; Maryknoll, N.Y.: Orbis Books, 1986); *Speaking the Truth: Ecumenism, Liberation, and Black Theology* (Grand Rapids: Eerdmans, 1986).

179. *Christian Faith in Black and White: A Primer in Theology from the Black Perspective* (Wakefield, Mass.: Parameter Press, 1973).

180. *Is God a White Racist? A Preamble to Black Theology* (Garden City, N.Y.: Anchor Press, 1973).

181. *Liberation Theology: Human Hope Confronts Christian History and American Power* (New York: Paulist Press, 1972); *Mary, the Feminine Face of the Church* (Philadelphia: Westminster Press, 1977); *Sexism and God-Talk: Toward a Feminist Theology* (Boston: Beacon Press, 1983).

182. *An Asian Theology of Liberation* (Maryknoll, N.Y.: Orbis Books, 1988).

183. See George W. Stroup, *The Promise of Narrative Theology: Recovering the Gospel in the Church* (Atlanta: John Knox Press, 1981), ch. 3.

184. James William McClendon, Jr., *Biography as Theology* (Nashville: Abingdon Press, 1974).

185. *The Christian Story*; vol. 1, *A Narrative Interpretation of Basic Christian Doctrine* (Grand Rapids: Eerdmans, 1978; rev. ed. 1984); vol. 2, *Authority: Scripture in the Church for the World* (ibid., 1987).

186. (Philadelphia: Westminster Press, 1959).

187. (Waco, Tex.: Word Books, 1976-83). Henry wrote a monograph on God and edited several symposia.

biblical hermeneutics and authority, science and Scripture, special revelation, sin, the Holy Spirit, Christology, and glorification, Walter Ralston Martin's (1928-) handbook geared to the refutation of cults,[188] Donald G. Bloesch's (1928-) two-volume *Essentials of Evangelical Theology*,[189] and John Jefferson Davis's (1946-) *Foundations of Evangelical Theology*.[190]

Some books on systematic theology do not lend themselves readily to such classification as has been attempted and seem either to be *sui generis* or to belong to a comprehensive category of Protestant theology. Such would seem to be true of the writings of Clarence Augustine Beckwith (1849-1931),[191] William Adams Brown (1865-1943),[192] Nathaniel Micklem (1886-1976),[193] Nels Fredrick Solomon Ferré (1908-71),[194] Charles S. Duthie (1911-),[195] Gordon Dester Kaufman (1925-),[196] John C. Meyer (1934-),[197] Thomas N. Finger,[198] and Kenneth Cauthen (1930-).[199]

From the study of the scope of systematic theology, both its relation to other theological disciplines and its own subdivisions, from some inquiry as to the sources Christian theologians do use and should use and as to the relative importance of these sources, and from a rather detailed review of various types of systematic theology that have come to be during the twentieth century, one should now have a somewhat clearer and more precise understanding of what systematic theology is.

188. *Essential Christianity: A Handbook of Basic Christian Doctrines* (Grand Rapids: Zondervan, 1962).
189. (San Francisco: Harper and Row, 1978, 1979). Bloesch also has produced monographs on the Trinity and on salvation.
190. (Grand Rapids: Baker Book House, 1984).
191. *Realities of Christian Theology: An Interpretation of Christian Experience* (Boston: Houghton, Mifflin, and Company, 1906).
192. *Christian Theology in Outline* (New York: Charles Scribner's Sons, 1916). A Presbyterian, Brown did not expound Reformed theology per se; he was more open to the Roman Catholic tradition than most Protestants of his day.
193. *The Creed of a Christian: Being Monologues upon Great Themes of the Christian Faith* (London: SCM Press, 1940).
194. Ferré authored numerous volumes of a doctrinal nature, including monographs on faith and reason, God, the person and work of Christ, good and evil, the Christian life and prayer, the church, and Christianity and religions.
195. *Outline of Christian Belief* (London: Lutterworth Press; Nashville: Abingdon, 1968).
196. *Systematic Theology: A Historicist Perspective* (New York: Scribner's, 1968).
197. *Christian Beliefs and Teachings* (Washington: D.C.: University Press of America, 1981).
198. *Christian Theology: An Eschatological Approach*, vol. 1 (Nashville: Thomas Nelson, 1985). Finger abandons the traditional order of topics, commences with eschatology, and provides an alternate sequence.
199. *Systematic Theology: A Modern Protestant Approach*, Toronto Studies in Theology, vol. 25 (Lewiston, N.Y.: Edwin Mellen Press, 1986).

PART I

Revelation and the Bible

CHAPTER 3

What Is "Revelation"?
General Revelation

Where should one begin the exposition of the doctrines of the Christian religion in a systematic theology, once one has completed the prolegomena? Some would affirm that one should commence with the existence and nature of God himself. Others would contend that one should begin with God's making himself known to humankind and thus how human beings know God. Good arguments can be advanced on behalf of each approach. We shall opt for the second approach, partly because the doctrine of revelation has been so very important for Christian theology during the twentieth century.

I. WHAT IS "REVELATION"?

The term "revelation," which is so basic to present-day Christian theological writings, may be defined by examining its etymology, its New Testament uses, and its modern theological significance.

A. ETYMOLOGY

The English term "revelation" is derived from the Latin noun *revelatio,* which is a translation of the Greek noun *apokalypsis.* Etymologically the term means an "unveiling" and hence a disclosure.

B. NEW TESTAMENT USAGES

1. The word appears in the title of the last book of our New Testament canon, and hence this book is called the Revelation, or the Apocalypse. By such a title the book is linked to the intertestamental and noncanonical "apocalyptic" writings of the Jews with their theme of sudden, decisive divine intervention.

2. The word is one of three Greek nouns used in the New Testament, chiefly by Paul, to refer to the second coming of Jesus Christ.[1]

---

1. See Part IX, Ch. 84.

3. The word did not become for the New Testament authors a comprehensive, oft-used term for God's action(s) of self-disclosure to human beings. The words of Emil Brunner serve as a clarifying reminder:

> Neither in the Old Testament nor in the New Testament is there a word that corresponds to our theological idea of 'revelation'. The Old Testament has a number of words for this: God allows Himself to be seen, to be known, to be discovered; above all, God speaks; revelation is also meant where the event is described purely from its subjective human aspect; a seeing, a hearing, a beholding, a knowing, a perceiving. . . . The same is true of the New Testament; not only *apokalyptein* and *phaneroun* but a number of other words describe that which we gather up under the one heading of 'revelation': *dēloun, gnōrizein, lalein, phōtizein,* and also nouns like *logos, phōs, alētheia*.[2]

C. THEOLOGICAL USAGE

1. The concept of revelation has been of great importance in modern Christian theology. Theologically the term means the self-disclosure of deity to humankind. John Baillie defined it as "the lifting of an obscuring veil, so as to disclose something that was formerly hidden."[3]

2. A claim to revelation is basic to many, if not to all religions. "Revelation is one of the fundamental words of religion. . . . The concept of revelation . . . is as widespread as the idea of God."[4] Even nontheistic religions claim that ultimate meaning or truth is disclosed or is discoverable.

3. Revelation involves both a Revealer and the recipients of the revelation. "By a revelation of himself we mean that somehow God has put himself within the range of man's knowing powers."[5] Divine revelation has come to humans in their total situation. Its recipients have lived amid their quest for meaning, their grandeur and misery, their conscience and guilt, their eagerness to know their origin and their destiny, their capacity for God and their kinship to the animals, and their mortality and yearning for life after death. But human self-understanding, including a grasp of one's origin, nature, and destiny, is actually dependent on a "breakthrough" from the outside; that is, it is dependent on what Christians speak of as "divine revelation."[6]

4. Revelation, in the distinctive Jewish, Christian, and Islamic senses of that concept, comes through the medium of history. This will become more evident in the examination of what has been called "special revelation" or "historical revelation." John Macquarrie has differentiated between " 'classic' or 'primordial' revelations on which communities of faith get founded, and the subsequent experience of the community in which

---

2. *Revelation and Reason,* p. 21, n. 4.
3. *The Idea of Revelation in Recent Thought* (New York: Columbia University Press, 1956), p. 19.
4. Brunner, *Revelation and Reason,* p. 20.
5. Conner, *Revelation and God,* p. 45.
6. *A New Catechism: Catholic Faith for Adults,* pp. 3-22.

the primordial revelation keeps coming alive, so to speak, in the ongoing life of the community so that the original disclosure of the holy is being continually renewed." The latter, according to Macquarrie, can be called " 'repetitive' revelation."[7]

5. Revelation, in the distinctive Christian sense, is not merely God's making available information about himself but the personal unveiling of God that transforms and reconciles the believing recipient of the revelation. Early in the present century E. Y. Mullins wrote: "On the human side revelation is primarily a spiritual transaction rather than mere illumination of the intellect."[8] Later in the century Protestants have engaged in extensive theological debate as to whether revelation is primarily or solely propositional or is primarily or solely relational. We will treat this issue in greater detail later in this volume.[9]

6. Protestant and Roman Catholic theologians have understood the mediation or transmission of revelation according to various models.[10]

II. GENERAL REVELATION

A. Its Definition and Differentiation from Special Revelation

"General" revelation is that disclosure of God which is available to all human beings through the created universe (nature) and in the inner nature of human beings (conscience).[11] On the contrary, "special" revelation is the historical disclosure of God to the people of Israel and in Jesus Christ. The distinctly Christian revelation of God is, therefore, special or historical revelation.

B. The Biblical Witness to General Revelation

Although the content and means of general revelation differ from those of that special revelation which is recorded in the Bible, the Bible itself does, strange as it may seem, bear witness to or teach the reality of general revelation. We will now examine in some detail the specific biblical texts that give witness to general revelation.

---

7. *Principles of Christian Theology,* pp. 80-81.
8. *The Christian Religion in Its Doctrinal Expression,* p. 141.
9. See Part I, Ch. 7, II, A, 3.
10. Avery Dulles, S.J., *Models of Revelation* (New York: Image Books, 1985), has differentiated five models: the doctrinal (Neo-Scholastics, Conservative Evangelicals); the historical (salvation history; universal history); the experiential (modernists, mystics); the dialectical presence (Neoorthodoxy); and the new awareness (Gregory Baum, Karl Rahner, Paul Tillich). Dulles has argued for another model: "symbolic mediation."
11. Somewhat different is the definition by William W. Stevens, *Doctrines of the Christian Religion,* p. 15, who tends to equate "general revelation" with "that which can be acquired by reason through a study of nature." Millard J. Erickson, *Christian Theology,* pp. 154-55, includes "history" as one of the avenues of general revelation, but in doing so he merely borrows from the content of the doctrine of providence and does not explain how the various histories of nations and cultures are revelatory.

1. Analysis of Biblical Texts That Seemingly Teach General Revelation

a. Revelation in and through the Created Universe

1) Psalm 19:1-6

The heavens declare the glory of God;
   the skies proclaim the work of his hands.
Day after day they pour forth speech;
   night after night they display knowledge.
There is no speech or language
   where their voice is not heard.
Their voice goes out into all the earth,
   their words to the ends of the world. (vv. 1-4, NIV)

The psalmist declares that the created universe embodies a manifestation or revelation of God. That revelation is not defined more explicitly than in the term "glory" and the name "God" ('*El*, the God of power). Verses 1-6 are joined to a context (19:7-11) in which the law of God is also discussed. Some contend that any apprehension of such a revelation through the heavens depended in the psalmist's time on being in covenant relation with Yahweh and hence having the Torah. Accordingly, only those who had special revelation (the Israelites) could apprehend general revelation. But verses 1-6 do not compel such an interpretation, and the Apostle Paul was much clearer as to universality.

2) Romans 1:18-32

Seven features of this passage are pertinent to the doctrine of general revelation.

a) Paul teaches that there is and has been a revelation of God through the created universe (v. 20a).

b) This revelation has existed since the creation of humankind and existed in Paul's day (v. 20). Hence this is not a revelation given only to unfallen Adam and Eve; it has indeed been given to all fallen humanity as well.

c) This revelation has been made to all humankind and hence is universal, as verse 18 implies.

d) This revelation embraces "the eternal power and deity" of God (v. 20).

e) This revelation carries with it a serious responsibility or accountability for one's response to it (v. 20c).

f) This revelation has not been accepted and implemented but rejected and corrupted by human beings in the context of the universality of sin (vv. 18, 21-32).

g) This revelation through the created universe, as also the revelation through the inner nature of human beings, does not provide an experiential knowledge of the true God despite one's sin but rather is the source of human idolatry (v. 25). "The sinful human being is a vessel in which the lees of sin transform the wine of the knowledge given by God into the vinegar of idolatry."[12]

3) Acts 14:17

In his sermon at Lystra, "his first to a pagan audience" according to Acts, Paul urged his hearers to turn from idolatry to the Creator God. The apostle acknowledged, " 'In past generations he [God] allowed all the nations to walk in their own ways' " (v. 16, RSV). He insisted: " 'yet he did not leave himself without witness, for he did good and gave you from heaven rains and fruitful seasons, satisfying your hearts with food and gladness' " (v. 17). The text suggests some revelation of God in and through nature. "It was not through the power of the fertility gods that they received their food," but through the one true God, "the controller of nature."[13]

b. Revelation in and through the Inner, Created Nature of Human Beings

1) Acts 17:26-28

In his sermon amid the Areopagus in Athens Paul, having referred to an altar " 'to an unknown God,' " proclaimed God as Creator of all, not living in human shrines or dependent on human ministrations, but the Giver of life and breath to all humans (17:23-25).

> And he made from one every nation of men to live on all the face of the earth, having determined allotted periods and the boundaries of their habitation, that they should seek God, in the hope that surely then they might feel after him and find him. Yet he is not far from each of us, for
>
> "In him we live and move and have our being";
> as indeed some of your poets have said,
> "For we are indeed his offspring." (vv. 26-28, RSV)

Paul was teaching that God created human beings so that they might seek and find him and documented this human quest by quoting Stoic authors. Taylor Clarence Smith (1915-) has concluded that Paul's first quotation "is possibly a modification of part of a poem by Epimenides, a sage of Greece in the sixth century B.C. who came from the island of Crete," and that his second is derived "from Aratus (*Phaenomena,* line 5), the poet from Tarsus in the fourth century B.C. who greatly influenced Stoic thought." Paul's point is simply this: "Since the Stoics themselves admit that man depends entirely upon God, why should they give credence to idols?"[14] The quotations, therefore, are designed to show the folly of idolatry, not the salvific or redemptive effect of this revelation of God.

---

12. Brunner, *Revelation and Reason,* p. 65.
13. T. C. Smith, *Acts,* vol. 10 of *Broadman Bible Commentary,* ed. Clifton J. Allen (Nashville: Broadman Press, 1970), p. 88.
14. Smith, *Acts,* p. 104.

2) Romans 2:14-16

> When Gentiles who have not the law do by nature what the law requires, they are a law to themselves, even though they do not have the law. They show that what the law requires is written on their hearts, while their conscience also bears witness and their conflicting thoughts accuse or perhaps excuse them on that day when, according to my gospel, God judges the secrets of men by Christ Jesus. (RSV)

This passage, according to Dale Moody,

> is intended to make clear that there is a type of law in general revelation apart from the Mosaic law in special revelation. . . . Gentiles may come to a knowledge of God through the light of creation (Rom. 1:19f) and conscience (2:14f). Paul . . . here has in mind the pagan conscience, despite Luther and Karl Barth. . . . Calvin was wiser than Luther on this point. . . . Paul's gospel declared that the final judgment would be by Jesus Christ. . . . The truth in creation and conscience by general revelation and the truth in the old covenant find fulfilment and will be finally judged in the light of the gospel of Jesus Christ.[15]

Bernard Ramm has called this "the inner moral dialogue,"[16] and G. C. Berkouwer has interpreted this passage to mean that "even in estrangement some connection remains between men and God."[17]

2. *Exposition of the Biblical Doctrine of General Revelation*

Having completed the analysis of the pertinent biblical passages, we must now seek an overview of the meanings of these texts in relation to the twentieth-century treatments of the concept of general revelation.[18] What are the proper conclusions to be drawn from the biblical texts?

a. The biblical writers did not seek to prove the existence of God by formal argument but rather assumed that God was on the scene of action. The biblical doctrine of God's revelation in the created universe and in human beings is that of a divine disclosure of the being and power of God, not a formal proof of the existence of God such as Thomas Aquinas utilized in the opening pages of his *Summa Theologica*.[19]

b. The revelation in the created universe and in human conscience

15. Dale Moody, *Romans*, vol. 10 of *Broadman Bible Commentary*, ed. Clifton J. Allen (Nashville: Broadman Press, 1970), pp. 175-76.

16. *Special Revelation and the Word of God* (Grand Rapids: Eerdmans, 1961), p. 17.

17. "General and Special Revelation," in Carl F. H. Henry, ed., *Revelation and the Bible* (Grand Rapids: Baker Book House, 1958), p. 20.

18. The most recent comprehensive study of general revelation is Bruce A. Demarest, *General Revelation: Historical Views and Contemporary Issues* (Grand Rapids: Zondervan, 1982), who contends that every human being "effably intuits (in the first moment of mental and moral self-consciousness)," apart from the will and with the help of "a general illumination," "eternal changeless truths, including the reality of God," that he "also infers the existence and character of God by rational reflection on the data of the created universe," and that he nevertheless "*consistently suppresses all forms of general revelation*" by turning from the worship and service of the Creator to idolatry (pp. 22-23, 228-29, 233, 241, 244-47).

19. 1.2.

ought to be differentiated from "natural theology." Admittedly there are various legitimate usages of the term "natural theology," and these will be listed in a later chapter.[20] Here we will consider only two definitions.

1) Two-story view

"Natural theology" has been used to refer to a natural and rationally discoverable foundation of the knowledge of God to which "supernatural revelation" has been added as the superstructure. Such a definition underlies the theology of Thomas Aquinas and the teaching of Vatican Council I.[21]

2) Competitive view

"Natural theology" has been defined by Emil Brunner as "the knowledge of God based on purely rational grounds, independent of the Christian revelation of salvation and therefore in competition with it. . . ."[22] General revelation, Millard J. Erickson has concluded, "cannot be used to construct a natural theology."[23] The opposite is also true: natural theology cannot be constitutive of general revelation.

c. General revelation helps "to explain the worldwide phenomenon of religion and religions."[24] The widespread occurrence of human beings as religious is explicable on the basis that they have an awareness, even if corrupted and misused, of God. The Christian missionary does not take the entire awareness of God to non-Christian peoples but wisely builds on that foundation.[25]

d. General revelation, therefore, affords "a common ground or a point of contact between the believer and the nonbeliever, or between the gospel and the thinking of the unbeliever."[26] Hence the Christian gospel is not to be flung at human beings as if they were inanimate objects or animals but instead addressed to "areas of sensitivity" such as one supreme deity, creation, human accountability, and the like.

e. General revelation is thus, as Paul argued in his Epistle to the Romans, the ground of or basis for the accountability of all human beings to God; for Paul, this was especially true of the Gentiles. The Pauline

---

20. See Part I, Ch. 5, II.

21. *Summa Contra Gentiles* 1.3.2; 1.9; *Summa Theologica* 1.12.12-13; Vatican Council I, *Dogmatic Decree on the Catholic Faith and the Church of Christ*, ch. 2.

22. *Revelation and Reason*, p. 61. Brunner and Karl Barth engaged in vigorous debate during the 1940s on issues centering in general revelation. Barth identified natural theology and general revelation as synonymous and rejected both as far as any true and efficacious knowledge of God is concerned. Brunner criticized Barth for failing to differentiate natural theology from general revelation and rationalistic systems from God's self-disclosure in the created universe and in the inner nature of human beings. Brunner taught general revelation and rejected natural theology (as he defined it).

23. *Christian Theology*, p. 171.

24. Ibid., p. 174.

25. This topic will be further treated in Part I, Ch. 4, V.

26. Erickson, *Christian Theology*, p. 173.

"without excuse" conclusion is basic to the thought of Romans and should inform a multicontinent Christian theology of missions at the end of the twentieth century.

f. General revelation, as received and applied, does not, according to Paul, furnish human beings with a sufficient, effective, and redemptive knowledge of God and his will.

1) This revelation has been darkened and corrupted by human sin. Humans do not in response live up to the light and truth of this revelation.[27]

2) This revelation provides some knowledge of God as the powerful Creator and the faithful Sustainer of the universe and of human existence, but it cannot and does not provide a transforming knowledge of the holy love and redeeming grace of God on behalf of sinful human beings.

3) Paradoxically, this revelation is sufficient for the condemnation of humans as sinners but not sufficient in itself for the redemption or salvation of humans from sin and into the fellowship of God.[28]

The foregoing exposition of the biblical doctrine of general revelation represents essentially the same view as was advanced by John Calvin[29] during the sixteenth century and has been articulated more fully by Emil Brunner during the twentieth century. But inasmuch as other approaches to general revelation have been advocated during the twentieth century, it is important now to examine such alternate positions.

C. OTHER CONTEMPORARY APPROACHES TO THE DOCTRINE OF GENERAL REVELATION

1. *Denial of the Existence or Occurrence of General Revelation (Karl Barth)*

a. Barth's Interpretation of Romans 1:18-32

How did Barth interpret this passage in his *The Epistle to the Romans*? Those "who hold the truth imprisoned in unrighteousness" are taken to be people who have exalted themselves in an idolatrous fashion so that God's righteousness is imprisoned or encased. For Barth, "That which may be known of God is manifest unto them" means the "truth concerning the limiting and dissolving of men by the unknown God, which breaks forth in the [final] resurrection," not the present knowledge of his "everlasting power and deity." The Swiss theologian understands "For the

---

27. This corruption is more pervasive than a mere second- and third-generation religious phenomenon, as Dallas Roark, *The Christian Faith,* pp. 45-46, has suggested.

28. See Brunner, *Revelation and Reason,* pp. 65-66.

29. The primary text is the first book of his *Institutes of the Christian Religion* (1559 ed.), although Calvin's teachings on how humans know God are also scattered throughout his writings. See Kenneth Sealer Kantzer, "John Calvin's Theory of the Knowledge of God and the Word of God" (Ph.D. diss., Harvard University, 1950), in which Kantzer (1917-) finds "common grace" rather than general revelation to be, for Calvin, the source of the unregenerate person's knowledge of God the Creator (esp. pp. 372-92).

invisible things of God are clearly seen" to refer to the rediscovery or remembrance of "the archetypal, unobservable, undiscoverable Majesty of God." Barth alludes here to animals, not to the total created universe. Paul's words "his everlasting power and divinity" are identified with "the gospel of the resurrection." "So that they are without excuse" means human "godlessness" and "unrighteousness." On and on the Barthian exegesis goes, and one gets the impression that for Barth Romans 1 either means a Platonic remembering of an eternity past or an anticipation of the Christian fulfillment of the last days, neither of which allows for general revelation in the present.[30]

In his *Church Dogmatics*[31] Barth held that Rom. 1:18-32 refers to those who have already received special revelation.

b. The Barthian Conclusion

Barth equated general revelation and natural theology and rejected both. Consequently, for Barth, since there is no general revelation of God whatsoever, the only kind of divine revelation is what others call special revelation. Hendrik Kraemer, the missiologist who was influenced by Barth, called the term "general revelation" "one of the most misleading and confusing terms possible" and stated that it "ought to be abolished." But Kraemer's objection arose from his recognizing that "general revelation" had so often been used as a synonym for "natural theology" and his holding that "natural theology" is far different from Rom. 1:18-32.[32]

2. *General Revelation as Being, at Least to an Extent, Salvific or Redemptive*

a. Biblical Texts Most Often Cited in Support

Advocates of this view tend to cite two texts among those already analyzed, namely, Acts 17:27, with emphasis on "and find him," and Rom. 2:15, with emphasis on "perhaps excuse them." They also cite and stress John 1:9, two translations of which are as follows:

> There was the true light, even the light which
> lighteth every man, coming into the world. (ASV)

> There was the true light which, coming into the
> world, enlightens every man. (NASV)

Certain questions have been raised regarding these texts. Does Paul's reference in his Areopagus sermon to seeking and finding God mean finding God's mercy, forgiveness, and grace apart from the historic

30. Trans. Edwyn C. Hoskyns (London: Oxford University Press, 1933), pp. 42-48.
31. II/1, trans. T. H. L. Parker, W. B. Johnston, Harold Knight, and J. L. M. Haire (Edinburgh: T. & T. Clark, 1957), p. 119.
32. *Religion and the Christian Faith*, pp. 340-59, esp. 342.

Jesus and his death? If the thoughts of human beings excuse them, does this mean that these persons have been excused by and reconciled to God? How does the Logos enlighten every human being? Do all humans effectively receive this enlightenment, or do only certain humans effectively receive it? Is this illumination by the universal Logos redemptive apart from the incarnation and death-resurrection of the Logos and a faith-response to the incarnate, crucified, and risen Jesus Christ? Those who hold to this third position concerning general revelation normally give affirmative and sympathetic answers to these questions.

b. Some Recent and Varied Statements of This View

1) Romans 1–2 as referring collectively, not individually, to the Gentiles (Hans Küng)

The general revelation taught by Paul in Romans 1–2 is said to have a collective, not an individual, significance.

> But this does not amount to a judgment on the salvation or damnation of an individual pagan. For the question being asked here is not about the fate of individual pagans before Christ but about the responsibility and guilt of both groups of pre-Christian mankind, Jews and gentiles alike.[33]

2) The faint revelation of God's mercy and the clear revelation of God's wrath (Eric C. Rust)

> The background of general revelation must not be viewed negatively. Man in his sin did grasp in his religious consciousness some significant aspects of the divine nature and purpose. His religious imagination did weave some images and patterns of the invisible reality which foreshadowed the truth that was to come. Even though he experienced the living God more as wrath than as grace, even though his religious consciousness was strangely perverted by sin, we cannot see secular history wholly in a negative way. Something of God was breaking through. God's mercy was being faintly recognized, and the light that lightens every man by coming into the world was dispelling man's darkness.[34]

3) The preexistent Logos and the Noahic covenant (John Baillie, 1888-1960, Dale Moody)

Baillie's argument may be summarized as follows. Since "in Hebrew thought revelation is always conceived as being given within a covenant relationship," since we have the record of a covenant which God made with Noah which included "the whole human race before it was divided into the Shemites, the Hamites, and the sons of Japheth," and since the Noahic covenant was the "most appealed to in later Judaism," the Noahic covenant, not Stoicism, stood behind Paul's thought in Romans 1–2. Thus

---

33. "The World Religions in God's Plan of Salvation," in Joseph Neuner, ed., *Christian Revelation and World Religions* (London: Burns & Oates, 1967), p. 43.

34. *Salvation History* (Richmond, Va.: John Knox Press, 1962), p. 33.

"any measure of authentic insight" in the sacred books of ethnic religions "was in fact the fruit of God's historical dealings with the souls of the peoples concerned."[35] Moody agreed with Baillie's position.[36]

c. Salvific Dimensions of This View

Certain individual Christian thinkers, notably Justin Martyr (?-165) in the second century and Ulrich Zwingli in the sixteenth, have taught the divine salvation of leading Greek philosophers. In the twentieth century the arena of effective divine salvation has been extended by some Christian thinkers to include modern leaders in or members of non-Christian religions, such as Mohandas Karamchand Gandhi (1869-1948). Hence among such thinkers the line of the "saved" outside biblical history and outside church history has been extended so as to run from Plato (c. 428-c. 348 B.C.) to Gandhi.

But the Christian churches have not, at least until Vatican Council II, pronounced on or clearly affirmed with certitude as salvific or redemptive the effects of general revelation. The issue has generally been left to the arena of the unknown dimension of the outworking of God's grace and providence. During the nineteenth and twentieth centuries, for Protestants especially, the missionary movement has both raised the possibility of such salvation apart from specific faith in the incarnate, crucified, and risen Jesus as the Son of God and reemphasized the exclusive character of salvation only through Jesus Christ.

This third option as to general revelation tends to give support to this wider line of salvation apart from the specifics of the Christian gospel.

D. CONCLUSIONS CONCERNING GENERAL REVELATION

The three major viewpoints among twentieth-century Protestant theologians about general revelation can be instructive for all who would seek to draw proper conclusions on this subject. The Barthian view is right in stressing that revelation must necessarily proceed from the initiative of God but seems wrongly to deny the genuineness of that general revelation which the Apostle Paul affirmed. The view of Küng, Baillie, and others is right in stressing that Christians should not limit unduly the theater of God's revelatory activity but seems to go beyond the New Testament in affirming the salvific character of general revelation. The view of Calvin and Brunner is right in stressing that God reveals himself both in creation and in redemption but seems not to provide an adequate answer to the problem as to a revelation that is adequate to condemn but not to save.

Yet the last view, that of Calvin and Brunner, though not without problems, seems to be most consistent with biblical teaching, especially that of Paul.

---

35. *The Idea of Revelation in Recent Thought*, pp. 125-33.
36. *The Word of Truth*, p. 61.

CHAPTER 4

Revelation, Religion, and Religions

The entire concept of a divine self-disclosure through the created universe and through conscience easily and naturally leads to the question as to whether various religions practiced among the peoples of mankind are to be connected essentially with such divine revelation. Hence the topic of revelation, religion, and religions seems to follow closely on general revelation.

I. SOME DEFINITIONS OF "RELIGION"

How ought one to understand the English word "religion," whose Latin root suggests the idea of binding? Definitions of the term "religion" are quite numerous, and it is not possible here to explore all of them. Instead we will note five definitions.

First, it is possible to define religion as the relationship of human beings to one Supreme Being. This is a theistic definition of the term that does not strictly apply to religions that have no concept of a God or of gods.

Second, one can define religion as the relationship of human beings to the object of their supreme devotion. This is a more inclusive definition than the first. Under such a definition, for example, Marxist-Leninism would be considered a religion, whereas under the first definition it would not.

Third, religion can be defined as "the response by the totality of man's being to the totality of existence."[1] Such a definition serves to emphasize the complete involvement of human beings in religious commitment but can also be used of pantheistic forms of religion.

Fourth, religion can be defined as "that complex of phenomena, permeated by symbol and expressed in creed-code-cult, which accompanies . . . the experience of the Transcendent."[2]

---

1. Kraemer, *Religion and the Christian Faith*, p. 38.
2. Paul Knitter, "Christianity as Religion: True and Absolute? A Roman Catholic Perspective," in Mircea Eliade and David Tracy, eds., *What Is Religion? An Inquiry for Christian Theology*, Concilium, vol. 136 (New York: Seabury Press, 1980), p. 12.

Fifth, religion is "the human attitude towards a world beyond, which is unquestionably assumed as the authentic and authoritative reality and the relation to which finds its expression in a body of myth, rite and individual and social behaviour."[3] Both the fourth and the fifth definitions focus on beliefs, ethics, and worship as being characteristic of religion.

Whatever definition or definitions of religion may be employed, it should be clearly recognized that religion is a widespread phenomenon among humankind, if not indeed absolutely universal.

II. THE ORIGIN OF RELIGION

The study of the origin of religion has not been confined to Christian theologians. Modern philosophers, sociologists, psychologists, and comparative religionists have entered into this arena, expounding diverse and varied theories as to this origin. Christian systematic theology hardly permits a detailed treatment of these many theories. Hendrik Kraemer, who treated these with careful specificity, differentiated naturalistic or immanental theories that find no transhuman factor in the origin, philosophical theories of various types, and theological theories, examples of which extend throughout Christian history from Justin Martyr to Vatican Council II.[4] The naturalistic theories are incompatible with general revelation. General revelation is most fully harmonizable with theological theories.

III. CHRISTIANITY'S CONFRONTATION WITH NON-CHRISTIAN RELIGIONS

Today there is a major crisis in the relation of the Christian revelation to non-Christian religions. In 1938 Hendrik Kraemer described the twentieth-century crisis as consisting of a "Western crisis," precipitated by the rise of relativism and secularism, and an "Eastern crisis," resulting from the penetration of the West into the East. "The Christian Church in the West and the East, despite the difference in background and history, is virtually confronted with the same fundamental problem: the relation to the world and all its spheres of life, and the same danger lest it solve it in the wrong way."[5]

In 1956 Kraemer more pointedly underscored the inevitability of a more thoroughgoing encounter of the Christian faith with religion and religions because of (a) the nature of the biblical message; (b) the present unprecedented interdependence of all parts of the world and the recognition of the fact of religious pluralism; and (c) the missionary character of

3. Kraemer, *Religion and the Christian Faith,* p. 37.
4. *Religion and the Christian Faith,* pp. 33-233.
5. *The Christian Message in a Non-Christian World,* pp. 1-30, esp. 30.

the Christian church. Now "for the first time since the Constantine victory in A.D. 312 and its consequences, the Christian Church is heading towards a real and spiritual encounter with the great non-Christian religions."[6]

Within the past one-third of a century this confrontation has become much more apparent. In addition to the factors cited by Kraemer, other developments have intensified the confrontation. Today the East is penetrating the West, as Muslims, Buddhists, Hindus, Sikhs, and others are emigrating to Western nations. Moreover, non-Christian religions are now sending their representatives (missionaries) to Western nations. This development is testing the commitment of Christians in the West to religious freedom for all.[7] Even more basically the increased confrontation has made imperative a new Christian theology of religions.

IV. ASSESSING THE CLAIMS OF NON-CHRISTIAN RELIGIONS TO AN AUTHENTIC REVELATION OF GOD

In order to investigate the possible connection between non-Christian religions and divine revelation, it is necessary to attempt to determine whether these religions actually claim to embody or convey a disclosure of deity and, if so, to seek to evaluate or assess such claims. In what follows we will examine the efforts of two twentieth-century Protestant theologians to cope with non-Christian religions.

A. JOHN MACQUARRIE'S CLASSIFICATIONAL APPROACH

Macquarrie held that variations in religions are due to at least three factors: (a) *"variation of symbolism"*; (b) variations in *"the psychology of the individual or group"*; and (c) *"variations in Being's own self-disclosure."* He sought to classify various religions under distinctive types, asserting that such classification must be on "a logical basis" and consistently applied and must be from a perspective. Macquarrie stated that his perspective was "the Christian one."[8] The following chart, most of which has been reproduced from his book,[9] will serve to clarify Macquarrie's classification of religions:

TYPICAL CONTRASTS

Immanent	Transcendent
Timeless	Eschatological
Quietist	Activist
Impersonal	Personal
Mystical	Rational

6. *Religion and the Christian Faith*, pp. 17-32, 35, 20.
7. See Edwin Luther Copeland, *Christianity and World Religions* (Nashville: Broadman Press, 1963), pp. 6-10, 131-32, 134-35.
8. *Principles of Christian Theology*, pp. 147-50.
9. Ibid., p. 151.

Limiting case: Fetishism ("vaguely diffused numinous power")	Limiting case: Atheism
Immanence Series	Transcendence Series
Type 4: Animism (being immanent in beings) Example: Primitive Religions	*Type 4: Deism* Examples: Confucianism, 17th- and 18th-Century Deism
Type 3: Polytheism (eternal return with no sense of history) Examples: Rig Veda, Egypt, Greece	*Type 3: Dualism* Examples: Zoroastrianism, Gnosticism, Manichaeism
Type 2: High Pantheism; Mysticism (change, multiplicity as illusions) Examples: Some Hinduism; Taoism	*Type 2: Sovereignty or Power* (more severe monotheism) Example: Islam
Type 1: Cosmic Order (no personal God but impersonal order with cycles) Examples: Hinayana Buddhism, Taoism, Stoicism	*Type 1: Monotheism* Examples: Religion of the Old Testament; Judaism

Existential-Ontological Theism
Examples: Christianity (doctrine
of incarnation), Mahayana
Buddhism (?)

The major mark of differentiation among non-Christian religions, according to Macquarrie, is whether the religion veers toward transcendence or toward immanence. It should also be noted from Macquarrie's analysis of variations that he has assumed that there may be the self-disclosure of Being in non-Christian religions.

B. EMIL BRUNNER'S EVALUATIVE APPROACH

Brunner's treatment of world religions was not so much in order to classify them according to types as to evaluate their claims to revelation in view of the revelation of God in Jesus Christ. He began with primitive religions.

> Every religion, however primitive, has *some* traces of the idea of revelation. . . . But no one seriously believes that the primitive religions have any claim to be an authentic revelation which could possibly be compared with the claim of the Christian revelation. . . . Even the most primitive religions have intercourse with divine powers, and thus presuppose that these powers, in some way or another, manifest themselves and can be encountered.

Yet these religions have

> no awareness of anything possessing universal validity; nor can the multiplicity of divine powers be combined with the strict sense of truth. These religions contain no traces of a truth or a bond which is holy and binding for all men, at all times, of an eternal divine Being, and of an eternal will of God.[10]

Brunner cited favorably John Calvin's view "that the *sensus numinis* is derived" from general revelation.[11]

Brunner then moved to the higher polytheistic religions of ancient Greece and modern India. These, he concluded, do not embody

> any revelation that could be a rival to the claims of Christian revelation. The element that distinguishes these religions from the primitive forms of religion is not anything essentially religious, but rather something rational or cultural. Religious feeling and religious imagination are here restrained and purified by the political, legal, social, moral, and scientific reason. . . . There is no trace here of a revelation that claims uniform and universal validity.[12]

Omitting such national or ethnic religions as Confucianism and Shintoism, Brunner proceeded to the higher forms of mysticism and Buddhism, which he deemed the border line between the lower religions and the religions that explicitly claim revelation. The higher mysticism by means of "esoteric instruction" initiates its adherents "into the right approach to the divine mystery," and it claims divine revelation as far as "the way to the experience of divine revelation, or the result of this experience itself," may be concerned.

> The way to the mystical experience is . . . exactly described, but the revelation itself, in its essentials, is inexpressible. Thus the mystic cannot, like the Prophet or the Apostle, proclaim as valid a revelation that has taken place. . . . The mystic's message does not claim the heart and life of the person in question; he cannot claim the person for the revelation itself; all he can do is to point to the way, open to all, of the experience of the revelation.[13]

According to Hinayana Buddhism, neither Buddha (557-477 B.C.) nor original Buddhism claimed to have "received a divine revelation." Buddha's "'illumination,' however, is understood as an event of a supernatural character, as a mystical experience, through which he received the ultimate truth about the nature of the world, the reason for suffering, and the possibility of escaping from the latter." For Brunner, the illumination of the Buddha can be described as "a supernatural intuition, but not as a revelation, because here no communicating, self-disclosing subject, no revealing God, is either believed or experienced."[14]

10. *Revelation and Reason*, pp. 222-23.
11. Ibid., p. 222.
12. Ibid., p. 213.
13. Ibid., p. 224.
14. Ibid., p. 225.

Mahayana Buddhism sees Buddha as a savior or deliverer, not merely a teacher or enlightened one. Buddhists are "trustfully" to call upon the name of Amita Buddha. But

> Amita Buddha is not God, the Creator and Lord, nor is he a historical revealer of God's will; he is a mythical figure, borrowing the name from the historical Buddha, but otherwise having nothing in common with him. . . . [H]e is a religious hero, who, after he had already entered into nirvana, out of pity for men sacrificed his bliss in order to become a helper to man. But his help does not consist in the fact that through him man shares in the hidden divine truth.[15]

Mahayana Buddhism shares with Hinayana "the same impersonal outlook," but in Mahayana "everything has been transformed from the pessimistic world-denying view into a more pantheistic world-affirming understanding of life."[16]

Then Brunner analyzed what he called the "prophetic religions," Zoroastrianism, Islam, and Judaism. Although it appears that Zoroaster (633-556 B.C.) was a prophet speaking for the Creator of heaven and earth and communicating his instruction and was the forerunner of a coming victorious Redeemer, Zoroastrianism was an ethical religion lacking any promise of forgiveness and mercy. It "is moralism projected into the sphere of metaphysics." "In the strict sense of the word, here there *can* be no question of revelation." This religion's "metaphysical dualism of the good and evil principles" makes the good god to be bound by the good, but he "is not himself the principle which separates good from evil."[17]

Islam clearly and distinctly sets forth "a claim to revelation of the highest kind. The Koran claims to be a book of divine revelation." The "giving of the Koran . . . is a special manifestation of the grace of Allah." According to Brunner, the Koran is lacking in "creative originality," being made up of Old Testament, Christian, and Arabian pagan elements. He charged that Islam's "prophetic claim does not seem to be in any way justified by the actual content of the revelations." Having rejected the revelation in Jesus Christ, Mohammed (570-632) "never dared to assert that he himself, in his own person, was a revelation of God." The Islamic faith "knows nothing of the revelation of a Person; it is first and foremost the religion of a book." Furthermore, it is "a religion of 'righteousness of works,' of moralism," lacking any "revelation of the gracious mystery."[18]

"Like Islam, Judaism, as distinguished from the Old Testament itself, is the religion of a Book; its revelation is the Sacred Book." With John the Baptist, "the Old Testament was finally closed."

15. Ibid., pp. 225-26.
16. Ibid., p. 226.
17. Ibid., pp. 227-28.
18. Ibid., pp. 229-31.

It is therefore incorrect to regard Judaism simply as the continuation of the revealed religion of the Old Testament. Through the rejection of Jesus as the Messiah the Jewish religion has taken its stand upon a particular interpretation of the Old Testament, namely, that Jesus cannot have been the Messiah.

Thus Jews "refuse to admit that the final revelation has taken place" and acknowledge "the temporary character of the revelation that has come to them."[19]

Brunner completed his evaluation of religions by discussing "Rational-Moralistic Theism," which he traced from Cicero (106-43 B.C.), Lucius Annaeus Seneca (4 B.C.-A.D. 65), and Marcus Aurelius (121-80) through Herbert of Cherbury and Immanuel Kant to more recent theists. He found its chief distinctive to be "the rejection of 'positive' revelation." "This Theism, both in its ancient and modern form, is the ultimate product of a movement of emancipation, of severance from the positive religions of the ancient world, and from Christianity." It has substituted "the moral law" for salvific revelation. Lacking "redeeming power," it "is the religion of self-redemption, . . . of the self-complacent *bourgeoisie*, and of the self-sufficient human reason." Hence it lacks a genuine "claim to revelation."[20]

By his evaluative approach Brunner is open to the criticism that he has permitted his own Christian commitment and perspective to govern and shape the entire evaluative process, and he likely would not have denied outright such criticism. Every evaluative approach to religions is made from a perspective or an overview or a faith-principle. Such is true even of Macquarrie's approach, for Macquarrie has assumed that ultimate Being self-discloses through various religions. Others who operate from the history of religion apply their own presuppositions, which are often quite different from the specifically Christian.

V. REVELATION AND THE EXISTENCE AND CLAIMS OF NON-CHRISTIAN RELIGIONS

Some of the world's religions, especially the animistic, polytheistic, and mystical types, do not make a clear, specific claim to the self-disclosure of deity, though they may teach or imply a coming into contact with ultimate reality. The great monotheistic religions (Islam, Judaism) do claim to be religions of divine revelation, especially religions of a sacred book.

Furthermore, the widespread and almost universal occurrence of religion among human beings seems to be related to a truth that we will treat subsequently, namely, that human beings are created by God with a capacity for fellowship with God and their own unfulfillment, as Augustine of Hippo said,[21] until they should be rightly related to the true and living God.

19. Ibid., pp. 231-32.
20. Ibid., pp. 232-34.
21. *Confessions* 1.1.

Edwin Luther Copeland (1916-) has assessed the human religious consciousness as follows:

> Regardless of how man's religion may have begun, from the standpoint of biblical faith, man is religious because God created him for fellowship with him as his child. Man's religious consciousness is a part of the divine image in which man is created. This religious consciousness apprehends the revelation of God as disclosed in nature, society, and the inner life of man. But, being itself distorted by sin, man's religious consciousness perverts the truth of God's revelation. Thus, the many religions, having been shaped by the fallen nature of man, are at once products both of divine revelation and human perversion (see Rom. 1:18-25). This is true of religions whenever they develop. Thus one may expect to meet with elements both of the divine and the demonic in religion, both of truth and falsity.[22]

Even idolatrous paganism, to say nothing of the more sophisticated or secular paganisms, affords an indirect witness to the existence of the true God as the proper object of human worship and allegiance. God does not reveal himself *as* the gods of various non-Christian religions, but the allegiance of human beings to these gods points to their own basic nature as worshiping beings and to the existence of One who is both the Author of such a worshiping or idolatrous humanity and the proper Recipient of the worship and obedient service of human beings.

VI. THE RELATION OF NON-CHRISTIAN RELIGIONS TO THE CHRISTIAN REVELATION OF GOD

How ought Christians to understand the relationship between non-Christian religions and the Christian revelation of God? Different answers have been given; we will note briefly the most frequently cited answers or theories.[23]

A. THE FULFILLMENT THEORY

According to this view the Christian revelation of God is a direct fulfillment of "what truth and revelation there are in other religions."[24] A leading exponent was J. N. Farquhar (1861-1929), who in *The Crown of Hinduism*[25] "tried to show how the various strands of Hindu belief and practice came to their real fulfilment in Christ and the Christian religion." Yet Farquhar "blurred the deep, unbridgeable differences between Hinduism and Christianity" and "failed to see that much of Hinduism would not be fulfilled, but destroyed and replaced when Hindus accepted Chris-

---

22. *Christianity and World Religions*, pp. 4-5.
23. Here we will rely on E. Luther Copeland's exposition of three theories in *Christianity and World Religions*, pp. 140-44.
24. Ibid., p. 141.
25. (London, New York: H. Milford, 1913).

tian faith."[26] There is an element of truth in the fulfillment theory, but there is also the dimension of judgment and replacement.

B. THE LOGOS THEORY

According to this view the relationship between non-Christian religions and the Christian revelation of God is to be understood by means of the concept of the Logos, that is, the preexistent and enlightening Logos (Word) of the Fourth Gospel (John 1:1, 9) that is active wherever the Christian gospel has never been preached. Developed during the age of the Church Fathers, this theory attributes elements of truth in non-Christian religions to the activity of the Logos. But, one must ask, is the Logos to be held responsible for the untruths and distortions to be found in these religions? The answer is obviously to be negative, but some other explanations must be supplied.

C. THE DISCONTINUITY THEORY

According to this view there is no "organic relation between the Christian revelation and man's religions," religions being the products of humankind and especially of the human religious consciousness. Consequently, common religious practices such as prayer and sacrifice are to be attributed to the human religious consciousness and not to a "common revelation" of God. The Christian revelation stands, therefore, "in utter uniqueness and unrelatedness."[27] This theory serves well the uniqueness of the Christian revelation, but does it adequately embody the fruit of the Christian doctrine of general revelation?

Whichever theory one may embrace, or even if one should have no explicit theory at all, Christians may be inclined to conclude with Copeland:

> Whatever fleeting glimpses men have of the true Light in original revelation are at best but dim, flickering lamps with blackened globes. The darkness in which they faintly glimmer can be illumined only by the brilliant, warm "light of the knowledge of the glory of God in the face of Jesus Christ." (2 Cor. 4:6)[28]

VII. THE QUEST FOR A COMMON DENOMINATOR, THE DRIFT TOWARD SYNCRETISM, AND INTERRELIGIOUS DIALOGUE

The topic of revelation and religions necessarily includes some consideration of those modern and contemporary trends in the interaction of the

26. Copeland, *Christianity and World Religions*, p. 141.

27. Ibid., p. 143. An exponent of this view, Hendrik Kraemer, *Religion and the Christian Faith*, esp. pp. 251-52, saw humankind's "dialectical condition," that is, his rebelling against and fleeing God and his groping toward and seeking God simultaneously, as "the constitutive element of man's religious consciousness."

28. *Christianity and World Religions*, p. 144.

world's major religions that are somewhat distinctive of the modern era and are impacting Christian theology today. Three of these warrant the attention of Christian theologians.

A. THE QUEST FOR A COMMON DENOMINATOR IN RELIGIONS

Nicholas (Krebs) of Cusa (1401-64) in his *De Pace Fidei* (1453) made a proposal for the unification of Judaism, Islam, and Christianity.[29] Since the era of the Enlightenment and of Deism a religious relativism has tended to prevail in the developing new discipline of comparative religion. Emil Brunner described such relativism in these words: "All religions contain an element of revelation, and no religion has any right to arrogate to itself a monopoly of revelation."[30] Whereas the Deists posited a "natural religion" without historical revelation and apart from the existing world religions, later comparative religionists searched for a common denominator within world religions. As a Christian theologian F. D. E. Schleiermacher held that "the essence of piety," that is, "the consciousness of being absolutely dependent," lies at the basis of all particular religions.[31] Thus, according to such a position, Christianity would be to religion as species to genus, and so would all other religions. During the twentieth century both Vedanta Hinduism and Baha'ism have been teaching that "all religions are essentially one," and yet each of these has been claiming that all other religions and their adherents should "merge" with them.[32]

Over against and contrary to this quest for a common denominator, Emil Brunner reasserted the uniqueness of the Christian revelation. He contended against the quest that "the exact opposite is true." Indeed, "it is the distinctive element that is essential, and all that the Christian faith may have in common with 'other religions' is nonessential."[33]

B. THE DRIFT TOWARD SYNCRETISM

During the past three decades there has been a pronounced drift or shift toward the recognition by avowedly Christian thinkers of the revelational and salvific character of non-Christian religions as being necessary to the present-day confrontation of Christianity with non-Christian religions and/or necessary to the compelling needs of humankind. Sometimes this drift has involved the quest for a common denominator in religions even while the goal of syncretism was being denied. We will now describe three examples of this drift.

29. An English translation is available in *Unity and Reform: Selected Writings of Nicholas de Cusa*, ed. John Patrick Dolan (Notre Dame, Ind.: University of Notre Dame Press, 1962), pp. 195-237.
30. *Revelation and Reason*, p. 219.
31. *The Christian Faith*, p. 12.
32. Copeland, *Christianity and World Religions*, p. 137.
33. *Revelation and Reason*, p. 220.

1. *The Call for Christianity to Surrender Its Claim to a Unique*
    Revelation of God (Arnold J. Toynbee) (1889-1975)

Toynbee called on "all the living higher religions" to "make a new
approach towards one another in face of a fearful common adversary,"
namely, "the worship of collective human power." He suggested that the
"common ground" might be found to be self-centered "human nature."
Toynbee advocated that Christianity be purged of its "traditional . . . belief
that Christianity is unique" and of "the exclusive-mindedness and intoler-
ance that follows from a belief in Christianity's uniqueness." The noted
historian argued on the basis of God's love that God must have made
various revelations other than that in Jesus and declared that "exclusive-
mindedness is a sinful state of mind," indeed "the sin of pride."[34]

2. *The Call for Christian Recognition of the Occurrence of Divine*
    Revelation (and Presumably of Salvation) in Non-Christian
    Religions (Neo-Henotheism) (John Macquarrie)

Macquarrie assumed "that in all religion there is some genuine
knowledge of God, genuine revelation, and genuine grace." He rejected
"the view that one religion is true and all the rest false." Rather he argued
that "one can commit oneself within one's own community of faith and
in terms of the symbols established in that community, and yet believe
that for a person in other circumstances, the same God reveals himself in
another community and under different symbols, and that there be nothing defective or inadequate about that person's commerce with God." One
should not, Macquarrie continued, "deny" that revelation has occurred in
another religion, though as an outsider one cannot truly affirm such either.
"The spiritual predicament of mankind today cannot be thought of in
terms of Christianity (or any other particular religion) against the rest, but
rather in terms of the contrast between the knowledge of God and of the
grace of holy Being on the one hand, and materialism and positivism on
the other."[35]

3. *The Call for the Nonevangelization of the Adherents of the Higher*
    Non-Christian Religions on the Ground That God's Grace Is
    Available to Them in and through Their Own Religions (Paul J.
    Tillich)

Tillich called for "a mutual judging" of religions that would "open
the way for a fair evaluation of the encountered religions." He agreed with
the tendency not to seek to convert Jews to Christianity and expressed the
hope that this attitude would be extended to Muslims. Tillich urged that
dialogue should replace conversion in the Christian relationship to non-

---

34. *Christianity among the Religions of the World* (New York: Charles Scribner's Sons,
1957), pp. 85, 95-96, 97.
35. *Principles of Christian Theology*, pp. 146, 155, 156, 158.

Christian religions. Christianity must break "through its own particularity" and "penetrate" into its own depth so that Christianity will lose its own "importance" as Christians become free to see God's presence "in other expressions of the ultimate meaning of man's existence."[36]

It is significant that each of these three, Toynbee, Tillich, and Macquarrie, drew the line of demarcation between true religion and false religion, not in terms of Christianity and other religions and philosophies but in terms of his own personal religio-philosophical postulate and views that would deny or obscure this. For Toynbee true religion is a faith that overcomes "the worship of collective human power." For Tillich true religion is that which expresses "the ultimate meaning of man's existence." For Macquarrie true religion is "the knowledge of God and of the grace of holy Being" as distinguishable from "materialism" and "positivism." In each case true religion is definable without reference to Jesus Christ. Tillich and Macquarrie had ontological interests that made it easy for them to absolutize "Being" or "the Ground of Being" and to connect true religion with such reality. Toynbee seemed to want the emerging world culture, presumably a single culture, to have allied religions strong enough to resist totalitarianism or other collectivisms. Although each of the three writers specifically denied that syncretism should be the goal, Toynbee urged the finding of "common ground" among all major religions, Tillich called on Christianity to break through "its own particularity" and for Christians to see "the spiritual presence" in other religions, and Macquarrie taught "that in all religion there is some genuine knowledge of God, genuine revelation, and genuine grace."[37]

C. INTERRELIGIOUS DIALOGUE

1. Rise and Growth of Interreligious Dialogue[38]

Formal dialogues between/among leaders of major world religions are a phenomenon of the twentieth century. Factors that may have contributed to the rise of such dialogues include the following: the World Parliament of Religions in Chicago in 1893; the American Protestant laymen's report in 1932 entitled *Re-thinking Missions;* the resurgence of Buddhism; and the increasing migration of adherents of non-Christian, non-Jewish religions to Western nations. For Roman Catholics interreligious dialogues began after Vatican Council II's adoption of *Nostra*

36. *Christianity and the Encounter of the World Religions* (New York: Columbia University Press, 1963), pp. 94-95, 97.

37. This paragraph, with certain variations in tenses, first appeared in the author's "Theological Foundations of Christian World Missions," prepared at the request of and submitted to the Missions Support Division of the Foreign Mission Board of the Southern Baptist Convention, September 1971, pp. 35-36. See also by the same author, "Three Present-Day Goliaths," *Western Recorder* 146 (25 March 1972): 3, 9.

38. Interreligious dialogue should be differentiated from ecumenical dialogue, which involves only religious bodies that are professedly Christian.

Aetate, the decree on non-Christian religions, and have been conducted under the Secretariat for Non-Christian Religions. For Protestants such dialogues have been chiefly but not solely conducted through the World Council of Churches.[39]

2. Present-day Trends in Interreligious Dialogue

Two fundamentally different trends or patterns respecting today's interreligious dialogues need to be identified and evaluated.

a. According to the first trend participants in dialogue should be equal partners fully open to the religious beliefs or insights of other participants, willing to acknowledge truth in the religions of others, ready to yield the absoluteness of Jesus Christ, and on the verge of undertaking a new syncretism or developing a "global theology." Comparative religionists who advocate and participate in this first trend include Wilfred Cantwell Smith (1916-) (Protestant, USA), John Harwood Hick (1922-) (Protestant, Great Britain), and Paul F. Knitter (1939-) (Roman Catholic, USA).[40]

b. According to the second trend participation in dialogue should be out of one's "common humanity," not out of any "common religiosity," should not necessarily be between total religious traditions, and, for Christians, should be predicated on the absoluteness of Jesus Christ. The second trend embodies the official posture of the World Council of Churches, although there are divergent views within the council.[41]

The first of these two trends poses quite serious problems for the integrity of Christian belief and teaching. Especially is this true for the doctrine of the person and work of Jesus, for the missionary role of present-day Christians—if dialogue is to replace witness to adherents of non-Christian religions—and for the future recognition of the uniqueness of the revelation/salvation of God in Jesus Christ if interreligious relativism is to prevail in the future. The second trend seems to pose fewer problems for the integrity of Christian belief and teaching, but it is not yet clear how this trend is to be related to Christian witness and missionary activity.

3. Interreligious Dialogue and Salvation in and through Non-Christian Religions

a. "Anonymous Christians"

Beginning in 1961, Karl Rahner, a Roman Catholic theologian, espoused the concept of the "anonymous Christian." This is the idea that persons who have adhered to non-Christian religions may "unknow-

---

39. John B. Cobb, Jr., *Beyond Dialogue: Toward a Mutual Transformation of Christianity and Buddhism* (Philadelphia: Fortress Press, 1982), pp. 15-25. The Interfaith Witness Department of the Southern Baptist Convention's Home Mission Board has been engaged in dialogues with Jews and Muslims.

40. John B. Cobb, Jr. (Protestant, USA), is not included because he is more Christocentric and allows for Christian witness beyond or after dialogue.

41. Cobb, *Beyond Dialogue,* pp. 36-47.

ingly" have "received the grace of Christ outside the [Christian] church."
Non-Christian religions can actually help such persons to receive such
grace, but after Christianity comes to such peoples, their non-Christian
traditions are "in principle superseded."[42]

b. Non-Christian Religions Themselves as Bearers of Divine Salvation for Their Adherents

Hans Küng has specifically taught that every world religion can be
the bearer or vehicle of divine salvation, even though it contains major
errors. The Christian Church is *"the 'extraordinary' way of salvation," and
world religions are "the 'ordinary' way of salvation for non-Christian* humanity."
Indeed,

> every man is intended to find his salvation within his own historical condi-
> tion. "Within his own historical condition" here means: within his particular
> individual and social environment, from which he cannot simply escape,
> and, finally, within the religion imposed on him by society. . . . A man is to
> be saved within the religion that is made available to him in his historical
> situation. Hence it is his right and his duty to seek God within that religion
> in which the hidden God has already found him. All this until such time as
> he is confronted in an existential way with the revelation of Jesus Christ.
>
> . . . .
>
> Every world religion is under God's grace and can be a way of salvation:
> whether it is primitive or highly evolved, mythological or enlightened,
> mystical or rational, theistic or non-theistic, a real or only a quasi-religion.
> Every religion *can* be a way of salvation and we hope that they all *are*.[43]

The soteriological teachings now common to the interreligious dialogues in which numerous Roman Catholics and mainline Protestants are
now involved are contrary to the soteriological teachings set forth by
evangelical Protestants in the past and in the present. Such a contemporary situation makes heavier the responsibility of today's evangelical
Protestants to maintain a high Christology and a Christ-based soteriology
and to articulate well their posture vis-à-vis non-Christian religions.

VIII. THE CHRISTIAN DOCTRINE OF SPECIAL REVELATION IN RELATION TO NON-CHRISTIAN RELIGIONS AND THEIR ADHERENTS

Although we have yet to discuss the doctrine of special revelation in
detail, we must reach forth to that topic in order to complete the consideration of revelation, religion, and religions.

42. Cobb, *Beyond Dialogue,* p. 23, based on Rahner, *Theological Investigations:* vol. 5,
Later Writings, trans. Karl- H. Kruger (Baltimore: Helicon Press; London: Darton, Longman
and Todd, 1966), ch. 6; vol. 14, *Ecclesiology, Questions in the Church, Church in the World,* trans.
David Bourke (New York: Seabury Press, 1976), ch. 17; vol. 16, *Experience of the Spirit: Source
of Theology,* trans. David Morland, O.S.B. (New York: Seabury Press, 1979), ch. 13.
43. "The World Religions in God's Plan of Salvation," pp. 51-52, 56-57. See also Cobb,
Beyond Dialogue, pp. 22-23.

A. Christianity, beginning with the apostles, has claimed that God's revelation has uniquely and supremely occurred in Jesus of Nazareth as Messiah, Son of God, and Lord and that this revelation has had a certain exclusive salvific character. "No one has ever seen God; the only Son, who is in the bosom of the Father, has made him known" (John 1:18, RSV). "I am the way, and the truth, and the life; no one comes to the Father, but by me" (John 14:6). "He who has seen me has seen the Father" (John 14:9c). "This is the stone which was rejected by you builders, but which has become the head of the corner. And there is salvation in no one else, for there is no other name under heaven given among men by which we must be saved" (Acts 4:11-12). Admittedly, Justin Martyr, Ulrich Zwingli, and others taught the salvation of certain Greek philosophers and sages. But Christian doctrine has emphasized that God's salvation is through Jesus Christ.

B. This Christian claim at its best is not a manifestation of human achievement and hence not an instance of human or "parochial" pride, but it points to the glorification of God in Jesus Christ. In the words of J. E. Lesslie Newbigin (1909-),

> It is because we have a message of judgment and mercy for the whole human race, a message from beyond death, that we can and must go to all men, not least to those whose ethical achievement dwarfs our own and tell them the gospel.[44]

C. Christianity's eras of advance or expansion, from the pre-Constantinian to the modern, have involved the presupposition of the uniqueness and sole sufficiency of God's revelation in Christ rather than any major syncretistic tendencies or the quest for the common denominator in religions or the pronouncement that other religions are true bearers of salvation. The cutting edge of the Christian message and its proclamation has been the uniqueness and sufficiency of Jesus Christ. Can there, therefore, be a surrender of the claim to the uniqueness of the Christian revelation without distortion of Christian teaching and practice and without major impairment of the missionary practice of churches? Ought not Christians to be warned of and alerted to syncretism and/or relativism as a "Trojan horse"?

D. Is it not possible and feasible that a *modus vivendi* between Christians and the adherents of non-Christian religions be actualized, such as through cooperation in humanitarian projects and efforts for international peace, without the Christian surrender of the uniqueness and indispensability of the revelation and redemption in Jesus Christ?

E. The proclamation of the gospel to all human beings and to all nations and peoples remains the task of Christians and of the Christian Church between the first and second advents of Jesus Christ (Matt. 23:14).

---

44. *A Faith for This One World?* (New York: Harper and Brothers, 1961), p. 71.

The dying and rising of Jesus constitutes an event beside which even the future existence of human civilization is a secondary question. The Christian claim is that that event has to be announced to the whole world as the one secret of reconciliation, first between man and his Maker and second between man and man.[45]

45. Ibid., p. 55.

CHAPTER 5

Natural Theology: Worldviews

In our treatment of general revelation (Ch. 3) we made an effort to differentiate general revelation from natural theology. Now it is fitting that we should give specific attention to natural theology. After taking note of the major attitudes in Christian history as to the relationship of philosophy with Christian theology and of several definitions of natural theology, we will examine some of the important worldviews in the light of the Christian revelation of God (Ch. 5) and the major arguments theism has employed in its effort to prove the existence of God (Ch. 6).

I. THE RELATIONSHIP BETWEEN PHILOSOPHY AND CHRISTIAN THEOLOGY

Throughout the history of Christianity various views have been advanced as to the proper or desired relationship between philosophy or philosophies and Christian theology. Millard J. Erickson has summarized such views in a fivefold manner.[1]

A. Christian theology should have no essential relation with or dependence on (chiefly Greek) philosophy (Tertullian, Martin Luther, 1483-1546).

B. Christian theology "can be elucidated by philosophy" (Augustine of Hippo, using Neo-Platonism).

C. Christian theology can "sometimes [be] established [or proved] by philosophy" (Thomas Aquinas, using Aristotle, 384-322 B.C.).

D. Christian "theology may . . . be judged by philosophy" (Deism; e.g., John Toland). Thereby some major Christian teachings were rejected.

E. Christian theology may have some of its content supplied by philosophy (Georg W. F. Hegel). With Hegel Christian truths were subordinated to and absorbed into idealistic philosophy.

In section III of this chapter we will relate the discussion of worldviews especially to the second and third views set forth by Erickson.

---

1. *Christian Theology*, pp. 40-42.

II. SOME DEFINITIONS OF "NATURAL THEOLOGY"

Julian Victor Langmead Casserley (1909-78) set forth four different but legitimate definitions of the term "natural theology."[2]

A. "Any intellectual movement of the mind which is conceived to lie in a Godward direction . . . [or] a movement of mind which he [a person] undertakes because he is a special kind of being—a being with an intellectual destiny which is oriented Godward."

B. "Some sort of argument, based upon naturalistic premises, for the validity of religious behavior, for the existence of God or of a spiritual realm."

C. "A theology of nature" or "an attempt to show that the theological categories of thought are adequate to the interpretation of nature and natural science."

D. "The tracing of an analogy between . . . 'natural' and 'evangelical' experience," such as in Joseph Butler's (1692-1752) *Analogy of Religion* and George Berkeley's (1685-1753) *Alciphron.*

In view of the forthcoming discussion of worldviews, it seems desirable and appropriate to construct yet another definition of "natural theology" that specifically relates to worldviews and to use that definition and Casserley's second definition in the consideration of worldviews and theistic arguments.

The newly constructed definition is as follows: Natural theology is humankind's effort, on the basis of reason (not merely "technical reason," but the totality of human powers and experience, including nature and history), to construct a worldview.

Casserley's second of four definitions tends to tie natural theology to theism, whereas the newly constructed definition can be related to and inclusive of various worldviews. If "natural religion" is to be taken to mean human striving and seeking after a favorable relationship with ultimate reality, whether God, or gods, or otherwise, then the working definition of "natural theology" should be just as comprehensive. Similarly Hendrik Kraemer declared that "all religions, all philosophies and world-views are the various efforts on the part of man to apprehend the totality of existence, often stirring in their sublimity and as often pathetic or revolting in their ineffectiveness."[3]

Therefore, the various worldviews are to be seen in a very broad sense as expressions of natural theology.

---

2. *The Scope and Variety of Natural Theology* (Washington, D.C.: n.p., 1953), pp. 2-3.
3. *Religion and the Christian Faith*, p. 44.

III. REPRESENTATIVE WORLDVIEWS

A. ATHEISM: THE DENIAL OF THE EXISTENCE OF GOD[4]

1. History

Atheism can be traced to the Sophists and materialists of ancient Greece. It is found among the Jainists in modern India. There has been a Western tradition of atheism since the Renaissance. In the twentieth century it has been allied with Marxist-Leninism, and in the United States, too, it has become an organized movement.

2. Types

a. Practical Atheism

This is a life-style conducted as if there were no God. Perhaps the psalmist had this kind of atheism in mind when he declared, "The fool says in his heart, 'There is no God' " (14:1a; 53:1a).

b. Postulatory Atheism

In Friedrich Nietzsche's (1844-1900) writings one finds these words: "If there were no gods, how could I bear it not to be a god? Thus there are no gods."[5] Here one finds a declaratory form of atheism that may not be more carefully delineated.

c. Theoretical Atheism

This is a more deliberate and formal effort to prove the nonexistence of God. Exemplars include Jean-Paul Sartre (1905-80), the French literary figure who denied that God ever lived, and Madalyn Murray O'Hair (1919-), the militant, politically oriented American atheist.

3. Result

Under atheism no knowledge of God in any positive sense is possible, and consequently there can be no revelation of God, only mistaken notions about nonexistent deity.

4. Critique

Atheism ignores or discounts the evidences of design in the universe, the import of widespread human testimony to religious experience, the strong evidence of human religious consciousness, and other considerations favorable to theism.

---

4. Atheism can be joined with certain other worldviews.
5. *Zarathustra* 2, "On the Happy Islands," quoted by Brunner, *Revelation and Reason*, p. 349.

5. *Value*

Atheism represents "the right to protest against the element of untruth which clings to every human formulation of divine truth, the 'all-too-human' and godless element in all theology."[6]

B. MATERIALISM: MATTER OR SOME MANIFESTATION OF MATTER AS ULTIMATE REALITY

1. *History and Types*

In ancient Greece Leucippus and Democritus taught materialism. In modern materialistic philosophy the focus has shifted from matter to energy.

Modern applications of the worldview of materialism include the regard for financial prosperity as the *summum bonum* and for modern technology and its many conveniences as the *summum bonum*.

Secularism, or the view that the only reality is that which pertains to "this age" *(hoc saeculum)* and "this world" *(hic cosmos)*, is a variation of materialism.

2. *Results*

According to materialism, God is nonexistent, for personality is only a temporary state, and what is called "soul" or "spirit" is a phase of material existence. Religion is at best superstition, and ethics is expediency. According to secularism life after death can be neglected if not fully denied, and God is not needed to explain the entire world order.

3. *Critique*

Materialism cancels out one set of realities, the spiritual, so as to exalt another set of realities, the material. It fails to account adequately for the transphysical dimensions in human life; for example, mind, memory, will, and freedom. Likewise, it offers no explanation of design in nature.[7]

4. *Value*

Materialism serves as a protest against the illusions of speculative argument, poetic imagination, dreams, visions, or hallucinations and as a witness to the tangible, though not ultimate, reality of what theists call the created order.

---

6. Brunner, *Revelation and Reason*, p. 350.
7. Mullins, *The Christian Religion in Its Doctrinal Expression*, pp. 109-10.

C. AGNOSTICISM: THE DENIAL OF THE POSSIBILITY OF KNOWING
   GOD WITH CERTAINTY (= *IGNORAMUS*)

1. *History and Types*

a. Eighteenth- and Nineteenth-Century Philosophers

1) Immanuel Kant (1724-1804), while allowing that human beings can know the "phenomenal" world, denied that they can know with any certainty the "noumenal" world *(Critique of Pure Reason)*. Full attainment of human moral goals, however, necessitates life after death and therefore the positing of God, freedom, and immortality *(Critique of Practical Reason)*.

2) David Hume (1711-76) taught that any meaningful statement "must be either rational or subject to the control of the five physical senses."[8] According to Hume, beliefs are "due to custom and instinct, not to reason," and hence have no "certain and demonstrable character."[9]

3) Herbert Spencer (1820-1903) argued that human minds are "necessarily shut out from a knowledge of ultimate reality," for they are, being relative and finite, incompetent to apprehend the Absolute, even though humans may "have a sort of vague, indefinite assurance" that the Absolute exists.[10]

4) Auguste Comte's Positivism, which became a religion of humankind as well as a philosophy, assumed that knowledge is limited to phenomena and taught three "stages" of human history as a sociological law. First, there was the theological stage, characterized by fetishism, polytheism, and monotheism. Second, there came the metaphysical stage, which coincided with the Enlightenment. Third, now humans are in the "positive" or scientific stage, wherein knowledge comes through the scientific method. Moreover, the methods of knowing employed during the first two stages are now passé.[11]

b. Logical Positivism

This philosophical movement arose from a seminar in 1923 at the University of Vienna led by Moritz Schlick and including Ludwig Wittgenstein (1889-1951) and Alfred Jules Ayer (1910-). It sought to limit meaningful or "representative" language to a priori or analytical or mathematical statements (e.g., "two plus two equals four") and to a posteriori or synthetic or factually informative or scientifically verifiable statements (e.g.,

8. John P. Newport, "The Unique Nature of the Bible in the Light of Recent Attacks," *Southwestern Journal of Theology* n.s. 6 (October 1963): 93.
9. Arthur Kenyon Rogers, *A Student's History of Philosophy* (3d ed.; New York: Macmillan, 1935), p. 345.
10. Ibid., p. 458b.
11. Ibid., pp. 435-42.

"[T]he stone in my left hand is heavier than the stone in my right hand"). Logical positivists allowed language to have a nonrepresentative or "emotive" usage (e.g., "Ouch!"), and for them theological statements rise no higher than the emotive level.[12]

c. Scientism

Similar to Comte's Positivism, scientism holds that the only valid knowledge is that which is derivable through the scientific method, that is, by observation, experimentation, and verification.

2. *Critique*

Agnosticism is self-contradictory, for it asserts "that there is an unknowable which cannot be known."[13] To know that it exists and that we cannot know it is considerable knowledge itself. Furthermore, like atheism and materialism, agnosticism takes a reductionist approach to all spiritual reality.

3. *Value*

Agnosticism represents "the truth that man cannot know God by his own efforts" and "that all rational knowledge of God is to the highest degree hypothetical and uncertain."[14]

D. PANTHEISM: THE IDENTIFICATION OF GOD AND THE MATERIAL WORLD ("GOD IS ALL")

1. *History and Types*

a. Polytheistic Pantheism

This is a "nonreflective" and "naive" form of pantheism.

For it is of the essence of paganism to fail to make a distinction between God and the world; the transition from the creature to the Creator is fluid. Nature is deified and God is drawn into the natural sphere.[15]

b. Reflective or Philosophical Pantheism

Baruch Spinoza (1632-77) held that God is the eternal, universal Substance and that extension and thought are his attributes.

c. Panentheism

This is a halfway house between pantheism and theism. Karl Christian Friedrich Krause (1781-1832), its early exponent, sought to combine the Absolutism of Schelling and Hegel and the subjectivism of Kant and

---

12. Erickson, *Christian Theology*, pp. 128-33.
13. Mullins, *The Christian Religion in Its Doctrinal Expression*, p. 108.
14. Brunner, *Revelation and Reason*, p. 357.
15. Ibid., p. 350.

Fichte.[16] According to this view, "God richly pervades nature and man yet is not identical with either."[17]

2. Results

God, for pantheism, is

> the impersonal intelligence and life which pervades the whole universe. God and nature are one. . . . Nature is simply a passing phase or manifestation of the Infinite Reality which we call God. . . . Therefore there is no personal God who transcends nature.[18]

Thus God is known as nature.

For the pantheist, God cannot be personal because personality means self-consciousness, or the ability to differentiate the self from the not-self, and such self-consciousness is contrary to pantheism's universality. Thus the Creator cannot be distinguished from the creature.

Prayer to God, the consciousness of sin against God, and the incarnation of the Son of God can have no objective reality under pantheism.[19]

3. Critique

a. Pantheism does not deal adequately with the evidence for personality in God and/or in human beings.

b. Pantheism does not offer a better explanation of the origin and order of the world than does theism.

c. Pantheism can be seen as expressive of "an exaggerated doctrine of the divine immanence."[20]

4. Value

Pantheism represents a "one-sided" development of the truth of "the omnipotence of the Creator" to the neglect of the relative independence of the creature. It is true that "God is the Ground of all" and the only one who exists in himself.[21]

E. DIALECTICAL MATERIALISM: THE HISTORICAL INTERACTION OF OPPOSITE ECONOMIC FORCES AS ULTIMATE REALITY

This worldview is a form of materialism, but it is materialism with "a purposive dialectic movement."

---

16. *The Encyclopedia Americana*, 1952 ed., 16:539.

17. Bernard L. Ramm, *Special Revelation and the Word of God* (Grand Rapids: Eerdmans, 1961), p. 23.

18. Conner, *Revelation and God*, pp. 39-40.

19. Ibid., p. 46; Mullins, *The Christian Religion in Its Doctrinal Expression*, pp. 52, 117.

20. Mullins, *The Christian Religion in Its Doctrinal Expression*, p. 138.

21. Brunner, *Revelation and Reason*, p. 351.

1. Exponents and Historical Sources

a. Exponents

The leading exponents have been Karl Marx (1818-83) and Vladimir Ilich Lenin (1870-1924).

b. Historical Sources

1) Its dialectic (thesis, antithesis, synthesis) was derived from G. W. F. Hegel (1770-1831). Also from Hegel came the ideas that the rational is the real and that the state is the divine idea on earth.[22]

2) Its materialism was derived from Ludwig Feuerbach (1804-72).[23]

3) Its concept of a goal at the end of history was seemingly derived from the Judaeo-Christian heritage.

2. Results

Under dialectical materialism there is no possibility of an ultimate spiritual Being and hence no possibility of his self-disclosure. Economics is the foundation of truth as well as of society. Religion, ethics, and social institutions are part of its superstructure. Hence religion is determined by economics and can be called "the opiate of the people."

3. Critique

Dialectical materialism shares the weaknesses of materialism and atheism, and its goal-oriented dimension can be better supplied by the Christian expectation of the last things.

4. Value

a. It represents the truth that humans cannot long survive without economic sustenance.

b. It represents the truth that history has meaning, for it has a goal or end toward which it is moving.

F. PRAGMATISM: THE MEANINGFULNESS OF AN IDEA DETERMINED BY ITS PRACTICAL RESULTS

1. Leading Exponents

Pragmatism is "perhaps the one distinctively American philosophy." Its leading exponents were Charles Santiago Sanders Peirce (1839-1914); William James (1842-1910), the author of *Varieties of Religious Experience;* and John Dewey (1859-1952), who was a major influence on American education.

---

22. R. N. Carew Hunt, *The Theory and Practice of Communism: An Introduction* (5th rev. ed.; New York: Macmillan, 1957), pp. 9, 16-20.

23. Ibid., pp. 9-10.

> Peirce concentrated on the repeatable experiments of the community of
> scientists. James . . . stressed the particular beliefs of the individual as a
> human being rather than as an intellectual investigator. . . . [Hence] the
> meaning (for Peirce) or the truth (for James) of a proposition is its experi-
> enceable consequences.

Dewey held to an "instrumentalism" that stressed the problem-solving
and moral-development benefits of any idea.[24]

2. Results

Pragmatism is not concerned with ultimate truth or reality but with
the experience of utility and practicality. For Dewey, religion is valuable
in "bringing persons together in a unity of communication, of shared life
and shared experience." Other forms of religion that are not so useful
should be rejected.[25]

3. Critique

Millard J. Erickson has raised three probing questions about pragmatism:

a. How ought expediency or practicality to be determined? Is not
some value-system apart from pragmatism needed?

b. Does not pragmatism unduly limit "the realm of true statements"?

c. What is the needed or proper "time span for the evaluation of
ideas"?[26]

4. Value

Pragmatism offers a valid protest against speculative or abstract
systems of thought that have little or no value for human life.

G. EXISTENTIALISM: TRUTH OBTAINABLE BY COMMENCING WITH THE CONCERNS OF THE SELF RATHER THAN WITH METAPHYSICS

According to this worldview, existence is prior to essence, and thus
by participating in existence one finds the mystery of existence, or truth.
Existentialism is irrational, individualistic, freedom-oriented, and subjective.[27]

1. History and Types

a. Atheistic

Its leading exponent has been Jean-Paul Sartre.

---

24. Erickson, *Christian Theology,* pp. 42, 43-44.
25. Ibid., p. 44.
26. Ibid.
27. Ibid., pp. 45-46.

b. Neutral, but Inclined to Atheism

This was the posture of Martin Heidegger (1889-1976).

c. Theistic

Its exponents include both its pre-twentieth-century pioneers and its twentieth-century exponents: Blaise Pascal (1623-62), who stressed the knowledge of the heart; Søren Kierkegaard (1813-55), who emphasized knowledge by appropriation; Karl Jaspers (1883-1969); and Gabriel Marcel (1889-1973).[28]

2. *Results*

Existentialism rejects propositional truth and holds to existential truth, realized through the leap of faith. For the atheistic type human existence leads to the denial of the existence of God. For the theistic type human existence leads to faith in the God who acts, not God as Being. This worldview "may be either a hindrance or a handmaid to faith depending on the point of pilgrimage in which one finds himself."[29]

3. *Critique*

Millard Erickson has focused three criticisms of existentialism:[30]

a. It excessively subjectivizes truth, making it the "truth for me," so that there is the danger that "the subjective experience becomes the end in itself."

b. It "has difficulty supporting its values and ethical judgments."

c. Its stress on "passion" may reflect "the anxiety of insecurity" and be utterly different from genuine Christian faith-commitment.

4. *Value*

a. Existentialism emphasizes as true the personal dimension of the human self in the apprehension and appropriation of truth.

b. Some of its themes parallel the themes of Christianity: the worth and uniqueness of human persons, "freedom and the necessity of choice," the passionate involvement needed for faith and truth, and the absurdity and despair of unbelief or noncommitment.[31]

28. Bernard L. Ramm, *A Handbook of Contemporary Theology* (Grand Rapids: Eerdmans, 1966), p. 46.

29. Moody, *The Word of Truth,* pp. 70-71.

30. *Christian Theology,* pp. 47-48.

31. Ibid., p. 47.

H. PROCESS PHILOSOPHY: PROCESS AS THE ULTIMATE REALITY WITH CHANGE AS THE CLUE TO ITS APPREHENSION

1. History and Types

a. Heraclitus of Ephesus (c. 500 B.C.) taught that all reality is to be seen as a constant flux.

b. Alfred North Whitehead (1861-1947), British-born mathematician and philosopher, fathered the modern process movement. Other philosophers espousing this worldview have included Charles Hartshorne (1897-) and Henry Nelson Wieman (1884-1975). Theologians who have sought to combine process philosophy and Christian theology include W. Norman Pittenger, John B. Cobb, Jr., and David Ray Griffin.

2. Concepts

Process philosophers refer to "occasions of experience" as the "units of process . . . characterized by enjoyment." Present occasions have a "prehension" or "feeling" for previous occasions. There is limited, though not complete, incorporation of the past into the present, as through memory.[32] A "nexus" is "the group of connections in a society of actual occasions."[33]

3. Results

God, according to process thought, "participates in the reality of all else."[34] God's Becoming is stressed more than God's Being, at least by Hartshorne. Defenders and critics differ as to whether this worldview can be an adequate base for the Christian revelation of God.

4. Critique

Erickson[35] has raised four critical questions about this worldview:

a. What is "the basis of identity" in the "moments of experience" if "not in a substance or a person"?

b. "What is the basis for evaluating change?" Surely not all change is good.

c. "Is there no middle ground between" viewing "change as the basic reality" and viewing "ultimate reality" as "a static, immovable, fixed substance"?

d. "How long is a moment" (in the "moments of experience")? "If there is an infinite number of these units," can one properly "speak of them as units at all"?

---

32. John B. Cobb, Jr., and David Ray Griffin, *Process Theology: An Introductory Exposition*, pp. 16-23.

33. Moody, *The Word of Truth*, p. 71.

34. Erickson, *Christian Theology*, p. 51.

35. Ibid., pp. 52-53.

5. *Value*

Process philosophy represents the truth that totally static apprehensions of reality are not adequate.

I. IDEALISM AND PERSONALISM: THE SELF OR PERSONHOOD, WHETHER DIVINE OR HUMAN, AS THE ULTIMATE REALITY

Speculative or absolute idealism and personalism can be coupled because of their similarities, but they need to be treated separately because of their differences.

1. *Speculative or Absolute Idealism*

This worldview holds that the divine Self and the human self are identical, for the human self is a spark from the divine Self.

a. History

1) Later Hindu Vedantism, sometimes described as "Theopanism," held to the identity of God and the human self and denied the reality of the external world.[36]

2) The "I" philosophy of Johann Gottlieb Fichte (1762-1814) taught that all philosophical knowledge derives from "the one principle of the consciousness of the indivisible Ego."[37]

3) More moderate forms of idealism are to be found in the philosophical systems of Plato, Immanuel Kant, and Gottfried Wilhelm Leibniz (1646-1716).

b. Results and Critique

Under absolute idealism God's creation of human beings is denied, human sin as rebellion against God is denied, and any knowledge of "God" is essentially knowledge of the self. Various basic Christian teachings seem to be incompatible with absolute idealism.

c. Value

Absolute idealism represents the truths that:

1) There is a "divine self-testimony in the human spirit," or that which we have earlier[38] described as God's self-disclosure through the inner nature of human beings.

2) "[M]an, as man, is always moved in his spirit by God."

3) "[H]uman existence cannot be severed from the divine self-revelation."[39]

---

36. Brunner, *Revelation and Reason*, pp. 352-53.
37. "Fichte, Johann Gottlieb," *The New Schaff-Herzog Encyclopedia of Religious Knowledge*, 4:309.
38. See Ch. 3.
39. Brunner, *Revelation and Reason*, pp. 353-54.

2. Personalism

This worldview holds that the divine Person and the human person are akin or similar. One may begin with a personal Spirit, who is the source of all things, and proceed to human beings as personal spiritual beings, or one may begin with human beings as spiritual persons and attribute personality to the ultimate reality.[40]

a. History

1) Rudolf Hermann Lotze (1817-81) set forth an anti-Hegelian "teleological idealism" with ethics as the "starting point" of metaphysics.[41]

2) A succession of professors at Boston University, namely, Borden Parker Bowne (1847-1910), Edgar Sheffield Brightman (1884-1953), and Peter Anthony Bertocci (1910-), together with Ralph Tyler Flewelling (1871-1960) of the University of Southern California, expounded "Boston Personalism."

b. Results and Critique

Both God and human beings are manifestly personal according to personalism. This worldview tends to validate religious experience. Yet its monism makes it difficult for personalism to allow for sin, judgment, the two natures of Jesus Christ, and certain other Christian teachings.

c. Value

Personalism represents the truth of the kinship of human beings as creatures and God as the personal Creator. It gives philosophical support to the idea that human beings are made for God.

J. DEISM AND THEISM: ONE SUPREME SPIRITUAL BEING AS THE ULTIMATE REALITY

Although Deism and theism are similar enough to be coupled, there are enough differences to warrant separate discussion.[42]

1. Deism

This worldview is a religion of the one supreme spiritual Being known solely as Creator and Judge (Punisher-Rewarder) and known naturally.

---

40. See Paul Deats, "Introduction to Boston Personalism," in Paul Deats and Carol Robb, eds., *The Boston Personalist Tradition in Philosophy, Social Ethics, and Theology* (Macon, Ga.: Mercer University Press, 1986), p. 2, who finds that personalism at Boston has identified the person as the ultimate reality and personality as the fundamental category.

41. Hubert Evans, "Lotze, Rudolf Hermann," *The New Schaff-Herzog Encyclopedia of Religious Knowledge,* 7:47.

42. Brunner, *Revelation and Reason,* pp. 232-34, did not differentiate Deism and theism.

a. History

The earliest exponent of Deism seems to have been Herbert of Cherbury (1583-1648). Among its eighteenth-century advocates were John Toland (1670-1722) and Matthew Tindal (1653(?)-1733) of England and Thomas Paine (1737-1809) in colonial America. They posited that human beings had had a natural knowledge of God ever since their creation and denied the historical or special revelation of God.

More recent interpretations of the earlier Deism have stressed the Deist concept of the absentee Creator under the analogy of the watchmaker and the watch, but Deism was more extensive than this theme.

b. Results and Critique

Deism posits one supreme spiritual Being and hence is theistic. However, it denies categorically any historical self-disclosure of God, whether in the faith of the Old Testament, in Christianity, in later Judaism, or in Islam. The Christian doctrines of incarnation and redemption are incompatible with Deism. Deism, therefore, is a competitor of the great monotheistic religions, even though one may trace a certain indebtedness of Deism to the Judaeo-Christian heritage.

c. Value

Deism represents the truth of the transcendence of God at the expense of the immanence of God and represents the truth of divine revelation through the creation at the expense of divine revelation through history.

2. *Theism*

This worldview is a religion of the one supreme spiritual Being, however he may act or be made known. In a sense theism is more inclusive than Deism, and yet it can serve as an alternative to Deism.

a. History

There were aspects of theism in ancient Greek and Roman philosophy. Theism has been a correlate of Christianity and Judaism. Emil Brunner argued that theism has usually prevailed "only upon the foundation of Christianity." It "has had a vigorous development only where the Christian theological tradition was living."[43]

b. Results

Theism posits one supreme spiritual Being. It has developed and utilized the theistic arguments for the existence of God. It has stressed that human beings are made in the image of God. Although it may confess to

---

43. Ibid., p. 358.

take into account only nonhistorical aspects of the knowledge of God, it has actually drawn on the Judaeo-Christian heritage.

c. Critique

Anthony Garrard Newton Flew (1923-) has charged that theism has no adequate criterion for its falsification.[44]

d. Value

Theism represents the truth of the existence of one supreme spiritual Being. It provides a philosophical framework for monotheistic religion without denying the claims relative to divine revelation through history.

IV. CHRISTIANITY AND WORLDVIEWS

A. The existence and the prevalence of numerous contradictory worldviews, especially in the Western religio-philosophical tradition, serve as persuasive evidence that there is no single "natural theology."

B. Such worldviews vary considerably in respect to their possible compatibility with the Christian revelation of God. Christian theologians and philosophers in the modern period from time to time have claimed that certain of these worldviews are quite compatible with the Christian faith-claims; especially has this been said of theism, personalism, and theistic existentialism, although some have made this claim for process philosophy as well. The degrees of effectiveness of such alliances between Christianity and specific worldviews will doubtless continue to be debated and reassessed.

---

44. "Theology and Falsification," in Flew and Alasdair MacIntyre, eds., *New Essays in Philosophical Theology* (London: SCM Press, 1955), pp. 96-99, 106-8; for the replies to Flew, see pp. 99-105, 109-30.

CHAPTER 6

Natural Theology: Theistic Arguments

Theism has produced several arguments for the existence of God, which may be regarded as evidences for the existence of God. Such arguments owe much to the Greek philosophical tradition. Their cogency is denied by those who hold to worldviews contradictory to theism.

These theistic arguments are usually thought to belong to the field of Christian apologetics, and indeed most Christian apologists have made use of them or at least treated them in considerable detail. Do these arguments also belong to Christian systematic theology? Those who emphasize the basic faith-orientation of theology may be inclined to answer in the negative. But systematic theologians have often answered affirmatively, and their inclusion of the arguments perhaps can best be justified by acknowledging that theologians wish to take into full account the relationship between the Christian gospel and theism.

We will now examine the several theistic arguments under two major categories, those arguments that are from the natural order and those arguments that derive from the nature, thought, experience, and destiny of human beings.

I. ARGUMENTS FROM THE NATURAL ORDER

A. COSMOLOGICAL: ARGUMENT FROM THE EXISTENCE OF THE COSMOS TO THE NECESSARY EXISTENCE OF GOD

This is an argument from an effect *(cosmos)* back to a necessary cause (God). It takes various forms:

1. *Argument from Motion to a First Mover*

This is the first argument advanced by Thomas Aquinas in his *Summa Theologica*.[1] He argued: "whatever is in motion must be put in motion by another." If this putting into motion should be carried to infinity (or, to eternity), there would be perpetual motion and hence no

---

1. I, q. 2, art. 3.

prime mover. But perpetual motion contradicts putting into motion. To explain putting into motion, one needs to posit a prime mover, or God.

Admittedly objections have been and can be raised against this form of the cosmological argument. Objectors can either posit an infinity or eternity of what we call motion or posit that motion arose "from nothing," or spontaneously.[2] But the second law of thermodynamics, the law of entropy, bespeaks of a decline in energy and seems to be contrary to perpetual motion in the universe.[3]

2. *Argument from Efficient Cause to a First Efficient Cause, or God*

This is the second argument set forth by Thomas Aquinas in his *Summa Theologica*.[4] Nothing is "the efficient cause of itself"; "for so it would be prior to itself, which is impossible." The chain of causality (efficient causes, intermediate causes, ultimate causes) cannot be infinite, for "to take away the cause is to take away the effect." Thus, "if there be no first cause among efficient causes, there will be no ultimate, nor any intermediate cause." Therefore, one must posit "a first efficient cause," or God.

Similarly, objectors may argue either that the "chain of causality" is eternal or that it "originated from nothing."[5] Furthermore, David Elton Trueblood (1900-) has raised two other questions. Can we trust "the whole principle of causality"? How do we know that the first cause is the same as the God who has been revealed in Jesus Christ?[6]

3. *Argument from Contingency, That Is, from Beings That "Do Not Contain in Themselves the Reason for Their Existence" to an External Reason or Being for Their Existence*

It has been argued that an external reason "must be an existent being," that is, one that "contains within itself the reason of its [own] existence" *or* one "which cannot not-exist." Such a being, therefore, is God.[7]

Objectors can either point to the eternality of contingent beings or insist that contingent beings have come from nothing.[8]

B. TELEOLOGICAL: ARGUMENT FROM PURPOSIVE DESIGN IN NATURE TO THE NECESSARY EXISTENCE OF A DESIGNER, OR GOD

This is the fifth argument set forth by Thomas Aquinas in his *Summa Theologica*.[9] Thomas identified it as the argument "from the governance of

2. J. Oliver Buswell, Jr., *A Systematic Theology of the Christian Religion*, 1:79.
3. Dallas M. Roark, *The Christian Faith*, pp. 5-6.
4. I, q. 2, art. 3.
5. Buswell, *A Systematic Theology of the Christian Religion*, 1:79.
6. *Philosophy of Religion* (New York: Harper, 1957), pp. 92-93.
7. F. C. Copleston, "A Debate on the Existence of God," *The Existence of God*, ed. John Hick (New York: Macmillan, 1964), pp. 168-69.
8. Roark, *The Christian Faith*, p. 7.
9. I, q. 2, art. 3.

things." Accordingly, it is said that planets, animals, and plants "work for an end" of which they seem to lack knowledge. The fact that they normally "attain their end" comes "by design, not by chance." Hence there must be "an intelligent being by whom all natural things are directed to their end."

William Paley (1743-1805) set forth this argument in classic form, but Immanuel Kant held that it "only argued for a divine architect and not for an infinite God."[10] The argument from or "to design" may be illustrated by "the snowflake, or the water crystal, or the amazing structure of the eye," but it must be directed "to a cosmic teleology." Reference is often made to the earth's distance from the sun and the moon's distance from the earth.[11]

The chief objection to the teleological argument arises from the problem of natural evil. Do not "the dysteleological facts in the world"— sickness and disease, one animal's devouring another for food, the arid deserts, the frozen polar regions, earthquakes, tornadoes, hurricanes, and volcanic eruptions—outweigh the evidences for design? Does not the Bible construe the natural order as participating in the fall of humankind and thus needing redemption (Gen. 3:17-18; Rom. 8:18-25)? Does the teleological argument allow enough room for freedom?[12]

Defenders of the teleological argument contend that God has set limits to freedom and "natural evil," that is, limits that permit humans to speak of design or purpose.[13] But Trueblood has asked whether Charles Darwin's principle of "natural selection" has invalidated the teleological argument by its explanation of changes by purely natural causes.[14]

It may be necessary, therefore, to recognize both the validity and the limits of the teleological argument. Blaise Pascal declared: "Nature has some perfections to show that she is the image of God, and some defects to show that she is only His image."[15]

II. ARGUMENTS FROM THE NATURE, THOUGHT, EXPERIENCE, AND DESTINY OF HUMAN BEINGS

A. MORAL: ARGUMENT FROM THE MORAL LAW OR THE HUMAN SENSE OF OUGHTNESS TO THE AUTHOR OF SUCH, OR GOD

Immanuel Kant argued in his *Critique of Practical Reason* that humans have "a sense of 'oughtness' or duty to pursue the highest good." In order "to be able and free" to pursue the highest good—whether "morality" or "happiness" or holiness—humans may need life after death. For there to

---

10. Ramm, *The God Who Makes a Difference* (Waco, Tex.: Word Books, 1972), p. 96.
11. Roark, *The Christian Faith*, p. 7.
12. Ibid., pp. 8-9.
13. Ibid., p. 9.
14. *Philosophy of Religion*, p. 93.
15. *Pensées*, 579, trans. W. F. Trotter (New York: Modern Library, 1941), p. 190.

be such life after death, one must necessarily assume the existence of God.[16]

Hastings Rashdall (1858-1924) argued from the fact that an "absolute Moral Law or moral ideal . . . can exist only in a Mind from which all Reality is derived."[17] Thus "objective Morality implies the belief in God."[18]

One may ask whether the Lawgiver is the Creator of the universe or the transcendent God. One may object that such a Lawgiver is only the projection of human desires, wishes, and fears. Furthermore, where there is considerable relativism in morality, as, for example, in the situation ethics of the 1960s, the moral argument may not be persuasive, for the moral law as objective reality has been downplayed, if not denied.

B. ONTOLOGICAL: ARGUMENT FROM THE HUMAN IDEA OF AN INFINITE AND PERFECT BEING TO HIS NECESSARY EXISTENCE

This is a syllogistic argument rather than an argument from effect to cause. Its first exponent, Anselm of Canterbury (1033-1109), expounded it in deductive fashion in his *Proslogium*. First, contended Anselm, a human being has in his mind the idea of an infinite and perfect being. Second, "[e]xistence is an attribute of perfection." Third, an infinite and perfect Being, therefore, must exist. Even in Anselm's own day the question was raised as to the truth or validity of the second premise. If one should have in his mind the idea of an island in the Atlantic Ocean, does that mean that that island necessarily exists? Anselm's reply was "that the case of God is a special one."[19] For him the ontological argument was "a necessary conclusion, not a contingent conclusion.[20]

Recently Norman Malcolm (1911-) has reinterpreted and defended a form of this argument. He finds Anselm to have been arguing that a "being whose nonexistence is logically impossible is 'greater' than a being whose nonexistence is logically possible."[21]

René Descartes (1596-1650) set forth the ontological argument both deductively and inductively. By the latter method he argued that "the idea of God, who is infinite and perfect, could not be produced [in human beings] by any finite object and must, therefore, be caused by God Himself."[22] Descartes himself stated: "The existence of God is demonstrated *a posteriori* from this alone, that his idea is in us."[23]

16. Roark, *The Christian Faith*, p. 11.
17. *The Theory of Good and Evil: A Treatise on Moral Philosophy*, 2 vols. (2d ed.; London: Oxford University Press, 1924), 2:211-13.
18. Roark, *The Christian Faith*, pp. 11-12.
19. *Reply to Guanilo*, 6; Anselm, 3-5; Roark, *The Christian Faith*, p. 9.
20. Ramm, *The God Who Makes a Difference*, p. 89.
21. "Anselm's Ontological Arguments," Hick, ed., *The Existence of God*, p. 52.
22. Trueblood, *Philosophy of Religion*, p. 91.
23. *The Meditations and Selections from the Principles of René Descartes*, trans. John Veitch (LaSalle, Ill.: Open Court Publishing Company, 1945), p. 220.

Does the ontological argument depend too much on the idea of God as a "necessary" idea? Does J. V. L. Casserley claim too much when he says that it demonstrates "that all rational beings believe in His [God's] existence"? According to Casserley, the ontological argument does not "prove" God's existence but rather proves "that essence involves existence, not always but in . . . God."[24] Trueblood has concluded that the ontological argument "does not carry conviction today, largely because it represents a prescientific mentality."[25]

C. RELIGIOUS: ARGUMENT FROM THE RELIGIOUS CONSCIOUSNESS OF HUMAN BEINGS OR FROM THE FACT OF EXTENSIVE CLAIMS TO RELIGIOUS EXPERIENCE AMONG ALL PEOPLES AND NATIONS TO THE NECESSARY EXISTENCE OF THE AUTHOR OF SUCH RELIGIOUS CONSCIOUSNESS OR THE TRUE OBJECT OF SUCH RELIGIOUS DEVOTION, OR GOD

1. *From the Religious Consciousness or Religious Nature of Human Beings*

This argument was implicit in the classic statement of Augustine of Hippo: "Thou hast made us for thyself, and our heart is restless till it finds rest in Thee, O God."[26] Augustus Hopkins Strong gave to it a modern formulation.

Man's emotional and voluntary nature proves the existence of a Being who can furnish in himself a satisfying object of human affection and an end which will call forth man's highest activities and ensure his highest progress.

Only a Being of power, wisdom, holiness, and goodness, and all these indefinitely greater than any that we know upon the earth, can meet this demand of the human soul. Such a Being must exist. Otherwise man's greatest need would be unsupplied, and belief in a lie be more productive of virtue than belief in the truth.[27]

Even idolatry bears witness to this religious consciousness.

2. *From the Fact of the Claims of Manifold Human Beings in Various Nations and Cultures to Having Had Religious Experiences*

Trueblood has pressed this argument in the twentieth-century context:

The fact that a great many people, representing a great many civilizations and a great many centuries, and including large numbers of those generally accounted the best and wisest of mankind, have reported direct religious experience is one of the most significant facts about our world. The claim which their reports make is so stupendous and has been made in such a widespread manner that no philosophy can afford to neglect it.[28]

---

24. *The Christian in Philosophy* (New York: Scribner, 1951), pp. 60, 64.
25. *Philosophy of Religion*, p. 92.
26. *Confessions* 1.1.
27. *Systematic Theology*, p. 83.
28. *Philosophy of Religion*, p. 145.

These two expressions of the religious argument may prove to be more persuasive and convincing to serious-minded persons today than the cosmological and teleological arguments.

D. WAGER: ARGUMENT THAT HUMAN BEINGS, OUT OF CONSIDERATION OF THE ETERNAL CONSEQUENCES OF SUCH A DECISION, OUGHT TO WAGER OR BET THAT GOD IS

An early form of this argument was expressed by Arnobius of Sicca in his *The Case against the Pagans*, written about A.D. 300-303.[29] Its most classic formulation was probably that of Blaise Pascal in his *Pensées*.[30]

If I bet that God is:

1. And he is, then I have gained all. Remember the stakes involve eternity.
2. And he is not, then I have lost nothing. (There is the possibility of gain if a good, moral, and "godly" life is valued more than an "immoral" one.)

If I bet God is not:

1. And he is, then I have everything to lose including everlasting happiness.
2. And he is not, then nothing is lost except the possibility of temporal happiness if through this conclusion one finds no meaning to life.

Therefore, if the odds are a billion to one, the reasonable person, the sensible person, would bet his life on God.

III. VALIDITY AND VALUE OF THE THEISTIC ARGUMENTS

A. THESE ARGUMENTS ARE NOT LOGICALLY DEMONSTRATIVE FOR ALL HUMAN BEINGS.

These arguments do not prove the existence of God in the sense of being infallible, indisputable, and utterly conclusive proofs that will convince any human being of God's existence, regardless of his inclinations, predispositions, or attitudes.

1. Since the various arguments are particularly dependent on certain philosophies or worldviews (that is, the cosmological, the teleological, and the moral on Aristotle; the ontological on Plato; the religious on psychology and history of religions; and the wager on existentialism), the tenability or cogency of a particular argument for a given human being or group of persons may depend on the attachment of the same to a particular philosophy, worldview, or discipline of learning.

29. 2:4 (ACW).
30. 233, as summarized and paraphrased by Roark, *The Christian Faith*, pp. 14-15.

2. Criticisms of, objections to, and probing questions concerning an argument for the existence of God must also be considered and evaluated. "These arguments (or 'proofs') stand—especially in our times—in the shadow of a great many 'proofs' *against* the existence of God."[31]

3. The inclination, presupposition, or attitude of a particular human being can play an even greater role in reference to the "convinceability" of the theistic arguments than the cogency of any argument. One's religious beliefs or unbeliefs are not founded on "pure reason," that is, reason devoid of inclination, feeling, or choice.

4. The arguments can be rejected *as arguments* without reflecting on the mental capacities of the rejector, and such rejection does not necessarily mean the rejection of Jesus Christ as the Son of God and as Lord and Savior.

B. These Arguments May Be Confirmatory and Corroborative of Christian Faith.

1. The arguments may create a climate favorable to belief in one supreme God.

> The most that can be said for any of the philosophical arguments, or for all of them put together, is that they point to a probability and create an intellectual interpretation of existence where the assumption of a God is not unreasonable. They do not, however, absolutely and irrefutable prove that God exists.[32]

These arguments may help to bring into focus the question as to what is the best worldview and may serve to point to theism or personalism or theistic existentialism or another worldview.

2. The arguments may furnish good reasons for believing in God so as either to serve the unbeliever who would become a Christian believer or to strengthen the faith of the Christian believer.

3. The arguments do not remove the absolute necessity for faith as the supreme and essential mode of knowing and being rightly related to God.[33]

---

31. Berkouwer, "General and Special Revelation," p. 17.

32. W. Burnet Easton, Jr., *The Faith of a Protestant* (New York: Macmillan, 1946), p. 18.

33. For a more extensive delineation of the "limitations" and "contributions" of the theistic arguments, see Yandall C. Woodfin, *With All Your Mind: A Christian Philosophy* (Nashville: Abingdon Press, 1980), pp. 47-55.

CHAPTER 7

Special Revelation to Israel and in Jesus Christ

The treatment of general revelation, which has been clearly differentiated from special revelation, has led to the consideration of the phenomenon of religion, non-Christian religions, worldviews, and theistic arguments. Now it is essential that special or historical or biblical revelation be explored in greater detail. Obviously there are two phases of biblical revelation, that which came to and through the people of Israel (Old Testament) and that which came in and through Jesus Christ (New Testament).

I. SPECIAL REVELATION TO AND THROUGH ISRAEL UNDER THE OLD COVENANT

A. THE BASIS OF DIVINE REVELATION UNDER THE OLD COVENANT[1]

The basis of revelation under the Old Covenant is God's choice[2] of a special people, Israel, out of God's sovereign love and with a view to the blessing of all humankind through Israel. Yahweh's choice of Israel was dramatized and particularized in his deliverance of Israel from Egypt (the Exodus), was symbolized and formalized by his covenant with Israel through Moses, and was to be fulfilled in the eschatological kingdom of God.

---

1. The recognition of the Old and the New Covenants as basic to special or biblical revelation is in effect a rejection of the concept of John Cocceius (or Koch) (1603-69) that the two basic biblical covenants were the Covenant of Nature *(foedus naturale)*, made with Adam and Eve and destroyed by the fall of humankind, and the Covenant of Grace *(foedus gratiae)*, found in both the Old and the New Testaments. See E. F. Karl Müller, "Cocceius, Johannes, and His School," *The New Schaff-Herzog Encyclopedia of Religious Knowledge*, 3:149-50. For a more recent exposition of the covenant of works (with Adam) and the covenant of grace, see Herman Hoeksema, *Reformed Dogmatics*, pp. 214-26, 285-336; Hoeksema called them "The Covenant with Adam" and "The *Pactum Salutis.*"
2. See Harold Henry Rowley, *The Biblical Doctrine of Election* (London: Lutterworth Press, 1952), esp. pp. 18-19.

The covenant[3] was intended to be a distinct blessing to Abram's seed[4] and to result in blessing to all peoples on earth (Gen. 12:1-3). The covenant, conditioned on obedience and covenant-faithfulness, was offered to the people of Israel through Moses and called for their affirmative response (Exod. 19:3-8). Israel was to know the presence of the invisible God (Exod. 33:12-23) and to receive the land of Canaan devoid of idolatry (Exod. 34:10-17). But Yahweh's choice of Israel as his people was not based on Israel's population or other qualifications but on his electing love and promises to the patriarchs (Deut. 7:6-11). This election did not exclude Yahweh's sovereignty over all the nations, as the Old Testament prophets often made clear. But the covenant must be renewed by subsequent generations of Israelites (Deut. 29; 2 Kings 23:1-3; also 2 Chr. 34:29-33).

In view of great ancient civilizations one may be prone to ask the question: Why not God's choice of China, of India, or of Egypt, with their cultures, history, religions, and people? Why tiny Israel? There seems to be no answer apart from the electing love and sovereign purpose of God.

B. Periods of Revelation under the Old Covenant

One should recognize that there were distinct periods or eras of revelation under the Old Covenant. To assert such periods is not to subscribe to any theory of the naturalistic evolution of Israel's religion. The Graf-Kuenen-Wellhausen approach to the Old Testament,[5] so dominant at the end of the nineteenth and the beginning of the twentieth centuries, seemed to presuppose a straight-line evolution of the religion of Israel from the lowest to the highest levels. Harry Emerson Fosdick in his *A Guide to Understanding the Bible*[6] popularized the same approach. John Bright has pointed out that the Graf-Kuenen-Wellhausen approach did have the value of showing that "revelation is not a picture gallery, but a process in history."[7]

Moreover, God's revelation was directed to Israel's situation and need.[8] But revelation advanced not only because Israel was willing or

3. Walther Eichrodt (1890-?), *Theologie des Alten Testaments* (Leipzig: C. Hinrichs, 1933, 1939), E.T. *The Theology of the Old Testament*, 2 vols., trans. J. A. Baker (Philadelphia: Westminster Press, 1961), was the first twentieth-century Old Testament theologian to make central the motif of the covenant.

4. Old Testament writers sometimes saw the covenant as issuing from Abraham's time and sometimes as issuing from Moses' time. See Rowley, *The Biblical Doctrine of Election*, pp. 19-36.

5. Julius Wellhausen, "Pentateuch and Joshua," *Encyclopedia Britannica*, 9th ed., 18:505-14; Robert H. Pfeiffer, *Introduction to the Old Testament* (New York: Harper and Bros., 1948), pp. 129-289, esp. 139-41. The author is indebted to Gleason L. Archer, Jr., for assistance in locating these materials.

6. (New York, London: Harper & Brothers, 1938).

7. *The Kingdom of God* (Nashville: Abingdon Press, 1953), pp. 9-10.

8. Conner, *Revelation and God*, p. 81.

ready to receive or perceive but also because God was ready and willing to disclose his nature and his will to Israel.

Consequently, one may identify as periods of revelation under the Old Covenant: the patriarchal, the Mosaic (Exodus, Law, and wanderings), the monarchical or early national (Samuel and the United Kingdom), the divided kingdom or prophetic, the captivity in Babylon, and the restoration or postexilic. From the perspective of the Old Testament canon one may say that the revelation under the Old Covenant embraces "the law (or Torah), the prophets (or Nebiim) and the writings (or Kethubim)."[9]

C. MODALITIES OF REVELATION UNDER THE OLD COVENANT

Many and diverse were the ways in which God revealed himself to Israel (Heb. 1:1). Bernard Ramm has utilized two adjectives to describe the modalities of biblical revelation, and they are especially applicable to the Old Testament. Ramm described biblical revelation as "anthropic" and as "analogical." By "anthropic" he means "marked by human characteristics throughout." Especially does this include what are called anthropomorphisms and the use of human languages. By "analogical" Ramm means the "bridge from the incomprehensibility of God to the knowability of God." "An analogy is that conceptual device whereby something in one universe of discourse is employed to explain, illustrate, or prove something in another universe of discourse."[10] Ramm's terms can serve as useful reminders of how thoroughly human and how filled with analogy was the revelation of God to and through Israel.

Emil Brunner has listed as modalities of revelation under the Old Covenant the following: theophanies, angels, dreams, oracles (such as Urim and Thummim), visions, locutions, natural phenomena, historical events, guidance to individuals and groups, and words and deeds of the prophets.[11] Ramm's list includes the following: the lot, Urim and Thummim (stones), deep sleep, dreams, visions, theophanies, and angels.[12] Erickson has stressed "historical events" and "divine speech."[13] One would think that the sacrifices and the moral mandates within the Torah should also be included.

Brunner also discussed revelation under the Old Covenant under four special categories: "the word of God," including teaching and the Law, "the acts of God," embracing narratives, signs, and acts of deliverance, "the name of God" as revelation itself, and "the Face of God," or theophanies.[14]

9. Stevens, *Doctrines of the Christian Religion,* p. 19.
10. *Special Revelation and the Word of God,* pp. 36-43.
11. *Revelation and Reason,* p. 21.
12. *Special Revelation and the Word of God,* pp. 44-48.
13. *Christian Theology,* pp. 181-90.
14. *Revelation and Reason,* ch. 7.

The Old Testament warns against two dangers concerning the modalities of divine revelation. First, there are dangers from false uses of true modalities, as one may see in the case of false prophets. Second, there are wrong kinds of modalities that are never to be trusted or heeded, such as witchcraft, astrology, and necromancy.[15]

D. THE UNIQUENESS OF THE REVELATION UNDER THE OLD COVENANT

1. The Events

The uniqueness of the religion of the Old Testament is to be found not only in the capacity of Israel's prophets to "see [the one] God in history" but also in the very events themselves. Thus prophetic insight alone does not account for the uniqueness of Israel's faith. Necessary to that uniqueness was the series of events that constituted Israel's history, which events we Christians by faith explain as God's self-disclosure to and through Israel.[16]

In the very recent past, Old Testament scholars have been divided concerning the issue of the locus of the uniqueness of the faith of Israel. First, certain Old Testament scholars such as Albrecht Alt (1883-1956), Martin Noth (1902-68), and Gerhard von Rad (1901-71), employing form criticism in the study of the Old Testament, have stressed Israel's own confession or interpretation of her faith. Von Rad, for example, has held that the subject matter of Old Testament theology "is simply Israel's own assertions about Yahweh." These assertions were founded on a "credo" around which numerous and various separate traditions were clustered. Accordingly, most of the Old Testament is an expansion of or commentary on this credo. Von Rad has denied that modern Christians, scholars or otherwise, can get behind these traditions to the bare events themselves.[17] Walther Eichrodt has criticized von Rad for cleaving or separating "the theological expressions of Israel's historical tradition and the facts of Israelite history."[18] Von Rad would accept some historical reality behind the traditions without making any effort to describe the "bare events."

Second, other Old Testament scholars such as Eichrodt, George Ernest Wright (1909-74), and Eric C. Rust have stressed the closer correlation of Israel's theology and the actual history of Israel so that the history is not relegated to uncertainty or nonimportance by the predominance of the credo or the kerygma. According to Eichrodt, there "must be an absolute refusal to surrender a real historical foundation to the faith of Israel, or to interpret the conflicts between the statements of the Old Testament version of history and that discovered by critical scholarship

15. Ramm, *Special Revelation and the Word of God*, pp. 49-52.
16. Conner, *Revelation and God*, pp. 81-83.
17. *Old Testament Theology*, trans. D. M. G. Stalker, 2 vols. (New York: Harper, 1962, 1965), 1:105.
18. *Theology of the Old Testament*, 1:512.

in a merely negative way as proof of the unimportance of the historical reference of religious statements."[19] Wright declared that biblical theology

> is a theology of recital or proclamation of the acts of God, together with the inferences drawn therefrom. These acts are themselves interpretations of historical events, or projections from known events to past or future, all described within the conceptual frame of one people in a certain historical continuum.[20]

If one should be inclined to agree with the second group of Old Testament scholars concerning the relation of historical events to faith-affirmations in the Old Testament, he should be aware of Millard Erickson's criticism of Wright's view within the context of a threefold typology of recent views as to the relation between divine revelation and historical events recorded in the Bible. Erickson sees the Neoorthodox view as that of "revelation through history." Accordingly, God has employed history as means or as "the shell" for his revelatory purpose, but revelation actually occurred in the past in experience (Abram, Moses, Isaiah, Paul) and occurs today whenever the reader or hearer of the Bible under the sovereignty of God has an encounter with God. Wright's view is labeled "revelation in history." Erickson interprets Wright's view to be that the mighty historical acts of God are the means of revelation but that the attributes of God are merely "inferred" from the mighty acts by the biblical writers and that modern Christians may have to correct or revise such inferences.[21] Finally, Erickson identifies the view of Wolfhart Pannenberg as that of "revelation as history," according to which the historical events of the Bible as God's mighty acts were indeed the revelation of God and clearly unfolded God's attributes.[22] Erickson has opted for Pannenberg's view.[23] Have not numerous conservative evangelical theologians in the Anglo-American sphere indeed taught essentially the same view?

2. The Concepts

Not only the events in Israel's history but also some of the concepts in Israel's apprehension of God were unique. Such concepts served to attract Gentile proselytes to the Jewish faith during the late intertestamental period and proved to be foundational to the faith of the New Testament. Four such concepts may be specified in particular.

---

19. Ibid., 1:516.
20. *God Who Acts: Biblical Theology as Recital*, Studies in Biblical Theology, vol. 8 (London: S.C.M. Press Ltd., 1952), p. 11.
21. The author is indebted to Thomas V. Brisco for the insight that Erickson's critique of Wright's view may not have taken into account all, and especially the later, writings of Wright and that in the latter one may find some balancing concerning the inferences.
22. *Christian Theology*, pp. 181-87.
23. Ibid.

a. The Significance of History

The sense of the significance of Israel's history, which came to be expressed in Israelite history writing, was not shared by contemporary nations.[24]

b. Monotheism

Israel alone was devoted to "the adoration of the one and only God."[25] This meant, in its maturity, that there was only one God for all humankind, not merely henotheism, or one deity for each nation or culture.

c. Attributes of Yahweh

Distinctive attributes were ascribed to Yahweh; for example, holiness, righteousness, love, faithfulness, etc.[26]

d. Messianism

Only in Israel was divine redemption seen to be from sin, in history, and through one from David's line, the Messiah.[27]

E. LIMITATIONS OF REVELATION UNDER THE OLD COVENANT

Neither an awareness of the unfolding character of revelation to Israel nor an acknowledgment of aspects of uniqueness in the revelation of God to and through Israel should prevent the frank acceptance of basic limitations within the revelation under the Old Covenant. Particularly should these limitations be viewed from the perspective of the postexilic or intertestamental era. Seven of these may be identified briefly.

1. The Law as Burdensome Code

Although it had been given as revelation and for Israel's good, the law, supplemented by a vast body of interpretation and application, became during the intertestamental period a burdensome code or system.

2. Inadequate Provision for Sin

Sacrifices for sin under the law had to be repeated. Moreover, they were effective only for sins of inadvertence (Lev. 4:2, 22, 27; 5:18; Num. 15:22-29), not for sins "with a high hand" (Num. 15:30).

3. Extreme Transcendence of God

Especially during the intertestamental era Yahweh was understood as quite transcendent, and thus Yahweh could be approached only through angels and mediaries.

24. *A New Catechism: Catholic Faith for Adults*, p. 41.
25. Ibid.
26. Norman H. Snaith, *The Distinctive Ideas of the Old Testament* (London: Epworth Press, 1944).
27. *A New Catechism: Catholic Faith for Adults*, pp. 40-41.

4. Unfulfilled Messianism

The Messiah had not yet appeared or come to the Jewish people, and thus all the associated expectations were as yet unrealized.

5. Dim Hope of Life after Death

The Hebrew doctrine of Sheol consisted of a shadowy, vague survival of human beings without any clear relationship to the living God.

6. Jewish Particularism

Although Israelite-Jewish history, especially with Ezra and the Maccabees, had been marked by the exclusion of the noncovenanted peoples, there had been exceptional Gentile inclusions (Ruth, Cyrus, Jonah to Nineveh). Although the exceptions continued (Gentile God-fearers and proselytes), Jewish particularism was so dominant as to prevent any Jewish mission to the Gentiles.

7. Repeated Covenant-Unfaithfulness of God's Covenant People

The wickedness and covenant-unfaithfulness that so repeatedly marked the rulers and the peoples of Israel and Judah served to obscure and to make less persuasive the revelatory features in Yahweh's covenant with this people.

II. SPECIAL REVELATION IN JESUS CHRIST UNDER THE NEW COVENANT

Christianity can be differentiated from Judaism by the Christian affirmation that God has made a new covenant in Jesus Christ that fulfills and in some ways supersedes the Old Covenant with Israel. Christianity can be differentiated from second-century and later forms of Marcionism by its affirmation that the Old Covenant was essential to salvation history and that the books of the Old Testament belong within and are integral to the canon of the Christian Scriptures.

In an effort to clarify what is meant by special revelation in Jesus Christ, we will examine it in terms of its modality or modalities, its fulfillment of the Old Covenant, its relation to the Holy Spirit and to apostleship, and its finality.

A. THE MODALITY OR MODALITIES OF REVELATION UNDER THE NEW COVENANT

1. One Modality

It is possible and indeed quite proper to conclude that under the New Covenant there is but *one* modality of revelation, namely, Jesus Christ himself. Erickson has identified "the incarnation" as "the most complete modality of revelation."[28] It is possible also to focus the modality in the person of Jesus Christ or in his death and resurrection. Any such answers mean that special revelation has only one modality.

2. Multiple Modalities

It is also possible to subdivide the modality so that one can conceive of a cluster of modalities through which God has revealed himself in Jesus Christ. The following delineation of such modalities is a recasting of Walter T. Conner's treatment.

a. The Death-Resurrection of Jesus

For post-Pentecostal Christianity of the first century A.D. no modality was of greater importance than Jesus' death and resurrection. By his resurrection Jesus was manifested as "Son of God in power" according to the Holy Spirit (Rom. 1:4). Following his resurrection he was exalted by God the Father and given "the name which is above every name" (Phil. 2:9). The One whom "God has made . . . both Lord and Christ" was the crucified Jesus (Acts 2:36). His crucifixion at "the hands of lawless men" was nevertheless both consonant with and expressive of God's purpose and plan (Acts 2:23). Jesus as crucified is both "the power of God and the wisdom of God" (1 Cor. 1:24). "God was in Christ reconciling the world to himself" (2 Cor. 5:19, RSV).[29] Paul saw in Jesus' death both a revelation of God's condemnation of human sin and a revelation of God's holy love for sinners (Rom. 8:3-4; 5:8).

b. Jesus' Claims concerning His Relationship with God the Father

Such claims by Jesus were threefold:

1) Jesus claimed to have been sent into the world with or on a divine mission by God the Father. "My food is to do the will of him who sent me, and to accomplish his work" (John 4:34, RSV). ". . . I seek not my own will but the will of him who sent me" (John 5:30). "For I have come down from heaven, not to do my own will, but the will of him who sent me" (John 6:38).

2) Jesus claimed to have a special, intimate, and unique knowledge of God the Father. He taught that "no one knows the Father except the Son" (Matt. 11:27c, RSV). "I know my own and my own know me, as the Father knows me and I know the Father" (John 10:14-15).

3) Jesus claimed to be the only conveyor or mediator of that special or unique knowledge of God to human beings. One should take note of the words: "and any one to whom the Son chooses to reveal him" (Matt. 11:27d, RSV).[30]

---

28. *Christian Theology*, pp. 190-91.
29. Conner, *Revelation and God*, pp. 115-18.
30. Ibid., pp. 114-15.

c. Jesus' Manifest Awareness of and Specific Teaching about God the Father

1) Jesus' conscious awareness of and fellowship with God the Father

This was the controlling factor in Jesus' life. His knowledge of the Father was direct and interpersonal, not based on argument or investigation or tradition. His relationship with the Father was unbroken by sin and continuous.

2) Jesus' teaching about God the Father

God was the center and subject of Jesus' teaching. His primary appellation for Yahweh God was the analogical name "Father." God the Father was characterized by love, grace, mercy, righteousness, power, wisdom, and similar qualities. Even those who deny Jesus' deity and the significance of his redemptive work acknowledge the superiority of his teaching about God.[31]

d. Jesus' Deeds and Actions

1) Miracles of healing

Jesus' miracles, called "signs" in the Fourth Gospel, manifested God's compassion and power and confirmed Jesus' divine mission (John 14:10-11).

2) Jesus' association with "sinners" (outcasts)

By associating with those persons who were religious and social outcasts Jesus manifested the Father's compassionate love for them.

3) Jesus' perfect embodiment of his own teaching

Jesus perfectly embodied his teaching about relationships with God the Father and with other human beings. He was sinless, being successfully resistant to temptation and not needing to repent of sin, as he had taught all others to do. Hence he was fully qualified to be the Redeemer or Savior of humankind.[32]

3. *Propositional Revelation or Relational Revelation?*

A major debate among Protestant theologians of the middle and latter twentieth century has been conducted between those who advocate propositional or conceptual revelation and those who advocate relational revelation. Although this debate pertains to biblical revelation under both testaments, the issue at stake is especially relevant for the New Testament, and hence it can be discussed under revelation under the New Covenant.

31. Ibid., pp. 111-13.
32. Ibid., pp. 113-14.

Propositionalism holds that revelation as propositions or concepts is either the primary or the sole characteristic of special revelation. Advocates of propositionalism include Cornelius Van Til,[33] Edward J. Carnell,[34] James I. Packer,[35] and Carl F. H. Henry.[36] Henry has provided a major statement and defense of propositionalism in his multivolume *God, Revelation, and Authority*.[37] The tenth of Henry's 15 theses is: "God's revelation is rational communication conveyed in intelligible ideas and meaningful words, that is, in conceptual-verbal forms."[38] According to Henry, revelational is mental, cognitive, meaningful, and propositional.[39]

Advocates of relational revelation include Karl Barth,[40] William Temple (1881-1944),[41] John Baillie,[42] Emil Brunner,[43] and William Hordern.[44] Building on "Søren Kierkegaard's distinction between objective and subjective truth" and Martin Buber's distinction between an I-Thou relationship and kind of knowledge and an I-it relationship and kind of knowledge, these theologians interpret revelation primarily, if not solely, as interpersonal, fiduciary, and encounter-centered.[45]

Must one choose sides in this debate? No, for there is some truth on both sides, and these truths need to be correlated. Propositionalism rightly stresses that God has employed human languages, including key words and concepts, in his self-disclosure through Israel and in Jesus Christ and that God has spoken and not merely acted in revelation with the result that revealed truth is not meaningless jargon. Relationalism rightly stresses that divine revelation is not dispensed information about God that does not transform the recipients with the result that revelation can never be rightly divorced from its liberating, saving, reconciling, and transforming effects on human beings. It is noteworthy that Carnell, classified above as a propositionalist, warned in 1959:

33. *The Protestant Doctrine of Salvation* (Ripon, Calif.: den Dulk Christian Foundation, 1967), p. 63.

34. *The Case for Biblical Christianity*, ed. Ronald H. Nash (Grand Rapids: Eerdmans, 1969), p. 169.

35. *"Fundamentalism" and the Word of God: Some Evangelical Principles* (London: Inter-Varsity Fellowship, 1958), pp. 91-94; *God Speaks to Man: Revelation and the Bible* (Philadelphia: Westminster Press, 1965), pp. 34, 49-58.

36. *God, Revelation, and Authority*, 3:455.

37. Ibid., 3:248-487.

38. Ibid., 2:12-13; 3:248.

39. Ibid., 3:248-487, et passim.

40. *The Doctrine of the Word of God: Prolegomena to Church Dogmatics*, I/1, pp. 124-35, 141-212; I/2, pp. 457-537.

41. *Nature, Man and God* (London: Macmillan, 1934), pp. 301-25, esp. 317, 319, 322.

42. *Our Knowledge of God* (London: Oxford University Press, 1939), pp. 35-43; *The Idea of Revelation in Recent Thought*, pp. 19-40.

43. *Revelation and Reason*, pp. 20-42.

44. *The Case for a New Reformation Theology*, pp. 54-75; *Speaking of God: The Nature and Purpose of Theological Language* (New York: Macmillan, 1964), pp. 142-46, 159-63.

45. Erickson, *Christian Theology*, pp. 191-96.

Protestants must recover the Reformation balance between revelation as a disclosure of God's *person* and revelation as a disclosure of God's *will*. The first is mystical and inward; the second, objective and propositional. If we drive a wedge between personal and propositional revelation, we evacuate Christian theology of its normative elements.[46]

Erickson has more recently declared:

Revelation is not *either* personal *or* propositional; it is *both/and*. What God primarily does is to reveal *himself*, but he does so at least in part by telling us something *about* himself.[47]

B. Revelation in Jesus Christ as the Fulfillment of the Revelation through Israel

"Think not that I have come to abolish the law and the prophets; I have come not to abolish them but to fulfil them" (Matt. 5:17, RSV). The leading aspects of this fulfillment coincide with the limitations characteristic of the revelation under the Old Covenant.[48]

1. *Law and Prophets*

The Law and the Prophets of the Old Covenant were fulfilled in him who was more than a prophet, the very Son of God, the Word of God, and the one who "ends the law and brings righteousness for everyone who has faith" (Rom. 10:4, NEB). "For the law was given through Moses; grace and truth came through Jesus Christ" (John 1:17).

2. *Forgiveness/Reconciliation*

The unresolved problem of human sin that necessitated repeated sacrifices under the Old Covenant has been solved in and by Jesus Christ. This was accomplished through his death as the Suffering Servant (Isa. 53) and as the High Priest who offered the once-for-all sacrifice for sin (Heb. 7:27; 9:12).

3. *Transcendence Balanced by Immanence*

Under the New Covenant the transcendent Yahweh has disclosed himself in and through the eternal Word "who became flesh and dwelt among us" (John 1:14). This Word could even be "heard" and "seen" and "touched" (1 John 1:1, NIV). He is superior to all angels (Heb. 1:4).

4. *Messianic Kingdom*

The promise and hope of the Messiah have been fulfilled by Jesus as the Messiah and, to use his preferred term, Son of Man, who heralded the

---

46. *The Case for Biblical Christianity*, p. 173. This half-chapter had originally been published as a book review in 1959.
47. Erickson, *Christian Theology*, p. 196.
48. See this chapter, I, E.

drawing near of the kingdom of God through his proclamation and ministry and its finalization at his second coming.

5. Life after Death

The expectation under the Old Covenant, dominated by the concept of Sheol and with occasional allusions to resurrection from the dead, has been clarified and made more specific by Jesus' resurrection from the dead and its serving as the basis for the final resurrection of humankind.

6. Particularism and Universalism

Although Jesus' own public ministry and that of the Twelve were focused on the people of the Old Covenant (Matt. 10:5-6), following Jesus' resurrection the good news concerning Jesus was proclaimed to Samaritans and Gentiles as well as Jews (Acts 8:4-25; ch. 10; 11:20-21). There began that missionary expansion of the Christian faith outside the boundaries of the Jewish people which issued from the belief that Jesus had died "for the sins of the whole world" (1 John 2:2b) and that "every [human] tongue [should] confess that Jesus Christ is Lord" (Phil. 2:11a) and from the specific commission by the risen Jesus (Matt. 28:18-20 and par.).

7. Revelation in the Obedient Divine-Human Person of Jesus Christ

Jesus by his submission to and obedience of the will of the Father, both in life and death and despite the allurements of temptation, perfectly fulfilled the New Covenant, thereby revealing the Father in unprecedented fashion and reconciling with singular effectiveness human beings to God.

C. REVELATION IN JESUS CHRIST AS ALSO REVELATION BY THE HOLY SPIRIT

God, or God the Holy Spirit, is, according to the New Testament, actively involved in the human reception of divine revelation. That reception is, of course, described as "believing" or "faith." But it is also described as the result of God's bestowal or initiative. Even the reception itself is due to the working of God, or, more explicitly, the working of the Holy Spirit. This divine agency in the reception of revelation is not always specifically attributed in the New Testament to the Holy Spirit. Sometimes it is ascribed to God the Father (Matt. 11:25; 16:17; Gal. 1:16).

There are New Testament texts in which the divine agency in the reception of revelation is specifically and clearly attributed to the Holy Spirit. Especially is this true of John 14–16 and 1 Corinthians. According to Jesus' promise or instruction, the Holy Spirit would "teach" the disciples "all things," "bring to . . . remembrance" all of Jesus' teaching (John 14:26, RSV), "bear witness" to Jesus (John 15:26), "guide" the disciples "into all the truth" (John 16:13, RSV), and "glorify" Jesus "by taking from

what is" Jesus' "and making it known" to the disciples (John 16:14, NIV).
Paul explicated the revelatory work of the Spirit in 1 Cor. 2:10-13, RSV:

> God has revealed to us through the Spirit. For the Spirit searches everything,
> even the depths of God. For what person knows a man's thoughts except
> the spirit of the man which is in him? So also no one comprehends the
> thoughts of God except the Spirit of God. Now we have received not the
> spirit of the world, but the Spirit which is from God, that we might under-
> stand the gifts bestowed on us by God. And we impart this in words not
> taught by human wisdom but taught by the Spirit, interpreting spriitual
> truths to those who possess the Spirit.

Similarly the same apostle declared that "no one speaking by the Spirit of
God ever says 'Jesus be cursed!' and no one can say 'Jesus is Lord' except
by the Holy Spirit" (1 Cor. 12:3, RSV).

D. REVELATION IN JESUS CHRIST ACCORDING TO THE WITNESS OF THE APOSTLES

All later Christians are dependent on the witness of the apostles to
Jesus Christ by the Holy Spirit. Their apprehension of Jesus Christ as
derivable through the New Testament depends on this apostolic witness.

1. The apostolic witness was post-Pentecostal, and hence the form
of this witness in the Acts and the epistles is different from its form in the
Gospels. Even so there is no basis for the anti-Pauline "Back to Jesus"
movement in Ritschlianism or for the Bultmannian overemphasis on the
early church's forming of the kerygma, or the proclaimed gospel.

2. The apostolic witness centered in the death-resurrection of Jesus,
not merely in his life and teachings.[49] It did include or use materials
incorporated in the four canonical Gospels.

3. The apostolic witness was that of irreplaceable eyewitnesses to
Jesus Christ. The apostles had a providential proximity to Jesus and were
personally selected and called by Jesus. Thus all later Christians are
necessarily dependent on their witness.[50] Yet, against Rudolf Bultmann,
it must be argued that the apostles did not "mythologize" the Christian
message.

4. Witness and mission[51] rather than rulership or dominion constituted the chief functions of the apostles, although they indeed exercised
apostolic authority. In the Catholic (Eastern Orthodox, Roman Catholic,
Anglo-Catholic) tradition the doctrine of apostolic succession from apos-

---

49. P. T. Forsyth, *The Principle of Authority* (London: Independent Press Ltd., 1952),
p. 87; C. H. Dodd, *The Apostolic Preaching and Its Developments* (Chicago: Willett, Clark &
Company, 1937), pp. 10-17, 22, 25, 48-51, 72-73.

50. Emil Brunner, *The Misunderstanding of the Church*, trans. Harold Knight (London:
Lutterworth Press, 1952), pp. 25-34; Stewart A. Newman, "The Ministry in the New Testa-
ment Churches," in Duke K. McCall, ed., *What Is the Church? A Symposium of Baptist Thought*
(Nashville: Broadman Press, 1958), pp. 52-53.

51. The term "mission" is linked through the Latin *mittere*, "to send," with the Greek
apostellein and *apostolos*.

tles to a line of bishops led those bishops to become rulers as well as teachers in the church, whereas for Irenaeus and Tertullian in the second and third centuries A.D. the emphasis was on the bishops' validation of apostolic truth.

5. The apostolic witness came to be embodied in the writings that we call "the New Testament." Thus the New Testament may be rightly construed as the successor to the apostles, even though every one of its books was not authored by an apostle. "The real successor of the Apostolate . . . was not the hierarchy but the canon of Scripture written to prolong their voice and compiled to replace the vanished witness."[52] Hans Küng has contended that "the whole Church" is successor to the apostles if its "witness" and "ministry" are apostolic.[53]

E. THE FINALITY OF THE REVELATION OF GOD IN JESUS CHRIST

1. The New Testament Witness

The New Testament writers bore witness to the finality or ultimacy of the revelation in Jesus Christ primarily by the use of the terms "image" and "Word." In 2 Cor. 4:4 Paul speaks of Christ as "the image of God," and in Col. 1:15 Christ is referred to as "the image of the invisible God." The Greek word for "image" (eikōn) is the same word that came later to be used in the Iconoclastic Controversy for "image" or "idol." In Heb. 1:3 (ASV) the author speaks of Christ as "the effulgence or outshining of God's glory and the express image of his substance." The word translated "image" here (charactēr) was used in the Greek in a manner similar to our modern English term used in engraving and printing, that is, the word "cut." Christ is the exact likeness of God even as the cut is the likeness of a human being. In John 1:1, 14-18 the Evangelist presents Jesus as the Word (logos) of God and as the incarnate Word. As the Word of God Jesus has "declared" or "exegeted" (exēgēsato) the Father. The finality of Jesus is also expressed by the sufficiency of his saving work. His work of reconciling the world is the work of God (2 Cor. 5:19), and his death as sacrifice is the "once-for-all" offering for sin (Heb. 9:12, 26; 10:12, 14).

2. The Contemporary Doctrine

The term "finality" needs to be understood in the sense of ultimacy and not in terms of chronological lastness. The finality of the revelation in Jesus Christ means that that revelation will not be abandoned, supplemented, or superseded.

---

52. P. T. Forsyth, *The Church and the Sacraments* (London: Independent Press Ltd., 1953), p. 64.
53. *The Church*, pp. 355-59.

a. Finality and the Person of Christ

The question as to the finality of special revelation in Christ depends on the finality of his person and work.[54] Any erosion as to the latter will inevitably affect the former. The cognitive aspect of revelation in Christ should never be severed from the redemptive or transformative aspect. The Christian claim is that revelation in Christ is ultimate, not to be superseded by Buddha or Krishna or Mohammed or Baha'u'llah (1817-92) or Joseph Smith, Jr. (1805-44), or Mary Baker Eddy (1821-1910) or Sun Myung Moon (1920-)!

b. Finality and the Universal Mission of Christianity

During the age of the Church Fathers the term "Catholic" came to mean not only geographical extensity, its original meaning, but also doctrinal authenticity, or, as Jaroslav Pelikan has stated, both "universality" and "identity."[55] Christianity has and will continue to have a "catholic" or universal mission. The gospel is to be taken to all human persons (demographic), "into all the world" (geographic), and "unto the end of the age" (chronological).

c. Finality and the General or Secular History of Humankind

Lesslie Newbigin has insisted that "the finality of Christ is to be understood in terms of his finality for the meaning and direction of history." He has asserted that the central question is not the Christian gospel vis-à-vis non-Christian religions (Will the pious Hindu be saved?) but rather Jesus Christ and universal history (Is Jesus the clue to all history?).[56] Wolfhart Pannenberg, writing over against Neoorthodoxy (Barth, Brunner) and the salvation-history school (Oscar Cullmann, 1902-), has insisted on directly relating the events crucial to the Christian gospel to general history.

d. Finality and Individual Human Destiny after Death

For centuries Christianity has connected "salvation" or "eternal life" with personal faith in Jesus Christ, his person and his work, so that individual destiny after death was governed by relationship with God through Jesus Christ. Today much of the theology and missiology of Roman Catholics and mainline Protestants has severed this relationship between the crucified and risen Jesus and personal destiny after death, with the result that only evangelical Protestants continue consistently to bear witness to the essentiality and necessity of personal faith in the incarnate, crucified, and risen Jesus for "salvation" or "eternal life."

54. Robert E. Speer, *The Finality of Jesus Christ* (New York: Fleming H. Revell Company, 1933).
55. *The Riddle of Roman Catholicism* (Nashville: Abingdon Press, 1959), pp. 22-23.
56. *The Finality of Christ* (London: SCM Press Ltd., 1969), pp. 8, 65.

In summary, special or biblical revelation consists both of revelation to and through Israel under the Old Covenant and of revelation in Jesus Christ under the New Covenant, and the latter is the proper and complete fulfillment of the former. "In the past God spoke to our forefathers through the prophets at many times and in various ways, but in these last days he has spoken to us by his Son . . ." (Heb. 1:1-2a, NIV).

CHAPTER 8

Biblical Inspiration

After exploring the Christian doctrine of revelation in confrontation with the claims of worldviews and non-Christian religions and as both general and special revelation, we must now turn to the relationship between that special revelation and the Bible, or the Holy Scriptures of the Old and the New Testaments. This new inquiry will involve the treatment of several different but related topics pertaining to the Bible. These will be the inspiration of the Bible, the canon of the Bible, the relation of the testaments, biblical criticism, the interpretation of the Bible, the Bible as the Word of God, the reliability of the Bible, and the place of the Bible in the total Christian concept of religious authority. The study can appropriately begin with the ancient and yet contemporary topic of the inspiration of the Bible.

I. SOME BASIC DISTINCTIONS AND DEFINITIONS CONCERNING BIBLICAL INSPIRATION

A. REVELATION AND THE BIBLE

Although some Christians have understood the two as synonyms, basic or primal revelation and the written Scriptures are related but not identical. In the words of W. T. Conner, "Revelation preceded the Bible. . . . The Bible is the product of revelation."[1] The revelation of God to Israel produced the Old Testament; the Old Testament did not produce God's revelation to Israel. Likewise, the revelation of God in Jesus Christ produced the New Testament; the New Testament did not produce the revelation of God in Jesus Christ. Francis Bruce Vawter (1921-) has asserted that Islam, Mormonism, and Christian Science are the products of their sacred books, delivered by their founders, but that "Israel and primitive Christianity definitely were not religions of this kind, for they were not brought into being by their sacred books."[2]

---

1. *Revelation and God*, pp. 78-79.
2. *Biblical Inspiration* (Philadelphia: Westminster Press; London: Hutchinson, 1972), p. 1. See Kelly, *Early Christian Doctrines*, pp. 29-79, for a summary of early Christian teachings both as to tradition, or the "canon of faith," and as to the Bible, or the canon of the Scriptures.

To pursue the distinction further, one should note that whereas revelation is God's self-disclosure to human beings, the Bible is the record of revelation. This distinction between revelation and the Bible does not prevent recognition that the Bible functions in the extension of the primal revelation and that for modern Christians the Bible has a necessary instrumental role in the testimony to and personal appropriation of revelation.

B. REVELATION AND INSPIRATION

Although closely related, revelation and inspiration are not identical. Revelation is God's working through events of history and human experiences so as to make himself known redemptively to human beings. On the other hand, inspiration is God's working through the biblical writers so as to secure an authentic declaration and record of the revelation. According to Harold Henry Rowley (1890-1969), "Revelation is . . . the divine self-unfolding, while inspiration lies in the use of human personality for the declaration of the divine message."[3] Thus inspiration is dependent on special revelation, yet inspiration enables special revelation to be extended to or made available to human beings in many nations and in different periods of human history. William James Abraham (1947-), however, has warned lest the distinction between revelation and inspiration be pressed too far. "As a matter of logic, inspiration is a unique activity of God that cannot be defined in terms of his other acts or activity, but as a matter of fact he inspires in, with, and through his special revelatory acts and through his personal guidance of those who wrote and put together the various parts of the Bible."[4]

C. THE TERM "INSPIRATION"

1. Etymology and Translation

The English term "inspiration" derives from the Latin noun *inspiratio* and means literally an "in-breathing." B. B. Warfield suggested that the English "spiration" would be a more proper term.[5] The Greek New Testament word used in 2 Tim. 3:16 is *theopneustos*, and its precise Latin equivalent would seemingly have been *spiratio Dei*. Thus an English word, "deispiration," yet to be coined or used, would probably be the ideal term. Abraham's assertion that the English "inspire" "supplies quite neatly what is required by the Greek"[6] is unconvincing. The word *theopneustos* is not from the Septuagint, according to Vawter, but "from the philosoph-

---

3. *The Faith of Israel: Aspects of Old Testament Thought* (London: SCM Press, 1961), p. 21.
4. *The Divine Inspiration of Holy Scripture* (New York: Oxford University Press, 1981), p. 67.
5. *The Inspiration and Authority of the Bible*, ed. Samuel G. Craig (London: Marshall, Morgan & Scott, 1951), p. 133.
6. *The Divine Inspiration of Holy Scripture*, p. 63. The author is indebted to Robert W. Bernard concerning Latin usage.

ico-religious vocabulary of classical Greece and of Hellenism," wherein it had ecstatic or mantic associations. But the meaning of the term in 2 Tim. 3:16 is based on Hebrew, not Greek thought.[7]

2. Definition

The definitions set forth for the term "inspiration" in reference to the Bible have been legion, and here it seems necessary to quote only two. The selection will deliberately exclude any definition that confines "inspiration" to human beings and refuses to apply it to biblical books. The definitions chosen are those by Augustus H. Strong and by Millard J. Erickson. According to Strong, "Inspiration is that influence of the Spirit of God upon the minds of the Scripture writers which made their writings the record of a progressive divine revelation, sufficient, when taken together and interpreted by the same Spirit who inspired them, to lead every honest inquirer to Christ and to salvation."[8] Erickson has defined inspiration as "that supernatural influence of the Holy Spirit upon the Scripture writers which rendered their writings an accurate record of the revelation or which resulted in what they wrote actually being the Word of God."[9] Both Strong and Erickson have mentioned the agency of the Holy Spirit; Strong emphasized the sufficiency of the Bible to lead human beings to Christ and salvation, whereas for Erickson it was important to state that by virtue of inspiration the Bible is the Word of God.

3. Principal Variant Usages

Quite significant differences in the usage of the term "inspiration" are to be found among Christian authors. Especially do these differences pertain to the objects of the inspiration, the focuses in respect to inspiration, and the methods used to formulate the concept.

a. Differing *Objects* of Inspiration

Some regard persons or authors only as the objects of the divine work of inspiration. Accordingly prophets, apostles, and other biblical writers themselves were divinely inspired, without any necessity that their writings be looked upon as inspired. Others reckon the writings, that is, the biblical books, to be inspired, and little or nothing is said about the inspiration of the writers. The two major texts pertaining to the inspiration of the Bible that appear in the New Testament reflect these two usages; 2 Pet. 1:20-21 refers to writers, and 2 Tim. 3:16-17 to writings.[10]

7. *Biblical Inspiration*, pp. 8, 10.
8. *Systematic Theology*, p. 196.
9. *Christian Theology*, p. 199.
10. Louis Gaussen, *The Divine Inspiration of the Bible*, trans. David D. Scott (Grand Rapids: Kregel Publications, 1971), pp. 24, 47, and William W. Stevens, *Doctrines of the Christian Religion* (Nashville: Broadman Press, 1967), p. 30, seem unduly to restrict inspiration to the writings.

b. Differing *Focuses* as to Inspiration

1) *On the process of inspiration*

How did inspiration occur? How were the divine and the human related? Those who have formulated detailed theories of inspiration have tended to major on the process. The various theories reflect in the main different efforts at describing the process.

2) *On the products of inspiration*

What are the evidences for inspiration, either from internal examination of the Bible or from its impact on human lives? What are the results of inspired Scripture? Such are the types of questions often posed by those intent on a focus on the results of inspiration. A. H. Strong preferred to define inspiration by its "result" rather than by its "method,"[11] and Russell Hooper Dilday, Jr. (1930-), has held that modern Christians can know the "purpose," "result," and "power" of inspiration even if they do not know for certain its method.[12]

c. Differing *Methods* of Formulating the Concept of Inspiration[13]

1) *Majoring on the biblical writers' statements about Scripture and their view of Scripture implied in the way by which they use it*

This is the deductive approach.[14] Biblical passages are collated so as to formulate the Bible's self-testimony, which is then applied to all the specifics of the Bible. This approach was espoused and utilized by the Princeton theologians Archibald Alexander Hodge (1823-86) and B. B. Warfield.[15] This method has characteristically given more emphasis to the divine agency than to human authorship in the production of the Bible.

2) *Majoring on the phenomena of Scripture, especially the nondidactic material and the so-called problems of Scripture*

This is the inductive approach.[16] A vast body of biblical texts that seem to pose problems as to how divine inspiration applies in specific cases is sometimes cited and discussed. This approach has become more common as a result of the rise and widespread use of the historical-critical method of Bible study. Exponents of this method have included Marcus Dods (1834-1909)[17] and Dewey Maurice Beegle (1919-).[18]

11. *Systematic Theology*, p. 196.
12. *The Doctrine of Biblical Authority* (Nashville: Convention Press, 1982), pp. 76-77.
13. See Erickson, *Christian Theology*, pp. 207-10.
14. Abraham, *The Divine Inspiration of Holy Scripture*, ch. 1.
15. Hodge, *Outlines of Theology* (rev. ed.; Grand Rapids: Eerdmans, 1949), pp. 69-71; Warfield, *The Inspiration and Authority of the Bible*, pp. 297-407.
16. Abraham, *The Divine Inspiration of Holy Scripture*, ch. 2.
17. *The Bible: Its Origin and Nature* (New York: Scribner's, 1905).
18. *Scripture, Tradition, and Infallibility* (Grand Rapids: Eerdmans, 1973), ch. 8.

4. Duration

Was the divine inspiration of prophets and apostles continuous or intermittent? Erickson, citing various Old Testament and New Testament texts concerning prophecy and spiritual gifts, has argued that inspiration was intermittent. Paul's correction of Peter (Gal. 2:14-21) is cited. Hence "inspiration was not a permanent and continuous matter tied inseparably to the office of prophet and apostle."[19]

II. INSPIRATION ACCORDING TO THE NEW TESTAMENT

It now becomes necessary to examine more fully that which New Testament writers state about the Old Testament and the wider testimony of these same writers concerning the divine inspiration and the human authorship of the Scriptures.

A. THE TWO PRINCIPAL TEXTS

1. Inspiration of the Old Testament Prophets or of All the Writers of the Old Testament

2 Pet. 1:20-21 (RSV) reads as follows:

First of all you must understand this, that no prophecy of scripture is a matter of one's own interpretation, because no prophecy ever came by the impulse of man, but men moved by the Holy Spirit spoke from God.

According to the context the eyewitnesses of Jesus, including Peter, were to be followed rather than "clearly devised myths." Indeed, the "prophetic word" was even "more sure." Did the author of these words intend the phrase "prophecy of scripture" to refer solely to the books of the Old Testament prophets? B. B. Warfield[20] and others have extended the meaning or application of this phrase so as to include all the canonical books of the Old Testament.

2. Inspiration of the Old Testament Scriptures

2 Tim. 3:16-17 reads as follows in the RSV:

All Scripture is inspired by God and profitable for teaching, for reproof, for correction, and for training in righteousness, that the man of God may be complete, equipped for every good work.

A careful examination of the Greek text shows that the first part of verse 16 is capable of being translated in at least four different ways:

a. Every Scripture is God-breathed and profitable. . . .
b. All Scripture is God-breathed and profitable. . . . ·
c. Every Scripture, God-breathed, is also profitable. . . .

---

19. *Christian Theology*, pp. 210-12.
20. *The Inspiration and Authority of the Bible*, pp. 135-36.

d. All Scripture, God-breathed, is also profitable. . . .

From the context we know that Timothy had from his childhood been familiar with the "sacred writings," which are instructive concerning salvation through Jesus Christ. The chief concern of the passage is that Timothy should be fully equipped as "the man of God." The intricacies that one may wish to probe concerning the manner of God's breathing of the Scripture have a lower priority for Paul.

B. OTHER RELATED TEXTS

Besides the two principal texts other passages in the New Testament may shed some light on the divine inspiration and human authorship of the biblical books. These passages have been assembled and interpreted by B. B. Warfield.[21]

1. Texts Relative to the Divine Inspiration or Authorship of the Scriptures

Paul declared that "the Jews are entrusted with the oracles of God" (Rom. 3:2, RSV), and Stephen in his sermon said that Moses had "received living oracles to give to us" (Acts 7:38, RSV). The author of Hebrews alludes to those who need to be taught again "the elementary truths of God's word" (5:12, NIV).

In the New Testament, Old Testament quotations are sometimes introduced by "it is said" instead of by "it is written" (Luke 4:12; Heb. 3:15). In other instances the Old Testament quotations are introduced by reference to what "He [God] says" or what "the Holy Spirit says" (Acts 13:35; Heb. 1:7; 3:7). Furthermore, Old Testament quotations are not uncommonly introduced by the subjectless verb "says" (Gal. 3:16; Rom. 15:10; 1 Cor. 6:16; 2 Cor. 6:12; Eph. 4:8; 5:14) with the implication that the subject should be God.

2. Texts Relative to the Human Dimension in the Inspiration of the Scriptures

Mark, in introducing the quotation of Ps. 110:1, stated: "David himself, inspired by the Holy Spirit, declared:" (12:36, RSV). Paul in his instructions to the Corinthian Christians about marriage made several comments that have some bearing on the human dimension of the New Testament books: "To the married, I give this command (not I, but the Lord)" (1 Cor. 7:10, NIV); "To the rest I say this (I, not the Lord)" (7:12); "Now about virgins: I have no command from the Lord, but I give a judgment as one who by the Lord's mercy is trustworthy" (7:25); and "I think that I too have the Spirit of God" (7:40b). In the same epistle Paul admonished: "If anybody thinks he is a prophet or spiritually gifted, let

21. Ibid., pp. 227-41, 297-407.

him acknowledge that what I am writing to you is the Lord's command" (14:37).

III. INSPIRATION IN THE HISTORY OF CHRISTIANITY

A. THE PATRISTIC AGE

In the writings of the Church Fathers there is great diversity as to the nature of biblical inspiration. No single view or theory predominates,[22] and modern scholarship has yet to provide a comprehensive treatment of the pertinent passages.[23] One can find extremely passive human participation in the writing of biblical books as well as more active and voluntary participation.

Some of the early Christian writers may have been influenced by the concept of Philo (c. 20 B.C.–c. A.D. 42), the Alexandrian Jew, that the prophets "lost consciousness" when God spoke through them.[24] The Montanists claimed that their prophet and two prophetesses were unconscious when they prophesied.[25] Athenagoras of Athens associated inspiration with a "state of ecstasy" and likened the divine inspiration of the Scriptures to a flute player's playing his flute,[26] while Theophilus of Antioch[27] referred to inspired men as "divine tools" and Hippolytus (d. 235) found a musical pick to be analogous to the inspired writers' being controlled by the Holy Spirit.[28] Irenaeus taught the verbal inspiration of the Scriptures yet ascribed to the human authors an active role such as in Paul's transposing the word order in his sentences.[29] Origen veered away from ecstasy and dictation and stressed the conscious powers and agency of the human authors.[30] In his *Commentary on John* he differentiated the divine element ("communication of a revealed word") and the human element ("commentary thereon by the scriptural author").[31] Yet the biblical books are clearly the product of the Holy Spirit.[32] John Chrysostom's (between 344 and 354-407) concept of condescension included the human authorship of the Scriptures.[33]

---

22. Maurice Wiles, *The Making of Christian Doctrine* (Cambridge: Cambridge University Press, 1967), p. 46.

23. Vawter, *Biblical Inspiration*, p. 21.

24. *Quis rer. div. haer.* 249-66 and *De spec. leg.* 4.48-49, as cited by J. N. D. Kelly, *Early Christian Doctrines* (New York: Harper and Bros., 1958), p. 62.

25. Epiphanius, *Haer.* 48.4ff., as cited by Kelly, *Early Christian Doctrines*, p. 62.

26. *Apology* 7, 9.

27. *To Autolycus* 2.9, as quoted by Vawter, *Biblical Inspiration*, p. 25.

28. *De Christo et Antichristo* 2, as cited by Vawter, *Biblical Inspiration*, p. 25. The dictation of the content of biblical books by the Holy Spirit to passive human amanuenses has been traced to 2 Esdras 14; see George Eldon Ladd, *The New Testament and Criticism* (Grand Rapids: Eerdmans, 1967), pp. 20-21.

29. *Against Heresies* 3.7.2, as cited by Otto W. Heick, *A History of Christian Thought*, 2 vols. (Philadelphia: Fortress Press, 1965-66), 1:84-85.

30. *Hom. in Ezek.*, frag. 6.1, as cited by Vawter, *Biblical Inspiration*, p. 26.

31. Vawter, *Biblical Inspiration*, p. 26.

32. *On First Principles* 4.9.

33. Vawter, *Biblical Inspiration*, pp. 40-42.

Jerome (347?-419) recognized stylistic and cultural differences among the biblical books,[34] and yet " 'every word, syllable, accent and point is packed with meaning.' "[35] Augustine of Hippo posited the use of personal reminiscences in the compilation of the Gospels.[36] Theodore of Mopsuestia (350-428) distinguished between the special inspiration of the Old Testament prophets and the "inferior grace of 'prudence' granted to Solomon"[37]—a distinction that rightly or wrongly modern scholars have tended to call levels of inspiration—and yet all biblical writers wrote under the influence of the Holy Spirit.[38]

B. The Middle Ages

Building on the foundation of patristic teaching, the Schoolmen applied to prophecy the "Aristotelian category of instrumental efficient causality."[39] The inspiration of biblical books was, according to Thomas Aquinas, a subordinate part of the larger subject of prophecy.[40]

C. The Reformation and Post-Reformation Eras

Martin Luther had a highly developed, multifaceted doctrine of Holy Scripture, but little of it was specifically focused on inspiration.[41] For John Calvin in his *Institutes of the Christian Religion* the internal testimony of the Holy Spirit concerning the Scriptures as validating the authority of the Scriptures was paramount; what he thought about biblical inspiration, that is, verbal inspiration with divine accommodation to differing human styles, must therefore be derived for the most part from his commentaries.[42] The Council of Trent in its delineation of the biblical canon reaffirmed that God is the "author" of both the Old and the New Testaments

34. *In Isa.*, prol., *In Jerem.*, prol., and *In Am.*, prol., as cited by Kelly, *Early Christian Doctrines*, p. 63.

35. *In Eph.* 2 (3.6), as quoted by Kelly, *Early Christian Doctrines*, p. 62.

36. *On the Harmony of the Evangelists* 3.30.

37. *In Job*, as quoted by Kelly, *Early Christian Doctrines*, p. 61.

38. *In Nah.* 1.1, as cited by Kelly, *Early Christian Doctrines*, p. 61.

39. Vawter, *Biblical Inspiration*, p. 48.

40. Ibid., pp. 52-57.

41. Paul Althaus, *The Theology of Martin Luther*, trans. Robert C. Schultz (Philadelphia: Fortress Press, 1972), ch. 9.

42. *Institutes of the Christian Religion*, 1559 ed., 1.7; Vawter, *Biblical Inspiration*, p. 30. On Calvin's teaching contrast: (1) A. Mitchell Hunter, *The Teaching of Calvin: A Modern Interpretation* (Glasgow: Maclehose, Jackson and Company, 1920), pp. 59-87; Edward A. Dowey, Jr., *The Knowledge of God in Calvin's Theology* (New York: Columbia University Press, 1952), pp. 90-124; Kenneth S. Kantzer, "Calvin and the Holy Scriptures," in John F. Walvoord, ed., *Inspiration and Interpretation* (Grand Rapids: Eerdmans, 1957), pp. 115-55; John Murray, *Calvin on Scripture and Divine Sovereignty* (Grand Rapids: Baker Book House, 1960), pp. 11-51; and John H. Gerstner, "The View of the Bible Held by the Church: Calvin and the Westminster Divines," in Norman L. Geisler, ed., *Inerrancy* (Grand Rapids: Zondervan, 1980), pp. 385-410, with (2) Wilhelm Niesel, *The Theology of Calvin*, trans. Harold Knight (Philadelphia: Westminster Press, 1956), pp. 22-39; T. H. L. Parker, *Calvin's Doctrine of the Knowledge of God* (Grand Rapids: Eerdmans, 1952), pp. 42-48; and H. Jackson Forstman, *Word and Spirit: Calvin's Doctrine of Biblical Authority* (Stanford, Calif.: Stanford University Press, 1962), pp. 49-65.

and declared that both the written Scriptures and "unwritten traditions" had been "dictated by the Holy Spirit."[43] A Lutheran, Matthias Flacius Illyricus (1520-75), first suggested the divine inspiration of the vowel points in the Hebrew Bible.[44] During the seventeenth century theologians of Lutheran and Reformed Orthodoxy, notably Johannes Gerhard (1582-1637), Johannes Andreas Quenstedt (1617-88), Johann Heinrich Heidegger (1633-98), and Francis Turretin (1671-1737), taught the utter passivity and sheer instrumentality of the biblical writers under the sway of the Holy Spirit, the dictation of biblical texts by the Holy Spirit, and the consequent inerrancy of the Bible.[45] Melchior Cano (1509-60) and Domingo Bañez (1528-1604), both Dominican theologians, were "maximalists" in that they affirmed divine dictation, even to the extent of the commas, whereas seventeenth-century Catholic theologians such as Francisco Suarez (1548-1617) and Richard Simon (1638-1712) were "minimalists" in that they held that "God provided negative assistance only to help the writers avoid errors in the text,"[46] a position similar to that of the Arminian Hugo Grotius (1583-1645).[47] The eighteenth-century practitioners of the new literary and historical (often called "higher") criticism of the Bible with their concepts of multiple authorship and redaction of biblical books abandoned any orthodox doctrine of inspiration; Johann Salomo Semler (1725-91) sought to retain the idea that the Bible evidenced "a consciousness of the power of God's word" and its mediation, but Johann Gottfried Herder (1744-1803), Johann David Michaelis (1717-91), and other critics disavowed any effort to retain any concept of the inspiration of the biblical writings.[48]

D. THE MODERN ERA

The nineteenth century witnessed the exposition of various and divergent views or theories of biblical inspiration; some of these had originated in earlier centuries, and for most of these there have been advocates during the twentieth century. In 1888 Basil Manly, Jr. (1825-92), a Southern Baptist, identified six different theories, some of which had variant forms.[49] In 1907 Augustus H. Strong listed only four major theories,[50] those same four theories were listed by Dewey M. Beegle in

43. *Canons and Decrees of the Council of Trent*, 4th session, 8 April 1546.
44. Bernhard Lohse, *A Short History of Christian Doctrine*, trans. F. Ernest Stoeffler (Philadelphia: Fortress Press, 1966), pp. 217-18.
45. Vawter, *Biblical Inspiration*, pp. 81-83; Robert Gnuse, *The Authority of the Bible: Theories of Inspiration, Revelation and the Canon of Scripture* (New York: Paulist Press, 1985), pp. 22-23.
46. Vawter, *Biblical Inspiration*, pp. 59-61; Gnuse, *The Authority of the Bible*, pp. 7-8.
47. Vawter, *Biblical Inspiration*, p. 82.
48. Ibid., pp. 83-89.
49. *The Bible Doctrine of Inspiration Explained and Vindicated* (New York: A. C. Armstrong and Son, 1888), pp. 44-60.
50. *Systematic Theology*, pp. 202-12.

1963,[51] and Millard Erickson listed five in 1983.[52] It is important to identify these theories and their major exponents.

1. Major Views or Theories

a. Verbal Inspiration with Inerrancy

Attempting to avoid the mechanical dictation, or amanuensis, theory of post-Reformation Lutheran and Reformed Orthodoxy, the advocates of this position have affirmed the divine inspiration of words, not merely ideas, and the total inerrancy of the Scriptures. They include F. S. R. Louis Gaussen (1790-1863), a Swiss Protestant whose book circulated widely in the English-reading world, Charles Hodge and B. B. Warfield of Princeton, and Popes Leo XIII, Pius X, and Benedict XV.[53] Those holding to this theory have had difficulty in avoiding the commonplace criticism of the dictational theory, namely, that the biblical writers are seen as "passive instruments or amanuenses—pens, not penmen, of God."[54]

b. Dynamic or Limited Verbal Inspiration View

This view has sought to emphasize the individuality and diversity of the biblical writers, especially respecting language, and although inspiration extends to the words, inerrancy is likely to be limited to matters of doctrine and ethics. Exponents have included James Orr (1844-1913), Abraham Kuyper (1837-1920), and G. C. Berkouwer among Protestants and Marie-Joseph Lagrange (1855-1938) among Roman Catholics.[55]

c. Different Levels or Degrees of Inspiration

Divine inspiration, according to this view, functioned differently on various levels. Four such levels have been reported;[56] from lowest to highest they are:

1) Superintendence: God's preventing the writer from embracing error
2) Elevation: God's giving loftiness to the thought of the human writer
3) Direction: God's instructing the writer what to include and what to omit
4) Suggestion: God's determining for the human writer both the thoughts and the words to be utilized

51. *The Inspiration of Scripture* (Philadelphia: Westminster Press), pp. 124-25.
52. *Christian Theology,* pp. 206-7.
53. Gnuse, *The Authority of the Bible,* pp. 23-24; Dewey Beegle, *Scripture, Tradition, and Infallibility* (Grand Rapids: Eerdmans, 1973), pp. 145-46, 231; Vawter, *Biblical Inspiration,* pp. 121-22, 138-41.
54. Strong, *Systematic Theology,* p. 208.
55. Ibid., p. 211; Gnuse, *The Authority of the Bible,* pp. 34-37.
56. Gaussen, *The Divine Inspiration of the Bible,* pp. 27-28, 107-8; Manly, *The Bible Doctrine of Inspiration,* pp. 52-54.

Seemingly Leonard Woods (1774-1854) and Salvatore di Bartolo advocated such an approach.[57]

d. Partial Inspiration

This perspective on biblical inspiration may be found in several forms, but the common element is that some aspect of the Bible is removed from the direct impact of divine inspiration. The more prevalent forms of this view have probably been those espousing inspiration of ideas and inspiration of persons. John Henry Newman (1801-90), Johannes Baptist Franzelin (1816-86), whose theology influenced Vatican Council I, and William Robertson Smith (1846-94) were exponents of the first view, according to which the ideas of biblical writers were inspired of God, but not their language, illustrations, quotations, or allusions. William Sanday (1843-1920), Harry Emerson Fosdick, and Charles Harold Dodd (1884-1973) were among the advocates of the inspiration of persons or authors, which inspiration was not extended to writings.[58]

e. Universal Christian Inspiration

This theory, also called the illumination theory, holds that the Bible was inspired by the Holy Spirit in the same way in which every Christian is illumined by the Holy Spirit. Hence there was no special divine agency in the production of the Christian Scriptures. Exponents of this position have included F. D. E. Schleiermacher, Samuel Taylor Coleridge (1772-1834), and James Martineau (1805-1900), a Unitarian theologian.[59]

f. Natural Inspiration, or Intuition

This is the view that the writers of the biblical books were inspired in no way distinctive from that in which poets, dramatists, philosophers, and geniuses such as Homer (9th cent. B.C.?), Plato, William Shakespeare (1564-1616), John Milton (1608-74), and Fyodor Dostoevsky (1821-81) were inspired. Accordingly, all human beings are inspired, and their inspiration differs only in degrees. Thus inspiration is seen as a type of religious and poetic genius. Advocates would find almost no uniqueness in the Bible when compared with other so-called sacred books. Theodore Parker (1810-60), an American Unitarian, adopted this view.[60]

The markedly liberal Protestant leadership during the nineteenth century normally accepted either the universal Christian or the natural view. The distinctly conservative Protestant leaders normally taught either the verbal inspiration with inerrancy view or the dynamic view.

---

57. Manly, *The Bible Doctrine of Inspiration*, p. 53; Vawter, *Biblical Inspiration*, p. 135.
58. Gnuse, *The Authority of the Bible*, pp. 42-47; Vawter, *Biblical Inspiration*, pp. 70-72, 96-100.
59. Strong, *Systematic Theology*, p. 204; Manly, *The Bible Doctrine of Inspiration*, pp. 56-59.
60. Strong, *Systematic Theology*, p. 202; Manly, *The Bible Doctrine of Inspiration*, pp. 54-56.

Other Protestants tended to opt for either of the other two views. Differences tended to be within and not merely between the denominations.[61] Among Roman Catholic theologians there were significant differences.

2. *Variations as to Language*

Writers dealing with the inspiration of the Bible during the modern era have not employed the key adjectives concerning inspiration in a uniform manner. Terms such as "plenary," "dynamic," "verbal," and "essential" have been used with different meanings. The term "plenary" has been accepted and joined with the inerrancy of the Bible.[62] The terms "plenary" and "verbal" have been accepted and the Bible's being "without error" affirmed but with mechanical dictation being denied.[63] The term "plenary" has been accepted and the term "verbal" rejected.[64] The term "plenary dynamical," meaning the Bible's trustworthiness in its secular history, has been rejected, whereas "religious dynamical," meaning the Bible's trustworthiness in religious matters, has been accepted.[65] The term "dynamical" has been applied both to writers and to writings, in an effort to recognize the individuality of the writers in environment, language, and expression, and has been joined with the terms "supernatural" and "plenary."[66] The term "plenary verbal" has been equated with mechanical dictation and both concepts rejected.[67] The terms "plenary," "verbal," and "dynamic" have been regarded as describing three different theories of inspiration.[68] It has also been held that no theory of the method of divine inspiration is needed, and hence no precision as to adjectives required.[69]

61. For example, see the author's "Representative Modern Baptist Understandings of Inspiration," *Review and Expositor* 71 (Spring 1974): 179-95.

62. Gaussen, *The Divine Inspiration of the Bible*, pp. 23, 34-35.

63. A. A. Hodge in A. A. Hodge and B. B. Warfield, *Inspiration* (reprint ed.; Grand Rapids: Baker Book House, 1979), pp. 18-29. Richard Riss, "Early Nineteenth-Century Protestant Views of Biblical Inspiration in the English Speaking World" (M.A. thesis, Trinity Evangelical Divinity School, 1986), as cited by Donald A. Carson, "Recent Developments in the Doctrine of Scripture," in Carson and John Woodbridge, eds., *Hermeneutics, Authority, and Canon* (Grand Rapids: Zondervan, 1986), pp. 12-13 and nn. 31-33, has cited six nineteenth-century Anglo-American authors of monographs on inspiration who did not differentiate "plenary inspiration" from "verbal inspiration."

64. Charles A. Briggs, *Presbyterian Review* 2 (1881): 550-79, as interpreted by Lefferts A. Loetscher, *The Broadening Church* (Philadelphia: University of Pennsylvania Press, 1954), p. 32.

65. Alvah Hovey, *Manual of Christian Theology* (New York: Silver, Burdett, 1900), pp. 85, 78-81.

66. Strong, *Systematic Theology*, p. 211.

67. J. Clyde Turner, *These Things We Believe* (Nashville: Convention Press, 1956), p. 3; Stevens, *Doctrines of the Christian Religion*, p. 32.

68. Dilday, *The Doctrine of Biblical Authority*, pp. 74-75.

69. W. T. Conner, *A System of Christian Doctrine* (Nashville: Sunday School Board of the Southern Baptist Convention, 1924), pp. 108-10; idem, *Revelation and God*, p. 84.

3. *Other Related Developments*

a. Catholic Modernists early in the twentieth century retained inspiration but affirmed biblical errancy, evoking the strong condemnation of Pope Pius X (1835-1914).[70]

b. Fundamentalist Protestants on the Anglo-American scene, building on the Princeton theology, conjoined inspiration and inerrancy of the autographs of the Bible and defended both.[71]

c. Neoorthodox Protestant theologians criticized verbal inspiration, which they reckoned to be identical with mechanical dictation, and themselves bypassed and became quite unspecific concerning inspiration.[72]

d. Alternative theologies vis-à-vis the Bible have been formulated: the salvation-history emphasis, focused on the mighty acts of God in biblical history (Oscar Cullmann);[73] the religious language school, stressing that God supplied the essential images, or language symbols, and not merely the events or truths that the images seek to describe (Austin Marsden Farrer, 1904-68);[74] and the socio-ecclesial view of inspiration, according to which inspiration is seen as that of the community of faith, especially in view of the work of scribes and redactors (Pierre Benoit, 1906-87, Karl Rahner, John Lawrence McKenzie, 1910- , Paul John Achtemeier, 1927-).[75]

e. Among Evangelical Protestants during the 1970s and 1980s, especially in the United States, inspiration has attained a new prominence as the ally of biblical inerrancy.[76]

IV. INSPIRATION AND TODAY'S CHRISTIANITY

For most of the centuries of Christian history the concept of the divine inspiration of the Bible was largely unchallenged through major objec-

70. Gnuse, *The Authority of the Bible*, pp. 11-12.

71. See George M. Marsden, *Fundamentalism and American Culture: The Shaping of Twentieth-Century Evangelicalism, 1870-1925* (New York: Oxford University Press, 1980), pp. 16-18, 103-8, 110-14, 119-22.

72. Emil Brunner, *Revelation and Reason*, pp. 118-30; idem, *Our Faith*, trans. John W. Rilling (New York: Charles Scribner's Sons, 1936), pp. 6-11; William Hordern, *The Case for a New Reformation Theology*, pp. 53-75.

73. Cullmann, *Christ and Time*; idem, *Salvation in History*; G. E. Wright, *God Who Acts*; E. C. Rust, *Salvation History*.

74. Farrer, *The Glass of Vision* (London: Dacre Press, 1948).

75. Karl Rahner, *Inspiration in the Bible*, trans. Charles Henkey and rev. Martin Palmer (2d rev. ed.; New York: Herder and Herder, 1964); Pierre Benoit, *Inspiration and the Bible*, trans. Jerome Murphy-O'Connor and M. Keverne (New York: Sheed and Ward, 1965); Paul J. Achtemeier, *The Inspiration of Scripture: Problems and Proposals*, Biblical Perspectives on Current Issues (Philadelphia: Westminster Press, 1980), pp. 114-18; Gnuse, *The Authority of the Bible*, pp. 50-62.

76. Jack B. Rogers, ed., *Biblical Authority* (Waco, Tex.: Word Books, 1977); Rogers and Donald K. McKim, eds., *The Authority and Interpretation of the Bible: An Historical Approach* (San Francisco: Harper and Row, 1979); John D. Woodbridge, *Biblical Authority: A Critique of the Rogers-McKim Proposal* (Grand Rapids: Zondervan, 1982).

tions, if not always clearly interpreted or precisely defined. Its major challenge has come in the modern period through the impact of literary and historical criticism of the Bible with its corresponding stress on the human aspects of the Bible. During the present century inspiration has been bypassed or downplayed by some and reasserted and somewhat reinterpreted by others who see it as central to authentic Christianity. Despite the fact that neither the teaching of Jesus (and accompanying interpretation by the Gospel writers) nor the major epistles of Paul nor the epistles of John contain the teaching of biblical inspiration, modern Christians cannot avoid the need to deal directly and responsibly with this topic.

The greatest single need with respect to the doctrine of inspiration is for balance between divine agency and human involvement in the coming to be of the books of the Old and the New Testaments. Even as in Christology, wherein extremes of emphasis on the divine to the neglect of the human or on the human to the neglect of the divine have led to heretical conclusions and serious theological conflict, so also extremes in respect to the divine and the human associated with the Bible need to be avoided. Neither a "docetism" nor a mere "humanitarianism" regarding the Bible can be adequate.[77]

Christians at the end of the twentieth century should also be increasingly aware that biblical inspiration cannot be studied or expounded effectively in isolation from related themes concerning the Bible—the canon, the relation of the testaments, biblical criticism, biblical hermeneutics, the concept of the Word of God, the dependability of the Bible, and the larger question of authority in Christianity. Rather it must be treated in fruitful conjunction with these related subjects. Hence it is now urgent that these closely related topics be explored.

---

77. Gnuse, *The Authority of the Bible,* pp. 30-31, 64; Berkouwer, *Holy Scripture,* pp. 17-20.

CHAPTER 9

The Canon of the Bible,
the Relation of the Testaments,
and the Unity of the Bible

To affirm that the Bible is the record of special divine revelation and that
it is divinely inspired while being also the product of human composition
is to need to ask further questions as to the scope of the Bible and the
relation of its various parts to the whole. Hence we now come to the study
of what is called the "canon" of the Old and the New Testaments, the
relation of the Old Testament and the New Testament, and the basic unity
of the Bible.

I. THE CANON OF THE BIBLE

The Greek word *kanōn*, translated into English as "canon," seems to have
had originally a general or secular usage, namely, a reed used for a
measuring rod or yardstick. Among Christians of the postapostolic era
this Greek word was, it seems, first used to refer to the Old Roman
Symbol (R)—what we now call the Apostles' Creed—and then later was
used in reference to accepted biblical books. By this second usage
"canon" came to be understood as the inclusive number and exact
identity of the books of the "New Testament," and subsequently as the
inclusive number and exact identity of those books which Christians had
received from Jews and now called the "Old Testament."[1] The history of
the process of canonization by Jews of that which Christians came to call
the Old Testament and of the process of canonization by Christians of
the New Testament cannot be pursued in great detail here, but it must
be presupposed from biblical studies. Greater attention must here be
given to those theological issues which pertain to canonization and the
continuing existence of the canon.

1. Heick, *A History of Christian Thought,* pp. 82-92, esp. 83.

A. The Canon of the Old Testament

Scholars do not fully agree concerning the stages in the canonization of the books of the Hebrew Bible, which stages must not be assumed to be identical with the times of writing of these books. Some have traced the beginning of the canonization of the Law prior to the Deuteronomic reform movement during King Josiah's reign in the late seventh century B.C.[2] Others have allowed for a possible sixth-century canon collection of the Prophets during the Babylonian exile, which collection correlated the prophecies of doom and the prophecies of salvation.[3] Still others have held that the Pentateuch did not attain full canonicity until the fourth century B.C. and the prophetic books not until about 200 B.C.[4] There has been greater agreement as to the probability that the third portion of the Hebrew Bible, the Writings, did not attain to full canonicity prior to the end of the first century A.D., though it is not clear whether this occurred at the rabbinic Council of Jamnia (A.D. 90).[5] It has been argued that this process of canonization, however, did not result in one universally accepted canon among all Jews. Instead the result was two canons. One was the Palestinian canon, which consisted only of the 22 books of the Hebrew Bible. According to this reckoning the books of Joshua-Judges, Samuel, Kings, Chronicles, and Ezra-Nehemiah were taken as five, and not ten, books, all the minor prophets were considered one book, and Ruth and Lamentations were counted as separate books. The other was the Hellenistic canon, which consisted of the 22 books of the Hebrew Bible, nine additional books, and some additions to the books of Daniel and Esther.[6] But now, on the basis of a reconsideration of the entire history of the Old Testament canon, David G. Dunbar has rejected the theory of closure at Jamnia and the theory of a distinctive Alexandrian or Hellenistic canon and has inclined to the conclusion that the canon closure occurred by about 100 B.C.[7] Roger T. Beckwith has pushed the closure back to the Maccabean age, 164 B.C.[8]

If this was in summary the role of the Jews in recognizing as canonical the books of their sacred writings, what did Christians do as to

---

2. Brevard Childs, *Introduction to the Old Testament as Scripture* (Philadelphia: Fortress Press, 1979), pp. 60-67.

3. Ronald Clements, "Patterns in the Prophetic Canon," in *Canon and Authority: Essays in Old Testament Religion and Theology,* ed. George Coats and Burke Long (Philadelphia: Fortress Press, 1977), pp. 42-55, esp. 52.

4. Ira M. Price, *The Ancestry of Our English Bible,* rev. William A. Irwin and Allen P. Wikgren (3d rev. ed.; New York: Harper & Brothers, 1956), pp. 16-17.

5. Gnuse, *The Authority of the Bible,* p. 107.

6. J.N.D. Kelly, *Early Christian Doctrines* (New York: Harper & Bros., 1958), pp. 53-54. Floyd V. Filson, *Which Books Belong to the Bible? A Study of the Canon* (Philadelphia: Westminster Press, 1957), pp. 82-83, expressed doubts, based on Philo's usage, as to the existence of two Jewish canons.

7. "The Biblical Canon," in Carson and Woodbridge, eds., *Hermeneutics, Authority, and Canon,* pp. 299-360, esp. 303, 308, 315.

8. *The Old Testament Canon of the New Testament Church and Its Background in Early Judaism* (London: S.P.C.K., 1985; Grand Rapids: Eerdmans, 1986), pp. 260-62, 316-18, 434-37.

the recognition as canonical of these same books? During the first and second centuries A.D. Christians were in no dispute on this question and tended to follow the so-called Hellenistic canon. By the fourth and fifth centuries, however, a perceptible difference had arisen. The Eastern, chiefly Greek, Church Fathers seemed to look upon those books included in the Hellenistic canon but excluded from the so-called Palestinian canon as "deuterocanonical," and hence as being less fully canonical than the other books. The Western or Latin Church Fathers, however, following the lead of Augustine of Hippo, adhered to the more inclusive canon of the Old Testament.[9] This Western pattern was continued in the West during the medieval period and then given conciliar sanction by the Council of Trent. On the other hand, the Protestant Reformers adopted the less inclusive canon of the Old Testament. Consequently, during the modern era Protestants and Eastern Orthodox[10] share a common canon, which is that of the Palestinian canon of the Jews, and Roman Catholics have a more inclusive canon, as was the Hellenistic canon of the Jews.

B. THE CANON OF THE NEW TESTAMENT

The canonization of the New Testament involved a process that extended from the second century A.D. until the later fourth century. During that period there were yet-to-be clarified views as to the extent of the canon and the precise identity of the canonical books. Some postapostolic Christian writings such as the Shepherd of Hermas, Clement of Rome's Epistle to the Corinthians, the Epistle of Barnabas, the Apocalypse of Peter, and the Acts of Paul were for a time recognized in some circles as being of equal value with the apostolic writings. Some of the books that comprise our canonical New Testament were not indisputably canonical until after the middle of the fourth century. Hebrews, James, and 2 Peter were slow to be accepted in the West, and in the East there was reluctance to receive Revelation.[11]

Why, one may ask, was it necessary to have a closed canon of the New Testament? Among the reasons or factors given for the necessity of a definitive canon have been the proliferation of Gnostic gospels and apocalypses, the challenge of the Montanist movement, the issuance of Marcion's canon (c. 140) with its truncated Gospel of Luke and ten Pauline letters, and the Syrian Church's use of the Peshito as its canon after the second century.[12]

9. Kelly, *Early Christian Doctrines,* pp. 54-56.
10. Whereas the Russian Orthodox Church in its confession of 1839 clearly rejected the Old Testament Apocrypha as noncanonical, Greek Orthodoxy has been more indecisive on this issue during the modern era. Filson, *Which Books Belong to the Canon?,* pp. 90, 95.
11. Alexander Souter, *The Text and Canon of the New Testament,* rev. C. S. C. Williams (2d ed.; London: Gerald Duckworth & Company Ltd., 1954), pp. 163-77.
12. Adolf Harnack, *Marcion: Das Evangelium vom fremden Gott: Eine Monographie zur Geschichte der Grundlagen der Katholische Kirche* (Leipzig: J. C. Hinrichs, 1921); E.T. *Marcion: The Gospel of the Alien God,* trans. John E. Steely and Lyle D. Bierma (Durham, N.C.: Labyrinth

Early in the second century the Gospels and Pauline epistles attained to an authority akin to that of the Old Testament. Late in that century, as evidenced in Irenaeus, the canonicity of the four Gospels was seemingly complete, and the Pauline epistles were theoretically equal to the Gospels. The full canonicity of the latter and of Acts surely came early in the third century. During the century between 250 and 350 1 Peter and 1 John were recognized as canonical, and 2 and 3 John, James, 2 Peter, and Jude were striving for canonicity, with Hebrews being accepted in the East and Revelation in the West. The Synod of Laodicea (363) recognized all our present New Testament with the exception of Revelation, and in the Festal Letter (367) of Athanasius one finds the oldest extant list of the precise books comprising the later New Testament. Synods at Hippo Regius (395) and Carthage (397, 419) formally adopted the closed canon. Some use of apocryphal books and of the shorter canon persisted. From its origin c. 431 the Nestorian Church never accepted Jude or Revelation. With this single exception the prevalent closed canon of the New Testament became the common heritage of all Christians.[13]

What were the internal factors that led to the canonization of some early Christian writings and to the noncanonization of others? Were there indeed tests or standards for canonicity, and is it possible to speak of a theology of canon formation? From patristic literature it seems impossible to derive any authentic lists or statements of such standards, and modern scholars have no widely accepted list. Inferences as to what likely were factors in canon formation can be drawn. Vawter has suggested that "the community tradition of a unique authority and character," not the content of the writing, was the key to canonicity.[14] But, one may ask, why did some writings have such "tradition of a unique authority" while others did not? Are not some more specific answers needed? Recent authors as different as Floyd Vivian Filson (1896-)[15] and Robert Laird Harris (1911-)[16] have

---

Press, in process), concluded that Marcion's canon was the decisive factor in producing the Catholic canon of the New Testament, whereas E. C. Blackman, *Marcion and His Influence* (London: S.P.C.K., 1948), pp. 32-35, downplayed the impact of Marcion's canon and upgraded the influence of Montanism. Hans von Campenhausen, *The Formation of the Christian Bible*, trans. J. A. Baker (Philadelphia: Fortress Press, 1972), while treating Marcion and his canon at length (pp. 147-209), concluded that Montanism was the "factor which brought about the concentration of a Canon in a 'New Testament'" (pp. 210-43, esp. 221). Denis M. Farkasfalvy, O.Cist., "The Early Development of the New Testament Canon," in William R. Farmer and Farkasfalvy, *The Formation of the New Testament Canon: An Ecumenical Approach* (New York: Paulist Press, 1983), pp. 99-103, 134-41, is critical of Harnack and others who would merely credit "Marcion with inventing the idea of the New Testament" and favors looking "for a multiplicity of causes and factors" relative to the canon of the New Testament.

13. Kurt Aland, *The Problem of the New Testament Canon*, Contemporary Studies in Theology, vol. 7 (London: Mowbray, 1962).

14. *Biblical Inspiration*, p. 7.

15. *Which Books Belong in the Bible?*, pp. 122-24.

16. *Inspiration and Canonicity of the Bible: An Historical and Exegetical Study* (rev. ed.; Grand Rapids: Zondervan, 1969), pp. 219-35. Harris stressed that in the canonized books of the New Testament there were claims to apostolicity.

made apostolic authorship or authorship by a disciple of an apostle the principal factor in canonization. But was it also not very probable that frequent reading of the writing when Christians gathered for worship was a criterion for final canonization? Moreover, would not the factor of content also have likely been retained?

Since the sixteenth century Roman Catholics have attached greater significance to the decisions of the late fourth-century and early fifth-century synods as to the scope and identity of the canon of the New Testament, whereas Protestants have given greater stress to the agency of the Holy Spirit and to the providence of God in canon formation.

Furthermore, during recent years the latest form of biblical criticism to be practiced has been the so-called "canonical criticism,"[17] which has as its focus the canon of the Bible and its relation to biblical interpretation.

C. THEOLOGICAL QUESTIONS CONCERNING THE CANON OF THE BIBLE

For the systematic theologian the most important consideration about the biblical canon may prove to be the cluster of questions that theologians are prone to ask about the canon, even though the answers to some of these questions must be left open-ended. Four of these questions should be considered.

1. One Canon of the Old Testament?

Can or will the Roman Catholic, the Eastern Orthodox, and the Protestant churches ever reconcile their centuries-long differences concerning the canon of the Old Testament? A Southern Baptist scholar has reopened the issue of the tenability of the Protestant position,[18] and a Presbyterian scholar has insisted that 1 and 2 Esdras and the Prayer of Manasseh not be restored to the Old Testament canon.[19]

2. The Canon of the New Testament: Closed or Open?

In view of the Qumran, the Nag Hammadi, and other important nineteenth- and twentieth-century discoveries of ancient documents related to the New Testament and the possibility of important future discoveries, would the canon of the New Testament be considered open if and when a newly discovered book should be widely recognized as having been written by an apostle of Jesus Christ? This question is

---

17. James A. Sanders, *Torah and Canon* (Philadelphia: Fortress Press, 1972); idem, *Canon and Community: A Guide to Canonical Criticism*, Guides to Biblical Scholarship (Philadelphia: Fortress Press, 1984).

18. Marvin E. Tate, "The Old Testament Apocrypha and the Old Testament Canon," *Review and Expositor* 65 (Summer 1968): 339-56. Edgar J. Goodspeed seems to have argued for inclusion. David L. Bartlett, *The Shape of Scriptural Authority* (Philadelphia: Fortress Press, 1983), p. 154, n. 35.

19. Filson, *Which Books Belong in the Bible?*, p. 95. David Dunbar, "The Biblical Canon," pp. 308-10, has found "no compelling reason to revise the historic Protestant evaluation of the Apocrypha."

different from the view of those who have expressed regret that the canon of the New Testament was ever closed.[20]

3. The Functioning Canon of the Bible

Do most Christians and most churches actually function with a "canon within the canon" of the Bible? Martin Luther elevated the Gospel of John, Romans, Galatians, Ephesians, the First Epistle of John, and the First Epistle of Peter to a centrist position in the New Testament canon.[21] The nineteenth-century "quest for the historical Jesus" and Ritschlian "back to Jesus" from Paul movement represented an inner canon within the canon. Such is also true of Ernst Käsemann's (1906-) elevation of Romans, 1 and 2 Corinthians, and Galatians and criticism of "early Catholicism" in other parts of the New Testament.[22] A collation of all sermon texts and all biblical passages read in worship services for a period of 15 or 20 years in a given congregation and a comparison of the total with the entire canon of the Bible would provide empirical evidence as to whether that congregation functions with a "canon within the canon."

4. A Third Canon of Postbiblical Christian Writings?

If Christian congregations should continue to read in their services of worship quotations from the writings of postbiblical Christian authors such as Augustine of Hippo, Francis of Assisi (1182-1226), Martin Luther, John Bunyan (1628-88), Dietrich Bonhoeffer (1906-45), Clive Staples Lewis (1898-1963), and Watchman Nee (1903-72), should there be delineated a third canon of such writings?

II. THE RELATION OF THE OLD AND THE NEW TESTAMENTS

Inasmuch as the Old and the New Testaments were composed in different languages, were derived from different communities of faith, and had distinguishable processes of canonization, one should not find it difficult to understand why Christian systematic theology would need to deal with the basic relationship between these two testaments. First we will state some negations of this essential relationship, and then we will discuss various attempts to explicate this relationship.

---

20. Robert Laurin, "Tradition and Canon," in *Tradition and Theology in the Old Testament,* ed. Douglas Knight (Philadelphia: Fortress Press, 1977), pp. 261-74.

21. Rupert E. Davies, *The Problem of Authority in the Continental Reformers: Study in Luther, Zwingli, and Calvin* (London: Epworth Press, 1946; Westpoint, Conn.: Hyperion Press, Inc., 1979), pp. 32-37; Althaus, *The Theology of Martin Luther,* pp. 82-85.

22. *New Testament Questions of Today,* trans. William John Montague and Wilfred F. Bunge (Philadelphia: Fortress Press, 1969), pp. 236-51.

A. Denials of the Fundamental Connection between or
Essential Unity of the Two Testaments

Floyd V. Filson's germinal article[23] surveying the prevalent twentieth-century denials of the coordinate integrity of the two testaments will
serve as the principal source and structure for this review of the denials.

1. Rejections of the Old Testament and Hence of the Integrity of the Two Testaments

a. Some have rejected the full canonicity of the Old Testament on the
basis of an asserted antithetical dualism within the attributes of God, that
is, a conflict between God's justice and his mercy, which leads to a doctrine
of two gods, one the just deity of the Old Testament and the other the good
God of the New Testament. These are the modern followers of the second-
century Marcion, who completely rejected the canonicity of the Old
Testament.

b. Some have downplayed the role and significance of the Old
Testament by making the Old Testament synonymous with law and the
New Testament synonymous with grace, with the result that the Old
Testament, as well as law, is deemphasized if not denied. This view
ignores aspects of divine love and mercy in the Old Testament and aspects
of divine wrath and judgment in the New Testament.

c. Some have challenged the canonicity of the Old Testament by
stressing the Hellenistic background of the New Testament to the neglect of the Old Testament as its background. Rudolf Bultmann represented this view, especially in his *Theology of the New Testament*,[24] and
the earlier Nazi rejection of the Old Testament as Semitic and non-Aryan
was an awesomely disastrous form of this view. The biblical theology
movement during the middle third of the present century sought to
correct this view.

d. Some may have unintentionally curtailed the relevance of the Old
Testament in their quest for shortened forms of it and selected portions
from it that would be more useful to Third World peoples today.[25]

2. Rejections of the New Testament and Hence of the Integrity of the Two Testaments

a. Present-day Jews who reject Jesus as the Messiah and whose
interpretation of the Hebrew Bible is in the light of rabbinic theology and
later Jewish tradition reject the New Testament as sacred Scripture.

b. Some have downplayed the significance of the New Testament by

23. "The Unity of the Old and the New Testaments," *Interpretation* 5 (April 1951):
134-37.
24. 1:108-21, 140-43, 148-49, 164-83, 201-3, 298-303; 2:3-69, 144-54.
25. Godfrey Edward Phillips, *The Old Testament in the World Church: With Special
Reference to the Younger Churches* (London: Lutterworth Press, 1942), esp. pp. 106-8, 121-23.
Filson may have somewhat misinterpreted the intentions of Phillips.

assuming that Jews and Christians today equally possess the Hebrew Bible (or Old Testament), that Jews and Christians both belong to the "Judaeo-Christian tradition," and that modern Judaism is also the rightful culmination of the Old Testament.[26] Such a perspective either concludes or implies that there are two equally valid routes: The Talmud and Rabbinic Judaism, and the New Testament and Christianity.

c. Some scholars, such as Albert Schweitzer (1875-1965), have undercut the importance of the New Testament, without necessarily intending to do so, by turning from their own highly apocalyptic reinterpretation of the New Testament to a philosophy of "Reverence for Life" with roots in Stoicism and Chinese thought.[27]

d. Some have made a de facto denial of parts of the New Testament and hence the essential unity of the New Testament by adoption of a "canon within the canon" of the New Testament.[28]

B. EFFORTS TO FORMULATE AN ADEQUATE CHRISTIAN VIEW OF THE RELATIONSHIP BETWEEN THE TWO TESTAMENTS

Some form of Christological interpretation of the Old Testament has been followed throughout the Christian era. In what follows we will examine four specific efforts to formulate the relationship between the two testaments.

1. Typology

This approach involves the location and usage of "types" in the Old Testament as "prefiguration by counterpart" of certain "antitypes" in the New Testament, especially antitypes that pertain to Jesus Christ. Typology is at the same time both a method of relating the two testaments and a method of interpreting the Old Testament. Typological interpretation has usually been the method used by those who have affirmed a complete identity of theological content in respect to the Old Testament and the New Testament.

During the modern period the effort to set limits on typological interpretation has been called Marsh's principle. Herbert Marsh (1757-1839),[29] Anglican bishop of Peterborough, led a school of interpretation based on the principle that only those Old Testament types which are specifically identified as types within the New Testament writings should be regarded as types by modern Christians. Such types would include

---

26. I. G. Matthews, *The Religious Pilgrimage of Israel* (New York: Harper and Bros., 1947), esp. ch. 15.

27. *Out of My Life and Thought: An Autobiography*, trans. C. T. Campion (New York: Henry Holt and Company, 1933), pp. 254-83. "Reverence for Life" included an emphasis on "Resignation, World- and Life-Affirmation, and the Ethical" (p. 269).

28. See above, I, C, 3.

29. *Lectures on the Criticism and Interpretation of the Bible* . . . (rev. ed.; Cambridge: C. and J. Ribington, 1828), pp. 440-65.

persons mentioned in the Old Testament and events in Old Testament history.[30] Marsh was reacting against the earlier school of John Cocceius, which had made much more extensive use of typology, allowing for "inferred" as well as "innate" types. An American exegete contemporary with Marsh, Moses Stuart (1780-1852), agreed with Marsh, but in Britain Patrick Fairbairn (1805-74) rejected Marsh's principle as being too restrictive.[31] In the latter twentieth century Bernard L. Ramm has declined to follow Marsh.[32] On the other hand, prior to the midpoint of this century there had been a renascence of typological interpretation among German Protestants in the work of Leonhard Goppelt (1911-73)[33] and Wilhelm Vischer (1895-).[34]

Some have reacted very strongly against all forms of typology and moved to the opposite extreme of radical discontinuity between the two testaments. Against such a view three considerations need to be offered: first, the extensive use of Old Testament quotations by New Testament writers; second, Paul's use of the "how much more" argument in 2 Cor. 3:7-11; and third, the total indebtedness of the New Testament to the Old Testament.

2. Homology

This approach to the relationship of the testaments finds a "correspondence" of "patterns" between the testaments. A leading exponent was William John Phythian-Adams (1888-1967).[35] He saw three stages in each testament: "redemption from bondage, consecration of the people by covenant, and gift of the inheritance." Both "testaments tell a literal story, but the two stories correspond closely." Filson criticized homology for magnifying the priestly at the expense of the prophetic in the Old Testament.[36]

3. Midpoint

This approach finds the relationship between the testaments to be explicable in terms of the once-for-all "Christ-event" as the "midpoint" of

---

30. Patrick Fairbairn, *The Typology of Scripture* (reprint ed.; Grand Rapids: Zondervan, 1963), p. 22, listed such types and provided references to the pertinent passages in both testaments.

31. Ibid., pp. 9-24, esp. 18-19, 11.

32. *Protestant Biblical Interpretation: A Textbook of Hermeneutics* (3d ed.; Grand Rapids: Baker Book House, 1970), pp. 218-21.

33. *Typos: Die typologische Deutung des Alten Testaments im Neuen* (Gutersloh, 1939; Darmstadt: Wissenschaftliche Buchgesellschaft, 1969); E.T. *Typos: The Typological Interpretation of the Old Testament in the New*, trans. Donald H. Madvig (Grand Rapids: Eerdmans, 1982).

34. *Das Christuszeugnis des Alten Testaments*, 2 vols. (Zollikon-Zurich: Evangelischer Verlag, 1946); E.T. *The Witness of the Old Testament to Christ*, vol. 1, trans. A. B. Crabtree (London: Lutterworth Press, 1949); F.T. *L'Ancien Testament Temoin du Christ*: vol. 2, *Les Premiers Prophètes*, trans. Pierre Klossowski (Neuchâtel: Delachaux et Niestlé, 1951).

35. *The Way of At-one-ment* (London: SCM Press, 1944).

36. Filson, "The Unity of the Old and the New Testaments," p. 146.

salvation history. Oscar Cullmann, the chief representative, took a linear view of biblical history and saw the "Christ-event," embracing his life, ministry, death, and resurrection, as the "midpoint" of that linear history.[37] Such an understanding enabled Cullmann to avoid both typology and allegory and still have a Christological interpretation of the Old Testament. The Old Testament prepared the way for the Christ-event, its redemptive history pointing toward the incarnation.[38]

4. Promise and Fulfillment

This approach reckons the Old Testament primarily in terms of promise and the New Testament primarily in terms of fulfillment. There have been some variations among the advocates of this approach. Arthur Gabriel Hebert (1886-1963) represented a "mystical" or spiritual interpretation of the Old Testament that was essentially fulfilled Messianism, not only in the person of the Messiah but also in the throne of David.[39] Emil Brunner employed promise and fulfillment as terms descriptive of the revelation under each of the covenants.[40] Filson has warned that this approach could fail "to come to grips with the reality of Old Testament history," could fail to recognize that "the Old Testament is not all promise," could miss the "element of surprise and novelty" in fulfillment, and could fail to see the New Testament as "a book of hope."[41]

III. THE UNITY OF THE BIBLE

A. ITS DENIAL AND ITS REAFFIRMATION

The unity of the Bible has been denied during recent decades not only by those who have downplayed or denied one of its two testaments and by those who have posited a radical disjuncture between the two testaments but also by those who have magnified the diversity within the New Testament writings to the point that diversity has been taken to mean contradictions. Such a conclusion would make impossible any meaningful unity of the Bible.

1. Diversity as Consisting of Contradictions That Make Theological Unity Impossible

We will survey the positions of three authors expressive of this stance about the writings of the New Testament.

37. *Christus und Zeit* (Zollikon-Zurich: Evangelischer Verlag, 1946); E.T. *Christ and Time: The Primitive Christian Conception of Time and History*, trans. Floyd V. Filson (Philadelphia: Westminster Press, 1941).
38. Filson, "The Unity of the Old and the New Testaments," pp. 149-50.
39. *The Throne of David: A Study of the Fulfilment of the Old Testament in Jesus Christ and His Church* (London: Faber and Faber Ltd., 1941).
40. *Revelation and Reason*, pp. 81-118.
41. Filson, "The Unity of the Old and the New Testaments," pp. 142-43.

a. Walter Bauer (1877-1960)

In a large volume first issued in 1934 Bauer, having studied second-century Christianity, concluded that "orthodox" and "heretical" parties or churches "existed side by side," the orthodox sometimes being in the minority, and that the orthodox churches prevailed in the end for primarily political reasons, there not being until very late a clearly defined difference between truth and error.[42]

b. James D. G. Dunn (1939-)

Accepting Bauer's conclusions and writing in 1977, Dunn took the idea of contradictory *kerygmata* back into first-century Christianity, that is, the New Testament writings. He found thoroughgoing diversity among these writings and also certain "unifying elements," denied the existence of a *"single normative form of Christianity in the first century"* or of any basic awareness of the difference between orthodoxy and heresy, and concluded that the only connecting link within the diverse New Testament writings is a rather general acknowledgment of *"the unity between Jesus the man and Jesus the exalted one."* For Dunn, therefore, the canonization of the New Testament meant the affirmation of the theological diversity of early Christianity, not of its unity.[43]

c. James Leslie Houlden (1929-)

Popularizing what were more intricate studies by Bauer and Dunn, Houlden criticized systematic theologians in the twentieth century for a clumsy use of the New Testament and for selecting overarching themes (e.g., Bultmann, existentialism; Pannenberg, resurrection; and Moltmann, Christian hope) so as to eliminate elements of diversity in the New Testament. He leveled a similar criticism at Cullmann, a New Testament scholar, for his choice and use of salvation history. Houlden found no "single pattern" in the New Testament "sufficiently coherent and comprehensive to serve as the basis for any modern attempt to reach a unified statement of doctrine." Hence the modern Christian theologian should do what the New Testament writers did, namely, from one's own perspective, mind-set, and circumstances to work out "the implications of a theism shaped and defined as a result of Jesus."[44]

---

42. *Rechtgläubigkeit und Ketzerei im ältesten Christentum* (Tübingen: J. C. B. Mohr, 1934); 2d ed. 1964; E.T. *Orthodoxy and Heresy in Earliest Christianity,* trans. by team and ed. Robert A. Kraft and Gerhard Krodel (Philadelphia: Fortress Press, 1971); D. A. Carson, "Unity and Diversity in the New Testament: The Possibility of Systematic Theology," in *Scripture and Truth,* ed. D. A. Carson and John D. Woodbridge (Grand Rapids: Zondervan, 1983), p. 66.

43. *Unity and Diversity in the New Testament: An Inquiry into the Character of Earliest Christianity* (Philadelphia: Westminster Press, 1977), esp. pp. 370, 373, 371, 377; Carson, "Unity and Diversity in the New Testament," pp. 72-73.

44. *Patterns of Faith: A Study in the Relationship between the New Testament and Christian Doctrine* (Philadelphia: Fortress Press, 1977), esp. pp. 4-5, 7, 71-72. See also John Charlot, *New*

There have been replies and refutations to the diversity-as-contradiction school, and these must now be examined.

2. *Diversity as Noncontradictory and as Embraced in an Overarching Unity of Truth, Which Is Distinguishable from Error or Heresy*

We will now investigate the views of four authors expressive of this position about the books of the New Testament.

a. Archibald Macbride Hunter (1906-)

In 1944 Hunter reported "a growing recognition of the essential unity of the New Testament and of the need for synthesis" among New Testament scholars. He attributed to the framers of the canon a recognition of a certain unity, and he made use of the German term *Heilsgeschichte* (salvation history) to express this unity. He then proceeded to expound the unitary message of the New Testament under three principal themes: "one Lord," "one church," and "one salvation."[45]

b. Harold Henry Rowley

Rowley's *The Unity of the Bible* (1953)[46] was directed more to the relation of the two testaments than to the unity of the New Testament, but it has important implications for the latter. Rowley noted the shift in biblical scholarship from a preoccupation with biblical diversity to an openness concerning biblical unity. What Rowley wrote about the two testaments is not inapplicable to the books of the New Testament: "It is unnecessary to close our eyes to the diversity in order to insist on the unity, or to close our eyes to the unity in order to insist on the diversity." Moreover, the Bible's unity is "dynamic," not "static." Variation in the Bible "does not spring from any variation in God, but from the variety of the levels of the persons whom He used." "Diversity and unity must be perceived together in the Bible, and neither can be sacrificed to the other."

c. Henry Ernest William Turner (1907-)

Turner, writing in 1954 a major answer to Bauer, according to D. A. Carson, "examined Bauer's work in ruthless detail and exposed its repeated arguments from silence, its sustained misjudgments concerning the theological positions of such figures as Ignatius and Polycarp, and its incautious exaggerations on many fronts."[47] Turner declared: "Christians lived Trinitarily long before the evolution of Nicene orthodoxy." He also

---

Testament Disunity: Its Significance for Christianity Today (New York: E. P. Dutton and Company, 1970).

45. *The Unity of the New Testament* (London: SCM Press, 1943); U.S. ed. *The Message of the New Testament* (Philadelphia: Westminster Press, 1944), esp. pp. 9, 11.

46. (Philadelphia: Westminster Press), esp. pp. 1-2, 3, 7-8, 29.

47. Carson, "Unity and Diversity in the New Testament," p. 71.

expounded eight characteristics of the "classical theory" of the nature and rise of heresy.[48]

d. Donald A. Carson (1946-)

In an article published in 1983,[49] Carson, after a critique of Bauer and Dunn, concluded that the "diversity in the New Testament very often reflects [either] diverse pastoral concerns, with no implications whatsoever of a different credal structure" or "the diverse personal interests and idiosyncratic styles of the individual writers." Hence "there is no intrinsic disgrace to theological harmonization, which is of the essence of systematic theology."[50]

The evidence in favor of the unity of the Bible, when coupled with recognition of elements of diversity, therefore, seems to outweigh the evidence in favor of the diversity of the Bible when diversities are regarded as contradictions that make impossible any unitary message of the Bible.

B. Its Nature

(1) The unity of the Bible is not to be found in the identity of all its concepts, on the assumption that a conceptual sameness prevails throughout the books of the biblical canon. Rather there is diversity of expression and emphasis amid an underlying unity.

The Old Testament must be interpreted and understood by Christians in the light of Jesus Christ and the New Testament. But the Old Testament does not present all New Testament truth in preview, as the extreme typological interpretation would seem to suggest. "It is right that we should view the Old Testament in terms of that to which it has led as well as that out of which it arose."[51]

The New Testament must be interpreted with full recognition of the aspects of diversity that responsible modern biblical study has located and investigated. Such diversities ought not to be smothered in an attempt to effectuate an unnecessary scheme of uniformity.

(2) The unity of the Bible is capable of being identified and expressed. Such unity may, for example, be found in the following:

---

48. *The Pattern of Christian Truth: A Study in the Relations between Orthodoxy and Heresy in the Early Church* (London: A. R. Mowbray, 1954), esp. pp. 28, 3-8.

49. "Unity and Diversity in the New Testament," esp. pp. 66-67, 71-77, 82-93.

50. See also Neil Alexander, "The United Character of the New Testament Witness to the Christ-Event," in *The New Testament in Historical and Contemporary Perspective: Essays in Memory of G. H. C. Macgregor*, ed. Hugh Anderson and William Barclay (Oxford: Basil Blackwell, 1965), pp. 1-33; Joachim Jeremias, *The Central Message of the New Testament* (New York: Charles Scribner's Sons, 1965); Werner Georg Kümmel, *The Theology of the New Testament: According to Its Major Witnesses: Jesus, Paul, John*, trans. John E. Steely (Nashville: Abingdon Press, 1973), esp. pp. 322-33; and Robert A. Kraft, "The Development of the Concept of 'Orthodoxy' in Early Christianity," in *Current Issues in Biblical and Patristic Interpretation: Studies in Honour of Merrill C. Tenney*, ed. Gerald F. Hawthorne (Grand Rapids: Eerdmans, 1975), pp. 47-59.

51. Rowley, *The Unity of the Bible*, p. 7.

a. The identity of the One who has been manifested under both covenants and in both testaments—Yahweh God, the God of Abraham, Isaac, and Jacob, who is the God and Father of Jesus Christ
b. The man Jesus, the promised and expected Messiah and the Messiah who has indeed come, who is also the incarnate Word and the eternal Son of God
c. The Spirit of God, who in both power and intimacy indwells and empowers persons under both covenants and in both testaments
d. The correlatable completeness of the work of the one God—in creation, in sustenance of that created, in redemption of a people, and in the consummation of all things, whether in judgment or blessedness—to which aspects of the work of God both testaments bear witness.

CHAPTER 10

Biblical Criticism
and Biblical Hermeneutics

The inspiration of the Bible and the canon of the Bible are topics that have been matters of theological concern for Christianity from the patristic age to the present time. The task of interpreting the many passages in the biblical books, together with the principles and methods of interpretation, can also be traced through the centuries to the early history of Christianity. But, in contrast, the application of textual, literary, and historical criticism to the Bible has been so distinctly a development within the modern era of Christianity that only in the modern era and especially during the twentieth century has biblical criticism become a viable or necessary topic to be addressed by the systematic theologian.[1] In this chapter, then, we will examine both biblical criticism and biblical hermeneutics, or interpretation, as parts of the ongoing exposition of the doctrines of revelation and Scripture.

I. BIBLICAL CRITICISM

How should we understand the term "biblical criticism"? According to Dale Moody, "Biblical criticism is the English term used to represent the application of historical science to the study of the Bible."[2] For George E. Ladd the term "means making intelligent judgments about historical, literary, textual, and philological questions which one must face in dealing with the Bible, in the light of all of the available evidence, when one recognizes that the Word of God has come to men through the words of men in given historical situations."[3] Probably it suffices to understand biblical criticism as the application of the principles of textual, literary, and historical criticism to the books of the Bible.

---

1. Erickson, *Christian Theology*, pp. 81-104, is one of the few systematic theologians to devote an entire chapter to biblical criticism.
2. *The Word of Truth*, p. 73.
3. *The New Testament and Criticism*, p. 37.

The rise and widespread usage of biblical criticism during the modern era is important not only in its own right but also, especially for systematic theology, because it has had a major impact on Christian views concerning the inspiration of the Bible, the interpretation of the Bible, the reliability of the Bible, and the authority of the Bible. We have already examined the first of these; we have yet to consider the other three.

A. METHODS OF BIBLICAL CRITICISM

The various major methods of biblical criticism that are employed today need to be defined and evaluated.

1. Textual (or Lower) Criticism

This is the science of ascertaining the true text of the Old Testament and of the New Testament in view of the variations and errors that crept in during the long period of the copying and transmission of manuscripts. Modern printing of the New Testament, commencing with Desiderius Erasmus early in the sixteenth century, began by the rather uncritical use of late manuscripts. Such a printed text has come to be known as the Textus Receptus. Textual criticism, probably traceable to the work of Origen in the third century A.D., studies all extant manuscripts and papyrus fragments of biblical books together with the early versions (Greek, Syriac, and Latin for the Old Testament; Syriac, Latin, Coptic, and Armenian for the New Testament). It posits the development of certain families in the transmission of the New Testament text and seeks to correct the Textus Receptus in the light of the great volume of textual evidence now available. A similar but more limited task is undertaken by Old Testament textual criticism. Actually only a small portion of the Bible is under any uncertainty as to its textual authenticity, and no major doctrine is imperiled by alternate textual readings. Some Christians who during the nineteenth or twentieth centuries have rejected as invalid literary criticism of the Bible and all other methods of biblical criticism have retained and employed textual criticism.[4]

4. See Ralph W. Klein, *Textual Criticism of the Old Testament: The Septuagint after Qumran* (Philadelphia: Fortress Press, 1974); Peter Kyle McCarter, Jr., *Textual Criticism: Recovering the Text of the Hebrew Bible* (Philadelphia: Fortress Press, 1986); Eberhard Nestle, *Introduction to the Textual Criticism of the Greek New Testament*, trans. William Eadie and ed. Allan Menzies (1st German ed. 1897; London: Williams and Norgate, 1901); Marvin R. Vincent, *A History of the Textual Criticism of the New Testament* (New York, London: Macmillan, 1899); Frederic G. Kenyon, *Handbook to the Textual Criticism of the New Testament* (London, New York: Macmillan, 1901); Caspar René Gregory, *Canon and Text of the New Testament* (New York: Charles Scribner's Sons, 1907), pp. 297-539; Souter, *The Text and Canon of the New Testament*, rev. ed., pp. 1-133; Archibald Thomas Robertson, *An Introduction to the Textual Criticism of the New Testament* (Nashville: Sunday School Board of the Southern Baptist Convention, 1925); Vincent Taylor, *The Text of the New Testament: A Short Introduction* (London: Macmillan, 1961); J. Harold Greenlee, *Introduction to New Testament Textual Criticism* (Grand Rapids: Eerdmans, 1964); Bruce M. Metzger, *The Text of the New Testament: Its Transmission, Corruption, and Restoration* (New York, London: Oxford University Press, 1964;

2. Literary (or Higher) Criticism

This is the study of the historical background, the authorship, the
date of writing, the recipients, the literary genre, the philology, and the
probable written sources, if any, used in the writing of the biblical books.
Some refer to the study of the written sources as "source criticism" and
hence differentiate "historical criticism," encompassing historical background, authorship, date, and recipients, from source criticism.[5] Literary
criticism of the Bible arose at least in part in the quest for explanations for
numerous facts and problems such as the following:

a. The usage by New Testament writers of quotations from the
   Old Testament
b. Variations in the style of writing of different biblical writers[6]
c. Variations among the Synoptic Gospels in recording the sayings
   of Jesus
d. Differences between the Synoptic Gospels and John's Gospel
e. Evidences for more than one author of a single biblical book
   (e.g., Isaiah)
f. Evidences for a date of writing different from the traditional
   date ascribed to a given biblical book (e.g., Daniel)
g. The place of human investigation and authorship in the writing
   of biblical books (e.g., Luke 1:1-4)

Source criticism has been employed chiefly in reference to the Pentateuch
and the Synoptic Gospels. Relative to the former the employment of
different divine names ("'Elohim" and "Yahweh") and other variations
served as clues of the source critics, and respecting the latter the numerous
variations in content and order opened the way for source criticism.[7]
Literary criticism of the Bible has served to magnify the human factor in
the Bible and to discredit those views of biblical inspiration in which the
authors were utterly passive amanuenses of the Holy Spirit. In defense of
literary criticism Marcus Dods wrote at the beginning of the present

---

2d ed. 1968); and Greenlee, *Scribes, Scrolls, and Scripture: A Student's Guide to New Testament
Textual Criticism* (Grand Rapids: Eerdmans, 1985).

5. Erickson, *Christian Theology*, pp. 83-84.

6. Dods, *The Bible: Its Origin and Nature*, pp. 113-15.

7. Beginning with Johann Gottfried Herder in 1797, Heinrich Ewald (1803-75) in
1848-49, and Heinrich Julius Holtzmann (1832-1910) in 1863, New Testament scholars held
the view that Mark's Gospel was the earliest of the Gospels, thus reversing the centuries-old
assumption, traceable to Augustine of Hippo, that Matthew's Gospel was the earliest.
Subsequently a two-source document hypothesis (Mk, Q) came to be widely accepted and
to be classically formulated by Burnett Hillman Streeter, *The Four Gospels, a Study of Origins:
Treating of the Manuscript Tradition, Sources, Authorship, and Dates* (London: Macmillan, 1924;
rev. ed. 1930). But in recent New Testament scholarship the priority of Matthew has been
reasserted on critical grounds. See William R. Farmer, *The Synoptic Problem: A Critical
Analysis* (New York: Macmillan, 1964), pp. 199-232, whose view is related to the work of
Johann Jakob Griesbach (1745-1812) (pp. 2-9, 16, 18, 30-31, 37, 44, 54, 55, 63, 67-69, 74-90,
and passim).

century: "To attempt to bar out criticism by affirming inspiration is a futile enterprise."[8] Yet Dods also recognized that biblical criticism can be destructive.[9] Hence all the warnings by opponents of methods other than textual criticism against "higher criticism" were not irrelevant. Indeed, more recent biblical studies have sought to correct the excessively analytical and atomistic approach of earlier biblical critics.[10]

3. Form Criticism

This is the study of the presumed oral forms of transmission that preceded various component parts of certain biblical books, especially the Gospels, but also the New Testament epistles and portions of the Old Testament, and the occasions or situations *(Sitzen im Leben)* under which and out of which these oral forms came to be used and ultimately included in a biblical writing. Hermann Gunkel (1862-1932), convinced that much of the Old Testament originated as folk literature, at the turn of the present century utilized form criticism as he classified what he regarded as the "legends" of Genesis, some of which he thought to be historical.[11] Karl Ludwig Schmidt (1891-1956),[12] Martin Dibelius (1883-1947),[13] and Rudolf Bultmann[14] applied form criticism to the Gospels after the end of World War I. They sought to learn the situations in the primitive church or churches that called for the use of certain kinds of oral tradition and to classify the "forms" of such segments of oral tradition (e.g., parable, miracle, narrative).[15] At its best, form criticism of the Gospels has focused on the period of the oral transmission of material later incorporated into a canonical Gospel. It has made clear, for example, that the Synoptic Gospels are not objectively scientific biographies of Jesus but rather the witness of the primitive church concerning Jesus Christ. It has helped to

8. Dods, *The Bible: Its Origin and Nature*, p. 173.

9. Ibid., p. 169.

10. See William A. Beardslee, *Literary Criticism of the New Testament* (Philadelphia: Fortress Press, 1970), and Norman C. Habel, *Literary Criticism of the Old Testament* (Philadelphia: Fortress Press, 1971).

11. *The Legends of Genesis: The Biblical Saga and History*, trans. W. H. Carruth (New York: Schocken, 1964), which "is a translation of the introduction to Gunkel's *Genesis* (Göttingen: Vandenhoeck und Ruprecht, 1901)." Edgar V. McKnight, *What Is Form Criticism?* (Philadelphia: Fortress Press, 1969), pp. 10-13; Gene M. Tucker, *Form Criticism of the Old Testament* (Philadelphia: Fortress Press, 1971), pp. 4-6, 11, 15, 18, 23-34, 46-50, 51, 56-57, 62-63, 65, 79-81.

12. *Der Rahmen der Geschichte Jesu: Literarkritische Untersuchungen zur ältesten Jesusüberlieferung* (Berlin: Trowitzsch und Sohn, 1919).

13. *Die Formgeschichte des Evangeliums* (Tübingen: J. C. B. Mohr, 1919; 2d ed. 1933); E.T. *From Tradition to Gospel*, trans. Bertram Lee Woolf (New York: Charles Scribner's Sons, 1935); 3rd German ed. 1959.

14. *Die Geschichte der synoptischen Tradition* (Göttingen: Vandenhoeck und Ruprecht, 1921; 2d rev. ed. 1931; 3rd ed. 1958); E.T. *History of the Synoptic Tradition*, trans. John Marsh (New York: Harper and Row, 1963).

15. Dibelius's categories were "paradigms" (didactic narratives), "tales" (miracle stories), "legends" (about holy men and women), and "myths" (interactions between mythological persons). Bultmann's categories were "apophthegms" (like the "paradigms" of Dibelius), "dominical sayings," "miracle stories," "historical stories," and "legends."

illuminate the situations in primitive Christianity that are identifiable
with various units in the Gospels.[16] On the other hand, form criticism has
received some negative evaluations. Under its impact the Gospels have
lost any semblance of chronology. Units of Gospel material are like pearls
that have been removed from a necklace and that no one knows how to
re-string properly. The doubt of form critics as to the ability and reliability
of the Gospel writers regarding historical matters seems contrary to the
exceptional quality of the Oriental memory. Why should miracle stories
and Christological texts be dated late? Several issues that were controversial in Paul's ministry (e.g., tongues, circumcision, meat offered to idols)
do not seem to be reflected in the choice of Gospel materials. Form critics
deemphasize written sources for the canonical Gospels and tend to ignore
the divine inspiration of the New Testament. Even the classifications of
"forms" have been highly suspect.[17] But some British and American
scholars have made more "cautious" and "productive use" of form criticism of the New Testament.[18] These include Burton Scott Easton (1877-
1950),[19] Vincent Taylor (1887-1968),[20] and Harvey Eugene Dana (1888-
1945) on the Fourth Gospel,[21] and Charles Harold Dodd[22] and Joachim
Jeremias (1900-),[23] a German, on the parables of Jesus.

4. Redaction Criticism

This is the study of the theological motivation of an author or compiler as
this is revealed in the collection, arrangement, editing, and modification of
traditional material, and in the composition of new material or the creation
of new forms within the traditions of early Christianity.[24]

Preceded by Wilhelm Wrede (1859-1906),[25] who contended in 1901
that Mark's Gospel gives evidence of theological presuppositions, Robert
Henry Lightfoot (1883-1953),[26] who in 1934 used the method without

16. Redlich, *Form Criticism*, pp. 79-80; McKnight, *What Is Form Criticism?*, pp. 1-3, 78.
17. Erickson, *Christian Theology*, pp. 88-95; Redlich, *Form Criticism*, pp. 77-79; Arthur W. Wainwright, *Beyond Biblical Criticism: Encountering Jesus in Scripture* (Atlanta: John
Knox Press, 1982), esp. pp. 11-19; Erhardt Güttgemanns, *Candid Questions Concerning Gospel
Form-Criticism: A Methodological Sketch of the Fundamental Problematics of Form and Redaction
Criticism*, trans. William G. Doty (Pittsburgh: Pickwick Press, 1979).
18. McKnight, *What Is Form Criticism?*, pp. 45, 51.
19. *The Gospel before the Gospels* (New York: Charles Scribner's Sons, 1928).
20. *The Formation of the Gospel Tradition* (London: Macmillan, 1933; 2d ed. 1935).
21. *The Ephesian Source: An Oral Tradition of the Fourth Gospel* (Kansas City, Kan.: Kansas
City Seminary Press, 1940).
22. *The Parables of the Kingdom* (New York: Charles Scribner's Sons, 1935; rev. ed. 1936,
1961).
23. *The Parables of Jesus*, trans. S. H. Hooke (New York: Charles Scribner's Sons, 1955).
24. Norman Perrin, *What Is Redaction Criticism?* (Philadelphia: Fortress Press, 1969),
p. 1.
25. *Das Messiasgeheimnis in den Evangelien* (Göttingen: Vandenhoeck und Ruprecht
1901; 2d ed. 1913; 3d ed. 1963); E.T. *The Messianic Secret*, trans. J. C. G. Greig (Cambridge:
J. Clarke, 1971).
26. *History and Interpretation in the Gospels* (New York, London: Harper & Brothers,
1934), pp. 206-25, esp. 208-10.

employing the term, and Ned Bernard Stonehouse (1902-62),[27] Günther Bornkamm (1905-),[28] Hans Conzelmann (1915-),[29] and Willi Marxsen (1919-)[30] launched redaction criticism, called by some "composition criticism," after World War II. Norman Perrin (1920-76) has connected the rise of redaction criticism with the "fall" of the hypothesis of Marcan priority, built as it was on the idea that Mark's Gospel was historical and free of theological presuppositions.[31] Thus far redaction criticism has been limited to the Synoptic Gospels. The method is too young for full assessment to be made of its work. The systematic theologian, however, cannot afford to be indifferent to this effort to ferret out and interpret the theological motivations of the Synoptists. Conservative evangelicals such as Grant Richard Osborne (1942-)[32] have found positive values in redaction criticism and such as Edward Earle Ellis (1926-)[33] have utilized the method. On the other hand, redaction criticism tends to be indifferent to historical facticity and to attribute too much theological expertise to the Evangelists.[34]

The most recently developed form of biblical criticism, canonical criticism, has been mentioned previously in the consideration of the canon of the Bible.[35]

B. ASSESSING BIBLICAL CRITICISM

In the various definitions offered for the differing methods of biblical criticism, one may take note that textual criticism was defined as a "science" and literary criticism, form criticism, and redaction criticism as "studies." This distinction recognizes that textual criticism deals with literary documents—manuscripts, papyrus fragments, and versions—and draws its conclusions largely on the basis of findings from existing documents. In the other branches of biblical criticism probable conclusions are drawn from projected source documents (J, E, D, and P for the Pentateuch; Q for the Synoptic Gospels), from projected classifications of

27. *The Witness of Luke to Christ* (London: Tyndale Press, 1951; Grand Rapids: Eerdmans, 1953); *Origins of the Synoptic Gospels: Some Basic Beliefs* (Grand Rapids: Eerdmans, 1963).

28. "End-Expectation and Church in Matthew" and "The Stilling of the Storm in Matthew," in Günther Bornkamm, Gerhard Barth, and Heinz Joachim Held, *Tradition and Interpretation in Matthew*, trans. Percy Scott, New Testament Library (London: SCM Press Ltd.; Philadelphia: Westminster Press, 1963), pp. 15-57.

29. *Die Mitte der Zeit* (Tübingen: J. C. B. Mohr, 1953; 5d ed. 1957); E.T. *The Theology of St. Luke*, trans. Geoffrey Buswell (New York: Harper and Row, 1960).

30. *Der Evangelist Markus: Studien zur Redaktionsgeschichte des Evangeliums* (Göttingen: Vandenhoeck und Ruprecht, 1956; 2d ed. 1959); E.T. *Mark the Evangelist: Studies on the Redaction History of the Gospel*, trans. James Boyce et al. (Nashville: Abingdon Press, 1969).

31. *What Is Redaction Criticism?*, pp. 3-13.

32. "The Evangelical and Redaction Criticism: Critique and Methodology," *Journal of the Evangelical Theological Society* 22 (December 1979): 305-22.

33. *The Gospel of Luke*, Century Bible, new ed. (London, Camden, N.J.: Thomas Nelson and Sons, 1966); rev. ed. New Century Bible (London: Marshall, Morgan and Scott, 1974).

34. Erickson, *Christian Theology*, pp. 99, 98.

35. See above, Ch. 9, I, B.

Gospel materials in their oral form, and from the probable theological presuppositions of the Gospel writers. The subjective factor seems to play a greater role under these methods than under textual criticism. Marcus Dods observed at the outset of the present century: "Our hope is in criticism free, fair, full. But we have yet to search with a lantern for the ideal critic."[36] Awareness of the subjective factor should help the ordinary student of the Bible to be able to weigh or evaluate some of the conclusions drawn by the experts in biblical criticism. Biblical criticism should not be regarded as a veritably infallible body of esoteric truth, the key to which is only in the hands of the experts. Rather the conclusions drawn in the various branches of biblical criticism must always be tested and retested in relation to other branches of biblical study, other theological disciplines, related secular disciplines, and the needs of the churches.

During the twentieth century it has been common for biblical critics and others to speak of "the assured results of biblical criticism." These words were designed to emphasize that certain findings of biblical critics had attained wide acceptance and could be regarded as no longer a matter of dispute or question. Such language, of course, has its place when used to refer to obviously accepted conclusions such as that Daniel and Revelation belong to the genre of apocalyptic writings, that the content of John's Gospel differs considerably from that of the Synoptic Gospels, and that the Apostle Paul seems not to have written the Epistle to the Hebrews. But such language needs to be coupled with the words "the criticism of criticism," by which is meant the continued testing, evaluation, and assessment of the conclusions advanced by biblical critics. The assessment process and the acceptance process can proceed concurrently, but both are needed. Furthermore, the assessment process can sometimes confirm the conclusions of biblical criticism and at other times invalidate such conclusions.[37]

Three examples can be cited wherein major conclusions by certain biblical critics during the modern era have been found subsequently to be untenable or to need to be balanced by other considerations. First, in the mid-nineteenth century Ferdinand Christian Baur (1792-1860) of Tübingen applied Hegel's dialectic to early Christian history. As a result he seemingly posited a clash between the Petrine party (thesis) and the Pauline party (antithesis) and concluded that the primitive church (synthesis) was the result of that clash. Baur's hypothesis was not universally accepted in his own time, and it has few advocates today if by "advocates" we mean those who would hold to it as a comprehensive explanation of early Christian origins.[38] Second, the source-document hypothesis (J, E, D, P) concerning the Pentateuch was shaped and defended by Old Testament scholars,

---

36. *The Bible: Its Origin and Nature*, p. 175.
37. See George Eldon Ladd, *The New Testament and Criticism*, p. 16.
38. Dunn, *Unity and Diversity in the Testament*, pp. 3-4. But Peter C. Hodgson, *The Formation of Historical Theology: A Study of Ferdinand Christian Baur*, Makers of Modern Theology (New York: Harper and Row, 1966), pp. 207-12, has insisted that Baur has been

notably K. H. Graf (1815-69), Abraham Kuenen (1828-91), and Julius Well-hausen (1844-1918). Although resisted by more conservative biblical scholars and by many Christian believers, this hypothesis was the regnant view of the origin of the Pentateuch among Old Testament critical scholars for half to three-fourths of a century. But today Old Testament critics themselves are emphasizing much more the oral transmission of Pentateu-chal materials and have modified the Graf-Kuenen-Wellhausen view.[39] Third, Rudolf Bultmann advocated a theory concerning the predominance of the Hellenistic and Gnostic backgrounds to the New Testament, espe-cially in reference to the Fourth Gospel. Such a theory entailed the rather late dating of some New Testament writings and involved a deemphasis on the Old Testament as the most important background to the New Testament.[40] But more recently Bultmann's approach has been counter-balanced by a greater stress on the Jewish background to the New Testa-ment and a movement toward the earlier dating of New Testament books. Joachim Jeremias showed the importance of the Aramaic language and rabbinical materials;[41] Robert McQueen Grant (1917-) clarified heretical Judaism, including Jewish forms of Gnosis and Gnosticism, thus making the theory of predominant Hellenistic influence less convincing;[42] Wil-liam Foxwell Albright (1891-1971) saw the Gospel of John as both very Jewish and historically reliable and concluded from Qumran organization and concepts of light and darkness at Qumran that a pre–fall of Jerusalem dating of many New Testament books was probable;[43] and John A. T.

---

misunderstood in that he actually taught three "moments" in the emergence of a Catholic Christian Church, namely, "conflict, gradual reconciliation, [and] accommodation," rather than "thesis, antithesis, and synthesis."

39. For recent statements of the source hypothesis, see Otto Eissfeldt, *The Old Testa-ment: An Introduction*, trans. Peter R. Ackroyd (New York: Harper and Row, 1965), pp. 182-212, who also posits a "Lay- source" or L; Ernst Sellin and Georg Fohrer, *Introduction to the Old Testament*, trans. David E. Green (Nashville: Abingdon Press, 1968), pp. 106-32, who posit G, a groundwork source, and N, a nomadic source; and Artur Weiser, *The Old Testament: Its Formation and Development* (New York: Association Press, 1961), pp. 69-142. For a recent critique of the four-source document hypothesis, see R. N. Whybray, *The Making of the Pentateuch: A Methodological Study*, Journal for the Study of the Old Testament Supplement Series, no. 53 (Sheffield: University of Sheffield, 1987), who has concluded that the Pentateuch is "the work of an ancient [that is, exilic] historian" who "may have intended it as a supplement (i.e., prologue) to the work of the Deuteronomistic Historian, which dealt with the more recent period of the national history" (p. 242). The author is indebted to Jerry Moye for assistance in locating these materials.

40. See above, Ch. 9, n. 24.

41. *New Testament Theology: The Proclamation of Jesus*, trans. John Bowden (New York: Charles Scribner's Sons, 1971), esp. pp. 3-8, 61-68.

42. *Gnosticism and Early Christianity* (New York: Columbia University Press, 1959), esp. chs. 1 and 2.

43. Albright, "Recent Discoveries in Palestine and the Gospel of St. John," in W. D. Davies and David Daube, eds., *The Background of the New Testament and Its Eschatology: In Honour of Charles Harold Dodd* (Cambridge: University Press, 1954; reprint ed. 1964), pp. 153-71; idem, "Toward a More Conservative View," *Christianity Today* 7 (18 January 1963): 3-5; idem, "Retrospect and Prospect in New Testament Archaeology," in E. Jerry Vardaman and James Leo Garrett, Jr., eds., *The Teacher's Yoke: Studies in Memory of Henry Trantham*

Robinson surprisingly pushed the cause of early dating.[44] Thus what Edgar
Martin Krentz (1928-) has referred to as the "self-correcting" aspects of
biblical criticism go on.[45]

II. BIBLICAL HERMENEUTICS

Consideration of inspiration, canon, and criticism must inevitably lead to
the principles and methods by which the biblical text ought to be interpreted. Biblical hermeneutics is the study of such principles. It may be
defined more extensively as the study of the approach(es) needed to bring
the true meaning of an ancient Israelite or Christian canonical writing to
the consciousness of the twentieth-century interpreter or reader so that he
(she) may hopefully discern, hear, and heed the Word of God. Also useful
may be a differentiation between "exegesis" and "interpretation." Exegesis is the more careful and detailed examination of all aspects of a biblical
text by use of the original language of that text. Interpretation is the more
practical effort to derive the meaning of the text, both for its author and
original recipients and for Christians or the church today. Both exegesis
and interpretation should proceed from some general or guiding principle
or principles. These constitute the hermeneutic of the exegete or the
interpreter.

A. OLDER METHODS OF BIBLICAL INTERPRETATION

First, it is desirable to examine the major methods of biblical interpretation that flourished or prevailed prior to the rise and prevalence of
the historical-critical method.

1. Typological Method

This is the hermeneutic of types and antitypes. "Types" are the
anticipated counterparts, prefigurations, or foregleams in the Old Testament of truths in the New Testament. "Antitypes" are those truths in the
New Testament which are anticipated by and matched with types. Earlier[46] we studied typology as a method of relating the two testaments; here
the focus is on typology as a hermeneutical method. Typology is to be
found among the Christian writings of the second century A.D.; the Epistle
of Barnabas contains numerous types and antitypes, and the Commentary on Daniel by Hippolytus of Rome, the oldest extant biblical commentary, uses typology. Such patristic use of types did not involve the elimi-
nation of the literal sense of the text.[47] Geoffrey William Hugo Lampe

---

(Waco, Tex.: Baylor University Press, 1964), pp. 27-41. The present author is indebted to E. J.
Vardaman for insights concerning the thought and writings of Albright.
  44. *Redating the New Testament* (Philadelphia: Westminster Press, 1976).
  45. *The Historical-Critical Method* (Philadelphia: Fortress Press, 1975), p. 66.
  46. See above, Ch. 9, II, B, 1.
  47. Kelly, *Early Christian Doctrines*, p. 71.

(1912-) has made as viable a case for typology in the postcritical age as any scholar. He has insisted that both type and antitype be firmly rooted in history and has rejected that typology which veers into allegory, having a correspondence "between the earthly and the heavenly, the shadow and the reality," rather than between "the past and the future, the foreshadowing and the fulfilment."[48] Whatever legitimate use may be made of typology today, it can hardly serve as the most basic hermeneutical principle.

2. Allegorical Method

This is the hermeneutic of the hidden spiritual meaning or meanings. Allegory, according to R. P. C. Hanson, "is a method of interpreting Scripture whereby the text is made to yield a meaning which is other than its literal or surface or historical meaning."[49] Allegorical interpretation is predicated on the concept of Scripture as "a vast ocean, or forest, of mysteries" or "a patchwork of symbolism."[50] Building on the foundation laid by Clement of Alexandria, Origen employed a threefold hermeneutic. Accordingly there are three possible meanings of a biblical text, although not every text indeed has three meanings. The first meaning is "the fleshly," literal, or historical meaning; the second is "the psychic," moral, or typological meaning; and the third is "the spiritual," or allegorical meaning.[51] Augustine of Hippo allowed for four possible meanings of a biblical text: the historical, the etiological (which sets forth a cause), the analogical (which would harmonize the testaments), and the allegorical or figurative.[52] Patristic and medieval interpreters commonly sought and explicated allegorical meanings in biblical texts. The fourfold sense used in the medieval period (literal, allegorical, moral, and anagogical) was still being employed by Nicholas of Lyra (c. 1270-1340).[53] John Wycliffe's (c. 1330-84) interpretation of the parable of the good Samaritan is a classic example of allegorical interpretation:

> The man who went down from Jerusalem to Jericho represents our first parents; the robbers are the fiends of hell; the priest and Levite who went by on the other side are the patriarchs, saints, and prophets who failed to bring salvation; the Good Samaritan is Jesus, pictured as of another nation because of his heavenly origin; the wine which he pours into the wounds is sharp words to prick men from sin, and the oil is hope; the Samaritan setting the man on his beast means Christ bearing man's sin in his body; the inn is

48. "The Reasonableness of Typology," in Lampe and K. J. Woollcombe, Essays on Typology, Studies in Biblical Theology, no. 22 (London: SCM Press Ltd., 1957), pp. 9-38, esp. 33.

49. "Allegory," in Alan Richardson, ed., A Dictionary of Christian Theology (Philadelphia: Westminster Press, 1969), p. 4.

50. Kelly, Early Christian Doctrines, pp. 73-74.

51. On First Principles 4.11-13.

52. On the Usefulness of Believing 5-8.

53. James D. Wood, The Interpretation of the Bible: A Historical Introduction (London: Gerald Duckworth and Company Ltd., 1958), pp. 72, 83.

the church, and the help received there sacraments and heavenly gifts; the following day, when he left the inn, is after the resurrection; the inn keeper is the clergy to whose care needy man is committed; and the twopence given to him represent Christ's Godhead and manhood to feed mankind to the day of doom.[54]

Although allegory is to be found in the New Testament (Gal. 4:22-31), Christians in the modern era would be well advised to be aware of the fanciful and imaginative extremes to which allegorical interpretation has led and the neglect of literal or historical meanings that it has often caused.

3. Dogmatic Method

This is the hermeneutic of dogmatic or doctrinal presuppositions. During the patristic, medieval, and Reformation periods this method was frequently and widely employed by such authors as Augustine of Hippo, Jerome, the Scholastic theologians, and various Protestant Reformers. An example of such interpretation may be found in the Christological exposition of Ps. 8:1 by Martin Luther. In explaining the words, "O Lord, our Lord," Luther stated that the first "Lord" is indicative of Christ's divinely given name and hence points to the deity of Jesus Christ, whereas the second "Lord" ('Adonai) is his humanly given name and points to the humanity of Jesus Christ. Yet he is one person.[55] It is difficult for the modern student of Luther to avoid the conclusion that Luther's interpretation of Ps. 8:1 was greatly influenced by the Chalcedonian Christology of the fifth century A.D. But one may raise a very legitimate question: Does the Bible not contain doctrinal teachings or emphases, and should not good interpretation always allow for such teaching to be faithfully exhibited? Yes, doctrinal teachings that are intended by the author and are endemic to the passage should be accurately reflected in the interpretation; but dogmatic hermeneutics involves bringing into the text and its interpretation doctrinal teachings derived from another biblical writer or from postbiblical Christian history.

4. Mystical Method

This is the hermeneutic of the way of the mystic. Mysticism is understood as "the theory of the direct contact of human consciousness with the realm of deity."[56] The mystical method may be used together with the allegorical method by the same interpreter. Some mystics have

54. Thomas Arnold, in *Select English Works of John Wyclif*, ed. Thomas Arnold, 1:31-33, sermon 13, as quoted by Harry Emerson Fosdick, *The Modern Use of the Bible* (New York: Macmillan, 1924), p. 81. Wyclif's interpretation was seemingly drawn from Augustine's *Quaestiones Evangeliorum* 2.19 (Migne, *PL*, vol. 35, col. 1321), according to Kelly, *Early Christian Doctrines*, p. 70, n. 2.
55. "Psalm 8," trans. Jaroslav Pelikan, in *Luther's Works*, 55 vols. (St. Louis: Concordia; Philadelphia: Muhlenberg, 1955-86), 12:97-103.
56. Harvey Eugene Dana, *Searching the Scriptures: A Handbook of New Testament Hermeneutics* (rev. ed.; Kansas City, Kan.: Central Seminary Press, 1946), p. 89.

denied the necessity for any historical revelation of God. Nevertheless the mystical method has been applied to the interpretation of the Bible. Hugh of St. Victor (1097?-1142) and Bernard of Clairvaux (1091?-1153) were representative of this method. Bernard in his interpretation of the Song of Solomon emphasized the love that Christ as the Bridegroom has for the redeemed soul.[57] Like the allegorical method, the mystical may downplay the literal or historical sense of the text. It may have difficulty in preserving the mediatorial office of Christ.

These methods of interpretation, the typological, the allegorical, the dogmatic, and the mystical, though they are not without their exponents and practitioners in the twentieth century, were largely displaced by and with the rise and widening acceptance of the historical-critical method of interpretation.

B. THE HISTORICAL-CRITICAL METHOD

Theodore of Mopsuestia, the prolific biblical commentator who was so very representative of the school of Antioch, and John Calvin, one of the two most prolific biblical commentators of the Protestant Reformation, worked in ways similar to what is now called the historical-critical method of biblical interpretation and may be said in some measure to have anticipated such a method.[58] With these exceptions, one may conclude that such a method gained widespread acceptance and was commonly practiced only during the modern era, namely, the eighteenth, the nineteenth, and the twentieth centuries. Indeed, the employment of modern biblical criticism has tended to validate and enthrone the historical-critical method of interpretation.

The historical-critical method seeks to interpret a text in view of lexical, grammatical, syntactical, comparative lexical, author-related, literary, comparative religious, secular historical, and other factors or to see the text, as far as possible, in the light of its total context and situation.

Before we make any inquiry as to the present use and status of this hermeneutical method, we should review some of the contributions made by this method.

---

57. *On the Song of Songs*, trans. Kilian Walsh, *Works of Bernard of Clairvaux*, vol. 2 (Spencer, Mass.: Cistercian Publications, 1971).

58. Dudley Tyng, "Theodore of Mopsuestia as an Interpreter of the Old Testament," *Journal of Biblical Literature* 50 (1931): 298-303, while denying that Theodore was a "modern" biblical interpreter "in the fifth century," did reckon him to have used a "literal and historical method," to have held to the single sense, and to have rejected allegory. Furthermore, his "spirit and method" were "revived" by John Calvin. James I. Packer, "Calvin's View of Scripture," in John Warwick Montgomery, ed., *God's Inerrant Word: An International Symposium on the Trustworthiness of Scripture* (Minneapolis: Bethany Fellowship, Inc., 1974), p. 95, has called Calvin "the father of modern critical and theological exegesis."

1. *Contributions of the Historical-Critical Method*

This method has brought to light or made more evident certain truths pertaining to the nature of revelation and of the Bible as historical. Included among those truths or values are the following:

a. Biblical interpretation should begin in the strange ancient world of the Bible, not in the traditions of later Christianity or the experience of present-day Christians. "Through the study of the geographical and historical context," Edgar Krentz has declared, "the life and history of Israel and the early church have been given new light." "Historical study prevents too rapid modernizing."[59] Other writers have warned of the danger of "modernizing" Jesus.[60]

b. Biblical interpretation needs to be done in context. A given biblical text or passage should be understood in reference to the preceding and succeeding verses and chapters. Either "proof-text" hunting or excessive biblical literalism can lead to misinterpretations of the Bible. According to Harry Emerson Fosdick, "to read the books of the Bible without thus knowing their vivid settings is like listening to one half of a telephone conversation."[61] Furthermore, the Old Testament should be interpreted in context and not merely in an effort to make the Old Testament say in advance precisely what the New Testament was later to say.

c. A biblical passage or text has only one meaning or sense, not several. By "meaning or sense" is meant that which was intended by the author or compiler. The Protestant Reformers, rejecting the medieval fourfold sense of Scripture, insisted on *unus simplex sensus* (one single sense) or *sensus historicus sive grammaticus* (the historical or grammatical sense).[62] Two important qualifications respecting the single sense of a biblical text need carefully to be noted. One is that the single sense in itself does not determine whether a given text should be taken literally or figuratively. Such a determination must be made on other grounds. The other is that the single sense does not preclude or prevent the making of multiple applications of the passage in the modern situation.

d. The historical revelation of God recorded in the Bible was situational; that is, God addressed himself to human beings in their personal, social, geographical, and chronological settings. Some theologians and biblical scholars, sometimes citing Heb. 1:1-3, Matt. 5:17, and Gal. 4:4, have gone on to assert that the revelation was "progressive" in nature. Such language may at times have been misused. "Progressive revelation" ought not to be used to mean progression from error to truth, a straight-line naturalistic evolution of religious concepts, or a view that denies or obscures Israel's disobedience or retrogressions concerning the revela-

---

59. *The Historical-Critical Method,* pp. 63-64, 65.
60. Henry J. Cadbury, *The Peril of Modernizing Jesus* (New York: Macmillan, 1937).
61. *The Modern Use of the Bible,* p. 20.
62. Krentz, *The Historical-Critical Method,* p. 64.

tion. If used, it should mean that God's revelation was conditioned on God's awareness of the condition of human beings, especially of the Israelites, and his willingness to disclose himself meaningfully and redemptively to human beings (Israelites) in their situations. The interpreter, however, must distinguish between God's will or God's ultimate ideal or God's fully revealed truth on the one hand and humankind's imperfect perception of or response to or obedience to the divine revelation on the other hand. Accordingly, Old Testament divorce practices (Matt. 19:3-12) and rejoicing at the destruction of the children of one's enemies (Ps. 137:8-9) are not to be taken as indications of God's perfect will but of imperfect and sinful Israelite perception and the accommodation of God's will in practice.[63]

e. In the biblical record of a historically mediated revelation of God a distinction must be made between the passing and the permanent, between the culturally restricted and the universally applicable. Two illustrations may help to clarify the nature of this distinction. Christians have made a distinction, which is traceable at least as far back as John Calvin,[64] between the ceremonial law and the civil law of the Pentateuch as passing and therefore not binding on the Christians and the moral law of the Pentateuch as permanent and binding on Christians. Such a distinction was, of course, without precedent in Judaism. The second illustration stems from present-day observance of church ordinances. Most Protestant denominations observe only two "sacraments" or "ordinances," baptism and the Lord's Supper. These they regard as practices to be observed in perpetuity during the Christian era, whether because of their symbolic and didactic functions vis-à-vis the death and resurrection of Jesus or for other reasons. The Brethren (Dunker) tradition, on the contrary, holds that the washing of disciples' feet is also to be practiced as a church ordinance. The rationale offered by other denominations to the Brethren for not observing footwashing today may rest on the premise that such a practice was in Jesus' times connected with the dusty roads and sandals worn in Palestine.[65]

These contributions of the historical-critical method of interpretation need to be remembered, especially when considering the criticisms of this method that have been and are being set forth.

2. *Alien Presuppositions Conditioning the Use of the Historical-Critical Method*

Some practitioners of the historical-critical method have assumed presuppositions for their work that are alien or hostile to the biblical

---

63. Conner, *Revelation and God*, pp. 89-90.
64. *Institutes of the Christian Religion*, 1559 ed., 2.7.
65. Conner, *Revelation and God*, p. 86. For statements of the Brethren position, consult the titles cited above in Ch. 2, II, B, 7.

revelation attested to and embodied in the Bible. Especially has this been true of presuppositions drawn from either positivism or historicism or both. Previously[66] we traced positivism to the three-stage theory of Auguste Comte, who defined it in such a way that it is virtually synonymous with scientism. Those who have employed the historical-critical method with positivist presuppositions have been antimetaphysical and antitheological, insisting that knowledge can come "only by observation and experience."[67] The result can easily be a totally human Bible and a humanized form of biblical religion.

Historicism is the view that the history of anything, pointing to its origins, can fully account for its nature and values. It has tended to be antisupernatural.[68] Building on Ernst Troeltsch's third principle, that is, that of correlation, which "allows only causation that is not theological or transcendent," historicism would expunge divine causation from the biblical record and deny the possibility of miracle. According to historicism, history cannot serve as the bearer of the unique or the eternal. "Historicism has falsely taught that one should accept as true and believe only what can be established by positive, rational proofs."[69]

To the extent that positivist and/or historicist presuppositions have shaped the work of some users of the historical-critical method, the criticisms and fears of the opponents of the method, especially Fundamentalists in the Anglo-American setting, have not been without foundation. Gerhard Maier (1937-) has contended that from Johann Salomo Semler in the eighteenth century onward some users of the historical-critical method have sought to put a "cleavage between Scripture and the Word of God."[70]

3. Recent Criticisms of the Historical-Critical Method

Within the last two decades substantive criticism of the historical-critical method has surfaced outside the repeated objections of Fundamentalists. Such has occurred among German Protestant scholars. Prior to such recent developments Karl Barth had limited historical criticism to a "preliminary" role in the task of biblical interpretation, wherein the Word of God addresses modern man, and Rudolf Bultmann had made an existentialist interpretation of the New Testament whereby faith can be separated from and made not to be dependent on history.[71]

66. See above, Ch. 5, III, C, 1.
67. R. W. Hepburn, "Positivism," in Alan Richardson, ed., *A Dictionary of Christian Theology* (Philadelphia: Westminster Press, 1969), pp. 260-61.
68. Bernard L. Ramm, *A Handbook of Contemporary Theology* (Grand Rapids: Eerdmans, 1966), pp. 59-60.
69. Krentz, *The Historical-Critical Method*, pp. 58, 67.
70. *Das Ende der historisch-kritische Methode* (Wuppertal: Theologischer Verlag Rolf Brockhaus, 1974); *The End of the Historical-Critical Method*, trans. Edwin W. Leverenz and Rudolph F. Norden (St. Louis: Concordia Publishing House, 1977), p. 50.
71. Krentz, *The Historical-Critical Method*, pp. 30-31.

In addition biblical theologians from the 1930s to the 1960s had supplied a theological dimension to supplement the historical and literary focus of the historical-critical method. But the recent criticism of the method has been more explicit than these earlier developments. Theologians and exegetes such as Friedrich Mildenberger, Wolfhart Pannenberg, Jürgen Moltmann, Peter Stuhlmacher (1932-), Ferdinand Hahn (1926-), and Martin Hengel (1926-) have participated in the critical reassessment of the historical-critical method.[72] One of the most thoroughgoing critiques, however, has been that of Gerhard Maier. Of his six criticisms of the use of the historical-critical method three are especially forceful: the method has not presented "a single 'divine' and 'human' Bible," has not been "able to grasp the person-structure of the Bible," and has tilted its conclusions against the reality of divine revelation.[73] Such increasing criticism of this major method of biblical interpretation would seem to place on all its contemporary users some responsibility for responding to and evaluating the new critiques.

4. Present Alternatives concerning the Historical-Critical Method

Two major options seem to be available to present-day employers of the historical-critical method of biblical interpretation. One would be to abandon the historical-critical method and to place in its stead some other method of biblical interpretation. The other would be to correct, reform, or redirect the existing or prevailing historical-critical method. A third option, not reckoned here as major or highly desirable, would be to continue, without reexamination or assessment, the present usage of the method.

a. Proposals for the Adoption of a New Hermeneutical Method in Place of the Historical-Critical Method

1) Existentialist method

Certain post-Bultmannian theologians during the 1960s and the 1970s advocated a new existentialist method of interpretation of the Bible.[74] Effort was made to take history somewhat more seriously than had Bultmann, but nevertheless the focus of interpretation became existentialist philosophy and the so-called situation of modern man. Less attention was given to the ancient biblical world. It is problematic as to

72. Ibid., ch. 5.

73. *The End of the Historical-Critical Method*, p. 25.

74. Gerhard Ebeling, *The Nature of Faith*, trans. Ronald Gregor Smith (Philadelphia: Muhlenberg; London: Collins, 1961); idem, *Word and Faith*, trans. James W. Leitch (Philadelphia: Fortress Press; London: SCM Press, 1963), esp. ch. 11; Ernest Fuchs, "The New Testament and the Hermeneutical Problem," in James M. Robinson and John B. Cobb, Jr., eds., *The New Hermeneutic*, New Frontiers in Theology, no. 2 (New York: Harper and Row, 1964), pp. 111-45; Paul J. Achtemeier, *An Introduction to the New Hermeneutic* (Philadelphia: Westminster, 1969).

whether the post-Bultmannians have escaped the criticism made of Bultmann himself, namely, that he had produced a "form of remythologizing"
through "his modern myth (of 'existential man')."[75]

2) Structuralist method

Building on the methods of Ferdinand de Saussure, a linguist, and of
Claude Lévi-Strauss (1908-), an anthropologist, structuralist exegesis assumes that language is ontological and that " 'significations are imposed
upon man' " and focuses on "the linguistic, narrative, or mythical structures of the text under consideration."[76] Admittedly the biblical interpreter
must learn all he can about literary genre and the structure of the text under
consideration, but to adopt the theory of a secular discipline as the primary
principle for biblical interpretation would seem to endanger the unique
message of the Bible that is expressed through genres and structures.

3) Maier's "Historical-Biblical" Method

Gerhard Maier's proposed new method involves six considerations:

a) Suspension of the principle of analogy in reference to the Bible
   and adoption of the view that the Bible as a book is *sui generis*
b) Stress on the sovereignty of God over against human
   intellectual reservations
c) Advocacy of the view that Scripture interprets itself, with a
   corresponding deemphasis on contemporary subjectivism
d) Emphasis on the congregation's spiritual experience of "all of
   Scripture as a unity"
e) Application of the principle that any given text is to be seen in
   the larger context of Scripture
f) Stress on that which through the text God wishes to say to all
   human beings.[77]

Even with the delineation of these six characteristics of Maier's
proposed method it is not altogether clear how Maier's method in practice
would differ from the use of the historical-critical method by those who
are free from positivist and historicist presuppositions.

To adopt the existentialist method, the structuralist method, Maier's
method, or any other in place of the historical-critical method would seem
to be a decision that should be made only if and when there is good
evidence that the new method is obviously superior to the historical-
critical method.

---

75. Wood, *The Interpretation of the Bible,* p. 173.
    76. Daniel Patte, *What Is Structural Exegesis?* (Philadelphia: Fortress Press, 1976), pp.
1, 14, 16. See also Edmund Leach and D. Alan Aycock, *Structuralist Interpretations of Biblical
Myth* (Cambridge: University Press, 1983), and David Greenwood, *Structuralism and the
Biblical Text,* Religion and Reason, no. 32 (New York, Berlin: Mouton Publishers, 1985).
    77. *The End of the Historical-Critical Method,* pp. 51-58, 84, 87.

b. Proposals for the Transformation or Reformation of the
   Historical-Critical Method

1) *George Eldon Ladd's advocacy of biblical critical work by evangelical
   scholars*

Ladd was fully aware of the naturalistic and humanistic presuppositions assumed by many of the shapers of the historical-critical method.
He knew that biblical criticism had "undermined confidence in the Bible
as the Word of God" and had "resulted in violent controversy in the
churches." But he declared that "biblical criticism *properly defined* is not an
enemy of evangelical faith, but a necessary method of studying God's
Word, which has been given to us in and through history." Hence he
admonished evangelical Protestant scholars to assume a greater portion
of the task of biblical criticism, the validity of which hinges on the fact that
the Bible is "*both* the words of men and the Word of God."[78]

2) *Edgar Krentz's endorsement of the self-critical reformulation of the
   historical-critical method*

Krentz has concluded:

. . . I remain convinced that the Reformation legacy of concern for the
historical sense of the Bible marked a decisive turn that culminated in
historical-critical methods of interpretation. . . . Scholars have been unceas-
ingly self-critical. Methods are refined, developed, and changed constantly.
This methodological flux is a mark of the health, vitality, and utility of
historical criticism. The utility of historical criticism can no longer be questioned.[79]

3) *John P. Newport's multiform hermeneutic centered in salvation
   history*

Newport has sought to combine the "grammatical, historical, theological, and practical principles of biblical interpretation" into a mosaic
and to take the "already-not-yet stream of redemptive history" as the
"guiding key" to the Bible.[80] This may be seen as a modification of the
historical-critical method when employed with positivist or historicist
presuppositions and a redirection of it in conjunction with concepts of
salvation history.

It is noteworthy that none of the newly proposed methods of biblical
criticism designed to replace the historical-critical method is a reiteration
of one of the major methods commonly used prior to the rise and prevalence of the historical-critical method. It has been suggested that the
exponents of the new methods are obligated to show clearly whether their
proposed new methods are indeed superior to the historical-critical

78. *The New Testament and Criticism*, pp. 31, 39, 53, 215, 24.
79. *The Historical-Critical Method*, p. 87.
80. *What Is Christian Doctrine?*, Layman's Library of Christian Doctrine (Nashville:
Broadman Press, 1984), chs. 4, 5.

method. The exponents of the proposals looking to the modification or redirection of the historical-critical method face a similar responsibility to demonstrate the viability and adequacy of their proposals. Moreover, we should not assume that all the proposals, either for new methods or for modifications, have yet appeared. Indeed, others are already being advanced.[81]

The task of interpreting the Bible goes on, even while discussion of principles and methods of interpretation takes place. Whatever decisions are to be made, the goal should continue to be the most accurate and responsible unfolding of the meaning of the biblical text so that human beings at the end of the twentieth century may hear and heed the Word of God.

---

81. On both the history of biblical hermeneutics and contemporary issues, see Moisés Silva, *Has the Church Misread the Bible? The History of Interpretation in the Light of Current Issues.* Foundations of Contemporary Interpretation, vol. 1 (Grand Rapids: Zondervan, 1987).

CHAPTER 11

The Bible as the Word of God; the Dependability of the Bible

If indeed the proper interpretation of the Old and the New Testaments is designed to enable the modern reader or hearer of the Bible to discern, hear, and heed the Word of God, it now becomes necessary to ask whether and in what sense Christians can and do affirm that the Bible itself is the Word of God and whether and to what extent the Bible is dependable, reliable, or truthful. First, then, we must examine the concept of the Bible as the Word of God.

I. THE BIBLE AS THE WORD OF GOD

The statement that the Scriptures of the Old and the New Testaments are "the Word of God" is more explicitly to be found in the documents of postbiblical Christianity than in the Scriptures themselves. This is true even when the focus is on what New Testament writers may have declared about the Old Testament writings.

The Old Testament prophets repeatedly[1] asserted that "the word of the LORD" had come to them so as to enable them to declare that word to Israel/Judah. But those assertions were not seemingly directed to the written form of the prophetic books. Psalm 119 repeatedly[2] refers to the "word" of the Lord.

In the New Testament the largest number of usages of the terms "the Word (*logos*) of God," "the word (*logos*) of the Lord," and "the word (*rhēma*) of God" apply to the "word of God" in the sense of the gospel, or the preached message concerning Jesus; the second largest number refer

---

1. See especially Amos 1:1; Mic. 1:1; Jon. 1:1; 3:1; Jer. 1:1-4; 2:1; 7:1; 11:1; 13:1, 3, 6, 8; 14:1, 11, 14; 16:1; 18:1; 21:1; 25:1, 15; 30:1; 32:1, 26; 34:8, 12; 35:1; 36:1; 37:6; 40:1; 46:1; 47:1; 48:1; Zeph. 1:1; Ezek. 1:3; 3:16; 6:1; 7:1; 12:1, 8, 17, 21, 26; 13:1; 14:12; 15:1; 16:1; 17:1, 11; 18:1; 20:45; 21:1, 18; 22:1, 17, 23; 23:1; 24:1, 15; 25:1; 27:1; 28:1, 11, 20; 29:1; 30:1; 31:1; 32:1, 17; 33:1; 34:1; 35:1; 36:16; 38:1; Hag. 1:1, 3; 2:1, 10, 20; Zech. 1:1; 6:9; 7:1, 4, 8; 8:1, 18; and Mal. 1:1.
2. Verses 9, 11, 16, 17, 25, 28, 37, 42, 43, 49, 65, 67, 74, 81, 89, 101, 105, 107, 114, 133, 147, 158, 161, 169, and 172.

to Jesus Christ himself as "the Word of God"; and the two passages that may possibly refer to the Old Testament Scriptures as "the word of God" are not indisputably clear. Hence there are three types of uses of the term "word of God" in the New Testament: the evangelical, the Christological, and possibly the scriptural.

The evangelical usages include both of the Greek terms translated "word": *logos* and *rhēma*.[3] The "word *(logos)* of the Lord" seems to refer to the gospel as preached by Paul and others in 1 Thess. 1:8; 2 Thess. 3:1; and Acts 13:44. The "word *(logos)* of God" in 1 Pet. 1:23 also refers to the gospel. In Luke 5:1 the same term refers to teaching by Jesus, and in 1 Tim. 4:5 probably to a blessing before the eating of food. The term "the word *(rhēma)* of God" seems to mean the gospel in Eph. 6:17 and in Heb. 6:5, whereas in Heb. 11:3 it refers to the divine word that issued in the creation. The "word *(rhēma)* of Christ" in Rom. 10:17 probably means preaching concerning Jesus Christ, and "the word *(rhēma)* of the Lord" in 1 Pet. 1:25, a quotation from Isa. 40:8b, appears in a context wherein the gospel has been mentioned. The Christological uses of God's Logos are found in the Johannine writings: John 1:1, 14 ("the Word"); 1 John 1:1 ("the Word of life"), from which some demur; and Rev. 19:13 ("the Word of God").

The only New Testament texts utilizing the term "the word of God" that can possibly refer to the Old Testament Scriptures are John 10:35 and Heb. 4:12, both of which use *logos,* but the former can also be understood as Yahweh's pronouncing Israel's judges as "gods" and the latter can also be understood as a reference to the gospel. 1 Tim. 3:16-17 and 2 Pet. 1:20-21 do not contain either the term "the word of God" or the term "the word of the Lord."[4]

The affirmation that the Bible "is the Word of God" was not as common during the patristic and medieval periods as during the Reformation and post-Reformation periods. When the early Fathers referred to the Bible as the Word of God,[5] according to Robert Preus, such a statement meant that "God is the real author [*auctor*] of the Scriptures" and that *auctor* "meant one who produces or effects something."[6] That same authorial dimension can be seen in Martin Luther, who declared:

---

3. Both of these nouns are derived from Greek verbs that mean "to speak."

4. James Orr in his lengthy article on "The Bible" in *The International Standard Bible Encyclopedia* (Grand Rapids: Eerdmans, 1955), 1:459-69, did not treat the Bible as the Word of God, and W. L. Walker in his brief article on "Word" did not include the Bible in his list of nine uses (ibid., 5:3105). Nor did J. Y. Campbell treat the Bible as the Word of God in "Word," in Alan Richardson, ed., *A Theological Word Book of the Bible* (New York: Macmillan, 1950), pp. 283-85.

5. See Tertullian, *Apology* 18; idem, *Against Marcion* 4.22; Origen, *Against Celsus* 59; Augustine, *Against Faustus* 15.1; idem, *Epistles* 8, 10.

6. "The View of the Bible Held by the Church: The Early Church through Luther," in Norman L. Geisler, ed., *Inerrancy* (Grand Rapids: Zondervan, 1980), p. 361.

> The Holy Scriptures are the Word of God, written and (I might say) lettered
> and formed in letters, just as Christ is the eternal Word of God veiled in the
> human nature.[7]

In his defense before the Diet of Worms Luther equated the Scriptures
with the Word of God.[8] For John Calvin no other writings can properly
share the title "the Word of God."

> Let this then be a sure axiom—that there is no word of God to which place
> should be given in the Church, save that which is contained, first, in the Law
> and the Prophets, and, secondly, in the writings of the Apostles. . . .[9]

Furthermore, Christians who by means of the "firm proofs" for the credi-
bility of the Bible "wish to prove to unbelievers that the Bible is the Word
of God are acting foolishly," inasmuch as only by the "inward persuasion
of the Holy Spirit" through faith "can this be known."[10] The explicit
confession of the Bible as the Word of God appeared more often in
Reformed confessions than in Lutheran, Anglican, or Eastern Orthodox
confessions. According to the First Helvetic Confession (1536), "The holy,
divine, biblical Scripture, which is the Word of God, delivered by the Holy
Spirit and brought forth to the world through the prophets and apostles,
is the most ancient, most complete, and highest of all teaching. . . ."[11] The
French Confession of Faith (1559) declared that "the Word contained in
these books has proceeded from God, and receives its authority from him
alone, and not from men."[12] In the Second Helvetic Confession (1566) one
reads: "We believe and confess the Canonical Scriptures of the holy prophets and apostles of both Testaments to be the true Word of God, and to have
sufficient authority of themselves, not of men. For God himself spoke to
the fathers, prophets, and apostles and still speaks to us through the Holy
Scriptures."[13] According to the Irish Articles of Religion (1615), "The
ground of our religion and the rule of faith and all saving truth is the Word
of God, contained in the holy Scripture."[14] The Westminster Confession of
Faith (1657) in its long article on the Bible stated that the church gives
testimony that Holy Scripture is "the Word of God" and that the Bible is
called "the Word of God written" because it has God as "the Author."[15]

During the modern period some usages of biblical criticism have led

7. W.A. 3.347, 262, as quoted by Preus, "The View of the Bible Held by the Church,"
p. 377.
8. W.A. 7.836-38; Luther's Works, 32:112.
9. Institutes of the Christian Religion, 1559 ed., 4.8.8, trans. Henry Beveridge (Grand
Rapids: Eerdmans, 1953), 2:394.
10. Ibid., 1.8.13, as quoted by James I. Packer, "Calvin's View of Scripture," in
Montgomery, ed., God's Inerrant Word, p. 109.
11. Art. 1, in Philip Schaff, The Creeds of Christendom, 3 vols. (Grand Rapids: Baker Book
House, 1966), 3:211.
12. Art. 5, in Schaff, Creeds of Christendom, 3:362.
13. Ch. 1, sect. 1, in Schaff, Creeds of Christendom, 3:237, 831.
14. Art. 1, in Schaff, Creeds of Christendom, 3:526.
15. Ch. 1, sects. 4, 5, 2, in Schaff, Creeds of Christendom, 3:601-3.

to the denial of the truth that the Bible is the Word of God and to a consequent conclusion that the Bible is essentially a human document. In response to that trend some other defenders of the divine inspiration, trustworthiness, and authority of the Bible have almost gone to the opposite extreme by downplaying, if not denying, that the Bible consists of the words of human beings. George E. Ladd has wisely warned that the "fact that the Bible is the Word of God does not mean that the human factor has been ignored nor the words of men bypassed." Hence the Bible is at the same time the Word of God and the words of human beings.[16]

II. THE DEPENDABILITY OR TRUTHFULNESS OF THE BIBLE

To select the terms "dependability" and "truthfulness" for use in reference to this topic means to prefer such terms to the other major alternative terms, namely, "reliability,"[17] "infallibility,"[18] and "inerrancy."[19] By such terms is meant that the books of the Bible are able to be depended on and are worthy of trust with respect to all that God intends in and through the Holy Scriptures. These terms mean at least that they are fully adequate and altogether sufficient to "make you wise for salvation through faith in Christ Jesus" (2 Tim. 3:15b, NIV).

Because so many contemporary theologians insist that the term "inerrancy" must be used for this topic, it will be helpful to examine what representative theologians who employ the term "inerrancy" mean by that term. Millard Erickson has defined "inerrancy" as "the doctrine that the Bible is fully truthful in all of its teachings."[20] According to Roger Robert Nicole (1915-), inerrancy means

> that at no point in what was originally given were the biblical writers allowed to make statements or endorse viewpoints which are not in conformity with objective truth. This applies at any level at which they make pronouncements. . . . Obviously, this does not confer a divine endorsement on all statements made by all the individuals who appear in the drama of the Bible. . . . Similarly, some written documents quoted in Scripture would not necessarily receive divine endorsement.[21]

16. *The New Testament and Criticism,* pp. 22, 20, 24.
17. Berkouwer, *Holy Scripture,* discussed "reliability" (ch. 9) as well as "certainty" (ch. 1), "clarity" (ch. 10), and "sufficiency" (ch. 11).
18. Stephen T. Davis, *The Debate about the Bible* (Philadelphia: Westminster Press, 1977); Paul Woolley, ed., *The Infallible Word: A Symposium by the Members of the Faculty of Westminster Theological Seminary,* 3d rev. ptg. (Philadelphia: Presbyterian and Reformed Publishing Company, 1967).
19. See, for example, John Warwick Montgomery, ed., *God's Inerrant Word: An International Symposium on the Trustworthiness of Scripture;* Roger R. Nicole and J. Ramsey Michaels, eds., *Inerrancy and Common Sense* (Grand Rapids: Baker, 1980); Geisler, ed., *Inerrancy.*
20. *Christian Theology,* p. 221.
21. "The Nature of Inerrancy," in Nicole and Michaels, eds., *Inerrancy and Common Sense,* p. 88.

Paul David Feinberg (1938-) has defined the term as follows:

> Inerrancy means that when all facts are known, the Scriptures in their original autographs and properly interpreted will be shown to be wholly true in everything that they affirm, whether that has to do with doctrine or morality or with the social, physical, or life sciences.[22]

Each of these definitions represents an increasingly specific and precise definition of "inerrancy," and some theologians and biblical scholars have raised the question as to whether the assemblage of all pertinent factual data about specific biblical texts and the specificity of any exacting definition of biblical inerrancy are fully harmonizable.

A. HISTORY OF THE DOCTRINE

Heightened interest in the subject of biblical inerrancy during the last two decades has led to greater curiosity concerning the history of this doctrine. Unfortunately there is still not available a comprehensive study or series of studies covering the entire history of Christian doctrine. There is general agreement that for many centuries Christians have held to the truthfulness of the Holy Scriptures. Few are likely to question Erickson's observation "that the general idea of inerrancy is not a recent development."[23] Augustine of Hippo in his Epistle 82 can be cited:

> Only to those books which are called canonical have I learned to give honor so that I believe most firmly that no author in these books made any error in writing.
>
> . . . .
>
> Holy Scripture in no part is disharmonious.[24]

Martin Luther can also be quoted:

> Natural reason produces heresy and error. Faith teaches and adheres to the pure truth. He who adheres to the Scriptures will find that they do not lie or deceive.[25]
>
> . . . .
>
> Scripture cannot err.[26]
>
> . . . .
>
> The Scriptures have never erred.[27]

Jack Bartlett Rogers (1934-) and Donald K. McKim (1950-) have produced a study of the history of the doctrine that focuses on the Reformed tradition,[28] and John Dunning Woodbridge (1941-) in a monograph writ-

22. "The Meaning of Inerrancy," in Geisler, ed., *Inerrancy*, p. 294.

23. *Christian Theology*, p. 226.

24. Sect. 1, as quoted by Preus, "The View of the Bible Held by the Church," p. 365; sect. 9, as quoted by Vawter, *Biblical Inspiration*, p. 33.

25. Martin Luther, *Sammtliche Schriften*, ed. J. G. Walch, 2d ed. (St. Louis: Concordia, 1881-1930), 11:162, as quoted by Preus, "The View of the Bible Held by the Church," p. 379.

26. *Sammtliche Schriften*, 14:1073, as quoted by ibid., p. 379.

27. Ibid., 15:1481; 9:356, as quoted by ibid., p. 379.

28. *The Authority and Interpretation of the Bible: An Historical Approach* (New York: Harper and Row, 1979).

ten to refute Rogers and McKim[29] has not covered much more than the
Reformed tradition. Biblical inerrancy as a theological issue today is much
more controversial among and receives much more attention from Evangelical Protestants than from Roman Catholics, Eastern Orthodox, or
Liberal Protestants. This fact alone may account for the lack of intensive
research concerning biblical inerrancy or dependability in all the Christian
communions. Nor does the citation of the Fathers and the Reformers alone
settle all the contemporary questions. What James I. Packer has written of
Calvin could also be applied to Augustine or to Luther:

> . . . Calvin did not have to face all the problems about the Bible that we face.
> He was not under pressure from epistemological problems about how God
> can be known and teach truths, nor from historical problems about the
> contents of biblical narratives, nor from problems raised by the account of
> this world which the natural sciences give, nor from theological problems
> about whether inspiration could extend to the very words used; nor was he
> up against the post-Kantian dualism which affirms God's presence in man's
> psyche but effectively denies his Lordship over the cosmos as such. . . .[30]

These manifold modern problems affect the way Christians think, speak,
and write concerning the Bible. One, therefore, need not be surprised to
encounter Erickson's statement that biblical inerrancy "has not been a fully
enunciated theory until modern times."[31] For those who advocate a tightly
drawn definition of biblical inerrancy, the doctrine is seen as the "corollary
of the doctrine of full inspiration" of the Bible and as "the completion of
the doctrine of Scripture."[32] For those who are more intent to dwell on the
problems posed by various biblical texts there is hesitation concerning the
necessity for and the propriety of a tightly drawn definition.

B. THE LEVELS ON WHICH THE DEPENDABILITY OF THE BIBLE MAY BE AFFIRMED

The question concerning the dependability of the Bible may be
raised on at least three basic levels, and the affirmations concerning its
dependability may thus be affirmed on the same three levels.

1. The Reliability of the Present-day Text of the Old Testament and the New Testament in Respect to Its Transmission as Books from the Hands of Its Human Authors

Textual-critical studies of the New Testament have led to an increasingly certain critically produced text of the Greek New Testament, and
textual-critical studies of the Old Testament, augmented by the discoveries at Qumran, have reached a similar result for the Hebrew-Aramaic text

---

29. *Biblical Authority: A Critique of the Rogers-McKim Proposal* (Grand Rapids: Zondervan, 1982).

30. "Calvin's View of Scripture," in Montgomery, ed., *God's Inerrant Word,* pp. 97-98.

31. *Christian Theology,* pp. 225, 221.

32. Ibid. See "The Chicago Statement on Biblical Inerrancy," *Journal of the Evangelical*

of the Old Testament. As noted earlier,[33] present-day Christians can have a very high level of certitude that the texts of both testaments now available to biblical scholars and from which contemporary translations are being made into various languages are dependably accurate reproductions of the originals or autographs. There are some who cling to the use of the Textus Receptus. Even so, the question of the reliability of the biblical text constitutes no substantive problem and no theological issue for Christians today, and the problems encountered by biblical scholars seem to be found both in the autographs and in the modern critical texts.

2. *The Reliability of the Bible in Respect to Its Basic Religious and Moral Message as the Truth of God: The Level of Doctrine and Ethics*

This is the aspect of the reliability or trustworthiness of the Scriptures that has received the greatest emphasis in the past. Reformed and Baptist confessions of faith are replete with affirmations and assurances that the Bible contains the saving truth of God and is the sufficient source for such truth.[34] Evangelical Protestants today give evidence of a high degree of unity on this aspect of biblical reliability. It is understandable, therefore, how the publication of Paul King Jewett's (1919-) *Man as Male and Female*, in which the Evangelical author concluded that the apostle Paul was wrong in teaching the subordination of wives to husbands,[35] would evoke criticism from Evangelicals and be seen as a departure from this canon of biblical dependability in the area of Christian ethics. Daniel Payton Fuller (1925-) offered a "corrective" to B. B. Warfield's position by suggesting that "verbal plenary inspiration involves accommodation to the thinking of the original readers in non-revelational [paleontological, cosmological, meteorological, and biological] matters."[36]

Theological Society 21 (December 1978): 289-96; "The Chicago Statement on Biblical Hermeneutics," ibid., 25 (December 1982): 397-401.

33. See above, Ch. 10, I, A, 1.

34. The Westminster Confession (1647) contained and the Second London Confession of Particular Baptists (1677) retained a threefold usage of the terms "infallible" and "infallibility" in respect to the Bible: (1) hermeneutical (difficult passages to be interpreted in the light of clear passages); (2) authoritative (the Bible as the supreme rule of doctrine and ethics); and (3) authenticating (the saving revelation recorded in the Bible is true over against all rival claims). These confessions did not address issues of chronology, geography, or science. The New Hampshire Baptist Confession's (1833) language, namely, that the Bible "has God for its author, salvation for its end, and truth, without any mixture of error, for its matter," has been retained in the Southern Baptist Convention's 1963 Statement on Baptist Faith and Message. William L. Lumpkin, *Baptist Confessions of Faith* (rev. ed.; Valley Forge, Pa.: Judson Press, 1969), pp. 361-62, 393. See the present author's "Biblical Authority according to Baptist Confessions of Faith," *Review and Expositor* 76 (Winter 1979): 43-54.

35. *Man as Male and Female: A Study in Sexual Relationships from a Theological Point of View* (Grand Rapids: Eerdmans, 1975), esp. pp. 112-19, 142-47.

36. "Benjamin B. Warfield's View of Faith and History," *Journal of the Evangelical Theological Society* 11 (Spring 1968): 75-83, esp. 82. But Fuller, writing against Edward J. Young, retained Warfield's stress that the *"indicia"* or "marks" of the Bible's divinity are known empirically, and hence one does not rely " 'solely upon the inward testimony of the Holy Spirit.' "

3. *The Reliability of the Bible in All Chronological, Geographical,*
    Literary, and Scientific Matters: The Level of Total or Complete
    Inerrancy

This third level of biblical reliability constitutes the crux of the
present-day controversy among Evangelical Protestants. Whereas there
is a high level of agreement as to biblical dependability on the first and
second levels, there are noteworthy differences as to the nature and
extent of dependability on this third level. Early in the twentieth century
B. B. Warfield and James Orr differed on this issue, the former affirming
and the latter denying biblical inerrancy on the third level.[37] The issue
was pressed even more vigorously during the 1970s and the 1980s as
Harold Lindsell,[38] Edward Joseph Young (1907-),[39] Kenneth Sealer
Kantzer,[40] Francis August Schaeffer (1912-84),[41] John Warwick Montgomery (1931-),[42] John H. Gerstner,[43] Clark Harold Pinnock (1937-),[44]
Carl F. H. Henry,[45] and James I. Packer[46] defended both the term and the
concept of total biblical inerrancy as a necessary and true Christian
doctrine and as Dewey M. Beegle,[47] Jack B. Rogers, Donald K. McKim,[48]
and William Sanford LaSor (1911-)[49] advanced arguments against such
a position and in favor of a more restricted or limited conclusion about
biblical dependability on the third level. As the debate has continued,

37. Warfield, *The Inspiration and Authority of the Bible,* ed. Samuel G. Craig (Philadel-
phia: Presbyterian and Reformed Publishing Company, 1970), pp. 208-26; Orr, *Revelation and
Inspiration* (New York: Charles Scribner's Sons, 1910), pp. 161-62, 164-65, 168-69, 179-81, 199,
212-17.
    38. *The Battle for the Bible* (Grand Rapids: Zondervan, 1976); *The Bible in the Balance*
(Grand Rapids: Zondervan, 1979).
    39. *Thy Word Is Truth: Some Thoughts on the Biblical Doctrine of Inspiration* (Grand
Rapids: Eerdmans, 1957), chs. 5–8.
    40. "Evangelicals and the Doctrine of Inerrancy," in James Montgomery Boice, ed.,
The Foundation of Biblical Authority (Grand Rapids: Zondervan, 1978), pp. 147-56.
    41. *No Final Conflict: The Bible without Error in All That It Affirms* (Downers Grove, Ill.:
InterVarsity Press, 1975); "Foreword: God Gives His People a Second Opportunity," in Boice,
ed., *The Foundation of Biblical Authority,* pp. 13-20.
    42. "Biblical Inerrancy: What Is at Stake?" in Montgomery, ed., *God's Inerrant Word,*
pp. 15-42.
    43. *Biblical Inerrancy Primer* (Grand Rapids: Baker, 1965); "The View of the Bible Held
by the Church: Calvin and the Westminster Divines," in Geisler, ed., *Inerrancy,* pp. 383-410.
    44. *A Defense of Biblical Infallibility* (Philadelphia: Presbyterian and Reformed Publish-
ing Company, 1967); *Biblical Revelation: The Foundation of Christian Theology* (Chicago: Moody
Press, 1971), pp. 69-86.
    45. *God, Revelation, and Authority,* 2:14-15; 4:162-255, 353-84.
    46. "Encountering Present-Day Views of Scripture," in Boice, ed., *The Foundation of
Biblical Authority,* pp. 59-82.
    47. *The Inspiration of Scripture* (Philadelphia: Westminster Press, 1963); republished as
Scripture, Tradition, and Infallibility.
    48. Rogers, "The Church Doctrine of Biblical Authority," in Rogers, ed., *Biblical
Authority* (Waco, Tex.: Word Books, 1977), pp. 15-46; Rogers and McKim, *The Authority and
Interpretation of the Bible.*
    49. "Life under Tension—Fuller Theological Seminary and 'The Battle for the Bible,' "
in *The Authority of Scripture at Fuller* (Pasadena, Calif.: Fuller Theological Seminary Alumni,
Theology, News and Notes, Special Issue, 1976), pp. 5-10, 23-28.

there is some evidence that among the former group of authors one can now see emerging some differences between strict or consistent inerrantists (Lindsell, Young, Kantzer, Schaeffer, Packer) and qualified inerrantists (Pinnock, Bernard L. Ramm[50]).

The present-day advocates of a strict or consistent biblical inerrancy on the third level have rather uniformly insisted that inerrancy applies only to the autographs, or originals, of the books of the Bible. This position is a reiteration of the stance taken by Archibald Alexander Hodge and B. B. Warfield more than a century ago.[51] But Beegle has pointed out that J. A. Quenstedt, a seventeenth-century Lutheran theologian, taught that the copies of the Old Testament that were used by the Apostle Paul were reckoned by Paul as *theopneustos* (2 Tim. 3:16), inasmuch as the autographs had been lost and yet "careful transcribing had preserved the precise sense and wording of the autographs."[52]

The most difficult issues connected with the current debate concerning inerrancy focus not, however, on the autographs of the Bible but rather on the various problems, yet not completely resolved, that biblical scholars have cited and discussed in reference to certain texts in the Bible. To such problems we must now turn.

C. THE DEPENDABILITY OF THE BIBLE AND THE PHENOMENA OF THE BIBLE: UNRESOLVED PROBLEMS ON THE THIRD LEVEL

Especially during the twentieth century biblical scholars have taken note of and made lists of problems, difficulties, or enigmas connected with specific passages in the Old and the New Testaments that, according to those listing such problems, have not been resolved or adequately explained. At the beginning of the century Marcus Dods listed some seven "irreconcilable discrepancies between the four [Gospel] accounts of some of our Lord's sayings and actions." These included variations in the title placed over the cross of Jesus, in the accounts of Jesus' postresurrection appearances, in the anointing of Jesus' body, as to the stone rolled away from the tomb, as to the date of the Last Supper and the crucifixion, and concerning the "except for fornication" phrase (Matt. 19:9) and the attribution of a text from Malachi to Isaiah and of a text in Zechariah to Jeremiah.[53]

Dewey Beegle in 1963 set forth and discussed in some detail problems connected with ten biblical texts, three in the Old Testament and three in the New Testament, with four problems related to texts in each

50. *Protestant Biblical Interpretation: A Textbook of Hermeneutics* (3d rev. ed.; Grand Rapids: Baker, 1970), pp. 201-14. David S. Dockery, "Can Baptists Affirm the Reliability and Authority of the Bible?" *SBC Today*, May 1986, pp. 10-11, has listed seven different forms of teaching about biblical inerrancy.
51. A. A. Hodge and B. B. Warfield, *Inspiration* (orig. publ. 1881; reprint ed.; Grand Rapids: Baker Book House, 1979).
52. *Scripture, Tradition, and Infallibility*, pp. 163-64.
53. *The Bible: Its Origin and Nature*, pp. 135-37.

testament. The Old Testament difficulties included the span of time for the genealogies of Genesis 5, the length of the reign of King Pekah of Israel, and the dating of the reign of King Hezekiah of Judah. The New Testament difficulties included the number of rooster crowings at the time of Peter's denial of Jesus, Jude's quotation of the intertestamental book of 1 Enoch as if it were the word of the Enoch of Genesis, and Jude's reporting that the archangel Michael contended with Satan for the body of Moses when the canonical Old Testament did not mention such but the noncanonical Assumption of Moses seemingly did. The difficulties spanning the testaments included the age of Terah when his son Abram left Haran, the burial place of Jacob, the length of the residency of the Israelite people in Egypt, and Paul's quotation (1 Cor. 3:19) of Eliphaz in the book of Job by stating "For it is written."[54] In 1976 William LaSor cited five difficulties not mentioned by Dods or Beegle: the dating of the Exodus, differences in numbers between Samuel/Kings and Chronicles, the measurements of the laver in Solomon's temple, variations in the two genealogies of Jesus, and the number of angels at Jesus' tomb.[55] In 1983 Millard Erickson added three more: differences among the Synoptists as to whether Jesus did or did not instruct his disciples to take a staff, verbal variations as to the cry of the multitude at the triumphal entry of Jesus, and the reconciliation of the teaching that God neither tempts nor is tempted (Jas. 1:13) with the report that God sent an evil spirit on King Saul so that Saul attempted to murder David (1 Sam. 18:10).[56]

Prior to the intensification of the debate about biblical inerrancy Evangelical Protestant authors had written monographs in which they sought to provide explanations or answers to the difficulties or "alleged discrepancies" found in the Bible: J. W. Haley,[57] Kenneth Anderson Kitchen,[58] and Raymond F. Surburg (1909-).[59] In 1980 Gleason Leonard Archer, Jr. (1916-), sought to refute in detail the alleged discrepancies cited by LaSor and by Beegle. More often Archer advanced alternative explanations of the data, but sometimes he attributed the discrepancy to scribal or transmissional error.[60]

54. *The Inspiration of Scripture*, pp. 41-60.
55. "Life under Tension—Fuller Theological Seminary and 'The Battle for the Bible,' " pp. 5-10, 23-28.
56. *Christian Theology*, pp. 229-30.
57. *An Examination of the Alleged Discrepancies of the Bible* (Andover, Mass.: W. F. Draper, 1875; reprint ed.; Nashville: B. C. Goodpasture, 1951). Haley discussed the origin, the design, and the results of these "alleged discrepancies" and then analyzed them under three categories: doctrinal, ethical, and historical.
58. *Ancient Orient and Old Testament* (Chicago: Inter-Varsity Press, 1966). Kitchen dealt chiefly with problems of dating, anachronism, relations with Near Eastern religions, and literary criticism.
59. *How Dependable Is the Bible?* (Philadelphia: Lippincott, 1972). See also Harris, *The Inspiration and Canonicity of the Bible*, pp. 107-10, 113-14, and George E. Ladd, *I Believe in the Resurrection of Jesus* (Grand Rapids: Eerdmans, 1975), pp. 79-103, esp. 91-93.
60. "Alleged Errors and Discrepancies in the Original Manuscripts of the Bible," in Geisler, ed., *Inerrancy*, pp. 55-82.

Since not everyone acknowledges that certain alleged difficulties have not been resolved and since not everyone is persuaded by the explanations or solutions provided, it is now necessary to examine the possible attitudes or stances that may be taken in regard to these biblical problems.

D. POSSIBLE ATTITUDES OR STANCES CONCERNING PROBLEMS OR DIFFICULTIES IN THE BIBLE VIS-À-VIS THE DEPENDABILITY OF THE BIBLE

At least five different attitudes or stances may be taken in regard to the difficulties or problems previously cited.

1. Denying the Existence of Such Problems

It is possible to deny the genuine existence of such problems, possibly on the assumption that they have been conjured up by extreme practitioners of biblical criticism, and hence ordinary Christians can dismiss these as nonexistent. This seems to be an unrealistic position for serious students of the Bible who are also earnest Christians with a high view of the Scriptures.

2. Ignoring Such Problems While Acknowledging That They Do Exist

Such a posture tends to postpone some responsible consideration of these matters. B. B. Warfield's stance may be so classified.[61] To declare that none of these problems is able to overthrow the Christian doctrine of Scripture may indeed be a true statement, but such a statement, made to sanction a refusal to give attention to the various problems raised, may constitute an inadequate strategy.

3. Pronouncing These Problems or Difficulties as Specific "Errors" in the Bible

This position has been commonly taken by representatives of Liberal Protestantism and Neoorthodox Protestantism, by some Roman Catholics, and by a few Evangelical Protestants such as Dewey Beegle. It tends to finalize critical judgments concerning these problems and to assume that there can be no solutions, either now or in the future. Primarily for Evangelical Protestants, with their teaching about the dependability of the Scriptures and their serious interest in the problems themselves, does this position constitute a major hurdle.

---

61. *The Inspiration and Authority of the Bible*, pp. 214-26. Donald A. Carson would classify Warfield under the fifth stance described below. But Warfield did not clearly differentiate inspiration and inerrancy, did not treat the "phenomena" in detail, and held that the difficulties were of "a progressively vanishing quantity" (p. 221).

4. *Working Out Some Theory of Harmonization between Biblical Inerrancy and the Problems or Difficulties*

Erickson has identified at last three types of theories of harmonization.[62]

a. There is "absolute inerrancy," according to which the Bible is seen as providing "a considerable amount of exact scientific or historical data" and the problems "can and must be explained." Exponents of this theory include Louis Gaussen,[63] Edward J. Young,[64] and Harold Lindsell.[65]

b. There is "full inerrancy," or the view that the Bible's references to historical and scientific matters are "popular descriptions" and "not necessarily exact" and yet "are correct." This view has been advanced by Roger Nicole.[66]

c. There is "source inerrancy," or the position that inspiration and inerrancy guarantee "only an accurate reproducing of the sources which the Scripture writer employed, but not a correcting of them." Such an explanation could serve as a theory of harmonization. Edward J. Carnell discussed this view.[67]

5. *Leaving the Problems Open for Future Study and Added Evidence without Reckoning Them as "Errors" and without Forced or Dubious "Solutions"*

This has been called the posture of "moderate harmonization." It encourages the resolution of any of the problems that can be truly resolved and is willing to leave for future resolution, especially through archaeological or other discovery and/or historical and philological research, the rest of the problems. Everett F. Harrison (1902-)[68] and Erickson[69] have opted for this approach. This posture can appropriate and put into a different context the words of the pastor-teacher of the Pilgrims, John Robinson (c. 1575-1625), who said that "the Lord had more truth and light yet to break forth out of his Holy Word."[70]

In conclusion, we need to make three statements. First, the depend-

62. *Christian Theology*, pp. 222-24.
63. *Inspiration of the Holy Scriptures*, pp. 207-70.
64. *Thy Word Is Truth*, chs. 5–8.
65. *The Battle for the Bible*, pp. 165-66.
66. "The Nature of Inerrancy," in Nicole and Michaels, eds. *Inerrancy and Common Sense*, pp. 82-86.
67. *The Case for Orthodox Theology* (Philadelphia: Westminster Press, 1959), pp. 109-11.
68. "Criteria of Biblical Inerrancy," *Christianity Today*, 20 January 1958, pp. 16-18.
69. *Christian Theology*, pp. 232-33.
70. "Parting Advice," quoted by Robert Ashton, "Memoir of Rev. John Robinson," in *The Works of John Robinson*, ed. Robert Ashton, 3 vols. (London: John Snow, 1851), 1:xliv. Henry, *God, Revelation, and Authority*, 4:362, has warned: "Whatever may be the predicament of biblical criticism, evangelicals must not exempt themselves from serious interest in the vexing problem passages of the Bible. These passages should be studied not primarily to expose compromise or concession in certain evangelical quarters, but rather to search the Scriptures as a matter of academic integrity."

ability of the Bible is an important Christian doctrine worthy of the serious and responsible attention of Christians. It helps to explain why Christians can rightly affirm that the Bible is the Word of God. Second, none of the problems or difficulties connected with specific biblical texts and posed in relation to dependability/trustworthiness/infallibility/inerrancy on the third level jeopardizes any basic Christian doctrine unless it should be inerrancy. Third, those who engage in theological controversy and warfare over these matters, insisting on the rightness of their own conclusions and the wrongness of those conclusions advanced by others, stand under the mandate of Jesus Christ concerning love for and among his disciples (John 13:34-35).

CHAPTER 12

Authority in Christianity

In an effort to explicate the doctrines of revelation and the Bible, we first studied general revelation through nature and the human conscience, then the phenomenon of religion and the claims of various non-Christian religions. Next, under the rubric of natural theology, we examined the major worldviews in relation to the Christian revelation of God and explored the theistic arguments for the existence of God. We saw that special revelation, as differentiated from general revelation, was first through Israel and then supremely and finally in Jesus Christ. Such special revelation, we noted, came to be inscripturated, or recorded authentically, in the Holy Scriptures of the Old and the New Testaments. We studied the divine inspiration of these biblical authors and biblical books along with the human authorship thereof. Following that we gave attention to the canon of these two testaments, the relationship between these testaments, and the unity of the Bible. Then we investigated and evaluated biblical criticism and explained and evaluated the major methods of biblical interpretation. Subsequently we explored the history and the meaning of the declaration that the Bible is the Word of God, after which we devoted attention to the dependability of the Bible.

We are now ready to address the last topic related to revelation and the Bible, namely, authority in Christianity. By such a term we do not mean ecclesiastical authority, or church polity or government; rather we mean the entire issue of religious authority according to the Christian religion. How is the authority of divine truth, which abides in and derives from God himself, transmitted or conveyed or shared with human beings? Conversely, what is the proper ranking of those channels for transmitting divine truth, including the Bible, which are available to Christians? Before we can adequately set forth the contemporary question, we need some historical perspective.

I. THE HISTORY OF THE PRINCIPLES OR PATTERNS OF RELIGIOUS AUTHORITY IN CHRISTIANITY

The New Testament contains various statements about the existence of a body of Christian beliefs or truths and their transmission. Reference is made to "the faith," probably in the sense of a body of teaching (Gal. 1:23; Col. 2:7; 1 Tim. 6:20c; Tit. 1:13; Jude 3), to "one faith" (Eph. 4:5), to "sound teaching" (2 Tim. 4:3; Tit. 1:9), to "the good teaching" (1 Tim. 4:6) and "the sure word according to the teaching" (Tit. 1:9), and, by way of contrast, to "another gospel of a different kind" (Gal. 1:8). Likewise the gospel (or a virtual synonym) is said to have been "passed down" or "transmitted" (Luke 1:2; 1 Cor. 11:2, 23; 15:3; Rom. 6:17; Jude 3), that which has been passed down or transmitted can be called "the traditions" (2 Thess. 2:15; 1 Cor. 11:2), and both the content and the fact of transmission together were called "what has been entrusted" (1 Tim. 6:20; 2 Tim. 1:14, RSV). The word "tradition" could also have a negative connotation vis-à-vis incipient Gnosticism (Col. 2:8).[1]

A. THE PATRISTIC AGE

What standards or channels of religious truth were recognized or utilized by the Christians of the middle or latter first century A.D.? The question is a difficult one because there is no extant document that precisely identifies such standards. Undoubtedly for a time the sayings of Jesus (Logia), together with accounts of his miracles and passion, circulated in oral form, as form criticism has strongly asserted, but how long this was true after the writing of the canonical Gospels is not clear. The proclaimed central message (*kērygma*) of early Christianity, centering in the death-resurrection of Jesus, also seems to have been regarded as having authority (1 Cor. 15:3-4). First-century Christians had the Hebrew Bible (Old Testament), especially in the form of the Septuagint, which they interpreted in relation to Jesus as the Messiah and which they deemed to be inspired by the Holy Spirit (2 Pet. 1:20-21). Certain Christian prophets claiming the guidance of the Holy Spirit were operative[2] and very likely heeded. Some ethical teaching (*didachē*), as distinct from the *kērygma* and as given in the latter parts of most of Paul's epistles, may have been circulating and recognized among first-century Christians. The books that would eventually comprise the New Testament were in existence, it seems, before the end of the century, but to what extent they may have been considered distinctive channels of religious authority is not clear.

By the end of the second century a threefold pattern of religious authority began to be expressed in the writings of Christian authors such as Irenaeus and Tertullian. This pattern presupposed that the Old Testament books were Christian Scriptures, most likely in the extended canon.

---

1. On the use of "the word of God" as the gospel, see above, Ch. 11, I.
2. See below, Ch. 57.

The pattern was itself formulated in response to the challenges posed by Gnosticism, Montanism, and Marcionism. It consisted of (1) the Christian Scriptures of the new covenant, which by the latter part of the second century clearly included the four Gospels and the Pauline epistles; (2) the "Rule of Faith," a triadic confession in a Trinitarian form with an expanded Christological section, the language of which was becoming more fixed;[3] and (3) the concept that those bishops or presbyters who served in direct succession to those apostles who had founded their particular churches had indeed received and transmitted apostolic truth in contrast to the falsehoods of the heretics.[4] In the face of heresy the church would find that the rule of faith and the apostolic teaching would serve as the key to interpretation of the Scriptures, and these would be coordinate channels of religious authority.[5] Hence a modern church historian, Karl Heussi (1877-1961), has declared:

> About [A.D.] 50, he was of the church who had received baptism and the Holy Spirit and called Jesus, Lord; about 180, he who acknowledged the rule of faith (creed), the New Testament canon, and the authority of the bishops.[6]

The orthodox claim about the "rule of faith" and apostolic teaching was that it was open and public, unlike the secret tradition claimed by the Gnostics and even claimed by such early third-century Christian teachers as Clement of Alexandria and Origen for the intellectually mature Christians. But even Clement and Origen held to the authority of the Scriptures,[7] and the Acts and the epistles were being recognized as canonical.

By the fourth century creeds and church councils had become a part of the pattern of authority.[8] Creeds, probably developed from baptismal and catechetical questions and certainly finalized amid theological controversy, came to be used as standards for true Christian beliefs and teaching,[9] and episcopal councils, both ecumenical and regional, became during the post-Constantinian era the normal means for resolving theological disputes. Although isolated texts can be cited in which the authority of the Catholic Church seems to have been put above the Scriptures,[10] the main thrust of the Church Fathers of the fourth and fifth centuries

---

3. Irenaeus, *Against Heresies* 1.10.1-2; 5.20.1; *Proof of the Apostolic Preaching* 6; Tertullian, *The Prescription against Heretics* 13; *On the Veiling of Virgins* 1; *Against Praxeas* 2; *Apology* 47.

4. Irenaeus, *Against Heresies* 3.2.2; 3.3.3; 3.4.1; Tertullian, *The Prescription against Heretics* 21, 28, 32; *Against Marcion* 4.5.

5. Kelly, *Early Christian Doctrines*, pp. 38, 39, 47.

6. *Kompendium der Kirchengeschichte*, p. 44, cited by Williston Walker, *A History of the Christian Church*, 3d ed. rev. by Cyril C. Richardson, Wilhelm Pauck, and Robert T. Handy (New York: Charles Scribner's Sons, 1970), p. 57.

7. Kelly, *Early Christian Doctrines*, pp. 37, 43, 42.

8. Ibid., p. 44.

9. J. N. D. Kelly, *Early Christian Creeds* (London: Longmans, Green and Company, 1950), esp. pp. 30-61.

10. For example, Augustine of Hippo, *Against the Epistle of Manichaeus Called Fundamental* 5.6; *Against Faustus the Manichaean* 28.2.

was toward the supreme authority of the canonical Scriptures.[11] By the time of the episcopate of Leo of Rome (bp. 440-61) more ecclesiastical authority was attributed to the bishop of Rome, even as Leo was setting forth the doctrine of Petrine primacy,[12] but this did not mean that he could dominate the ecumenical councils being held in the East. Appeal was also being made to the teaching common among the earlier Fathers; Vincent of Lérins in the middle of the fifth century affirmed the sufficiency of the Scriptures and laid down a threefold criterion of church tradition,[13] and Gregory the Great (bp. 590-604) was appealing to the authority of the teaching of the early Fathers and of the first four ecumenical councils.[14]

B. EASTERN ORTHODOXY

The appeal to the Scriptures and to apostolic tradition through the Fathers and the councils was made normative in the Chalcedonian and non-Chalcedonian churches of the East, which espoused continuity, not change. This position was affirmed in the seventh century by Maximus Confessor (c. 580-662), for whom, in Jaroslav Pelikan's words, "The lamp of Scripture could be seen only when it stood on the lampstand of the church."[15] In later centuries the Orthodox Church reckoned as seven— from Nicaea I (325) through Nicaea II (787)—the number of recognized and hence authoritative ecumenical councils.[16] Orthodoxy accepted the shorter canon of the Old Testament, and the Nestorian Church never received Jude or Revelation into its canon of the New Testament.[17] Orthodoxy and the non-Chalcedonian churches rejected the Western elevation of the authority of the bishop of Rome.[18]

C. THE MEDIEVAL WEST

Medieval Western Christianity had a concept of authority quite similar to the later patristic view. The Scriptures and church tradition, not

11. George Duncan Barry, *The Inspiration and Authority of Holy Scriptures: A Study in the Literature of the First Five Centuries* (London: S.P.C.K., 1919); Woodbridge, *Biblical Authority*, pp. 31-48.

12. See Basil Studer, "Italian Writers until Pope Leo the Great," in Angelo di Berardino, ed., *Patrology*, vol. 4, trans. Placid Solari, O.S.B. (Westminster, Md.: Christian Classics, Inc., 1986), pp. 607-10.

13. *Commonitories* 2. The test was "that which everywhere, always, and by all has been believed."

14. *Epistles* 1.25; 4.38; 6.2.

15. *The Spirit of Eastern Christendom (600-1700)*, Christian Tradition, vol. 2 (Chicago: University of Chicago Press, 1974), p. 18.

16. Ibid., p. 30.

17. See above, Ch. 9, I, A, B.

18. John Meyendorff, *The Orthodox Church: Its Past and Its Role in the World Today*, trans. John Chapin (n.p.: Pantheon Books, 1962), pp. 27- 38, 208-15; idem, *Orthodoxy and Catholicity* (New York: Sheed and Ward, 1966), esp. pp. 49-90; Nicolas Zernov, *Orthodox Encounter: The Christian East and the Ecumenical Movement* (London: James Clarke and Company, Ltd., 1961), pp. 18-37.

in unwritten form but as patristic writings, were both authoritative. Hugo of St. Victor in the twelfth century was a representative exponent:

> All divine Scripture is contained in the two Testaments, the Old and the New. Each Testament is divided into three parts. The Old contains the Law, the Prophets, the Historians. The New contains the Gospel, the Apostles, the Fathers. . . . In the last category (*i.e.* the Fathers) the first place belongs to the Decretals which are called canonical, that is, regular. Then there come the writings of the holy Fathers, of Jerome, Augustine, Ambrose, Gregory, Isidore, Origen, Bede and the other Doctors; these are innumerable. Patristic writings, however, are not counted in the text of the divine Scriptures. Likewise in the Old Testament, some books are not in the Canon, yet they are read, like the Wisdom of Solomon and others. The whole body, as it were, of the text of the divine Scriptures is contained in thirty main books. Twenty-two belong to the Old Testament and eight to the New, as has been shown above. The other writings are, so to say, added to them and implied in them. . . . In the wonderful plan of the divine dispensation, the full and perfect truth resides in each Scripture, yet none is superfluous.[19]

No description of the medieval conception of authority can refuse to ask to what extent the church as institution with its hierarchical structure participated in the actual shaping of religious authority, and this would include both the papal office[20] and those councils held in the West and recognized as ecumenical by the West, though not by the East.[21] Georges Henri Tavard (1922-) has contended that not until the fourteenth century—the teachings of Henry of Ghent (1217-93), Gerald of Bologna (?-1397), Marsilius of Padua (c. 1271-1342), William of Ockham (1300-1359), and John Wycliffe—was there the breakdown of the doctrine of the coinherence of the Scriptures and church tradition and the result of that breakdown, the idea that tradition was oral and pluriform, that is, traditions.[22] But Protestant and other authors have disagreed, tracing the idea of numerous extrabiblical traditions back as far as Tertullian.[23] During the fifteenth century writers as diverse as Peter d'Ailly (1350-1420), a Conciliarist; Thomas Netter (c. 1377-1430), an opponent of Wycliffe and Hus; and John of Turrecremata (1388-1468), an opponent of

---

19. *De Scriptura et Scriptoribus Sacris* 6 (*PL*, 175:15-16), as quoted by Georges H. Tavard, *Holy Writ or Holy Church: The Crisis of the Protestant Reformation* (New York: Harper and Bros., 1959), p. 16.

20. Walter Ullmann, *The Growth of Papal Government in the Middle Ages: A Study in the Ideological Relation of Clerical to Lay Power* (3d ed.; London: Methuen and Company Ltd., 1970), esp. pp. 413-46.

21. Hubert Jedin, *Ecumenical Councils of the Catholic Church,* trans. Ernest Graf, O.S.B. (Glen Rock, N.J.: Paulist Press, 1960); Francis Dvornik, *The Ecumenical Councils,* Twentieth Century Encyclopedia of Catholicism, vol. 82 (New York: Hawthorn Books, 1961); Philip Hughes, *The Church in Crisis: A History of the General Councils, 325-1870* (Garden City, N.Y.: Doubleday and Company, Inc., 1961).

22. *Holy Writ or Holy Church,* pp. 22-43.

23. Kelly, *Early Christian Doctrines,* p. 39. Even Yves M.-J. Congar, O.P., *Tradition and Traditions: An Historical and Theological Essay,* trans. Michael Naseby (New York: Macmillan, 1967), cited more than a dozen Church Fathers who listed various unwritten traditions.

Conciliarism, espoused the transmission of authoritative oral or nonwritten traditions.[24]

D. THE PROTESTANT REFORMATION

It has been stated now and again that the Protestant Reformation was characterized by a shift from the authority of the Church to the authority of the Scriptures, without the Old Testament Apocrypha. Likewise, the supreme authority of the Scriptures has been called "the formal principle" of the Reformation. It has been called "the fundamental issue of the Reformation," and the same author declared that "the question of authority came to the front more prominently" in the age of the Reformation "than at any other point of history, before or since."[25] But not every Protestant leader or movement in the sixteenth century took the same stance on authority.

Among the magisterial Reformers the level of unity on authority was fairly high. Luther, Zwingli, Melanchthon, Martin Bucer (1491-1551), and Calvin affirmed the Scriptures as the Word of God and placed them above popes, councils, and creeds. In his conflict with ecclesiastical and imperial authorities Luther made his defense on the basis of the supreme authority of the Scriptures, yet his tendency to posit a "canon within the canon" of the New Testament meant that some biblical books such as the Epistle of James did not share in that supreme authority. Zwingli was not so driven to his view of the Scriptures by his own religious conversion (i.e., justification by faith) as was Luther, and Calvin included within his doctrine of authority the internal testimony of the Holy Spirit. These Reformers, when explicating the Trinity or Christology, drew heavily upon the first four ecumenical councils.[26]

The radical Reformers stood with the magisterial Reformers in the rejection of "the medieval synthesis of Scripture, tradition, and papal authority." Anabaptists elevated the New Testament, which they interpreted literally as a kind of "new law," above the Old Testament, including the Old Testament Apocrypha, which they interpreted typologically and allegorically. For the Spiritualists authority centered in the relationship of the Son of God or the Holy Spirit to the inner Word and/or to the inner spirit of human beings. Faustus Socinus (1539-1604) taught that the

24. Tavard, *Holy Writ or Holy Church*, pp. 54-61.
25. Davies, *The Problem of Authority in the Continental Reformers: A Study in Luther, Zwingli, and Calvin*, p. 11.
26. Ibid., pp. 29-55, 68-89, 105-46, 154; on Luther see Althaus, *The Theology of Martin Luther*, pp. 72-102; on Calvin see J. K. S. Reid, *The Authority of Scripture: A Study of the Reformation and Post-Reformation Understanding of the Bible* (New York: Harper and Brothers, 1957), pp. 29-55, and Hunter, *The Teaching of Calvin*, pp. 59-87; on Luther and Calvin, see Woodbridge, *Biblical Authority*, pp. 49-67; on Bucer see W. P. Stephens, *The Holy Spirit in the Theology of Martin Bucer* (Cambridge: University Press, 1970), pp. 129-55; Melanchthon did not have a section on Scripture or authority in his *Loci Communes*, but he seems not to have deviated significantly from the other magisterial Reformers.

Bible "may contain things above reason" but "does not contain anything contrary to reason" and hence the "Bible reader must be at pains to ascertain the rational sense of Scripture."[27] The New Testament stands above the Old Testament because it announces immortality and has a higher ethic.[28]

The Council of Trent adopted a doctrinal decree on the written Scriptures and the unwritten traditions that constituted the Roman Church's response to the Protestant Reformation's challenge respecting authority. The Tridentine bishops declared that the gospel, which had been "first promulgated" by Jesus "with His own mouth" and which Jesus had commanded the apostles to preach "to every creature," is the "fountain" of all "saving truth and moral discipline." Seeing that such truth and discipline

> are contained in the written books, and the unwritten traditions which, received by the Apostles from the mouth of Christ himself, or from the Apostles themselves, the Holy Ghost dictating, have come down even unto us, transmitted as it were from hand to hand; (the Synod) . . . receives and venerates with an equal affection of piety, and reverence, all the books of the Old and the New Testament—seeing that one God is the author of both—as also the said traditions, as well those appertaining to faith as to morals, as having been dictated, either by Christ's own word of mouth, or by the Holy Ghost, and preserved in the Catholic Church by a continuous succession.[29]

For four centuries this decree was strictly interpreted as teaching two distinct sources of authority, written Scriptures and unwritten traditions.

E. THE POST-REFORMATION ERA

During the seventeenth century Lutheran and Reformed theologians gave expression to a form of theological orthodoxy, sometimes called Protestant Scholasticism, in which the Bible was held to be the Word of God, "for God speaks to us in Scripture" and God speaks to Christians today only through the Scriptures, divinely inspired by the Triune God as revelation put to writing. This inspiration accordingly was plenary, so as to apply to all of Scripture, verbal, so that every word came by the suggestion of God, applicable to contemporary texts as well as to the autographs, and dictational, but in the sense that God accommodated to the stylistic differences of the human penmen. The autographs of the inspired Scriptures only were inerrant in all areas (not just doctrine and ethics), and there is harmony between the two testaments and among the books of the Bible. The Scriptures, moreover, are intrinsically authorita-

27. George Huntston Williams, *The Radical Reformation* (Philadelphia: Westminster Press, 1962), pp. 816-32, 750-51.

28. O. Zöckler, "Socinus, Faustus, Socinians," *The New Schaff-Herzog Encyclopedia of Religious Knowledge*, 10:490-91.

29. 4th Session, 8 April 1546, as trans. by J. Waterworth in Schaff, *Creeds of Christendom*, 2:79-80.

tive, having both internal and external evidences of such authority and indeed also the internal witness of the Holy Spirit, so that, contra Rome, the Scriptures do not have to be validated by the church. The text of the Scriptures is authentic even to the extent of the Hebrew vowel points. Hence the Scriptures are the only "source" of "supernatural theology" and are "the only norm of Christian doctrine."[30]

Very different indeed were the concepts of authority common to English Deism and the Continental Enlightenment. Here in progressive steps or stages, revealed or biblical truth was held to be supplementary and superior to the truths obtained through reason, not to be contrary to the judgment of reason, and finally to be subject to and hence overruled by the demands of reason.[31]

Other movements such as Puritanism, Pietism, and Wesleyanism maintained the supreme authority of the Bible for Christian doctrine but interpreted biblical authority so that it evoked and undergirded Christian piety or experience. According to one recent study of representative Puritans, Richard Sibbes (1577-1635) used the figurative language of the Scriptures in his plain, spiritual preaching; Richard Baxter (1615-91) majored on biblical promises about the heavenly rest in providing guidelines for Protestant meditation; Gerrard Winstanley (1609–after 1660), taking the Bible as a " 'report' " of the revelations by the Spirit to prophets and apostles, saw it as authorizing his call for the common people to plant the common land; John Milton championed the clarity, plainness, power, and veracity of the Scriptures in contrast to tradition and hierarchical and ceremonial religion and coupled with these marks the renovating work of the Spirit; and John Bunyan skillfully employed the metaphors and events of the Bible so "as to give shape and meaning to the spiritual life" of his readers from justification by faith all the way to the New Jerusalem.[32] Among Pietists the Bible must be properly read and that means prayerfully read (Philip Jacob Spener, 1635-1705),[33] the Bible as God's Word, containing both law and gospel, is designed to lead human beings to the new birth (August Hermann Francke, 1663-1727),[34] and the

---

30. Robert Preus, *The Inspiration of Scriptures: A Study of the Theology of the Seventeenth Century Lutheran Dogmaticians* (Mankato, Minn.: Lutheran Synod Book Company, 1955), pp. 13, 17, 28-29, 31, 33, 39, 47-49, 53, 60, 62-64, 77, 85-86, 88-89, 106-18, 93-106, 134-46, 1-4, 118-30.

31. Gerald R. Cragg, *Reason and Authority in the Eighteenth Century* (Cambridge: University Press, 1964), pp. 28-92, has presented two stages: "the authority of reason confirmed by revelation" (Latitudinarianism) and "the authority of reason independent of revelation" (Deism). John Redwood, *Reason, Ridicule, and Religion: The Age of Enlightenment in England, 1660-1750* (Cambridge, Mass.: Harvard University Press, 1976), pp. 198-212.

32. John Ray Knott, Jr., *The Sword of the Spirit: Puritan Responses to the Bible* (Chicago: University of Chicago Press, 1980).

33. Spener, *The Necessary and Useful Reading of the Holy Scriptures* (1694) in Peter C. Erb, ed., *Pietists: Selected Writings,* Classics of Western Spirituality (New York: Paulist Press, 1983), pp. 71-75.

34. F. Ernest Stoeffler, *German Pietism during the Eighteenth Century,* Studies in the History of Religions, vol. 24 (Leiden: E. J. Brill, 1973), pp. 16-17.

Word of God is Jesus Christ, and the Scriptures "form a most reliable and precious system of divine testimonies" whose very text is to be carefully studied (Johann Albrecht Bengel, 1687-1752).[35] John Wesley (1703-91) recognized the supreme authority of the Bible but attributed to reason a secondary role as "the handmaid of faith, the servant of revelation."[36]

F. THE MODERN ERA

Beginning with Schleiermacher, Liberal Protestantism shifted the locus of authority from the objective Scriptures to the religious consciousness or religious experience. For Schleiermacher religion was not belief or morality but the feeling of absolute dependence on God. The Bible is a sourcebook for those affirmations that are expressed by and consonant with dependence on God.[37] The Ritschlian school emphasized value-judgments in Christianity,[38] and the French Protestant Louis August Sabatier (1839-1901), rejecting the religions of authority—whether of the church or of the Bible—espoused a religion of the Spirit.[39]

Vatican Council I (1869-70), reaffirming the primacy of Peter and of the Church at Rome and the finality of his judgments and restating the two-level view of natural theology derived from reason and supernatural theology obtained through faith, declared that the teaching authority (*magisterium*) of the Catholic Church reaches its climax in the exercise by the pope of infallibility. Specifically,

> the Roman Pontiff, when he speaks *ex cathedra,* that is, when in discharge of the office of pastor and doctor [teacher] of all Christians, by virtue of his supreme Apostolic authority, he defines a doctrine regarding faith or morals to be held by the universal Church, by the divine assistance promised to him in blessed Peter, is possessed of that infallibility with which the divine Redeemer willed that his Church should be endowed for defining doctrine regarding faith or morals, and . . . therefore such definitions of the Roman Pontiffs are irreformable of themselves, and not from the consent of the Church.[40]

Reacting against Liberal Protestantism and that thoroughgoing form of it which both Roman Catholics and Protestants at the beginning of the twentieth century were calling Modernism, Protestant Fundamentalism, especially in the United States, rejected the "Higher Criticism" of the Bible

---

35. *Gnomon of the New Testament*, in Erb, ed., *Pietists: Selected Writings*, pp. 255-71.

36. William R. Cannon, *The Theology of John Wesley: With Special Reference to the Doctrine of Justification* (New York: Abingdon-Cokesbury Press, 1946), pp. 156-60, esp. 159.

37. Hugh Ross Mackintosh, *Types of Modern Theology: From Schleiermacher to Barth* (London: Nisbet and Company Ltd., 1937), pp. 44-50, 60- 68, 74-83, 94-100; Rupert E. Davies, *Religious Authority in an Age of Doubt* (London: Epworth Press, 1968), pp. 34-56.

38. Mackintosh, *Types of Modern Theology,* pp. 153-55, 174-75.

39. *Religions of Authority and the Religion of the Spirit,* trans. Louise Seymour Stoughton (New York: Hodder and Stoughton, 1904).

40. "Dogmatic Constitution on the Catholic Faith" (24 April 1870), chs. 2–4; "First Dogmatic Constitution on the Church of Christ" (18 July 1870), chs. 1–4, in Schaff, *The Creeds of Christendom,* 2:240-51, 256-71.

and reasserted the plenary verbal inspiration of the Bible, the inerrancy of the autographs of biblical books, and the supreme authority of the Bible for Christian doctrine and life together with certain doctrines related to Jesus Christ as the Son of God.[41]

In Britain Peter Taylor Forsyth (1848-1921) asserted that authority rests ultimately in "the grace of a holy God" in Jesus Christ or in his redemptive act in Christ so that his redemption is the content of Christian experience.[42] The Continental Neoorthodox theologians, rejecting much of the theology of Liberal Protestantism, affirmed the authority of the Word of God—not in the sense that the Bible itself can be fully and rightly called the Word of God but in the sense that the Bible may become the Word of God when God speaks by encounter to modern man through it. They had no place for plenary verbal inspiration or for biblical inerrancy.[43]

Vatican Council II (1962-65), while reaffirming the decrees of Trent and Vatican I, put less emphasis on a twofold approach to the Scriptures and unwritten traditions, preferring to speak of "Tradition" (singular), and declared that both "make up a single sacred deposit of the word of God, which is entrusted to the Church." Likewise, without undercutting papal infallibility, the council affirmed that the bishops, gathered in an ecumenical council, can also exercise infallible teaching authority when they concur among themselves and when the pope agrees.[44]

II. THE MAJOR OPTIONS CONCERNING RELIGIOUS AUTHORITY

According to the Christian revelation of God, ultimate truth and the authority of that truth rest in God himself, Father, Son, and Holy Spirit. Jesus as the Son of God is the supreme earthly and historical embodiment of divine truth (John 14:6), and Jesus both attributed truth to God the Father (John 3:34-35; 5:36b-37a) and promised that it would be made available through "the Spirit of truth" (John 16:13). For Christians, therefore, the controverted theological issue is not whether truth does indeed rest in and derive from God, but instead how and where this divine truth is faithfully and responsibly transmitted or communicated to humans, and especially to Christians. The "how and where" question has elicited

41. *The Fundamentals: A Testimony to the Truth,* ed. R. A. Torrey, A. C. Dixon, et al., 4 vols. (Los Angeles: Bible Institute of Los Angeles, 1917), vol. 1 (in its entirety); vol. 2, chs. 1–7.

42. *The Principle of Authority* (2d ed.; London: Independent Press Ltd., 1952), esp. pp. 10-13, 26-30, 57-59, 67, 78, 184-86, 364-65.

43. Brunner, *Revelation and Reason,* pp. 118-36, 164-84, 412-22; Barth, *Church Dogmatics,* I/1, pp. 98-162, 213-83; I/2, pp. 457-740.

44. *Dogmatic Constitution on Divine Revelation* (18 November 1965), paras. 7-10; *Dogmatic Constitution on the Church* (21 November 1964), para. 25, in Austin Flannery, O.P., gen. ed., *Vatican Council II: Conciliar and Post Conciliar Documents: Study Edition* (Northport, N.Y.: Costello Publishing Company, 1987), pp. 753-56, 379-81; Geiselmann, *The Meaning of Tradition.*

differing answers, thus making the quest for the true channel or channels of religious authority a significant theological issue.

A. CHURCH AND TRADITION: CATHOLIC CHRISTIANITY

Catholic Christianity, whether Roman Catholic or Eastern Orthodox or Old Catholic or Monophysite, has placed high on the list of channels of religious authority the historic or institutional church in perpetuity and what may be called ecclesiastical tradition and authority. This is not to say that Catholic Christianity has officially and unambiguously placed church and tradition above the Scriptures in the order of channels of religious authority. Rather the authority of the Bible is normally qualified by the authority of church and tradition in Catholic Christianity. Eastern Orthodoxy, while affirming the authority of the Old and the New Testaments, holds to the special and unique authority of seven early ecumenical councils: Nicaea I (325), Constantinople I (381), Ephesus (431), Chalcedon (451), Constantinople II (553), Constantinople III (680-81), and Nicaea II (787). Roman Catholicism, while recognizing the authority of 21 ecumenical councils—Vatican II (1962-65) being the twenty-first—stresses the present-day *magisterium* (teaching authority) of the church as that reaches its climax in the office of the pope, to whom is ascribed infallibility when functioning as the supreme pastor and teacher. Both the canonical Scriptures and unwritten traditions are held to be authoritative, along with the *magisterium*.

B. THE SCRIPTURES OF THE OLD AND THE NEW TESTAMENTS: CLASSICAL PROTESTANT CHRISTIANITY

Protestant Christianity in its more classical forms has placed at the top of the list of channels of religious authority the Bible, or the canonical Scriptures. The Protestant Reformation, as has been noted, brought about a restoration of the primacy of biblical authority. Protestants sometimes have acknowledged the work of the Church Fathers in formulating such doctrines as the Trinity and the person of Jesus Christ. Protestants have framed and utilized confessions of faith, but these same confessions have repeatedly affirmed the supreme or final authority of the Bible, always above any creeds or confessions of faith or church councils or private religious experiences or opinions.[45]

C. THE DIVINE-HUMAN ENCOUNTER: VARIOUS MOVEMENTS

A third channel of religious authority in Christianity may be identified by the all-embracing term "the divine-human encounter." Its advocates include Catholic mystics, Quakers, Liberal Protestants, existentialists, and others. They stress an immediate transference of divine truth with a self-authenticating principle of authority. When elevated to the first position among the channels of religious authority, the divine-human

45. Schaff, *The Creeds of Christendom*, vol. 3, passim.

encounter judges both the Scriptures and churchly tradition. Medieval Western Catholic mystics stressed the mystical and sometimes nonhistorical path to God; notable among these were Hugh of St. Victor, Bernard of Clairvaux, and Meister Eckhardt (c. 1260–c. 1327). Quakers, or Friends, have described the encounter as "the Inner Light." Robert Barclay (1648-90), the early Quaker theologian, taught the continued existence of "divine inward revelations"—"by the Spirit"—which do not "contradict" the Scriptures and do not need to be "subjected" to the Scriptures or to "natural reason," for they "serve as their own evidence."[46] Liberal Protestants, especially during the nineteenth century, stressed either the religious consciousness ("the feeling of absolute dependence upon God," according to F. D. E. Schleiermacher), human value-judgments in religion (according to Albrecht Ritschl), or the unfettered religion of the Spirit (according to August Sabatier). Existentialist theologians such as Rudolf Bultmann and Gerhard Ebeling have emphasized the leap of faith and the transformation of historical—even if it still can be called that—revelation into personal experience. If and when present-day practitioners of the spiritual gifts of speaking in tongues and prophecy should allow the exercise of their gifts to be a more authoritative source of religious truth than the written Scriptures, they would need to be reckoned under the divine-human encounter.

In summary, the advocates of the authority of the Bible normally rank the Bible first among the channels of religious authority and the advocates of the authority of the divine-human encounter tend to rank that encounter first among the channels but the advocates of the church and tradition do not formally assert that church and tradition should rank first among the channels but instead allow it to modify the authority of the Scriptures or to become de facto the primal channel.

III. THE QUEST FOR A VIABLE PATTERN OF RELIGIOUS AUTHORITY

The issue as to religious authority among Christians today is not so much the question, "Which channel of religious authority is valid and to be recognized?" as it is the question, "What ranking is proper to the different channels of authority?" Bernard L. Ramm has referred to "a mosaic of authority" or "a chain of authority."[47] Some may express doubt concerning such a statement inasmuch as they may contend that Protestants have held to *sola Scriptura*, or the Bible as the only or sole channel of religious authority. Did not Luther assert *sola Scriptura*, and did not other major Reformers agree with his assertion? Must not today's Protestants who would be faithful to their Reformation heritage hold to *sola Scriptura*?

46. *An Apology for the True Christian Divinity*, prop. 2, ed. Dean Freiday (Elberon, N.J.: editor, 1967), p. 40.
47. *The Pattern of Authority* (Grand Rapids: Eerdmans, 1957), p. 18.

James I. Packer has restated the case for the absolute necessity of *sola Scriptura*,[48] but in a context in which he was explaining and defending the Reformers' entire doctrine of Scripture. Some of Packer's reasons for insisting on *sola Scriptura* can be met as well by *suprema Scriptura*, or the Bible as the supreme or highest channel of religious authority. Rejection of the *magisterium* of the Roman Catholic Church, nondependence on popes and church councils for the interpretation of the Bible, vivid awareness of the Bible as the Word of God, and rightful judging of what the church in each age has taught can also be derived from *suprema Scriptura*. Only the having of a single channel for revealed truth would seem to necessitate *sola Scriptura*. Moreover, to defend *sola Scriptura*, Packer finds it necessary to reckon such differences as those between divine sovereignty and human freedom, between believer's baptism and infant baptism, and among various millennial views as "secondary" issues about which controversy "sprang from insufficient circumspection in exegesis." In Robert Charles Sproul's (1939-) defense of *sola Scriptura*,[49] in which he has made Luther's doctrine of *sola Scriptura* to be a corollary of his doctrine of the inerrancy of the Bible, Sproul has interpreted the Reformers' *sola Scriptura* to mean that the Bible is not "the only authority in the church," to be "the supreme norm of ecclesiastical authority," and to allow for general revelation. Sproul indeed has defined *sola Scriptura* so as to mean *suprema Scriptura*. Similarly, Bernard Ramm, in an essay[50] in which he warns that certain present-day followers of the Hodge-Warfield heritage are in effect trying to make *sola Scriptura*, or more precisely a certain doctrine of inspiration and inerrancy, to be "the essence of Christianity," also has interpreted *sola Scriptura* to mean *suprema Scriptura*. According to Ramm, *sola Scriptura* means that "only Scripture" has "the final word on a subject" and that the Bible "is the supreme and final authority in theological decision-making." Both Sproul and Ramm acknowledge that the Reformers respected and made use of the Church Fathers. In fact, Luther's treatise *On the Councils and the Churches* (1539)[51] is marked evidence that Luther agreed with and recognized the validity of the doctrinal decisions of the early ecumenical councils. Furthermore, Lutheranism's formulation and use of confessions of faith and catechisms are compatible with *suprema Scriptura*.

The argument points to the conclusion that *suprema Scriptura*, not a quite literal and restricted *sola Scriptura*, provides the most representative and accurate Protestant answer to the question as to the ranking of

48. " 'Sola Scriptura' in History and Today," in Montgomery, ed., *God's Inerrant Word*, pp. 43-62.
49. "*Sola Scriptura*: Crucial to Evangelicalism," in Boice, ed., *The Foundation of Biblical Authority*, pp. 101-19, esp. 104, 106, and 107.
50. "Is 'Scripture Alone' the Essence of Christianity?" in Rogers, ed., *Biblical Authority*, pp. 107-23, esp. 112, 119, and 122.
51. Trans. Charles M. Jacobs and rev. Eric W. Gritsch, *Luther's Works*, 41:3-178.

channels of religious authority. This means that the Bible always ranks and stands above church and tradition, the divine-human encounter, and any other possible channel of religious authority. The question then comes to be that of evaluating and ranking the other channels of religious authority in relation to the supreme channel, the Bible. All the channels are designed to convey the authoritative truth of God in Jesus Christ. If and when, however, these nonbiblical channels should contradict the Scriptures, they must be rejected or corrected by the Scriptures. Yet at the same time we must be prepared to acknowledge that our very interpretation of texts of the Bible may have been influenced by one or more of the other channels of authority—church and tradition, the divine-human encounter, or a specific human culture or civilization. Furthermore, in the ranking of the nonbiblical channels the more churchly forms of Christianity normally put the church and tradition in second place, and the more individualistic forms of Christianity normally put the divine-human encounter in second place.

If Protestantism in general can be said to be served best by a carefully constructed concept of *suprema Scriptura*, is this also true of specific denominations such as the Baptists? The great majority of the Baptist confessions of faith and the great majority of writing Baptist theologians have held to the Bible as the supreme authority for doctrine, conduct, and polity and not to a strictly defined *sola Scriptura*. Among the writers of popular monographs on Baptist beliefs some have held to sole authority and some to supreme authority.[52] The 1925 and the 1963 Statements of the Baptist Faith and Message adopted by the Southern Baptist Convention affirm both concepts without explaining how this can be so. The preamble to these statements contains an avowal of *sola Scriptura*, and article 1 on the Bible affirms the Bible's role as the supreme standard.[53] Baptists who emphasize the use of Baptist confessions of faith and who insist on a clearly articulated doctrine of the Trinity, often using terms easily traceable to the patristic age, would do well to affirm *suprema Scriptura*.

IV. THE NATURE OF BIBLICAL AUTHORITY[54]

If indeed the Bible is to be reckoned as the supreme standard or highest ranking channel of religious authority for Christians, how ought the authority of the Bible to be understood?

A. The Bible is authoritative primarily as a book of religion or of divine revelation. It is not a textbook on the natural sciences or a record of all ancient history. This is not to impute error to the Bible in matters not

---

52. James Leo Garrett, Jr., "Sources of Authority in Baptist Thought," *Baptist History and Heritage* 13 (July 1978): 41-49.

53. SBC *Annual*, 1925, p. 71; 1963, pp. 270-71.

54. This section presupposes, builds on, and amplifies Conner, *Revelation and God*, pp. 95-99.

essentially religious; it is rather to stress the essentially religious purpose and character of the Bible. The Bible is the record of a historically mediated revelation of God centered in the mighty words and acts of God, and it derives its authority from the self-revealing and self-authenticating God.

B. The authority of the message of the Bible transcends the societal, geographical, and chronological matrix of the biblical books, and, contrary to the recent school of cultural relativism[55] that alleges that the message of the Bible cannot be communicated to another nonbiblical culture, the message of the Bible can and does show itself to be communicatable to and applicable in numerous present-day cultures.

C. The authority of the Bible is that of the sovereign God, who commands and persuades but does not coerce human beings and who redeems or liberates but does not enslave human beings. When the nature and the authority of the Bible are rightly understood, there is no valid basis for the accusation that Christians engage in and are guilty of "Bibliolatry."[56] Moreover, the Christian doctrine of the Scriptures is markedly different from the Islamic doctrine of the Koran and the Mormon teaching about the Book of Mormon.

D. The Bible is authoritative as it is accurately and faithfully interpreted in its historical context and by the criterion of Jesus Christ,[57] who as the promise and the fulfillment is the central personage and theme of the Bible.

E. The Bible is authoritative as the Holy Spirit bestows illumination as to the significance and application of specific texts within and specific books of the Old and the New Testaments. According to Bernard Ramm, the Protestant principle of authority is "the Holy Spirit speaking in the Scriptures."[58]

In this chapter we have traced the history of the principles or patterns of religious authority in Christianity from the New Testament to the twentieth century, identified the major present-day options concerning such authority, made a case for *suprema Scriptura* rather than *sola Scriptura*, and described the nature of biblical authority. Now we must turn to the doctrine of God.

---

55. See James Barr, *The Bible in the Modern World* (London: SCM Press Ltd., 1973), ch. 3. Barr does not fully agree with but is willing to tolerate the claims of the cultural relativists.

56. Brunner, *Revelation and Reason*, pp. 127-28, 133-35, 273-75; John Marsh, *The Fulness of Time* (New York: Harper and Bros., 1952), p. 5.

57. "Statement of Baptist Faith and Message," art. 1, SBC *Annual*, 1963, p. 270.

58. *The Pattern of Authority*, p. 28.

PART II

God the Holy and Loving Father; the Trinity

CHAPTER 13

The Existence of God;
the Name and the Names of God

Now that we have studied revelation and the Bible, it is imperative that we investigate the entire concept of the being of God. Who is the God revealed in nature and conscience and more fully through the people of the Old Covenant and supremely in Jesus Christ, the Mediator of the New Covenant? Who is the God of whom the Bible speaks?

The teaching about God or the gods is central to and significant for any religion. Religions do not rise to heights above their conception of deity. Christian theology has no more basic task than the explication of the being of God. Karl Barth has written:

> Dogmatics, in each and all of its divisions and subdivisions, with every one of its questions and answers, with all its biblical and historical assertions, with the whole range of its formal and material considerations, examinations and condensations, can first and last, as a whole and in part, say nothing else but that God is.[1]

Similarly, a Methodist theologian has declared:

> God is not one of our religious beliefs; he is *the* belief. He is not one doctrine; he is the heart of all doctrine.[2]

The doctrine of God, according to Christian theologians, usually consists of at least two aspects: the attributes, qualities, or perfections of God, and the inner or Trinitarian relationships within the being of God.[3] We will treat these in the chapters that follow.

Ought the study of the doctrine of God to begin with the works or deeds of God and then proceed to the qualities of the divine being? Or should it commence with the qualities of the divine being? Philip Melanchthon during the Reformation enunciated the dictum, namely,

---

1. *Church Dogmatics*, II/1, p. 258.
2. H. F. Rall, *The Meaning of God* (Nashville: Cokesbury, 1925), pp. 6-7.
3. Among theologians of the Reformed tradition it is common to insist on a third aspect, namely, the decrees of God.

"This is to know Christ, to wit, to know his benefits."[4] If applied to God
the Father as well as to Jesus Christ, this dictum would call for commencing with the deeds. Karl Barth has criticized Melanchthon's bypassing of
God's being and his later turning to nonrevelational materials for his
doctrine of God.[5] In the study of revelation and the Bible (Chs. 3–12) we
have given considerable attention to the mighty acts of God or the events
of salvation history. It should now be evident that special or biblical
revelation is inseparable from the major events of biblical history and thus
that God's being must be seen in the light of God's actions. Having come,
then, to the doctrine of God, we need not hesitate to proceed with the
qualities or attributes that belong to God. But before we enter into a
discussion of divine qualities or attributes we must deal with some prior
considerations. The first of these is the existence of God.

I. THE EXISTENCE OF GOD

The topic of God's existence, including both the denials and the affirmations thereof, undoubtedly belongs to Christian apologetics. Indeed,
Christian apologists during the twentieth century have necessarily given
major attention to this topic. So widespread have been the exponents and
adherents of atheism in this century that the Christian theologian does not
wisely bypass this topic or merely refer it to his apologetic colleagues.

A. THE CHALLENGE OF MODERN ATHEISM TO THE CHRISTIAN FAITH

During the nineteenth and twentieth centuries atheism has had its
major exponents and has advanced major arguments for its distinctive
conclusion.

1. Leading Exponents

Ludwig Feuerbach (1804-72) set forth an "anthropological" form of
atheism. The idea of God was merely the projected wish of human beings.
Therefore, what is claimed about God (theology) is only the extension of
what is known about humans (anthropology). Karl Marx expounded a
"sociopolitical" form of atheism, as our earlier inquiry[6] into dialectical
materialism showed. From a materialistic base he saw in the history of
class conflicts religion as a human fabrication and as "opiate" serving the
"vested interests" of those in power. Sigmund Freud represented "psy-
choanalytic atheism." Belief in God is illusory or wishful thinking that
marks the infantile stage of human development.[7] Jean-Paul Sartre was

4. *Loci Communes* (1521 ed.), trans. Charles Leander Hill (Boston: Meador Publishing
Company, 1944), p. 68.
5. *Church Dogmatics*, II/1, pp. 259-60.
6. See above, Ch. 5, III, A.
7. Hans Küng, *Does God Exist? An Answer for Today*, trans. Edward Quinn (Garden
City, N.Y.: Doubleday and Company, Inc., 1980), ch. C, has treated in detail Feuerbach, Marx,
and Freud.

an atheistic existentialist. For him human beings become through free decision-making. Life is absurd and meaningless except as humans create their own values. For God to exist, according to Sartre, would mean that human freedom be curtailed, and this cannot be.[8]

2. Major Arguments for Modern Atheism

Sylvester Paul Schilling (1904-), after an extensive reading of atheistic authors and interviews with leading living atheists, identified and interpreted seven major arguments or "bases" used by modern atheists in denying belief in the existence or reality of God. It will be helpful to allow Schilling to state clearly these seven arguments:

(1) Belief in God . . . *can be explained as an objectification of purely human ideals, wishes, longings, or needs. . . .*
(2) [Belief in God] . . . *is in one way or another inconsistent with scientific method and the scientific view of reality. . . .*
(3) [Belief in God usually means that] . . . *the term 'God' lacks clear, univocal meaning which can be unambiguously communicated. . . .*
(4) [Belief in God] . . . *is irreconcilable with the extent and intensity of human suffering. . . .*
(5) [Belief] . . . *in the sovereignty of God is inconsistent with recognition of the worth, freedom, and full responsibility of man. . . .*
(6) [Belief in God] . . . *produces passivity in the presence of injustice and opposition to social change. . . .*
(7) [Belief in God seems untenable, for many persons today] . . . *who are seriously committed to the highest human values, have no personal awareness of God.*[9]

These basic arguments for atheism, to summarize, are drawn from projectionism, scientism, linguistic philosophy, the problem of suffering, responsible humanism, social injustice, and the experience of the absence of God.

B. A CRITIQUE OF AND REPLY TO MODERN ATHEISM

1. Some Specific Criticisms of Atheism

Hans Küng has directed four criticisms toward atheism:

a. All *proofs or arguments of the eminent atheists* are certainly adequate to raise doubts about the existence of God but not to make God's nonexistence unquestionable. . . .
b. The constantly varied *arguments, based on philosophy of history or of culture, for an end of religion* involve an ultimately unsubstantiated extrapolation into the future. . . .

8. S. Paul Schilling, *God in an Age of Atheism* (Nashville: Abingdon Press, 1969), pp. 65-69.
9. Ibid., pp. 115-34.

c. The continually varied *individual or social-psychological arguments for religion as projection* are based on a postulate that is neither methodically nor objectively substantiated. . . .

d. Atheism, too, lives by an undemonstrable faith. . . .[10]

2. Forbidden Responses to Atheism

In addition to specific arguments against atheism as a worldview Küng wisely cautions Christians and other theists that not every possible attitude toward or assessment of atheism ought to be adopted or pursued. First, atheism should not "be indiscriminately morally condemned as deliberate apostasy from God," for it often results from a "merely half-considered participation in the philosophical, scientific, cultural spirit of the age" and hence is "more a drift away from than an abandonment of faith." Perhaps this is basically a pastoral or evangelistic concern, not primarily an apologetic one. Second, atheism ought not to be considered as "hidden 'belief in God' . . . as if atheists were 'secret' believers in God" or " 'anonymous Christians.' " Third, atheism "is not to be toyed with, flattered, [or] acquiesced in," as by participating in the "death of God" movement of the 1960s.[11] Küng's warnings, therefore, focus on how Christians and other theists are to understand and identify atheists and on theists' dabbling in the language and concepts of atheism.

3. A Christian Apologetic vis-à-vis Atheism

We may put forth seven considerations in an effort to show the viability of belief in the existence of God.

a. Many human beings in today's world actually do believe in God. Hence there are limits to the atheistic assertions about the experience of the absence of God.

b. Human beings, when they have rejected or failed to exercise faith in a personal God, tend to absolutize or make idolatrous something(s) or someone else. Whence comes this proclivity to worship?

c. Christian martyrs and other believers in God have suffered for and given witness to their faith in God, especially through his Son Jesus Christ—often when renunciation would have prevented their deaths or alleviated their sufferings. The twentieth century has been the century of the awesome Holocaust and the century in which, it is reported, more Christians have been put to death on account of their faith than in any

10. *Does God Exist?*, p. 329.

11. Ibid., p. 339. Concerning the history of and for a critique of the death-of-God theology, see Helmut Thielicke, *The Evangelical Faith*, 1:221-311. Paul Tillich's assertion "God does not exist" must be understood in relation to Tillich's concepts of the Ground of Being, essence, and existence. Tillich insisted:

The ground of being cannot be found within the totality of beings. . . . God does not exist. He is being-itself beyond essence and existence. Therefore to argue that God exists, is to deny him. *Systematic Theology*, 1:205.

preceding century of the Christian era. Is such suffering and martyrdom to be explained as due to an illusion or the projection of human wishes?

d. Christian missionaries have given and do give their entire adult lives to the sharing of their faith in God with other human beings, usually crossing the barriers of language and culture.

e. Christians believe in God despite close contact with Marxist-Leninism and in spite of persecution, discrimination, and pressures from Marxist-Leninist governments. There have been notable converts to Christianity from Marxist-Leninism (e.g., Nicolai Berdyaev, 1874-1948, and Aleksandr Solzhenitsyn, 1918-). Christians continue in their faith and continue to share their faith while living under Marxist-Leninist regimes.

f. Christian believers have been for centuries and are presently engaged in various ministries designed to meet human need and alleviate human suffering. Included are hospitals, children's homes, homes for the aged, and agencies for famine and disaster relief.

g. Christian believers have been and are at work to help to effect societal reforms. Examples include prison reform, the abolition of slavery, child labor laws, the turning of tribal dialects into written languages, literacy work, Christian schools, the abolition of the Hindu practice of suttee, and the Christian witness against war.

Like the various theistic arguments for the existence of God, the arguments against atheism will not convince every human being regardless of his/her attitudes or presuppositions, but they do provide a viable alternative to atheism for thinking people.

C. THE BIBLICAL WITNESS TO THE EXISTENCE OF GOD

1. The biblical writers did not seek to prove the existence of God by formal argument. Rather they assumed the existence of God.

2. The psalmist rejected the denial of the existence of God: "The fool says, in his heart, 'There is no God'" (14:1; 53:1, NIV). Some interpret the psalmist to refer to practical or life-style atheism rather than to formal or theoretical atheism.

3. According to the author of the Epistle to the Hebrews, belief in the existence of God is essential to a right relation with God: "And without faith it is impossible to please God, because anyone who comes to him must believe that he exists and that he rewards those who earnestly seek him" (11:6, NIV).

II. THE NAME AND THE NAMES OF GOD

The method of the older systematic theologies in the commencement of their discussion of the doctrine of God was to treat in some detail the various names of God, especially those found in the Old Testament, most of which were built on the Hebrew 'El. Without disparaging such a study we should take note of the emphasis that Louis Berkhof and Emil Brunner have placed during the present century on the name (singular) of God as a theological topic.

A. THE NAME OF GOD

Berkhof posed the issue as follows:

> The Bible often speaks of the name of God in the singular, as for instance, in Ex. 20:7 and Ps. 8:1. When it does this, it does not refer to any special designation of God, but uses the term in a very general sense to denote His self-revelation.[12]

Brunner viewed the name of God as a neglected theme among theologians. He found that the phrases "the name of God" and "the name of the Lord" and their variants were used in nearly 100 passages in the Old Testament and in more than 200 passages in the New Testament.[13] Examples of such usages are the following: "You shall not take the *name* of the LORD your God in vain" (Exod. 20:7); "[I] will proclaim before you my *name*, 'The LORD' . . ." (Exod. 33:19); "How excellent is thy *name* in all the earth" (Ps. 8:1); "Hallowed be thy *name*" (Matt. 6:9); "I have come in my Father's *name*" (John 5:43); and "I have manifested thy *name* to the men whom thou gavest me out of the world" (John 17:6, RSV). According to Brunner, the name of God "gathers up . . . certain decisive elements in the reality of revelation"; the name itself stands for the selfhood of God, and the manifestation of God's name stands for the action of God. The Swiss theologian identified three of these "decisive elements":

1. The name of God means the possibility of divine revelation. "God is known only where He Himself makes His name known."

2. The name of God manifests the nature of God as Person. The naming of God suggests that God is a "Thou" and not an "it." "It is the prerogative of persons to possess a name." The God who manifests his name is described in the biblical books by means of anthropomorphisms, that is, ways of speaking about God after the form of human beings.

3. The naming of God is designed to lead human beings into communion or fellowship with God. To communicate one's name is to disclose oneself; for God to manifest his name is for him to call on human beings to seek him and to enter into fellowship with him.[14]

To Brunner's three "decisive elements" a fourth may be added:

4. The name of God intensifies the seriousness of blasphemy and cursing. In the Septuagint blasphemy "always refers finally to God." "In the New Testament the concept of blasphemy is controlled throughout by the thought of violation of the power and majesty of God."[15]

---

12. *Manual of Christian Doctrine* (Grand Rapids: Eerdmans, 1933), p. 58.
13. *The Christian Doctrine of God*, trans. Olive Wyon, Dogmatics, vol. 1 (London: Lutterworth Press, 1949), pp. 128-32.
14. Ibid., pp. 120-24.
15. Hermann W. Beyer, *"blasphēmeō, blasphēmia, blasphēmos,"* in Gerhard Kittel, ed.,

B. THE NAMES OF GOD

Along with an awareness of the theological significance of the name of God in the Bible some knowledge of the specific biblical names for God is needed.

1. The Old Testament

The two most frequently used names for God in the Old Testament are the general Semitic name for God, 'El, and the special or covenant name, Yahweh.

a. 'El and Its Variants

'El meant the strong or powerful God. It "belonged to the entire Semitic world, being found in Babylonian, Phoenician, Aramaic, and Arabic writings, no less than in Hebrew."[16] The name 'El Shaddai, or God Almighty, is used in Gen. 17:1; 28:3; 35:11; 43:14; 48:3; 49:25; and Exod. 6:3. The name 'El 'Elyon is found in the Melchizedek passage (Gen. 14:18, 19, 20, 22). The term 'El Hai, or the living God, is used in Deut. 5:26; Josh. 3:10; 1 Sam. 17:26, 36; 2 Kings 19:4, 16 (par. Isa. 37:4, 17); Hos. 1:10b; Jer. 10:10 and 23:36; and Ps. 42:2 and 84:2. The plural 'Elohim has been said to be "the plural of majesty or eminence," or "more accurately the plural of fulness or greatness."[17]

b. Yahweh

The etymology of this word is somewhat uncertain, but it seems to be a form of the Hebrew verb "to be" (hāyāh). Old Testament theologians and other theologians differ somewhat in their definitions of the basic meaning of "Yahweh." For Andrew Bruce Davidson (1831-1902), the term had redemptive rather than ontological significance. "It does not describe God on the side of His nature, but on that of His saving operations, His living activity among His people, and His influence upon them."[18] For Carl F. H. Henry "it is not the idea of continuous existence—existence self-complete, but of God's coming to man, which is here conspicuous."[19] According to Emil Brunner, the term, especially in Exod. 3:14, connotes God as "the Mysterious One, . . . the Incomparable."[20] Edmund Jacob (1909-) found the key idea in the name Yahweh to be God's presence with his people.[21] Walther Eichrodt

---

Theological Dictionary of the New Testament, trans. Geoffrey W. Bromiley, 10 vols. (Grand Rapids: Eerdmans, 1964-76), 1:621-25.

16. Carl F. H. Henry, Notes on the Doctrine of God (Boston: W. A. Wilde Company, 1948), p. 87, n. 7.

17. A. B. Davidson, The Theology of the Old Testament, International Theological Library (Edinburgh: T. and T. Clark, 1904), pp. 40-41.

18. The Theology of the Old Testament, p. 47.

19. Notes on the Doctrine of God, pp. 82-83.

20. The Christian Doctrine of God, p. 120. A. H. Strong, Systematic Theology, pp. 256-57, interpreted Exod. 3:14 as implying the "self-existence" or "aseity" of God, that is, God's "having the ground of his existence in himself," for God's is a "necessary," not a "contingent" existence.

21. Theology of the Old Testament, trans. Arthur W. Heathcote and Philip J. Allcock (London: Hodder and Stoughton, 1958), pp. 52-54.

declared that "the most natural interpretation remains that which equates the Tetragrammaton with 'He is,' 'He exists,' 'He is present.' "[22]

Certain translations of the Bible into English have employed the word "Jehovah" instead of rendering Yahweh as "the LORD." Moreover, the name Jehovah has come to be used in various English-language hymns. What is the relation of Jehovah to Yahweh? Some historical facts are required to answer that question. After the Babylonian Captivity the Jews ceased to pronounce Yahweh orally, presumably out of their great reverence for that name, when they read aloud the Hebrew Bible, but instead they used the circumlocution 'Adonai, or the Lord. About A.D. 1520 Christians, following the lead of the Vatican, began to join the consonants from Yahweh with the vowels from 'Adonai to form the hybrid word "Jehovah."

2. The New Testament

The name "God" prevails in the New Testament without any distinction comparable to the usage of 'El and Yahweh in the Old Testament. Yet in the New Testament the great analogical names for God, which were first used in the Old Testament, come to prominence. Among the analogical names are Father,[23] Shepherd, Redeemer or Savior, Judge, King, and Lord. The term Creator is less properly to be reckoned as analogous since the Hebrew word translated "to create" (bārā') means "to bring into existence that which has not existed."

3. Philosophical Usage

There is a marked contrast between the analogical terms for God used in the Bible, which serve to magnify the personal nature of the God of the Bible, and the more impersonal terms for deity used in the Western philosophical tradition.

> The great philosophic writings are, indeed, studded with names for God—Socrates' Daimon, Plato's Idea of the Good, Aristotle's Prime Mover, Plotinus' One, Spinoza's Causa Sui, Hegel's Absolute, and Spencer's Unknowable.[24]

Sometimes theologians have joined with philosophers in opting for impersonal language for God. Eunomius of Cyzicus, a fourth-century Arian, contended that the only name for God should be Ungenerated (i.e., without origin).[25] The tension between the more personal and the more impersonal names for God continues even to the present.

22. Theology of the Old Testament, 1:189.
23. For an argument that fatherhood does not provide an analogical name, see J. K. Mozley, The Doctrine of God (London: Society for Promoting Christian Knowledge, 1933), pp. 54-55.
24. Henry, Notes on the Doctrine of God, p. 75.
25. John Courtney Murray, The Problem of God (New Haven, London: Yale University Press, 1965), p. 61. The name used by Eunomius was Agennētos.

Thought that has been fed on philosophical abstractions therefore finds the concept of the Name of God, and the revelation of the Name, to be an anthropomorphic degradation, making God finite, which cannot be permitted.[26]

A twentieth-century Jewish theologian, Martin Buber (1878-1965), told how a friend had rebuked him regarding his use of the name of God. The friend said:

> How can you bring yourself to say 'God' time after time? . . . What you mean by the name of God is something above all human grasp and comprehension, but in speaking about it you have lowered it to human conceptualization. What word of human speech is so misused, so defiled, so desecrated as this! All the innocent blood that has been shed for it has robbed it of its radiance. All the injustice that it has been used to cover has effaced its features. When I hear the highest called 'God,' it sometimes seems almost blasphemous.

Buber replied to his friend as follows:

> Yes, it is the most heavy-laden of all human words. None has become so spoiled, so mutilated. Just for this reason I may not abandon it. Generations of men have laid the burden of their anxious lives upon this word, and weighed it to the ground; it lies in the dust and bears their whole burden. . . . Where might I find a word like to describe the highest! If I took the purest, most sparkling concept from the inner treasure-chamber of the philosophers, I could only capture thereby an unbinding product of thought. I could not capture the presence of Him whom the generations of men have honoured and degraded with their awesome living and dying. I do indeed mean Him whom the hell-tormented and heaven-storming generations of men mean. . . . But when all madness and delusion fall to dust, when they stand over against Him in the loneliest darkness and no longer say 'He, He' but rather sigh 'Thou,' shout 'Thou,' all of them the one word, and when they add 'God,' is it not the real God whom they all implore, the One Living God, the God of the children of man? . . . And just for this reason is not the word 'God,' the word of appeal, the word which has become a *name*, consecrated in all human tongues for all time?[27]

26. Brunner, *The Christian Doctrine of God*, p. 124.

27. Buber, *Eclipse of God: Studies in the Relation between Religion and Philosophy* (New York: Harper and Bros., 1952), pp. 16-17. Following the death of Buber in Jerusalem in 1965, at a memorial service for Buber in New York City Paul J. Tillich declared:

> Going back through four decades from this last to our first meeting, I remember the conference of Religious Socialists in Germany in the year 1924. Our movement, founded after the First World War, tried to heal the catastrophic split between the churches and labor in most European countries. It was my task to elaborate adequate concepts from the theological, philosophical, and sociological sides. This meant that I had to replace traditional religious terms, including the word 'God,' with words which could be accepted by the religious humanists who belonged to our movement. After I had finished, Martin Buber arose and attacked what he called the 'abstract facade' I had built. With great passion, he said that there are some aboriginal words like 'God,' which cannot be replaced at all. He was right and I learned the lesson. I don't believe that concepts like 'ultimate reality' or 'unconditional concern,' which are much used in my systematic writing, appear in the three volumes of my sermons. This awareness, produced by Martin Buber, enabled me, I believe, to preach at all.

"Martin Buber, 1878-1965," *Pastoral Psychology*, September 1965, p. 52

CHAPTER 14

God as Personal and Present; the Attributes of God

Having treated the existence of God and the naming and the names of God, we must next ask whether God can be rightly described as a "Person" and in what sense God can be said to "be present" and then address the question of the attributes or qualities that belong to God as God.

I. GOD AS PERSONAL

A. IS IT BIBLICAL? NOT A BIBLICAL TERM, BUT A BIBLICAL IDEA

1. *The Language of the Bible*

The terms "person" and "personal" do not appear in the Old and the New Testaments, as a brief perusal of a biblical concordance will verify. The Bible does speak of "the living God."[1] Many modern Christian thinkers, however, are persuaded that these terms in modern use signify something quite basic to the biblical understanding of God, namely, that God, who is distinguishable from human beings, nature, and the universe, is to be understood under the analogy of the selfhood of human beings.

The problem is similar to that connected with the term *homoousios* during the fourth century A.D., when opponents of the Nicene position contended that *homoousios* was not a biblical term and hence need not be subscribed to by fourth-century Christians and the Nicene defenders in turn replied by arguing for its consonance with and representation of biblical truth about the relationship of the Son of God to God the Father.

2. *The Nature of the Predication*

John Macquarrie has insisted that

this adjective "personal" is predicated of God symbolically, not literally.... We can certainly assert that God is not less than personal, and that the

---

1. See above, Ch. 13, II, B, 1, a.

dynamic diversity-in-unity of personal life affords our best symbol of the mystery of God. But it cannot exhaustively comprehend this mystery.[2]

According to John Kenneth Mozley (1883-1946), "one of the real drawbacks to speaking of God as a Person" is that it "suggests that God belongs to a class though doubtless in that class He is the greatest." "It would be far better to say that God is *the* Person."[3]

3. The Apologetic Challenge

The use of the terms "Person" and "personal" in reference to God has been made very desirable, if not necessary, by Christian apologetical considerations during the modern era. Specifically, the denial of the personal aspects of God by idealistic pantheism and by process philosophy and the prevalence of these philosophies have caused Christians increasingly to employ and rely on the terms "Person" and "personal." More will be said in this chapter about this apologetic challenge.

4. Old Testament Evidence That God Is Personal

A. C. Knudson identified and proposed[4] three major evidences from the Old Testament that the God of Israel was understood to be, in modern terms, personal. One of these is the covenant name for God, Yahweh, which conveys the qualities of personal being. Another is Yahweh's free and sovereign relationship to both nature and history. Israel's faith was unlike the fertility cult and season-oriented religion of the Canaanites and unlike the cyclical view of history common among the Greeks. Yahweh was Lord of nature and of history. A third evidence from the Old Testament of a personal God is the repeated and deliberate use of anthropomorphism, or the representation of God under the form of the human.

Adrio König (1936-) in a rather intensive study of biblical anthropomorphisms[5] has classified these under three subcategories. First, there are physical anthropomorphisms. Reference is made to the face of God,[6] the eyes of God,[7] the ears of God,[8] the mouth of God,[9] the nose of God,[10] the lips and tongue of God,[11] the arms of God,[12] the hands of God,[13] the

---

2. *Principles of Christian Theology,* p. 187.

3. *The Doctrine of God,* p. 53.

4. *The Religious Teaching of the Old Testament* (New York: Abingdon Press, 1918), ch. 2.

5. *Here I Am!: A Believer's Reflection on God* (London: Marshall, Morgan and Scott; Grand Rapids: Eerdmans, 1982), pp. 60-61.

6. Gen. 4:14; 32:30; Exod. 33:11; Num. 6:25; Deut. 5:4; Ps. 27:8-9; Mic. 3:4; Matt. 18:10; 1 Cor. 13:12.

7. Deut. 11:12; 1 Kings 8:29; Ps. 11:4; 1 Pet. 3:12.

8. 2 Kings 19:16; Isa. 59:1; Jas. 5:4.

9. Num. 12:8; Isa. 1:20; Matt. 4:4.

10. Exod. 15:8; 2 Sam. 22:9, 16; Ps. 18:15.

11. Isa. 30:27; Job 11:5.

12. Exod. 6:6; Deut. 4:34; 5:15; 33:27; Isa. 52:10; Job 40:9; Luke 1:51.

13. Exod. 9:3; 13:9; Num. 11:23; Deut. 7:8; Ps. 89:13; Isa. 59:1; John 10:29; Acts 4:30; Rom. 10:21; Heb. 1:10; 10:31.

feet of God,[14] the heart of God,[15] and the voice of God.[16] Second, there are
psychological anthropomorphisms. God is said to love,[17] to repent,[18] to
have no pleasure in,[19] to laugh,[20] to be glad or to rejoice,[21] to be jealous,[22]
to be angry or wrathful,[23] to hate,[24] to be merciful,[25] and to have compassion.[26] Third, there are actional anthropomorphisms. According to the Old
Testament, God sees,[27] hears,[28] speaks,[29] whistles,[30] rests and is re-
freshed,[31] descends,[32] smells,[33] walks or strolls,[34] and sits on his throne.[35]
Both inside and outside biblical thought there have been objections to
anthropomorphisms. Xenophon (c. 430 B.C.-after 355 B.C.) objected to these
as applied to the gods and goddesses of Greece. Philo had difficulty with
the Old Testament usage of anthropomorphisms. Certain Church Fathers
objected to anthropomorphisms on the basis that they violate the changelessness of God.[36] König has defended the biblical usage: "The anthropomorphisms in the Bible are intentionally used to speak appropriately
about God, in contrast to Israel's neighbours."[37] Modern Christians find
it easy to connect that intentionality with God's being personal.

5. New Testament Evidence That God Is Personal

At least three types of evidence may be cited. First, the teaching of
Jesus concerning God was filled with personal or analogical names for
God; for example, "Father," "Shepherd," and "Lord."[38] Second, Jesus'
own personal communion with God the Father and his praying to the
Father were such as to indicate a personal God. Surely this is true of his

14. Ps. 2:11-12; 99:5; 132:7; Isa. 66:1; Matt. 5:35; 1 Cor. 15:25, 27.

15. Gen. 6:6; 8:21; 1 Sam. 2:35; Acts 13:22.

16. Gen. 3:8; Deut. 4:33; 5:25; Josh. 24:24; 1 Sam. 15:22; Ps. 29:3-5; Ezek. 10:5; Job 40:9;
Mark 1:11; 9:7; John 12:28.

17. Deut. 7:8; 10:15; Hos. 11:1; Isa. 43:4; John 3:16, 35; 2 Cor. 9:7; 1 John 4:9-10, 16.

18. Gen. 6:6-7; Num. 23:19; 1 Sam. 15:11, 35; Jer. 4:28; Heb. 7:21.

19. Isa. 1:11; 65:12; Heb. 10:6, 10, 38.

20. Ps. 2:4; 37:13; 59:8.

21. Deut. 28:63; 30:9; Luke 15:7, 10.

22. Exod. 20:5; 34:14.

23. Exod. 4:14; Num. 11:10; Deut. 6:15; Judg. 2:14; Isa. 5:25; Jer. 4:8; Rom. 1:18; 9:22.

24. Lev. 26:30; Amos 5:21.

25. Exod. 34:6; Deut. 4:31; Ps. 103:8; Hos. 1:6-7; Jon. 4:2; Neh. 9:17, 31; Rom. 9:15-16;
Phil. 2:27.

26. Deut. 13:17; 30:3; 2 Kings 13:23; Ps. 86:15; Jer. 12:15; Rom. 9:15.

27. Gen. 16:13; 31:42; Exod. 3:4; Matt. 6:4, 6, 18.

28. 2 Sam. 22:7; 1 Kings 8:30; John 11:41-42.

29. Gen. 8:15; 46:2; Exod. 7:8; Num. 12:4; Isa. 8:11; Mark 12:26; Acts 18:9.

30. Isa. 5:26; 7:18.

31. Gen. 2:2-3; Exod. 31:17.

32. Gen. 11:5, 7.

33. Gen. 8:21.

34. Gen. 3:8.

35. Rev. 4:2; 5:1.

36. König, Here I Am!, pp. 60, 63-66, 84.

37. Ibid., p. 97.

38. See above, Ch. 13, II, B, 2.

High-Priestly Prayer (John 17), and it may also be seen in his teaching of the Model Prayer (Matt. 6:9-13; Luke 11:2-4). Third, the apostolic experience with God is highly suggestive of the modern terms "Person" and "personal." Note especially Peter's sermonic reference to "the God of Abraham and of Isaac and of Jacob, the God of our fathers" (Acts 3:13, RSV), Paul's description in Athens of the Creator who gives life as personal (Acts 17:24-25), Paul's declaration about "the light of the knowledge of the glory of God in the face of Christ" (2 Cor. 4:6), and the Petrine allusion to the love for and joyful trust in the ascended, invisible Christ (1 Pet. 1:8).

B. GOD AS PERSONAL: THE APOLOGETIC TASK

We have already made reference to the impact of idealistic pantheism and process philosophy on the Christian usage of terms such as "Person" and "personal" concerning God, making such usage highly desirable, if not necessary. The nature of the Christian interaction with these movements needs to be clarified.

1. Idealistic Pantheism: Spinoza, Schelling, and Hegel

a. Baruch Spinoza

An excommunicated Jew and a philosopher, Spinoza taught that God is

> a being absolutely infinite, that is, substance consisting in infinite attributes, of which each expresses eternal and infinite essentiality. . . . God is the only substance, and substance is identified with God. . . . God is the immanent cause of the universe but not its creator. . . . Moreover, there is no real metaphysical distinction between God and the universe.[39]

b. Friedrich Wilhelm Joseph von Schelling (1775-1854)

A professor of philosophy at various German universities and one who was under the influence of the philosophy of J. G. Fichte, Schelling "made no absolute separation between the subject and the object, between the ego and the non-ego." Both subject and object are combined in the Absolute. There "is no reality in individual Beings," for "they are merely modes of the Absolute."[40]

c. Georg Wilhelm Friedrich Hegel

Also a professor of philosophy at various German universities, Hegel developed the concept of the Absolute.

> The Absolute is not the thing-in-itself; it is not a transcendent force, nor is it a subjective ego. The Absolute is the world process itself, . . . characterized

---

39. Frederick Mayer, *A History of Modern Philosophy* (New York: American Book Company, 1951), pp. 134, 135-36.
40. Ibid., pp. 342, 344.

> . . . by activity. The Absolute represents a process which . . . reaches a complete expression in the Hegelian philosophy.

This is not the God of theism.

> The Absolute does not stand beyond human history, nor does the Absolute change the laws of history.

Thus

> we have in Hegel a rational world process, which he described as the Absolute Idea.[41]

Hegel served as the bridge between the earlier German idealism and the later Anglo-American process philosophy.

2. *Process Philosophy: Whitehead and Hartshorne*

a. Alfred North Whitehead

A British-born mathematician and Harvard University professor of philosophy, Whitehead was the father of modern process philosophy. He rejected the Hebrew-Christian doctrine of divine creation in favor of the Greek idea of process. This process is continuing, and the process itself is reality. Man as cocreator partakes of divinity and thereby attains to a general immortality. Whitehead feared anthropomorphism but attributed to God awareness, the capacities to relate, to communicate, and to influence and to be influenced, freedom of choice within consistency, and intention or purpose.[42]

b. Charles Hartshorne

Professor of philosophy at the University of Texas in Austin, Hartshorne developed the term "bipolar" to describe the concepts of God as *being* and *becoming,* with emphasis on the latter.[43]

In a critical evaluation of process philosophy Eric C. Rust has concluded that Whitehead's system is "a veiled pantheism of the Spinozoistic variety" and that Hartshorne, seeking to avoid both classical theism and classical pantheism, has come ultimately to "panentheism."[44]

The modern Christian affirmation that God is "personal" is at least partly designed to be an apologetic response to the pantheistic tendencies in modern Western philosophy.

---

41. Ibid., p. 357.
42. Based on Whitehead's statement made six weeks before his death, quoted by Norman Pittenger, *Alfred North Whitehead* (Richmond, Va.: John Knox Press, 1969), pp. 296-97, 35-36.
43. Pittenger, *Alfred North Whitehead,* p. 35.
44. *Evolutionary Philosophies and Contemporary Theology* (Philadelphia: Westminster Press, 1969), pp. 113, 178.

C. GOD AS PERSONAL: ESSENTIAL TO THE PERSONHOOD OF HUMAN BEINGS

At least from the time of John Calvin, if not from an earlier time, Christian thinkers have seen human selfhood as derivative of, dependent on, and coordinate with God's personhood. At the outset of his *Institutes of the Christian Religion* (1559), Calvin declared:

> Our wisdom . . . consists almost entirely of two parts: the knowledge of God and of ourselves. But as these are connected together with many ties, it is not easy to determine which of the two precedes, and gives birth to the other. For, in the first place, no man can survey himself without forthwith turning his thoughts towards the God in whom he lives and moves. . . . Every person, therefore, on coming to the knowledge of himself, is not only urged to seek God, but is also led as by the hand to find him.
>
> On the other hand, it is evident that man never attains to a true self-knowledge until he have previously contemplated the face of God, and come down after such contemplation to look into himself.[45]

Calvin's stress, therefore, was on the interconnectedness of our knowledge of God and our knowledge of ourselves.

Francis A. Schaeffer has addressed this issue in the latter twentieth-century setting and with a more apologetic purpose:

> Either there is a personal beginning to every thing or one has what the impersonal throws up by chance out of the time sequence. The fact that the second alternative may be veiled by connotation words makes no difference. The words used by Eastern pantheism; the new theological words such as Tillich's "Ground of Being"; the secular shift from mass to energy or motion, all eventually come back to the impersonal, plus time, plus chance. If *this* is really the only answer to man's personality, then personality is no more than an illusion, a kind of sick joke which no amount of semantic juggling will alter. Only some form of mystical jump will allow us to accept that personality comes from impersonality.
>
> . . . .
>
> This is the crux of the matter; either an intrinsically personal "what is" in the sense of a creation by the personal God, or John Cage's devilish din![46]

Thus, the personal nature of human beings stands or falls with the personhood of God.

Millard Erickson has delineated some of the consequences for modern Christians of the personhood of God. The Christian's relationship with God "has a dimension of warmth and understanding," for "God is not a bureau or a department; he is not a machine or a computer that automatically supplies the needs of people." Moreover, this relationship is reciprocal. "God is to be treated as a being, not an object or force," and hence God "is not something to be used or manipulated." Finally, "God is an

---

45. 1.1-2, trans. Henry Beveridge (Grand Rapids: Eerdmans, 1958), pp. 37-38.
46. *The God Who Is There: Speaking Historic Christianity into the Twentieth Century* (Chicago: Inter-Varsity Press, 1968), pp. 88, 91.

end in himself, not a means to an end," and thus he "is of value to us for what he is in himself, not merely for what he *does.*"[47]

D. GOD AS PERSONAL: DISTINCT FROM THE "PERSONS" OF THE TRINITY

All affirmations that God is personal, which seem to be necessary to distinguish the Christian understanding of God from the pantheistic and process philosophies, must be carefully and even painstakingly differentiated from the historic usage of the term "Person" (Latin *persona;* Greek *hypostaseis*) as a Trinitarian word to demarcate the Father, the Son, and the Holy Spirit. The latter term can be traced to its secular use as a Latin word, whereby it could mean the mask or the face that an actor wore in a drama. Seemingly, as originally applied in the third century A.D. to the Father, the Son, and the Spirit, the term did not mean, as the modern word "person" often means, a fully individuated being.[48]

In reference to the Christian doctrine of the Trinity "Person" means the essential differentiation within the Godhead. In reference to the Christian doctrine of God vis-à-vis modern philosophies, "Person" and "personal" refer to the being of God as somewhat analogous to human beings as they are individually differentiable from other beings and from nature and from history. These two differing usages must be clearly and continually kept in mind.

II. GOD AS PRESENT

Ought we to speak of the "omnipresence" of God or of the "presence" of God? The former term is derived from the Latin *omnipraesentia,* which was used by the medieval Schoolmen. A. H. Strong expressed the traditional, postmedieval approach when he used the term "omnipresence" and meant by it that "God ... penetrates and fills the universe in all its parts." Indeed, "the whole of God is in every place," but his presence is "not necessary, but free."[49] Herman Bavinck (1854-1921), retaining the term "omnipresence," sought the Augustinian balance between transcendence and immanence.[50] Emil Brunner was rather critical of the centuries-long impact of the Scholastic doctrine of omnipresence, for he saw it as very susceptible to pantheism, but he still retained the use of the term.[51] Karl Barth also retained the term but defined it so as to avoid some of the dangers of past usage.[52] Erickson has treated the presence of God as

47. *Christian Theology,* p. 270.
48. See below, Ch. 23, I, B.
49. *Systematic Theology,* pp. 279-82.
50. *The Doctrine of God,* trans. William Hendriksen (Grand Rapids: Eerdmans, 1955), pp. 157-64, esp. 158.
51. *The Christian Doctrine of God,* pp. 256-61.
52. *Church Dogmatics,* II/1, pp. 461-90.

subsidiary to the discussion of transcendence and immanence, and he has insisted that transcendence and immanence "should not be regarded as attributes of God," for "they cut across the various attributes."[53]

A. THE BIBLICAL CONCEPT OF THE PRESENCE OF GOD

The biblical teaching concerning the presence of God involves different aspects or degrees of the presence of God.

1. The Extensive or General Presence of God

God's presence is sometimes described extensively in the sense that no human creature can escape the divine presence or in the sense that there is no divine absence. Expressive of this usage are the words of Ps. 139:7-10 (RSV):

> Whither shall I go from thy Spirit? Or whither shall I flee from thy presence? If I ascend to heaven, thou art there! If I make my bed in Sheol, thou art there! If I take the wings of the morning and dwell in the uttermost parts of the sea, even there thy hand shall lead me, and thy right hand shall hold me.[54]

The psalmist is not engaging in speculative omnipresence. Rather he is faced with his inability to commit sins and wrongs outside the presence of God. There is indeed no place where God is completely absent. Human beings, even in their desperation, can never ultimately flee from the presence of God.

2. The Intensive or Special Presence of God

God's presence is sometimes held to be such an intimate or special presence that it can be differentiated from the general presence of God. One thinks of the divine promise to Jacob at Bethel: "Behold, I am with you and will keep you wherever you go, and will bring you back to this land; for I will not leave you until I have done that of which I have spoken to you" (Gen. 28:15, RSV). There are the twin promises of Jesus: "For where two or three are gathered together in my name, there I am in the midst of them" (Matt. 18:20), and ". . . and lo, I am with you always, to the close of the age" (Matt. 28:20). James admonished: "Draw near to God and he will draw near to you. Cleanse your hands . . . and purify your hearts" (4:8). As used in the Bible, nearness and distance can have nonspatial meanings. God's distance and presence can be in hiddenness and in revelation, in wrath or in grace. Three meanings of the special presence can be identified.

a. The presence of God is essential to the full revelatory and redemptive work of God in history. Specifically this means the incarnation of the Word or Son of God: "and his name shall be called 'Emmanuel' (which means, God with us)" (Matt. 1:23b, RSV), and "the Word became flesh and dwelt [or, tabernacled] among us" (John 1:14a). It also means the advent

53. *Christian Theology*, pp. 301-19.
54. See also Jer. 23:23-24.

of the Holy Spirit: "But you shall receive power when the Holy Spirit has come upon you" (Acts 1:8a).

b. The presence of God means the removal of the distance wrought by sin (or the distance from God that is sin) and the restoration of nearness (through forgiveness of sin) and communion, for Gentiles as well as for Jews, through the new covenant (Acts 2:39; Eph. 2:13, 17).

c. The presence of God, for Christians, means the indwelling of or by the Holy Spirit. This can be in the physical bodies of individual Christians (1 Cor. 6:19), and it can be in the Christian community as "the temple of God" (Eph. 2:20b-21; 1 Cor. 3:16).

3. The Unique, Full, and Particular Presence of God

This presence is to be found only in Jesus Christ, the Son of God. "For in him all the fulness of God was pleased to dwell" (Col. 1:19, RSV).

B. ALTERNATIVE NONBIBLICAL CONCEPTS

Two alternative concepts of divine presence can be differentiated, but these are at the same time closely related.

1. The Philosophical Concept of Omnipresence

According to this view, God's presence consists of a neutral and almost static presence of God everywhere in the spatial order. It seems to favor the spatial distribution of God. This concept is constantly in danger of losing the relative independence of the creatures and the created order and thus of falling into pantheism.

2. The Mystical Concept of Divine Presence through the "Divine Spark" in Human Beings

Some forms of mysticism posit the existence of a "divine spark" within human beings. By turning to this spark within, humans can realize intuitively the nearness and presence of God. The divine presence, accordingly, is not dependent on God's taking the initiative to reveal himself and to act savingly in the larger arena of human history. Special or biblical revelation and redemption are made unnecessary by the thoroughgoing mystical answer.

III. THE ATTRIBUTES OF GOD

Having considered the naming and the names of God, God's nature as personal, and God's presence, we now turn to an inquiry concerning the attributes or characteristics that belong to God according to the Christian revelation. A preliminary or general study of divine attributes is needed prior to the explication of particular attributes.

A. THE NATURE AND POSSIBILITY OF THE ATTRIBUTES OF GOD

1. *Some Definitions of Divine Attributes*

Christian theologians who have discussed the attributes of God normally have offered some general definition of such attributes. Three samples of such definitions will suffice to provide a clearer understanding of the term. A. H. Strong defined the attributes of God as "those distinguishing characteristics of the divine nature which are inseparable from the idea of God and which constitute the basis and ground for his various manifestations to his creatures."[55] Similarly, according to Millard Erickson, God's attributes "are ["permanent"] objective characteristics of his nature" that are "inseparable from the being or essence of God" and belong to "the entire Godhead."[56] W. T. Conner defined attributes as "those qualities or characteristics of the divine Being, by virtue of which he is distinguished from all created beings and without which he would not be worthy of the worship and service of man."[57]

2. *Some Hesitations about Divine Attributes*

Some have expressed caution and have been hesitant about divine attributes despite such definitions as have been quoted.

a. Are the attributes that are ascribed to God more the product of the mental projections of theologians than they are the proper formulations of the data of revelation? One should, of course, always acknowledge the all-too-human factor in identifying and describing divine attributes. The fact that there is no list of universally accepted divine attributes is suggestive of this human factor. But, on the other hand, when theologians submit to the pattern of religious authority that Christians hold to be normative and carry out their theological work accordingly, ought not the results to be seen as much more than the projections of theologians?

b. Do the formulating and use of divine attributes not tend to rob Christians of the sense of the mystery of God that stands behind all revelation? Eunomius of Cyzicus, a nominalist who held that "a name either designates the essence of a thing or . . . is merely an empty sound," claimed: "I know God as God knows himself."[58] Responsible theologians today would not make such claims for our knowledge of God and would not reckon humanly stated attributes of God as fully identifiable with the very essence of God. A touch of realism and a dose of humility help to relieve this second hesitation about divine attributes.

55. *Systematic Theology*, p. 244.
56. *Christian Theology*, p. 265.
57. *Revelation and God*, p. 214.
58. John Courtney Murray, *The Problem of God, Yesterday and Today*, p. 61. William of Ockham advocated the opposite extreme, namely, that the divine attributes are not founded or based on the being of God but are "the product of the human intellect." Alister E. McGrath, *Iustitia Dei: A History of the Christian Doctrine of Justification*, 2 vols. (Cambridge: University Press, 1986), 1:68-69.

B. THE SOURCES OF THE ATTRIBUTES OF GOD

From what sources do Christian theologians obtain the terms or the concepts that they affirm to be characteristics of God? First, the most extensively used source is the Bible, including both testaments. Quite a number of the attributes ascribed to God by Christian theologians are biblical words and may be found easily in a biblical concordance. Examples of such include holiness, wrath, righteousness, love, faithfulness, mercy, and grace. Second, some attributes ascribed to God are expressed by terms that are traceable to Greek philosophy; for example, the impassibility of God, or his inability to suffer, was likely borrowed by the Church Fathers from the legacy of Greece. Moreover, recent objections to this particular attribute have been at least partly based on the argument that impassibility is a Greek, but not a biblical concept. Third, some attributes are traceable to the medieval Schoolmen. Particularly is this true of the three "omni" attributes: omnipotence, omniscience, and omnipresence. Finally, some attributes may be traceable to modern worldviews such as theism; such may be true of infinity, immensity, and aseity.

C. PATTERNS OF CLASSIFICATION OF THE ATTRIBUTES OF GOD

Several different patterns have been adopted and followed in an effort to classify meaningfully the attributes of God.

1. Negative, Positive, and Causative Attributes

This somewhat classic scheme can be traced to Clement of Alexandria. First, there are those negative statements that can be made about God, or more specifically, about what God is not. These attributes, as stated in English, usually have the negative prefix "in" or "im" and conclude with "able" or "ible." Hence God is said to be immutable, incomprehensible, invisible, impassible, etc. The Greek Orthodox have called this "apophatic theology," based on the Greek word for "denial." Second, there are positive statements about God in which he is said to have certain attributes in a supreme or eminent way. Thus God is most holy, most wise, most loving, most compassionate, etc. Third, there are statements about God's contingent relations with the world; for example, God is eternal (respecting time) and immense (respecting space).[59]

2. Incommunicable and Communicable Attributes

This pattern has been used especially by modern Reformed theologians. Incommunicable attributes are those in which there is no divine sharing and no reflex in human beings, whereas communicable attributes

59. Charles Bigg, *The Christian Platonists of Alexandria* (Oxford: Clarendon Press, 1886), pp. 62-64; John Patrick, *Clement of Alexandria* (Edinburgh, London: William Blackwood and Sons, 1914), pp. 69-75. Louis Berkhof, *Systematic Theology*, 4th rev. and enl. ed., 1979, pp. 52-53, ascribed to the Schoolmen a threefold classification: causative, negative, and eminental or positive.

are those in which there is divine sharing and a reflex in human beings. Herman Bavinck placed under the "incommunicable" independence, immutability, eternity, omnipresence, unity, and simplicity. Under the "communicable" he placed spirituality, invisibility, omniscience, wisdom, veracity, goodness, righteousness, holiness, will, omnipotence, perfection, blessedness, and glory.[60] Louis Berkhof made a similar classification.[61]

3. Absolute and Relative Attributes

A. H. Strong advocated the twofold classification: the "absolute" or "immanent" attributes and the "relative" or "transitive" attributes. The former are those "which respect the inner being of God, which are involved in God's relation to Himself, and which belong to his nature independently of his connection with the universe." Included were life, personality, self-existence, immutability, unity, truth, love, and holiness. The latter are those "which respect the outward revelation of God's being, which are involved in God's relation to the creation, and which are exercised in consequence of the existence of the universe and dependence upon him." Strong cited eternity, immensity, omnipresence, omniscience, omnipotence, veracity and faithfulness, mercy and goodness, and justice and righteousness. While attempting to subsume holiness under this twofold pattern, Strong was so insistent that "holiness is the fundamental attribute in God" that holiness became de facto a third type of attribute.[62]

4. Natural and Moral Attributes

E. Y. Mullins differentiated "natural" attributes, or those "pertaining to God's nature," and "moral" attributes, or those "pertaining to his moral character and relations." Under the former he placed self-existence, immutability, omnipresence, omniscience, omnipotence, eternity, and immensity. Under the latter he included holiness, righteousness, love, and truth.[63] Millard Erickson's use of the two categories, the "greatness" and the "goodness" of God, is quite similar to Mullins's classification.[64]

5. Attributes of Mystery, Overwhelmingness, Dynamism, and Holiness

John Macquarrie has employed a fourfold system of classifying the attributes. The attributes of "mystery" include God's being incomparable, incomprehensible, suprarational, and personal. Under "overwhelmingness" he placed immensity, infinity, eternity, omnipotence, omniscience, and omnipresence. Faithfulness or immutability, selfhood, perfection, and goodness were grouped under "dynamism," and wrath, righ-

60. *The Doctrine of God*, pp. 113-251.
61. *Systematic Theology*, pp. 55-81.
62. *Systematic Theology*, pp. 243-303.
63. *The Christian Religion in Its Doctrinal Expression*, pp. 222-43.
64. *Christian Theology*, pp. 263-300.

teousness, justice, grace, love, and mercy under "holiness." According to Macquarrie, God is "holy Being," yet love "has a supreme place."[65]

6. Bipolar Attachment to Leading Attributes

Some theologians have chosen to gather the various divine attributes in clusters around those attributes that are thought to be primary. Usually the primary attributes have been two in number. Emil Brunner chose holiness and love as the primary attributes for an informal clustering.[66] Karl Barth treated three pairs of attributes under the "perfections of the divine loving" and three pairs of attributes under the "perfections of the divine freedom."[67] Martin Luther[68] and John Dillenberger (1918-)[69] made "God hidden" and "God revealed" the stackpoles for other attributes. Somewhat different was Hendrikus Berkhof's pairing of an attribute of transcendence with an attribute of condescension *ad seriatum*.[70]

7. Rejection of Classifications in Favor of Stress on One Central Attribute

The Swedish Lundensian theologians elevated *agapē* to the status of central and controlling divine attribute, as the writings of Anders Nygren,[71] Gustav E. H. Aulén,[72] and the American Nels F. S. Ferré[73] make clear. Peter Taylor Forsyth tended to regard holiness as the central attribute.[74]

D. CORRELATION OF THE ATTRIBUTES OF GOD

An awareness of the various patterns for classifying the attributes of God and some knowledge of the history of the treatment of divine attributes can lead to the recognition of the need for proper correlation of the attributes. Such correlation or the lack thereof can have a profound effect on the rest of one's theology. Two dangers as to correlation are worthy of brief comment. First, one should avoid that antithetical juxtaposing of divine attributes which suggests that there is a conflict or internal warfare going on inside the being of God. Marcion (?-c. 160) posited such an antithesis between justice and love and came ultimately to believe in two gods.[75] Second, one should avoid emphasizing one

65. *Principles of Christian Theology*, pp. 186-93.
66. *The Christian Doctrine of God*, pp. 157-289.
67. *Church Dogmatics*, II/1, pp. 351-677.
68. Althaus, *The Theology of Martin Luther*, pp. 20-34, 274-86.
69. *God Hidden and Revealed* (Philadelphia: Muhlenberg Press, 1953).
70. *Christian Faith*.
71. *Agape and Eros*, trans. Philip S. Watson (London: S.P.C.K., 1954).
72. *The Faith of the Christian Church*, pp. 120-53.
73. *The Christian Understanding of God* (London: SCM Press, 1952), pp. 15-46.
74. *God the Holy Father* (London: Independent Press, Ltd., 1957).
75. Blackman, *Marcion and His Influence*, pp. 66-73; F. J. Foakes-Jackson, *Christian Difficulties in the Second and Twentieth Centuries: A Study of Marcion and His Relation to Modern Thought* (Cambridge: W. Heffer and Sons; London: Edward Arnold, 1903), pp. 46-82.

attribute or group of attributes so as to downplay, minimize, or deny another attribute or group of attributes. Late medieval popular theology, if not the writings of the best theologians, so totally identified the *justitia Dei* with punishment that it could not be connected with salvation.[76] Nels F. S. Ferré's absolutizing of *agapē* seemingly led him to embrace eschatological universalism.[77] Every attribute may not deserve the same emphasis as every other, but a responsible correlation of divine attributes is a mark of good Christian theology.

---

76. On the history of the medieval doctrine of the righteousness of God see McGrath, *Iustitia Dei*, 1:51-70.
77. *The Christian Understanding of God*, pp. 114-18.

CHAPTER 15

God as Holy

Through our previous discussion of various patterns for classifying the divine attributes, we have tried to make clear that the method to be employed in arranging and interpreting these attributes is quite important. In fact, the method can affect the content of the attributes. In the ensuing treatment of the divine attributes holiness, the much emphasized attribute in the Old Testament, and love, the much emphasized attribute in the New Testament, will constitute the organizing centers. Around each of these, other related attributes will be clustered, and righteousness will serve as a "bridge" attribute between holiness and love. We will especially devote attention to those attributes which have been specifically expressed in the Bible.

I. THE OLD TESTAMENT USAGE AND MEANINGS OF THE TERM "HOLY"

A. THE TERM AND ITS ETYMOLOGY

The Hebrew verb *qāḏaš* in the Kal stem means "to be holy" and in the Piel and Hiphil stems means "to make holy, sanctify, hallow, consecrate, or dedicate." The Hebrew adjective *qāḏôš* means "holy"; as a substantive it means "the Holy One." The Hebrew noun *qōḏeš* means "holy thing" or "holiness." This family of words is used in the Old Testament to convey the concept that God is indeed holy.

The earliest or original meaning of *qāḏaš* and its cognates has probably been lost. The word is thought to have had a physical or nonreligious meaning in Hebrew and other Semitic languages. The only extant usages, however, are of a religious nature. Old Testament scholars have frequently suggested that the root idea of *qāḏaš* was "to cut off, to be separated," and hence "to exalt."[1]

---

1. Snaith, *The Distinctive Ideas of the Old Testament,* pp. 21-32.

208

B. HOLINESS AS SEPARATENESS OR TRANSCENDENCE

From their earliest usage in the Old Testament the terms "holy" and "holiness" seem to have carried the idea of separateness or transcendence. Holiness meant that which was uniquely, distinctively, and transcendently other than humankind. Emphasis on God as holy kept the Old Testament writers from succumbing to pantheism or to immanentism. But we should not understand the Old Testament concept of divine holiness merely in the negative sense of being "separated from"; rather it should also be reckoned in a positive sense as being "separated to." "God is separate and distinct because he is God."[2] The Holy One is the Wholly Other.

C. HOLINESS AS A SYNONYM FOR DEITY

The term "holy" and its cognates were used as synonyms for deity in the Old Testament and also in pagan religions. In such usage "holy" does not indicate a particular attribute or characteristic of deity but rather the essential fact or being of deity.

1. In the book of Isaiah the term "the Holy One of Israel," meaning the God of Israel, is used 27 times.[3] Thirteen of these usages are in chs. 1–39; 12 are in chs. 40–55; and two are in chs. 56–66. The term "Holy One of Israel" is used in Ps. 89:18, and the term "the Holy One in your midst" in Hos. 11:9 (NEB).

2. Another indication that holiness in Hebrew thought could be a synonym for deity may be seen by comparing Amos 6:8, "The LORD God has sworn by himself" (NEB), with Amos 4:2, "the LORD has sworn by his holiness" (NEB).[4] Pertinent to the same usage is Hos. 11:9 (NEB): "for I am God and not a man, the Holy One in your midst."

3. In the book of Daniel the words "the spirit of the holy gods" are used (4:8, 9; 5:11), and an extant Phoenician inscription uses the term "Holy Gods."[5]

D. HOLINESS AS APPLIED TO HUMAN BEINGS, PLACES, AND
   RELIGIOUS INSTITUTIONS

In a secondary or derived sense holiness came to be applied to certain human beings, places, and institutions connected with the faith of the Israelites. These were said to be "holy" in the sense that they were dedicated or sanctified to Yahweh, the God of Israel. The nation of Israel was said to be "holy" (Exod. 19:6; Deut. 7:6), and the Sabbath to be a "holy"

2. Ibid., p. 30.
3. 1:4; 5:19, 24; 10:17, 20; 12:6; 17:7; 29:19; 30:11, 12, 15; 31:1; 37:23; 41:14, 16, 20; 43:3, 14, 15; 45:11; 47:4; 48:17; 49:7; 54:5; 55:5; and 60:9, 14. The "Holy One of Jacob" is used in 29:23.
4. Davidson, *The Theology of the Old Testament*, p. 155.
5. Knudson, *The Religious Teaching of the Old Testament*, p. 138.

day (Exod. 20:8-11; 31:14-15). The tabernacle (Exod. 40:9), the holy place and the most holy place in the tabernacle (Exod. 26:33), the priests (Lev. 21:6) and their garments (Exod. 28:2, 4), and the anointing oil (Exod. 30:25) were also "holy." Similarly, the tithe (Lev. 27:30, 32), the vessels in the tabernacle (1 Kings 8:4), and the ark of the covenant (2 Chr. 35:3) were called "holy." The same was said of Jerusalem (Isa. 52:1; 66:20; Neh. 11:1), Mount Zion (Ps. 2:6), the temple (Ps. 11:4; 65:4; 79:1), the covenant (Dan. 11:28, 30), and the angels (Job 5:1; Ps. 89:5, 7).

This derived usage did not connote anything moral or ethical about the persons to whom the term "holy" was applied.[6] There are at least three evidences for such a statement. First, the application of the term "holy" to nonpersonal things was in itself an indication that no inherent moral or ethical meaning was implied. Second, the term was applied to pagan deities, to which their devotees did not ascribe high ethical qualities. Third, the fact that a term from the same Hebrew root was used to denominate temple prostitutes and sodomites is major evidence that the applied or secondary usage of holiness connoted no basic moral or ethical meaning.[7]

E. HOLINESS AND CEREMONIAL CLEANNESS

In the Old Testament the "holy" was set in contrast with the "profane" (ḥalil), a word derived from the verb ḥalal, meaning "to desecrate, to detract from holiness." Hence cleanliness came to be associated with holiness, though the two were not synonymous. The "profane" or "unclean" could not be made holy.[8] But cleanness is "only a condition of holiness, not holiness itself."[9]

F. HOLINESS AS DIVINE AVERSION TO HUMAN SIN

In Isaiah 6 Isaiah's vision of Yahweh as "holy" involved the prophet's acute awareness of his own religio-moral uncleanness and that of the people of Judah and of Yahweh's forgiveness of iniquity and commissioning of Isaiah. Holiness in this passage is distinctly related to sin and evil; it is more than transcendence and more than a synonym for deity. The "thoughts" and "ways" of "the Holy One of Israel" are on a plane far above the "thoughts" and "ways" of human beings (Isa. 55:5, 8, 9). "But the LORD of Hosts sits high in judgement, and by righteousness the holy God shows himself holy" (Isa. 5:16, NEB).

---

6. Davidson, *The Theology of the Old Testament*, p. 145.
7. Knudson, *The Religious Teaching of the Old Testament*, p. 151.
8. Snaith, *The Distinctive Ideas of the Old Testament*, pp. 41-43.
9. Davidson, *The Theology of the Old Testament*, p. 152.

II. THE NEW TESTAMENT USAGE AND MEANINGS OF THE TERM "HOLY"

In the New Testament one finds the adjective *hagios,* meaning "holy," the verb *hagiazein,* "to make holy, to sanctify," and the noun *hagiosynē,* "holiness." This family of words, however, is not used as frequently with reference to God in the New Testament as the parallel family of Hebrew words is used in the Old Testament. This apparent lack of New Testament emphasis on God as holy is balanced by the rather developed New Testament teaching as to the Holy Spirit.[10]

The idea of holiness as transcendence is not absent from the New Testament. One may detect such meaning in Matt. 6:9, "Hallowed [or, Sanctified] be Thy name," and in Jesus' reference to "Holy Father" in his High-Priestly Prayer (John 17:11). Sometimes the term "holy" seems to connote the ethical perfection of God, as in 1 Pet. 1:15-16, which is a quotation and application of the more ceremonial Lev. 11:44. In such a context the holiness of God is the standard for the holiness of Christians. In 1 John 2:20, wherein the term "the Holy One" is difficult to define, the term may be a synonym for deity.

III. REPRESENTATIVE MODERN DEFINITIONS OF "HOLINESS"

Do the results of biblical theology as to the meanings and usages of "holy" as applied to God translate into a uniform, fully agreed upon modern theological definition? The answer is not an affirmative one, for there are several different definitions of divine holiness, representative expressions of which we will now examine.

A. THE NONRATIONAL OR EXTRARATIONAL FACTOR IN GOD

Rudolf Otto (1869-1937), Protestant theologian of Marburg, in a well-known monograph explored and interpreted "the holy" as the nonrational or extrarational aspect of God. To represent this reality, Otto coined the term "numinous," derived from the Latin noun *numen,* meaning a "nod" or "beckoning of the hand" and hence "the divine will, command, or majesty." "The Holy" is described as *"mysterium tremendum."* The *"tremendum"* is characterized by "awefulness," "overpoweringness," and "energy" or "urgency." The *"mysterium"* is characterized by "fascination" and is the "Wholly Other."[11]

---

10. Brunner, *The Christian Doctrine of God,* p. 157.
11. *The Idea of the Holy: An Inquiry into the Non-Rational Factor in the Idea of the Divine and Its Relation to the Rational,* trans. John W. Harvey (London: Oxford University Press, 1923; 2d ed. 1950). The German original, *Das Heilige,* was published in 1917.

B. THE PURITY OF GOD

Not a few modern Christian theologians have made purity the central meaning of God's holiness. According to Charles Hodge, "Freedom from impurity is the primary idea of the word."[12] Making holiness the central attribute of God and the ground of human moral obligation, A. H. Strong defined it as the "self-affirming purity" of God.[13] J. K. Mozley stated that holiness is "the moral transcendence of God" or "the purity" of God or "that spiritual aspect of His transcendence wherein is given the idea of the absolute contradiction between God and evil."[14] According to Donald G. Bloesch, holiness is "separation from all that is unclean." God as holy "must be intolerant of sin and can only demand purity of heart on the part of his subjects."[15] Millard Erickson has defined holiness as God's "uniqueness" or separateness and as "his absolute purity or goodness," but he has given emphasis to the latter by classifying holiness under the attributes of "moral purity."[16]

C. BOTH THE SUPRARATIONAL MYSTERY AND THE PURITY OF GOD

Aiden Wilson Tozer (1897-1963) combined the first and the second definitions of holiness. The term means both the "awesome," "incomprehensible," "suprarational" Mystery, as in Otto, and "personality and moral content," with "an infinite, incomprehensible fullness of purity," as in the Bible.[17]

D. THE DIVINE ATONING NATURE AND ACTIVITY VIS-À-VIS HUMAN SIN AND SINNERS

Peter Taylor Forsyth understood divine holiness in connection with atonement for sin.

> He is the father of pity to human weakness, still more father of grace to human sin, but chiefly father of holy joy to our Lord Jesus Christ. . . . Fatherhood in the Old Testament neither demands sacrifice nor makes it, but in the New Testament the Holy Father does both. The holiness is the root of love, fatherhood, sacrifice, and redemption. . . . The divine Father is the holy. And the Holy Father's first care is holiness. The first charge on a Redeemer is satisfaction to that holiness. The Holy Father is one who does and must atone. . . . You can go behind love to holiness but behind holiness you cannot go.[18]

---

12. *Systematic Theology*, 1:413.
13. *Systematic Theology*, p. 268.
14. *The Doctrine of God*, pp. 67, 68, 65.
15. *Essentials of Evangelical Theology*, 1:33.
16. *Christian Theology*, pp. 284-86.
17. *The Knowledge of the Holy* (New York: Harper and Brothers, 1961), pp. 110-14.
18. *God the Holy Father* (reprint ed.; London: Independent Press Ltd., 1957), pp. 3-5. The book was originally published in 1897.

E. The Unity of Seeming Opposites

For both Karl Barth and Emil Brunner divine holiness embraced and united what seem to be opposite or contradictory characteristics or movements. Barth declared: "The holiness of God consists in the unity of His judgment with His grace. God is holy because His grace judges and His judgment is gracious." Barth treated both grace and holiness under "perfections of the divine loving." Both grace and holiness "in characteristic though differing fashion point to the transcendence of God over all that is not Himself."[19] Emil Brunner affirmed that "in the concept of the Holiness of God there is a twofold movement of the Divine Will—at first sight a contradictory movement, namely, a movement of withdrawal and exclusion, and a movement of expansion and inclusion."[20]

F. The Transcendence or Moral Absoluteness of God

Other theologians, taking their clue from the otherness of God, have concluded that transcendence or separateness or moral transcendence is the most adequate general definition of God's holiness. According to E. Y. Mullins, holiness

> is found sometimes in connection with the exercise of his natural attributes. But usually holiness is the manifestation of his moral attributes. It is thus a general term descriptive of the moral perfection of God. . . . The holiness of God, then, is his supreme moral excellence in virtue of which all other moral attributes have their ground in him.[21]

Concerning holiness W. T. Conner wrote:

> [It] is the quality of infinity, absoluteness or transcendence that belongs to God. . . . Holiness is the moral perfection of God considered from the point of view of his absoluteness and transcendence. Righteousness is God's holiness in relation to man as a responsible moral agent. . . . Love is the holiness of God as interested in man as weak and sinful.[22]

Norman H. Snaith (1898-1982) emphasized transcendence.

> God was from the beginning transcendent in that He was different from man, but that He was by no means transcendent in that He was remote from man. . . . Transcendence does not mean remoteness. It means otherness. . . . Still less among the Hebrews does transcendence imply *static* remoteness, or any type of passivity. . . . It is therefore not enough to say that it stands for the separation between God and man. It comes to stand for the positive activity of that Personal Other, whom the Hebrews recognized as Jehovah.[23]

Otto's definition of divine holiness, which rightly affirms awesomeness and incomprehensibility, fits the New Testament less well than it

19. *Church Dogmatics*, II/1, pp. 363, 360.
20. *The Christian Doctrine of God*, p. 162.
21. *The Christian Religion in Its Doctrinal Expression*, p. 230.
22. *Revelation and God*, pp. 243-47.
23. *The Distinctive Ideas of the Old Testament*, pp. 47, 49.

does the Old Testament. Purity as the definition of holiness, as also the concept of sanctification, is hard to reconcile with Jesus' utterance, "For them I sanctify myself" (John 17:19a, NIV), if his sinlessness is to be maintained. Forsyth is doubtless right in saying that atoning is what the holy God does, but is that the best definition of holiness? Holiness should hardly be a bridge attribute, for it needs to have its centrality and uniqueness expressed, although Brunner's two movements have validity. Transcendence, though not above criticism, seems to offer more advantages as a basic definition of what it means to say that God is "holy."

> Holy, holy, holy! Lord God Almighty!
> All Thy works shall praise Thy name, in earth,
>   and sky, and sea;
> Holy, holy, holy; merciful and mighty!
> God in three Persons, blessed Trinity![24]

CHAPTER 16

Attributes Related to Holiness

Following our study of God as holy, it is fitting that we investigate those attributes of God which can appropriately be gathered or clustered around God's holiness. Although each of these has its own distinctive meaning and is not to be fused into a melting pot of attributes, these can be seen in connection and correlation with the truth that God is holy. The attributes to be considered are the eternity of God, the changelessness of God, the wisdom of God, the power of God, the jealousy-anger-wrath of God, and the glory of God.

I. THE ETERNITY OF GOD

A. BIBLICAL MATERIALS

In the Old Testament the Hebrew word 'ôlām is used to convey the everlastingness of Yahweh, and in the New Testament the Greek word aiōnios is used to convey the concept that God is eternal. According to the psalmist, "Before the mountains were brought forth, or ever thou hadst formed the earth and the world, from everlasting to everlasting, thou art God" (Ps. 90:2, RSV). Indeed, "thou art the same, and thy years have no end" (Ps. 102:27). In Isaiah Yahweh's sole deity was affirmed so as to imply his eternity (43:10c; 44:6b). Habakkuk asked the question: "Art thou not from everlasting, O LORD my God, my Holy One? We shall not die" (1:12a). In the New Testament "the King of kings and Lord of lords . . . alone has immortality," and to him is to be ascribed "eternal dominion" (1 Tim. 6:15b-16). To "the only God" are to be attributed "glory, majesty, dominion, and authority, before all time and now and for ever" (Jude 25). A similar threefold formula appears in Rev. 1:8: " 'I am the Alpha and the Omega,' says the Lord God, who is and who was and who is to come, the Almighty."

B. THEOLOGICAL INTERPRETATION

1. God, according to the Bible, is conscious of and vitally related to the temporal order. The eternal God is not divorced from the world of time

215

and space. This means that the biblical concept of God's eternality is not identical with Platonic timelessness and the negation of time,[1] or time "as the shadow of the eternal."[2] It also means that the biblical concept of time is not necessarily to be identified with Søren Kierkegaard's concept of the infinite qualitative distinction between eternity and time. God transcends and is not limited by time, but God relates to the temporal order in creation, sustenance, and redemption. In Jesus Christ God "took time and made it His own . . . [and] was able Himself to be temporal."[3] "For, among the ancient traditions, it was the Hebrew-Christian movement alone which assigned an important role to time, without making time the ultimate explanation or ground of the universe, and without placing God in time."[4]

2. The biblical concept of God as eternal, together with God's creatorship, leads to the conclusion that time has been created by God. Contrary to this conclusion was the view of Origen, who held that time is the product of the fall of eternally preexistent spirit beings.[5] But mainstream Christian thinkers followed not after Origen but rather after Augustine of Hippo, who wrote:

> With the motion of creatures, time began to run its course. It is idle to look for time before creation, as if time can be found before time. . . . We should, therefore, say that time began with creation rather than that creation began with time. But both are from God.[6]

3. The concept of God as eternal means that God was before time and God will be after time. This was the testimony of the psalmist (90:2). According to Paul, God "decreed" his wisdom "before the ages" (1 Cor. 2:7) and "chose us in him before the foundation of the world" (Eph. 1:4). Moreover, God will continue after the Son of God has delivered the rule to him (1 Cor. 15:28). "For from him and through him and to him are all things. To him be glory forever" (Rom. 11:36, RSV). Fitting indeed is the definition of eternity by Anicius Manlius Severinus Boethius (c. 480-524), an ancient Christian philosopher: "Eternity is the complete, simultaneous, and perfect possession of interminable life."[7] Karl Barth emphasized the aspect of simultaneity:

> The being is eternal in whose duration beginning, succession and end are not three but one, not separate as a first, a second and a third occasion, but one simultaneous occasion as beginning, middle and end. Eternity is the simultaneity of beginning, middle and end, and to that extent it is pure duration. . . . Eternity is just the duration which is lacking to time. . . .[8]

---

1. Brunner, *The Christian Doctrine of God*, pp. 266-67.
2. Henry, *Notes on the Doctrine of God*, p. 126.
3. Barth, *Church Dogmatics*, II/1, p. 617.
4. Henry, *Notes on the Doctrine of God*, p. 125.
5. *On First Principles* 3.5.4.
6. *The Literal Meaning of Genesis* 5.5.12.
7. *De consol. phil.* 5.6, as quoted by Barth, *Church Dogmatics*, II/1, p. 610.
8. *Church Dogmatics*, II/1, p. 608.

But, it may be asked, is the concept of eternity as "infinitely extended time" an adequate concept and is it the biblical concept of eternity? Oscar Cullmann asserted that such a linear view of time and eternity was the biblical concept,[9] but John Marsh (1904-), answering negatively, insisted that in the Bible eternity is "qualitatively different from time" because in the incarnation the eternal has entered history, thus making it impossible to think of eternity as linear or successive.[10] Carl Henry found that both Cullmann and Marsh had denied the true ontological base for God's eternity,[11] and James Barr found that both Cullmann and Marsh had stretched the biblical data, the former concerning time and eternity and the latter concerning time.[12] Millard Erickson has connected eternity with the will of God.

> There is a successive order to the acts of God and there is a logical order to his decisions, yet there is no temporal order to his willing. His deliberation and willing take no time. He has from all eternity determined what he is now doing.[13]

II. THE CHANGELESSNESS OF GOD

Christian theologians have identified this attribute of God by means of differing terms. Karl Barth referred to God's *Beständigkeit*, a term translated as "constancy,"[14] and Millard Erickson adopted the latter word.[15] Adrio König used "faithfulness,"[16] and E. Y. Mullins the "self-consistency" of God.[17]

A. BIBLICAL MATERIALS

In Balaam's second oracle one finds a declaration and a question: "God is not a man, that he should lie, nor a son of man, that he should change his mind. Does he speak and then not act? Does he promise and not fulfill?" (Num. 23:19, NIV). According to the psalmist, "The counsel of the LORD stands forever, the thoughts of his heart to all generations" (Ps. 33:11, RSV). In contrast to the heavens and the earth, "you remain the same, and your years will never end" (102:27, NIV). In a context of the postponement of punishment and a call to repentance Malachi records the words: " 'I the LORD do not change. So you, O descendants of Jacob, are not destroyed' " (3:6, NIV). The Epistle to the Hebrews refers to God's

9. *Christ and Time*, rev. ed. 1962, p. 65.
10. *The Fulness of Time*, pp. 139-43.
11. *God, Revelation, and Authority*, 5:243-51.
12. *Biblical Words for Time*, Studies in Biblical Theology, no. 33 (2d rev. ed.; London: SCM Press, 1969), pp. 21-85.
13. *Christian Theology*, p. 275.
14. *Church Dogmatics*, II/1, pp. 490-522.
15. *Christian Theology*, pp. 278-81.
16. *Here I Am!*, pp. 89-91.
17. *The Christian Religion in Its Doctrinal Expression*, p. 224.

showing to "the heirs of the promise the unchangeable character of his purpose" (6:17, RSV). According to James, "Every good endowment and every perfect gift is from above, coming down from the Father of lights, with whom there is no variation or shadow due to change" (1:17, RSV).

B. Theological Interpretation

1. God's changelessness is consistent with biblical anthropomorphisms. Objection has been raised against divine changelessness on the ground that certain anthropomorphisms show that God does change. Take, for example, the statements that "the LORD repented" concerning something: making Saul king of Israel (1 Sam. 15:11); judgments by locusts and by fire (Amos 7:3, 6); of calamity if the nation should turn from evil (Jer. 18:8); the fall of Jerusalem to the Babylonians (Jer. 42:10); imminent punishment of Ninevites (Jon. 3:9). Do not these texts, it has been asked, make it impossible to conclude that the Old Testament teaches that God is changeless? No, these texts rather bear out the truth that God "changes in response to" or "reacts" to the changing attitudes and actions of human beings. "God's behavior alters according to the behavior of men. For this very reason He is the living God, in contrast to the divinity of abstract thought."[18] Indeed, God "has changed" and "does change" in the creation, in the incarnation, in reconciliation, and in answer to petitions and intercessions. Adrio König has referred to the incarnation as "a *humiliating change*" in God.[19]

2. God's changelessness should not be equated with immobility. E. Y. Mullins warned that immutability, when ascribed to God, should not be taken to mean immobility.[20] König has warned against a "metaphysical immutability."[21] God is free to initiate new actions; in this sense God "changes."

3. Changelessness, on the other hand, is denied by process philosophy and the theologies built on process thought. A. N. Whitehead with his "organismic" view of the universe as process interpreted God as "the Principle of Concretion in Creativity" that is responsible for "the selection of eternal objects for ingression into the process as subjective aims" and "limiting the multiplicity of possible worlds to the one which is actualized in the process of becoming." God is "the first emergent of Creativity" but is not the Creator. "God has both a mental and a physical pole." "The becoming of the world is thus, at the same time, the becoming of God." "Indeed, the world creates God as much as God creates the world. God and the world are mutually necessary." God is so identifiable with the process of becoming, for Whitehead, that there is no enduring character

---

18. Brunner, *The Christian Doctrine of God*, p. 269.
19. *Here I Am!*, p. 88.
20. *The Christian Religion in Its Doctrinal Expression*, p. 223.
21. *Here I Am!*, pp. 86-87.

and nature of the faithful God.[22] Charles Hartshorne adopted panentheism, holding that God is both being and becoming. According to Eric C. Rust, insofar as Hartshorne has regarded God as "unchanging in his essence but constantly surpassing himself in his advancing experience," he may have retained something of the biblical concept of God. But whether for Hartshorne God is the free and sovereign Creator and Lord is not altogether clear.[23] Donald G. Bloesch is doubtful, quoting Hartshorne's definition of the absolute as " 'the totally relative.' "[24]

4. The changelessness of God means that God's fundamental character and his overall purpose abide or persist without alteration or deviation. Emil Brunner commented: "A God who is constantly changing is not a God whom we can worship, He is a mythological Being for whom we can only feel sorry."[25] Hendrikus Berkhof wrote of "the changeable faithfulness" of God.[26] König has related God's changelessness and his decision-making in a paradoxical way:

> . . . God's faithfulness is not something automatic. As the living God he decides how and where he will fulfill his promises—but not arbitrarily. There is a fixed pattern. This can be read, among many places, in Jeremiah 18:7-10. This is the unchangeableness of God, that he always unchangingly, changes in this way.[27]

III. THE WISDOM OF GOD

A. BIBLICAL MATERIALS

The Old Testament uses the Hebrew word *ḥokmāh* for "wisdom" in the sense of skill or steadfastness. The wisdom of God is a recurring theme in Proverbs, Psalms, and Job. Closely associated with *ḥokmāh* are the terms for "understanding" *(tebûnāh)* and for "knowledge" *(daʿat)*. "The fear of the LORD is the beginning of knowledge; fools despise wisdom and instruction" (Prov. 1:7, RSV). "The LORD by wisdom founded the earth; by understanding he established the heavens; by his knowledge the deeps broke forth, and the clouds drop down the dew" (Prov. 3:19-20). "O LORD, how manifold are thy works! In wisdom hast thou made them all; the earth is full of thy creatures" (Ps. 104:24). Job asked: " 'But where shall wisdom be found? And where is the place of understanding? . . . God understands the way to it, and he knows its

---

22. Rust, *Evolutionary Philosophies and Contemporary Theology*, pp. 102-19, esp. 110, 111, 113, 119.

23. Ibid., pp. 185-97, esp. 188-90, 192.

24. *Essentials of Evangelical Theology*, 1:28. Paralleling the impact of process philosophy on Western Christian theology is the likely impact of the Chinese *I Ching* (Book of Changes) on Asian Christian theology; both interpret God as "Change-itself" or "Becoming." See Jung Young Lee, "Can God Be Change Itself?" *Journal of Ecumenical Studies* 10 (Fall 1973): 752-70.

25. *The Christian Doctrine of God*, p. 269.

26. *Christian Faith*, pp. 140-47.

27. *Here I Am!*, p. 91.

place' " (Job 28:12, 23). "It is he who made the earth by his power, who established the world by his wisdom, and by his understanding stretched out the heavens" (Jer. 10:12).

Wisdom is said to be obtainable from Yahweh (Prov. 9:10; Ps. 111:10; Job 28:28). Of special importance has been the teaching of Proverbs 8 concerning the wisdom of Yahweh. Some have noted that wisdom is hypostatized inasmuch as voice, lips, and mouth are ascribed to wisdom (vv. 1, 4, 6-8). The Church Fathers tended to identify the Wisdom of Proverbs 8 either with the preexistent Logos or with the Holy Spirit. Advocates of the former included Justin Martyr,[28] Tertullian,[29] Origen,[30] and Cyprian,[31] whereas advocates of the latter included Irenaeus[32] and Hippolytus.[33] But the fact that Prov. 8:22 can be translated "The LORD created me at the beginning of his work" (RSV), although it has also been translated, "The LORD possessed me at the beginning of his work" (NIV), tends to discourage full identification with the Logos or the Spirit. Favoring the translation "possessed," Karl Barth has contended that the Old Testament knows no "independent attempt at world interpretation," no idea of wisdom as "an intermediary between God and the world," and no "conception of an immanent divine wisdom accessible to and recognizable by man of himself."[34]

Whereas the Old Testament tends to magnify the relation of God's wisdom to creation, the New Testament relates wisdom primarily to redemption through Jesus Christ—his cross and his church. The Greek New Testament term for "wisdom" is *sophia*, a word that conveyed the ideas of tact or skill. Wisdom is the major theme of 1 Cor. 1:18–2:16. Therein the message of the cross, reckoned by Greeks as "foolishness" (1:23b), is seen to be the Spirit-empowered truth of God in contrast to the worldly wisdom of Greek philosophy and the miracle-seeking unbelief of Jews. In the passage wisdom is attributed to God in respect to the cross of Christ (1:21), Jesus Christ is said to be God's gift of "wisdom" to human beings (1:30), and God's message of wisdom has been revealed by the Holy Spirit (2:6-10). Elsewhere, Paul declared that "all the treasures of wisdom and knowledge" are hidden in Christ (Col. 2:3, RSV), that in God's wisdom the mystery of God's will has been set forth in Christ (Eph.

28. *Dialogue with Trypho* 61, 129.

29. *Against Praxeas* 6.

30. *On First Principles* 1.2.1-5, 8, 12.

31. *Testimonies against the Jews* 2.2.

32. *Against Heresies* 4.20.1, 3; *Proof of the Apostolic Preaching* 5.

33. *Against Noetus* 10-11.

34. *Church Dogmatics*, II/1, pp. 427-32. On the problem of translation in Prov. 8:22, see William McKane, *Proverbs: A New Approach*, Old Testament Library (Philadelphia: Westminster Press, 1970), pp. 351-54, and R. B. Y. Scott, *Proverbs*, Anchor Bible (Garden City, N.Y.: Doubleday, 1965), p. 73, per Harry B. Hunt, Jr. But wisdom is not to be understood as a goddess, as by Susan Cady, Marian Ronan, and Hal Taussig, *Sophia: The Future of Feminist Spirituality* (San Francisco: Harper and Row, 1986).

1:9), and that "through the church the manifold wisdom of God might now be made known" to supramundane beings (Eph. 3:10). If humans lack wisdom, they are to ask God for it (Jas. 1:5a). "To the only wise God be glory for evermore through Jesus Christ!" (Rom. 16:27).

B. THEOLOGICAL INTERPRETATION

Divine wisdom, according to the wisdom writings of the Old Testament, was closely connected with "knowledge" and "understanding" and was the apex of Hebrew faith and culture. According to Paul, the wisdom of God was not to be identified with the worldly wisdom of his day but with the "foolishness" of Jesus' death on the cross. Karl Barth was probably correct in interpreting divine wisdom as the absence of "impulsiveness" or whimsical caprice in God's bestowal of grace.[35] It should also be noted that wisdom is one of the communicable attributes of God. Barth defined God's wisdom as "the inner truth and clarity with which the divine life in its self-fulfillment and its works justifies and confirms itself and in which it is the source and sum and criterion of all that is clear and true."[36] Since Barth did not treat "truth" or "truthfulness" as a major attribute of God, he seems to have subsumed these under wisdom and hence has defined wisdom in terms of truth. In this volume "truthfulness" will be treated in connection with the "faithfulness" of God.

IV. THE POWER OF GOD

A. BIBLICAL MATERIALS

1. Old Testament Terms and Passages

The use of the name "the Almighty God"[37] has been treated in the section on the names of God.[38] The term "the Almighty" is found frequently in the book of Job. The noun *gᵉbûrāh*, meaning "power" or "might," was ascribed to God. "Thy *power* and thy righteousness, O God, reach the high heavens" (Ps. 66:7a, RSV). David prayed: "Thine, O LORD, is the greatness, and the *power*, and the glory, and the victory, and the majesty" (1 Chr. 29:11a).[39] The substantive *'ābîr*, meaning "the Mighty One," was used "of Jacob" (Gen. 49:24c; Ps. 132:2, 5; Isa. 49:26c; and 60:16c) and "of Israel" (Isa. 1:24a) as a synonym for the God of Jacob/Israel. The common adjective *gibbôr*, meaning "mighty," was used of God. "For the LORD your God is God of gods and Lord of lords, the great, the *mighty*, and the terrible God" (Deut. 10:17a, b).[40] A more generally used noun for power,

35. *Church Dogmatics*, II/1, p. 425.
36. Ibid., p. 426.
37. See Gen. 17:1; 28:3; 35:11; 43:14; 48:3; 49:25; and Exod. 6:3.
38. See above, Ch. 13, II, B, 1, a.
39. See also Ps. 21:13b; 65:6; 106:8a; and 145:11b.
40. See also Ps. 24:8; Isa. 9:6d; 10:21; Jer. 20:11a; 32:18c; Zeph. 3:17a; Neh. 9:32a.

kōaḥ, appears in various passages in a dozen Old Testament books. Sometimes the reference is to God's power as demonstrated in the Exodus (Exod.
9:16; 15:6a; 32:11c; Deut. 4:37b; 9:29b; 2 Kings 17:36). Elsewhere, especially
in Jeremiah, the reference is to God's power in creation (Isa. 40:26c; Jer.
10:12a; 27:5a; 32:17; 51:15a). Still other passages involve a more general
ascription of power to God (Num. 14:17; Job 36:22a; Ps. 111:6; 147:5; Nah.
1:3a; 1 Chr. 29:12b; 2 Chr. 20:6c; 25:8b; Neh. 1:10). Another noun for divine
"power" or "strength," *ʿōz,* was employed especially in the Psalms.[41] Also
the adjective *ḥāzāq,* meaning "strong, mighty, or hard," was frequently used
of God's power, especially in the formula that Yahweh had "brought Israel
out of Egypt with a *mighty* hand" (Exod. 32:11c; Deut. 6:21c; 7:8b; 9:26d;
34:12; and Dan. 9:15a), and also with "an outstretched arm" (Deut. 4:34b;
5:15b; 7:19a; 11:2d; 26:8a), but there were also more general usages (Deut.
3:24a; Josh. 4:24; Ezek. 20:33; and 2 Chr. 6:32). In summary, the following
patterns predominate in the Old Testament: power or might in fullness is
ascribed to God through the names and titles of God that connote power;
power is ascribed to God especially in the Exodus and in the creation; and
power is more generally ascribed to God.

2. *New Testament Terms and Passages*

The Greek word *dynamis,* meaning "ability" or "power," was used
especially by Luke and by Paul in various contexts: the virginal conception
of Jesus (Luke 1:35), the gift of the Holy Spirit on the Day of Pentecost
(Luke 24:49), the enthronement of the Son of Man (Luke 22:69), the content
of general revelation (Rom. 1:20), the nature of Paul's preaching (1 Cor.
2:4-5) and of his ministry (2 Cor. 6:7; Eph. 3:7), and the keeping of believers
unto final salvation (1 Pet. 1:5). Paul emphasized the greatness of God's
power (2 Cor. 4:7; Eph. 1:19), especially for the Christian life (Eph. 3:16;
Col. 1:11). The word *kratos,* meaning "strength, power, or dominion," was
used by Paul (Eph. 6:10; Col. 1:11; 1 Tim. 6:16) and in Revelation 5:13.
Another term for "strength" or "might," *ischys,* may be found in Eph. 6:10
and 2 Thess. 1:9. The substantive *pantokratōr,* meaning "the all-powerful
One" or "the Almighty," was repeatedly used in Revelation (1:8; 4:8; 11:17;
15:3; 16:7, 14; 19:15; and 21:22) and appeared in 2 Cor. 6:18. The verb
dynamai, meaning "to be able, to have power, to be powerful," was
frequently used to express the power of God. God "*is able* from these
stones to raise up children to Abraham" (Matt. 3:9b, RSV), and Jesus could
restore sight to the blind (Matt. 9:28). The power of Christ is all-controlling
(Phil. 3:21) and, when the divine power is "at work" within Christians,
God "*is able* to do far more abundantly than all that we ask or think" (Eph.
3:20). The living Christ "*is able* to keep those who are tempted" (Heb. 2:18),
"to keep" believers "from falling" (Jude 24), and "for all time to save" them
(Heb. 7:25). According to the New Testament, God's power is sufficient

---

41. See Ps. 59:16a; 62:11c; 63:2b; 66:3b; 78:26c; Hab. 3:4c.

for his saving or redemptive purpose. He is able to do whatever his saving purpose requires.

B. THEOLOGICAL INTERPRETATION

The framers of the Old Roman Symbol, better known as the Apostles' Creed, juxtaposed God's fatherhood and his almightiness, perhaps in order to answer Gnostics and Marcionites, by means of the familiar affirmation, "I believe in God the Father Almighty. . . ."[42] The almighty Creator is indeed the Father of Jesus Christ.

Medieval theologians normally ascribed to God *omnipotentia*, meaning his all-powerful nature. Sometimes discussions of omnipotence led to fanciful, speculative questions as to what God can and cannot do. Such discussions could be unrelated to specific biblical teachings about the power of God and might veer toward a pantheistic denial of the relative independence and moral responsibility of human beings.

What the medieval Schoolmen had done with omnipotence helped to lead Emil Brunner to differentiate Scholastic omnipotence from the biblical understanding of the power of God. Relative to the biblical teaching he contended that divine power always allowed for the relative independence of creatures. For Brunner divine omnipotence "means that He is free to deal with the universe He has created when and how He wills."[43] Karl Barth discussed both the knowledge of God and the will of God as "the positive characteristics of the divine omnipotence."[44]

An adequate concept of the power of God should include the fullness or plenitude of his power to execute and fulfill his purpose, but the doctrine should not be pressed into speculative excesses or made to support a view that makes humans helpless and irresponsible puppets of God.

V. THE JEALOUSY, ANGER, AND WRATH OF GOD

Because of the close relationship between these three attributes—jealousy, anger, and wrath—especially in the Old Testament, it will be helpful to present a somewhat coordinated discussion of the three.

A. THE JEALOUSY OF GOD

1. *Biblical Materials*

a. Old Testament Terms and Passages

The Hebrew verb *qānā'*, meaning "to be jealous, to be zealous," was not used in the Kal stem but rather in the Piel and Hiphil stems. This verb, the adjective *qannā'*, meaning "jealous," and the noun *qin'āh*, meaning

---

42. The Latin for "Almighty" was *omnipotentem*, and the Greek *pantokratora*.
43. *The Christian Doctrine of God*, p. 252.
44. *Church Dogmatics*, II/1, pp. 543-607.

"jealousy," were used of God's jealousy in the Old Testament. The jealous Yahweh will punish to the third and fourth generation those hating him and will show steadfast love to the thousandth generation of those who love him and keep his commandments (Exod. 20:5-6; Deut. 5:1-10). His jealousy was particularly directed to the covenant people when they consorted with false gods worshiped by neighboring peoples (Exod. 34:14; Num. 25:11; Deut. 6:1-15; Josh. 24:19; Ezek. 16:42). Such is true also when the covenant people engaged in idolatry (Deut. 4:24; Ezek. 8:2-3, 5). But Yahweh's jealousy was evoked in defense of Judah when invaded, plundered, or threatened (Ezek. 36:5-6; 38:19) and in behalf of rebuilding and the remnant (Zech. 1:14; 8:2).

b. New Testament Term and Passages

The Greek verb relative to divine jealousy is *zēloun*, which means "to be jealous," and the compound verb *parazēloun* is also used. The number of uses of these verbs in reference to God in the New Testament, however, is minimal. Paul, when contrasting the table of the Lord and the table of demons, asked, "Shall we provoke the Lord to jealousy?" (1 Cor. 10:22, RSV). The only other usage is somewhat indirect. "I feel a divine jealousy for you, for I betrothed you to Christ to present you as a pure bride to her husband" (2 Cor. 11:2). The term, therefore, was obviously less central to New Testament thought than to that of the Old Testament.

2. Theological Interpretation

Divine jealousy, according to the Old Testament, was affirmed both in the context of warnings against the harlotry of worshiping false gods and in the context of defending the covenant people against her enemies. The "jealous 'El" stood over against the Canaanite pantheon! Whereas the Homeric gods of Greece took away benefits from the Greek people, Yahweh blessed unto multiplied generations those who worshiped and served him alone.[45] God's jealousy is not, as some would have us to conclude, a very primitive religious concept, for indeed polytheism and henotheistic religion were tolerant of the worship of other gods. Rather it is a corollary of monotheism. The jealousy of God is, therefore, the intensity of his holiness in demanding and expecting the ready and undivided allegiance of his human creatures, especially those in covenant with him.

B. THE ANGER OF GOD

1. Biblical Materials

a. Old Testament Term and Usage

The Hebrew word for divine anger is *'ap*, a noun derived from the verb *'ānap*, which means "to breathe, or breathe through the nostrils."

45. König, *Here I Am!*, pp. 95-96.

Thus 'ap is an onomatopoetic word that is related to the heavy breathing that accompanies anger. The KJV sometimes translates 'ap as "anger" and sometimes as "wrath," but the NASV and NIV almost always render 'ap as "anger." At least 130 times the word 'ap conveys the idea of God's anger in the Old Testament. These usages are scattered through the Pentateuch, the Prophets, and the Writings. In the Pentateuch, the prophetic books, and the historical books the usages of anger are normally associated with some particular historical situation, quite often the disobedience of the covenant people, whereas in the Psalms the usages are of a more general nature so that it is difficult to identify any historical situation. Perhaps the most common expression of God's anger in the Old Testament is the burning of his anger. Sometimes God's anger is said to continue (Isa. 10:4; Jer. 23:20; 30:24); sometimes it is said to be "turned away" (Hos. 14:4; Isa. 12:1; 2 Chr. 12:12; Ezra 10:14); and sometimes it is said to be "held back" or delayed (Isa. 48:9) or "restrained" (Ps. 78:38b).

b. New Testament

The writings of the New Testament do not apply the term "anger" to God in the manner and with the frequency of the Old Testament usage,[46] but much of the idea is conveyed in the New Testament usage of "wrath" in reference to God.

2. *Theological Interpretation*

The anger of God, together with some uses of "wrath," is the principal Old Testament expression of God's holiness in reaction to the sins of Israel the nation and the sins of individuals, especially the nation's leaders.

What role, if any, should the anger of God have in a contemporary Christian doctrine of God? Some assume that to affirm the love and grace of God is to eliminate or reject God's anger. Emil Brunner has offered an alternative answer:

> Because God takes Himself, His love infinitely seriously, and in so doing also takes man infinitely seriously, He cannot do otherwise than be angry, although "really" He is only Love. His wrath is simply the result of the infinitely serious love of God.[47]

C. THE WRATH OF GOD

1. *Biblical Materials*

a. Old Testament Terms and Passages

Three different Hebrew nouns are used in the Old Testament to express the wrath of God. The word *qeṣep*, which can also mean "twigs"

---

46. See Rev. 14:10.
47. *The Christian Doctrine of God*, p. 170.

and "splinters," normally conveyed divine wrath in respect to specific historical situations (Num. 16:46c; Jer. 50:13a; 2 Chr. 29:8; 32:26; Ps. 38:1). *Ebrāh,* derived from a verb meaning "to pass over, go beyond" and suggesting an outpouring of anger or wrath, also related wrath to specific situations (Hos. 5:10; 13:11; Isa. 9:19a), though it could also be used generally (Ps. 90:9, 11) and of a future "day of the wrath of the LORD" (Zeph. 1:15a, 18a, RSV). *Hēmāh,* meaning wrath in the sense of "heat" or "fury," was also used vis-à-vis specific occasions of disobedience (2 Kings 22:13b, 17b; 2 Chr. 36:16).

b. New Testament Terms and Passages

Two Greek nouns are employed to express the wrath of God in the New Testament. *Orgē,* meaning "wrath, anger, or indignation," is the more generally used term and is to be found especially in Romans and in Revelation. Sometimes this wrath is specifically directed at unbelievers or the disobedient (John 3:36; Rom. 1:18; Eph. 5:6; Col. 3:6). Law with its consequent disobedience brings forth wrath (Rom. 4:15), divine wrath expresses vengeance (Rom. 12:19), and such wrath can even be executed by civil rulers (Rom. 13:4c, 5). Elsewhere the reference is to future wrath (Matt. 3:7; 1 Thess. 1:10; 5:9; Rom. 2:5, 8; 5:9). *Thymos,* meaning "glowing, ardor, passion, or angry heat," is found only in Revelation, where its usages are eschatological (14:10, 19; 15:1, 7; 16:1; 18:3a), as is also true of the uses of *orgē* in Revelation (6:16-17; 11:18a; 16:19; 19:15).

2. *Theological Interpretation: History of Christian Doctrine*

Like the term "anger," the term "wrath" expresses in the Bible the reaction of God as holy against human sin. The concept of divine wrath has received different interpretations and has been correlated with other attributes differently during the history of Christian doctrine.

a. Wrath as God's "Strange Work" (Martin Luther)

Luther spoke of God's wrath as his *opus alienum* ("strange work") and of God's love as his *opus proprium* ("proper work"). The two are coupled in contrast. Commenting on Ps. 2:9, wherein he referred also to Isa. 28:21, Luther wrote:

> Although He is the God of life and salvation and this is His proper work, yet, in order to accomplish this, He kills and destroys. These works are alien to Him, but through them He accomplishes His proper work. For He kills our will that His may be established in us.[48]

Indeed, God's "strange work" is strange "because it does not spring from the essential will of God, but because it is forced upon Him by the sinful resistance of man."[49]

---

48. "Psalm 2," *Luther's Works,* 14:335.
49. Luther, *W.A.,* 42:356, as quoted by Brunner, *The Christian Doctrine of God,* p. 169.

b. Neglect of or Denial of God's Wrath (Liberal Protestant Theologians)

F. D. E. Schleiermacher treated three divine attributes related to the consciousness of sin: God is holy, just, and merciful. He did not specifically deal with "wrath," but he did discuss justice as "retributive."[50] Albrecht Ritschl had little to say of divine wrath,[51] and for Nels F. S. Ferré a predominant emphasis on God's *agapē* excluded divine wrath.[52]

c. Deattributization of the Wrath of God (C. H. Dodd)

Dodd noted that only three times (Rom. 1:18; Eph. 5:6; Col. 3:6) did Paul use the full term "the wrath of God." For Dodd wrath was "not a certain feeling or attitude of God towards us" but rather "an inevitable process of cause and effect in a moral universe." "Wrath is the effect of human sin: mercy is not the effect of human goodness, but is inherent in the character of God."[53] Dodd's view was refuted by Leon Morris (1914-).[54]

d. God's Wrath as God's Wounded Love (Gustav Friedrich Oehler, 1812-72, Adrio König)

According to Oehler, "the wrath of God is the highest strained energy of the holy will of God, the zeal of His wounded love."[55] Similarly König has affirmed that the wrath of God, being his reaction to sin, is his "injured love." "He *became* angry, but he *is* love."[56]

VI. THE GLORY OF GOD

A. BIBLICAL TERMS

The Old Testament and the New Testament terms for the "glory" of God had somewhat distinct linguistic backgrounds, as Emil Brunner noted.[57] The Hebrew term *kābôd*, when first applied to deity, referred to lightning, thunderstorms, and the like. It came to mean a "weight" or "difficulty." The word had an objective meaning. In Old Testament usage it connoted the "majestic self- manifestation of God." The Greek term *doxa*,

50. *The Christian Faith*, pp. 341-54.
51. *The Christian Doctrine of Justification and Reconciliation*, trans. H. R. Mackintosh and A. B. Macaulay (reprint ed.; Clifton, N.J.: Reference Book Publishers, Inc., 1966), pp. 45, 321-22, 571-72. Ritschl's mentioning of the wrath of God normally occurred when he was discussing the views of other theologians.
52. *The Christian Understanding of God*, pp. 114-18.
53. *Romans*, Moffatt New Testament Commentary (London: Hodder and Stoughton, 1949), pp. 21, 23.
54. *The Apostolic Preaching of the Cross* (London: Tyndale Press, 1955), pp. 129-36; *The Cross in the New Testament* (Grand Rapids: Eerdmans, 1965), pp. 189-92; *New Testament Theology* (Grand Rapids: Zondervan, 1986), p. 63.
55. *Theology of the Old Testament*, trans. Ellen D. Smith. 2 vols. (Edinburgh: T. & T. Clark, 1880), 1:166. The German original was published in 1873.
56. *Here I Am!*, pp. 94, 95.
57. *The Christian Doctrine of God*, pp. 285-87.

on the other hand, was derived from the verb *dokein*, which means "to think, seem, appear," and hence *doxa* came to mean an "opinion" or a "reputation." With a more subjective meaning, it connoted human perception of the divine majesty.

B. BIBLICAL USAGES

The *kāḇôḏ* of Yahweh was manifested among all mankind, both by the heavens (Ps. 19:1) and throughout the earth (Ps. 72:19; Isa. 6:3; Hab. 2:14). It was also manifested particularly to and among the people of Israel (Exod. 15:6, 11; 40:34).

The *doxa* of God was manifested in Jesus Christ: in his preexistence (John 17:5), in his incarnation (John 1:14), in his transfiguration (Luke 9:32), in his death and resurrection (John 12:28; 17:1, 5), and in revelation to believers (2 Cor. 4:6). Likewise it was to be manifested in the final or eschatological aspect of God's redemption (1 Cor. 15:43; 2 Cor. 3:18; Rom. 5:2; 8:18; Col. 1:27; 1 Pet. 5:1).

C. THEOLOGICAL INTERPRETATION

Whether taken from its more objective or from its more subjective aspect, the glory of God is the majestic manifestation and recognition of God as holy and worthy of worship and praise. Although found in virtually all Christian traditions, the glorification of God has had a special function in the Eastern Orthodox tradition.

Summary: Eternity is the duration of God's holiness. Changelessness is the continuing stability or constancy of God's holiness. Wisdom is the truth of God's holiness. Power is the strength of God's holiness. Jealousy, anger, and wrath are the reaction of God's holiness to sin. Glory is the recognized manifestation of God's holiness as majesty.

CHAPTER 17

God as Righteous

The concept of righteousness as applied to God is prominent in both the Old Testament and the New Testament and has been significant during the postbiblical history of Christianity, especially during the Protestant Reformation. In the present study the righteousness of God serves as a bridge between holiness and the attributes related to it and love and the attributes related to it. Righteousness can have such a role partly because of the diversity of meanings it has.

I. THE OLD TESTAMENT

A. TERMS

The concept of righteousness in the Old Testament is expressed principally through one family of words. The verb *ṣādaq*, probably having as a general or secular meaning "to be straight," came to have a religious meaning, namely, "to be right or righteous." The adjective is *ṣaddîq*, meaning "righteous," and the nouns are *ṣedeq*, which is usually translated "righteousness" or "justice," and *ṣedāqāh*, meaning "rightness, justice."

Closely associated with *ṣādaq* and its cognates and sometimes expressive of righteousness was the verb *šāpaṭ*, "to judge," and the noun *mišpāṭ*, meaning "judgment," which words more often convey the ideas of judgment and justice.

B. USAGES

1. Universal Righteousness

In certain Old Testament passages the contexts show that "righteousness" or "justice" has a universal meaning. Especially is this true of Yahweh's kingly rulership of the nations. Early in the Pentateuch one finds the question: "Will not the Judge of all the earth do right?" (Gen. 18:25b, NIV). The idea appears in the Psalms: "Say among the nations, 'The LORD reigns.' . . . he will judge the peoples with equity" (96:10a, c). "He will judge the world in righteousness and the peoples in his truth" (96:13b). "The heavens proclaim his righteousness, and all the peoples see his glory" (97:6). Of both Judah and her neighboring peoples Jeremiah recorded: "'I am the LORD, who exercises kindness, justice and righteousness on earth, for in these I delight,' declares the Lord" (9:24b).

2. Covenantal Righteousness

The great majority of usages of the righteousness of God pertain to the covenant people: God is righteous in all his dealings with Israel/Judah. Although it has not been true among Old Testament theologians, certain Baptist systematic theologians have formulated and utilized a threefold differentiation of covenantal righteousness.[1] Such a differentiation seems to be consistent with the various passages under examination and will therefore be used here.

a. Mandatory Righteousness

In some Old Testament passages God is said to be "righteous" in the sense that his law is righteous and places righteous demands on the covenant people for their obedience to it. Hence Yahweh's "righteousness" mandates or makes imperative Israelite obedience of the law. In contrast to towns inhabited by the wicked, obedient Israelites should obey Yahweh, "keeping all his commands" and "doing what is right in his eyes" (Deut. 13:18, NIV). The righteous character of the law is affirmed in the Psalms: "The precepts of the LORD are right, giving joy to the heart. . . . The ordinances of the LORD are sure and altogether righteous" (19:8a, 9b).

> Righteous are you, O LORD, and your laws are right. The statutes you have laid down are righteous; they are fully trustworthy. . . . Your righteousness is everlasting and your law is true. . . . Your statutes are forever right; give me understanding that I may live. (119:137-38, 142, 144)

b. Retributive or Punitive Righteousness

Not a few Old Testament passages contain the idea that as the "righteous" God Yahweh punishes or brings retribution on his sinful, disobedient people. Such passages seem to suggest that because Yahweh is "righteous" he must inflict such punishment. Sometimes God's righteousness is connected with Yahweh's accusing the people because of their sins. Along with the punishment of the wicked, in the context we read: "For the LORD is righteous, he loves justice; upright men will see his face" (Ps. 11:7, NIV). Also connected with woes and judgment is the statement: "the holy God will show himself holy by his righteousness"

---

1. Mullins, *The Christian Religion in Its Doctrinal Expression*, pp. 233-34; Conner, *Revelation and God*, pp. 248-63; Herschel H. Hobbs, *Fundamentals of Our Faith* (Nashville: Broadman Press, 1960), pp. 34-35. A. H. Strong, *Systematic Theology*, pp. 290-95, differentiated "righteousness" as "mandatory" from "justice" as "retributive" but did not identify the redemptive aspect. The author is indebted to Ralph Lee Smith for insights concerning Old Testament theologians.

(Isa. 5:16). Against those who had plotted to kill him Jeremiah wrote: "But, O LORD Almighty, you who judge righteously and test the heart and mind, let me see your vengeance upon them, for to you I have committed my cause" (11:20). The words of Jerusalem, in agony and remorse, are cast in the first person: "The LORD is righteous, yet I rebelled against his command" (Lam. 1:18a). That Jerusalem deserved punishment is reflected in the words: "The LORD within her is righteous; he does no wrong. Morning by morning he dispenses his justice, and every new day he does not fail, yet the unrighteous know no shame" (Zeph. 3:5). The book of Daniel reflects the same usage of righteousness in Daniel's prayer: "LORD, you are righteous, but this day we are covered with shame—the men of Judah and people of Jerusalem and all Israel, both near and far, in all the countries where you have scattered us because of our unfaithfulness to you" (9:7). "The LORD did not hesitate to bring the disaster upon us, for the LORD our God is righteous in everything he does; yet we have not obeyed him" (9:14). Ezra connected God's righteousness with the remnant: "O LORD, God of Israel, you are righteous! We are left this day as a remnant. Here we are before you in our guilt, though because of it not one of us can stand in your presence" (9:15). Neh. 9:33 expresses a similar thought.

c. Redemptive or Saving Righteousness

There are also numerous passages, chiefly in the Psalms and in Isaiah 40–66, in which the righteousness of Yahweh is clearly depicted in association with his redemption of his people. The texts seem to imply that because Yahweh is "righteous" he redeems or saves his people. God's saving righteousness is affirmed in a context of forgiveness and removal of transgressions (Ps. 103:6; also vv. 3, 12). The righteous God is compassionate and loving toward all his creatures, especially those who cry to him (Ps. 145:17; also vv. 8-9, 19). There is prayer for salvation in God's "righteousness" (71:2), and prayer for deliverance from trouble on the basis that God is righteous (143:1, 11). Yahweh's saving righteousness can be sung about (51:14); indeed salvation and righteousness are synonyms (98:2).

In Isaiah 40–66 the redemptive or saving aspect of God's righteousness is even more explicit. The covenant people are to be strengthened and helped by God's "righteous right hand" (41:10b, NIV). The Servant of Yahweh is "called in righteousness" to become "a covenant for the people and a light for the Gentiles" (42:6). Yahweh the only God is "a righteous God and a Savior," and the "ends of the earth" are to turn to him to "be saved" (45:21-22). Four times "righteousness" and "salvation" are coupled in synonymous parallelism (46:13; 51:5a; 51:6c; 61:10).

The saving righteousness of Yahweh is expressed elsewhere in the Old Testament. Divine righteousness is joined with the betrothal of Israel unto faithfulness (Hos. 2:19-20), and when Judah's leaders humble themselves in repentance, confessing that "Yahweh is righteous," subjection to the king of Egypt is averted (2 Chr. 12:5-8).

God's righteousness, therefore, in the Old Testament was universal in dimension and particularized with the covenant people, and in the latter sphere it was expressed with mandatory, punitive, and redemptive significance.

II. THE NEW TESTAMENT

The Greek New Testament word for "righteous" is *dikaios*, and the word for "righteousness" is *dikaiosynē*. These words are closely related, especially in the letters of Paul, to the verb *dikaioun*, meaning "to justify." The idea that God is "righteous" is a Pauline and Johannine teaching, and the use of "righteousness" in reference to God is primarily a Pauline teaching.

A. GOD AS "RIGHTEOUS"

God is addressed as "righteous Father" in Jesus' High-Priestly Prayer (John 17:25), and 1 John identifies both Jesus Christ (2:1b) and God the Father (3:7b) as "righteous." Paul in speaking of the last judgment alludes to God as "the Lord, the righteous judge" (2 Tim. 4:8). In Rev. 16:5 God is said to be "righteous" in the "judgments" connected with the bowls of wrath in language that seems to have been a quotation of Ps. 119:137.

B. THE "RIGHTEOUSNESS OF GOD"

Although the term *hē dikaiosynē theou* or its equivalent is to be found occasionally in the non-Pauline books of the New Testament, as in Jesus' statement, "But seek first his kingdom and his righteousness" (Matt. 6:33, NIV), and in "a faith of equal standing with ours in the righteousness of our God and Savior Jesus Christ" (2 Pet. 1:1b, RSV), it is primarily a Pauline term. In Paul's usage the meaning most often expressed is that God's righteousness is his gift through the gospel of Jesus Christ (Rom. 1:17; 3:21-22; 10:3; Phil. 3:9). But the term can also refer to an attribute of God (Rom. 3:25-26) and to Christians' becoming through Jesus' death "the righteousness of God" (2 Cor. 5:21; also Eph. 4:24).

The history of exegesis, however, shows that exegetes and theologians have found it difficult to agree on the meaning or meanings of "the righteousness of God." Some, taking the phrase as a subjective genitive, have insisted that the term refers only to an attribute or quality of God and has no other meaning. Ambrose[2] during the patristic age held that position. Others, taking the phrase as a genitive of origin, have concluded that it refers only to the gift that God bestows in Christ through faith on

---

2. *Flight from the World* 3.14.

sinful human beings. Augustine of Hippo,[3] Martin Luther,[4] John Calvin,[5] John Gill (1697-1771),[6] Richard Charles Henry Lenski (1865-1936),[7] Anders Nygren (1890-?),[8] and Ernst Käsemann[9] have represented that view. Thirdly, still others have held that the term can mean both attribute and gift. Among the advocates of this position have been Johann Albrecht Bengel,[10] William Sanday and Arthur Cayley Headlam (1862-1947),[11] Charles Harold Dodd,[12] W. T. Conner,[13] Paul Althaus (1888-1966),[14] and Charles Ernest Burland Cranfield (1915-).[15] The third position seems to be capable of defense on the basis of Rom. 3:21-26, wherein the dual meaning can be seen in separate texts and even in the same verse. In 3:25-26 "the righteousness of God" is a divine attribute, in 3:21-22 it is the gift of God through Jesus Christ, and in 3:26, wherein the noun, the adjective, and the verb are used, both meanings can be found.

The fact that "the righteousness of God" is God's gift through Jesus' death makes its use as a divine attribute consistent with God's saving activity. In fact righteousness, according to Paul, is, as in Psalms and Isaiah, a redemptive attribute. The same is true in the Johannine writings. God saves or forgives sinners, not in spite of his being righteous but because he is "righteous" (1 John 1:9).

3. *On the Spirit and the Letter* 15 (9).

4. *Lectures on Romans*, re 1:17 and 3:26, *Luther's Works*, vol. 25. John Reumann, *"Righteousness" in the New Testament: "Justification" in the United States Lutheran–Roman Catholic Dialogue* (Philadelphia: Fortress Press; New York: Paulist Press, 1982), p. 66, has interpreted Luther as holding to an "objective genitive" in the sense of "the righteousness which is valid before God."

5. *Commentaries on the Epistle of Paul the Apostle to the Romans*, trans. John Owen (Grand Rapids: Eerdmans, 1947), re 1:17 and 3:21, 22.

6. *An Exposition of the New Testament*, 6 vols. (reprint ed.; Grand Rapids: Baker Book House, 1980), vol. 6, re Rom. 1:17 and 2:21, 22.

7. *The Interpretation of St. Paul's Epistle to the Romans* (Columbus: Wartburg Press, 1936), re 1:17.

8. *Commentary on Romans*, trans. Carl C. Rasmussen (Philadelphia: Muhlenberg Press, 1949), pp. 159-62.

9. *New Testament Questions of Today*, trans. W. J. Montague (Philadelphia: Fortress Press, 1969), pp. 168-82.

10. *Gnomon of the New Testament*, 5 vols., vol. 3, trans. James Bryce (Edinburgh: T. and T. Clark, 1866), re Rom. 1:17.

11. *A Critical and Exegetical Commentary on the Epistle to the Romans*, International Critical Commentary (5th ed.; Edinburgh: T. and T. Clark, 1902), pp. 82-83, 90-91.

12. *The Epistle of Paul to the Romans* (London: Hodder and Stoughton, 1932), pp. 59-60.

13. *The Faith of the New Testament* (Nashville: Broadman Press, 1940), pp. 268-73.

14. *Der Brief an die Römer*, Das Neue Testament Deutsch (Göttingen: Vandenhoeck und Ruprecht, 1970), pp. 13-16, esp. 13. Althaus referred to "the apparent double meaning" *(scheinbare Doppeldeutigkeit)* of "the righteousness of God" but then said that it was "thoroughly one in meaning" *(durchhaus eindeutig)*.

15. *A Critical and Exegetical Commentary on the Epistle to the Romans*, International Critical Commentary, n.s., 2 vols. (Edinburgh: T. and T. Clark, 1975), 1:202, 211-13.

III. THE HISTORY OF CHRISTIAN DOCTRINE

A. Late medieval Roman Catholicism tended to obscure or deny the righteousness of God as gift by equating righteousness with justice *(iustitia)* and through its doctrine of human merits, both condign and congruous. The Council of Trent (1545-63) clarified the Roman doctrine of justification, retaining the teaching that eternal life is both "grace" and "reward."[16]

B. Martin Luther's celebrated tower discovery *(Turmerlebnis)* in the monastery at Wittenberg was seemingly his coming to realize on the basis of Rom. 1:17 and passages in the Psalms that "the righteousness of God" *(dikaiosynē, iustitia)* was a redemptive attribute and gift, not merely the exercise of retribution or punishment.[17]

C. Some high Calvinists and others may have understood God's righteousness solely as retributive justice ("God *must* punish sin because he is righteous; he *may* redeem or forgive the sinner") and thus have obscured the redemptive aspect of divine righteousness.[18]

D. Systems of philosophical ethics such as hedonism, or the ethic of pleasure, and utilitarianism, or the ethic of usefulness, have contradicted the theocentric ethics of Christianity, according to which the nature of God as righteous is the ultimate basis for the distinctions between right and wrong.

E. Liberal Protestant theologians, by subsuming righteousness under the divine love and/or by denying the reality of any retribution— some even affirming eschatological universalism—downgraded righteousness as a theme and tended to remove its retributive aspect. Rightly interpreted, retributive righteousness is not sheer vindictiveness but the characteristic reaction of the Holy One who is righteous toward sin.

In the Old Testament God is said to be "righteous" in relation to all humankind and in relation to the covenant people. Under the latter "righteousness" is variously employed with mandatory, retributive, and redemptive meanings. In the New Testament, especially in Paul, God's righteousness is both his attribute and his gift bestowed on human beings through Jesus Christ. During postbiblical history God's righteousness has been wrongly preempted by human merits, pressed to mean only retribution, denied as the ground of ethics, and demoted by an overemphasis on love.

---

16. *Canons and Decrees of the Council of Trent,* 6th session, 13 January 1547.

17. Uuras Saarnivaara, *Luther Discovers the Gospel: New Light upon Luther's Way from Medieval Catholicism to Evangelical Faith* (St. Louis: Concordia Publishing House, 1951); Gordon Rupp, *The Righteousness of God: Luther Studies* (London: Hodder and Stoughton, 1953), pp. 121-256.

18. Charles Hodge, *Systematic Theology,* 1:416-27; Strong, *Systematic Theology,* pp. 290-95.

CHAPTER 18

God as Love

From God's holiness and those attributes which can be clustered around holiness and the "bridge" attribute of righteousness we turn now to that other focal attribute, God's love. Love has been said to be the most communicable of all the communicable attributes of God. Some, however, have insisted that love is not an attribute of God, for, since there is a biblical teaching that "God is love" (1 John 4:8b), love ought only to be considered as the very nature of God. One should not, however, seek to make a major theological distinction solely on the basis of the difference between the use of a noun ("God is love") and the use of adjectives ("God is holy," "God is righteous," and "God is merciful").

I. THE OLD TESTAMENT

Some seemingly have assumed that there is no doctrine of God's love in the Old Testament, but the evidence against such an assumption should be convincing to any serious student of the Old Testament.

A. PRINCIPAL TERMS FOR DIVINE LOVE

1. *The Verb* 'āhab *and the Noun* 'āh^abāh

a. This verb-noun family is the most comprehensive set of terms for love in the Old Testament. It was "used of any and every kind of love," both "secular" and "religious." The root idea of the stem, found also in other Semitic languages, seems to have been "to burn, kindle, or set on fire." Among the secular usages in the Old Testament some few pertain to "inanimate things" such as food, sleep, and wisdom, but the majority apply to persons. Most frequently these personal usages involve the attitude of a superior to an inferior, but, when rarely used of the attitude of an inferior to a superior, it is a "humble, dutiful love." Among the religious usages of the family, both verb and noun, 27 involve God's loving human beings and 24 have to do with humans' loving God.[1]

---

1. Snaith, *The Distinctive Ideas of the Old Testament*, pp. 131-33.

235

b. When used of God, '$\bar{a}h^ab\bar{a}h$ signified "election-love," or "an uncon-ditioned sovereign love," according to Norman Snaith.[2] Israel's election was, therefore, due to the '$\bar{a}h^ab\bar{a}h$ of Yahweh, not to any merit or inherent worth among the Israelites. "It was not because you were more in number than any other people that the LORD set his love upon you and chose you" (Deut. 7:7, RSV). Rather, it was "because he loved your fathers and chose their descendants after them, and brought you out of Egypt . . ." (Deut. 4:37; see also Deut. 10:15). Because of Yahweh's love Balaam's curse was turned into blessing (Deut. 23:5). " 'When Israel was a child, I loved him, and out of Egypt I called my son'" (Hos. 11:1). Covenant-making love was ex-pressed in Ezekiel's allegory of unfaithful Jerusalem (16:8). The meaning of electing love is partly to be seen through the contrast between '$\bar{a}hab$, "to love," and $s\bar{a}n\bar{e}$', "to hate," as in "Jacob I loved, but Esau I hated" (Mal. 1:3). Against the charge that Yahweh's electing love is "irrational," Snaith contended that such a term should mean that "man cannot find a reason" and not "contrary to reason."[3] In bestowing his electing love Yahweh provided an "over-plus" beyond his "general love for mankind."[4]

2. *The Noun* Hesed

a. This word is derived from a Semitic root that presumably means "eagerness," "keenness," or "ardent desire." Its etymology is complicated by the fact that a few times in the Old Testament it means "shame, reproach, defilement." In most of the older English translations of the Old Testament, probably beginning with that of Miles Coverdale, hesed was rendered by "mercy" or "lovingkindness." This choice was likely due to the facts that the Septuagint had translated it with *eleos,* meaning "pity" or "mercy," and that the Latin Vulgate had rendered it by *misericordia,* also meaning "pity" or "mercy."[5] Present-day Old Testament scholars, however, tend to hold that the correct meaning of this Hebrew noun, when applied to God, is "covenant-love," "loyalty-love," "troth," "bond-affection," or, as the RSV translators determined, "steadfast love."

b. Hesed had in the Old Testament what Snaith called a "double development." When applied to God, the term had the connotations just specified by possible English translations. But, when used of human beings, the term developed into the concept of "piety" or "godliness," as the name of the later Jewish party, the Chasidim, would indicate. This "double development" was possible because originally hesed denoted "that attitude of loyalty and faithfulness which both parties to a covenant should observe towards each other."[6] That Yahweh expected the covenant people to have hesed toward him is clear in the prophets. Hosea lamented the absence of *ḥeseḏ* in the land (4:1); indeed, the people's *ḥeseḏ* was like the disappearing morning mist (6:4), for Yahweh desired "*ḥeseḏ*, not sacrifice" (6:6). True religion, for Micah, included loving *ḥeseḏ* (6:8). The adjective *ḥasîḏ* was used in the Psalms and the postexilic writings of the pious, devoted, or loyal ones.[7] The people's *ḥeseḏ* should be the knowledge of Yahweh that issues in loyalty in worship and faithfulness in duty.

c. When used of Yahweh, *ḥeseḏ* meant his determined faithfulness to his covenant. It was the means whereby the covenant was sustained, and it stood in contrast to the unfaithfulness of Israel/Judah. "*'Ahabah* is the cause of the covenant; *chesed* is the means of its continuance. Thus *'ahabah* is God's Election-Love, whilst *chesed* is His Covenant- Love."[8] In this sense *ḥeseḏ* is used in Exodus, Hosea, Micah, Jeremiah, and the Psalms. The covenant-making God of the Decalogue showed his *ḥeseḏ* to a thousand generations of those loving him and keeping his commands (Exod. 20:6). Yahweh's betrothal of Israel to himself was to be "in *ḥeseḏ*" (Hos. 2:19), even as he had showed his *ḥeseḏ* to Abraham (Mic. 7:20). Yahweh's *ḥeseḏ* "endures for ever" (Jer. 33:11b; Ps. 100:5, RSV) or all the days of one's life (Ps. 23:6a).

B. IDEAS OR ANALOGIES RELATED TO GOD'S LOVE

The intimate connection between Yahweh's covenant with Israel and his love for Israel has been made clear through the study of the two principal terms. Furthermore, the husband-wife analogy was also applied to divine love. Hosea represented Israel as the "wayward wife" of Yahweh; Yahweh commanded him to love wayward Gomer even as Yahweh loved wayward Israel (3:1-3). Similarly, Jeremiah saw Judah as "a woman unfaithful to her husband" (3:20a, NIV). Moreover, God's *ḥeseḏ* was coupled with the father-son relationship. The divine promise to David was that his son Solomon would have a filial relationship with Yahweh:

> When he does wrong, I will punish him with the rod of men, with floggings inflicted by men. But my love [*ḥeseḏ*] will never be taken away from him, as I took it away from Saul. . . . (2 Sam. 7:14b, 15a, b, NIV)

C. EXTENT OF DIVINE LOVE

The texts related to divine love do not specifically deny that God's love was extended to non-Israelites or non-Jews, but the implications of election-love and covenant-love clearly limited Yahweh's love to the people of the covenant. Moreover, the major universalistic texts in the Old Testament do not employ the two major terms for divine love.

---

7. Ibid., pp. 123-27.
8. Ibid., p. 95.

II. THE NEW TESTAMENT

A. PRINCIPAL TERMS FOR DIVINE LOVE

The New Testament uses two verbs for divine loving, *agapaō*, and *phileō*, but only one noun for love, *agapē*. The verb *phileō*, which connotes the love of friendship, is used a few times in the Gospel of John. It refers to God the Father's love for the Son of God (5:20a), the Father's love of Jesus' disciples (16:27a), Jesus' love of Lazarus (11:3, 36), and Jesus' love of the Apostle John (20:2). The New Testament does not use the noun *philia* or the noun *erōs*.

The New Testament usage of *agapaō* and *agapē* to express divine love and whatever nuances they have that *phileō* does not have can hardly be determined by strictly philological inquiry, but rather they need to be explicated through exegetical and doctrinal study. Exegetes and theologians have not agreed about the relationship between these two words. William Evans found *agapaō* to be "the highest, most perfect kind of love" and *phileō* to be "natural" and sentimental love, especially in John 21:15-19, but James Moffatt (1870-1944) warned against "forced and fanciful" distinctions between these words since they had been synonyms in classical Greek. Ethelbert Stauffer (1902-) found that *agapaō* and *agapē* had acquired a "new" meaning by being the preferred translations for *'āhab* and *'āhabāh* in the Septuagint, and Gustav Stählin (1900-) wrote of the restricted usage of *phileō* in the New Testament.[9] Anders Nygren was even more specific in identifying and elaborating upon the meaning of *agapaō-agapē*. Nygren, in the words of Philip S. Watson, taught that God's *agapē* is "entirely independent of external stimulus and motivation," "neither kindled by the attractiveness nor quenched by the unattractiveness of its object," and "opposed to all forms of selfishness."[10] In Nygren's terms *agapē* is "spontaneous and 'unmotivated,' " " 'indifferent to value,' " "creative," and "the initiator of fellowship with God."[11]

B. MEANING OF DIVINE LOVE

The teaching about divine love in the New Testament is mostly to be found in the Gospel and First Epistle of John and in the epistles of Paul.

1. Divine love in the New Testament includes the love that belongs to and is expressed by God the Father. Repeatedly the love of God the Father is said to be for the Son of God (John 3:35; 10:17; 15:9; 17:24, 26). The Father also loves humankind, and that love is expressed in the giving of his Son unto death (John 3:16; Rom. 5:8; 1 John 4:10). Historically that

9. Evans, "Love," *International Standard Bible Encyclopedia,* 1955 ed., 3:1932; Moffatt, *Love in the New Testament* (London: Hodder and Stoughton, 1929), pp. 44-48; Stauffer, *"agapaō, agapē, agapētos," Theological Dictionary of the New Testament,* 1:21-55, esp. 39; Stählin, *"phileō, kataphileō, philēma, philos, philē, philia,"* in ibid., ed. Gerhard Friedrich, 9:113-46, esp. 128.

10. "Translator's Preface," in Anders Nygren, *Agape and Eros,* trans. Philip S. Watson (London: S.P.C.K., 1954), pp. ix, xiii.

11. Nygren, *Agape and Eros,* pp. 75-81.

fatherly love has been an electing love toward Jacob (Rom. 9:13), and presently it is the Father's love for Jesus' disciples (John 14:21, 23; 2 Thess. 2:16). The Father's love is directed to both the Son of God and "the world" (John 17:23c). His love is likewise expressed in believers' becoming his children (1 John 3:1) and in God's chastening of his children (Heb. 12:6).

2. Divine love in the New Testament embraces the love that belongs to and is expressed by the Son of God. The Son loves God the Father (John 14:31), and his love for humankind is manifested in his cross (Gal. 2:20; Eph. 5:2; 1 John 3:16). Jesus' love for his disciples is both a continuing love (John 13:1, 34) and a constraining love (2 Cor. 5:14), and there will be no ultimate separation of believers from the love of God expressed in Jesus Christ (Rom. 8:38-39).

3. The New Testament does not so specifically express the love belonging to and expressed by the Holy Spirit, but God's love is said to have been poured into the hearts of believers through the given Holy Spirit (Rom. 5:5). In a more general sense, initiative in loving comes from God (2 Cor. 13:14; 1 John 4:7, 10), and the very nature of God is love (1 John 4:8).

In view of all that has been said about divine love and in the light of the preceding comment about love's being the most communicable of the communicable attributes of God, it is proper to conclude that the love of God is both a divine attribute and a divine gift to human beings.

III. THEOLOGICAL INTERPRETATION

A. DIVINE LOVE AND NON-CHRISTIAN RELIGIONS

The biblical doctrine of God's *agapē* is unique among the world's religions and philosophies. Neither Zeus (Jupiter), nor Brahma, nor Ahura Mazda, nor Vishnu, nor Allah is said to be a God of self-giving love. For Plato the divine was good but not loving.[12]

The "nearest analogy to Christian love" is to be found in the bhakti form of Hinduism, which originated during the eleventh and twelfth centuries A.D. In its nobler forms one finds in bhakti "some approximation to a synthesis of the divine love for man, man's love for God in return, and man's love for his fellow-man as in some sense the outcome of both." But bhakti assumes that there must be "successive incarnations" of avatars, and its monotheism was compromised by a subordinate polytheism.[13]

B. DIVINE LOVE AND THE TRINITY

God's *agapē* is basic to the inner Trinitarian relationships of the Father, the Son, and the Holy Spirit. Augustine of Hippo taught that the

---

12. Brunner, *The Christian Doctrine of God*, p. 183.
13. James Moffatt, *Love in the New Testament* (London: Hodder and Stoughton, 1932), pp. 11-13.

Holy Spirit is especially called "love" and is the "communion" and conveys the common love between the Father and the Son.[14] Claude Welch (1922-) has written of "an eternal communion or 'communityness' of love between Father, Son and Holy Spirit." "The love of Father and Son is . . . an inner procession of self-giving love, which is the ground of God's outward *agapē* and therefore of creation and redemption."[15]

C. DIVINE LOVE AND THE ANTHROPIC APPROACH

Anders Nygren developed the hypothesis that *agapē*, from the New Testament, and *erōs*, from Plato and other Greeks, being fundamentally distinct and opposed, were in a three-way competition with *nomos*, or law, during the early patristic age and that these three came to be embodied in a synthesis in Augustine's concept of acquisitive love. The Augustinian synthesis consisted of *caritas*, or the upward love of God and the eternal, and *cupiditas*, or the downward love of the world and the temporal. According to Nygren, after medieval writers continued to build on the Augustinian synthesis, a renewal of the *agapē* motif came with Martin Luther.[16] An important expression of the medieval concept of love was the four "degrees" or stages of Bernard of Clairvaux: human beings' love of themselves for their own sake, love of God for their own benefit, love of God for God's sake, and love of themselves for God's sake.[17] Bernard's anthropocentric approach stands in marked contrast to the theocentrism of the First Epistle of John.

D. LOVE AS THE DOMINANT ATTRIBUTE

Love as an attribute of God has been elevated to a dominant and all-possessing role in the nature of God by Nels F. S. Ferré. Holiness is subordinate to love, for Ferré, and from this dominance of *agapē* he has rejected eternal hell and posited universal eschatological salvation.[18] On the other hand, Hugh Ross Mackintosh clearly sought the correlation of holiness and love. He discerningly declared that "to assert unflinchingly that love and holiness are one in God, despite their seeming antagonism, is as much the business of a true theology as to assert that deity and manhood are one in Christ."[19]

---

14. *On the Trinity* 15.17.29, 31; 15.19.37; 5.11.12; 15.17.27.
15. *In This Name: The Doctrine of the Trinity in Contemporary Theology* (New York: Charles Scribner's Sons, 1952), pp. 286, 288.
16. *Agape and Eros*, esp. pp. 30-34, 476, 483.
17. *On Loving God*, trans. Gillian R. Evans, *Bernard of Clairvaux: Selected Works*, CWS (Mahwah, N.J.: Paulist Press, 1987), pp. 173-205, esp. 192-97.
18. *The Christian Doctrine of God*, pp. 115-17, 227-28.
19. *Types of Modern Theology: Schleiermacher to Barth* (London: Nisbet, 1937), p. 159.

CHAPTER 19

Attributes Related to Love

Following our study of God as love, it is proper that we investigate those attributes of God which can appropriately be gathered or clustered around the love of God. Our purpose is not to fuse attributes or to force attributes to become synonyms; rather, it is to pursue the meaning of each and to identify its relation to love. The attributes we will consider are the patience-forbearance of God, the faithfulness of God, the mercy-compassion-kindness of God, the grace of God, and the passibility of God.

I. THE PATIENCE OR FORBEARANCE OF GOD

A. OLD TESTAMENT

In the Old Testament one finds the recurring assertion that God is "slow to anger" (*'erek 'ap*), which literally means "long of face or of anger." The deferral of divine anger in specific human situations has the effect of describing God as forbearing or patient. These affirmations about God can be found in various segments of Old Testament literature; often Yahweh's being "slow to anger" formed a part of a mosaic or cluster of attributes being ascribed to the God of the covenant. He is said to have been "slow to anger" in the giving of the two new stone tablets (Exod. 34:6b) and in response to the cowardly unbelief at Kadesh-barnea (Num. 14:18). Joel (2:13c), Jonah (4:2c), and Nahum (1:3a) acknowledged this characteristic of Yahweh, and it is also found in the Psalms (86:15b; 103:8b; 145:8b) and in Nehemiah (9:17c).

B. NEW TESTAMENT

The most frequently used New Testament word for divine patience is the noun *makrothymia*, which literally and picturesquely means "distance of wrath," but which is most often translated "forbearance" or "patience." In the conversion of Paul, Christ is said to have displayed "his unlimited patience as an example for those who would believe on him and receive eternal life" (1 Tim. 1:16b, NIV). God's "patience" was expressed "in the days of Noah while the ark was being built" (1 Pet. 3:20a), and Christians were assured that "our Lord's patience means salvation" (2 Pet. 3:15a). But the noun could also be used of God's bearing "with great patience the objects of his wrath—prepared for destruction" (Rom. 9:22). The verb *makrothymeō*, "to be longsuffering, patient," was used in juxtaposition with God's "not wanting any to perish, but everyone to come to repentance" (2 Pet. 3:9b).

Twice in the New Testament Paul used of God the word *anochē*, which was derived from the verb *anechō*, "to hold up, sustain, bear with, or endure," and which means "tolerance" or "forbearance." Unbelieving Jews ought not to "show contempt for the riches" of God's "forbearance" (Rom. 2:4, NIV), and Jesus' death was intended "to show God's righteousness, because in his divine forbearance he had passed over former sins" (Rom. 3:25b,[1] RSV). Paul expressed a similar idea in other words in his Athenian sermon (Acts 17:30, RSV): "The times of ignorance God overlooked, but now he commands all men everywhere to repent."

C. THEOLOGICAL INTERPRETATION

The patience or forbearance of God means that he does not forthwith destroy his people (Num. 14:18; Rom. 9:22), that for a time God "passes over" the sins of human beings (Rom. 3:25), and that he desires that all sinners should repent (2 Pet. 3:9). According to Karl Barth, the patience of God is

> ... His will, deep-rooted in His essence and constituting His divine being and action, to allow to another ... space and time for the development of its own existence, thus conceding to this existence a reality side by side with His own, and fulfilling His will towards this other in such a way that He does not suspend and destroy it as this other but accompanies and sustains it and allows it to develop in freedom.[2]

Emil Brunner declared that "the longsuffering of God is nothing less than the *possibility* of *history*."[3] Hence the very extension of the temporal order, in contradistinction from the immediate exercise of full and final punitive judgment, depends on the patience or forbearance of God. This divine patience, Barth asserted, is, "like His mercy," "a specific form of the divine majesty."[4]

II. THE FAITHFULNESS OF GOD

A. OLD TESTAMENT

The principal Hebrew word expressive of the faithfulness of God is the noun *'emûnāh*, meaning "faithfulness" or "stability" and derived from

1. 3:26a in Greek New Testament (UBS).
2. *Church Dogmatics*, II/1, pp. 409-10.
3. *The Christian Doctrine of God*, p. 274.
4. *Church Dogmatics*, II/1, p. 411.

the verb *'āman*, "to be faithful, to be steady." In Psalm 89 *'ĕmûnāh* is a recurring emphasis. "Faithfulness" surrounds Yahweh (v. 5), is firmly "established . . . in heaven itself" (v. 2b, NIV), and is coupled with his "steadfast love" in behalf of David (v. 24a, RSV). Hence the psalmist desires to "proclaim" Yahweh's "faithfulness to all generations" (v. 1b, RSV) and is confident that Yahweh will never "be false" to his "faithfulness" (v. 33b, RSV). Elsewhere in the Psalms Yahweh's faithfulness is proclaimed (40:10b; 92:2b) and its enduring celebrated (119:90a); his faithfulness is the basis for a prayerful plea for mercy (143:1b). Israel was betrothed to Yahweh "in faithfulness" (Hos. 2:20a), and even in the literature of distress that faithfulness is said to be "great" (Lam. 3:23). The substantive form of *'āman*, translated "the faithful," is used of God (Deut. 7:9; Isa. 49:7).

B. NEW TESTAMENT

The Greek adjective *pistos*, meaning "faithful" or "steady," was used of God in the New Testament epistles. God as "faithful" will keep believers (1 Thess. 5:24), and "the Lord," in what may be a reference to Jesus Christ, "will strengthen and protect you from the evil one" (2 Thess. 3:3, NIV). God is "faithful" in giving spiritual gifts as well as in keeping "to the end" (1 Cor. 1:7-9, NIV) and in not letting believers be tempted beyond their strength (1 Cor. 10:13b). Moreover, God as "faithful" will forgive the sins of those who confess them (1 John 1:9) and will keep his promises and confirm hope (Heb. 10:23b).

C. THEOLOGICAL INTERPRETATION

God's faithfulness is the reliability of his nature and purpose as made known by historical revelation and especially through the keeping of his promises. "For those who trust in this faithfulness, deliverance, not deserved ruin, not the righteous judgment of condemnation, is certain."[5] Millard Erickson has differentiated but correlated the genuineness of God (against the nonexistence of false gods), the veracity of God (his not lying), and the faithfulness of God (his promise-keeping).[6]

"Great is Thy faithfulness!
Great is Thy faithfulness!"
Morning by morning new mercies I see;
All I have needed Thy hand hath provided—
"Great is Thy faithfulness," Lord, unto me.[7]

---

5. Brunner, *The Christian Doctrine of God*, p. 272.
6. *Christian Theology*, pp. 289-92.
7. Thomas O. Chisholm

III. THE MERCY OR COMPASSION AND KINDNESS OF GOD

A. OLD TESTAMENT

The Old Testament word *hesed*, which in the older English translations was normally rendered "lovingkindness" or "mercy," is, as was
noted above,[8] probably better translated as "steadfast love," "covenant-
love," or "loyalty-love." Hence we have treated it in connection with the
love of God.

Another family of Hebrew words conveyed more precisely the
concept of God's mercy or compassion. The verb *rāham*, which generally
meant "to glow" or "to feel warm" and which came from the same root
as the Hebrew word for "womb," suggested a maternal or fraternal
feeling. In the Old Testament it normally was used to mean "to show or
have mercy on" another. Yahweh assured Moses: " 'I . . . will show mercy
on whom I will show mercy' " (Exod. 33:19c, RSV). Hosea declared that
Yahweh would "have pity on the house of Jacob" (1:7a), and Isaiah that
he would "have compassion on Jacob" after the Babylonian captivity
(14:1a). That same mercy or compassion was promised in regard to future
restoration (Isa. 54:8b; Jer. 33:26d). The noun for "compassion, mercy,"
rahªmîm, was used of God in connection with the killing of the inhabitants
and the destruction of the plunder of Canaanite towns (Deut. 13:17c). The
adjective *rahûm*, meaning "compassionate, merciful," appears in the
Psalms in relation to forgiveness of sins (78:38a), protection from enemies
(86:15a), remembrance of Yahweh's great deeds (111:4b), and praise of
Yahweh (145:8a). Although *rāham* had associations with the womb, it and
its cognates were used to express the divine or fatherly compassion or
mercy of Yahweh.

Related to, but distinct from the terms for mercy were the Hebrew
noun *tôb*, meaning "goodness," and its cognates. Sometimes the emphasis
was on "the goodness" of Yahweh (Exod. 33:19a; Ps. 27:13b; 31:19a; 145:7a;
2 Chr. 6:41c; and Neh. 9:25d, 35). At other times, especially in the Psalms,
Yahweh is said to be "good" (Ps. 25:7c, 8a; 34:8a; 73:1; 86:5; 100:5a; 119:68a;
135:3a; 145:9a; Nah. 1:7a).

B. NEW TESTAMENT

Paul used the Greek verb *eleeō*, meaning "to be merciful to," when
quoting Exod. 33:19c, d (Rom. 9:15) and when interpreting the same theme
of sovereign mercy (Rom. 9:18). The noun *eleos*, "mercy," was utilized to
express divine mercy in the salvation (Tit. 3:5), the making alive (Eph. 2:4),
and the being born again (1 Pet. 1:3b) of believers.

Divine mercy was also expressed in the New Testament through two
terms for the human bowels. Paul used *oiktirmos*, a noun meaning
"bowels, pity, or merciful compassion," when he appealed to the Chris-

---

8. See above, Ch. 18, I, A, 2.

tians at Rome "by the mercies of God" (Rom. 12:1, RSV) and when he referred to God as "the Father of mercies" (2 Cor. 1:3). The verb *splanch-nizomai*, meaning "to have the bowels yearning" and also "to be moved with compassion toward" or "to have compassion on," was repeatedly used in the Synoptic Gospels: of Jesus' healing of a leper (Mark 1:41), of his raising of the son of the widow of Nain (Luke 7:13), of crowds without a shepherd (Matt. 9:36), of the crowds before the feeding of the five thousand (Mark 6:34 par. Matt. 14:14) and of the four thousand (Mark 8:2 par. Matt. 15:32), of the healing of a boy with an evil spirit (Mark 9:22), and of the healing of two blind men at Jericho (Matt. 20:34).

The noun *chrēstotēs*, meaning "kindness" or "goodness," having been used as the normal Septuagint translation for the Hebrew *tôb*, was utilized by Paul; he coupled it with "forbearance and patience" (Rom. 2:4, RSV), with the "severity" *(apotomia)* of God (Rom. 11:22), with the grace of God (Eph. 2:7), and with the "lovingkindness" *(philanthrōpia)* of God (Tit. 3:4).

C. THEOLOGICAL INTERPRETATION

The biblical terms for divine mercy or compassion convey the warmth and emotion of God's very nature in the forgiving, healing, and restoring of human beings, especially sinful human beings. For Karl Barth, God's mercy was best understood as his sympathetic sharing of our human "distress."

> The mercy of God lies in His readiness to share in sympathy the distress of another, a readiness which springs from His inmost nature and stamps all His being and doing. It lies, therefore, in his will, springing from the depths of His nature and characterizing it, to take the initiative Himself for the removal of this distress. . . . In concrete the mercy of God means . . . His compassion at the sight of the suffering which man brings upon himself, His concern to remove it, His will to console man in this pain and to help him to overcome it.[9]

IV. THE GRACE OF GOD

A. OLD TESTAMENT

The Hebrew noun *ḥēn,* meaning "grace" or "favor," stood for the unmerited favor of a superior toward an inferior. The characteristic or prevailing usage of *ḥēn* in the Old Testament, however, was with respect to a person's finding or obtaining favor with God or with another human being, and only rarely did it mean God's bestowal of favor on human beings (Ps. 84:11b). The verb *ḥānan,* "to be gracious," was used in reference to God about 13 times in the Old Testament (Gen. 33:5c, 11b; 43:29c; Exod. 33:19c; Num. 6:25; 2 Sam. 12:22; 2 Kings 13:23a; Amos 5:15b; Isa. 30:18a,

---

9. *Church Dogmatics,* II/1, pp. 369, 371-72.

19b; 33:2a; Ps. 77:9a; Mal. 1:9a). The adjective *hannûn*, meaning "gracious," was used 11 times to refer to God, and always it was coupled with the adjective "compassionate" or its cognate (Exod. 34:6b; Joel 2:13b; Jon. 4:2c; Ps. 86:15a; 103:8a; 111:4b; 116:5; 145:8a; 2 Chr. 30:9b; and Neh. 9:17c, 31b).

B. New Testament

1. *Synoptic Gospels*

Luke knows only the Old Testament sense of "favor" (1:30; 2:40, 52).

2. *Pauline Epistles*

The noun *charis*, translated "grace," is principally, though not exclusively, a Pauline term. Its most central meaning seems to have been unmerited favor. This grace is the grace of God and of Jesus Christ (2 Thess. 1:12) that "has appeared for the salvation of all men" (Tit. 2:11, RSV). Even the promise to Abraham rested "on grace" (Rom. 4:16). Human beings are justified by grace (Rom. 3:24; Tit. 3:7); they are saved by grace, not by works of which they can boast (Eph. 2:8). There is "a remnant, chosen by grace" (Rom. 11:5). Through Jesus Christ human beings have "access to this grace" (Rom. 5:2). It is "glorious grace" (Eph. 1:6), grace that extends to more and more people (2 Cor. 4:15), surpassing grace (2 Cor. 9:14), and grace describable in terms of "riches" (Eph. 1:8). The grace of the preexistent Christ was demonstrated in his becoming poor (2 Cor. 8:9) and is the supreme motive for Christian giving. Through grace human beings are given "eternal comfort and good hope" (2 Thess. 2:15), and such grace abounds more than does sin and reigns to "eternal life" (Rom. 5:20-21). Paul frequently attributed his apostolic ministry to the grace of God (Gal. 1:15; 2:9; 1 Cor. 15:10; Rom. 15:15; Eph. 3:2, 7; Acts 20:24). God's grace was sufficient amid Paul's "thorn in the flesh" (2 Cor. 12:9).

3. *Acts of the Apostles*

In Acts there are various allusions to the grace of God (13:43; 14:26) and to the grace of Christ (15:11, 40).

4. *Gospel of John*

Grace is both the characteristic (1:14) and the gift (1:16-17) of the Word that "became flesh."

5. *Epistle to the Hebrews*

It was by God's grace that Jesus died for every human being (2:9). Hence believers should come boldly in prayer to "the throne of grace" to "find grace to help in time of need" (4:16). No one should fail to obtain the grace of God (12:15), and deliberate sinning leads to outraging "the Spirit of grace" (10:29).

6. Epistles of Peter

The coming of grace was prophesied (1 Pet. 1:10). Christians are to be "good stewards of God's varied grace" respecting gifts (4:10, RSV), for indeed this grace has been given "to the humble," not "to the proud" (5:5). The "God of all grace" will restore believers after their persecution (5:10), for their hope is set "upon the grace that is coming ... at the revelation of Jesus Christ" (1:13). Christians should "grow in the grace and knowledge" of Jesus Christ (2 Pet. 3:18).

From the preceding explication of the concept of grace in the New Testament it should be clear that grace, like righteousness and like love, is presented both as an attribute of God and as the gift of God to human beings.

C. HISTORY OF CHRISTIAN DOCTRINE

The doctrine of grace has been a major issue in certain noteworthy theological controversies during the postbiblical history of Christianity. In such controversies it has been grace as gift more than grace as attribute that has been at issue, though obviously there have been implications in such controversies concerning grace as attribute.

1. Augustine of Hippo versus Pelagius and the Pelagians (Fifth Century)

Augustine taught that the grace of God is absolutely necessary for sinful human beings, both for the forgiveness of their sins and for their enablement to salvation. Under pressure of controversy he insisted that divine grace is irresistible. Augustine's doctrine of God's grace is closely related to other doctrines taught by Augustine: divine sovereignty, the predestination of the elect, original sin, the loss of human *libertas* (freedom), though not of the *liberum arbitrium* (free will), and the gift of perseverance.[10]

Pelagius (c. 354-?), Caelestius (?-430s?), and Julian of Eclanum (c. 386-454) gave a diversified or unfocused interpretation to grace. It was identified as human free will, as the natural law, as the law of Moses, and as the teachings of Jesus. Grace was reckoned as supplemental to human freedom and ability.[11] The Pelagian view was condemned by the Council of Carthage (418) and by the Second Council of Orange (529).

Reaching beyond the controversy with the Pelagians, Albert Cook

---

10. G. F. Wiggers, *An Historical Presentation of Augustinism and Pelagianism from the Original Sources* (Andover, Mass.: Gould, Newman and Saxton, 1840; reprint ed.; Ann Arbor, Mich., London: University Microfilms International, 1979), pp. 194-218; Eugène Portalié, S.J., *A Guide to the Thought of Saint Augustine*, trans. Ralph J. Bastian, S.J. (Chicago: Henry Regnery Company, 1960), pp. 177-84, 190-229; Kelly, *Early Christian Doctrines*, pp. 366-69.

11. Wiggers, *An Historical Presentation of Augustinism and Pelagianism*, pp. 177-94, 219-28; Portalié, *A Guide to the Thought of Saint Augustine*, pp. 184-89; Robert F. Evans, *Pelagius: Inquiries and Reappraisals* (New York: Seabury Press, 1968), pp. 109-13; Kelly, *Early Christian Doctrines*, pp. 359-60.

Outler (1908-89) has summarized Augustine's entire doctrine of grace as follows:

> The central theme in all Augustine's writings is the sovereign God of grace and the sovereign grace of God. Grace, for Augustine, is God's freedom to act without any external necessity whatsoever—to act in love beyond human understanding or control; to act in creation, judgment, and redemption; to give his Son freely as Mediator and Redeemer; to endue the Church with the indwelling power and guidance of the Holy Spirit; to shape the destinies of all creation and the ends of the two human societies, the 'city of earth' and the 'city of God.' Grace is God's unmerited love and favor, prevenient and occurrent. It touches man's inmost heart and will. It guides and impels the pilgrimage of those called to be faithful. It draws and raises the soul to repentance, faith, and praise. It transforms the human will so that it is capable of doing good. It relieves man's religious anxiety by forgiveness and the gift of hope. It establishes the ground of humility by abolishing the ground of human pride. God's grace became incarnate in Jesus Christ, and it remains immanent in the Holy Spirit in the Church.[12]

Western medieval Catholicism tended to distort the meaning of grace by interpreting it as a quasi-substantial and supernatural reality, a thing to be obtained by means of the sacraments and also by merits gained through good works.

2. High Calvinists of the Synod of Dort versus Arminians or Remonstrants (Early Seventeenth Century)

The High Calvinists taught predestination as the eternal divine predetermination of the elect humans and the nonelect humans apart from any prescience of the human responses; particular atonement, or the doctrine that Christ's death intended to and actually did provide atonement only for the sins of the elect; the irresistibility of grace; faith and repentance as the gifts of God; and the gift of perseverance to the elect only.

On the contrary, the Arminians taught election as God's prescience of which human beings would repent and believe and hence the divine choice of them; general atonement, or the doctrine that Christ's death intended to and does make available atonement for the sins of all humankind; the resistibility of grace; faith as a human response to the regenerating work of the Holy Spirit; and the possibility of lapse from the grace of God by true believers.[13]

The Calvinist-Arminian controversy was not decisively settled

---

12. "Introduction," in Outler, ed., *Augustine: Confessions and Enchiridion*, LCC, vol. 7 (Philadelphia: Westminster Press, 1955), pp. 14-15.

13. George L. Curtiss, *Arminianism in History, or the Revolt from Predestinationism* (Cincinnati: Cranston and Curts; New York: Hunt and Eaton, 1894), esp. ch. 1; Clarence A. Beckwith, "Arminius, Jacobus, and Arminianism," *New Schaff-Herzog Encyclopedia of Religious Knowledge*, 1:296-98; Archibald Harold Walter Harrison, *Arminianism* (London: Duckworth, 1937); Carl Bangs, *Arminius: A Study in the Dutch Reformation* (Nashville: Abingdon Press, 1971), esp. chs. 13–15, 25–26.

during the seventeenth century but produced differing theological traditions that have survived to the present.

3. Jansenists versus Jesuits (Seventeenth and Eighteenth Centuries)

Cornelius Jansen (1585-1638) and his associates taught in the Roman
Catholic Church a new Augustinianism that was similar to the position
of the High Calvinists but different from the then prevailing teaching in
his own church. The Jesuits resisted Jansenism, especially its doctrines of
predestination and perseverance, magnified human faith and works, and
prevailed over the Jansenists, although some Jansenist teachings have
been upheld by the Dominicans.[14]

Not as an extension or a renewal of these controversies, although his
sympathies with Augustine and the High Calvininsts would likely not be
disputed, Karl Barth magnified the doctrine of the grace of God, particularly in respect to the divine condescension.

> Grace is the distinctive mode of God's being in so far as it seeks and creates
> fellowship by its own free inclination and favour, unconditioned by any
> merit or claim in the beloved, but also unhindered by any unworthiness or
> opposition in the latter—able, on the contrary, to overcome all unworthiness
> and opposition. . . . But grace means a turning, not in equality, but in
> condescension. The fact that God is gracious means that He condescends,
> He, the only One who is really in a position to condescend, because He alone
> is truly transcendent, and stands on an equality with nothing outside
> Himself. His inmost being in grace is that He wills not to remain in this
> position. . . . His condescension is free, i.e., conditioned only by His own
> will. . . . It is thus a gift in this strictest sense of the term.[15]

V. THE PASSIBILITY OF GOD

By "passibility" is meant the ability or capacity of God to suffer or to
experience pain or sorrow. If there is such a thing as the passion or
suffering of God, then obviously God has the ability or capacity to suffer.
The crucial question, therefore, is: Does God suffer?

For many centuries orthodox Christian theology has asserted the
impassibility of God.[16] The inability of God to suffer was a Hellenistic idea

---

14. Paul Tschackert, "Jansen, Cornelius, . . . Jansenismus," *Realencyklopädie für protes-
tantische Theologie und Kirche*, 24 vols. (Leipzig: J. C. Hinrichs, 1900), 8:589-99; idem, "Jansen,
Cornelius, Jansenism," *New Schaff-Herzog Encyclopedia of Religious Knowledge*, 6:95-98; J. Forget, "Jansenius and Jansenism," *The Catholic Encyclopedia*, 16 vols. (New York: Robert
Appleton Company, 1907-14), 8:285-94; Nigel J. Abercrombie, *The Origins of Jansenism* (Oxford: Clarendon Press, 1936), part 1; L. J. Cognet, "Jansenism," *New Catholic Encyclopedia*, 17
vols. (New York: McGraw-Hill, 1967), 7:820-24; Dale Van Kley, *The Jansenists and the Expulsion
of the Jesuits from France, 1757-1765* (New Haven: Yale University Press, 1975), pp. 6-36;
W. Davish, "Jansen, Cornelius Otto" and "Jansenism," *Encyclopedic Dictionary of Religion*, 3
vols. (Washington, D.C.: Corpus Publications, 1979), 2:1867-68.

15. *Church Dogmatics*, II/1, pp. 353-55.

16. J. K. Mozley, *The Impassibility of God: A Survey of Christian Thought* (Cambridge:
University Press, 1926), traced the history of this doctrine and its modern rejection.

that first penetrated Christian thought during the patristic age, during which time various Church Fathers embraced and defended it.[17] It was repeated and widely accepted as being essential to the transcendence of God. The suffering of Jesus, especially in the crucifixion, was reserved for his human nature, and conversely it was denied that he suffered in his divine nature. Impassibility has its advocates today.[18]

During the twentieth century various Christian thinkers have critically reassessed impassibility and insisted that God has suffered or does suffer. Geoffrey Anketell Studdert-Kennedy (1883-1929), a British army chaplain,[19] and Bertrand R. Brasnett, an Episcopal theologian in Scotland,[20] posed the question after World War I, and Kazoh Kitamori (1916-), a Japanese Christian theologian who perhaps was influenced by the Buddhist concept of *Dukka* (suffering), explicated the pain of God after World War II.[21] The passion of God has become a significant theme in Protestant theology.[22]

But does passibility have any basis in the Bible? Kitamori cited Jer. 31:20c (NIV), "Therefore my heart *yearns* for him [Ephraim]; I have great compassion for him," and 1 Pet. 2:24c, "By his *wounds* you have been healed." But is not Christ's suffering the focus of the latter text?

At least two questions about the passion of God need to be raised. First, can the passion of God the Father be postulated and defended apart from and in addition to the suffering of Jesus Christ as the Son of God? To establish the passion of God, one must do more than assert that Jesus suffered on the cross. Second, can a modern Christian doctrine of God's suffering escape the pitfall of second-century Patripassianism, also called Modalism, which said that God the Father suffered and died on the cross? Can modern exponents of God's passion avoid saying or implying that the Father was crucified? To say with Paul that "God was in Christ reconciling the world to himself" (2 Cor. 5:19, NASV) does not mean that God the Father was Christ or that Christ was God the Father.

Despite the attendant problems and questions, it seems to be neces-

17. George Leonard Prestige, *God in Patristic Thought* (London: S.P.C.K., 1952), pp. 6-9, 11-12.

18. Richard E. Creel, *Divine Impassibility: An Essay in Philosophical Theology* (Cambridge: University Press, 1986).

19. *The Hardest Part* (London: Hodder and Stoughton, 1919), pp. 12-14, 41-47, 61-62, 67-72, 114-15, 132-35, 138, 147-48, 153, 187, 193, 201; *The Sorrows of God and Other Poems* (New York: Richard R. Smith, Inc., 1930), pp. 12-14, 121-26.

20. *The Suffering of the Impassible God* (London: S.P.C.K., 1928).

21. *Theology of the Pain of God,* trans. unspecif. (Richmond, Va.: John Knox Press, 1965). Kitamori repeatedly referred to "love rooted in the pain of God," but esp. on pp. 111-12, 117-27, 160-67.

22. Charles Ohlrich, *The Suffering God: Hope and Comfort for Those Who Hurt* (Downers Grove, Ill.: Inter-Varsity Press, 1982); Terence E. Fretheim, *The Suffering of God: An Old Testament Perspective* (Philadelphia: Fortress Press, 1984); Warren McWilliams, *The Passion of God: Divine Suffering in Contemporary Protestant Theology* (Macon, Ga.: Mercer University Press, 1985); John W. de Gruchy, *Standing by God in His Hour of Grieving: Human Suffering, Theological Reflection, and Christian Solidarity* (Pretoria: University of South Africa, 1986).

sary to affirm that God has the capacity to suffer, for he has participated in suffering.

Summary: Patience or forbearance is the persistence of God's love. Faithfulness is the reliability of God's love. Mercy-kindness is the deep compassion of God's love. Grace is the free and undeserved condescension of God's love. Suffering is the assumed and endured pain of God's love.

CHAPTER 20

God as Father

In a previous treatment of the names of God we noted that "Father" was one of the analogical names used of God in the Bible, especially in the New Testament.[1] Now that we have interpreted and correlated the various attributes of God, it becomes necessary, prior to consideration of the Father, the Son, and the Holy Spirit in their Trinitarian relationship, to investigate the nature and viability of the concept of God as Father.

I. THE OLD TESTAMENT

In all three major divisions of the Hebrew Bible Yahweh was referred to as Father. This paternal relationship applied particularly to the covenant people of Israel rather than to individuals or to all humankind.

Yahweh's fatherly relation to the Israelites was expressed both in Egypt and in the wilderness: "And you shall say to Pharaoh, 'Thus says the LORD, Israel is my first-born son, and I say to you, "Let my son go that he may serve me"; and if you refuse to let him go, behold, I will slay your first-born son'" (Exod. 4:22-23, RSV). Both in Egypt and in the wilderness, Moses declared, "you have seen how the LORD your God bore you, as a man bears his son, in all the way that you went until you came to this place" (Deut. 1:31). "Know then in your heart that, as a man disciplines his son, the LORD your God disciplines you" (Deut. 8:5). The laws of clean and unclean foods were prefaced with the declaration, "You are the children of the LORD your God" (Deut. 14:1a). The question, "Is he not your father, who created you, who made you and established you?" (Deut. 32:6b), probably referred to the creation of the covenant people.

According to Hosea, "in the place where it was said to them, 'You are not my people,' it shall be said to them, 'Sons of the living God'" (1:10b). Historically, "When Israel was a child, I loved him, and out of Egypt I called my son" (Hos. 11:1). A Son of David text that is usually interpreted messianically contains the title "Everlasting Father" (Isa. 9:6c). "For thou art our Father, though Abraham does not know us and Israel

---

1. See above, Ch. 13, II, B, 2.

252

does not acknowledge us; thou, O LORD, art our Father, our Redeemer from of old is thy name" (Isa. 63:16). "I thought you would call me, My Father, and would not turn from following me" (Jer. 3:19b). Judah will be restored, "for I am a father to Israel, and Ephraim is my first-born" (Jer. 31:9c). "Have we not all one father? Has not one God created us?" (Mal. 2:10a) seems to refer to the fatherly creation of the covenant people.

In the Psalms divine fatherhood is an analogy rather than a title. "Father of the fatherless and protector of widows is God in his holy habitation" (68:5). "As a father pities his children, so the Lord pities those who fear him" (103:13).

George Angus Fulton Knight (1909-) set forth the dubious hypothesis that the Father-Son principle is part of the essence of God and thus eternal and that God tried to bestow sonship on Israel, but his plan was wrecked by Israel's disobedience.[2] Joachim Jeremias concluded that in the Old Testament God was never addressed in prayer as "Father." Jeremias found a few examples of such in postcanonical Diaspora Judaism.[3]

II. THE NEW TESTAMENT

A. SYNOPTIC GOSPELS

1. *Jesus' Usage in General*

Jesus' favorite designation of God was "Father."[4] Jesus did not "break new ground" but made this truth a living reality as never before.[5] Jesus, according to W. T. Conner, did three things for the concept of God as Father.

> He made fatherhood the controlling idea in God's relation to men. . . . He put a new ethical quality into the idea of fatherhood as applied to God. . . . And he made this a living conception as applied to the relation between the individual worshiper and God.[6]

2. *Jesus' Term*

Jesus evidently used the Aramaic term "'*abbā*'" (Mark 14:36; compare Gal. 4:6; Rom. 8:15). According to Jeremias, the Jews did not use '*abbā*' in reference to God,[7] but it seems to have been Jesus' common term of address in praying to God.

---

2. *A Biblical Approach to the Doctrine of the Trinity*, Scottish Journal of Theology Occasional Papers, no. 1 (Edinburgh: Oliver and Boyd, 1953), pp. 66-73.

3. *New Testament Theology*, pp. 63-64.

4. Conner, *The Faith of the New Testament*, p. 96.

5. Henry Maldwyn Hughes, *The Christian Idea of God* (London: Duckworth; New York: Charles Scribner's Sons, 1936), ch. 5.

6. *The Faith of the New Testament*, p. 96.

7. *New Testament Theology*, pp. 63-67.

3. Specific Texts

a. Sermon on the Mount (Matthew)

The word *patēr* was used five times with the singular adjective "thy Father" or "your Father" (6:4, 6, 18). It was used three times with the plural adjective "your Father" (5:45; 6:1, 15b). The term "your heavenly Father" was employed four times (5:48; 6:14, 26, 32). Once we find "your Father who is in heaven" (7:11b). In addition to and in distinction from the foregoing 13 usages of "Father" in reference to Jesus' disciples, there are two others in the Matthean form of the Sermon on the Mount, namely, "Our Father who art in heaven" (6:9), and "my Father who is in heaven" (7:21).

b. Miscellaneous Synoptic Sayings

Matthew included a saying that reminds the modern reader of the Johannine materials:

> "I thank thee, Father, Lord of heaven and earth. . .; yea, Father, for such was thy gracious will. All things have been delivered to me by my Father; and no one knows the Son except the Father, and no one knows the Father except the Son and any one to whom the Son chooses to reveal him." (11:25-27, RSV)

The one who " 'does the will of my Father in heaven is my brother, and sister, and mother' " (Matt. 12:50). Not a single sparrow " 'will fall to the ground without your Father's will' " (Matt. 10:29). Jesus " 'will acknowledge before my Father who is in heaven' " every human being who acknowledges him before others, and conversely he " 'will deny before my Father who is in heaven' " everyone who denies him before others (Matt. 10:32-33). The same Father in heaven has revealed to Simon Peter that Jesus is the Messiah (Matt. 16:17). If evil humans, said Jesus, give "good gifts" to their children, " 'how much more will the heavenly Father give the Holy Spirit to those who ask him!' " (Luke 11:13). Jesus' disciples are not to address other humans as "father," " 'for you have one Father, who is in heaven' " (Matt. 23:9). At the final judgment the "sheep" are to be addressed as " 'blessed of my Father' " (Matt. 25:34).

c. Passion Sayings of Jesus

In the Gethsemane narrative "My Father" is used twice with regard to the possible avoidance of the "cup" of suffering (Matt. 26:39, 42). The same term is used in the saying about possible help from angels (Matt. 26:53). Two of the seven sayings of Jesus issued while on the cross contain the name "Father," used in the vocative: " 'Father, forgive them; for they know not what they do' " (Luke 23:34), and " 'Father, into thy hands I commit my spirit' " (Luke 23:46).

B. PAULINE EPISTLES

Paul alluded to God as Father in his epistolary salutations and in connection with the adoption of believers as sons to God. Among the epistolary salutations reference is made to "God the Father" (1 Thess. 1:1; 2 Thess. 1:2; Gal. 1:1; 1 Tim. 1:2; 2 Tim. 1:2; Tit. 1:4), to "God our Father" (1 Cor. 1:3; 2 Cor. 1:2; Rom. 1:7; Eph. 1:2; Phil. 1:2; Col. 1:2), to "the God and Father of our Lord Jesus Christ" (2 Cor. 1:3; Eph. 1:3), and to "God, the Father of our Lord Jesus Christ" (Col. 1:3). When Paul referred to the adoption of believers as sons to God, he declared that believers call God 'abbā' at the instigation of and with the confirmation of the Holy Spirit (Gal. 4:5-6; Rom. 8:15-16).

C. JOHANNINE WRITINGS

The emphasis in the Gospel and the First Epistle is on the Father-Son relationship. Therein the Father is almost exclusively Father to the Son of God or the only Son, Jesus.

1. Gospel of John

a. The Son vis-à-vis the Father

The Son (Logos) was in the beginning with the Father, was God, is the only Son from the Father (1:1, 14, 18; compare 3:16-18), and has his being in the Father (14:20). The Son knows the Father even as the Father knows the Son (10:15). The Son has been sent by, or is on mission from, the Father (5:36b, 37, 38; 6:57; 10:36-38; 13:3; 20:21), and the Son comes in the Father's name (5:43). The Son depends on the Father (5:19), singularly sees the Father (6:46), honors the Father (8:49), and obeys and loves the Father (14:31). He knows "the righteous Father" in contrast to the world's not knowing him (17:25).

The Son speaks on the Father's authority (8:27-28, 38), utters the word of the Father (14:24) and the command of the Father (12:49-50), and speaks plainly of the Father apart from figures (16:25). The Son is the mediator of the knowledge of the Father as the only way of entry to the Father and as the adequate revealer of the Father (14:6-9). The works of the Son done in the Father's name call for faith (10:31) and bear witness to the Son (10:25). The Son and the Father "are one" (10:30).

The Son prays to the Father for the glorification of the Father's name (12:27-28) and for the Father's glorification of the Son so that the Son may glorify the Father with the Son's preexistent glory (17:1, 5). The Son prays to the Father for the giving of the Holy Spirit (14:16-17), and the Son is to send from the Father to believers the Spirit, who proceeds from the Father (15:26). The Son prays that the "Holy Father" may keep those given to him by the Father so that these may be one as the Father and the Son are one (17:11). The Son likewise prays for the unity of present and future believers after the analogy of the unity of the Father and the Son "so that the world may believe that" the Father has sent the Son (17:20-21). Moreover, the Son prays that believers may be with the Son in order to behold the Father's eternal glorification of the Son (17:24).

The Son is to drink the cup given to him by the Father (18:11) and is to take again his life with the power and authority of the Father (10:18). The Son has not yet ascended to the Father (20:17), yet he is about to leave the world and go to the Father, who is greater than the Son (13:3; 14:28; 16:10, 17, 28). Moses, not the Son, is to accuse unbelievers before the Father (5:45), and the Son will vivify "whom he will" and administer that final judgment given to him by the Father (5:21-22).

b. The Father vis-à-vis the Son

The Father gives the "true bread from heaven" (6:32) and is present with the Son (16:32). The Father loves the Son "and shows him all that he himself is doing" (3:35a; 5:20a), sets his seal on him (6:27), and glorifies him (8:54). He gives all things into the hand(s) of the Son (3:35b; 13:3), for all that which belongs to the Father belongs to the Son (16:15). The temple in Jerusalem is "my Father's house" (2:16). The Father bears witness to the Son (8:18-19) and draws believers to the Son (6:44-45; compare 6:65). The Father, who indwells the Son, performs such works as call for human believing (14:10-11). The Father hears the Son's prayer regarding Lazarus (11:41), and prayer in the name of the Son is to be granted in order that the Father may be glorified (14:12-14; 15:16; 16:23). The Father is to send the Holy Spirit in the name of the Son (14:26). The Father's love of the Son is attributed to the Son's giving of his life (10:17). The Father has a heavenly "house" (14:2).

c. Believers/Disciples vis-à-vis the Father and the Son

Those given by the Father to the Son will come to the Son, believe in him, and have "eternal life" (6:37, 40). Disciples are to worship "the Father in spirit and truth" (4:21-24). Those who have God as their Father will love the Son, who proceeded from the Father (8:42). The one who loves the Son is beloved by the Father (14:21, 23), and the Father honors the one who serves the Son (12:26). The Father loves disciples because they have loved the Son and have believed that the Son came from the Father (16:27). The Son makes known to his disciples all that the Son has heard from the Father (15:15). The Father as the vinedresser is glorified by the fruit-bearing of disciples, by their loving the Son, and by their obeying the Son (15:1, 8-10). Believers are to perform greater works than the works of the Son because the Son will go to the Father (14:12). No one shall snatch away the Son's "sheep" out of the hand of the Father, who is "greater than all" (10:29). Persecutors of the disciples have known neither the Father nor the Son (16:3), and the one who hates the Son hates the Father also (15:23-24).

References to God as "Father" or "the Father" are found in at least 62 different passages in the Gospel of John. In only four chapters (7, 9, 19, 21) is there no reference. Unquestionably divine fatherhood is a major theme in this gospel.

2. *First Epistle of John*

In 11 usages the term is uniformly "the Father." Sometimes the Father-Son relationship is prominent, as in the Son's eternal presence with the Father (1:2b), in the Father's sending of the Son (4:14), and in denial or confession (2:22b-23). In other contexts the Father loves the "children of God" (3:1) and Jesus is "an advocate with the Father" (2:1b). Elsewhere, the focus is on disciples' knowing the Father (2:13c), loving the Father (2:15b), having fellowship with the Father and the Son (1:3c), and abiding in the Son and the Father (2:24b).

III. THE HISTORY OF CHRISTIAN DOCTRINE

A. APOSTLES' CREED

The term "Father" was used in the initial or first confession of the Old Roman Symbol (R), or the Apostles' Creed: "God the Father Almighty, Maker of heaven and earth." The fact that power and creatorship were closely associated with fatherhood may have been the result of anti-Gnostic considerations.

B. ARIAN CONTROVERSY

The term "Father" as applied to God figured prominently in the fourth-century Arian controversy, but chiefly in respect to the Son's relationship to the Father, not to the scope of God's fatherhood respecting human beings.[8]

C. TWENTIETH-CENTURY LIBERAL PROTESTANTS AND EVANGELICAL PROTESTANTS

The fatherhood of God has been a divisive issue between Liberal and Evangelical Protestants during the present century. Three areas of disagreement can be identified:

1. Is God's fatherhood respecting its scope universal or particular? Liberal Protestants have normally affirmed it as universal, whereas Evangelical Protestants have taught that it is particular. Liberals have appealed to the parable of the prodigal son (Luke 15:11-32), asserting that the prodigal never ceased to be his father's son while in the "far country." They cite Matt: 5:45, a text about love of enemies: "so that you may be sons of your Father who is in heaven; for he makes his sun to rise on the evil and on the good, and sends rain on the just and on the unjust" (RSV). According to William Newton Clarke (1841-1912), "in the parable the natural relation

---

8. For a more detailed treatment of the history of this doctrine prior to the twentieth century, see John Scott Lidgett, *The Fatherhood of God* (Edinburgh: T. and T. Clark, 1902; Minneapolis: Bethany House Publishers, 1987), pp. 72-149 (1987 ed.); William Boothby Selbie, *The Fatherhood of God* (New York: Charles Scribner's Sons, 1936), pp. 63-81.

of father and son was never altered."[9] Evangelicals, on the other hand, have stressed that the New Testament emphasis is on God as "the Father of our Lord Jesus Christ" and as the Father of the regenerate, or Christians, and that a specific text that clearly teaches universal fatherhood is lacking. Evangelicals have cited the Pauline texts concerning adoption as sons and the following passages: Matt. 13:38; John 1:12; 8:44; and Gal. 3:26. According to Carl F. H. Henry, "divine fatherhood" is not "an automatic derivative" from monotheism, for "[n]either Judaism . . . nor Mohammedanism . . . developed a conviction of divine fatherhood which commends itself to the New Testament mood." Indeed, "it is only in trinitarian theism, and not in the philosophical theisms or the religious theisms which argue for a unipersonal deity, that there has arisen a concept of divine fatherhood which possesses the warmth of the Biblical view."[10]

There have been efforts to harmonize or reconcile the universal divine fatherhood and the particular, the universal sonship to God and the particular. In addition to the thoroughgoing positions on either side, that is, the exclusively universalistic and the exclusively particularistic, E. Y. Mullins listed three efforts at harmonization. First, some would hold that God's fatherhood is universal but that sonship among human beings is particular. Hence the unchangeable God is Father to all humankind, but only Christians are "sons of God." But one may ask whether some reciprocity is not essential to a genuine father-son relationship. Second, others would differentiate natural sonship and spiritual sonship. Hence "all men are natural sons of God, but only believers in Christ are true spiritual sons." Can these two categories always and precisely be separated? Third, yet others would differentiate potential sonship and actual sonship, so that "all men are constituted for sonship to God, and . . . God desires all men to become sons," but only Christians are the actual or real sons of God. Accordingly, unregenerate humans have "a filial character" or "constitution," but the "relation" has been lost through sin. Thus a potential son can become an actual son only by being born anew through faith or by adoption as sons. Mullins favored the third view.[11]

2. Is divine fatherhood grounded primarily in creation or in redemption? The answers to this second question tend to be correlatable with the answers to the first question. Those who have stressed universal fatherhood have tended to ground fatherhood in creation, whereas those who have stressed particular fatherhood have tended to ground fatherhood in redemption. Clarke found the basis for divine fatherhood in creation,[12] and Henry held that it was mainly grounded in redemption.[13]

3. Is divine fatherhood somewhat antithetical to divine sovereignty,

9. *The Christian Doctrine of God* (Edinburgh: T. and T. Clark, 1912), p. 156.
10. *Notes on the Doctrine of God*, pp. 94-95.
11. *The Christian Religion in Its Doctrinal Expression*, pp. 401-6.
12. *The Christian Doctrine of God*, p. 161.
13. *Notes on the Doctrine of God*, pp. 98-100.

or can these two be correlated? Clarke sought a harmonization of the two by asserting that "sovereignty is grounded in the true Father's right and power to govern his spiritual offspring" and limiting his sovereignty "over men" to "a manner accordant with his own nature."[14] Some interpreters of divine fatherhood as universal have turned divine love toward sentimentality and God's fatherhood into an indulgent grandfatherhood.[15] The Jewish concept of fatherhood contemporaneous with Jesus involved roles of family leadership and discipline, and such a factor helps to make possible the rightful correlation of fatherhood and sovereignty, at least in the New Testament setting.[16]

IV. THE CONTEMPORARY DOCTRINE

The Christian doctrine of God as Father faces today various challenges to its tenability so that the task of the Christian theologian is not merely expository but also apologetic. In modern Western civilization, especially during the nineteenth and twentieth centuries but also earlier, there have been revolts against or rejections of the entire concept of divine fatherhood. W. A. Visser 't Hooft has traced these rejections. He reaches back to Baruch Spinoza's *"Deus sive natura"* (god or nature) and to François Marie Arouet de Voltaire's (1694-1778) rejection of divine providence. He cites Percy Bysshe Shelley's (1792-1822) revolt against Jupiter in *Prometheus Unbound*, the projectionism of Marx, Friedrich Wilhelm Nietzsche, and Freud, and the thought of the anarchists (Pierre Joseph Proudhon, 1809-65, and Michael Bakunin, 1814-76), who held that "faith in God the Father was not merely an illusion or a malady" but "the source of all evil in current society."[17] As a sequel to these rejections, Hubertus Tellenbach (1914-), a German psychiatrist, has contended that "the father figure has all but vanished from the western psyche."[18]

It is now desirable to examine in greater detail three forms of the contemporary rejection of divine fatherhood.

A. FREUDIAN PSYCHOANALYSIS

Sigmund Freud taught the Oedipus theory, according to which the Greek mythological Oedipus killed his father and married his mother, with disastrous consequences, and this deed is relived in every human being's struggle for independence from parents. Freud also reinterpreted Israelite history by positing that Moses was murdered by the Israelites and that Israelites suppressed the account thereof. Hence the memory of the

---

14. *The Christian Doctrine of God*, pp. 167, 168.
15. For a refutation of such a view, see Hughes, *The Christian Idea of God*, p. 139.
16. Ibid., pp. 113-19; Henry, *Notes on the Doctrine of God*, ch. 7.
17. *The Fatherhood of God in an Age of Emancipation* (Philadelphia: Westminster Press; Geneva: World Council of Churches, 1982), ch. 11.
18. Quoted by Robert Hamerton-Kelly, *God the Father: Theology and Patriarchy in the Teaching of Jesus* (Philadelphia: Fortress Press, 1979), p. 4.

murder of their father figure Moses has brought guilt on Jews. For Freud God as Father "is only a human memory, rather than a divine being," and consequently rejection of divine fatherhood is "essential for human maturity and sanity."[19] The Freudian perspective militates against any positive appropriation of biblical imagery about divine fatherhood.

B. Child Abuse and Neglect

The viability and usefulness of fatherhood as a leading analogy for God has been severely challenged, especially in Western and industrialized societies, by the widespread occurrence of child abuse and child neglect by human fathers. Because human fathers have perpetrated such deeds and have been guilty of such neglect and abandonment, the concept of God as Father does not convey for these children the positive connotations of care, protection, love, sacrifice, and wholesome discipline. This is the testimony of clinical psychologists, family counselors, social workers, and others.

C. Women's Liberation Movement

The radical wing of the Women's Liberation movement has challenged and rejected the use of paternal language in reference to God. Paternal language is seen as indicative of a patriarchal human fatherhood that suppresses women and denies to them their legitimate role and rights.[20] Mary Daly (1928-) has called for the "liberation," "castration," and "exorcism" of the language of the doctrine of God, charging that patriarchy has led to "rape, genocide, and war."[21]

What should be the Christian response to such rejections of the concept of God's fatherhood? Christians can seek to "de-patriarchalize" the language and concept of God as Father and yet to preserve the abidingly valid dimensions of divine fatherhood. To do this, Christians need to be reminded of Jesus' use of the term 'abbā', the filial consciousness toward God that he manifested in giving the Lord's Prayer, his placement of discipleship above family ties, his teaching and associating with women, his parables of the laborers in the vineyard and of the prodigal son, and his teaching and example concerning servanthood, not domination. Patriarchalism, on the other hand, "is resistance to the process of emancipation," competition for power between father and son, "the abuse of a father's power," and treatment of women "as second-rate beings." Hence, according to Visser 't Hooft, the "revolt against the Father-God is . . . to a very considerable extent a revolt against a caricature of the true God whom we come to know through Jesus."[22]

---

19. Hamerton-Kelly, *God the Father*, pp. 7-13, 18.

20. Langdon Gilkey, *Message and Existence*, ch. 4, has revised the Apostles' Creed so as to read: "I believe in God the Parent Almighty."

21. *Beyond God the Father: Toward a Philosophy of Women's Liberation* (Boston: Beacon Press, 1973), pp. 7-11, 114-22; Hamerton- Kelly, *God the Father*, pp. 5, 118.

22. *The Fatherhood of God in an Age of Emancipation*, pp. 119-27.

In response to the radical feminism of the latter twentieth century, is it necessary to affirm the motherhood of God? First, it should be noted that there are some biblical texts, especially in Isaiah, in which maternal features are ascribed to God. Indeed, "as little mother birds hovering so will Jehovah of hosts protect Jerusalem" (Isa. 42:14, George Adam Smith). Following a time of restrained silence "now I will cry out like a woman in travail, I will gasp and pant" (Isa. 42:14, RSV). "'Can a woman forget her sucking child that she should have no compassion on the son of her womb?'" (Isa. 49:15). "'As one whom his mother comforts, so will I comfort you'" (Isa. 66:16).[23] "'O Jerusalem, Jerusalem, killing the prophets and stoning those who are sent to you! How often would I have gathered your children together as a hen gathers her brood under her wings, and you would not!'" (Luke 13:34). Second, it should be remembered that biblical religion, being confronted with the fertility goddesses of surrounding nations—"Ishtar of Babylonia, Cybele, the Great Mother of Phrygia, Astarte and Asjeria of Syria, Anoth of Canaan," and Diana of the Ephesians—with their accompanying ritual prostitution, maintained "a clear reticence with regard to symbolism which could be interpreted as describing God as a mother goddess." That same reticence was characteristic of the Church Fathers, who confronted the Gnostic use of Helena as the consort of Simon Magus, the ascription of femininity to the Holy Spirit, and the ethical extremes of asceticism and promiscuity.[24] Third, late twentieth-century Christians, recalling how both the Shakers under Ann Lee (1736-84)[25] and Christian Science under Mary Baker Eddy[26] espoused the concept of a Father-Mother God, should "maintain a certain reserve in speaking of the motherhood of God."[27]

Visser 't Hooft has concluded:

> God transcends the difference of the sexes. We call him Father because Jesus has taught us to do so, and to cease so to call him is to cease to pray as Jesus enjoined us. To refuse to use any reference to God as "He" and to choose terms such as "the divine being" or "the Deity" is to depersonalize God. The fatherhood of God is however not a closed or exclusive symbolism. It is open to correction, enrichment, and completion from other forms of symbol, such as "mother," "brother," "sister," and "friend."[28]

23. Compare Ps. 17:8; 36:7; and 63:7.

24. Visser 't Hooft, *The Fatherhood of God in an Age of Emancipation,* pp. 130-32.

25. Shakers after the death of Ann Lee taught a "dual messiahship" (Jesus, Ann Lee), two "Heavenly Parents" (Jesus, Ann Lee), and even a "quaternity" (God the Father, the Son of God, Holy Mother Wisdom, Daughter Ann Lee), according to Edward Deming Andrews, *The People Called Shakers: A Search for the Perfect Society* (enl. ed.; New York: Dover Publications, 1963), pp. 97, 154-58, 222. See also the various excerpted passages from nineteenth-century Shaker authors about the Father-Mother God and the editor's introduction to these texts in Robley Edward Whiston, ed., *The Shakers: Two Centuries of Spiritual Reflection,* CWS (New York: Paulist Press, 1983), pp. 207-57.

26. Mary Baker Eddy, *Science and Health with Key to the Scriptures* (1913 ed.), pp. 16, 331, 332, 335, 569, 577, 592, 691-92.

27. Visser 't Hooft, *The Fatherhood of God in an Age of Emancipation,* p. 132.

28. Ibid., p. 133.

CHAPTER 21

The Trinity:
Introduction and Biblical Materials

Before we undertake any explication of the Christian doctrine of the
Trinity, including an investigation of the biblical materials related to this
significant subject, it is appropriate that we ask and answer two basic and
preliminary questions. One of these concerns the location or positioning
of the doctrine of the Trinity in a systematic theology, and the other
pertains to the relation between the doctrine of the Trinity and the phenomenon of divine revelation.

I. INTRODUCTION TO THE TRINITY

A. WHERE IN A CHRISTIAN SYSTEMATIC THEOLOGY SHOULD THE DOCTRINE OF THE TRINITY BE LOCATED?

F. D. E. Schleiermacher placed the Trinity in the final subsection
of *The Christian Faith*.[1] Albrecht Ritschl did not treat the Trinity in
systematic fashion.[2] On the other hand, Charles Wesley Lowry (1905-)
stated that "the most important question that a theologian can ask is: 'Is
the Christian Religion a Trinitarian Religion?' "[3] Karl Barth in his *Church
Dogmatics* placed the Trinity at the very beginning of his system (ch. 2),
or at least immediately after the doctrine of the Word of God (ch. 1).[4]
Barth protested against the plan of treating the doctrine of revelation,
the existence of God, and the divine attributes in detail and then of
proceeding to treat the Trinity. His major objection to such a plan was
as follows:

> It is the doctrine of the Trinity which fundamentally distinguishes the
> Christian doctrine of God as Christian—it is it, therefore, also, which marks

1. Pp. 738-51.
2. *The Christian Doctrine of Justification and Reconciliation;* Claude Welch, *In This Name:
The Doctrine of the Trinity in Contemporary Theology* (New York: Scribner, 1952), p. 19.
3. *The Trinity and Christian Devotion* (New York, London: Harper and Brothers, 1946),
p. 47.
4. I/1, chs. 2, 1.

off the Christian concept of revelation as Christian, in face of all other possible doctrines of God and concepts of revelation.[5]

Barth further defended his prioritizing of the Trinity.

The problem of the doctrine of the Trinity meets us in the question put to the Bible about revelation. When we ask, Who is the self-revealing God? the Bible answers us in such a way that we are impelled to consider the Three-in-oneness of God.[6]

In addition to being aware of the radical divergence between Barth and Liberal Protestants as to the placement of and emphasis on the doctrine of the Trinity, one needs to know that numerous other systematic theologians have placed the Trinity in locations between the prioritizing of Barth and the making an addendum of Schleiermacher. Moreover, in the present study a *via media* will be sought in the placement of the Trinity. We are placing it early in our system but after the treatment of revelation and Scripture and of the existence, personhood, attributes, and fatherhood of God. Thus our treatment of the Trinity will precede that of creation, the person and work of Jesus Christ, the person and work of the Holy Spirit, and all other doctrines.

B. What Is the True Relationship between the Phenomenon of Divine Revelation and the Doctrine of the Trinity?

On this question twentieth-century theologians have been divided, as the noteworthy study by Claude Welch has made clear.[7]

1. Karl Barth taught that the Three-in-Oneness of God is "an immediate implication of revelation, and therefore . . . [is] essentially identical with the content of revelation."[8] Consequently for Barth Trinitarian truth did not await some later patristic or conciliar formulation but was immediately derived from God's revelatory activity in Christ and by the Spirit. For Barth there is no Christian apprehension of God that is not Trinitarian.

2. Emil Brunner regarded the Trinity as "an ultimate theoretically necessary implication of the primary data of faith and . . . a synthesis of those data" or as "a theologically defensive doctrine *(Schutzlehre)* for the biblical and ecclesiastical faith-center."[9] Hence, for Brunner, the Three-in-Oneness of God was not immediately derived from the phenomenon of revelation in Christ and by the Spirit but was like a protecting wall erected against heresies by the Church Fathers. Similarly, for Leonard Hodgson (1889-1969), the Trinity is the "product of rational reflection on those particular manifestations of the divine activity which center in . . . Jesus Christ and . . . the Holy Spirit."[10]

---

5. Ibid., I/1, p. 346.
6. Ibid., p. 348.
7. *In This Name.*
8. Ibid., p. 161.
9. *The Christian Doctrine of God,* p. 206.
10. *The Doctrine of the Trinity* (London: Nisbet and Company, 1955), p. 25.

3. Conservative and Fundamentalist Protestants and traditional pre–Vatican Council II Roman Catholic dogmaticians normally looked on the Trinity as a doctrinal truth derived from apostolic truth. The Protestants saw the Trinity "as one of the truths revealed in the Bible." Because of its biblical base, therefore, it belonged to Protestant theology. The Roman Catholics accepted the Trinity as part of the "eternal deposit of truth" preserved in the Bible and "entrusted to" and "infallibly defined by the [Roman Catholic] Church."[11]

Some evaluation of these three approaches to the relationship between the phenomenon of revelation and the doctrine of the Trinity is necessary. First, the third view rightly allows the Three-in-Oneness of God to be a revealed truth but fails to stress that the term "trinity" does not appear in the Bible and that the shaping of the doctrine came during the patristic age. Second, the second view, while rightly acknowledging the contribution of the Church Fathers, by reckoning the Trinity to be a defensive weapon against heresy or a rational reflection of the divine manifestations in Jesus and by the Spirit tends to lose the Three-in-Oneness that is implied in various New Testament passages. Third, the first view rightly interprets the Christian doctrine of God as Trinitarian but limits too severely its transmission to an "immediate implication of revelation" and does not differentiate the Three-in-Oneness in various New Testament passages from the fully formulated patristic doctrine of the Trinity.

By giving attention initially to the question as to the location of the doctrine of the Trinity in a Christian systematic theology and to the issue as to how the phenomenon of divine revelation is to be related to the doctrine of the Trinity, we will now hopefully be able to enter into the investigation and explication of the doctrine itself with keener anticipation and deeper insights.

II. THE BIBLICAL WITNESS TO THE TRIUNE NATURE OF GOD

A. OLD TESTAMENT

1. *Is There an Old Testament Witness to or Apprehension of the Threefold Nature of the One God?*

a. Certain passages are often quoted to suggest that there is an Old Testament "doctrine" of the Trinity, but such texts seemingly do not specifically teach such. These passages may be identified as the "us" and "our" texts. " 'Let us make man in our image, after our likeness...' " (Gen. 1:26, RSV). " 'The man has now become like one of us, knowing good and evil' " (Gen. 3:22, NIV). " 'Come, let us go down, and there confuse their

11. Welch, *In This Name*, pp. 94, 100.

language . . .' " (Gen. 11:7, RSV). " 'Whom shall I send, and who will go for us?' " (Isa. 6:8, RSV).[12]

1) Such texts may be understood as expressive of the plural of majesty, as some understand the plural form of 'El, that is, 'Elohim. Walther Eichrodt referred to the usage of 'Elohim as the "abstract plural" or the "plural of intensity."[13] Theodorus Christian Vriezen (1899-) rejected the idea that Gen. 1:26 involves a still lingering "polytheism" and held that in Isa. 6:8 "us" means Yahweh as "surrounded by angels."[14] Umberto Cassuto (1883-1951),[15] Bruce Vawter,[16] and Claus Westermann (1909-)[17] have preferred a plural of exhortation. But G. A. F. Knight rejected the plural of majesty and held instead to the "quantitative plural."[18]

2) These texts may also be regarded as consonant with the New Testament's differentiation of the Father, the Son, and the Holy Spirit for the Christian interpreter of the Old Testament.

3) Yet it is very doubtful that such texts should be understood as teaching, by the intention of their authors, the Three-in-Oneness of God. How can we be certain that the "us" and "our" in these texts were intended to refer to three and not to four or to more?

b. The Old Testament concepts of "Word," "Spirit," and "Wisdom" anticipated the concept of the Trinity by being pointers toward hypostatization, but the Old Testament teachings about these three were hardly constitutive of Trinitarian teaching per se for the authors, the compilers, or the users of the Old Testament books. According to Robert Sleighthome Franks (1871-1963), "Word" was hypostatized in Ps. 147:15-18 and "Spirit" was hypostatized in Ps. 104:30,[19] but even more complete hypostatization occurred with "Wisdom" in Proverbs 8 and in the noncanonical Wisd. of Sol. 7:22-23. If, however, Prov. 8:22 should be correctly interpreted as teaching that Wisdom was created,[20] then it is difficult to press such a passage as a prooftext for the Trinity. There have been those who have concluded that the Old Testament does teach a doctrine of the Trinity but have based such a conclusion on materials other than the "us" and "our" texts quoted above. Those materials have normally included

12. This effort began with the Church Fathers. Arthur W. Wainwright, *The Trinity in the New Testament* (London: S.P.C.K., 1962, 1982), p. 18.
13. *Theology of the Old Testament*, 1:185-86.
14. *An Outline of Old Testament Theology*, trans. S. Neuijen (Wageningen: H. Veeneman, 1958; Boston: C. T. Branford Company, 1960), pp. 179-80.
15. *A Commentary on the Book of Genesis*, trans. Israel Abrahams, 2 vols. (Jerusalem: Magnes Press of Hebrew University, 1961, 1964), 1:55-56.
16. *On Genesis: A New Reading* (Garden City, N.Y.: Doubleday, 1977), p. 54.
17. *Genesis 1–11: A Commentary*, trans. John J. Scullion (Minneapolis: Augsburg Publishing House, 1984), pp. 144-45; also Harry B. Hunt, Jr., to whom the author is indebted for assistance.
18. *A Biblical Approach to the Doctrine of the Trinity*, p. 20.
19. *The Doctrine of the Trinity* (London: Gerald Duckworth, 1953), pp. 20-21.
20. See a review of contemporary interpretations in William McKane, *Proverbs: A New Approach*, Old Testament Library (Philadelphia: Westminster Press, 1970), pp. 351-54.

the nature and activity of the Word and of the Spirit of Yahweh. Antonio
Neves de Mesquita, having collected materials from seven periods of Old
Testament literature, concluded that the Old Testament teaches both the
deity and personality of the Messiah and the deity and personality of the
Spirit of God.[21] Aubrey Rodway Johnson (1901-85) stressed that the
"extension of personality," as in the Achan story, and "collective per-
sonality," as seen in the actions of the Spirit and of the Word, apply to
God as well as to humankind in the Old Testament.[22]

It is, therefore, one thing to conclude that the Old Testament contains
pointers toward the differentiation of the Father, the Son, and the Holy
Spirit that are consistent with the Christian doctrine of the Three-in-Oneness of God. It is quite another thing to assert that the writers of the Old
Testament intended to speak about and explicate this doctrine. It seems,
therefore, that the former option rather than the latter must be taken.

2. *The Old Testament Teaches and the New Testament Retains the*
    Teaching That God (Yahweh) Is One and the One God for All
    Humankind.

a. The Old Testament Teaching

There are two strands of teaching or two motifs, namely, that
Yahweh is unique, possibly a henotheistic teaching, and that Yahweh is
the sole deity, necessarily a monotheistic teaching.[23]

1) *Yahweh is unique or incomparable ("none like me")*

The plague of frogs in Egypt was designed to show Pharaoh that
"there is no one like the LORD our God" (Exod. 8:10, RSV). The same was
true of the plague of hail (Exod. 9:14). Elijah's contest with the prophets
of Baal and Asherah on Mount Carmel sought to make clear who was
"God in Israel" (1 Kings 18:36-37, 39). "To whom then will you liken God,
or what likeness compare with him? . . . To whom then will you compare
me, that I should be like him? says the Holy One" (Isa. 40:18, 25).

2) *Yahweh is the sole deity ("none besides me")*

The "great and awesome deeds" that constituted the Exodus from
Egypt were made known to the Israelites so that they would know that
"besides him [Yahweh] there is no other" (Deut. 4:34-35). He is God of
both heaven and earth (Deut. 4:39). "Hear, O Israel, the LORD our God is
one LORD" (Deut. 6:4a). The Shema is "the fundamental article of the
Jewish faith" and "the cry which for centuries has been recited twice each

21. "The Doctrine of the Trinity in the Old Testament" (Th.D. diss., Southwestern
Baptist Theological Seminary, 1922).
22. *The One and the Many in the Israelite Conception of God* (Cardiff: University of Wales
Press, 1961), pp. 6-26.
23. In place of henotheism Dale Moody, *The Word of Truth,* pp. 62-63, 90-94, prefers
the term "monolatry."

day in the Jewish liturgy."[24] "I, I am the LORD, and besides me there is no savior" (Isa. 43:11). "I am the LORD, and there is no other, besides me there is no God" (Isa. 45:5a). "And there is no god besides me, a righteous God and a Savior; there is none besides me" (Isa. 45:21c).

The two motifs, Yahweh is unique and Yahweh is sole deity, both appear in Isa. 46:9: "for I am God, and there is no other; I am God, and there is none like me."

b. The New Testament Retention of the Old Testament Teaching of the Oneness and Sole Deity of God

1) In Jesus' reiteration and application of the Shema the oneness and sole deity of the Lord are reaffirmed: "And the scribe said to him, 'You are right, Teacher; you have truly said that he is one, and there is no other but he'" (Mark 12:32).

2) The unity of the moral law rests on the oneness of the Lawgiver: "For he who said, 'Do not commit adultery,' said also, 'Do not kill'" (Jas. 2:11a).

3) The oneness of God is connected with mediation. Moses as the "mediator" of the law did not "represent just one party; but God is one" (Gal. 3:20, NIV). "For there is one God, and there is one mediator between God and men, the man Christ Jesus" (1 Tim. 2:5, RSV).

4) The one God and the one Lord stand in contrast to polytheism.

> Hence, as to the eating of food offered to idols, we know that "an idol has no real existence," and that "there is no God but one." For although there may be so-called gods in heaven or on earth—as indeed there are many "gods" and many "lords"—yet for us there is one God, the Father, from whom are all things and from whom we exist, and one Lord, Jesus Christ, through whom are all things and through whom we exist. (1 Cor. 8:4-6)

Furthermore, the early Christians were not charged by unbelieving Jews with polytheism or idolatry.

B. NEW TESTAMENT

1. The Advents of Jesus and of the Holy Spirit

Three-in-Oneness in God is made explicit in the New Testament by virtue of the advent, the "personhood," and the deity of Jesus and by the advent, the "personhood," and the deity of the Holy Spirit. According to R. S. Franks, the doctrine of the Trinity "sprang from the reaction upon Jewish monotheism of belief in the Divine mission of Jesus Christ and the experience of the power of the Holy Spirit in the Christian Church."[25]

24. Wainwright, *The Trinity in the New Testament*, p. 15. Vriezen, *An Outline of Old Testament Theology*, pp. 175-76, has held that Israelites came to affirm such oneness not only by rejecting the polytheism of other nations but also out of their own practice of worshiping at various local shrines.
25. *The Doctrine of the Trinity*, p. 2.

a. Jesus

1) Jesus is distinct from the Father.

Both in the Synoptics and in John this distinction is made clear. Indeed, "no one knows the Son except the Father, and no one knows the Father except the Son and any one to whom the Son chooses to reveal him" (Matt. 11:27, RSV). "For the Father loves the Son. . . . The Father judges no one, but has given all judgment to the Son" (John 5:20, 22). Jesus promised, "I will pray the Father, and he will give you another Counselor" (John 14:16). The prayers of Jesus were addressed to God the Father. The distinction is clearly seen in the cry of dereliction, " 'My God, my God, why hast thou forsaken me?' " (Matt. 27:46).

2) Jesus is divine and one with the Father.

"In the beginning was the Word, and the Word was with God, and the Word was God . . . [and] we have beheld his glory, glory as of the only Son from the Father" (John 1:1, 14b). "I and the Father are one" (John 10:30).

b. The Holy Spirit

1) The Holy Spirit is distinct from the Father and from the Son.

In Jesus' Farewell Discourse the distinctiveness of the Counselor is evident. Jesus will ask the Father to give "another Counselor" (John 14:16), the Father will send the Counselor in Jesus' name (14:26), and this Spirit "proceeds from the Father" (15:26). Jesus will go to the Father, and then the Counselor will come (16:7-11), and "the Spirit of truth" will teach what belongs to the Father and the Son (16:13-15).

2) The Holy Spirit is God.

Paul implied the deity of the Spirit. "God has revealed to us through the Spirit. For the Spirit searches everything, even the depths of God. For what person knows a man's thoughts except the spirit of the man which is in him? So also no one comprehends the thoughts of God except the Spirit of God" (1 Cor. 2:10-11). Relative to spiritual gifts Paul alluded to "the same Spirit," "the same Lord," and "the same God" (1 Cor. 12:4-6).

2. *Distinctions of Father, Son, and Holy Spirit Are Recognized in the New Testament*

a. Some passages merely mention the Father, the Son, and the Spirit in the same context but without any statement or implication of the significance of their being three yet one.

1) Synoptic Gospels

At Jesus' baptism the Spirit of God descended like a dove and a heavenly voice declared, " 'This is my beloved Son' " (Matt. 3:16-17). Jesus expelled demons "by the Spirit of God" so that "the kingdom of God has come upon you" (Matt. 12:28, NIV). Jesus rejoiced in the Holy Spirit that the Father had revealed his truth to "babes" instead of the wise (Luke 10:21, RSV).

2) Acts

Jesus charged his disciples to remain in Jerusalem "to wait for the promise of the Father" and hence shortly to "be baptized with the Holy Spirit" (1:4-5). Stephen, "full of the Holy Spirit, gazed into heaven and saw the glory of God, and Jesus standing at the right hand of God" (7:55).

3) Pauline Epistles

At the outset of his first Thessalonian letter Paul alluded to "our God and Father," "our Lord Jesus Christ," and "the Holy Spirit" in an extended statement (1:3, 5). Also, "this is the will of God in Christ Jesus for you. Do not quench the Spirit" (5:18b-19). The apostle gave thanks to God for brethren beloved by the Lord [Jesus], whose salvation was "through sanctification by the Spirit" (2 Thess. 2:13). God and Christ are mentioned in connection with the sealing of the Spirit and the Spirit as "down payment" (2 Cor. 1:21-22). Paul had been liberated from "the law of sin and death" through "the law of the Spirit of life in Christ Jesus" and by God's sending of his Son (Rom. 8:2-3). In the same passage reference is made to "the Spirit of him who raised Jesus from the dead" (Rom. 8:11a). In one of his prayers Paul mentioned "the Father," his "Spirit," and "Christ" (Eph. 3:14, 16, 17). Believers are to "be filled with the Spirit" and to give "thanks to God the Father for everything, in the name of our Lord Jesus Christ" (Eph. 5:18, 20). Furthermore, "God our Savior," "the Holy Spirit," and "Jesus Christ our Savior" are named in a salvation text (Tit. 3:4-6).

4) General Epistles

In a context pertaining to Jesus' death reference was made to "the blood of Christ," "the eternal Spirit," and "God" (Heb. 9:14). The elect of God "have been chosen according to the foreknowledge of God the Father, through the sanctifying work of the Spirit, for obedience to Jesus Christ and sprinkling by his blood" (1 Pet. 1:2, NIV).

5) John's Gospel and First Epistle

Of Jesus who "comes from heaven" it was said: "For he whom God has sent utters the words of God, for it is not by measure that he gives the Spirit" (John 3:34, RSV). The same distinctions may be found in John 16:7-11, 13-15. " 'As the Father has sent me, even so I send you.' ... 'Receive the Holy Spirit' " (John 20:21b, 22b). Christians "have confidence before God," "believe in the name of his Son Jesus Christ," and know his abiding presence "by the Spirit" given to them (1 John 3:21, 23, 24). "By this you know the Spirit of God: every spirit which confesses that Jesus Christ has come in the flesh is of God" (1 John 4:2). "We know that we live in him and he in us, because he has given us of his Spirit. And we have seen and testify that the Father has sent his Son to be the Savior of the world" (1 John 4:13-14, NIV).

6) Revelation

John was "on the island called Patmos on account of the word of God and the testimony of Jesus" and "was in the Spirit on the Lord's day" (1:9b-10a, RSV). In the letters to the churches in Sardis and in Laodicea there are contexts in which Jesus, the Father, and the Spirit are mentioned (3:5b-6, 21-22).

b. Other passages present the Father, the Son, and the Holy Spirit, although not always in that order, so as to imply a relationship among the three. These passages are of special importance for ascertaining to what extent Three-in-Oneness is found in the New Testament writings. They are quoted from the RSV:

F	S	Sp	Matt. 28:19: "Go therefore and make disciples of all nations, baptizing them in the name of the Father and of the Son and of the Holy Spirit."
Sp	S	F	1 Cor. 12:4-6: "Now there are varieties of gifts, but the same
	(L)	(G)	Spirit; and there are varieties of service, but the same Lord; and there are varieties of working, but it is the same God who inspires them all in every one."
S	F	Sp	2 Cor. 13:14: "The grace of the Lord Jesus Christ and the
(L)	(G)		love of God and the fellowship of the Holy Spirit be with you all."
F	S	Sp	Eph. 1:1a, 5a, 6c, 13b: "Blessed be the God and Father of our
	(B)		Lord Jesus Christ. . . . He destined us in love to be his sons through Jesus Christ . . . the Beloved. . . . In him you also . . . were sealed with the promised Holy Spirit. . . ."
S	Sp	F	Eph. 2:18: "for through him [Christ] we [Jews and Gentiles]
(Ch)			both have access in one Spirit to the Father."
Sp	S	F	Eph. 4:4-6: "There is one body and one Spirit, just as you
	(L)		were called to the one hope that belongs to your call, one Lord, one faith, one baptism, one God and Father of us all, who is above all and through all and in all."
S	F	Sp	John 14:16-17a: "And I will pray the Father, and he will give
(I)			you another Counselor, to be with you forever, even the Spirit of truth. . . ."

Sp F S   John 14:26: "But the Counselor, the Holy Spirit, whom the
    (my   Father will send in my name, he will teach you all things,
   name) and bring to your remembrance all that I have said to you."

Sp S F   John 15:26: "But when the Counselor comes, whom I shall
(Csl) (I)   send to you from the Father, even the Spirit of truth, who
Sp F S   proceeds from the Father, he will bear witness to me."
    (me)

Among these New Testament texts quoted in the latter group every
possible order of the three is employed except the one order: Father, Spirit,
and Son. The latter order can be found among the texts cited in the former
group.

The New Testament writings did not use the term "Trinity."
Theophilus of Antioch (c. A.D. 180) was seemingly the first Christian writer
to use the Greek term *trias* of the Godhead.[26] Tertullian, writing after A.D.
213, was presumably the first Christian writer to use the Latin term *trinitas*
of the Godhead.[27]

The New Testament writers did bear witness to a relationship involving Father, Son, and Holy Spirit, but they did not define or elaborate
on the precise nature of that relationship.[28] They bore witness to the
Three-in-Oneness of God in his historical activity or manifestation. But
Leonard Hodgson has insisted that "Christianity began as a trinitarian
religion with a unitarian theology."[29] This was true in the sense that
Christians inherited from Judaism and retained a basic monotheism. But
the alteration of what Hodgson called "unitarian theology" into Trinitarian theology had already begun with the New Testament writers, especially Paul and John.

Arthur William Wainwright (1925-) has made the case strongly for
Three-in-Oneness in the New Testament. He prefers to speak of the
"problem" of the Trinity in the New Testament rather than the "doctrine"
of the Trinity in the New Testament.

> A statement of doctrine is an answer to a doctrinal problem. There is no
> formal statement of trinitarian doctrine in the New Testament as there is in
> the Athanasian Creed or in Augustine's *De Trinitate*. It will be argued that
> the problem of the Trinity was in the minds of certain New Testament
> writers, and that they made an attempt to answer it. None of their writings,
> however, was written specifically to deal with it, and most of the signs that
> a writer had tackled the problem are incidental. There was no elaborate or
> systematic answer to the problem. For this reason the word "problem" has
> been preferred to the word "doctrine." But it must be understood that the

26. *To Autolycus* 2.15.
27. *Against Praxeas* 2-3.
28. Frank Stagg, "Southern Baptist Theologians Today: Interview with Frank Stagg,"
Theological Educator 8 (Fall 1977): 26-27, warning of tritheism, seems to conclude from the
absence of the word "Trinity" in the New Testament that there is no Three-in-Oneness taught
in the New Testament.
29. *The Doctrine of the Trinity*, p. 103.

New Testament writers did not entirely neglect to answer the problem, although other matters occupied most of their attention. In so far as a doctrine is an answer, however fragmentary, to a problem, there is a doctrine of the Trinity in the New Testament. In so far as it is a formal statement of a position, there is no doctrine of the Trinity in the New Testament.[30]

Whether one adopts Wainwright's term "problem" or not, his recognition that Three-in-Oneness was acknowledged by the writers of the New Testament but that the formal formulation of the doctrine came later during the patristic age is a position that the facts seem to make tenable.

Charles W. Lowry has concluded:

The doctrine of the trinity is the one all-comprehensive Christian doctrine. It gathers up into the seam of a single grand generalization with respect to the being and activity of God all the major aspects of Christian truth. It is the formulation which the Christian facts in their totality compel.[31]

Now that we have investigated the biblical materials relative to the one God—Father, Son, and Holy Spirit—it becomes necessary to identify and assess the major alternatives posed against the Christian doctrine of the Trinity during the postbiblical history of Christianity prior to a consideration of the theological significance of the Trinity in the contemporary setting.

30. *The Trinity in the New Testament*, p. 4.
31. *The Trinity and Christian Devotion*, p. 52.

CHAPTER 22

The Trinity: Contrary Views

The task of formulating the Christian doctrine of the Trinity in its more precise and complete form was the work of the early centuries of the Christian era, that is, chiefly the patristic era. We will consider various positive aspects of the doctrine, as formulated by the Church Fathers, in the subsequent systematic formulation. In this chapter we will investigate the principal alternatives to Trinitarian doctrine, most of which also appeared early in Christian history.

Before examining these alternative or contrary views, however, we should take note of the differing answers that have been given to a basic question: How should twentieth-century Christians evaluate the patristic doctrine of the Trinity? Admittedly, the Fathers employed their own cultural tools, namely, the language and thoughts of Hellenistic metaphysics. First, some have regarded the patristic dogma of the Trinity and the Nicene and Constantinopolitan creeds as a Hellenistic alteration, if not a perversion of that original Christianity which had been basically Jewish Christian. Adolf Harnack was representative of this perspective.[1] To Harnack's critics his Galilean gospel seemed to have the characteristics of Liberal Protestantism. Harnack and others probably failed to take note of the soteriological concern that impelled Athanasius and others to affirm that the Son is coeternal and "consubstantial" with the Father. Second, others have seen the patristic doctrine as a necessary defensive doctrine, that is, *eine Schutzlehre*, to use Emil Brunner's term, against erroneous teachings, that is, the very contrary views about to be discussed. This posture has already been evaluated as more viable as to the patristic developments and somewhat defective as to the New Testament writings.[2] Third, still others have eagerly embraced and gratefully commended the patristic doctrine of the Trinity. Its value is viewed as transcending the

---

1. *What Is Christianity?*, trans. Thomas Bailey Saunders (2d rev. ed.; New York: G. P. Putnam's Sons; London: Williams and Norgate, 1902). The more general case for the decisive influence of Hellenism on Christianity was made on pp. 205, 214-24, 225-28, and 233-62; in one of Harnack's two specific allusions to the Trinity he saw the dogma of the Trinity as based on the Greek conception of redemption as deification and immortalization (pp. 250-51).

2. See above, Ch. 21, I, B, 2.

cultural context in which it was shaped. Emile Cailliet (1894-1981) was representative of this attitude.[3] It should perhaps face more directly the need for recognizing how Hellenistic the patristic doctrine of the Trinity is and for probing how adequate it is in other cultural contexts.

At the very least it may be said that most modern Christians owe much more to the patristic formulation of the Trinity than most of them have acknowledged.

I. THE UNITARIAN VIEW

This basic view, formulated at different times during Christian history and with varying descriptive labels, interprets Jesus of Nazareth in such a way that he does not belong within the nature and being of God and thus interprets God as unipersonal, or without internal differentiations.

A. DYNAMIC, OR DYNAMISTIC, MONARCHIANISM

This view, which originated in the second century A.D., was preceded by Ebionitism, which had regarded Jesus as the Jew selected as the Messiah by God, and by the Alogi, or Alogoi, who had rejected any developed Logos doctrine and any doctrine of the Holy Spirit, seemingly allowing no place for any differentiation within God. According to Dynamic Monarchians, there was in the human Jesus an impersonal power (*dynamis*) derived from God. This power did not constitute any personal differentiation between God and the human Jesus, but it was the impersonal indwelling of the one God.[4]

Theodotus, the leather seller of Byzantium who went to Rome and was excommunicated there about A.D. 195, stressed the human nature and life of Jesus and the Synoptic record and taught that Jesus was endowed at his baptism with a supernatural power. He even accepted his miraculous birth and his resurrection but seems to have refused to apply the title "God" to Jesus. Artemon of Rome acknowledged the supernatural birth, the superior virtue and sinlessness, and the unique dignity of Jesus but concluded that he was a human being, not God.[5] Dynamic Monarchianism reached its fullest expression in Paul of Samosata, the bishop of Antioch whose teaching was condemned by a synod in Antioch in 269.

3. Although it may not appear in his published works, the following statement was made by Cailliet in his classroom at Princeton Theological Seminary during 1948-49: "The ancient creeds are clusters of assurance in terms of Hellenistic metaphysics sealed until Christ comes again."

4. Justo L. González, *A History of Christian Thought*, 3 vols. (Nashville: Abingdon Press, 1970-75), 1:124-28; J. F. Bethune-Baker, *An Introduction to the Early History of Christian Doctrine to the Time of the Council of Chalcedon* (London: Methuen and Company, 1903), pp. 96-98; Pelikan, *The Emergence of the Catholic Tradition (100-600)*, p. 24; Heick, *A History of Christian Thought*, 1:66-67.

5. Bethune-Baker, *An Introduction to the Early History of Christian Doctrine*, pp. 98-100; Kelly, *Early Christian Doctrines*, pp. 115-17.

He affirmed the unipersonality of God and denied any *hypostasis* of the logos or of the wisdom of God. Logos, son, and spirit were seen as attributes of God. Logos, an impersonal *dynamis* projected from God from eternity, abode in Jesus and grew in the course of his development until finally through it as a medium Jesus attained a certain divine status. The only union, however, between Jesus and God was moral.[6]

B. ARIANISM

This expression of the unitarian view derived from the teaching of Arius (c. 250-c. 336), a presbyter in Alexandria, who began in 318 to publish his views about the nature of the Logos. He was suspended from office by Alexander, his bishop, but was supported by Eusebius, the bishop of Nicomedia. His views were the key issue at the Council of Nicaea I (325) and were condemned by that council and also later by the Council of Constantinople I (381).

For Arius God was utterly transcendent, "the unoriginate source of all reality," whose essence "cannot be shared or communicated," and who is thus indivisible and changeless. Furthermore, the Logos or Son is a creature of God, created prior to the creation of the universe. "There was when he was not," Arius repeatedly asserted. The Logos has no communication with God or the Father and is dissimilar to the Father. He "must be liable to change and even to sin," though the Father gave to him the grace to prevent his sinning. By courtesy only can the Logos be called "God" or "Son of God." Thus he is a kind of "demigod," more than human but less than God.[7]

C. SOCINIANISM

In the teaching of Faustus Socinus, or Sozzini, as expressed in the anti-Trinitarian, anabaptist, immersionist, and communal community of Rakow in Poland at the beginning of the seventeenth century, we find another expression of the unitarian view. The Racovian Catechism (1605) denied the divine nature of Jesus Christ, as that doctrine had been formulated by the Council of Chalcedon (451) in terms of two natures in one person, while allowing that the Holy Spirit indwelt Jesus. The man Jesus was virgin-born, was "sent into the world by the Father," became by his resurrection immortal like God, and by his "dominion and supreme authority over all things" resembled or even equaled God.[8] Most Socinians allowed Christ to be invoked and worshiped, but Francis David (c. 1510-79)

6. Bethune-Baker, *An Introduction to the Early History of Christian Doctrine*, pp. 100-102; González, *A History of Christian Thought*, 1:147-48; Kelly, *Early Christian Doctrines*, pp. 117-19; Pelikan, *The Emergence of the Catholic Tradition (100-600)*, pp. 176, 198; Heick, *A History of Christian Thought*, 1:148-49.

7. Kelly, *Early Christian Doctrines*, pp. 227-30.

8. *Racovian Catechism*, trans. Thomas Rees (reprint ed.; Lexington, Ky.: American Theological Library Association, 1962), ch. 1.

in Transylvania led the nonadorantist branch. According to David, "the one God is the Father of the Lord Jesus Christ; . . . the Word was not, prior to the incarnation, the Son of God; and . . . the Holy Spirit was only the power of God." Faustus Socinus seems to have taught that Jesus became at his ascension the adopted Son of God.[9] For him Jesus Christ had been given "*divinitas* of function as distinct from *deitas* of nature."[10]

D. ANGLO-AMERICAN UNITARIANISM

The man who organized the Unitarian Society in Great Britain in 1791, Thomas Belsham (1750-1829), considered the Arian worship of Jesus Christ to be idolatrous.[11] American Unitarianism arose more directly in reaction to the Calvinistic doctrine of humankind. William Ellery Channing (1780-1842) held to an Arian view and taught the sinlessness, the miracles, and the resurrection of Jesus.[12] Ralph Waldo Emerson (1803-82) in his "Divinity School Address" (1838) claimed that historical Christianity "has dwelt . . . with noxious exaggeration about the *person* of Jesus" and has not "explored as the fountain of the established teaching in society" the moral law.[13] Theodore Parker in his sermon on "The Transient and Permanent in Christianity" (1841) defined Christianity as "absolute, pure morality; absolute, pure religion" and called on Christians to "worship as Jesus did, with no mediator, with nothing between us and the Father of all."[14] American Unitarianism bifurcated during the nineteenth century, with the major branch becoming subject to humanism and the scientific worldview and separating from historic Christianity and with the lesser branch seeking to retain or reestablish its connection with historic Christianity. According to the major branch, Jesus is not to be reckoned as more than or other than a mere human.

The Dynamic Monarchian, the Arian, the Socinian, and the Anglo-American Unitarian movements have shared a basic understanding of Jesus Christ that has placed him outside the being and nature of God, that has attributed to God unipersonality, and that has denied the triune nature of God.

9. George Huntston Williams, *The Radical Reformation* (Philadelphia: Westminster Press, 1962), pp. 718, 753.

10. Herbert John McLachlan, *Socinianism in Seventeenth-Century England* (London: Oxford University Press, 1951), p. 13.

11. Earl Morse Wilbur, *A History of Unitarianism*, 2 vols. (Boston: Beacon Press, 1945), 2:343.

12. David S. Schaff, "Channing, William Ellery," *The New Schaff-Herzog Encyclopedia of Religious Knowledge*, 3:4.

13. *Complete Works of Ralph Waldo Emerson*, 12 vols. (Boston: Houghton, Mifflin and Company, 1903; 2d reprint ed.; New York: AMS, 1979), 1:130, 134.

14. In H. Shelton Smith, Robert T. Handy, and Lefferts A. Loetscher, *American Christianity: An Historical Interpretation with Representative Documents*, 2 vols. (New York: Charles Scribner's Sons, 1960, 1963), 2:144, 145.

II. THE MODALIST VIEW

This view, formulated classically during the second and third centuries A.D. and later held by other individuals and groups, has interpreted the Son and the Holy Spirit as well as God the Father as divine by nature, has held that God is one, and has concluded that there are no "personal" or hypostatic distinctions within God. Its ancient formulation is usually called Modalistic Monarchianism. It shared with Dynamic Monarchianism the common belief that God is unipersonal but differed from Dynamic Monarchianism by affirming that the Son and the Spirit are God. Modalism lays stress on the offices, modes, or operations of the Father, of the Son, and of the Holy Spirit. Such offices or modes are what differentiate the Father, the Son, and the Spirit, not personal or hypostatic distinctions. We will now examine some of the thought of representative modalists.

A. NOETUS OF SMYRNA (LATE SECOND OR EARLY THIRD CENTURY)

Noetus, "perhaps the earliest modalist of appreciable influence,"[15] taught that the Father submitted to birth, became the Son, and then suffered and died. The term "Logos" is

> only a designation of God when He reveals Himself to the world and to man. The Father, so far as he deigns to be born, is the Son. He is called Son for a certain time . . . [and] the Son, or Christ, is therefore the Father veiled in flesh. . . .[16]

It is not difficult to understand, therefore, why the teaching of Noetus has been called Patripassianism.

B. PRAXEAS (EARLY THIRD CENTURY)

Having gone from Asia Minor to Rome and then later to Carthage, Praxeas was accused by Tertullian (c. A.D. 210) of doing "two jobs for the Devil at Rome": "He drove out prophecy and introduced heresy; he put to flight the Paraclete and crucified the Father."[17] The charge was that Praxeas opposed Montanism and embraced Patripassianism. In defense of Praxeas, James Franklin Bethune-Baker (1861-1951) has contended that the Modalistic Monarchians at Rome,

> while denying the existence of any real distinction in the being of God Himself . . . seem to have admitted a distinction [dating at least from the creation] between the invisible God and God revealed in the universe, in the theophanies of the Old Testament, and finally in the human body in Christ.[18]

One was the Father; the other was called the Logos or Son. If Bethune-Baker is correct, then Praxeas may not have been a full-fledged modalist.

15. Robert L. Calhoun, *Lectures on the History of Christian Doctrine* (New Haven, Conn.: Yale Divinity School, 1948; for private distribution only), p. 82.
16. Bethune-Baker, *An Introduction to the Early History of Christian Doctrine*, p. 104.
17. *Against Praxeas* 1 (ANF, 3:597).
18. *An Introduction to the Early History of Christian Doctrine*, pp. 103-4.

C. SABELLIUS (THIRD CENTURY)

A Libyan condemned and excommunicated at Rome, Sabellius represented full-orbed Modalism. He referred to God by the name *huiopatōr*, "Son-Father."[19] "He differed from Noetus and Praxeas in this, that . . . he gave the Holy Spirit a place with the Father and the Son."[20] His view has been called a "more sophisticated modalism."[21] God is essentially one. The Trinity is one of manifestation but not of essence. These manifestations are modes: Father, Son, and Holy Spirit. Sabellius used *prosōpa* to mean "role," not "person," and seemingly he understood the modes as successive. Zephyrinus (bp. 199-217) and Callistus (bp. 217-22), bishops of Rome, protected Modalists, for which they were criticized by Hippolytus of Rome. Later Callistus excommunicated both Sabellius and Hippolytus.[22] Callistus spoke of the Father's "suffering *jointly with* the Son" but used the term "Son" only to refer to Jesus' humanity.[23]

D. MICHAEL SERVETUS (1511-53)

In his *On the Errors of the Trinity* (1531) Servetus referred to the "three wonderful dispositions of God." He also identified the Holy Spirit as an angel and held that the Word no longer exists. He was critical of Hellenistic terms used in the doctrine of the Trinity. Wrongly called an "Anti-Trinitarian," for he was neither Arian nor Unitarian, Servetus was closest to Sabellius, with distinctives of his own.[24]

E. CYRIL CHARLES RICHARDSON (1909-76)

An Episcopal churchman and patristic scholar, Richardson in a monograph on the Trinity declared:

> The terms [Father, Son, Holy Spirit] do not denominate precise persons in the Trinity. They are ways of thinking about God from different points of view. And while they point beyond themselves to the necessity of making distinctions in the Godhead, they themselves are *not* the actual distinctions and cannot fittingly express them.

Richardson then proceeded to identify various "antinomies" or "paradoxes" concerning God and to conclude that "the doctrine of the Trinity" is an artificial construct.[25] His statements seem to warrant the conclusion that he has espoused modalism in some form.

Not every author who has favorably employed such terms as "modes of being" and "modal" is necessarily a modalist. Karl Barth's

---

19. Kelly, *Early Christian Doctrines*, p. 122, based on Arius, *Ep. ad Alex.*, and Epiphanius, *Haer.* 69.7.

20. Heick, *A History of Christian Thought*, 1:111.

21. Kelly, *Early Christian Doctrines*, p. 121.

22. Bethune-Baker, *An Introduction to the Early History of Christian Doctrine*, pp. 105-6.

23. Justo L. González, *A History of Christian Thought*, 1:239.

24. Earl Morse Wilbur, "Introduction," in Michael Servetus, *On the Errors of the Trinity* (1531), trans. Wilbur, Harvard Theological Studies, no. 16 (Cambridge, Mass.: Harvard University Press, 1932), p. xviii.

25. *The Doctrine of the Trinity* (New York: Abingdon Press, 1958), pp. 145-48.

preference for "modes of being" *(Seinsweise)* did not mean that the Swiss theologian had embraced modalism in its classical sense.[26] Charles Lowry used "Sabellianism" to identify modalism and employed "modal" to refer to the social analogies applied to the Trinity by the Cappadocian Fathers.[27]

Modalism can quote assuringly the saying of Jesus, "I and the Father are one" (John 10:30), but it has very great difficulty in explaining why and how Jesus prayed to the Father.

III. THE TRITHEISTIC VIEW

This view, never the acknowledged teaching of any major body of Christians, has persisted as the dangerous extreme that is common to much popular thought and speaking about the Father, the Son, and the Holy Spirit. These three are regarded as fully individuated beings, and hence there are three Gods. The basic oneness of God is disposed of in favor of threefold[28] deity. What is allowed is a generic unity underlying the Father, the Son, and the Spirit; they all are Gods or divine.

Roscelin (c. 1050-1125), an early nominalist and the teacher of Peter Abelard (1079-1142), by his philosophical rejection of universals seemed to teach three separate Gods, that is, tritheism. His teaching was condemned by the Council of Soissons in 1092.[29]

Present-day usage of language such as "cooperation within the Godhead," "conferring among persons of the Trinity," and "the councils of eternity" can easily lead to a tritheistic interpretation. Furthermore, some present-day usage of the historic term "person" in reference to Father, Son, and Holy Spirit, when devoid of understanding about its patristic origin, tends to fall into the trap of tritheism.

In summary, the unitarian view sacrifices the deity of Jesus Christ and indeed of the Spirit for the unipersonal oneness of God the Father. The modalist view sacrifices the personal differentiations of Father, Son, and Holy Spirit for the unipersonal oneness of God. The tritheistic view sacrifices the oneness of God for the triune differentiations of Father, Son, and Spirit, who become three Gods. These are sacrifices that are not demanded by integrated Christian truth. Those who are seeking to contextualize Christian theology in the Third World, as well as those in the older centers of Christian theology in Europe and North America, need to learn important lessons from the Christian past, especially from the inadequate answers as to the Father, the Son, and the Holy Spirit.

26. *Church Dogmatics*, I/1, pp. 407-23.

27. *The Trinity and Christian Devotion*, pp. 98-101.

28. Augustine of Hippo rejected the Latin term *triplex*, "threefold," but accepted *trinitas*, "Trinity." See also the writings of Anselm of Canterbury against Roscelin: *To John the Monk, To Fulco, Bishop of Beauvais*, and *The Incarnation of the Word* in *Anselm of Canterbury*, 4 vols., ed. and trans. Jasper Hopkins and Herbert Richardson (Toronto: Edwin Mellen Press, 1976), 3:1-37.

29. Jaroslav Pelikan, *The Growth of Medieval Theology (600-1300)*, The Christian Tradition, vol. 3 (Chicago: University of Chicago Press, 1978), pp. 264, 266; González, *A History of Christian Thought*, 2:162-64.

CHAPTER 23

The Trinity: Systematic Formulation

"What will it avail thee to argue profoundly of the Trinity, if thou be void of humility, and are thereby displeasing to the Trinity?"[1] This probing question put forth by a fourteenth-century Christian writer serves to remind any Christian who would probe the depths of the mystery of the Three-in-Oneness of God of the need for humility and for the recognition of one's own finite apprehension of this great truth.

We will now examine seven aspects of the doctrine of the Trinity.

I. THE THREENESS IN THE THREE-IN-ONENESS OF GOD

A. The fourth-century Cappadocian Fathers (Basil of Caesarea, Gregory of Nazianzus, and Gregory of Nyssa)[2] and some modern Anglicans[3] either assumed or taught that the threeness is the beginning point for explicating the Trinity. In support of this view it may be argued that threeness is the very point where Christian belief was and is to be differentiated from Jewish belief and that the threeness should therefore be the initial step in moving toward a comprehensive doctrine of the Trinity.

B. The entire history of interpreting the threeness in the Three-in-Oneness of God has centered around the problem of language, that is, the Latin term *personae*, the Greek term *hypostaseis*, the English term "person," etc. Tertullian first employed *tres personae* in reference to the Christian doctrine of the Father, the Son, and the Holy Spirit.[4] Among its usages as a term in the Latin language *persona* had been employed of the mask worn by an actor and of the different characters in a drama. Only slowly and with the help of the Cappadocian Fathers[5] did the Greek *hypostaseis*

---

1. Thomas à Kempis [or Gerard Groote?], *The Imitation of Christ*, 1.1.3.
2. Johannes Quasten, *Patrology*, 3 vols., vol. 3, *The Golden Age of Greek Patristic Literature from the Council of Nicaea to the Council of Chalcedon* (Westminster, Md.: Newman Press; Utrecht: Spectrum Publishers, 1960), pp. 228-29, 249-50, 285-87.
3. Hodgson, *The Doctrine of the Trinity*, began with the threeness and gave attention to the nature of the unity as the central problem. Lowry, *The Trinity and Christian Devotion*, began with the three "persons."
4. *Against Praxeas* 2.
5. Quasten, *Patrology*, 3:228-29; Kelly, *Early Christian Doctrines*, pp. 263-66.

become the standard Greek equivalent for the Latin *personae* vis-à-vis the Trinity. The question facing modern students of Christian theology is this: Did *personae* mean for Latin-speaking Christians during the third century A.D. the same thing as or something quite different from the twentieth-century English term "person" (or its equivalent in modern European languages) when applied to the Trinity?

Karl Barth was representative of those who in the twentieth century have insisted that these meanings do markedly differ. Accordingly, the modern use of "person" and "personality" connotes self-consciousness and individuation, whereas the patristic usage of *personae* connoted something less than full individuation. Hence, Barth himself, turning from "persons," preferred to use the term "modes of being" *("Seinsweise")* but without a Sabellianist meaning.[6] Karl Rahner similarly favored the term "distinct manners of subsisting" in place of "persons."[7] Georges Henri Tavard has offered a critique of the choices made by Barth and by Rahner and has defended the continued use of the term "person."[8]

Clement Charles Julian Webb[9] (1865-1954) and Leonard Hodgson,[10] on the other hand, were representative of those Anglicans and others who have insisted that the usage of *personae* has not significantly changed between the patristic and the modern eras. Webb affirmed that until the modern era only heretics would affirm "the Personality *of* God"; rather, the orthodox would refer to "Personality *in* God."[11]

Whatever may be concluded and established as to change and continuity in the meaning of *personae* and "persons," the term "persons" must not be used of the Father, of the Son, and of the Holy Spirit so as to mean three individual deities. Meanwhile, the search goes on for a satisfactory alternative term for "person." Charles W. Lowry has suggested the term "centers of consciousness, will, and activity."[12] Such a lengthy term, however adequate it may be for theological discussion, can hardly serve as a substitute for "God in three Persons, Blessed Trinity," in the well-known hymn, "Holy, Holy, Holy."

C. As previously noted,[13] the English term "person" must in present-day usage do double duty both as an antipantheistic term and as a Trinitarian term, and these usages must not be confused.

D. The threeness in the Three-in-Oneness of God means furthermore

---

6. *Die kirchliche Dogmatik,* 5 vols. in 13 (Zollikon: Verlag der Evangelischen Buchhandlung, 1932-70; *Church Dogmatics,* I/1, p. 379; *Church Dogmatics,* I/1, pp. 412-13.

7. *The Trinity,* trans. Joseph Donceel (New York: Herder and Herder, 1970), pp. 109-15.

8. *The Vision of the Trinity* (Lanham, Md.: University Press of America, 1981), p. 131.

9. *God and Personality* (London: Allen and Unwin; New York: Macmillan, 1919), p. 61.

10. *The Doctrine of the Trinity,* pp. 78-83, 154-56.

11. *God and Personality,* pp. 61-65. Webb suggested that the first usage of the term "Personality of God" by orthodox Christians would likely be found in the eighteenth century.

12. *The Trinity and Christian Devotion,* p. 106.

13. See above, Ch. 14, I, D.

that the Trinity involves a union of "persons," not the union of "members of a species" in an impersonal sense, or the union of the bond of "love or friendship," or the "union of members of a group."[14]

II. THE ONENESS IN THE THREE-IN-ONENESS OF GOD

A. Augustine of Hippo regarded the oneness or the unity of God as the proper beginning point for the explication of the Trinity. "And this Trinity is one God; and none the less simple because a Trinity."[15] Moreover, "we do not say that the very supreme Trinity itself is three Gods, but one God."[16] In support of this approach is the fact that the oneness of God is Christianity's essential debt to and link with Jewish monotheism.

B. Interpreting the oneness in the Three-in-Oneness of God has involved the question as to the nature and meaning of that oneness or unity. How can there be oneness if there be threeness? The fifth-century[17] so- called *Athanasian Creed* (or *Quicumque*), which expounded in creedal form Augustine's doctrine of the Trinity, declared that Father, Son, and Spirit "are not three eternals," "not three uncreated," not "three incomprehensibles," "not three Almighties," "not three Gods," and "not three Lords," "but one God" and "one Lord."[18] Even so, when one speaks of such oneness in God, vis-à-vis his threeness, what kind of oneness should one have in mind? Should it be primarily an *arithmetical* unity or oneness, that is, without regard to fractions and hence the oneness of the integer? Karl Barth has answered in the affirmative because, he has contended, God is the one God only as he triply repeats himself.[19] But, on the contrary, Leonard Hodgson has held that *organic* unity, rather than mathematical unity, should be the model for the doctrine of the Trinity. Mathematical unity, despite fractions, is characterized by an "absence of inner multiplicity," whereas the organic unity of a cell "exists by virtue of an inner multiplicity." The doctrine of the Trinity, according to Hodgson, needs mathematical unity only when contrasting monotheism with polytheism.[20]

C. The oneness or unity in the Three-in-Oneness of God also pertains to the work of the triune God. The work of the Father, of the Son, and of the Spirit can be identified and even differentiated, but the work of each is not exclusive. The work of each is in a sense the work of the Godhead. God the Father may be called Creator, but the Son and the Spirit are not excluded from the work of creation. God the Son may be called Redeemer,

14. Lowry, *The Trinity and Christian Devotion*, p. 87.
15. *On the City of God* 11.10 (Marcus Dods trans., Modern Library, p. 354).
16. *On the Trinity* 5.9 (NPNF, 1st ser., 3:91).
17. J. N. D. Kelly, *The Athanasian Creed* (New York: Harper & Row, 1964), p. 113.
18. Arts. 11, 12, 14, 16, 18, in Philip Schaff, *The Creeds of Christendom*, 3 vols. (New York: Harper & Brothers, 1919), 2:67.
19. *Church Dogmatics*, I/2, p. 402.
20. *The Doctrine of the Trinity*, pp. 105, 107.

but the Father and the Spirit are not excluded from the work of redemption. The Holy Spirit may be called Sanctifier, but the Father and the Son are not excluded from the work of sanctification. Some of the Church Fathers, notably John of Damascus (c. 675-c. 749), expounded a doctrine of divine coinherence (Greek *perichōrēsis*;[21] Latin *circumincessio*),[22] whereby the Father, the Son, and the Spirit "condition and permeate one another mutually with such perfection, that one is as invariably in the other two as the other two are in the one."[23] Jürgen Moltmann has referred to the "circulatory character of the eternal divine life."[24]

III. THE TRINITY AS ETERNAL, ESSENTIAL, AND IMMANENTAL

A. The triune nature of God needs to be understood as more than merely a Trinity of historic self-manifestation, or what some have called an "economic"[25] Trinity.

Some acknowledge a certain three-in-oneness of God in the advent of Jesus Christ among human beings and in the manifestation of the Holy Spirit on the Day of Pentecost but deny or are reluctant to affirm that this three-in-oneness in God reflects the eternal being of God. Albrecht Ritschl and Ritschlian theologians of the pre–World War I era, for example, referred to Jesus Christ as having the value of God for Christian believers and made much of the kingdom of God but were reluctant to affirm the participation of the Son of God in an eternal triune Godhead.[26]

The crucial question is this: Is the Three-in-Oneness of God that is manifested in the events to which the New Testament bears witness a true reflection or disclosure of an eternal and immanental Three-in-Oneness? The factor of divine revelation argues for an affirmative answer.

B. The triune nature of God needs to be understood as more than a triplex of divine attributes.

Peter Abelard was condemned by the Council of Soissons (1121) for his views concerning the Trinity. Reportedly his teaching was tritheistic

---

21. This noun was derived from the classical Greek verb *perichōreō*, meaning "to go round, rotate, or come to in succession."

22. The Latin term means literally "movement in and around."

23. Barth, *Church Dogmatics*, I/1, p. 425.

24. *The Trinity and the Kingdom: The Doctrine of God*, trans. Margaret Kohl (San Francisco: Harper & Row, 1981), pp. 174-76.

25. The term is derived from the Greek noun *oikonomia*, "household management" or "stewardship."

26. Ritschl, *The Christian Doctrine of Justification and Reconciliation*, avoided the doctrine of the Trinity. Wilhelm Herrmann, *Systematic Theology*, pp. 151-52, and idem, *The Communion of the Christian with God*, trans. J. Sandys Stanyon (London: Williams and Norgate, 1895), provided a minimal treatment of the Trinity. But Theodore Haering, *The Christian Faith*, 2:913-24, though placing the Trinity at the end of his treatment of eschatology, had more respect for the traditional doctrine of the Trinity.

in nature. In actual fact he seems to have held to a Sabellianism of divine attributes. God is essentially Power, Wisdom, and Goodness or Love. Hence this distinction of attributes seems to have stood in place of a distinction of persons.[27] Mary Baker Eddy taught that "Life, Truth, and Love" are the distinctions or marks of the pantheistic God.[28] In the hymn "Thou, Whose Almighty Hand," one finds the suggestion of the attributal distinctions "Truth, Love, and Might."[29]

C. The triune nature of God needs to be understood as more than merely an equality of rank, station, or power for the Father, the Son, and the Spirit that lacks also an equality of being, essence, or nature.

Concerning Phil. 2:6 Michael Servetus (1511-53) declared: "for the expression, *equally* denotes not his nature but his station; and he [Jesus] could pronounce himself on an equality with God in power, who promises that he can do all things soever that the Father does [Matt. 11:27; John 3:35; 5:19; 13:3]."[30] The New Testament admittedly does, especially in John 17, refer to the preincarnate and postincarnate station and glory of the Son of God, but in its books one finds no usage of station or glory as a substitute for divine being or essence.

D. Rather the doctrine of the triune nature of God is "the projection into eternity of this essential relationship, [indeed] the assertion that eternally the Divine life is a life of mutual self-giving to one another."[31]

The doctrine of an eternal, essential, and immanental Trinity has been built on various affirmations that were first made during the patristic age:

1. The eternal generation of the Son from the Father (Origen)
2. The consubstantiality of the Son with the Father and hence his coeternity and coequality (Nicaea I, Athanasius)
3. The consubstantiality of the Holy Spirit with the Father and the Son (Gregory of Nazianzus, c. 330-c. 90)
4. The procession of the Holy Spirit from the Father through the Son (Cappadocian Fathers)
5. The procession of the Holy Spirit from the Father and from the Son (Western insertion of *filioque*)
6. The coinherence of the Father, the Son, and the Holy Spirit (John Chrysostom, John of Damascus)

According to Charles Lowry, the Apostles' Creed, "rightly understood, implies" the Trinity; the Nicene Creed "is intelligible only on the assump-

27. A. C. McGiffert, *A History of Christian Thought,* 2 vols. (New York: Charles Scribner's Sons, 1954), 2:212.
28. *Science and Health with Key to the Scriptures* (Boston: Allison V. Stewart, 1913), p. 331.
29. *Baptist Hymnal,* ed. Walter Hines Sims (Nashville: Convention Press, 1956), no. 461.
30. *On the Errors of the Trinity* (1531), 1:26. Servetus also taught that the eternal Logos preexisted as an idea in God and only became personalized in Jesus. H. C. Sheldon, *History of Christian Doctrine,* 2 vols., 4th ed. (New York: Eaton & Mains, 1906), 2:100.
31. Hodgson, *The Doctrine of the Trinity,* p. 68.

tion that the one God . . . is also in some sense three"; and the so-called Athanasian Creed "states explicitly the doctrine of the Trinity."[32]

Conceived in more intimate terms, the "doctrine of the Trinity is the teaching that God, who as the Father hath made me and all the world, who as the Son hath redeemed me and all mankind, and who as the Holy Spirit sanctifieth me and all the people of God, is within the unity and perfection of His eternal being Three as well as One, and that the Divine Three are mutually and personally related to one another."[33]

E. The essential or immanental Trinity is, therefore, important for the Christian worship of God.

Christians worship the one God—Father, Son, and Holy Spirit—on the basis that the historical self-manifestation of this God is a true and valid, if not perfect, reflection of the eternal and essential being of this God. Jürgen Moltmann has expounded "the doxological Trinity."[34]

IV. ANALOGIES TO THE TRINITY?

Many and varied are the analogies that Christians have applied to the Trinity in an effort to illustrate the Trinity or to bring the Trinity into the range of human experience. But one should not be too sanguine concerning the effectiveness or adequacy of these efforts.

A. PSYCHOLOGICAL ANALOGIES

Augustine of Hippo taught that there are numerous "vestiges" of the Trinity, especially in human beings themselves. He explored the possibility of numerous psychological analogies. In the field of optics one has the object of vision, the human representation of the object, and intentional focusing.[35] Augustine saw the possible analogy of memory, internal memory image, and intention of the will[36] and also that of the sound of words in the memory, mental recollection, and will of the person who remembers and thinks that unites the other two.[37] The bishop of Hippo also thought of human being, knowing, and willing;[38] of memory, understanding, and will;[39] and of the mind, the mind's knowledge of itself, and the mind's love of itself.[40] It seems, however, that Augustine regarded as the most satisfying analogy to the Trinity the human mind as remembering, knowing, and loving God.[41] In the twentieth century Karl

32. *The Trinity and Christian Devotion*, p. 19.
33. Ibid., p. 77.
34. *The Trinity and the Kingdom*, pp. 151-61.
35. *On the Trinity* 11.2-5.
36. Ibid. 11.6-7.
37. Ibid. 13.20.26.
38. *Confessions* 13.11.
39. *On the Trinity* 10.17-19.
40. Ibid. 9.2-8.
41. Ibid. 14.11–end.

Barth employed a psychological analogy (Revealer, revelation, revealed-ness),[42] and so did Dorothy Leigh Sayers (1893-1957) (idea, energy, and power for the creative writer).[43]

B. NATURAL ANALOGIES

Other analogies to the Trinity have been drawn from nature. Ter-tullian mentioned three: (1) the root, the tree, and the fruit; (2) the fountain, the stream, and the lake; and (3) the sun, the ray, and the apex.[44] Augustine of Hippo, perhaps influenced by Tertullian, suggested (4) the fountain, the river, and the lake and (5) the root, the trunk, and the branches.[45] Anselm of Canterbury reiterated (6) the fountain, the river, and the lake[46] and utilized (7) the sun, brightness, and heat.[47]

C. MODAL ANALOGY

Still others have utilized the differing functions or roles of a human being as analogous to the Trinity. Theodore Roosevelt (1858-1919) was at the same time president, sportsman, and playmate to the young.[48]

D. HUMAN ANALOGIES

Even human beings have been employed in the effort to locate adequate analogies to the Trinity. Gregory of Nazianzus cited Adam, Eve, and Seth,[49] and the opponents of Gregory of Nyssa (c. 335-c. 94) used Peter, James, and John.[50] Augustine of Hippo referred to the lover, the beloved, and love,[51] and Karl Barth to Begetter, Begotten, and begottenness.[52]

E. WHAT OF THE ANALOGIES?

The human analogies to the Trinity prove to be analogies to tritheism rather than to the Three-in-Oneness of God. Adam, Eve, and Seth have the bond of a common humanity and the added tie of family relationship but are essentially three individuated human beings. Peter, James, and John have the bond of a common humanity and the added commonality of apostleship but are three distinct human beings. The

42. *Church Dogmatics*, I/1, pp. 344, 415-17, 426-27.
43. *The Mind of the Maker* (London: Methuen and Company, 1941), pp. 26-35.
44. *Against Praxeas* 8.
45. *On Faith and the Creed* 9.17.
46. *De fide Trin.* 8, as cited by Sheldon, *History of Christian Doctrine*, 1:338; *The Incarnation of the Word* 13; *The Procession of the Holy Spirit* 9, in *Anselm of Canterbury*, 3:32-34, 211-14.
47. *The Procession of the Holy Spirit* 8, in *Anselm of Canterbury*, 3:207-9.
48. Henry Pitney Van Dusen, *Spirit, Son and Father: Christian Faith in the Light of the Holy Spirit* (New York: Charles Scribner's Sons, 1958), pp. 173-74, citing Harry Emerson Fosdick.
49. *Orations* 31.11.
50. On "Not Three Gods" (NPNF, 2d ser., 5:331).
51. *On the Trinity* 8.12–9.2.
52. *Church Dogmatics*, I/1, p. 417.

alternatives offered by Augustine and by Barth tend to illustrate binitarianism.

The modal analogy centering in the differing roles or functions of a single human being is perfectly adapted to the modalistic alternative to the Trinity but does not allow for hypostatic differentiations among the Father, the Son, and the Spirit. The analogies from nature tend to involve either organic growth in plant life, differing states of water, or differing aspects of light. Such natural analogies function in a manner similar to the modal analogy in that they illustrate three stages or phases of one reality, not that which is basically both one and three.

The psychological analogies also illustrate three functions of the human self. The result is that oneness of being and diversity of functions are that which is being illustrated, and there is no analogy to the threeness of persons.

However widespread and recurrent the usage of analogies to the Trinity and whatever elements of true analogy one may detect in them, it must be concluded that the efforts to locate or identify the all-satisfactory analogy have not been successful. The Christian preacher who yearns for the perfect illustration of the Trinity for his sermon is destined to be disappointed or to misuse analogy. As we will learn from the subsequent study of the divine creation of all things, the Three-in-Oneness of God is unique and hence without parallel.

V. THE TRINITY AND THE NON-CHRISTIAN RELIGIONS

Efforts have been made to locate and identify triune features or parallels to the Christian doctrine of the Trinity in non-Christian religions. Are there indeed instances of three-in-oneness among non-Christian deities? Several so-called instances have been identified. In ancient Egyptian religion Osiris (the father), Isis (the mother), and Horus (the son) have been cited, and in contemporary Hinduism Brahma (the ultimate reality), Siva (the destroyer), and Vishnu (the restorer). These instances, however, seem to be tritheistic rather than trinitarian. Likewise, in the religious philosophy of the Neo-Platonist Plotinus (205-70), one finds the Good, Intelligence *(nous)*, and the World-Soul. These three, however, are states or stages in modalistic emanation, not the simultaneous Three-in-Oneness of God.[53] Hence the Christian belief in and affirmation of the Three-in-Oneness of God, Father, Son, and Holy Spirit, seems to be a distinctive of Christianity.

53. Van Dusen, *Spirit, Son and Father*, pp. 151-53.

VI. THE TRINITY AND THE CHRISTIAN DENOMINATIONS OR CONFESSIONS

The doctrine of the Trinity constitutes significant common theological ground among the various Christian denominations or confessions. There is no distinctively Baptist doctrine of the Trinity as distinct from the Presbyterian or Methodist or Lutheran doctrines of the Trinity. Here Protestants, Roman Catholics, and Eastern Orthodox can find much common ground. Differences concerning the understanding of the Trinity today tend to be within denominations more than between denominations, although some rather distinctive Anglican emphases have been noted. Rejection of the Trinity is basic to the Unitarian-Universalists and the Jehovah's Witnesses. These differences in teaching and these rejections tend to be a repetition of views first set forth during the patristic or medieval or even Reformation eras rather than completely new positions. Although there is no distinctive Baptist doctrine of the Trinity, Baptists, as indeed also members of other Christian denominations, can unduly neglect or deemphasize the Trinity in theological study,[54] church curriculum, congregational worship, or personal piety.

VII. THE TRINITY: MYSTERY AND WORSHIP

The doctrine of the Trinity points to the mystery of the Divine Being whom Christians worship and serve and who by their confession is at work in their lives. As a truth the Trinity has baffled the most astute Christian thinkers throughout the history of Christianity. It defies normal human logic and transcends our human, modal, natural, and psychological analogies. Karl Rahner has declared: "The dogma of the Trinity is an *absolute mystery* which we do not understand even after it has been revealed."[55] Yet the Trinity has been regarded as basic to the Christian understanding of God's reality. In creeds and confessions of faith Christian theologians have sought to bear witness to and to demarcate, if not to explain, the Trinity. Christian musicians, architects, and artists have attempted to celebrate and illustrate the Trinity. Amid all their limitations of knowledge and understanding, Christians have continued to teach about and to worship and praise the Triune God—Father, Son, and Holy Spirit.

54. *Review and Expositor*, the theological journal of Southern Baptist Theological Seminary, after 86 years of publication, *Southwestern Journal of Theology*, the theological journal of Southwestern Baptist Theological Seminary, after 40 years of publication, *Theological Educator*, the journal of New Orleans Baptist Theological Seminary, after 22 years of publication, and *Faith and Mission*, the theological journal of Southeastern Baptist Theological Seminary, after seven years of publication, have never issued a thematic issue on the doctrine of the Trinity.
55. *The Trinity*, p. 50.

PART III

Creation, Providence, and Suprahuman Beings

CHAPTER 24

Creation: Biblical Witness
and Theological Formulation

What do we mean when we use the word "creation"? Is our answer obvious and unambiguous? Christian theologians have tended to use the term in either or both of two ways: in reference to the *activity* of God in creating, and/or in reference to the *result* of God's creative activity.

A. H. Strong and Karl Barth were among those theologians who employed the term "creation" to mean God's creative activity. Strong offered two definitions illustrative of this trend. "Creation is designed origination, by a transcendent and personal God, of that which itself is not God." Furthermore, creation is "that free act of the triune God by which in the beginning for his own glory he made, without the use of preexisting materials, the whole visible and invisible universe."[1] According to Barth, "Creation comes first in the series of works of the triune God, and is thus the beginning of all the things distinct from God Himself."[2] Thus, chronologically and logically creation is the first of the mighty acts of God.

E. Y. Mullins utilized the term "creation" in reference to the result of divine activity. "By creation is meant all that exists which is not God."[3] Accordingly "creation" becomes the synonym of "created universe" and "the whole creation." In a distinctly eschatological passage in the Gospels, which involves a very Hebraic manner of speaking, both of these uses seem to be evident: "from the beginning of the creation which God created until now" (Mark 13:19, RSV).

The activity of creating that results in the created universe involves, according to the Bible and to Christian tradition, a personal Creator, God. Essential to the doctrine of creation is the role and office of the divine Creator. The Bible opens (Gen. 1:1) by declaring his role, and the Apostles' Creed initially affirms belief in "God the Father almighty, Maker of heaven and earth."

1. *Systematic Theology,* p. 371.
2. *Church Dogmatics,* III/1, trans. J. W. Edwards, O. Bussey, and Harold Knight (Edinburgh: T. and T. Clark, 1958), p. 42.
3. *The Christian Religion in Its Doctrinal Expression,* p. 251; see W. W. Stevens, *Doctrines of the Christian Religion,* p. 65.

I. THE BIBLICAL WITNESS TO CREATION

The task of explicating the Christian doctrine of creation at the end of the twentieth century does not begin with scientific observation or with philosophical speculation or with legislative maneuvering; rather it begins with the exegesis of pertinent texts in the Old and the New Testaments and their proper correlation. The Bible bears witness to the creative activity of God, and that witness is fundamental to anything that Christians today can believe and teach about creation.

A. THE OLD TESTAMENT

1. *The Pentateuch (Torah)*

a. The Early Genesis Accounts (1:1–2:4a and 2:4b-25)

1) *Their distinctive features*

a) Genesis 1:1–2:4a

Looking in the pages of Holy Scripture, we find Genesis 1:1 declaring the creation of the heaven and the earth; Genesis 1:2 stating that the earth was in an unformed condition. In Genesis 1:3ff. we have a narration of six days in which the earth is formed, and plant, fish, bird, and mammal life is created, climaxed with the creation of man.[4]

At least from the time of Basil of Caesarea (c. 330-79) and Ambrose of Milan (c. 339-97)[5] Christian authors have been attracted to the task of expounding the "six days of creation" account. Modern expositors have undertaken this task vis-à-vis the teachings of the geological, anthropological, and biological sciences. We may summarize the basic elements of that exposition as follows:

(1) Creation of "the heavens and the earth"
(2) Speaking of light into existence and separation of the light and the darkness (day and night) (first day)
(3) Making of a firmament for the separation of the upper and lower waters (second day)
(4) Separation of the dry land (earth) from the waters (seas) (third day)
(5) Earth's yielding of seed-bearing plants and trees (third day)
(6) Making of the sun, moon, and stars for chronology and for light (fourth day)
(7) Creation of fish and fowl (fifth day)

---

4. Bernard L. Ramm, *The Christian View of Science and Scripture* (Grand Rapids: Eerdmans, 1954), p. 172.

5. Basil's *Hexaemeron* (The Six Days of Creation), written before 370, may be found in the translation by Blomfield Jackson in NPNF, 2nd ser., 8:52-107. Ambrose's *Hexameron*, probably written in 387, may be found in Ambrose, *Hexameron, Paradise*, and *Cain and Abel*, trans. John J. Savage, Fathers of the Church, vol. 42 (New York: Fathers of the Church, Inc., 1961), pp. 3-283.

(8) Making of cattle, creeping things, and wild animals (sixth day)
(9) Creation of man, male and female, in the image / likeness of
    God with dominion (sixth day)
(10) Rest (seventh day)

Latin theologians distinguish between God's *opus divisionis* (work of division) during the first three days (Gen. 1:3-13) and his *opus ornatus* (work of ornamentation) during the fourth, fifth, and sixth days (Gen. 1:14-31).[6] Whereas the chronology advanced by James Ussher (1581-1656) concluded that creation occurred in 4004 B.C., Bernard Ramm has written: "There is no date nor time element in the record except the expression 'in the beginning.' The account is simple, brief, majestic, and monotheistic."[7]

b) Genesis 2:4b-25

This account stressed the formation of humankind "of dust from the ground" and with "the breath of life," the Edenic garden, the Adamic naming of the animal creation, and a distinct formation of woman from man. Some consider this account to be more anthropomorphic, that is, more expressed in human categories, than Gen. 1:1–2:4a.

Those who hold strictly to a source documentary view concerning the Pentateuch usually conclude that the P and J documents arose in Judah and included creation accounts, whereas the E and D documents, originating in Israel, placed less emphasis on creation.[8]

2) The Genesis accounts and the Babylonian Enuma elish

Soon after its discovery George Smith (1840-76) published a monograph with translated texts of *Enuma elish* under the title *The Chaldean Account of Genesis*.[9] For more than a century scholars have debated whether and how much the Genesis accounts were dependent on the Babylonian epic.[10] At the turn of the twentieth century James Orr was emphatic about the differences:

> The Babylonian cosmogonies are, without exception, polytheistic, mythological, fantastic in character to the highest degree. The Biblical story is the opposite of all this: serious, orderly, monotheistic, rational, the vehicle of the very noblest ideas about God and His world.[11]

6. William G. Heidt, O.S.B., *The Book of Genesis, Chapters 1–11*, Old Testament Reading Guide, no. 9 (Collegeville, Minn.: Liturgical Press, 1967), p. 9; Moody, *The Word of Truth*, pp. 144-45.

7. *The Christian View of Science and Scripture*, p. 172.

8. Bernard W. Anderson, *Creation versus Chaos: The Reinterpretation of Mythical Symbolism in the Bible* (New York: Association Press, 1967), pp. 55-60, 68-69.

9. (London: Sampson Low, Marston, Searle, and Rivington, 1876; rev. ed. A. H. Sayce, 1880).

10. Moody, *The Word of Truth*, p. 144.

11. *God's Image in Man and Its Defacement in the Light of Modern Denials* (London: Hodder and Stoughton, 1905), p. 38.

Although some have pressed the similarities and hence the dependence of Genesis, noting, for example, that Tiamat, the Babylonian monster of chaos, is similar to $t^eh\hat{o}m$, the term in Genesis for "the deep," the radical differences between polytheism and monotheism and between "chaotic instability" and orderly progression argue for a minimum of dependence.[12] According to Eric Charles Rust, *Enuma Elish* "is a representation of the rhythm of the cosmos and not of its creation," and in Genesis the Creator and the created are clearly differentiated without compromising the sovereignty of the Creator.[13] William George Heidt (1913-) has concluded that *Enuma Elish* "is not a 'creation account' at all . . . , but," in view of its having been a Sumerian epic into which Babylonian deities were inserted, "a justification for the political hegemony of Babylon during the era history associates with Hammurabi" and hence a "splendid piece of political propaganda."[14]

3) The Genesis accounts and the language of "myth," "symbol," and "saga"

During the twentieth century it has not been uncommon for Christian theologians to apply to the Genesis accounts of creation, together with Genesis 3, terms such as "myth," "symbol," and "saga" in an effort to emphasize the distinctive character of these accounts. Whether such usage has been strongly influenced by cultural anthropology and/or literary criticism is an open question. Three examples of the use of "myth" in relation to Genesis 1–3 may be cited. Emil Brunner referred to "the mythical idea of a Primitive State in Paradise."[15] Eric C. Rust declared: "The Old Testament begins with two myths of creation, both of which reflect elements from the pagan mythology of the surrounding peoples but both of which are also permeated by the transforming influence of the covenant faith."[16] Langdon B. Gilkey defined "religious myth" as "a symbolic story expressing the religious answer to man's ultimate questions." Furthermore, myth "has no direct relation to scientific theories."[17] This employment of the term "myth" in an intended favorable light to refer to biblical events of the remote past—or indeed also of the future— has encountered both contrary biblical usage and popular Christian resistance. In every New Testament usage—almost all in the Pastoral Epistles[18]—of the word "myths"[19] the connotation is uniformly negative.

---

12. Moody, *The Word of Truth*, pp. 144-45.
13. *Nature and Man in Biblical Thought* (London: Lutterworth Press, 1953), pp. 24, 35-36.
14. *The Book of Genesis, Chapters 1–11*, pp. 37-40.
15. *The Christian Doctrine of Creation and Redemption*, p. 74.
16. *Nature and Man in Biblical Thought*, p. 20.
17. *Maker of Heaven and Earth: A Study of the Christian Doctrine of Creation* (Garden City, N.Y.: Doubleday, 1959), p. 34.
18. 1 Tim. 1:4; 4:7; 2 Tim. 4:4; Tit. 1:14; 2 Pet. 1:16.
19. Joseph Henry Thayer, *Greek-English Lexicon of the New Testament* (reprint ed.; Lafayette, Ind.: Book Publisher's Press, Inc., 1981), p. 419, defined *mythos* as "a fiction," "a

The popular Christian mind can hardly be convinced that a term that has only negative nuances in the New Testament can ably serve as the tool of modern theologians for classification of the Genesis accounts of creation.

Somewhat more promising has been Karl Barth's use of the term "saga." The Swiss theologian explained:

> The history of creation is 'non-historical' or, to be more precise, pre-historical history. . . . And for this very reason it can be the object only of a 'non-historical,' pre-historical depiction and narration. . . . I am using saga in the sense of an intuitive and poetic picture of a pre-historical reality of history which is enacted once and for all within the confines of time and space.[20]

Geoffrey William Bromiley (1915-) and Thomas Forsyth Torrance (1913-) wrote of Barth's usage: "Saga, or more simply 'story,' is the telling of a historical event which cannot be historiographically expressed."[21] Strong early in the century had favored "the pictorial-summary interpretation" of the Genesis accounts.[22] Indeed, some special term is needed in the human and Christian effort to describe the awesome, unique activity of God in creation, of which no human was an eyewitness.

b. Other Pentateuchal Passages

The creation is not a prominent theme in the remainder of the Pentateuch. In the Melchizedek passage (Gen 14:19, 22) 'El 'Elyon is said to be the "maker of heaven and earth." In Deut. 4:32, RSV, allusion is made to "the day that God created man upon the earth." Deut. 32:6 is probably a reference to the "creation" of Israel as a covenant people rather than to the creation of all things.

2. The Prophetical Books

> For lo, he who forms the mountains, and creates the wind, and declares to man what is his thought, who makes the morning darkness, and treads on the heights of the earth—the Lord, the God of hosts, is his name!

These words are found in the prophecy of Amos (4:13, RSV). According to Jeremiah, Yahweh "made the earth," including human beings and animals (27:5), "established the world," and "stretched out the heavens" (10:12); indeed, Yahweh "formed all things" (10:16). In a lament concerning the king of Tyre, Ezekiel alluded to "the day you were created" and blamelessness until sin was committed (28:13, 15, RSV). In Isaiah 40–55 the Hebrew verb *bārā'*, "to create," is used 16 times.[23] "Wherever this latter

---

fable," or "a falsehood"; in the plural, those "of the Jewish theosophists and Gnostics, esp. concerning the emanations and orders of the aeons."

20. *Church Dogmatics*, III/1, pp. 80, 81.
21. "Editors' Preface," ibid., p. viii.
22. *Systematic Theology*, p. 393.
23. Isa. 40:26, 28; 41:20; 42:5; 43:1, 7, 15; 45:7 (twice); 45:8, 12; 45:18 (twice); 48:7; 54:16 (twice). Concerning the other Hebrew verbs associated with creation, see Erickson, *Christian Theology*, p. 368.

verb appears in the Old Testament, God is always the subject, and it surely refers to a unique creative action which he alone can perform."[24] "Have you not known? Have you not heard? The LORD is the everlasting God, the Creator of the ends of the earth" (40:28a, b, RSV). Yahweh "created the heavens" (42:5; 45:18), or "stretched out the heavens" (42:5; 44:34; 45:12), or "spread out the heavens" (48:13). He "spread forth the earth" (42:5), or "made the earth" (45:12, 18), or "formed the earth" (45:18), or "laid the foundation of the earth" (48:13). He "created man" (45:12), or gave "breath" and "spirit" to humans (42:5). "I [Yahweh] form light and create darkness, I make weal and create woe" (45:7, RSV) so that there has been no eternal dualism wherein evil has coexisted with God. He "did not create it a chaos" (45:18), for he has cut to pieces Rahab the monster and "dried up . . . the waters of the great deep" (51:9b, RSV). His creative work was so comprehensive as to include both the "blacksmith" and the "destroyer" (54:16).[25]

3. The Wisdom Writings

In poetic words ascribed to Job (26:7-14) God's comprehensive work of creation was celebrated, and Yahweh questioned Job (38:4-11) as to his whereabouts when the foundation of the earth was laid. Prov. 8:22-31 affirms that wisdom was "brought . . . forth as the first of his [Yahweh's] works" (NIV), prior to any other activity of creation. Psalm 8 is a celebration of the creation of humankind with dominion over the heavens as well as the earth. Yahweh made the heavens (Ps. 96:5) and founded the world on subterranean seas (Ps. 24:1-2). He "established the mountains" (Ps. 65:6), created south and north (Ps. 89:12), the depths and the heights, the sea and the dry land (Ps. 95:4-5), and the sun, the moon, and the stars (Ps. 74:16; 136:7-9; 147:4; 148:3-6). Creation was wrought by "the word of Yahweh" (Ps. 33:6), and the eternal God preceded and will succeed his creative work (Ps. 90:2; 102:25-27). God's mighty work of creation is celebrated in Ps. 77:16-19, and Psalm 104 unites God's work of creation and his sustenance of the created order. In the Psalms (74:13-15) and in Job (26:12), as well as in Isa. 51:9b, Yahweh is said to have overpowered the sea monster Rahab or Leviathan.

B. THE NEW TESTAMENT

Passages in the New Testament that refer specifically to creation are fewer in number than in the Old Testament, but the writers assume the reality of creation, and creation is mentioned in each of the four principal types of New Testament literature.

---

24. James Muilenburg, "Introduction [Isaiah], Chs. 40–66," *The Interpreter's Bible*, 12 vols. (New York, Nashville: Abingdon Press, 1951-57), 5:401.
25. Isa. 43:1, 5 and Ps. 100:3 probably refer to the creation of Israel as a covenant people, and Isa. 48:7a to Yahweh's creation of "new things" for that people. Concerning dualism, see below, Ch. 25, I, A, and Ch. 29, III, B.

1. Gospels

Allusions to creation appear in a strongly eschatological text (Mark 13:19) and in a Logos text (John 1:3), in which the agency of the Logos in creation is emphasized.

2. Acts

A Creator formula was used in Acts, namely, the God "who made the heaven and the earth and the sea and everything in them" (NIV). It was used by Peter and John in Jerusalem (4:24b), by Paul in Lystra (14:15c), and by Paul in condensed form in Athens (17:24). This Creator, according to Paul, " 'gives to all men life and breath and everything' " and indeed " 'made from one every nation of men to live on all the face of the earth' " (17:25b, 26a, RSV).

3. Epistles

Paul quoted the commandment of light in creation (Gen. 1:3; 2 Cor. 4:6), put idolatry as creature-worship in stark contrast to the intended worship and service of the Creator (Rom. 1:25), and referred to Abraham's God as the one "who gives life to the dead and calls into existence the things that do not exist" (Rom. 4:17c, RSV). He mentioned the Creator in connection with the divine plan of the ages (Eph. 3:9) and in relation to the image-renewal that brought the new nature in Christ (Col. 3:10). In Col. 1:16-17 one finds the most detailed statement in the New Testament concerning the role of Jesus Christ in creation and in the sustenance of all things. According to Peter, the persecuted can "entrust their souls to a faithful Creator" (1 Pet. 4:19, RSV), and in the roll call of faith (Heb. 11:3, RSV) we read: "By faith we understand that the world was created by the word of God, so that what is seen was made out of things which do not appear."

4. Apocalypse

In an exalted scene God is acclaimed as worthy of worship because he "create[d] all things" and by his will "they existed and were created" (4:11, RSV). The Creator formula of Acts appears in slightly altered form in Rev. 10:6.

C. THE RELATION OF BIBLICAL TEXTS TO THE DOCTRINE OF CREATION

The biblical texts that speak of creation have posed a special problem for some Christian theologians during the modern era. Hence we need to address the question as to whether and to what extent these texts should be used in formulating the Christian doctrine of creation. F. D. E. Schleiermacher, after noting certain New Testament passages, called for the rejection of "any more definite conception of the Creation."[26] Quite re-

---

26. *The Christian Faith*, p. 150.

cently Hendrikus Berkhof expressed the same skepticism as to the doctrinal value of these texts. After citing ten passages in the Old Testament[27] as being the "most important statements about creation in the Old Testament," he then opined that the biblical concepts of creation were on a "secondary level" and concluded that the systematic theologian cannot "make direct use of any biblical statement on creation for the construction of his doctrine of creation."[28] What can be said in response to such a claim? First, one should acknowledge that theologians should handle biblical texts responsibly, recognizing context and literary genre and utilizing the best results of the work of biblical exegetes. Admittedly that has not always occurred in the past. Second, skepticism regarding the doctrinal import of biblical texts on creation, if applied widely to other doctrines of the Christian religion, would soon make impossible any Christian theological system with deep roots in the Bible. With such dire consequences in mind, one may ask, then, what is so very special about the doctrine of creation. Third, biblical statements about creation are essentially religious,[29] no matter in what literary form they are expressed, and whenever they are brought into dialogue with the findings of the geological, anthropological, and biological sciences or with modern philosophies of origins, this essential religious nature must be preserved and recognized. One ought, then, without skepticism but with care to proceed to build on the foundation of the biblical texts.

II. A FORMULATION OF THE CHRISTIAN DOCTRINE OF CREATION

The Christian doctrine of creation must not only be built on the foundation of biblical affirmations but also take into account the history of Christian doctrine, both its contributions and its challenges. First, then, we will explore the multifaceted nature and significance of creation. Second, we will make inquiry as to the purpose of creation. Finally, we will give attention to the role of the Triune God in creation.[30]

A. THE NATURE AND SIGNIFICANCE OF CREATION

1. Dependence of the Created Order

By its very nature the created order is dependent. It is not eternal or ultimate. Nothing created "is absolute."[31] The creature is finite and

---

27. Gen. 1:1–2:4a; 2:4b-7; Job 26:12-13; 38:8-11; Ps. 74:13-14; 89:10-11; 104:5-9; Prov. 8:29; Isa. 27:1; 51:9-11.

28. *Christian Faith: An Introduction to the Study of the Faith*, pp. 157-59.

29. See Henry C. Sheldon, *System of Christian Doctrine*, pp. 228-29.

30. Some twentieth-century Christian theologians have chosen not to discuss the doctrine of creation with the same thoroughness characterizing their treatments of other Christian doctrines; for example, Walter T. Conner, Lewis Sperry Chafer, L. Harold DeWolf, and Helmut Thielicke.

31. H. Berkhof, *Christian Faith*, p. 161.

mortal, like the grass and flowers (Isa. 40:6-8). Consequently, idolatrous worship of the creaturely is sinful (Rom. 1:25). Instead creation should point to the eternal sovereignty of God (Ps. 90:1-2). But created existence as dependent is nevertheless real existence. Christians, in answer to pantheism, have insisted on the genuineness of creaturely existence.[32] According to Harold Barnes Kuhn (1911-), the created order has "a *conferred* reality."[33]

2. Creation as the Free Activity of God

Creation is an expression of the free activity of God as Creator. Strictly speaking, creation was not necessary. God did not create in order to bring himself to completion. Nor did he create because he was driven to do so by external compulsion. Rev. 4:11 bears witness to the voluntary nature of God's creative work. The Christian doctrine of creation is contrary to any necessitarian view, whether that of ancient Babylonian myths or that of modern pantheism. This doctrine helps us to understand God's "freedom, His self-sufficiency, and His uniqueness as an eternal Existent."[34]

3. Creation out of Nothing (creatio ex nihilo)

Creation, at least as taught in the New Testament, involved bringing into existence that which had not previously existed. It was not merely the reshaping or re-formation of existent materials. Eric C. Rust has contended that in the Genesis accounts of creation there is "no indication of a *creatio ex nihilo*." Instead "already a primeval chaos existed," and God created "the world out of this formless world-stuff." The teaching of *creatio ex nihilo* in Jewish writings, therefore, did not become "explicit" until the time of the Maccabees (2 Macc. 7:28).[35] On the other hand, J. Oliver Buswell has held that creation *ex nihilo* was implicit in the Hebrew verb *bārā'*.[36] Two New Testament texts (Rom. 4:17; Heb. 11:3) seem to teach that creation was without the use of preexistent materials. The term *creatio ex nihilo* was chosen by Christian thinkers in response to Christianity's encounter with various dualisms, especially Greek and Gnostic. Not every early Christian author taught creation *ex nihilo*. Theophilus of Antioch[37] did teach the doctrine, but Justin Martyr[38] and Clement of

---

32. Gilkey, *Maker of Heaven and Earth*, pp. 58-63. Christian theologians, according to Gilkey, have taught that created beings are "not illusory shadows whose real substance or reality was God. Rather each creature" is "a real existent, not identical with God but separate from Him, an existing thing with an intrinsic being, an essential structure, and certain natural powers" (p. 62).

33. "Creation," in Carl F. H. Henry, ed., *Basic Christian Doctrines* (New York: Holt, Rinehart, and Winston, 1962), p. 58.

34. Ibid., p. 56.

35. *Nature and Man in Biblical Thought*, pp. 29, 43.

36. *A Systematic Theology of the Christian Religion*, 1:135-37.

37. *To Autolycus* 2.4.

38. *1 Apol.* 59.

Alexandria[39] taught Plato's doctrine "that the universe was made from pre-existent matter."[40] In embracing creation *ex nihilo* early Christian thinkers were not only rejecting the Platonic view but also the theory that all things issued or evolved from God himself, whether Gnostic emanationism or Hindu monism.[41] In the present century process philosophy/theology seems to deny creation *ex nihilo*.[42]

4. The Goodness of Creation

Creation was in the beginning in such a state as to be pronounced "good" by the Creator (Gen. 1:4, 10, 12, 18, 21, 25, 31). The "gap" theory concerning Gen. 1:1-2 finds it necessary to interpret this goodness as applying to a reordering or restoration of a created order that had fallen into disorder, but such a theory has weak exegetical support. Against all dualisms that would make the created order to be evil or the product of an evil or angry deity, be they Marcionite, Gnostic, or Manichean, the Christian teaching has insisted on the goodness of creation. Thus "nothing in existence can be intrinsically evil."[43]

5. Creation and Redemption

Creation is the background for and the correlate of redemption. The God who redeemed Israel and who redeems in Jesus Christ is the same God who has created the entire universe, including humankind. In both the Old Testament and the New Testament God's creatorship followed from the covenant or from redemption: the God of the covenant was said also to be the Creator. Both redemption and creation are major themes in Isaiah 40–55 and in Col. 1:13-17. The biblical authors did not merely infer from God's creative work that he was also the Redeemer of mankind. Faced with the threat of the Gnostics and of Marcion, Irenaeus repeatedly insisted during the second century A.D. that the God of the Old Testament is the God of the New Testament, that the Creator is the Redeemer.[44] The one God had chosen in his Son to redeem/reconcile sinning human creatures. All attempts, from Marcion and the Gnostics onward, to divorce creation from redemption have ultimately been taken to be contrary to the biblical and distinctively Christian viewpoint. Furthermore, any present-day tendency to fuse creation and redemption by interpreting redemption as being only the recognition of the created origin and state of human beings is equally deficient in respect to the biblical perspective.[45]

39. *Stromateis* 5.14.
40. Moody, *The Word of Truth*, p. 144.
41. A. T. Hanson and R. P. C. Hanson, *Reasonable Belief: A Survey of the Christian Faith*, p. 16.
42. Erickson, *Christian Theology*, p. 370.
43. Gilkey, *Maker of Heaven and Earth*, p. 52.
44. *Against Heresies*, passim.
45. John R. Claypool, *Opening Blind Eyes* (Nashville: Abingdon Press, 1983), pp. 59, 88, 92, 97, 100, 113.

6. *Creation as History, but Not Ordinary Recorded History*

Creation may be said to belong in a sense to the category of history, but not to history in the ordinary sense of recorded history. Eyewitnesses there were for the Exodus and for the death of Jesus, but not for creation. Creation is not reportable by ordinary methods of history writing, and hence divine revelation and inspiration are essential. Augustine of Hippo was the first Christian thinker to teach clearly that time originated with creation.[46] Hence creation cannot be "explained" by human and historical analogy.[47]

7. *Creation an Affirmation of Faith*

Creation is an affirmation or article of faith; that is, it is known through faith. The Apostles' Creed meaningfully commences with the words, "I believe in God the Father almighty, Maker of heaven and earth." The Christian acknowledgment of creation as the work of God cannot ultimately rest or depend on deduction from metaphysics or induction from science. It is an affirmation of religious faith. This fact does not mean that issues posed by the sciences and/or philosophy do not have to be faced by present-day Christians; rather it means that they are to be faced from the stance of faith. Creation is a faith-affirmation of Christianity, Judaism, and Islam. In the early Christian centuries the biblical doctrine of creation was "a scandal to the pagan mind."[48] So it may be today.

B. The Purpose of Creation

Christians have commonly and understandably raised the question as to why God did create all things. They have sought answers even though there are biblical texts (e.g., Rom. 11:33-35) that can be taken to discourage such quests. The Bible itself, however, is not replete with statements that clearly seek to answer why God created.

The most frequently given answer is that creation occurred for the glory of God himself. Isa. 43:7b ("whom I created for my glory") seems clearly to offer that answer. God is glorified by the created order (Ps. 19:1) and by both creation and sustenance (Ps. 104:31). The final subordination of the Son of God to the Father is to have the result "that God may be all in all" (1 Cor. 15:28), and even when human beings cannot fathom the mind and ways of God, God is to receive "the glory forever" (Rom. 11:36). A. H. Strong set forth an elaborate statement of the idea that creation was for the glory of God, citing numerous biblical texts and advancing five rational arguments.[49] Charles Hodge[50] earlier and F. A. O. Pieper[51] later

46. *On the City of God* 11.6; *Confessions* 11.10-13.
47. Gilkey, *Maker of Heaven and Earth*, pp. 54, 64-71.
48. Kuhn, "Creation," p. 57.
49. *Systematic Theology*, pp. 397-402.
50. *Systematic Theology*, 1:567-68.
51. *Christian Dogmatics*, 1:479.

supported the same position. Strong was quite certain that God's "supreme end" in creation could not be the "happiness" or "holiness" of his creatures and that true divine glory is not "selfishness" or "vain-glory." "He who constitutes the centre and end of all his creatures must find his centre and end in himself."[52]

A second answer is to be found in God's having created in order to give expression to his own nature. Such an answer must be separated from any necessitarian view of creation. Augustine of Hippo, agreeing with Plato, emphasized the goodness of God as "the most sufficient reason" for the good creation.[53] According to Henry C. Sheldon, creation expressed God's "nature as holy love" in that God ultimately will have brought "many sons to glory" (Heb. 2:10).[54] If according to glorification God is essentially passive, this second answer sees him as very active.

Others have identified the purpose of creation as God's provision of fellowship with his creatures, especially human beings. According to E. Y. Mullins, "the end of God was the communication of his own life and blessedness to created beings," but Mullins coupled this with the divine glory.[55]

Whatever answer or answers are adopted, God's purpose in creation must be kept in tandem with his purpose in redemption (Eph. 3:9-11).

C. THE TRIUNE GOD AND CREATION

1. God the Father

The Old Testament refers to Yahweh or 'Elohim as the Creator. In the New Testament most of the references to God as Creator can be understood as allusions to the Father. The Apostles' Creed identifies creation with God the Father. Present-day Christians tend to speak and think of creation primarily in reference to God the Father. A reminder is needed, therefore, that the full consequence of biblical teaching is that the Triune God is the Creator of all things.

2. The Son of God, or the Logos

Not only the first Genesis account (1:3, 6, 9, 14, 20, 24, 26) but other Old Testament passages (Ps. 33:6; 148:5; Isa. 48:13) specified that creation occurred through the Word of God. In the light of the advent and saving work of Jesus Christ the New Testament writers specifically attributed to him a role in creation. In Col. 1:15-17, in a context in which he likely was countering an early form of Gnosticism, Paul declared the Son of God, who preceded and stands over the created order, to be the agent of creation, the sustainer of the creation, and the goal or end of creation. Heb.

52. *Systematic Theology,* pp. 398, 400, 401.
53. *On the City of God* 11.21.
54. *System of Christian Doctrine,* p. 236.
55. *The Christian Religion in Its Doctrinal Expression,* p. 253.

1:3 (NIV) identified the Son of God as the one "through whom" God "made the universe." According to the Johannine prologue "all things were made" through the eternal Logos, who "was with God in the beginning" (1:2, 3a, NIV). "God's instrument of creation was the Word of power in which He uttered Himself."[56]

3. The Spirit of God

Basic to the first Genesis account of creation is the declaration that "the Spirit of God was hovering over the waters" (1:2b, NIV). It is appropriate to ask to what extent there was hypostatic distinction of the Spirit from God in the mind of Moses and the shapers of Genesis. Ps. 104:30 connects the Spirit of God with the sustenance of the created order, though not with creation. The New Testament does not develop this theme. Eric C. Rust has articulated a doctrine of the Holy Spirit as the immanent agent of evolution, speaking even of "the Kenosis (self-emptying) of the Spirit."[57]

4. The Triune God

Christian theologians have been prone to want to allocate or specify the roles of the Father, the Son, and the Spirit in creation. For example, Strong identified "the Father as the originating, the Son as the mediating, [and] the Spirit as the realizing cause" of creation.[58] The more classical approach was enunciated by Pieper: "Creation as an *opus Dei ad extra* is the work of the Triune God."[59]

After exploring two basic usages of the term "creation," we have sought in this chapter to investigate the biblical witness to creation and to formulate the Christian doctrine of creation, depending heavily on that very biblical witness and using the results of Christian history. We have found creation to be a theme enunciated in various ways in all three major parts of the Hebrew Bible. In particular we have given attention to the two accounts of creation early in Genesis, especially their distinctive features, their relation to Babylonian literature, and their being subsumed under such categories as "myth" or "saga." Then, too, we have found creation to be a theme in all four types of New Testament literature. In explicating the doctrine of creation we have given major emphasis to its nature and significance, discussing such themes as the dependence of the created, the freedom of God, creation out of nothing, the goodness of creation, creation and redemption, creation and history, and creation and faith. We have

56. G. H. C. Macgregor, *The Gospel of John*, Moffatt New Testament Commentary (Garden City, N.Y.: Doubleday, Doran and Company, Inc., 1929), p. 5. For an incisive treatment of these texts, see Rust, *Nature and Man in Biblical Thought*, pp. 210-24.

57. *Science and Faith: Towards a Theological Understanding of Nature* (New York: Oxford University Press, 1967), pp. 182-200.

58. *Systematic Theology*, p. 373.

59. *Christian Dogmatics*, 1:479.

devoted less attention to the purpose of creation and to the role of the Triune God in creation.

Now it is advisable that we turn to various alternative answers that have been given in the Western religious and philosophical tradition to the question of origins.

CHAPTER 25

Contrary Views about Origins; Creation and Contemporary Issues

The Christian doctrine of creation has from the early Christian centuries been confronted with competing explanations of the origins of all things, whether philosophic or religious. Some of these explanations are not being vigorously advocated today, while others offer vigorous competition to the Christian teaching. Especially is this true of forms of evolutionary theory. In this chapter we will survey various competing views and then treat certain contemporary issues in greater detail.

I. CONTRARY VIEWS ABOUT ORIGINS[1]

A. DUALISM

At least three types of dualism have drawn conclusions contrary to the Christian doctrine of the divine creation of all things. These types need to be differentiated.

1. Metaphysical Dualism

This is the view that God and matter are "two self-existent principles," "distinct from and coeternal with each other." Accordingly, the material universe is in no sense derived from God, regardless of how matter is explained. Yet matter can be "subordinate to God" and serve as "the instrument of his will."[2] Hermogenes the Gnostic, according to the interpretation by Hippolytus,[3] taught "that God made all things out of coeval and unregenerated matter" and "subject to His design." There was, however, a portion of matter that "remains wild, and is denominated chaotic matter." In the books sacred to the Church of Jesus Christ of

---

1. At the beginning of this century Strong, *Systematic Theology*, pp. 378-91, provided a clear delineation of these views. The treatment here is built on and is an updated adaptation of Strong's presentation.
2. Ibid., p. 378.
3. *Refutation of All Heresies* 8.10; 10.24.

Latter-day Saints one finds the teaching that God organized the heavens and the earth and that matter was and is eternal.[4]

2. Moral Dualism

Although this view is not without metaphysical implications, it holds basically that "two antagonistic spirits, one evil and the other good," presumably both divine, have eternally existed, and matter is "either the work [product] or the instrument" of the evil spirit or being.[5] Manichaeism, a religion founded by Mani, or Manes (c. 215-75), in Persia, posited two eternally antagonistic spirits, the Light and the Darkness, both uncreated, coequal, and having separate kingdoms. Matter, or Hyle, was also unoriginated but belonged to the kingdom of Darkness. Yet the Light was able to produce worlds, elements, and Primordial Man.[6] On the contrary, in Zoroastrianism matter was looked upon as "pure" and as the product of the good deity, Ahura Mazda, not of the evil deity, Ahriman.[7]

3. Demiurgic Dualism

This is the view that matter and all the universe derive from the work of a demiurge, or a secondary or subordinate agent of creation, who himself had been created by God. This view is not strictly, only relatively dualistic. Marcion in the second century A.D. taught that Yahweh or the "just" God, who was quite distinct from the Stranger or Father of Jesus Christ or "good" God, created the world out of preexistent matter. In a sense Marcion was tritheistic, making the two gods and matter eternal, as E. C. Blackman has suggested. Moreover, Marcion's was not strictly a demiurgic view, since Yahweh was not created by the Father of Jesus, though Yahweh is supposed to disappear at the end of the age.[8] Valentinus, a prominent Gnostic, taught that the world came into existence through Sophia, the last of the 30-member pleroma, or body of aeons;[9] and Basilides, according to the interpretation given by Irenaeus,[10] posited the emanation of 365 heavens before the 365th one was able to make our world.

According to metaphysical dualism matter is eternal, according to moral dualism matter may or may not be eternal, and according to demiurgic dualism matter derives from a secondary creator.

4. *Doctrine and Covenants* 93.33; *Book of Abraham* 4.1.

5. Strong, *Systematic Theology*, pp. 381-82.

6. Geo Widengren, *Mani and Manichaeism*, trans. Charles Kessler (New York: Holt, Rinehart and Winston, 1965), esp. pp. 43-46.

7. Often thought to be the perfect example of dualistic religion, Zoroastrianism may have been less than the perfect example in that both Ahura Mazda and Ahriman were said to be begotten by Zervan, "an hermaphrodite space-time godhead." Ibid., p. 44.

8. Blackman, *Marcion and His Influence* (London: S.P.C.K., 1948), esp. pp. 71-80; R. Joseph Hoffman, *Marcion: On the Restitution of Christianity: An Essay on the Development of Radical Paulinist Theology in the Second Century*, American Academy of Religion Academy Series, no. 46 (Chico, Calif.: Scholars Press, 1984), pp. 192-210.

9. Irenaeus, *Against Heresies* 1.1-14, esp. 5.

10. Ibid. 1.24.

B. Monistic Emanationism

This is the view that "the universe is of the same substance with God and is the product of successive" overflowings or outflowings from the nature or being of God.[11] In more colloquial language it means that all things came about through a sloughing off of God. Basilides, according to Hippolytus,[12] taught that all things derived from God through a world-seed, which proliferated into a "threefold Sonship" and begat the Great Archon, the head of the world, who in turn begat a son and created the entire celestial order. Another derived Archon created the noncelestial universe. Neo-Platonism, represented by Plotinus, taught the emanation of all from the One, or the Good, through the Mind and the World-Soul and the later reabsorption of all that has derived into the One. "The process of division is not that of bisection, but is like the unfolding of wrappings."[13] John Milton in his *Christian Doctrine*[14] denied creation *ex nihilo* and affirmed that God "produced all things . . . out of himself." Milton avoided "the charge of pantheism" by emphasizing that God granted free will to the "centres of finite existence."[15] According to Emanuel Swedenborg (1688-1772), God

> creates from Himself, or by an efflux of Himself from Himself. . . . He creates always and incessantly. Whatever is exists by a perpetual and ever present efflux from Him. The work of creation is always now. . . . God creates the universe from Himself; but He creates it other than Himself. He creates it for His creatures, and He gives it to them. He makes it to be theirs. . . . God creates from Love.[16]

Emanationism often leads to pantheism since that which has emanated is looked upon as "still divine."[17] Today it is being taught by the New Age movement.

C. Creation from Eternity

This is the view that creation was "an act of God in eternity past."[18] It disconnects creation from the beginning of time and tends toward dualism in that the eternal process of creating is tantamount to positing that matter is eternal. There are, however, two distinct types of this theory.

---

11. Strong, *Systematic Theology*, p. 383.

12. *Refutation of All Heresies* 10.10.

13. Thomas Whittaker, *The Neo-Platonists: A Study in the History of Hellenism* (2d ed.; Cambridge: University Press, 1918; reprint ed.; Freeport, N.Y.: Books for Libraries Press, 1970), p. 63.

14. Bk. 1, ch. 7, in *Complete Prose Works of John Milton*, gen. ed. Don M. Wolfe (New Haven: Yale University Press), vol. 6, ed. Maurice Kelley (1973), p. 310.

15. Strong, *Systematic Theology*, p. 385.

16. Theophilus Parsons, *Outlines of the Religion and Philosophy of Swedenborg* (rev. ed.; New York: New Church Press, Inc., 1876), pp. 54, 55, 56.

17. Erickson, *Christian Theology*, p. 377.

18. Strong, *Systematic Theology*, p. 386.

1. Creation of Matter from Eternity by God

Accordingly, matter is eternal but somehow created by God or deity. Aristotle in *Physica* came to this conclusion from the eternity of motion.[19] Various later thinkers embraced this basic view.[20]

2. Creation of Spirit Beings from Eternity by God

Origen taught that a world of spiritual beings or rational spirits has been eternally or nontemporally created by God. Such beings are "originate" and "generate" and thus derive from God. They are unstable, and such instability led them away from God and toward nonbeing so that they diversified and became embodied in our physical world, which is not eternal. Such an eternal world of spirits, according to Origen, was necessary if God was to be omnipotent.[21] In the modern period the Church of Jesus Christ of Latter-day Saints teaches that all human beings once had a preexistent life as spirit beings, that Satan and one-third of these spirits rebelled and were cast down to earth in a nonbodily existence, and that the earth was created so that other preexistent spirits would have a dwelling place.[22] Unlike Origen and the Mormons, mainstream Christian thinkers have rejected the idea of the preexistence of the souls of human beings.

D. CONTINUOUS PRESENT CREATION

This is the view that "regards the universe as from moment to moment the result of a new [divine] creation."[23] Emanationism, as previously discussed, was found to contain the concept of the progressive coming-to-be of all things out of God's own being. The theory of continuous creation also has a durative element, but that which is being created is other than God, and the process is so broken into momentary units as to threaten any continuity. Certain New England theologians in colonial America held to this view, substituting continuous creation for preservation or sustenance of the created universe. Jonathan Edwards, Sr. (1703-58), asserted that "God's *preserving* created things in being is perfectly equivalent to a *continued creation*, or to his creating those things out of nothing at *each moment* of their existence."[24] Karl Heim (1874-1958), a German Protestant theologian who wrote on Christianity and science, asserted that something centuries old is

---

19. 4.12.221-22; 8.1.250-52, trans. R. P. Hardie and R. K. Gaye, in vol. 2, *The Works of Aristotle*, ed. W. D. Ross (Oxford: Clarendon Press, 1930).

20. Stoics, John Duns Scotus (c. 1264-1308), Giordano Bruno (1548-1600), Spinoza, and Hegel, according to Hendrikus Berkhof, *Christian Faith*, p. 154.

21. *On First Principles* 1.5; A. C. McGiffert, *A History of Christian Thought*, 2 vols. (New York: Charles Scribner's Sons, 1932-33), 1:223-24; Richard A. Norris, *God and World in Early Christianity* (New York: Seabury Press, 1965), pp. 119-26.

22. *Book of Abraham* 3.22-28; LeGrand Richards, *A Marvelous Work and a Wonder* (rev. ed.; Salt Lake City: Deseret Book Company, 1966), pp. 282, 285, 303.

23. Strong, *Systematic Theology*, p. 415.

24. *Original Sin* 4.3, ed. Clyde A. Holbrook, vol. 3, *The Works of Jonathan Edwards* (New Haven: Yale University Press, 1970), p. 401.

> a continuous series of successive acts of preservation by which from moment
> to moment it is decided afresh that this thing shall retain this particular form.
> Thus all maintenance is a continuous re-creation.[25]

The continuous view, therefore, holds that the universe is "continually
ceasing to be, and [that] God is continually calling it back into existence."[26]
Strong acknowledged that this view rightly assumes "that all force is will"
but pointed out that it erroneously maintains "that all force is *divine* will,
and divine will in *direct* exercise," thus downplaying both human wills
and the "forces of nature."[27]

E. ATHEISTIC EVOLUTION

This view, identified by Strong as "spontaneous generation,"[28] holds
that the universe, including all forms of life, has been derived without any
divine agency from a "natural process still going on—matter itself [or
energy] having in it the power, under proper conditions, of taking on new
functions, and of developing into organic forms."[29] This view is also
known as "evolutionary naturalism."[30] Representative of this view have
been Thomas Henry Huxley (1825-95),[31] an English biologist; Ernst Heinrich Philipp August Haeckel (1834-1919), a German zoologist; Julian Sorell
Huxley (1887-1975), an English biologist; and George Gaylord Simpson
(1902-84), an American paleontologist. It should be clearly recognized that
in drawing their conclusions these authors engaged in philosophy outside
the parameters of the scientific method. Haeckel, in an effort to span the
chasm between cosmic evolution and organic evolution, claimed that

> the cell consists of matter called protoplasm, composed chiefly of carbon
> with an admixture of hydrogen, nitrogen and sulphur. These component
> parts, properly united, produce the soul and body of the animated world,
> and suitably nursed became man. With this single argument the mystery of
> the universe is explained, the Deity annulled and a new era of infinite
> knowledge ushered in.[32]

Simpson concluded that

25. *God Transcendent: Foundation for a Christian Metaphysic*, trans. Edgar Primrose
Dickie (New York: Charles Scribner's Sons, 1936), pp. 181-85.

26. Erickson, *Christian Theology*, pp. 391-92.

27. *Systematic Theology*, p. 416.

28. The term has been more recently used by William J. Schmitt, S.J., "Creation and
the Origin of Life," *Science and Religion: New Perspectives on the Dialogue*, ed. Ian G. Barbour
(London: SCM Press, 1968), pp. 182-92.

29. Strong, *Systematic Theology*, p. 389.

30. Ian G. Barbour, *Issues in Science and Religion* (Englewood Cliffs, N.J.: Prentice-Hall,
Inc., 1966), pp. 408-14.

31. T. H. Huxley's position is best identified as "agnosticism" rather than theoretical
atheism, according to Gavin de Beer, "Huxley, Thomas Henry," *Encyclopedia Britannica*, 1969
ed., 11:916-18.

32. Quoted by W. S. Lilley in *Fortnightly Review* 39 (1886): 35, and requoted by Loren
Eiseley, *Darwin's Century: Evolution and the Men Who Discovered It* (rev. ed.; Garden City, N.Y.:
Doubleday and Company, 1961), p. 346.

there was no anticipation of man's coming. He responds to no plan and fulfills no supernal purpose. He stands alone in the universe, a unique product of a long, unconscious, impersonal, material process, with unique understanding and potentialities. These he owes to no one but himself, and it is to himself that he is responsible. He is not the creature of uncontrollable and undeterminable forces, but his own master.[33]

Full-fledged dualism posits the eternity of the material universe. Emanationism posits that all things are the efflux of God himself. Creation from eternity past lifts creation to prehistory, whereas continuous creation makes creation to be a moment-by-moment process. Atheistic evolution posits that matter or energy and all forms of life issued from primal energy without the agency of God. Over against these the Christian doctrine of creation teaches that the one eternal, Triune God created *de novo* out of nothing the entire universe and its forms of life, including human beings, and also sustains this created order toward the end or goal that he has chosen.

II. CREATION AND CONTEMPORARY ISSUES

It would be impossible to treat exhaustively the many present-day issues or problems related to the Christian doctrine of creation. Instead of attempting to list or locate these many issues, we choose rather to focus attention on four problem areas: creation and astrophysical theories about the origin of the universe, creation and geological data about the age of the earth, creation and evolutionary views about the origin of human beings, and creation and the contemporary religious movement known as "creation science."

Before we examine these four problem areas, however, it is necessary to reiterate[34] that the Christian doctrine of creation is primarily an affirmation of faith based on the biblical teachings about creation and informed by insights derivable from the history of Christian doctrine. It is also advisable to take note of some differing attitudes prevalent today among those who give attention to the intersection of the Christian doctrine of creation and the findings of the astrophysical, geological, biological, and anthropological sciences.

First, some in the scientific community see dialogue with Christian theologians and church leaders as useless since "scientific" conclusions have invalidated any role of God as Creator. Second, among Christians, especially Fundamentalist Protestant Christians, there are those who see dialogue with scientists as useless since all major scientists are thought to have embraced atheistic evolution and/or the Christian doctrine of creation has been so interpreted as to rule out any development of forms of

---

33. *Life of the Past: An Introduction to Paleontology* (New Haven: Yale University Press, 1953), p. 155.
34. See above, Ch. 24, II, A, 7.

life. These two groups by no means encompass the majority and may indeed constitute the extremes. Third, some theologically conservative Christians, Protestant and Roman Catholic, have concluded that a full harmonization of Christian teachings and scientific conclusions about origins has already occurred and these results simply need to be shared more widely. Fourth, still other Christian thinkers, especially in the neoorthodox and existentialist movements, see religious affirmations and scientific conclusions as being so very different that they, as it were, run on different tracks and never really meet one another. These four perspectives include a widening circle. Fifth, there are those, chiefly but not exclusively Christian believers, who, being aware of the differing roles of religion and the sciences, nevertheless see the need for continuing dialogue, respectful interchange, and critical analysis between the two realms and who seek greater correlation, if not harmonization, wherever legitimate and possible. The section that follows sympathizes with the fifth perspective.

A. CREATION AND ASTROPHYSICAL THEORIES ABOUT THE ORIGIN OF THE UNIVERSE

Astrophysicists and astronomers hold three principal theories as to the origin of the universe. First, there is the instantaneous or "big bang" theory of George Gamow (1904-). Accordingly, some "ten to fifteen billion years ago, the universe began from a small volume" but a very high density of energy and matter.[35] From a nucleus of neutrons it exploded into atoms, into elements, and ultimately into stars.[36] Second, there is the "steady state" of the universe theory of Fred Hoyle (1915-). Avoiding "infinite density at zero time,"[37] this view holds that throughout time and space matter has been uniformly coming into existence as "atoms continually condense into stars," which either die or move out of the range of observation.[38] Third, there is the "oscillating universe" theory of Ernst Jules Öpik (1893-). Accordingly the universe began in a smaller volume, has been increasing but is now increasing less rapidly, some billions of years later will actually cease to expand and will decrease its size, and then will begin its expansion anew.[39] According to David L. Dye (1925-), the data of the Christian revelation of God "neither intrinsically support nor preclude any of" these cosmological theories, and thus he sees no major problem between the two.[40] For Ian Graeme Barbour (1923-) the cosmological theories "are capable of either a naturalistic or a theistic interpretation." Hence Christians need not decide among the theories since the

---

35. David L. Dye, *Faith and the Physical World: A Comprehensive View* (Grand Rapids: Eerdmans, 1966), p. 129.
36. Barbour, *Issues in Science and Religion*, p. 366.
37. Dye, *Faith and the Physical World*, p. 130.
38. Barbour, *Issues in Science and Religion*, p. 366.
39. Dye, *Faith and the Physical World*, p. 131.
40. Ibid., p. 135.

"religious content of the idea of creation" can be harmonized with any of the theories.[41] Cosmological theories may pose, therefore, few problems for the Christian faith. Not so in other areas.

B. Creation and Geological Data about the Age of the Earth

For more than a century it has become increasingly evident that geological science was interpreting its expanding data so as to conclude that the earth is several billion years old, not several thousand years old, as Christian interpreters of Genesis have for centuries been accustomed to conclude. In the resultant confrontation of fossils and faith, therefore, does one face two irreconcilable positions, or is there an adequate way to reconcile the two?

Bernard L. Ramm in 1954 identified and evaluated nine different theories or views that had been set forth in an effort to resolve this issue.[42] In what follows we will interpret these and three additional theories. First, what Ramm called the "naive-literal view" teaches that creation occurred in six, successive 24-hour periods about 4004 B.C. That date was based on the chronology of Archbishop James Ussher and the computation of the Hebraist and biblical critic, John Lightfoot (1602-75). Although its advocates make various efforts to explain fossils, this view seems to be contradicted by the very great age of the earth, for geologists claim that the earth is from four to five billion years old. Second, the "religious-only" theory emphasizes that "Genesis states the origin of the universe in religious or theological terms, and . . . it is the province of science to declare *how* it happened." Again this is the two-track view of religion and science, and by its very definition it in effect throws the question under discussion out of court. Ramm criticized it as a "deistic" concession to science.

Third, the theory of flood or catastrophe geology, which was commonly held during the sixteenth, seventeenth, and eighteenth centuries, majors on the evidence of animal and vegetable life in the strata of the earth and attributes such to the flood in Noah's time. During recent decades this view has been reasserted by Seventh-day Adventists under the caption of the "new diluvialism." Geologists, however, reject this view on the basis of evidence that animal and vegetable life could not have been produced during a short span of time but rather was produced over a much longer period of time. Fourth, the idea of successive catastrophes and creations provided another theory. Advocated by Georges Cuvier (1769-1832), French founder of comparative anatomy, and Louis Rodolphe Agassiz (1807-73), Swiss-born professor of natural history at Harvard, it posits a series of floods and/or catastrophes and a series of

41. *Issues in Science and Religion*, pp. 367, 368.
42. *The Christian View of Science and Scripture* (Grand Rapids: Eerdmans, 1954), pp. 173-229. The reader is referred to Ramm's book for the documentation he supplied for the nine views discussed. Only those titles that have been added appear in the footnotes below.

new creations in order to account for the geological evidence that fossils were produced over a long period of time. Fifth, John Pye Smith (1774-1851) in 1840 localized the Genesis accounts of creation by limiting the action to Mesopotamia. The "six days" refer to the divine reorganization or rehabilitation of a small portion of the earth's surface; the "earth" of Genesis 1 is identical with the "garden" of Genesis 2. Presumably the earth as a whole could be much older.

Sixth, Philip Henry Gosse (1810-88), British naturalist and member of the Plymouth Brethren, in 1857 set forth a "pro-chronic or ideal time" theory based on a sharp differentiation between two ways of understanding time, namely, real time and ideal time. Presumably all objects of creation would have both kinds of time. Adam at creation, for example, could be said to have had the real time of zero but the ideal time of perhaps 30 years. Similarly, the earth could be said to have the real time of six to ten thousand years and the ideal time of millions of years. Geologists, however, unimpressed by such a philosophical distinction, insist that real time and ideal time must be identical. Seventh, there is the theory of creation–ruination–re-creation, or the restitution theory, popularly known as the "gap" theory. Advocated by Thomas Chalmers (1780-1847), Scottish Presbyterian leader, and expressed in the *Scofield Reference Bible*, it interprets Gen. 1:2 to mean that original creation was ruined and had to be restored or re-created. Ramm criticized the theory for being an aberration in the history of exegesis, with no basis in the Hebrew text, for eisegeting an elaborate angelology and demonology, and for failing to engage geology in a significant way.

Eighth, the "age-day" theory, also known as the theory of concordism, takes the "days" of Genesis 1 to be symbolic of and exactly parallel to the periods in the geological and biological history of the earth and of life on the earth. Advocates of this nonliteral approach to the "days" included James Dwight Dana (1813-95), professor of natural history and geology at Yale; John William Dawson (1820-99), a Canadian geologist; and Russell R. Byrum,[43] Church of God (Anderson, Indiana) theologian, who reckoned the order of Genesis and the order of geology-biology to coincide. Millard Erickson has found the "most satisfactory" view to be "a variation of the age-day theory."[44] Ramm agreed with this theory's metaphorical interpretation of Genesis 1 but concluded that it had not established exact concordance. Ninth, an American Mennonite theologian, John C. Wenger, set forth the theory that creation occurred in six ordinary but not immediately successive days,[45] and Robert C. Newman and Herman J. Eckelmann, Jr., have recently espoused the same view, but with the idea that most of God's creative activity occurred between the

43. *Christian Theology,* pp. 238-44.
44. *Christian Theology,* p. 382.
45. *Introduction to Theology,* p. 75.

"days."[46] Tenth, Davis Alan Young (1941-), a geologist at Calvin College, has interpreted Genesis 1 to mean that the life-forms specified were chiefly, but not exclusively, created on one of the six days so indicated, thus allowing for a given life-form to appear on more than one of the six days.[47] Eleventh, Percy John Wiseman (1888-?) set forth the view that the six 24-hour days of Genesis 1 were the time within human history when God revealed or "told the story of creation to man." Consequently, these days "are not related to the age of the earth or the age of man."[48]

Twelfth, there is the "pictorial day theory," or the "theory of moderate concordism." Advocated by Ramm, this view finds the main purpose of Genesis to be religious or theological (i.e., to evoke the worship of the Creator and to prohibit idolatry), advocates a metaphorical interpretation of the "days" of Genesis 1 so that they are pictorial or revelatory days, regards Genesis 1 as more topical than chronological and as prescientific, and opts for a moderate, not an exact, concordism.

Conrad Hyers (1933-), a Protestant theologian, has recently offered a critique of Ramm's position, labeling it "a form of the 'God of the gaps' hypothesis," in which Genesis 1 is surrendered to science and turned "into a scientific allegory." Hyers is probably correct in pointing out the symbolic and hence religious significance of numbers in Genesis 1, but his own two-track approach to religion and science can lead to a schizophrenia that may cause one to ask whether the God of Genesis is the same deity as the God of scientific endeavor.[49]

The age of the earth continues to be an issue for scientists and for Christian interpreters of Genesis.

C. CREATION AND/OR THE EVOLUTION OF HUMAN BEINGS

Since the publication of Charles Darwin's *The Origin of Species* in 1859, divine creation versus the evolution of human beings has been a major issue for Christians and for Western civilization. A veritable avalanche of writings has come forth from numerous perspectives. It is possible here only to identify the major views, and in doing so one needs to recognize that there are no universally agreed upon categories or labels by which to identify these major views. We have treated one of these major views, atheistic evolution, earlier in this chapter and will not need to include it in the present discussion. Moreover, it cannot be considered in any sense as an option for Christians. We will employ three major catego-

46. *Genesis One and the Origin of the Earth* (Grand Rapids: Baker Book House, 1977), pp. 64-65, 74.
47. *Creation and the Flood: An Alternative to Flood Geology and Theistic Evolution* (Grand Rapids: Baker Book House, 1977), pp. 116-17.
48. *Creation Revealed in Six Days: The Evidence of Scripture Confirmed by Archaeology* (London: Marshall, Morgan and Scott, Ltd., 1948); Roark, *The Christian Faith*, pp. 177-78.
49. *The Meaning of Creation: Genesis and Modern Science* (Atlanta: John Knox Press, 1984), pp. 73-92, esp. 86, 91, 74-80. Unfortunately Ramm has not revised his book in the light of discussions since 1954.

ries in an effort to identify the other options: fiat or instantaneous creation, theistic evolution, and progressive creation.

1. Fiat or Instantaneous Creation

This view holds that the divine creation of all things occurred within a relatively short segment of time. Usually its proponents give a literal and time-oriented interpretation to the six "days" of Genesis 1. Furthermore, this view concludes that such creation brought about an immediate fixity of species and that there has been no subsequent change or development within these species. It would be difficult indeed to find many practicing scientists today who fully embrace this view, and its proponents are drawn from the Christian community. A leading exponent is Henry Madison Morris (1918-).

2. Theistic Evolution

Here the problem of terminology becomes serious. There is no uniform sense of meaning for the term "theistic evolution." Millard Erickson prefers to differentiate "deistic evolution" from "theistic evolution" when dealing specifically with the creation of humans, using the former to mean the view that "God began the process of evolution" and then withdrew to become "Creator emeritus" and reserving the latter for the view that, whereas "man's physical nature is a product of the process of evolution," "God specially created the spiritual nature of Adam."[50] More often "theistic evolution" has been used more broadly to encompass all those understandings of origins that limit God to an initiatory role, and so it will be in the present discussion. Accordingly, theistic evolution means that God is at best immanent in the process of evolution that he somehow began, but that immanence does not limit natural selection or enable the coming to be of new life-forms. It would be difficult to place under theistic evolution the "creative evolution" advanced by Henri Louis Bergson (1859-1941), who held that evolution was under the guidance of élan vital, or a vital impulse, which is a nonpersonal but purposive force,[51] or the emergent evolution of Samuel Alexander (1859-1938)[52] and Conwy Lloyd Morgan (1852-1936),[53] according to whom an impersonal God is both identifiable with the present world and also a future emerging force. Neither of these perspectives has any commonly accepted view of a personal God. But the position of the French Jesuit paleontologist Pierre Teilhard de Chardin (1881-1955) seems definitely to belong under theistic evolution, even though God for him is more a future emergent, Omega, than an initiator of evolution.[54]

---

50. *Christian Theology*, pp. 480-81.
50. *Christian Theology*, pp. 480-81.
51. *Creative Evolution*, trans. Arthur Mitchell (New York: H. Holt and Company, 1911).
52. *Space, Time, and Deity*, 2 vols. (London: Macmillan, 1920).
53. *Emergent Evolution* (London: Williams and Norgate, 1923).
54. *The Phenomenon of Man*, trans. Bernard Wall (New York: Harper and Bros., 1959); *The Vision of the Past*, trans. J. M. Cohen (New York: Harper and Row, 1966).

3. Progressive Creation

This view holds that God as Creator not only was active in the initiation of a process that is most often called "evolution" but also was directly active at crucial stages or thresholds to bring forth new forms of life. Although the matter is not without dispute, it seems best to reckon the views of Augustine of Hippo and Thomas Aquinas as belonging under the category of progressive creation.

Augustine discussed creation in five of his writings.[55] As to the time of creation he taught both that creation took place on the several "days" of Genesis 1 and that it occurred simultaneously.[56] But Augustine's concept of the manner of creation has attracted the attention of modern scholars, especially since Darwin's time. God, according to the bishop of Hippo, implanted "causal reasons" (*rationes seminales, rationes primordiales*) in the created order in the beginning.[57] Ramm interpreted Augustine's view as follows:

> . . . God sowed *seminal principles* in Nature or matter and they taking root, as it were, developed the world of animals and plants. God . . . did not create them in seminal form. From seminal form, *under the guidance of God*, the final creatures were realized.[58]

Augustine seemed to posit a proliferation of life-forms from divinely created "seeds" but under the guidance of the Creator.

Thomas Aquinas rejected the Aristotelian view that matter is eternal but created by the Prime Mover[59] and also rejected the view that creation occurred eternally[60] so as opt for God's willing the existence of the world. To what extent did Thomas envision process in the creation? Ramm summarizes as follows:

> Evolution is but the *modus operandi* by which the ideas or forms or universals are realized in the animal and plant world. God as the cause of all motion is the spiritual and intelligent force behind evolution, and evolution occurs solely because there is a God, and because Nature is constituted in the terms described by Aquinas.[61]

Those in the nineteenth and twentieth centuries, especially Roman Catholic theologians and scientists, who have held that Adam's body was derived from prehuman beings but his soul or mind was directly created by God should be reckoned as progressive creationists. Examples would

55. *De Genesi contra Manichaeos libri duo* (A.D. 388); *De Genesi ad litteram imperfectus liber* (393-94); *Confessions* (397-400), bks. 12-13; *The Literal Meaning of Genesis* (401-15) [re: Gen. 1–3]; and *The City of God* (413-26), bk. 11 (417).
56. *The Literal Meaning of Genesis* 4.33 (51, 52), 34 (53); 6.6 (9).
57. Ibid. 4.33 (51); 6.5 (8); *The Trinity* 3.8 (13).
58. *The Christian View of Science and Scripture*, pp. 263-64.
59. *Summa Theologica* 1.44.2.
60. Ibid. 1.46.1.
61. *The Christian View of Science and Scripture*, p. 263.

include the Catholic zoologist St. George Mivart (1827-1900)[62] and the Catholic botanist Philip Gilbert Fothergill (1908?-), author of *Evolution and Christians*.[63] The work of Pierre Lecomte du Noüy (1883-1947),[64] who offered a critique of chance evolution and pointed out non sequiturs in the scientific case for evolution, may also be placed here.

Admittedly there are few clear and unambiguous conclusions vis-à-vis creation and evolution. Progressive creation seems to offer more promise than the other major options. Millard Erickson, favoring it, understands it "as a combination of a series of *de novo* creative acts and an immanent or processive operation." He allows for "microevolution" or " 'intrakind' development" but denies "macroevolution" or " 'interkind' development."[65]

4. Creation and "Creation Science"

In view of the regnant role of naturalistic or antitheistic philosophies of evolution, especially in university circles, with their assumption of the earth as being several billions of years old and human beings as having been derived from subhuman or prehuman mammals without divine creation, it is not surprising that there would be some new kind of reaction to this dominant perspective from the Christian community. Such a reaction indeed has come in the United States in the form of the "creation science" movement, which involves a significant number of scientists who are Christians and which has been led by Henry Madison Morris, onetime professor of hydraulic engineering, Virginia Polytechnic Institute, and more recently director of the Institute for Creation Research, San Diego. The author and editor of nearly a dozen and half books,[66] Morris has been the principal ideologue for the movement.

The basic teachings of the movement may be summarized as follows: (a) the militant rejection of all forms of evolution and evolution-

62. *On the Genesis of Species* (New York: D. Appleton and Company, 1871), pp. 294-307.
63. (London: Longmans, Green and Company, Ltd., 1961), esp. pp. 303-6, 334.
64. *Human Destiny* (New York: Longmans, Green and Company, 1947).
65. *Christian Theology*, pp. 481-82. Norman L. Geisler and J. Kerby Anderson, *Origin Science: A Proposal for the Creation-Evolution Controversy* (Grand Rapids: Baker Book House, 1987), esp. pp. 13-18, have recently proposed that "origin science," which would deal with "unobserved singularities in the past," be differentiated from "operation science," which would deal with recurring events in the present.
66. *That You May Believe* (Chicago: Good Books, 1946); (with John C. Whitcomb, Jr.) *The Genesis Flood: The Biblical Record and Its Scientific Implications* (Philadelphia: Presbyterian and Reformed, 1961); *The Twilight of Evolution* (Grand Rapids: Baker, 1963); *The Remarkable Birth of Planet Earth* (Philadelphia: Presbyterian and Reformed, 1964; Minneapolis: Dimension Books, 1972); *Studies in the Bible and Science: or, Christ and Creation* (Grand Rapids: Baker, 1966); *Evolution and the Modern Christian* (Grand Rapids: Baker, 1967); (ed. with Donald W. Patton) *A Symposium on Creation*, 6 vols. (Grand Rapids: Baker, 1968-77); *Biblical Cosmology and Modern Science* (Grand Rapids: Baker, 1970); (with W. W. Boardman, Jr., and R. F. Koontz) *Science and Creation* (San Diego: Creation-Science Research Center, 1971); *Many Infallible Proofs: Practical and Useful Evidences of Christianity* (San Diego: Creation-Life Publishers, 1974); (ed.) *Scientific*

ism;[67] (b) a hermeneutic of Genesis 1 that takes it as a literal, historical narrative;[68] (c) reckoning the Bible as "a textbook on science";[69] (d) the fiat creation in six consecutive 24-hour periods of all things in their present form;[70] (e) the interpretation of the flood of Noah's time as worldwide and as occurring between three and five thousand years before Abraham;[71] (f) the rejection of uniformitarianism in geology and the advocacy of catastrophism;[72] and (g) the advocacy of the teaching of "scientific creation" without any biblical or theological implications in public schools.[73]

During the 1980s there have been several critiques or refutations of "creation science." Davis A. Young, an evangelical Christian, used arguments from sedimentation, radiometrics, the earth's magnetic field, and geochemistry to refute the concept of the "young earth."[74] Gathering a collection of essays from the past and present, designed in varying degrees to refute creation-science, editor Roland Mushat Frye (1921-) provided a religious overview that was marred, though not flawed, by an establishmentarian bias.[75] Conrad Hyers rejected creation science's viewing the Bible as science and Genesis 1 as a " 'straightforward historical narrative,' " the intention of which was to give information about the method of creation. Differentiating "creation" and "creationism," he charged that "creation science," as identical with the latter, made scientific investigation "subservient to a theory of biblical exegesis" and hence its resultant scientific views were being "rejected by the vast majority of scientists." Moreover, the movement "compromises the religious meaning of Genesis and is an accommodation to scientific language and method"; Hyers labeled this a "modernistic" approach.[76] Langdon Gilkey, writing on the Arkansas creation-science case in federal court, noted that creation-science's chief defenders were scientists, not persons trained in religion, who sought to present creation science as science and as the only alternative to evolution science, evolution itself being allegedly outside the sphere of empirical science. Gilkey countered by contending that creation-

Creationism (San Diego: Creation-Life Publishers, 1974); *The Genesis Record: A Scientific and Devotional Commentary on the Book of Beginnings* (Grand Rapids: Baker, 1976); *The Scientific Case for Creation* (San Diego: Creation-Life Publishers, 1977); *King of Creation* (San Diego: Creation-Life Publishers, 1980); (with Gary E. Parker) *What Is Creation Science?* (San Diego: Creation-Life Publishers, 1982); *Science, Scripture, and the Young Earth: An Answer to Current Arguments against the Biblical Doctrine of Recent Creation* (El Cajon, Calif.: Institute for Creation Research, 1983); and *The Biblical Basis of Modern Science* (Grand Rapids: Baker, 1984).

67. *The Twilight of Evolution.*

68. *Studies in the Bible and Science,* ch. 3.

69. Ibid., ch. 11.

70. *The Remarkable Birth of Planet Earth,* p. vi; *King of Creation,* pp. 9-10.

71. *The Genesis Flood,* p. 489.

72. *Biblical Cosmology and Modern Science,* ch. 2.

73. *King of Creation,* p. 230.

74. *Christianity and the Age of the Earth* (Grand Rapids: Zondervan, 1982), chs. 6–11.

75. *Is God a Creationist? The Religious Case against Creation-Science* (New York: Charles Scribner's Sons, 1983).

76. *The Meaning of Creation: Genesis and Modern Science,* pp. 23-29.

science's "content" was religious.[77] Howard Jay Van Till (1938-), Davis Young, and Clarence Menninga (1928-) have offered evidence against creation science's assertions about a "shrinking sun," minimal dust on the moon, the rates of influx of elements into the ocean floors, and the nonexistence of missing strata in the Grand Canyon.[78]

Earlier in this section we issued a warning against the absolute separation of revealed truth and scientific knowledge so that never the two would meet. Now, even while the arguments for and against "creation science" continue, a counterwarning needs to be given against that too facile harmonization of revelation and science, of Genesis and geology, anthropology, and biology so that legitimate scientific investigation may be hindered or ignored and biblical writings put to uses never intended by their human authors or by God.

In this chapter we have examined four present-day issues involving creation: creation and astrophysical theories about the origin of the universe; creation and geological data about the age of the earth; creation and the biological teachings about the evolution of human beings; and creation and the contemporary American movement known as "creation science." It should be quite evident that we have not obtained final answers in this brief quest, but Christians should recognize anew the truth and centrality of the doctrine of creation and seek to apply it to all areas of life.[79]

77. *Creationism on Trial: Evolution and God at Little Rock* (Minneapolis: Winston Press, 1985), pp. 20-23, 29, 31.

78. *Science Held Hostage: What's Wrong with Creation Science and Evolutionism* (Downers Grove, Ill.: InterVarsity Press, 1988), chs. 3–6.

79. James Macintosh Houston, *I Believe in the Creator* (Grand Rapids: Eerdmans, 1980), chs. 7–9, has developed the themes of "living wisely before the Creator," enjoying God's world, and "living hopefully before the Creator."

CHAPTER 26

Providence as Sustenance, Sovereignty, and Theodicy

"I still believe in the providence of God." These are words that have often been uttered by Christians when facing one of the exigencies of life or death. What is meant by the term "providence" when applied to God, and what difference does it make if one believes that God acts in respect to his providence? Can this term, which may seem very archaic, be significant for Christians today? Such questions as these necessarily lead to a more detailed inquiry into the entire Christian doctrine of providence.

I. THE MEANING, SCOPE, AND USEFULNESS OF THE TERM "PROVIDENCE"

A. ETYMOLOGY

The word "providence" is derived from the Latin verb *providere*, which means "to see at a distance" and hence "to prepare for, to take precautions about."[1] "Providence" is associated with the English word "provide" and connotes "seeing ahead." "By an interesting juxtaposition of English usage it means also 'to look after.' "[2] Christian theologians have used the term to signify God's working out or effecting his purpose despite all hindrances in the world that he has created. Another term sometimes associated with providence is "preservation," which has been used by Christian theologians to signify God's sustenance or maintenance of all that he has created.

B. DEFINITIONS, SCOPE, AND RELATIONSHIPS

1. Some theologians, especially Baptist theologians, have defined and treated "providence" and "preservation" as distinctly separate terms and subjects. A. H. Strong employed the following definitions:

---

1. The Latin word *pro,* used also as a prefix, can mean "before," "in behalf of," or "far, at a distance." The third of these meanings applies in *providere*.
2. Georgia Harkness, *The Providence of God* (New York: Abingdon Press, 1960), p. 17.

> Providence is that continuous agency of God by which he makes all the events of the physical and moral universe fulfill the original design with which he created it.[3]

> Preservation is that continuous agency of God by which he maintains in existence the things that he has created. . . .[4]

Similarly E. Y. Mullins defined these terms as follows:

> By the providence of God we mean his control or direction of the universe toward the end which he has chosen.[5]

> Preservation is God's action in sustaining the universe he has made.[6]

Mullins, however, did not make a sharp distinction between the terms and treated both topics in the same chapter. W. T. Conner treated preservation as part of the doctrine of God and providence under the doctrine of the Christian life, utilizing the following definitions:

> By providence we mean that God is working out a purpose in the life of man.[7]

> [T]he preservation of the universe . . . [is] one of the specific functions of God in relation to the world . . . [for the] world could no more continue of its own accord than it could bring itself into existence at first.[8]

Dale Moody differentiated "the preservation of creation" and "the purpose of creation (providence),"[9] and Henry C. Thiessen[10] and William W. Stevens[11] made the same basic distinction. There seem to be no essential reasons, however, based on the Baptist understanding of the Christian gospel, why such a distinction must be made by Baptist theologians. Furthermore, a Methodist[12] and a Mennonite[13] theologian had employed the same distinction.

2. Other theologians have defined and treated "providence" without any significant emphasis on divine preservation of the world of nature. According to Georgia Elma Harkness, a Methodist theologian,

> The providence of God means the goodness of God and His guiding, sustaining care. Belief in providence in the most general sense implies the goodness as well as the power of God in the creation, ordering, and maintaining of his world, embracing the entire world of physical nature, biological life, and human persons. However, it is in the destinies of human

---

3, *Systematic Theology,* p. 419.
4. Ibid., p. 410.
5. *The Christian Religion in Its Doctrinal Expression,* p. 265.
6. Ibid.
7. *The Gospel of Redemption,* pp. 224-25.
8. *Revelation and God,* p. 270.
9. *The Word of Truth,* pp. 137-41, 151-56.
10. *Introductory Lectures in Systematic Theology,* pp. 173-88.
11. *Doctrines of the Christian Religion,* pp. 67-69.
12. Henry C. Sheldon, *System of Christian Doctrine,* pp. 246-54.
13. John C. Wenger, *Introduction to Theology,* pp. 108-12.

individuals that belief in providence centers. . . . In a word, to believe in divine providence is to believe that God sees the way before us and looks after us as we seek to walk in it.[14]

3. Still other theologians have defined the providence of God so as to make God's preservation of the universe an aspect of providence. John Calvin declared that the Creator

is also everlasting Governor and Preserver—not only in that he drives the celestial frame as well as its several parts by a universal motion, but also in that he sustains, nourishes, and cares for everything he has made, even to the least sparrow.[15]

According to Charles Hodge, "Providence . . . includes preservation and government."[16] John Leadley Dagg (1794-1884)[17] and James Petigru Boyce (1827-88),[18] both Southern Baptist theologians, included preservation under providence. John Miley (1813-95),[19] a Methodist; William Greenough Thayer Shedd (1820-94),[20] a Presbyterian; Russell R. Byrum,[21] the Church of God (Anderson, Indiana) theologian; and H. Orton Wiley[22] of the Church of the Nazarene all followed the same pattern. Emil Brunner defined providence so as to include both preservation and government. Accordingly, providence deals with "the relation between God and Nature, between the divine action and the course of History, between divine and human action, between human freedom and divine over-ruling, between events which are determined by human aims, and those controlled by the Divine Purpose."[23] G. C. Berkouwer treated the providence of God in considerable detail under three rubrics: sustenance, government, and concurrence (or cooperation).[24]

Because this third approach to the scope of the doctrine of providence is more integrative and creates no major problem for the biblical materials basic to the doctrine, we will follow it in the remainder of this chapter.

C. USEFULNESS

Whether the term "providence" can be said to be useful or at least tenable depends mainly on one's response to the question as to whether

---

14. *The Providence of God*, p. 17.
15. *Institutes of the Christian Religion* (1559 ed., trans. F. L. Battles) 1.16.1.
16. *Systematic Theology*, 1:575.
17. *A Manual of Theology* (Charleston, S.C.: Southern Baptist Publication Society, 1857), pp. 115-37.
18. *Abstract of Systematic Theology* (Philadelphia: American Baptist Publication Society, 1887), pp. 179-91.
19. *Systematic Theology*, 2 vols. (New York: Hunt and Eaton; Cincinnati: Cranston and Curts, 1892, 1894), 1:309-49.
20. *Dogmatic Theology*, 3 vols. (New York: Charles Scribner's Sons, 1888-94), 1:527-32.
21. *Christian Theology*, pp. 253-62.
22. *Christian Theology*, 1:477-87.
23. *The Christian Doctrine of Creation and Redemption*, ch. 6, esp. p. 148.
24. *The Providence of God*, trans. Lewis B. Smedes, Studies in Dogmatics (Grand Rapids: Eerdmans, 1952). See also Erickson, *Christian Theology*, pp. 387-405.

the concept of providence itself is tenable. During the nineteenth century in Western thought there tended to be a general or widespread acceptance of a providential and benevolent order of things. The German philosopher G. W. Leibniz had taken the position that this is the best of all possible worlds.[25] The concept of evolution was being applied to history, and there was a commonly accepted belief in progress. Divine providence seemed to fit into that scheme of things. But in the twentieth century, as G. C. Berkouwer has pointed out, in the face of two great world wars, the Holocaust, atomic and hydrogen bombs, and the like, grave doubts have arisen as to divine providence even as secularization has increased. These doubts have led some to despair, pessimism, and even nihilism. They have led others to adopt substitutes for divine providence, notably forms of the neo-occult such as Spiritism, astrology, and parapsychology.[26] The task of formulating the Christian doctrine of providence may indeed be a more sobering and difficult task today than in the days of our spiritual forebears, but it is no less important.

With the meaning of the term "providence" somewhat clarified, it is now expedient to proceed with the explication of the doctrine under three distinct divisions: providence as sustenance (God and nature); providence and sovereignty (God and history); and providence and theodicy (God and suffering).

II. PROVIDENCE AS SUSTENANCE (GOD AND NATURE)

A. BIBLICAL TEACHINGS

1. Old Testament

In addition to those texts which speak of divine creation, the Old Testament contains specific passages in which the theme of Yahweh's sustenance of the natural or physical order is set forth. For the prophet Amos sustenance is expressed in terms of "the rising and falling of the Nile" River (9:5-6).[27] One of the most complete and majestic of these texts is Ps. 104:24-30 (NIV):

> How many are your works, O LORD!
> In wisdom you made them all;
>   the earth is full of your creatures.
> There is the sea, vast and spacious,
>   teeming with creatures beyond number—

25. *Essais de théodicée sur la bonté de Dieu, la liberté de l'homme et l'origine du mal,* 2 vols. (Amsterdam, 1710).
26. *The Providence of God,* ch. 1. "The Providence doctrine was often used as another way of stating man's belief in progressive evolution. God was discernibly leading the world to His own benevolent end" (p. 11). "The confession of God's Providence has become, now more than ever, a stone of stumbling" (p. 13).
27. Moody, *The Word of Truth,* p. 138.

living things both large and small.
There the ships go to and fro,
    and the leviathan, which you formed to frolic there.
These all look to you
    to give them their food at the proper time.
When you give it to them,
    they gather it up;
when you open your hand,
    they are satisfied with good things.
When you hide your face,
    they are terrified;
when you take away their breath,
    they die and return to the dust.
When you send your Spirit,
    they are created,
    and you renew the face of the earth.

"The 104th Psalm is a long hymn to the preserving power of God, who keeps alive all the creatures of the deep, both small and great."[28] The Lord preserves "both man and beast" (Ps. 36:6), supplies rain (Ps. 68:8-9; 147:8-9) and snow (Ps. 147:16-17), and provides food for beasts and fowl (Ps. 147:9). "The eyes of all look to you, and you give them their food at the proper time. You open your hand and satisfy the desires of every living thing" (Ps. 145:15-16, NIV). In the Israelite confession of sins in Ezra's time Yahweh was acknowledged not only as Creator but also as the one who "preserves" or "gives life" to all that has been created (Neh. 9:6).

2. New Testament

In the teaching of Jesus one finds the declaration that the heavenly Father "makes his sun rise on the evil and on the good, and sends rain on the just and on the unjust" (Matt. 5:45, RSV). His disciples were not to pray as the Gentiles did, "for your Father knows what you need before you ask him" (Matt. 6:8). They were not to be "anxious," for "the birds of the air," "the lilies of the field," and "the grass of the field" are cared for by the heavenly Father, who knows all human needs, whose kingdom is first of all to be sought, and who will provide "all these things" as well (Matt. 6:25-34, RSV). No sparrow "will fall to the ground apart from the will" of the heavenly Father, and even human hairs are numbered (Matt. 10:29-30, NIV). Paul cited approvingly the poetic words, probably from Epimenides, " 'In him we live and move and have our being' " (Acts 17:28, RSV). Paul himself wrote of the all-wise God, "For from him and through him and to him are all things" (Rom. 11:36), and referred to him as the one "who gives life to all things" (1 Tim. 6:13, RSV). More specifically, in Christ

28. Strong, *Systematic Theology*, p. 412.

"all things hold together" (Col. 1:17, RSV). In the Epistle to the Hebrews the Son of God is said to be "sustaining all things by his powerful word" (1:3b, NIV).

B. MEANING

1. Sustenance, or preservation, is distinct from creation, though dependent on creation. Otto Weber has argued for the distinction between creation and preservation by asserting that the latter "by no means takes place 'out of nothingness,' but conserves created existence as something already extant and active and thus presupposes it."[29]

2. Sustenance is "a positive agency" of God, not mere refraining from destruction.[30] As such it is a free activity of God that is not "ontologically necessary."[31] John Calvin was quite sure that God is no "idle" God.[32]

3. Sustenance involves divine "concurrence" with secondary causes. God is thus immanent in the operation of natural phenomena according to natural law, though never so immanent as to preclude miracle. "In pantheism the second causes are identified with God, while in deism the second cause is divorced from the first cause, that is, God."[33] The Christian doctrine of sustenance, therefore, avoids the extremes and therefore the errors of both deism and pantheism.

4. How sustenance is related to earthquakes, tornadoes, hurricanes, and other such natural occurrences can be found in section IV below.

C. CONTRARY VIEWS

1. Deism

Deism, especially in its later form, denied divine sustenance by positing the absenteeism of the Creator from the created order and holding that the universe operates as a "self-sustained mechanism."[34] Various naturalistic philosophies in the twentieth century have agreed with the deistic view of the universe without acknowledging a Creator.

2. Continuous Creation[35]

Continuous creation theory denies God's sustenance of all things by substituting continuous creation for sustenance. Herman Bavinck used the term "continuous creation" (creatio continua) in a favorable sense so as to emphasize that sustenance is as great and important a work as creation.[36] Otto Weber distinguished between "continued creation" (creatio

---

29. Foundations of Dogmatics, 1:505.
30. Strong, Systematic Theology, p. 411.
31. Weber, Foundations of Dogmatics, 1:503.
32. Institutes of the Christian Religion, 1559 ed., 1.16.4, trans. F. L. Battles, LCC, 20:202.
33. Berkouwer, The Providence of God, p. 137.
34. Strong, Systematic Theology, p. 414.
35. See above, Ch. 25, I, D.
36. Gereformeerde Dogmatiek, 2:566-68, as cited by Berkouwer, The Providence of God, p. 62.

continuata), of which he found dependent and ontological subtypes, and "continuing creation" *(creatio continua)* but rejected both and advocated instead "the concept of 'the Creator continuing His own work' *(creator opus suum continuans)."*[37] Continuous creation theory can be incorporated into pantheistic and process philosophies.

III. PROVIDENCE AS SOVEREIGNTY (GOD AND HISTORY)

Almost all Christian theologians acknowledge that God's sovereign guidance of human history is a topic that belongs under the providence of God. Secularistic philosophies deny that there is any such thing as providential sovereignty.

Is belief in divine providence basic to all religions, or is it peculiar to Christianity? Christian theologians have not agreed in answering this question. Herbert Henry Farmer (1892-1981) held that the general concept of providence is basic to all forms of religion,[38] whereas G. C. Berkouwer claimed that providence is a uniquely Christian or biblical idea.[39] It is difficult to see how the working out of divine purpose could be meaningfully held in nontheistic and polytheistic religions; with mystical religions the concept would be pantheistic; with Judaism and Islam, Farmer's argument is more persuasive.

By divine sovereign guidance of human history we mean that the Triune God is exercising a caring rulership over both the broad sweep and the particulars of human affairs and destiny even in the face of human resistance to that rule and will bring that rulership to fulfillment in the consummated kingdom of God.

A. BIBLICAL PASSAGES AND CONCEPTS

It seems better to treat the materials from both testaments in relation to the major themes than to deal with the teachings of each testament separately.

1. *God's Overall Direction of History*

a. Universal Divine Rulership

The Old Testament presents Yahweh as the king of Israel (Num. 23:21; Deut. 33:5; 1 Sam. 12:12b), and even Solomon was said "to sit on the throne of the kingdom of God over Israel" (1 Chr. 28:5, NIV; see also 1 Chr. 29:23; 2 Chr. 9:8; 13:8). But in the Psalms, the hymnbook of Israel, Yahweh's kingship is repeatedly affirmed as universal (Ps. 103:19). He rules over all the earth (Ps. 47:2, 7; 97:9), over the kings of the earth (Ps. 47:9; 97:1, 5), and

---

37. *Foundations of Dogmatics,* 1:503-5.
38. *The World and God: A Study of Prayer, Providence and Miracle in Christian Experience* (London: Nisbet and Company, Ltd., 1935), p. 99.
39. *The Providence of God,* p. 48; see Dale Moody, *The Word of Truth,* p. 151.

over the nations (Ps. 96:10; 99:1-2). He foils the plans and purposes of peoples and nations (Ps. 33:10-11), and his rulership is eternal (Ps. 66:7; 93:2; 146:10). This universal kingship does not rule out Israel's being chosen by Yahweh (Ps. 47:3-4). Yahweh frustrated Pharaoh and resisted Sennacherib's attack on Jerusalem but employed Cyrus as his servant.[40] The numerous pronouncements of divine judgment on Israel's neighbors made through the prophets constitute further confirmation of this universal rulership.

b. Divine Action in History Centered in Jesus Christ

Christians interpret the Old Testament promises concerning the advent of the Son of David—the Son of Man—the Anointed One as having been fulfilled in the advent, ministry, death, resurrection, and ascension of Jesus. For Christians the clue to the meaning of history is to be found in Jesus as the Messiah and Son of God. "But when the time had fully come, God sent forth his Son" (Gal. 4:4, RSV), and "the Word became flesh and dwelt among us" (John 1:14a). Oscar Cullmann called "the Christ-deed" the "mid-point" of salvation history.[41] According to Paul, God purposes, under the headship of Christ, "to bring all things in heaven and on earth together" (Eph. 1:10b, NIV). Theologians of the salvation-history school and Wolfhart Pannenberg have differed as to how the unique happenings involving Jesus ought to be related to the general history of mankind,[42] but there is no disagreement concerning Jesus as the focal point of all history. God is no deistic absentee Creator missing from the world of nature; neither is he on vacation from the drama of human history. Hinduism and Buddhism have no comparable understanding of God's active role in history, and Judaism and Islam have rejected him who is history's clue and hope.

c. History's Goal or End

God works not only in history but toward the fulfillment of history, the full realization of his kingly rule and manifestation of his glory. Providence means the attainment of God's *telos*. Indeed, "to him [God] are all things" (Rom. 11:36). He is "Omega" as well as "Alpha" (Rev. 1:17c, KJV). The Son will deliver the kingly rule to the Father (1 Cor. 15:24-28), and, despite the power of evil both human and suprahuman (Eph. 6:12), God will be victorious (1 Cor. 15:57).

The mention of sin suggests that providence must address and deal realistically with sin if God's kingly rule over history is to be finalized.

40. See Berkouwer, *The Providence of God*, pp. 88-89, 94-95.

41. *Christ and Time: The Primitive Christian Conception of Time and History*, trans. Floyd V. Filson (rev. ed.; London: SCM Press, 1962), pp. 121-30.

42. Cullmann, *Salvation in History*, trans. Sidney G. Sowers et al. (New York: Harper and Row, 1967), esp. pp. 57-59; Eric C. Rust, *Salvation History*, chs. 1-2; Pannenberg, "Dogmatic Theses on the Doctrine of Revelation," in Pannenberg, ed., *Revelation as History*, trans. David Granskou (New York: Macmillan, 1968), pp. 123-58.

2. God's Agency in Reference to Human Sin

Does not the stubborn fact of human sin and its persistence constitute a stumbling block across the path of God's providential design? Can we really believe both in the reality of sin and the outworkings of divine providence? These are often the sincere questions of earnest people, and they do call for answers. A. H. Strong's delineation of this topic still can serve as a useful framework for its presentation.[43] According to Strong, God's providence is related in four ways to the occurrence of human sin. First, it can be preventive. God may prevent some sin that would otherwise be committed. Yahweh's word to King Abimelech through a dream was: "You have done this in the integrity of your heart, and it was I who kept you from sinning against me . . ." (Gen. 20:6, RSV). The psalmist prayed: "Keep your servant also from willful sins; may they not rule over me" (19:13, NIV). This preventive aspect is subsumed by Dutch Reformed theologians under the doctrine of "common grace."[44] Second, God's providence may be permissive respecting sin. He may allow human beings to cherish and continue in their sin. "Ephraim is joined to idols; leave him alone" (Hos. 4:17, NIV). Concerning Israel Yahweh declared: "So I gave them over to their stubborn hearts to follow their own devices" (Ps. 81:12). Surveying the Gentile world, Paul asserted that "God gave them over in the sinful desires of their hearts to sexual impurity" and "gave them over to a depraved mind" (Rom. 1:24a, 28b). Third, God's providence vis-à-vis human sin may be directive. He may direct "the evil acts of men to ends unforeseen and unintended by the agents."[45] Joseph's words to his brothers constitute a clear example: "As for you, you meant evil against me; but God meant it for good, to bring it about that many people should be kept alive, as they are today" (Gen. 50:20, RSV). Assyria was said to be the "rod" of Yahweh's "anger" and "the club" of his "wrath" (Isa. 10:4, NIV). According to Peter and John, when Herod Antipas, Pontius Pilate, Gentiles, and Jews gathered for the crucifixion of Jesus, they did what God's "power and will had decided beforehand should happen" (Acts 4:28, NIV). Fourth, God in his providence as it affects sin may be "limitarian."[46] He may set the bounds or limits to be reached by sin and its effects. The Israelites claimed that by Yahweh's help the attack of their enemies had been blunted (Ps. 124:1-5), and according to Paul God will not allow Christians to be tempted beyond their capacity to bear it and will even provide a "way of escape" (1 Cor. 10:13, RSV). Jesus drove out demons by the Holy Spirit (Matt. 12:28), the eschatological

43. *Systematic Theology*, pp. 423-25.
44. See Louis Berkhof, *Manual of Christian Doctrine* (Grand Rapids: Eerdmans, 1933), pp. 223-29; Cornelius Van Til, *Common Grace and the Gospel* (Nutley, N.J.: Presbyterian and Reformed Publishing Company, 1972).
45. Strong, *Systematic Theology*, p. 424.
46. Strong's term was "determinative." *Systematic Theology*, p. 425.

"man of lawlessness" is being restrained (2 Thess. 2:6-7), and Satan's binding is "for a thousand years" (Rev. 20:2).

Following our treatments of providence in relation to history and to sin, it is fitting that we ask how the Christian doctrine of providence is related, if at all, to the philosophical issue of determinism and free will. Otto Weber has called determinism "the experience of conditionedness" and indeterminism "the experience of personhood or of 'should-ness.'" Because of the influence of the Stoic concept of fate and of Aristotle's concept of the First Cause, Christian theology has tended to subject God to determinism, with the result that God came to be viewed as the "unfree" "epitome" of "inviolable law." For this reason Weber rejected the concept of divine "omnicausality," a form of omnipotence.[47] Likewise, because of the influence of Stoic fatalism and because of forms of interpretation of the Christian doctrines of predestination and fore-ordination, Christian theology has tended to subject human beings to determinism, with the result that the responsible human decision-making as to sinning/not sinning and obedience/disobedience which is so evident in the Bible is obscured or denied. Omnicausality is to be rejected for human considerations as well as divine. For Paul "it is God who works in you to will and to act according to his good purpose" (Phil. 2:13, NIV).

3. God's Care of All His Creation, Especially His Redeemed People

In the letters of Paul and Peter assurances are given as to God's sufficient care for his redeemed people. Veritably God's love is expressed not only as grace in the forgiveness of sins but also as providential care. God's care is an antidote to anxiety (1 Pet. 5:7), for believers are to have a prayerful, nonanxious trust in the garrisoning God (Phil. 4:6-7), whose supply of needs is indeed sufficient (Phil. 4:19). For the called ones God is working all things unto the good of Christlikeness (Rom. 8:28-29). This is "special" providence and not merely "general" providence. God's re-deemed are not his pampered favorites to the neglect of the rest of humankind but are under his fatherly care, even when this involves the sufferings and ills of life, that they may become like Jesus Christ, the image of God.

B. CONTRARY VIEWS

That divine providence is not widely accepted outside Christian circles may be seen through a brief examination of five major alternative or contrary views. These views constitute objections to the doctrine of providence as sovereignty or government, although some of them are also objections to providence as sustenance.

---

47. *Foundations of Dogmatics*, 1:508, 506-7, 509.

1. Mechanism

According to a strict mechanistic view of the world, not only the inorganic realm but also the organic and the human and even the historical realms are thought to be governed by a necessity inherent in the most elementary forces of nature. It may be called "pancausalism." Emil Brunner described this view as "determinism from below."[48]

Is mechanism defensible? Even its adherents do not follow its implications, for they expect their fellowmen to treat them ethically. This view "forcibly imposes an artificial theory of unity upon the graduated qualitative variety of reality."[49] While it may be applicable in physics and astronomy, it cannot be properly applied to the organic and human levels. The organic is inexplicable merely in terms of the inorganic or mechanistic. The human is inexplicable merely in terms of the organic. The divine is inexplicable merely in terms of the human. Furthermore, science is the product of human discoveries under the providence of God, and its discoveries and inventions show that mind is superior to things. Christians affirm that the universe is governed by God according to natural law, not by impersonal force or sheer necessity. Nature's regularities are seen as evidence of God's faithfulness and benevolence.[50]

2. Nontheistic Humanism

Adherents of this view would join with those of the Christian view in objecting to a purely mechanistic interpretation of reality but are unwilling to rise above the level of human causality. The latter is taken to be adequate for explaining all reality.

Such an attitude or philosophy seeks to exalt human beings by denying to God his rightful place. Although catastrophic world events earlier in the twentieth century shook the confidence of many in such humanism, not a few still espouse its cause. It does not, however, truly exalt humans, for it only makes them subject to the destructive forces resulting from evil—human and suprahuman—from the evil that the humanist refuses to acknowledge.[51]

3. Fatalism

This view holds that the world order, including human beings, is governed by impersonal fate or world-reason. The ancient Stoics set forth the idea of *pronoia*. Instead of a personal God working out his purpose in nature and history, fatalism poses an impersonal, deterministic, nonteleological, and very general force governing all of nature and history. The Stoics invented "a necessity out of the permanent causal nexus (*perpetuus*

---

48. *The Christian Doctrine of Creation and Redemption*, pp. 164-71, esp. 170.
49. Ibid., p. 170.
50. Conner, *The Gospel of Redemption*, pp. 226-28.
51. Dale Moody, *The Word of Truth*, pp. 155-56, has criticized Paul Tillich's concept of destiny as the selfhood for decision-making as an expression of humanism. See Tillich, *Systematic Theology*, 1:184-85.

nexus causarum) and a kind of immanent series which is supposed to be included in Nature."[52] There are parallels between ancient Stoicism and modern astrology.

Emil Brunner has labeled fatalism "determinism from above."[53] Ulrich Zwingli as a Christian theologian seemingly went too far toward embracing fatalism as he interpreted providence.[54] Fatalism is not to be identified with providence; it offers no mercy or comfort to human beings faced with pain, disappointment, guilt, or death.

4. Projectionism

This view counters the Christian doctrine of providence by claiming that providence as a belief is merely the projection of human wishes and desires for fatherly concern and support and has no basis in reality beyond such longings and desires. Providence, for projectionists, is a grand religious delusion. Projectionism has its roots in the thought of Ludwig Feuerbach, Karl Marx, and Sigmund Freud.

Because belief in providence cannot be tested scientifically and can be objected to philosophically, it is vulnerable to the view of projectionism. Also, the same projectionist objection can be and has been laid against the existence of God. Faith in God's providence today is based on God's rulership and faithfulness in the past, and hence special or historical revelation is crucial to overturning the projectionist objection. If Jesus went to his cross out of a sense of obedience to the purpose of God, was not crucifixion too great a price to pay for a projectionist illusion?

5. General Providence

This view allows for God's direction over the major movements of human history but denies that divine providence is individual, particular, or special. God may indeed have been at work at the battles of Tours, Waterloo, and Dunkirk, but providence is hardly more. It applies only to nations and groups.[55]

Jesus' various utterances about the Father's care are amazingly and convincingly particular; they seem to demand special providence.

IV. PROVIDENCE AS THEODICY (GOD AND SUFFERING)

The term "theodicy" seems to have been coined by G. W. Leibniz in 1710.[56] It means the justification of God, especially in reference to pain or suffering—what some would call "natural evil." Theodicy deals with the age-

---

52. Brunner, *The Christian Doctrine of Creation and Redemption,* pp. 155-57.
53. Ibid., p. 170.
54. *On the Providence of God,* ch. 3.
55. The opposite view is also possible, namely, that providence applies to the personal human arena but not at all to "the inanimate physical universe"; for an analysis, see William G. Pollard, *Chance and Providence: God's Action in a World Governed by Scientific Law* (New York: Charles Scribner's Sons, 1958), pp. 31-35.
56. Rudolf Eucken, "Leibniz," *New Schaff-Herzog Encyclopedia of Religious Knowledge,* 6:444.

old "problem of evil," which may be stated concisely as follows: Can God be concurrently both good and almighty in view of the existence of natural evil? Christian philosophers and theologians have differentiated "moral evil" and "natural evil." Accordingly, "moral evil" is "that which man *does*," and "natural evil" is "that which man *endures*."[57] For clarification one would need to add that "moral evil" is that evil which has been done for which the human doer is religiously and morally responsible, and that the recipient of "natural evil" has no comparable direct responsibility. In addition, the "moral evil" committed by some human beings can be for other humans "natural evil," as a bomb planted on a commercial airliner by a terrorist that results in massive loss of life would readily illustrate.

What does the Bible have to say about suffering or "natural evil"? Let us now locate and examine four strands of emphasis in the Old Testament and five such strands in the New Testament.

A. BIBLICAL TEACHINGS

1. *Old Testament*

a. Toil and Pain as the Consequence of the Advent of Human Sin

Gen. 3:16-19 alludes to the intensification of pain in childbirth and woman's submission to her husband as well as to man's having to engage in "painful toil" (v. 17b, NIV) through the "sweat" of his "brow" on an infested earth in order to obtain needed food. A traditional interpretation of the text is that the pain and toil (natural evil) were the retributive or punitive result of the sin of Adam and Eve (moral evil) and that the natural evil began only after the commission of moral evil.[58] Indeed, the use of the word "because" in v. 17 (see also a similar use in v. 14) seems to indicate a cause-effect relationship between sin and suffering. Some Christians have asked whether we should understand this text to mean that there was no suffering whatever or no potential for suffering prior to the commission of human sin. Put in vivid terms the question is: If Adam before sinning had fallen down a steep cliff, would he have injured himself? W. T. Conner contended that "there is no clear teaching any-where in the Bible to the effect that all suffering, animal death, and all natural evil, are the consequences of man's sin," though some have inferred such from the text under consideration and from Rom. 8:19-22 and 2 Pet 3:13. Conner went on to assert that

> it is not necessary to hold that man's sin preceded in the order of time the appearance of natural evil in the world. . . . Perhaps the disorder of the physical universe is intended as a reflection of the disorder of the moral universe. . . . The imperfections and disorders of the physical [universe] may

57. Andrew Martin Fairbairn, *The Philosophy of the Christian Religion* (5th ed.; London: Hodder and Stoughton, 1907), p. 134.
58. Even so, it is difficult to locate such an interpretation in the English-language commentaries on Genesis.

have been of the nature of "anticipative consequences." God could have made the physical universe to correspond to the foreknown condition of the moral world. . . . It is no more necessary to hold that thorns and thistles first began to grow after man sinned than it is to hold that God changed the laws of the refraction of light after the flood so that the rainbow should appear. . . . The history of the natural world would indicate that animal death was operative before man appeared in the world, and there is no good reason for holding that the Scriptures teach differently.

Conner clearly acknowledged that "specific forms of suffering are at times the direct or indirect result of man's sin" and that "this suffering is of the nature of a penalty for man's sin."[59]

b. Sufferings of the Righteous amid the Prosperity of the Wicked

Certain of the Psalms (esp. 10, 13, 37, 73, and 109) contrast the prosperity of the wicked and the sufferings and troubles of the righteous. The wicked are often seen as the enemies of the righteous, and frequently the psalmist (the righteous) calls on Yahweh to vindicate the righteous. Modern interpreters may be inclined to assert that the preoccupation of the Israelites with an inherited land and their looking on material prosperity as an indication of spiritual favor with God intensified the problem and the distress of the righteous. Even so, the problem is modern as well as ancient, for in modern societies the unjust, the dishonest, and the unscrupulous often accumulate more material possessions than the honest and the devout.

c. Suffering and Vindication of an Innocent Man

The book of Job presents in classic form the problem of the sufferings of a man innocent of deeds commensurate with such suffering and of his ultimate vindication before his accusers and of his trust in God.

d. Vicarious Suffering of the Servant of Yahweh

The fourth of the Servant Songs of Isa. 40–55 (52:13–53:12) describes the vicarious suffering of the Servant of Yahweh and his exaltation.[60]

2. New Testament

a. Suffering of the Righteous Jesus for Unrighteous Humankind

A theme central to the message of the New Testament is that Jesus, being righteous, suffered, especially in his crucifixion and death, for the sins of other human beings, who are unrighteous (2 Cor. 5:21; 1 Pet. 3:18a). Later we will examine these texts in reference to the meaning of the saving work of Jesus.[61] Here they are to be seen, even as with the suffering of the Servant of Yahweh, as pointing to a unique, once-for-all type of suffering.

---

59. *The Gospel of Redemption*, pp. 44-46.
60. See below, Ch. 46, for a discussion as to whether this vicarious suffering was thought to be only representative or also substitutionary.
61. See below, Ch. 46.

b. Suffering as the Persecution of Jesus' Disciples

Some suffering endured by Jesus' disciples was inflicted by their persecutors, even as Jesus himself had warned.

> "Blessed are those who are persecuted for righteousness' sake, for theirs is the kingdom of heaven. Blessed are you when men revile you and persecute you and utter all kinds of evil against you falsely on my account." (Matt. 5:10-11, RSV)

Paul's words about suffering and persecution were autobiographical.

> We are afflicted in every way, but not crushed; perplexed, but not driven to despair; persecuted, but not forsaken; struck down, but not destroyed; always carrying in the body the death of Jesus, so that the life of Jesus may also be manifested in our bodies. (2 Cor. 4:8-10, RSV)

The same apostle rejoiced in his sufferings in behalf of Colossian Christians, declaring that he was completing "what remains of Christ's afflictions for the sake of his body, that is, the church" (1:24, RSV). Persecution of Christians is a recurring theme in the First Epistle of Peter, where it is said to bring "blessedness" (3:14a; 4:14) and to be connected with the work of "the devil" (5:8-10).

c. Suffering Not Always the Direct Consequence of Specific Sin

In referring to certain Galileans who had been put to death by Pontius Pilate, Jesus denied that they were "worse sinners than all the other Galileans, because they suffered thus" (Luke 13:2, RSV). Jesus made the same kind of statement about the 18 on whom the tower of Siloam had fallen, causing their death (Luke 13:4). Even more explicit were his words about the man blind from birth who had been healed by Jesus at the pool of Siloam: " 'It was not that this man sinned, or his parents, but that the works of God might be made manifest in him' " (John 9:3, RSV).

d. Suffering for the Sake of Testing/ Discipline

Paul taught that suffering, presumably that by Christians, "produces endurance" (Rom. 5:3-4a, RSV) or "perseverance" (NIV) and that "endurance" or "perseverance" "produces character" (RSV). He interpreted his own "thorn in the flesh" as having been the occasion through which he had learned the sufficiency of God's grace and Christ's power as manifested in his own weakness (2 Cor. 12:7-9). The author of the Epistle to the Hebrews, following his exhortation about running the race of the Christian life (12:1-3), quoted Prov. 3:11-12:

> "My son, do not make light of the LORD's discipline,
>   and do not lose heart when he rebukes you,
> because the Lord disciplines those he loves,
>   and he punishes everyone he accepts as a son." (12:5-6)

The author then interpreted and applied this text. Suffering is a part of filial discipline (v. 7), and the absence of suffering suggests illegitimate sonship

(v. 8). Discipline is normal for earthly fathers (v. 9), but the heavenly Father has an even higher purpose, namely, "our good" (v. 10). Discipline, finally, "produces a harvest of righteousness and peace" (v. 11, NIV).

e. Suffering and the Goal of Christlikeness

There is a teleological aspect to the New Testament teaching about suffering. This is specifically taught in Paul's often-quoted Rom. 8:28-29. The apostle does not declare that "all things" are "good" but rather that God works "all things unto or for good." This assurance is not given to all humankind but to the "called according to his purpose" (RSV, NIV). The "good" is that "the called" should become like unto Jesus Christ. Hence suffering can be seen as designed to aid in the attainment of that goal. "For this slight momentary affliction is preparing for us an eternal weight of glory beyond all comparison" (2 Cor. 4:17, RSV).

Even as we had to contrast providence as sustenance and providence as sovereignty with certain other major alternative views, so also we need now to examine the major "solutions" to the problem of evil other than the Christian.

B. Alternative "Solutions"

1. Those Which Deny or Are Silent about the Goodness and Love of God

a. Buddhism

According to Buddhism, suffering grows out of the very nature of existence and attachment to existence. The remedy for suffering is the destruction of desire. To overcome suffering, therefore, the desire to exist must be eradicated. Buddhism offers the way or path for the attainment of this goal. There is nothing in Buddhism comparable to the suffering love of Jesus Christ. Divine love and goodness play no role in the Buddhist "solution" to suffering.

b. Stoicism

Stoics called on human beings to face natural evil by yielding to the inevitables of blind impersonal fate. Such yielding is to be marked by an impassionate or unemotional submission and endurance. No personal God and certainly no God of suffering love is involved in the Stoic "answer."

c. Naturalism

According to this view, pain is a biochemical indication that something is wrong in the human organism. It functions as a danger signal. Suffering is thus something quite natural and is to be borne with courage. Presumably the sufferer is not to raise questions about the why of suffering. Naturalism does not address the pain that human beings inflict on other human beings. In itself naturalism has no word about the goodness and love of God.

Erickson has cited Gordon Haddon Clark (1902-) as an example of a Christian philosopher who has in his philosophical teachings sacrificed the divine goodness for the sake of divine power.[62]

2. Those Which Deny the Almighty Power of God

a. Moral Dualism

As we noted earlier,[63] moral dualism affirms two uncreated and eternal Beings, the one good and the other evil. The evil God is the author or at least the controller of natural evil. Not all dualisms give a clear answer as to whether the good God will ultimately triumph. Dualism seems not to provide any assurance of personal victory over or through suffering.

b. Philosophy of Nonbeing

According to this view, moral and natural evil may be traced to the *Ungrund*, or "Divine Nothing," or Nonbeing. The Russian Orthodox philosopher Nicolai Berdyaev set forth this view. Both God and freedom were born out of the *Ungrund*; hence God is not responsible for the freedom of angels/humans, which gave rise to moral evil. Natural evil is chiefly the result of moral evil.[64] It seems that this "solution" assumes that God is impotent in the face of freedom-derived moral evil, and hence it must be traced to another source.

c. Theology of a Finite God

This view, espoused by the American philosopher Edgar S. Brightman,[65] holds that there is in the very being of God an extrarational and extravolitional aspect or "surd" or "the Given." This "surd" God himself cannot control, and it accounts for the occurrence of natural evil or suffering. The "surd," therefore, is an obstacle to God's realization of his purpose. God is limited by an uncontrollable something within his own being, and hence God is finite, not infinite.

3. That Which Denies the Reality or Seriousness of Natural Evil While Holding to the Goodness of God

Christian Science, or the teachings of Mrs. Mary Baker Eddy, being based on a pantheistic and idealistic philosophy, denies the reality of natural evil (suffering, illness, death) as well as the reality of moral evil (sin) and the reality of matter. The movement has discouraged the use of medical doctors, and its leaders conduct graveside burial services for those who, according to the official teaching, have not died. During her

62. *Christian Theology*, pp. 417-19.
63. See above, Ch. 25, I, A, 2.
64. *The Destiny of Man*, trans. Natalie Duddington (London: Geoffrey Bles, 1937), esp. pp. 25-33, 117-22.
65. *The Problem of God* (New York: Abingdon Press, 1930), pp. 96-98, 113-38; *The Finding of God* (ibid., 1931), p. 150; *A Philosophy of Religion* (Englewood Cliffs, N.J.: Prentice-Hall, Inc., 1940), pp. 276-341.

lifetime Mrs. Eddy found it necessary to posit "Malicious Animal Magnetism" to explain the activities of her opponents, even though this postulate was contradictory to her own teaching.[66]

C. The Christian "Solution"

1. Various Functions of Suffering

As the examination of biblical texts has suggested, the Bible ascribes various functions to suffering, and Christian theology has elaborated on these.

a. Suffering can be *retributive* or punitive, either for one's own sins or, indirectly, for the sins of others (Gen. 3:3; Deut. 30:15; 2 Cor. 5:10).

b. Suffering can be *disciplinary* as a legitimate aspect of sonship to God (Prov. 3:11-12; Heb. 12:5-11).

c. Suffering can be *probationary*, or a form of testing (Isa. 48:10; Job 2:3, 6, 9-10).

d. Suffering can be *revelational* in that God's nature and purpose can be made manifest through suffering (Jeremiah, Hosea, the exemplary dimension in Jesus' suffering).

e. Suffering can be *vicarious* or substitutionary in that Jesus' death was in behalf of and instead of others.

f. Suffering can be *testimonial* in that Christians by dying for or suffering greatly for their faith in and obedience to Jesus Christ are thereby witnesses for Christ, as the recent history of Christianity in the People's Republic of China and elsewhere clearly shows.

g. Suffering can be *eschatological*, or a characteristic of the end times (Matt. 24:8).[67]

2. Suffering Ordained and Suffering Permitted

Christian teaching normally maintains a distinction between that which God ordains and that which God permits. This distinction is needed in view of the freedom of created human beings to choose contrary to God's purpose, or the highest human good. Not all suffering permitted by God is necessarily ordained by God.

3. Suffering without Karma

Christian belief has no place for a doctrine of karma, built on strict distributive justice.[68]

---

66. *Science and Health with Key to the Scriptures* (Boston: Trustees under the Will of Mary Baker G. Eddy, 1934); teachings as to no evil (pp. 327, 330, 480, 526), no death (pp. 164, 251, 292, 427, 584), no matter (pp. 124, 171, 586, 591), and no medicine (pp. 142ff.); Edwin F. Dakin, *Mrs. Eddy: The Biography of a Virginal Mind* (New York: Charles Scribner's Sons, 1929), pp. 159-67, 185-87, 212-16, 501-5 (on Malicious Animal Magnetism).

67. Six of these seven functions have been taken from H. Wheeler Robinson's treatment of suffering according to the Old Testament and set in a larger context: *Suffering, Human and Divine* (New York: Macmillan, 1939), pp. 33-48.

68. Farmer, *The World and God*, pp. 242, 245.

4. Limits to the Phenomenon of Healing

Most contemporary Christians do not accept the teaching found among some Pentecostals and neo-Pentecostals, namely, that all pain, disease, bodily infirmity, and suffering can be eliminated by claiming the healing promised in the atoning or saving work of Christ (Isa. 53:5d) and by the exercise of full and genuine faith. Paul's "thorn in the flesh" seems to be biblical evidence against this view. Colin Brown (1932-) has argued that the new covenant in Christ mandates the forgiveness of sins but not in the same way bodily healing.[69]

5. Solvitur Patiendo through Christ

The Christian "solution" to suffering is not so much an intellectual rationale for suffering as it is the experience of suffering itself in the grace and power of Jesus Christ. H. Wheeler Robinson rightly claimed *solvitur patiendo* (it is solved through suffering).[70] H. H. Farmer has written on the same theme:

> But concerning those darker aspects of evil, wherein suffering and sin seem to take a form, or to produce consequences, definitely dysteleological in relation to human personality, its [Christian faith's] claim has never been to explain them philosophically, but rather to enable the individual through Christ to have fellowship with the living God in them, in such wise that the necessity for anything in the nature of a complete explanation, in respect either of his own life or of the lives of others, disappears. . . . This does not mean, however, that the Christian experience and faith shed no light at all on the problem of evil, as though it were merely a matter of being blindly and unintelligently optimistic about everything. To have victory over evil, through fellowship with God in it, must mean to understand it a little better as part of the wisdom of an utterly trustworthy divine love, even though much still remains in mystery. . . . There is light on evil, but it is not complete light, and it is hardly light at all to any who are not in some measure living within that world of reconciliation with God which is its source.[71]

To sum up, providence, as God's foreseeing and directing all things to his intended end, involves sustenance (God and nature), sovereignty (God and history), and theodicy (God and suffering).

---

69. *That You May Believe: Miracles and Faith* (Grand Rapids: Eerdmans; Exeter: Paternoster, 1985), pp. 202-3.

70. *Suffering, Human and Divine*, pp. 201-24.

71. *The World and God*, pp. 240-41.

CHAPTER 27

Miracles

Closely associated with the doctrine of providence and often discussed as a segment of that doctrine are miracles. The miracles associated with the Christian doctrine of miracles are primarily those recorded in the Old and New Testaments, but the discussion can also embrace postbiblical and even contemporary miracles. When we employ the term "miracle," is there universal or at least widespread agreement as to its basic meaning?

Definitions of "miracle" by twentieth-century Christian theologians have tended to emphasize that miracles constitute a considerable variation from natural law or natural processes. Both J. Gresham Machen[1] and W. T. Conner[2] defined "miracle" in terms of the transcending of natural law. According to Norman Leo Geisler (1932-),[3] it "is a divine intervention into, or an interruption of the regular course of the world that produces a purposeful but unusual event" that "cannot be predicted by natural means." For Clive Staples Lewis a "miracle" is "an interference with Nature by supernatural power."[4] Other authors have insisted on pressing beyond transcendence of natural law to other basic characteristics. A miracle is "an event of an extraordinary kind, brought about by a god, and of religious significance" (Richard Swinburne).[5] It is "that particular category of wonders which can be attributed to the intervention of a God who is unique and distinct from the world, such as the God of the Christians" (Joseph de Tonquédec, S.J.).[6] It is not only a supernatural "source of wonder" but also an event that is claimed to be revelatory of "God, his power, his activity, indeed his concern and love" (M. A. H. Melinsky).[7]

1. *Christianity and Liberalism* (New York: Macmillan, 1923), p. 103.
2. *Revelation and God*, p. 274.
3. *Miracles and Modern Thought* (Grand Rapids: Zondervan, 1982), p. 13.
4. *Miracles: A Preliminary Study* (London: Geoffrey Bles, 1947), p. 15.
5. *The Concept of Miracle* (London: Macmillan, 1970), p. 1.
6. *Miracles,* trans. Frank M. Oppenheim (West Baden, Ind.: West Baden College, 1955), p. 3.
7. *Healing Miracles: An Examination from History and Experience of the Place of Miracle in Christian Thought and Medical Practice* (London: A. R. Mowbray and Company Ltd., 1968), p. 2.

Inasmuch as the word "supernatural" has been employed in definitions of "miracle," one is prone to ask whether the two words are theological synonyms. That they are not necessarily so is evident, for example, from the fact that the new birth, or regeneration, is often described as a "supernatural" event but does not involve a transcending of the laws of the physical universe.

With such definitions in mind we turn now to a consideration of miracles as recorded in the Bible.

I. BIBLICAL MIRACLES

A. OLD TESTAMENT

Exodus contains more miracle narratives than any other book in the Old Testament. These include the turning of Aaron's rod into a snake that swallowed other rods (7:8-13), the ten plagues of Egypt (7:14–11:10), the pillar of cloud and pillar of fire (13:21-22), the deliverance through the Red Sea (14:21-22, 29), the manna (16:4-5, 13-19), and the water from the rock at Rephidim (17:6-7). Numbers contains the accounts of healing through the elevated serpent (21:8-9) and of the speaking by Balaam's donkey (22:28, 30). In Joshua there is the crossing of the Jordan River by the Israelites on dry ground (3:14-17). The books of Kings contain accounts of the raisings of the son of the widow of Zarephath (1 Kings 17:19-23) and of the son of the Shunammite woman (2 Kings 4:32-35) and of the healing of Naaman (2 Kings 5:14).[8]

Three principal Hebrew nouns are used in the Old Testament to identify miracles: 'ôt, môpēt, and niplā'ôt. The word 'ôt, normally translated "sign," appears 29 times in the Old Testament; of these uses 25 refer to the plagues of Egypt, or to the plagues, the Exodus, and other related miracles. The word appears repeatedly in Exodus (4:8-9, 17, 28, 30; 7:3-4; 8:23; 10:1-2) in reference to the ten plagues. When the word is used in Deuteronomy (4:34; 6:22; 7:19; 26:8; 29:3; 34:11), Joshua (24:17), Jeremiah (32:20-21), Psalms (78:43; 105:27; 135:9), and Nehemiah (9:10), it is usually joined together with môpēt, translated "wonders" or "miracles," and sometimes seems to refer to the Exodus as well as the plagues. But it could be used of a future prophet-dreamer (Deut. 13:1-3).

The word môpēt, a plural form, was probably derived from the verb yāpa', meaning "to shine, to be bright." Hence môpēt were "splendid deeds" or "wonders" or "miracles." Such happenings served to evoke awe in the ones who recognized in them the working of God. Môpēt appears 36 times in the Old Testament; of these usages 19 refer to the plagues of Egypt or to the plagues and the Exodus. Although the term sometimes stands alone (Exod. 4:21; 7:9; 11:9-10; 15:11; 1 Chr. 16:12), it more often is coupled with

8. See A. Allen Brockington, *Old Testament Miracles in the Light of the Gospel* (Edinburgh: T. and T. Clark, 1907).

'ôṯ to form the expression "signs and wonders" (Exod. 7:3; Deut. 4:34; 6:22; 7:19; 26:8; 29:3; 34:11; Jer. 32:20-21; Ps. 78:43; 105:27; 135:9; Neh. 9:10).

The word *niplā'ôṯ*, the niphal plural substantive of the verb *pālā'*, which means "to separate" or "to be wonderful," conveys the idea of "things done wonderfully" or "marvels." The events to which this term was applied in the Old Testament were always extraordinary, but not all of them were miraculous. *Niplā'ôṯ* was used of the plagues (Ps. 78:12) and probably of the plagues and the Exodus (Ps. 105:5; 1 Chr. 16:12, 24). In Ps. 105:5 one may study the usage of both *môpēṯ* and *niplā'ôṯ*, and in Ps. 105:27 one may examine the usage of both 'ôṯ and *môpēṯ*. Dale Moody has contended that the accounts of the ten plagues and the Exodus are "a blend of the natural and the supernatural."[9]

In Wisd. of Sol. 19:6-8 the crossing of the Red Sea was interpreted as a refashioning of the created order.[10]

B. NEW TESTAMENT

Alan Richardson (1905-75) has prefaced his study of the miracles in the Gospels with an exposition of the power of God, especially the power of God in Jesus Christ.[11] Reginald Horace Fuller (1915-), asserting that the "foundation miracles" of each of the testaments were the Exodus and the death-resurrection of Jesus, claimed that each of these had both "preliminary" and "accompanying" miracles. For the Exodus the preliminary miracles were the plagues, and the accompanying miracles were "the dividing of the Red Sea, the pillar of fire by night and the cloud by day, the water from the rock, and the manna." For the death-resurrection of Jesus the preliminary miracles were the healings, exorcisms, and nature miracles performed by Jesus, and the accompanying miracles included the virginal conception, the transfiguration, and the resurrection appearances.[12] The canonical Gospels assumed the historicity of the miracles recorded; questions about historicity or the philosophical possibility of miracles came later.

1. Terms

Four Greek words were repeatedly used in the New Testament to convey the concept of miracle.

a. The noun *dynamis*, which can also mean "power" in general, was used in the Synoptics, Paul, Acts, and Hebrews to mean "mighty deed or work" or "miracle." The term could refer to miracles performed by Jesus (Mark 6:2e; Matt. 11:20a; Luke 19:3b; Acts 2:22b) or by his disciples (Mark 9:39c), to the nonperformance of miracles by Jesus (Mark 6:5; Matt. 13:58), to apostolic miracles (2 Cor. 12:12; Acts 8:13b; 19:11; Heb. 2:4), and to the gift of working miracles (Gal. 3:5; 1 Cor. 12:10a, 28d).

9. *The Word of Truth*, pp. 162, 163.
10. Melinsky, *Healing Miracles*, pp. 13-15.
11. *The Miracle-Stories of the Gospels* (London: SCM Press Ltd., 1941), pp. 1-19.
12. *Interpreting the Miracles* (Philadelphia: Westminster Press, 1963), p. 10.

b. The noun *erga*, meaning "works," is distinctively a Johannine term whenever it connotes a miracle. Although *erga* can refer to the miracles as wrought by Jesus (John 7:3b; 15:24a), more often they are said to be by or from the Father (5:20b, 36b, c; 9:3-4a; 10:25b, 32, 37-38a; 14:10c-11).

c. The noun *sēmeion*, translated "sign" and quite similar in meaning to the Hebrew *'ôt*, was used in all four Gospels, Paul, Acts, and Hebrews. It referred to a physical or material transformation that had spiritual significance. The term was applied to those miracles which Pharisees and others were seeking of Jesus (Mark 8:11-12; par. Matt. 12:38-39; 16:1, 4; Luke 11:29; John 4:48b; 6:30b), to miracles performed by Jesus (John 20:30; Acts 2:22b; 4:30b), to apostolic miracles (2 Cor. 12:12; Rom. 15:19a; Acts 2:43b; 5:12a; 6:8; 8:13a; 14:3; 15:12b; Heb. 2:4), to miracles wrought by Moses (Acts 7:36), and to pretended eschatological miracles (2 Thess. 2:9).

d. The noun *teras*, normally translated "wonders," was never used alone in the New Testament to refer to miracles wrought by Jesus. It was, apart from other terms, used of deeds of false Christs (Mark 13:22 par. Matt. 24:24). *Teras*, when joined with *sēmeion* to form the expression "signs and wonders," was repeatedly used in reference to Jesus' miracles. It was applied to those miracles sought of Jesus (Acts 4:48), to miracles performed by Jesus (Acts 2:22; 4:30b), to apostolic miracles (Rom. 15:19a; Acts 2:43b; 5:12a; 6:8; 14:3; 15:12b; Heb. 2:4), to Moses' miracles (Acts 7:36), and to pretended eschatological miracles (2 Thess. 2:9).

Three other nouns, commonly used in pagan literature, are found in single occurrences in the New Testament. These are *paradoxa*, "remarkable things" (NIV), in Luke 5:26; *thaumasia*, "wonderful things" (NIV), in Matt. 21:15; and *aretai*, "wonderful deeds" (RSV), in 1 Pet. 2:9b, although it may be argued that in the last text miracles are not necessarily the referent.[13]

2. Classification

Various efforts have been made to classify the miracles reported in the Gospels. Edwin Basil Redlich (1878-1960) employed a twofold scheme: miracles of nature, and miracles of healing.[14] Hendrik van der Loos in his massive study followed the same division,[15] and Leopold Sabourin placed the raisings among the nature miracles.[16] Dale Moody, reaching beyond the Gospels, added miracles of history (Exodus, death-resurrection of Jesus) to the two categories of Redlich and van der Loos.[17] C. S. Lewis proposed two patterns of classification, the one more elaborate and the

13. Fuller, *Interpreting the Miracles*, p. 17.
14. *Form Criticism: Its Value and Limitations* (London: Duckworth, 1939), pp. 115-34.
15. *The Miracles of Jesus*, Supplements to *Novum Testamentum*, vol. 9 (Leiden: E. J. Brill, 1968), pt. 4.
16. *The Divine Miracles Discussed and Defended* (Rome: Officium Libri Catholici, 1977), chs. 6-7.
17. *The Word of Truth*, pp. 163-65.

other twofold. According to the first pattern, there were six kinds of miracles related to Jesus:

> Miracles of Fertility
> > Conversion of water into wine at Cana
> > Feeding of the five thousand
> > Feeding of the four thousand
> > Multiplication of fish
> > Virginal conception of Jesus
> Miracles of Healing (numerous examples)
> Miracle of Destruction
> > Withering of fig tree
> Miracles of Dominion over the Inorganic
> > Stilling the tempest
> > Walking on the water
> Miracles of Reversal
> > Raisings from the dead
> Miracles of Perfecting or Glorification
> > Transfiguration of Jesus
> > Resurrection of Jesus
> > Ascension of Jesus

Lewis's second scheme, involving miracles "of the Old Creation" and miracles "of the New Creation," combines the categories of the first scheme. Those miracles listed under the first three categories and the stilling of the tempest are the miracles "of the Old Creation," whereas the walking on the water and the miracles listed under the last two categories are the miracles "of the New Creation." The former are miracles that reproduce God's natural operations on the universe in a special way, and the latter are miracles that "focus at a particular point . . . God's . . . future operations on the universe." Yet, with all these efforts at classification, Lewis concluded that "the Grand Miracle" was the incarnation of Jesus Christ. Moreover, "[e]very other miracle prepares for this, exhibits this, or results from this."[18]

Not only have efforts been made to classify all the miracles in the Gospels but also New Testament scholars have found special configurations of miracle stories in the Gospels. Especially has this been true of the Gospel of John, wherein seven miracle stories seem to be associated with "the Book of Signs": water into wine at Cana (2:1-11), the healing of the official's son (4:46-54), the healing of the lame man at the pool of Bethesda (5:1-9), the feeding of the five thousand (6:1-13), walking on the water (6:16-21), the healing of the man blind from birth (9:1-34), and the raising

---

18. *Miracles*, pp. 131-95. Colin Brown, *That You May Believe*, pp. 48-49, has suggested that Lewis had moved from his natural theology of a personal "cosmic mind" to "the miracle-working God of the New Testament" only "by a leap of faith."

of Lazarus (11:1-44). Some hold that the Fourth Evangelist borrowed and adapted these stories from a book that had come into existence after the Synoptics had been written.[19]

3. Purposes

In studying the miracles recorded in the New Testament one finds it easy to raise basic questions about purpose. Why did Jesus perform miracles? Why were miracles performed through the apostles? Why were the miracle stories given such a prominent place in the New Testament, especially the Gospels?

a. Of Jesus' Miracles

On this topic there have been differences of interpretation and no little dispute. First, let us lay out the various answers that can be drawn from the New Testament. Second, let us identify and evaluate modern Christian understandings of these purposes.

1) Purposes Connected with New Testament Texts

a) Glorification

In the accounts of six different healings in the Gospels (Mark 2:12; Luke 7:16; 13:13; 17:15; 18:43; John 11:4) specific mention is made that either the one healed, those beholding the healing, or both gave glory and praise to God. Does this recurring expression of praise and glory constitute one of the purposes for the performance of Jesus' miracles?

b) Compassion

In the accounts of three different healings (Mark 1:41; Luke 7:13; Matt. 20:34) specific mention is made that Jesus had "compassion" or "pity" on those being healed. Does this factor need to be included in the statement of purposes of Jesus' healings?

c) Signification

In the "Book of Signs" within John's Gospel miracles are clearly seen to serve as "signs" or attestations of the power and saving activity of God in and through Jesus as the Son of God. In the Synoptics miracles are connected with the drawing near of the kingdom of God. In John 9:3, 38 restoration of sight seems to be a step toward faith in Jesus as the Messiah. Wherever miracles are taken to be "signs," they are seen as integral to the mission and ministry of Jesus. Can this purpose be excluded from any listing of the purposes of Jesus' miracles?

---

19. Fuller, *Interpreting the Miracles*, pp. 88-109, esp. 90. Fuller also has found "five groups" of miracles in Mark, a total of ten miracles in Matthew, and miracles to have been for Luke "the most important aspect of Jesus' ministry" (pp. 69-87, esp. 69, 77, and 84). See also Ray Summers, *Behold the Lamb: An Exposition of the Theological Themes in the Gospel of John* (Nashville: Broadman Press, 1979), p. 14.

2) Modern Understandings of These Purposes

The earlier orthodox view, as expressed by William Paley (1743-1805),[20] was that the miracles of Jesus were absolute proofs of his deity. Then came the Liberal Protestant view that they were expressions of power in the service of humanitarian compassion.[21] Form Criticism, represented by Rudolf Bultmann and Martin Dibelius, thought that the miracle stories yielded the primary view of Jesus as a powerful wonder-worker.[22] More recently, European New Testament scholars have brought forth a new emphasis on the miracles as signs, not absolute proofs, of the kingdom of God as drawing near in the person, ministry, and death-resurrection of Jesus.[23]

In the face of such diverse statements, what ought to be concluded about the purpose or purposes of Jesus' miracles? Paley's proofs cannot be taken so as to exclude faith as an essential response to Jesus' miracles. The compassion of Jesus need not be taken solely as representative of humanitarianism, for it can be seen as the divine compassion in the work of the God-man. The form-critical preoccupation with wonder-working fails to integrate miracles with the entire mission and ministry of Jesus. The newer emphasis on signs has much in its favor, but it need not rule out other purposes such as the divine compassion and the glorification of God.

b. Of Apostolic Miracles

The purpose of miracles wrought through the apostles has been a much less controversial issue. Most often these have been explained as signs of the kingdom of God or as confirmatory of the coming of the Holy Spirit on the Day of Pentecost.

c. Of Miracle Stories in the New Testament

But why, one may ask, were so many miracle stories included in the New Testament? In the Gospel of Mark, 31 percent of the verses are devoted to miracle accounts.[24] What purposes led to such extensive inclusion of materials related to miracles? Alan Richardson has under-

---

20. *The Evidences of Christianity*, pt. 1, ch. 6; pt. 3, chs. 4 and 5, in *The Works of William Paley, D.D.* (London: William Smith, 1838), pp. 222-24, 354, 359.

21. Vincent Taylor, *The Formation of the Gospel Tradition* (2d ed.; London: Macmillan, 1935), p. 133; William Barclay, *The Mind of Jesus* (New York: Harper and Brothers, 1961), p. 81.

22. Bultmann, *The History of the Synoptic Tradition*, trans. John Marsh (2d rev. ed.; Oxford: Basil Blackwell, 1972), pp. 209-44, esp. 219, 226, who saw healing miracles as expressing divine power and exorcisms as showing messianic authority; and Dibelius, *From Tradition to Gospel*, trans. Bertram Lee Woolf (New York: Charles Scribner's Sons, 1965), pp. 70-103.

23. Richardson, *The Miracle-Stories of the Gospels*; Edwyn C. Hoskyns, *Cambridge Sermons* (London: S.P.C.K., 1938; reprint ed. 1970), pp. 56, 60; William Manson, *Jesus the Messiah: The Synoptic Tradition of the Revelation of God in Christ, with Special Reference to Form-Criticism* (London: Hodder and Stoughton, 1943), pp. 43-46.

24. Melinsky, *Healing Miracles*, p. 15.

taken a detailed answer. First, the primitive church had the conviction that the powers associated with the drawing near of the kingdom of God had been manifested in Jesus as Messiah and Lord. Miracles, being expressive of such powers, were parallel to Jesus' teachings about the kingdom and were "the manifestation of the activity of the Spirit." As "signs" miracles were "enacted parables, not mere 'wonder-stories,' or occasional works of charity . . . or mere historical reminiscences." Second, miracle stories served a didactic purpose. They teach Jesus as healer, exorcist, and bringer of the forgiveness of sins and provide material for Christian "instruction and exhortation." Third, the miracle accounts provided the occasions for the Evangelists to make spiritual applications beyond the accounts themselves, and here Richardson is less than persuasive.[25] One should add, as Anton Fridrichsen (1888-1953) has done, that the apostolic miracles were most likely included in the Acts and the epistles as part of the Christian mission. Thus "the miracles manifest that divine power which sustains the mission, acts through it, and has created all things new in the ethical and material realms."[26]

In summary, we have found that Jesus' miracles were performed primarily as signs of the drawing near of the kingdom of God or the messianic age but have allowed such secondary purposes as divine compassion and the glorification of God. Apostolic miracles were performed as signs of the messianic age and the coming of the Holy Spirit. The inclusion of numerous miracle stories in the Gospels and in the Acts and the epistles is explicable in terms of the purposes of the miracles themselves and the needs of the early Christian community.

II. MIRACLES ACCORDING TO THE HISTORY OF CHRISTIAN DOCTRINE

A. PATRISTIC AGE

Colin Brown has recently posed the question as to whether the Palestinian Jews of Jesus' day understood Jesus to be in fulfillment of Deut. 13:1-5, according to which a future prophet-dreamer, who would announce and perform "a miraculous sign or wonder" (NIV), should be put to death lest Israelites be led to follow other gods.[27] However that question may be answered, it is not difficult to find evidence that Jews during the first and second centuries A.D. accused Jesus of having used magic to perform miracles. Justin Martyr, Origen, Arnobius, and Lactan-

---

25. *The Miracle-Stories of the Gospels*, pp. 38-99. Fuller, *Interpreting the Miracles*, p. 67, has stressed that whereas Jesus interpreted his miracles as "signs of the inbreaking of the final Reign of God," the primitive church interpreted them, in the light of his resurrection, "as signs that he was the Messiah."
26. *The Problem of Miracle in Primitive Christianity*, trans. Roy A. Harrisville and John S. Hanson (Minneapolis: Augsburg Publishing House, 1972), pp. 56-63, esp. 60.
27. *That You May Believe*, pp. 107, 115-17.

tius wrote of this accusation and framed an apologetic defense against it. Fridrichsen thought that this Jewish accusation helps to explain why second- and third-century Christian writers were slow to use Jesus' miracles to prove the validity of his mission.[28] But later Athanasius did see in these miracles the proclamation of Jesus' lordship over nature, and Gregory of Nyssa magnified them as "greater than nature." Augustine of Hippo has been said to have been "the first to draw up a systematic doctrine of miracle." But Augustine, according to Melinsky,

> puts so much emphasis on the sign-value of miracle that he almost neglects its transcendence. He sees divine intervention not so much as an act of God's creative power as an awakening of seeds already planted in things by the hand of Providence.[29]

Augustine did address the question of natural and supernatural in *The City of God:*

> For how is that contrary to nature which happens by the will of God, since the will of so mighty a Creator is certainly the nature of each created thing? A portent, therefore, happens not contrary to nature, but contrary to what we know as nature.[30]

B. MEDIEVAL ERA

With Thomas Aquinas and the rediscovered Aristotle, when theology had become a science, the emphasis concerning miracles shifted from the purpose of miracles and the human faith-response to "the nature of the divine intervention in a miraculous event." "The sign value" yielded to "the transcendence of God's act of power."[31] Thomas could still write about both, but the aspect of power was dominant:

> Two things may be considered in miracles. One is that which is done: this is something surpassing the faculty of nature, and in this respect miracles are called *virtues* [acts of power]. The other thing is the purpose for which miracles are wrought, namely the manifestation of something supernatural; and in this respect they are commonly called *signs:* but on account of some excellence they receive the name of *wonder* or *prodigy*, as showing something from afar.[32]

C. POST-REFORMATION AND MODERN PERIODS

Because miracles were not a leading issue during the Protestant Reformation, we will now give attention to the later periods. With the advent of Deism and the Enlightenment and the concurrent development of the natural and physical sciences, miracles became a major bone of contention, and especially was this true of the historicity or facticity of

28. *The Problem of Miracle in Primitive Christianity*, pp. 87-95.
29. *Healing Miracles,* pp. 38-42, esp. 41.
30. 21.8.2, trans. Marcus Dods.
31. Melinsky, *Healing Miracles,* pp. 42-43.
32. *Summa Theologica,* 2-2.178.1, reply obj. 3, trans. Fathers of the English Dominican Province.

biblical miracles. This "great debate" on miracle has within the recent past been traced in great detail by at least three authors: John Stewart Lawton,[33] who traced it from the early Deists in the seventeenth century to the work of Alan Richardson (1941); Robert M. Burns (1942-),[34] who reviewed it from Joseph Glanvill (1681) through David Hume (1750); and Colin Brown,[35] who scrutinized it from Baruch Spinoza (1670) to Rudolf Bultmann (1919) and Paul Tillich (1953). As important as were the major rejectors of miracles (Anthony Collins, Thomas Woolston, David Hume, T. H. Huxley, J. M. Thompson) and the major defenders of miracles (William Paley, John Wesley, Samuel T. Coleridge, J. B. Mozley, Richard C. Trench, B. F. Westcott, D. S. Cairns) and their respective arguments, it is not possible here to trace these in detail. Rather we will treat some of the concepts paramount in that prolonged debate subsequently under the major objections to miracles.[36]

III. THE VALIDITY OF MIRACLES

Although it would be an awesome, if not impossible task to list every conceivable objection to biblical miracles or even every one that has been issued in published form, it is feasible to give attention to some of the major lines of objection to biblical miracles.

A. MIRACLES AND NATURAL LAW: OBJECTION OF THE EIGHTEENTH-CENTURY DEISTS

Beginning with the Deists, the objection has been raised that miracles are an impossibility because they violate natural law. Sometimes it has been said that the ancients believed in miracles because they did not know the laws of nature but that modern people, aware of such laws, must therefore refuse to admit miracles.

Under such considerations, how is the term "natural law" to be defined? C. S. Lewis has noted that there are at least three possible definitions. First, natural law could mean "mere brute facts [of nature], known only by observation, with no discoverable rhyme or reason about them." Second, it could mean "applications of the law of averages" so that "'impossible events'" would be "so overwhelmingly improbable—by actuarial standards—that we do not need to take them into account." Third, natural law could mean "'necessary truths'" so that "the opposite would be meaningless nonsense."[37] There are, of course, other definitions,

33. *Miracles and Revelation* (New York: Association Press, 1960).
34. *The Great Debate on Miracle: From Joseph Glanvill to David Hume* (Lewisburg, Pa.: Bucknell University Press, 1981).
35. *Miracles and the Critical Mind* (Grand Rapids: Eerdmans, 1984), esp. pp. 31, 248-51, 172.
36. See below, section III.
37. *Miracles*, pp. 67-68.

such as that of Georgia Harkness, which is correlatable with the second of Lewis: "the formulation of an observed regularity in natural events."[38] Lewis argued that neither his first nor his second definition provides any "assurance against miracles," but he noted that the third "seems at first sight to present an insurmountable obstacle to miracle." Taking as his example two billiard balls that might be seen to have the same destinations, he showed how "a rough place in the cloth" and help from a cue can constitute "interferences" that lead to different destinations. So, in miracle God provides the special or interfering agency. "A miracle," Lewis concluded, "is emphatically not an event without cause or without results. Its cause is the activity of God: its results follow according to Natural Law."[39] But Harkness warned against a deistic interpretation of miracle in which God intrudes from the outside as if he had nothing to do with natural processes,[40] and Harry Emerson Fosdick by his definition of miracle sought to address the issue of natural law: "A miracle is God's use of his own law-abiding powers to work out in ways surprising to us his will for our lives and for the world."[41]

Care must also be taken lest natural law be seen as fate or as a force that does the governing of the natural order. Rather God utilizes what human beings call natural law. It is a statement of nature's regularities, and miracle is a deviation from or transcending of natural law, but not a violation of natural law.[42] Furthermore, Patrick Nowell-Smith (1914-) has suggested that miracles may be indications in the midst of the changing sciences of scarcely known or yet to be clarified natural laws.[43]

B. MIRACLES AND SYNOPTIC CRITICISM: OBJECTION OF NINETEENTH-CENTURY BIBLICAL CRITICISM

New Testament literary criticism moved during the nineteenth century toward certain widely accepted conclusions. Among these were the historical unreliability of the Gospel according to John and the source-document hypothesis for the origin of the Synoptic Gospels (Mk, Q, M, L).[44] Some New Testament critics and others assumed that Synoptic studies would lead to the conclusion that the earliest views of Jesus and his ministry were without miracles. Such persons tended to assume that they could eradicate the miracles from the Synoptic portrait of Jesus.

Source criticism of the Gospels, however, did not yield such ex-

---

38. *The Providence of God,* p. 151.
39. *Miracles,* pp. 60-64.
40. *The Providence of God,* pp. 150-51, 156.
41. *The Modern Use of the Bible,* p. 162.
42. Conner, *Revelation and God,* p. 273.
43. "Miracles," in Flew and MacIntyre, eds., *New Essays in Philosophical Theology,* pp. 243-53.
44. Mark's Gospel was regarded as a source for Matthew and Luke; a teachings source, Q, was said to have been used by all three Synoptists; Matthew employed his own special source, M; and Luke used his own special source, L.

pected conclusions. Mark's Gospel, considered with Q the earliest materials, contains references to some 18 miracles, not counting the transfiguration and resurrection of Jesus. Q, presumably a collection of the sayings or teachings of Jesus, contains one miracle account, the healing of the dumb demoniac (Matt. 9:32-34). Efforts to date miracle narratives late and to ascribe these to the later fantasy of the primitive church or of the Gospel writers contradicted the then accepted early date of Mark with its abundance of miracle stories. Efforts to expunge the miracle accounts from Mark on the basis that these had not been a part of the original Gospel of Mark were lacking in support from textual criticism. The attempts to discover a nonmiraculous Jesus in the Synoptic Gospels failed except by methods that were unhistorical and/or uncritical. "The effort to get back to a non-miraculous Christ has signally failed."[45]

Not only the canonical Gospels but also, to use Lewis's term, "the grand miracle,"[46] the incarnation, points toward miracles. "Supernatural works are the natural expression of a supernatural person."[47] "Healing was an inseparable part of the pattern of his work and of the pattern of the work of his apostles."[48]

C. Miracles and Scientific Testings: Objection of Twentieth-Century Naturalism/Scientism

Much contemporary rejection of biblical miracles has stemmed from the idea that modern science invalidates miracles. It is often said that only that which can be tested scientifically can be accepted as valid. Such a statement assumes both that scientific testing is based on all existent data and that scientific testing always results in an absolute uniformity of occurrence. By the same line of thinking, of course, objection can be made to the existence of God. Such conclusions, however, are not, strictly speaking, drawn from the use of the scientific method of observation and verification alone but rather from its being overshadowed by the philosophy of scientism, which excludes any possibility of knowledge from another source and knowledge of another kind. Scientific observation and verification do not embrace all data and do not result in absolute uniformity of occurrence. Such testing is necessarily far removed in time from the biblical miracles, though not from contemporary miracles. Although it may deal with occurrences not readily explicable in scientific terms, scientific testing has no means for taking into account the redemptive or re-creative purpose and activity of God.

---

45. Conner, *Revelation and God,* p. 279.
46. *Miracles,* ch. 14.
47. Conner, *Revelation and God,* p. 281.
48. William Barclay, *The Mind of Jesus,* p. 67.

D. MIRACLES AND THE TECHNIQUE OF MENTAL HEALING: INTERPRETATION OF TWENTIETH-CENTURY PSYCHOTHERAPY

Previously discussed objections to biblical miracles have been efforts entirely to invalidate those miracle accounts, but this one seeks to reinterpret those accounts. This viewpoint applies specifically to the healing miracles of Jesus. Such healing incidents are interpreted as mind-cures, or forms of mental healing, wherein Jesus is said to have mastered the technique of mental healing—a technique that modern humans can also employ. In the latter nineteenth century Mrs. Eddy's Christian Science and the parallel New Thought movement began to claim to be able to dispel the illusions of illness and suffering from the minds of those who suffered and to effect "healing." Beyond these movements, there have been those who have claimed that the healing accounts in the Gospels were early examples of mind-cures that have been repeated many times in later centuries. S. Vernon McCasland (1896-)[49] developed the thesis that demon possession in the New Testament was "an ancient expression for mental illness" and that it has its parallels in other ancient and modern cultures. Hence exorcisms in the New Testament are taken to be mental healings with no reference to evil spirits or demonic beings. The psychotherapeutic approach to the healings by Jesus puts little or no emphasis on the power of God or on miracles as signs of the kingdom of God. Furthermore, those who take this approach to the healings of Jesus can deny all other biblical miracles on naturalistic or other premises.

E. MIRACLES AND DEMYTHOLOGIZING: OBJECTION OF TWENTIETH-CENTURY BULTMANNIANISM

Rudolf Bultmann's demythologization of the New Testament was based on a definition of "mythology" that included the miraculous in the mythical. "Mythology is the use of imagery to express the other worldly in terms of this world and the divine in terms of human life, the other side in terms of this side."[50] It seems that this definition by Bultmann necessarily embraces the language of miracles, since miracles involve the interaction of the divine and the human. It was the task of demythologization to reinterpret the miracle stories of the Gospels by putting them into the categories of an existentialist self-understanding.[51] The resurrection of Jesus was included in the scope of demythologization, for, unlike the death of Jesus, it was detached from history and reduced to the faith of Christian believers in a continuing Jesus.

Bultmann's demythologization is the radical application to the New

---

49. *By the Finger of God: Demon Possession and Exorcism in Early Christianity in the Light of Modern Views of Mental Illness* (New York: Macmillan, 1951), esp. p. v.
50. "New Testament and Mythology," in Hans W. Bartsch, ed., *Kerygma and Myth*, p. 10, n. 2.
51. Ibid., p. 12.

Testament Gospels of that bifurcation between the phenomenal or objective world and the noumenal or subjective world that Immanuel Kant introduced to modern philosophy and that has dominated so much of German theology and philosophy from Kant's day to the present. A valid and tenable approach to biblical miracles calls for and indeed necessitates a more unified interpretation of reality than afforded by the Kantian heritage.[52]

Some, like William Barclay (1907-78), have in the recent past attempted a spiritualizing of the New Testament miracles that is akin to Bultmannian demythologization. Concerning the raising of Lazarus (John 11) Barclay wrote of Jesus' forgiving of a great sin by Lazarus—a sin that had brought Lazarus a grief like unto death, and thus Barclay did not speak of a raising of Lazarus from death. According to Barclay, the stories of Jesus' miracles "tell, not of things which *happened*, but of things which *happen*."[53]

In summary, Deists and others have raised major objections to biblical miracles in terms of natural law, biblical critics and others in terms of Synoptic criticism, naturalists and the devotees of scientism in terms of scientific testing, and the Bultmannian school in terms of demythologization, and psychotherapists have set forth an alternative approach to Jesus' healings. We have given answers to these views in support of the validity of biblical miracles.

IV. MIRACLES: POSTAPOSTOLIC AND CONTEMPORARY?

Have genuine miracles occurred during the postapostolic history of Christianity, and do they occur today? If so, for what purposes and with what results do they occur? These are questions on which Christians today are by no means agreed.

A. THE QUESTION OF OCCURRENCE

Christian denominations or confessions and individual Christians have held to three basic views.

1. Biblical Era View

According to this view, miracles occurred only during the biblical era and as part of salvation history recorded in the Old and New Testaments. Presumably a major argument in favor of this view is the interpretation of Jesus' miracles and of apostolic miracles as "signs" of the drawing near of the kingdom of God in the person, ministry, deeds, and death-resurrection

---

52. A German biblical scholar, Gerd Theissen, *The Miracles Stories of the Early Christian Tradition,* trans. Francis McDonagh and ed. John Riches (Philadelphia: Fortress Press, 1983), p. 299, has recently observed:

> Where Goethe could still assert that the miracle was faith's favorite child, modern exegetes instead give the impression that miracle is faith's illegitimate child, whose existence they try embarrassedly to apologize for. The ancient Church's pride in the miracles has turned into the opposite.

53. *The Mind of Jesus,* pp. 84-88, esp. 88.

of Jesus. The signs would not be needed in later centuries as they were in the first. Benjamin B. Warfield held that miracles, designed for "authentication of the Apostles as messengers from God," ceased to occur after the death of the disciples of the apostles.[54] Accordingly, all events that have been claimed to be miraculous in later centuries were not so.

2. Biblical and Patristic Era View

Certain Anglicans have held that miracles continued to occur during the age of the Church Fathers and ceased to occur early in the fourth century A.D. This conclusion is derivative from and dependent on a certain view of the special importance of the patristic age.[55]

3. Unlimited Era View

This view refuses to limit the occurrence of miracles to a specific age and insists on the occurrence of contemporary miracles as well as miracles during preceding centuries. Roman Catholics, Pentecostals, and Neo-Pentecostals in the latter twentieth century strongly affirm this view, but others undoubtedly hold it, if with less insistence. Not a few denominations have never taken any overt action with reference to any of these three views. One may search in vain, for example, for any reference to this question in Baptist confessions of faith from the seventeenth century through the twentieth.[56]

B. THE CITING OF EXAMPLES

1. Roman Catholic Marian and Hagiological Miracles

Numerous claims have been made and testimonies given with reference to healings among Roman Catholics through the intercession of the Virgin Mary and the canonized saints of the Roman Catholic Church. These have especially been cited during the nineteenth and twentieth centuries, prior to Vatican Council II, and in connection with well-known Marian shrines such as Lourdes in France, Ste. Anne-de-Beaupré in the province of Quebec in Canada, and Guadalupe in Mexico.[57] Certain Protestants and other non-Roman Catholics reacted critically to such testimonies, labeling these events as "miracle mongering." Miracles occasioned by the intercession of those saints not yet canonized have also been deemed necessary to the procedure for canonization.[58]

---

54. *Counterfeit Miracles* (New York: Charles Scribner's Sons, 1918; reprint ed.; London: Banner of Truth Trust, 1972), ch. 1, esp. pp. 21, 23-24.
55. In ibid., pp. 6-8, Warfield cited as exponents of the Anglican view Conyers Middleton, John Tillotson, Nathaniel Marshall, Henry Dodwell, Daniel Waterland, John Chapman, William Whiston, and John Wesley.
56. William L. Lumpkin, *Baptist Confessions of Faith*, passim.
57. Sabourin, *The Divine Miracles Discussed and Defended*, pp. 151-64.
58. Ibid., pp. 164-72; John F. Sullivan, *The Externals of the Catholic Church*, rev. John C. O'Leary (New York: P. J. Kenedy and Sons, 1951), pp. 332-37.

2. Pentecostal and Neo-Pentecostal Miracles

During the twentieth century numerous claims relative to divine healing have been made by persons in Pentecostal churches and in the Neo-Pentecostal movement that began during the 1960s. Especially were these miracles said to have occurred through the agency of persons exercising the spiritual gift of healing, and often such healings were said to have occurred in public healing services. Leaders who have asserted the exercise of the gift of healing have included John Alexander Dowie (1847-1907),[59] William Marian Branham (1909-65),[60] Gordon Lindsay (1906-73),[61] Granville Oral Roberts (1918-),[62] Kathryn Kuhlman (1907-76),[63] and Morris Cerullo (1931-).[64]

3. Trans-medical Miracles of Healing through Prayer

Claims have also been made, usually apart from any organized effort vis-à-vis healing, as to the occurrence of miraculous divine healing after and in response to intercessory prayer and beyond the resources of God-given medical science and practice.

It should be carefully noted that all assertions concerning miraculous divine healings in the contemporary era are subject to scientific testing and medical review. One should also be aware that there has been a paucity of claims to present-day miracles of nature or history.

C. THE PROPOSAL OF PURPOSES

If contemporary miracles do indeed occur, as so many have claimed, what may be said to be the purposes of such, so far as we may know? It seems necessary to reexamine those purposes previously identified for biblical miracles:[65] signs of the kingdom, divine compassion for human need, and glorification of God. It may be difficult to see how contemporary healings can be significant signs, unless it be in settings in which the Christian gospel is being introduced, but no such difficulty seems to apply to compassion or glorification. In a sea of callous humankind and amid religious movements that show little of the glory and power of the one God, miracles may be part of God's contemporary doings.

---

59. Gordon Lindsay, *The Life of John Alexander Dowie* (n.p.p.: Voice of Healing Publishing Company, 1951).

60. Gordon Lindsay, *William Branham: A Man Sent from God* (Jeffersonville, Ind.: William Branham, 1950).

61. Gordon Lindsay, *The Gordon Lindsay Story* (Dallas: Voice of Healing Publishing Company, n.d.).

62. David Edwin Harrell, Jr., *Oral Roberts: An American Life* (Bloomington: Indiana University Press, 1985), esp. pt. 2.

63. Allen Spraggett, *Kathryn Kuhlman: The Woman Who Believes in Miracles* (New York: World Publishing Company, 1970).

64. On all these leaders, see David Edwin Harrell, Jr., *All Things Are Possible: The Healing and Charismatic Revivals in Modern America* (Bloomington: Indiana University Press, 1975).

65. See above, I, B, 3.

In this chapter we have examined biblical miracles in respect to their terminology, classification, and purposes; we have identified certain aspects of the history of the doctrine of miracles; we have explained and answered major objections to miracles raised within the last three centuries; and we have examined the issue of postapostolic and contemporary miracles. In the midst of such detailed studies we would do well to take note of the words of Georgia Harkness, written in reflection on "Augustine's saying that man is a greater miracle than any of his works":[66]

> Man *is* a miracle, for he is the high point of God's wonderful creation. Yet the greatest miracle of all is Jesus Christ, the God-man, bearer of God's power and love and forgiving, saving mercy. So great is this miracle that before the wonder of Jesus all others seem inconsequential.[67]

---

66. See *The City of God* 10.12.
67. *The Providence of God,* pp. 165-66.

CHAPTER 28

Suprahuman Beings: Angels

In connection with providence and miracles some theologians have chosen to discuss prayer, particularly from the standpoint of the relation of petitionary and intercessory prayer to the providential sovereignty of God. Although such a pattern is fitting and legitimate, we will follow another course in this study, namely, the treatment of prayer as an aspect of the Christian life. We will examine prayer as a privilege and as a discipline of being the children of God by faith in Jesus Christ rather than as a problem in the correlation of the divine and the human. Consequently, we must now give attention to the suprahuman beings spoken of so frequently in the Bible, both good and evil. First, we will investigate the subject of angels, and then Satan and evil spirits.

I. ANGELS ACCORDING TO THE BIBLE AND THE INTERTESTAMENTAL WRITINGS

A. THE OLD TESTAMENT TERMS AND TEXTS

1. *Terms Clearly Referring to Angelic Beings*

a. *Mal'ak,* "Messenger" or "Angel"

The Hebrew noun *mal'āk* was derived from the root *l'k,* meaning "to send," but the verb "is not found in extant Hebrew but in Arabic and Ethiopic literature." It is by far the "most frequently used term to designate angel beings" in the Old Testament.[1] Although the word is used to refer to human prophets (2 Chr. 36:15-16; Isa. 42:19; 44:26; Hag. 1:13), to human priests (Eccl. 5:5; Mal. 2:7), and to the winds (Ps. 104:4), its predominant usage is in reference to suprahuman messengers of God. *Mal'āk* is translated by the English word "angel" 111 times in the KJV Old Testament,[2] but this total includes the references to "the angel of Yahweh." Thirty of these

---

1. William George Heidt, O.S.B., *Angelology of the Old Testament: A Study in Biblical Theology,* Catholic University of America Studies in Sacred Theology, 2d series, no. 24 (Washington, D.C.: Catholic University of America Press, 1949), p. 8.
2. Robert Young, *Analytical Concordance to the Bible,* 22nd Amer. ed. rev. by William B. Stevenson (Grand Rapids: Eerdmans, n.d.), p. 37.

occurrences are in the Pentateuch, 59 are in the Former and Latter Prophets, and 22 are in the Writings. According to Genesis angels made a visit to a human household (19:1, 15), helped to procure a wife for Isaac (24:7, 40), and were both seen in Jacob's vision at Bethel and active in his life (28:12; 31:11; 32:1; 48:16; compare Hos. 12:4). According to Exodus an angel went before and behind the Israelite army (14:19) and before the advancing children of Israel (23:20, 23; 32:34; 33:2). In the books of Samuel and Kings an angel is used in similes (1 Sam. 29:9; 2 Sam. 14:17, 20; 19:27), is said to have destroyed Jerusalem through a plague (2 Sam. 24:16-17), and speaks to an old prophet (1 Kings 13:18). According to the Psalms there are both destroying angels (78:49) and guardian angels (91:11), and in the single reference in Job (4:18) angels are said to be charged by God with error. In Zechariah we find recurrent angelic appearances to and conversations with the prophet himself (1:9, 11-14, 19; 2:3; 4:1, 4-5; 5:5, 10; 6:4-5), and in Daniel the rescue of Shadrach, Meshach, and Abednego (3:28) and the shutting of the mouths of lions in Daniel's behalf (6:22) are attributed to angels.

b. Cherub (*kerûḇ*) (plural, cherubim [*kerûḇîm*])

The second most frequently employed term for angelic beings is *kerûḇ*, it being found in a dozen texts. Of the various theories concerning its etymology, W. G. Heidt has favored an Assyrian origin by which it meant those who interceded "at the court of king or god."[3] Yet the actual uses in the Old Testament point in other directions. Cherubim are placed as guardians of the Garden of Eden (Gen. 3:24). Hammered golden likenesses of the cherubim with extended wings are placed on the top of the ark in the tabernacle (Exod. 25:18-20), and later Solomon causes wooden cherubim overlaid with gold to be placed in the holy of holies in the new temple and carved cherubim to be placed on its walls and doors (1 Kings 6:23-28, 29, 32, 35). Repeatedly Yahweh is said to have been "enthroned between the cherubim" (1 Sam. 4:4; 2 Sam. 6:2 par. 1 Chr. 13:6; Ps. 80:1b; 99:1b; Isa. 37:16). Ezekiel 10 portrays the cherubim at the throne of God and identifies them with the "four living creatures" seen by the prophet (1:5). Poetically David sees Yahweh mounting the cherubim and riding on them (2 Sam. 22:11; Ps. 18:10).

c. Holy Ones (*qāḏôšîm*)

The term *qāḏôš*, "holy one," is used in five texts of angelic beings. Its etymology is the same as that of the term when applied to God.[4] "Most aptly is the word applied to angels who are so far removed from worldly imperfections, so completely set apart for the service of the all-holy One."[5] The "assembly" (KJV) or "council" (NIV) of the "holy ones" reverences

---

3. *Angelology of the Old Testament*, p. 7.
4. See above, Ch. 15, I, A.
5. Heidt, *Angelology of the Old Testament*, p. 14.

God (Ps. 89:7). According to the theology of Eliphaz, Job cannot turn to any of "the holy ones" (15:15). These "holy ones" will accompany Yahweh on "the day of Yahweh" (Zech. 14:5), and Daniel records his having heard a "holy one," who was being addressed by another "holy one" (8:13).

d. Heavenly Host, or Hosts of Heaven (ṣābā')

The Hebrew ṣābā', which is used of the stars, seemingly connotes angels in 1 Kings 22:19 par. 2 Chr. 18:18, Ps. 103:21, and Ps. 148:2. Neh. 9:6 seems more debatable. W. G. Heidt concluded that this root does not suggest military forces but rather bondage or servitude assigned by One who is free.[6]

e. Watcher ('îr)

Only in Daniel is the Hebrew word 'îr used, derived from a verb meaning "to rouse oneself, awake."[7] It appears three times in the same passage (4:13, 17, 28), twice in the singular and once in the plural, and twice joined with the term "holy one."[8]

f. Sons of God (bᵉnê 'Ĕlōhîm, bᵉnê 'Ēlîm)

There is widespread agreement that "sons of 'Elohim" in Job 1:6 and 2:1 means angelic beings, and the same may be said of "a son of the gods" in Dan. 3:25. It is probable that "sons of 'Elim" in Ps. 29:1 and 89:6 refers to angels. It is possible, as A. B. Davidson suggested,[9] that "'Elohim" in Ps. 8:5 and Ps. 97:9 and "'Elim" in Exod. 15:11, and even Ps. 82:6, may be understood as referring to angels. But what of "sons of 'Elohim" in Gen. 6:1-2, 4? Is that text to be taken to refer to angels so that it involves the marriage of angels and human women? Because the same text has been invoked in support of fallen angels, it will be necessary to treat the text in the subsequent chapter on Satan and evil spirits.[10] In anticipation of that more detailed treatment, we need here only to extrapolate the conclusion, namely, that the preferable interpretation seems to be that Genesis 6 refers to the marriages between Sethite men and Cainite women.

g. Seraphim (śᵉrāpîm)

The word śᵉrāpîm is used only once in the Old Testament (Isa. 6:2-3). There have been many conjectures concerning its etymology, and thus there has been little agreement. Heidt has contended that "the casual way in which our author introduces them without any further explanation is sufficient evidence that the concept was familiar to his readers."[11]

---

6. Ibid., pp. 11-12.
7. Ibid., p. 10.
8. The term is also used in 1 Enoch 12:4; 13:10; 15:9.
9. "Angel," *A Dictionary of the Bible*, ed. James Hastings, 5 vols. (Edinburgh: T. and T. Clark, 1898-1904), 1:93-97.
10. See below, Ch. 29, I, A, 2, a.
11. *Angelology of the Old Testament*, p. 14.

h. Other Rarely Used Common Nouns or Substantives

Certain Hebrew terms such as are translated "the mighty," "media-tor," and "ministers" are also used of angels in the Old Testament but used only once or twice.[12]

i. Gabriel

In two instances, both in the book of Daniel, specific angels are given personal names in the Old Testament. Gabriel, meaning literally "a man of God," appears to Daniel, first for the interpretation of his dream (8:16) and subsequently while Daniel is praying for the bestowal of "insight and understanding" (9:21-22, NIV). As we will note shortly, Gabriel also is mentioned in the New Testament.

j. Michael

The angel Michael is thrice mentioned in Daniel (10:13, 21; 12:1), and each time he has a princely function. He is called "one of the chief princes," "your prince," and "the great prince." Some interpret 12:1 to mean that Michael was to serve as guardian angel for the Jewish people.[13]

2. "The Angel of Yahweh," "The Angel of God"

In the interpretation of the Old Testament one of the major enigmas seems to have been the identity of the one was is called "the Angel of Yahweh." This specific term may be found in the following passages:

Gen. 16:7, 9	2 Kings 1:3, 15
Gen. 22:11, 15	2 Kings 19:35
Exod. 3:2	1 Chr. 21:12, 15-16, 18, 30
Num. 22:22-27, 31-32, 34-35	Ps. 34:7
Judg. 2:1, 4	Ps. 35:5, 6
Judg. 5:23	Isa. 37:36
Judg. 6:11-12, 20-22	Zech. 3:1, 5-6
Judg. 13:3, 13, 15-17, 20-21	Zech. 12:8

In addition, "the angel of God" is used in Gen. 21:17; 31:11; and Exod. 14:19; "the angel who has delivered me from all harm" in Gen. 48:16, NIV; "my angel" in Exod. 32:34, and "the angel of his presence" in Isa. 63:9.[14]

There have been four major theories as to the identity of the Angel of Yahweh; it is now necessary only to state the central idea and supporting considerations of each.

---

12. See ibid., pp. 1-2, 9-10, for a treatment of these.

13. Michael is mentioned in Jude 9 and Rev. 12:7. Another named angel, Raphael, is mentioned in Tobit 8:2-3.

14. This list is not identical with but rather different from that of Heidt, *Angelology of the Old Testament*, p. 70.

a. Logos Theory

This thesis is that the Angel of Yahweh is the preexistent Logos who would later become incarnate in Jesus Christ. Some would even refer to the Angel as "the second person of the Trinity." This view was popular among the Church Fathers and has had its adherents through the centuries. Early in the present century Arno Clemens Gaebelein (1861-1945) held to this view,[15] and E. Y. Mullins found it difficult to move away from it.[16] Heidt reported in 1949: "No one in recent years has advocated this view; it may be considered obsolete."[17] But in 1975 William Franklin (Billy) Graham (1918-)[18] and G. B. Funderburk[19] advocated it.

b. Angelic Theory

This view holds that the Angel of Yahweh was an angel and therefore a created spiritual being who acted in special ways as the ambassador or representative of Yahweh. It appeals as being a literalist view of the matter. It often claims that this angel was received and listened to as a divine ambassador. Heidt cited modern Catholic, Protestant, and Jewish authors who have taken this position, but he argued against it partly because there are no claims in these passages that the Angel is an inferior representing his superior.[20]

c. Interpolation Theory

This theory, the product of biblical criticism, holds that during the long history of Israel and her sacred books some came to realize that certain passages referred to Yahweh in such anthropomorphic terms that these passages were in need of alteration and hence redactors inserted "Angel of" into such texts. M.-J. Lagrange was a principal exponent of this theory.[21] It makes of the Angel of Yahweh a literary device and thereby bypasses the question as to whether God or a special angel is intended.

---

15. *The Angels of God* (New York: Our Hope, 1924), p. 19.

16. *The Christian Religion in Its Doctrinal Expression,* p. 279.

17. *Angelology of the Old Testament,* p. 97.

18. *Angels: God's Secret Agents* (Garden City, N.Y.: Doubleday and Company, 1975), pp. 33, 105, 106; rev. ed. (Waco, Tex.: Word Books, 1986), pp. 36, 85.

19. "Angel," *The Zondervan Pictorial Encyclopedia of the Bible,* gen. ed. Merrill C. Tenney, 5 vols. (Grand Rapids: Zondervan, 1975), 1:162.

20. *Angelology of the Old Testament,* p. 99, n. 90; p. 99. According to Claus Westermann, *God's Angels Need No Wings,* trans. David L. Scheidt (Philadelphia: Fortress Press, 1979), p. 69, the angel of Yahweh/of God "acts very much like the guardian or guiding angel who is encountered in still other contexts [see Genesis 24] and who cannot be sharply distinguished from God himself." Edward Langton, *The Ministries of the Angelic Powers according to the Old Testament and Later Jewish Literature* (London: James Clarke and Company, n.d.), pp. 21-27, favored the view that the angel of Yahweh was a special angel "who is not God" but who "is a form of Divine revelation."

21. Heidt, *Angelology of the Old Testament,* pp. 100-101.

d. Instrumental Theory

This view, described by Heidt as the "identity theory,"[22] regards the Angel of Yahweh as "the visible or audible phenomenon through which God manifests himself and communicates with the person or persons concerned."[23] The Angel is thus the instrument of divine communication. A. B. Davidson understood these passages as theophanic,[24] D. M. G. Stalker declared that the Angel "is . . . Yahweh himself, in so far as he reveals himself,"[25] and Dale Moody has identified the Angel as "the personal presence of the Lord."[26] This view seems to pose fewer difficulties and to have more convincing appeal than the others.

B. The Intertestamental Jewish Writings

In the books of the Old Testament Apocrypha and of the Pseudepigrapha, most of which were written during the second and first centuries B.C. and the first century A.D., the conceptions of the nature and activities of angelic beings found in the Old Testament were both continued and expanded. Among the expanded concepts were specific accounts of the creation of angels and more specific ideas about angel guardians over individuals and over nations and about orders or ranks of angels, especially the role of named archangels, either seven or four in number.

In the rabbinical literature, consisting of the Targums, the Midrashim, and the Talmud, a similar pattern is found. New concepts include Metatron as the highest of the archangels, a council or company of angels, 70 (or 72) angels over the nations, and angels as occupying the highest of the seven heavens but not as near to God's throne as righteous humans.

It is not possible here to explore these materials in detail; for more information one may turn to Edward Langton's (1886-?) detailed study.[27]

C. The New Testament Term and Its Many Uses

The term for angels in the New Testament is *angelos*, which literally means "messenger" or "agent." According to Gaebelein, the New Testament mentions angels 165 times.[28] A count of the uses of *angelos* translated as "angel" in the KJV, listed by Young, totals 179.[29] The numerous uses of *angelos* can be found in every type of New Testament literature. Although occasionally *angelos* is used for human messengers (Luke 7:24; 9:52; Jas.

---

22. Ibid., p. 70.
23. Ibid., p. 70, n. 4.
24. "Angel," p. 94.
25. "Exodus," *Peake's Commentary on the Bible*, ed. Matthew Black and H. H. Rowley (London: Thomas Nelson and Sons, 1962), p. 211.
26. *The Word of Truth*, pp. 166-67.
27. *The Ministries of the Angelic Powers*, chs. 2–3.
28. *The Angels of God*, p. 12.
29. *Analytical Concordance to the Bible*, pp. 37-38.

2:25) and for John the Baptist as the "messenger" promised by Malachi
(Mal. 3:1; Mark 1:2; Matt. 11:10), the overwhelmingly predominant usage
is in reference to suprahuman beings.[30]

1. Synoptic Gospels

The angel Gabriel announced the birth of John the Baptist to his
father Zechariah (Luke 1:11-20) and the birth of Jesus to Mary the virgin
(Luke 1:26-38). An angel announced to Joseph the virginal conception of
Mary's child (Matt. 1:20-25), an angel gave to Jesus his name before his
conception (Luke 2:21), and angels praised God at the birth of Jesus (Luke
2:9-15).[31] An angel appeared to and instructed Joseph in Egypt after
Herod's death (Matt. 2:19-20). Angels ministered to Jesus after his wilderness temptations (Mark 1:13 and par.).

In the parable of the tares the "reapers are angels" and will gather
up evildoers (Matt. 13:39); according to the parable of the net, angels will
come forth at the end of the world to separate the wicked from the
righteous (Matt. 13:49); in the parable of the lost coin angels in heaven are
said to rejoice "over one sinner that repents" (Luke 15:10); and in the
parable poor Lazarus is carried by angels to Abraham's bosom (Luke
16:22). Angels in heaven do not marry (Mark 12:25 and par.), but they
"behold" the face of God the Father (Matt. 18:10). The Son of Man will
come in glory "with the holy angels" to be ashamed of those now ashamed
of him and to acknowledge those who acknowledge him (Mark 8:38 and
par.; Luke 12:8-9; Matt. 25:31), and he will send forth his angels to gather
the elect (Mark 13:27 and par.). But angels in heaven do not know "the
day and hour" of Jesus' Parousia (Mark 13:32 and par.).

While Jesus was in Gethsemane, "an angel from heaven" appeared
to him to strengthen him (Luke 22:43), and God the Father was said to be
able to send in Jesus' behalf "more than twelve legions of angels" (Matt.
26:53). An angel rolled away the stone before the tomb in which Jesus'
body had been placed, sat on it, and then spoke to the women who came
early in the morning on the first day of the week to Jesus' tomb (Matt.
28:2-5; compare Luke 24:23).

2. Gospel of John

Jesus spoke to Nathanael of a vision of "the angels of God ascending and descending upon the Son of man" (1:51). Mary Magdalene saw

---

30. Gerhard Kittel, "*angelos* in the NT," in Kittel, ed., *Theological Dictionary of the New
Testament*, trans. Geoffrey W. Bromiley, 10 vols. (Grand Rapids: Eerdmans, 1964-76), 1:83.

31. Macquarrie, *Principles of Christian Theology*, p. 216, contrasts Luke's approach,
wherein "angels seem to be represented as actual personal beings who come and go as
bearers of divine messages," with Matthew's approach, wherein angels "appear in dreams,
and it is the dream that is the vehicle for the communication." Edward Langton, *The Angel
Teaching of the New Testament* (London: James Clarke and Company, Ltd., n.d.), pp. 13-42,
finds the evidence to favor angelic presence and activity prior to and at the birth of Jesus, in
his wilderness temptations, in Gethsemane, and after his resurrection.

two angels in white sitting where Jesus' body had lain in the tomb (20:11-13).

3. Acts of the Apostles

An "angel of the Lord opened the prison doors" for the release of the apostles (5:19). According to Stephen, an angel had appeared to Moses at the burning bush (7:30, 35, 38) and had delivered the law to men (7:53). An angel directed Philip to go on the road from Jerusalem to Gaza (8:26). An angel also appeared to Cornelius in Caesarea and directed him to send for Peter in Joppa (10:3-7, 22; 11:13). An angel helped Peter to escape from prison (12:7-11), but some of the Christians insisted mistakenly that the one appearing was Peter's "angel" (12:15). The Sadducees disbelieved in angels, whereas the Pharisees believed in angels (23:8-9). Paul testified that during a storm at sea "an angel of the God to whom I belong and whom I worship" stood by him (27:23).

4. Pauline Epistles[32]

The Lord Jesus will be "revealed from heaven with his mighty angels" for judgment (2 Thess. 1:7). Even if "an angel from heaven" should preach to Galatian Christians a different gospel, they should not accept such (Gal. 1:8). The law "was ordained by angels through an intermediary" (Gal. 3:19). The apostles had "become a spectacle" "to angels" (1 Cor. 4:9). Christians "are to judge angels" (1 Cor. 6:3), women are to wear veils on their heads "because of the angels" (1 Cor. 11:10), and human beings who speak with angelic eloquence and have not love are "nothing" (1 Cor. 13:1-2). "Satan disguises himself as an angel of light" (2 Cor. 11:14), and angels will not be able to separate Christians "from the love of God in Christ Jesus" (Rom. 8:38). The "worship of angels" is rejected (Col. 2:18). Jesus was "seen by angels" (1 Tim. 3:16), and Paul charged Timothy in "the presence" "of the elect angels" (1 Tim. 5:21).

5. General Epistles

Jesus is superior to angels (Heb. 1:4-7, 13; 2:5-7), though angels have declared valid messages (Heb. 2:2). Only for "a little while was [Jesus] made lower than the angels" (Heb. 2:9). In his incarnation Jesus was "concerned" primarily "with the descendants of Abraham" rather than with angels (Heb. 2:16). The heavenly Jerusalem contains "innumerable angels" (Heb. 12:22). Hospitable Christians may have "entertained angels unaware" (Heb. 13:2).

Angels were interested in the prophets' announcement of the Messiah (1 Pet. 1:12). God committed to Tartarus until final judgment the

32. Kittel found in Paul a tendency "to emphasize the comparative unimportance of angelology," especially since, for Paul, angels are overshadowed by Jesus Christ and warning must be issued against the worship of angels (Col. 2:18). Ibid., p. 85.

sinning angels (2 Pet. 2:4; Jude 6), and angels do not judge sinful humans (2 Pet. 2:11). But angels are ultimately subject to the risen Jesus Christ (1 Pet. 3:22).

6. Apocalypse

The word "angel" appears 76 times in the Apocalypse, that is, in every chapter except 4, 6, and 13. But in chapters 2–3 "the angel of the church" seemingly refers to pastors or elders.[33]

D. THE SIGNIFICANCE OF ANGELS IN THE BIBLE

1. Creaturehood

The Bible assumes the existence of angels. The specific divine creation of angels, although assumed in the doctrine of the creation of all things, is not formally taught in the Bible, unless Ps. 148:2-5 does imply such:

Praise him, all his angels,
    praise him, all his heavenly hosts.
Praise him, sun and moon,
    praise him, all you shining stars.
Praise him, you highest heavens
    and you waters above the skies.
Let them praise the name of the LORD,
    for he commanded and they were created. (NIV)

As created beings angels are not to be worshiped, even though incipient Gnosticism may enjoin such (Col. 2:18). They are subordinate to Jesus the Son of God (1 Pet. 3:22; Heb. 1:4-6), who only in his incarnation and crucifixion was "made a little lower than the angels" (Heb. 2:9, NIV).

2. Multiplicity

The biblical concept of angels seems to include great numbers and varieties of angelic beings. The Hebrew term ṣābā', "host of heaven," although more often used of the sun, moon, and/or stars, sometimes is indicative of angels. Micaiah the prophet saw "the LORD sitting on his throne with all the host of heaven standing around him on his right and on his left" (1 Kings 22:19b, NIV; par. 2 Chr. 18:18). In Ps. 103:21a and 148:2 "heavenly hosts" refers to angels. In Daniel "the Ancient of Days" is described as follows: "Thousands upon thousands attended him; ten thousand times ten thousand stood before him" (7:10b, NIV). At the birth of Jesus "a great company of the heavenly host appeared with the angel" (Luke 2:13, NIV). The "heavenly Jerusalem" is said to have "thousands

33. Kittel, however, has taken these as angels rather than as bishops or church leaders (ibid., pp. 86-87). Langton, The Angel Teaching of the New Testament, pp. 186-214, has classified the angelic phenomena of the Apocalypse under seven headings: the seven spirits, the angels of the seven churches, the 24 elders, the four living creatures, "angels set over the elements," Michael's angels, and miscellaneous.

upon thousands of angels" (Heb. 12:22b), and before the exalted Lamb of God "many angels, numbering thousands upon thousands, and ten thousand times ten thousand" will sing their praises to the Lamb (Rev. 5:11a).

3. Functions

a. Worship of God

The worship of God is undoubtedly one of the major angelic functions. In Isa. 6:1-3 the seraphim call to each other: " 'Holy, holy, holy is the LORD Almighty [or, LORD of hosts]; the whole earth is full of his glory' " (NIV). According to Heb. 1:6, "when God brings his firstborn into the world, he says, 'Let all God's angels worship him' " (Deut. 32:43).

b. Obedient Service of God

This role of angels is specifically stated in Ps. 103:20 (NIV) and implied in virtually all the other angelic functions:

> Praise the LORD, you his angels,
>> you mighty ones who do his bidding,
>> who obey his word.

c. Interpretation of the Word and Will of God

The cherubim, who are seen by Ezekiel as "four living creatures," helped to communicate the message that the "glory" had departed from the temple of Yahweh (1:4-24; 10:1-22). A "watcher" appeared to give instructions about the tree in the tree-dream of King Nebuchadnezzar (Dan. 4:13-23). The angel Michael helped Daniel to interpret the vision of a man dressed in linen (10:4-21), and Gabriel helped Daniel to interpret the dream of a ram and a goat (ch. 8) and announced the births of John the Baptist (Luke 1:11-20) and of Jesus (Luke 1:26-38). A similar annunciation was made to Joseph (Matt. 1:20-25), who also received angelic instruction while in Egypt (Matt. 2:19-20).

d. Special Agency vis-à-vis Salvation History

In the New Testament Stephen alluded to an angel's having appeared to Moses at the burning bush near Mount Sinai (Acts 7:30, 35), and both Stephen and Paul referred to an angelic presence with Moses at the giving of the ten "living words" (Acts 7:38; Gal. 3:19). Angels are said to have assisted Jesus during his wilderness temptations (Mark 1:13; Matt. 4:11), to rejoice over repentant sinners (Luke 15:10), to have strengthened Jesus while in Gethsemane (Luke 22:43), and to have performed various functions at the empty tomb of Jesus (Matt. 28:2-5; John 20:11-13). In the Acts of the Apostles angels are said to have been involved in the release of the apostles from prison (5:19), in directing Philip on the road to Gaza (8:26), in causing Cornelius to send for Simon Peter (10:3-7, 22; 11:13), in Peter's escape from prison (12:7-11), and in encouraging Paul while in a storm at sea (27:23-26).

e. Guardianship of Human Beings

Does the Bible teach that particular angels act as guardians to specific human beings? Certain New Testament texts seem to provide an affirmative answer. Jesus indicated that little children have "their angels in heaven" (Matt. 18:10b, NIV). In the parable of the rich man and Lazarus "the angels carried him [Lazarus] to Abraham's side" (Luke 16:22), and after Peter's release from prison most of the disciples thought that the reappearing Peter was Peter's "angel" (Acts 12:15).

II. ANGELS ACCORDING TO THE HISTORY OF CHRISTIAN DOCTRINE

A. PSEUDO-DIONYSIUS THE AREOPAGITE

The most developed doctrine of angels during the patristic age came late in the period in *The Celestial Hierarchy,* written by a pseudonymous fifth- or sixth-century Christian author. "Dionysius" took nine different names for angelic beings from the Bible and set them in a hierarchical order, borrowed from his teacher Hierotheus and consisting of three triads or choirs with three different types of angels in each. This hierarchy was taken to be "a sacred order, a state of understanding, and an activity approximating as closely as possible to the divine," the goal of which was "to enable beings to be as like God as possible and to be at one with him." The very blessedness of God consists of purification, illumination, and perfection, and the descending order of angels is designed to enable divine blessedness to be received from above and transmitted to beings below.[34] The nine parts of the angelic hierarchy are as follows:

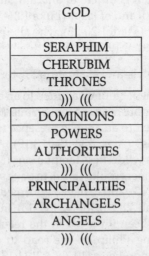

```
                    GOD
                     |
          ┌─────────────────────┐
          │      SERAPHIM        │
          │      CHERUBIM        │
          │      THRONES         │
          └─────────────────────┘
                   ))) (((
          ┌─────────────────────┐
          │     DOMINIONS        │
          │      POWERS          │
          │    AUTHORITIES       │
          └─────────────────────┘
                   ))) (((
          ┌─────────────────────┐
          │   PRINCIPALITIES     │
          │    ARCHANGELS        │
          │      ANGELS          │
          └─────────────────────┘
                   ))) (((
```

34. 6.2; 3.1, 2; 7.3; 10.2, in *Pseudo-Dionysius: The Complete Works,* trans. Colm Luibheid et al., CWS (New York: Paulist Press, 1987), pp. 143-91, esp. 160-61, 153-55, 164-65, 173-74.

B. THOMAS AQUINAS

In his somewhat detailed treatment of angels, Thomas Aquinas, known as "the angelic doctor," concentrated on the being of angels, their relation to space, the knowledge had by angels, the will or volition of angels, the love exercised by angels, the creation of angels, and their perfection unto beatitude.[35] It was indeed an otherworldly interpretation, and neither "Dionysius" nor Thomas made any serious effort to interpret the role of angels in the history of redemption.

C. TWENTIETH-CENTURY AUTHORS[36]

1. John Macquarrie: Angels as Necessary in the Order of Creation in the Service of Being

Among the twentieth-century authors who have dealt with angels, Macquarrie is probably closer to "Dionysius" and Thomas than any. He can speak of "creation . . . as a hierarchy of beings." For him, the concept of angels "stands for the unity and order of the whole creation in the service of Being; not merely at the level of cosmic process, but at the level of conscious and free cooperation." Negatively, angels are not to be models or mediators for humanity. Humans are not to embrace "angelism," or their own preoccupation with their spiritual and intellectual being to the neglect of their bodily nature. Like the cherubim outside the Garden of Eden, angels can constitute the limits for human beings, especially when tempted to undertake "lane-jumping." Positively, angels afford evidence that human beings are not alone in the cosmos and can point to the vastness of the created order.[37]

2. Karl Barth: Angels as God's Heavenly Ambassadors to Earth

Barth wrote a lengthy discussion of angels, placing it between a chapter on "God and Nothingness" and his treatment of demons. In the fine print he provided a veritable history of the doctrine, giving special attention to "Dionysius," Thomas, and the Continental Protestant dogmaticians. Barth clearly avowed to be expounding a biblical angelology. For him the angels belong essentially to the heavenly kingdom or realm and serve obediently as God's ambassadors or witnesses to the earthly realm.[38]

On the teaching about angels by Gregory the Great, Isidore of Seville, John of Damascus, Anselm of Canterbury, Bernard of Clairvaux, Peter Lombard, and Albert the Great, see Edward Langton, *Supernatural: The Doctrine of Spirits, Angels, and Demons, from the Middle Ages until the Present Time* (London: Rider and Company, 1934), pp. 25-52.

35. *Summa Theologica* 1.50-62.
36. Moody, *The Word of Truth*, pp. 165-69.
37. *Principles of Christian Theology*, pp. 215-18.
38. *Church Dogmatics*, III/3, trans. G. W. Bromiley and R. J. Ehrlich (Edinburgh: T. and T. Clark, 1961), pp. 369-519. For a noteworthy statement as to what angels cannot do, see p. 460.

3. Karl Rahner: Conscious, Created, Finite Beings Subordinated to Christ/God

Rahner emphasized the late appearance of the concept of angels in the Old Testament writings, alleging its rootage in non-Israelite religions and contending that it did not result from any event in salvation history. In the postexilic period it was both magnified (Job, Daniel) and minimized by silence (Priestly code). The Sadducees were influenced by Hellenistic rationalism to reject angels, but Jewish apocalypticism embraced belief in angels "but with a strict regard for the transcendence of God." Jesus was accompanied by angels in his wilderness temptations, in Gethsemane, and at his resurrection, and the Apocalypse abounds in references to angels. Angelology should be a subdivision of Christology. Much of past angelology can be considered optional now, but Rahner retained the Catholic veneration of good angels and the role of guardian angels. Rahner sought to avoid two extremes: one, the demythologization of angels or their being "trivialized into abstract ideas"; the other, the exaggeration of angels "in a Gnostic or Manichean way." Recognition of angels causes a person to realize that "he stands in a more comprehensive community of salvation and perdition than that of mankind alone." Moreover, if people today expect that there are "intelligent living beings outside the earth," why should they "reject angels outright as unthinkable"?[39]

4. Billy Graham: Angels as Taught in Scripture, Confirmed by Experience, and Active Today

Taking his title from modern military intelligence, Graham explained that he had written on this subject because of the paucity of recent books on the theme, even though many had been written on Satan. He wanted to accentuate "the positives of the Christian faith," and indeed the biblical references to angels "far outnumber references to Satan" and demons. Graham gave two reasons why he believed in the existence and activity of angels:

> I believe in angels because the Bible says there are angels; and I believe the Bible to be the true Word of God.
> I also believe in angels because I have sensed their presence in my life on special occasions.

Graham stressed the differences between angels and human beings, angels as God's messengers and as pointers to but not preachers of the gospel, angels as agents of protection and deliverance, of passage in death, and of judgment and fulfillment of prophecy, and the spectator role of angels.[40]

39. "Angel," in *Sacramentum Mundi: An Encyclopedia of Theology*, 6 vols. (New York: Herder and Herder; London: Burns and Oates Ltd., 1968-70), 1:27-35.
40. *Angels: God's Secret Agents*, rev. ed., esp. pp. 9, 26, 23, 30, 24.

III. PRESENT-DAY ATTITUDES TOWARD ANGELS

Finally, it is important to specify and focus on those attitudes toward angels, their existence and their functions, which tend to prevail among present-day Christians.

A. REJECTION

Since the era of the Enlightenment many Christians have been influenced by that rationalistic antisupernaturalism which finds no possibility of the existence of supramundane or suprahuman beings, whether good or evil. Other naturalistic and secularizing influences may have augmented that influence, and in addition Bultmannian demythologization may have had its impact. Specific reasons for rejecting the existence and work of angels may include the following:

1. The concept of angels is a relic of primitive beliefs that is totally unacceptable in a scientific age.

2. Jesus accommodated to the prevailing Jewish belief in angels, making no issue over its validity, and hence Jesus' authority should not be invoked in defense of angels.[41]

3. The existence of angels and evil spirits is not taught or demanded by the sources of revelation.[42]

4. Belief in angels has stimulated the formation of related myths and hence may need to be demythologized.[43]

B. INDIFFERENCE

A second and widely prevalent attitude toward angels is that of indifference, based either on an uncertainty about the existence of angels or on the assumed irrelevance of angels to the important issues facing modern Christians or on some other basis. Schleiermacher at the outset of the modern era expressed the attitude of indifference:

> The only tenet which can be established as a doctrine concerning angels is this: that the question whether the angels exist or not ought to have no influence upon our conduct, and that revelations of their existence are now no longer to be expected.[44]

C. ACCEPTANCE

What are the basic reasons why some Christians do positively accept the doctrine of angels?

1. The existence and activity of angels are assumed and described in numerous books of the Old and the New Testaments. A high view of the

41. See in Mullins, *The Christian Religion in Its Doctrinal Expression*, p. 277.

42. Piet J. A. M. Schoonenberg, *God's World in the Making* (Pittsburgh: Duquesne University Press, 1964), pp. 8-9.

43. Brunner, *The Christian Doctrine of Creation and Redemption*, pp. 133, 146. For additional causes for the modern rejection of angels, see Langton, *Supernatural*, pp. 113-18.

44. *The Christian Faith*, p. 159.

inspiration and authority of the Scriptures seems to call for the attitude of acceptance.

2. The acceptance of the reality and work of angelic beings serves to limit arrogance as to mankind's being the solitary climax of all creation.[45]

3. Belief in angels can strengthen the faith of Christians in the power and providence of God.[46]

4. The existence and activity of angels is consonant with the possibility of living beings on planets other than the earth.[47]

45. Brunner, *The Christian Doctrine of Creation and Redemption*, p. 134.
46. Strong, *Systematic Theology*, p. 462.
47. Rahner, "Angel," p. 29.

CHAPTER 29

Suprahuman Beings:
Satan and Evil Spirits

The study of angels leads naturally to the investigation of Satan and evil spirits. In such an examination we need to exercise caution lest we presume popular and/or literary conceptions of such beings to be the same as the biblical doctrine. On this topic, as with the consideration of angels, we must not only provide an exposition of the biblical and the postbiblical materials but also deal with the issue of their validity in the face of modern objections.

I. BIBLICAL AND INTERTESTAMENTAL TEACHINGS

A. THE OLD TESTAMENT

1. *The Term "Satan"*

a. Etymology

The Hebrew verb *śāṭan* means "to oppose" or "to be or act as an adversary." Edward Langton has found it to be "a pure Semitic word in early use among the Israelites."[1]

b. The Common Noun

The noun *śāṭān* is used in the Old Testament to refer to human adversaries. Philistine commanders were suspicious that David would be their "'adversary'" in battle with King Saul's army (1 Sam. 29:4b), and David later found that "the sons of Zeruiah" were acting as his "adversaries" in wanting Shimei to be put to death (2 Sam. 19:22b). When he was about to build the temple, Solomon thought that he had no "adversary" (1 Kings 5:4), but later his adversaries were Hadad the Edomite and Rezon of Zobah (1 Kings 11:14a, 23a). Even the "angel of Yahweh" could be an "adversary" to Balaam and his donkey (Num. 22:22).

---

1. *Essentials of Demonology: A Study of Jewish and Christian Doctrine; Its Origin and Development* (London: Epworth Press, 1949), p. 53.

c. The Proper Noun

One may be surprised to discover that *Śāṭān* as a proper Hebrew noun for a suprahuman being is used only three (or four) times in the Old Testament. Finding such texts is like looking for "a needle in a haystack."[2] Two of these passages are in Job (1:6-12; 2:1-7). There the article "the" is used before "Satan," but Satan is manifestly personal as "the adversary."[3] In Job nothing is written about the Satan as a fallen angel, and there is no concept that the Satan is chief of a kingdom of evil spirits. Rather, he is "one of the angel-ministers of Yahweh" who accuses Job before God and brings natural evils upon him. "He never acts without God's permission, and his ministry is evidently included in the Divine will." Even so there is "an element in the character of Satan which is contrary to the will of God," for seemingly Satan "would be pleased if he could prove that God's confidence in Job was misplaced."[4] In Zech. 3:1-2 the article "the" also appears before "Satan," which is not yet fully a proper name. The Satan is said to have accused Joshua the high priest, and Yahweh's response is one of rebuke for the Satan's harshness toward Jerusalem. In 1 Chr. 21:1 Satan—without the article and probably a proper name—is said to have "incited David to take a census of Israel" (NIV). His accusatory role has been turned into that of tempter, and David confesses that his census-taking was a sin (21:8).[5] It should be noted that the word "Satan" is not used in Genesis 3 and that Satan and the serpent are identified in Christian theology chiefly because they are identified in Rev. 12:9 and 20:2.[6]

2. *Other Possible Names for Satan and Possible Passages in Which He Is Mentioned*

a. "Sons of God" (Gen. 6:1-4)

This text refers to the marriages of "the sons of God" and "the daughters of men" and to their progeny as physical giants or heroes (v. 4) but spiritually wicked (v. 5). Although other interpretations have been given to this passage,[7] two major interpretations have prevailed during the centuries-long effort to understand these verses. One of these interpretations takes "the sons of God" as a term for angels and hence concludes that angels married human women and had offspring. This interpretation has a long history and claims the support of Philo, Josephus,

---

2. William Robinson, *The Devil and God* (London: Lutterworth Press; New York: Abingdon-Cokesbury Press, 1945), p. 48.
3. Langton, *Essentials of Demonology*, p. 53.
4. Ibid., pp. 53-54.
5. In the parallel passage (2 Sam. 24:1) Yahweh is said to have incited David to take the census.
6. Robinson, *The Devil and God*, pp. 50-51.
7. The only other interpretations sufficiently important to mention are (1) the view that these were marriages of patrician men and plebeian women (Targums, Symmachus, Samaritan versions, Baruch Spinoza, and J. G. Herder), and (2) the view that these were marriages of second-rank gods and human women (Claus Westermann).

Justin Martyr, Tertullian, Cyprian, Ambrose, Lactantius, Wilhelm Gesenius, G. H. A. Ewald, Franz Delitzsch, August Dillmann, Henry Alford, S. R. Driver, John Skinner, A. C. Gaebelein, Edward Langton, Gerhard von Rad, G. Henton Davies, and Bruce Vawter. Normally this interpretation assumes that the angels referred to in Gen. 6:1-4 were evil or wicked angels, who had a corrupting influence on their wives and children. Intertestamental Jewish writings seemingly connected this text with fallen angels so that it became a proof-text for the whole concept of fallen angels. The other major interpretation understands "the sons of God" to have been Sethite men and "the daughters of men" to have been Cainite women, and consequently these were human marriages having no direct reference to angels, fallen angels, or Satan. Its exponents have included Julius Africanus, Ephrem the Syrian, Theodoret of Cyrus, John Chrysostom, Augustine of Hippo, Cyril of Alexandria, Jerome, Martin Luther, Philip Melanchthon, John Calvin, E. W. Hengstenberg, G. F. Oehler, J. F. K. (also C. F.) Keil, J. P. Lange, W. H. Green, B. H. Carroll, C. I. Scofield, W. H. G. Thomas, and H. C. Leupold.[8]

b. "Morning Star" (Isa. 14:12-20)

This passage constitutes a portion of an extended taunt against the king of Babylon (14:3-23). The "morning star" (NIV) or "star of the morning" (NASV) or "day star" (ASV, RSV, JB) is said to "have fallen from heaven" and to "have been cast down to the earth." This one "once laid low the nations" and "made kingdoms tremble" but then sought to make himself like God. Consequently, because he has "destroyed" his "land" and "killed" his "people," he has been "brought down to the grave" and has been "cast out" of his own "tomb" (NIV). Although the context strongly inclines one to conclude that all these words were intended by the author to refer to the king of Babylon, this text has often been taken by Christians as a reference to Satan. The KJV rendering of "morning star" as "Lucifer," a Latin derivative meaning "light- bearer," with the implication that the term can be taken as a proper name, has helped to fuel such an interpretation. As a result not a few sermons on Satan have been preached from this text, when numerous undisputed texts were readily available. The interpretation of the "morning star" as a clear reference to Satan seems to be traceable to Tertullian[9] and Gregory the Great[10] in the patristic age, with its augmentation due largely to the *Inferno* of Dante

8. On these listings of advocates of each interpretation, see Franz Delitzsch, *A New Commentary on Genesis,* trans. Sophia Taylor (Edinburgh: T. and T. Clark, 1888); August Dillmann, *Genesis Critically and Exegetically Expounded,* trans. William B. Stevenson (Edinburgh: T. and T. Clark, 1897); and Merrill F. Unger, *Biblical Demonology: A Study of the Spiritual Forces behind the Present World Unrest* (5th ed.; Wheaton, Ill.: Scripture Press Publications, Inc., 1963), pp. 46-47.

9. *Against Marcion* 5.11, 17.

10. *Dialogues* 3.4; *Epistles* 18, 21.

Alighieri (1265-1321) and John Milton's *Paradise Lost*.[11] But John Calvin was very specific in his rejection of the Satanic interpretation, holding rather that the text alluded to a human tyrant.[12] The prevailing pattern among modern commentators on Isaiah (Albert Barnes, Franz Delitzsch, Conrad Orelli, T. K. Cheyne, John Skinner, George Adam Smith, Owen C. Whitehouse, George B. Gray, H. C. Leupold, Edward J. Young, Page H. Kelley, Otto Kaiser, John D. W. Watts) has been to interpret the taunt to refer to the king of Babylon and not to mention or deal with Satan.[13]

c. Guardian Cherub in Eden Expelled from the Mount of God and Destroyed (Ezek. 28:11-19)

This passage constitutes a lament concerning the king of Tyre, following prophecies against and another lament for Tyre (Ezek. 26:1–28:10). The one addressed in the lament is said to have been created by God, to have been in the Garden of Eden, adorned with precious stones, and "anointed as a guardian cherub." But because of his pride and dishonest and violence-ridden trade he has been driven from "the mount of God," "consumed" with fire, "reduced" to "ashes," and brought to "a horrible end" so that he "will be no more" (NIV). The overwhelming majority of modern commentators on Ezekiel (Patrick Fairbairn, E. W. Hengstenberg, C. F. Keil, F. W. J. Schröder, A. B. Davidson, W. F. Lofthouse, George A. Cooke, Walther Eichrodt, H. J. van Dijk, John Bernard Taylor, Walther Zimmerli, John T. Bunn, Keith W. Carley, John W. Wevers, Peter C. Craigie, Aelred Cody, O.S.B.)[14] have interpreted the passage to refer to the king of Tyre, have often taken the paradise elements as portrayal of the king, and have made no mention of Satan in their comments on the passage. Certain recent interpreters (Taylor, Carley, Wevers, Craigie) have stressed the parallels between Adam and the king of Tyre and their typifying the whole human story. But, on the contrary, American Dispensationalist commentators have had their own hermeneutic of Ezek. 28:11-19. A. C. Gaebelein[15] and Henry Allan Ironside (1876-1951)[16] understood the passage to refer to Satan, who is "the power behind the throne of the Tyrian king" (Gaebelein) and who "can

---

11. Conrad Orelli, *The Prophecies of Isaiah*, trans. J. S. Banks, Clark's Foreign Theological Library (Edinburgh: T. and T. Clark, 1889); Edward Joseph Young, *The Book of Isaiah* (Grand Rapids: Eerdmans, 1969); Page H. Kelley, "Isaiah," *Broadman Bible Commentary* (Nashville: Broadman Press, 1971), vol. 5.

12. *Commentary on the Book of the Prophet Isaiah*, trans. William Pringle, 4 vols. (Grand Rapids: Eerdmans, 1956-61).

13. Edward J. Young, Page H. Kelley, and John D. W. Watts, *Isaiah 1–33*, Word Biblical Commentary (Waco, Tex.: Word Books, 1985), did treat the Satanic interpretation but did not accept it. No documentation is offered here for each of these commentaries; the pertinent material is to be found where the authors have treated Isaiah 14.

14. No documentation is offered here for each of these commentaries; the pertinent material is to be found where the authors have treated Ezekiel 28.

15. *The Prophet Ezekiel: An Analytical Exposition* (2d rev. ed.; New York: Loizeaux Bros., 1972; first published in 1918).

16. *Expository Notes on Ezekiel the Prophet* (New York: Loizeaux Bros., 1949).

hardly be distinguished from the king of Tyre" (Ironside). Slightly different were the views of F. C. Jennings, Charles Lee Feinberg, and Paul P. Enns (1937-). For Jennings the king of Babylon was "a representative" of Lucifer, the true name of him who was later called Satan.[17] According to Feinberg, Ezekiel saw behind the king of Tyre "the motivating force and personality who was impelling him in his opposition to God," namely, Satan;[18] and for Enns,[19] Satan "is the real power behind the king of Tyre." F. B. Huey, Jr. (1925-), has clearly identified, therefore, the four hermeneutical options: (1) the "literal history" of Satan's fall; (2) the king of Tyre as "a satanic person"; (3) the king or kingdom of Tyre under judgment, couched in the language of the familiar paradise story; and (4) the fall of the king or kingdom of Tyre as parallel to the fall of Adam (and Eve).[20]

From the foregoing examination of Gen. 6:1-4, Isa. 14:12-20, and Ezek. 28:11-19 it should be evident that the building of the biblical doctrine of Satan should be on the foundation of biblical passages that clearly and evidently involve references to Satan and not on the disputed texts.

3. Demonic Beings

Does the Old Testament have a doctrine of demonic beings or evil spirits? Langton has answered in the negative respecting a formulated doctrine, but he has concluded that in certain Old Testament passages "supernatural evil beings are referred to or described which, when examined, are found to correspond to demons among other [esp. Egyptian, Arabic, Assyrian, Babylonian, and Persian] peoples."[21] Some of these beings took animal forms, while others took human forms. To be specific, there were the "fiery serpents,"[22] the "he-goats" or hairy demons,[23] the scapegoat,[24] Lilith the night demon,[25] and "demons" who seemingly had been considered gods.[26]

In summary, the Old Testament has a concept of "Satan," expressed in three passages, as one of the angel-ministers of Yahweh who tests and tempts human beings. It contains three other texts that some, despite very strong evidence to the contrary, wish to see as referring to Satan. It has in the process of formation some ideas concerning demons. The Old Testa-

---

17. *Studies in Isaiah* (New York: Bible Truth Press, n.d.).

18. *The Prophecy of Ezekiel: The Glory of the Lord* (Chicago: Moody Press, 1969).

19. *Ezekiel: Bible Study Commentary* (Grand Rapids: Zondervan, 1986). The Dispensationalist interpretation of Ezek. 28:11-19 could claim the support of Origen and Cyril of Jerusalem. Langton, *Satan, a Portrait: A Study of the Character of Satan through All the Ages* (London: Skeffington and Son, Ltd., 1945?), pp. 52, 58.

20. *Layman's Bible Book Commentary*, vol. 12, *Ezekiel, Daniel* (Nashville: Broadman Press, 1983).

21. Langton, *Essentials of Demonology*, p. 35.

22. Num. 21:6; Deut. 8:15; Isa. 14:29; 30:6.

23. Lev. 17:7; Isa. 13:21; 34:14; 2 Chr. 11:15.

24. Lev. 16:8-10, 15, 18, 20-22, 26.

25. Isa. 34:14.

26. Deut. 32:17; Ps. 106:37. Langton, *Essentials of Demonology*, pp. 37-52.

ment contains no unambiguous accounts either of Satan's creation or of Satan's sin or fall. Langton concluded:

> So far as the teaching of the Old Testament is concerned, Satan can scarcely be said to belong to the sphere of demonology; for he possesses none of those demonic characteristics. . . . Nevertheless we are able to trace here the first small beginnings of that stream of Hebrew thought concerning a supernatural enemy of God and man which was destined to exercise a predominating influence upon the whole body of Jewish and Christian teaching concerning God and man in all the succeeding centuries.[27]

Because of the great importance of the Jewish intertestamental writings for the New Testament doctrine of Satan and evil spirits, it is important that we include such writings in the present study.

B. Jewish Intertestamental Writings and Concepts[28]

1. Old Testament Apocrypha and Pseudepigrapha

Although it would be possible to arrange and discuss the pertinent texts according to the chronological order of these writings, such a chronological method would be hampered by the fact that most of these writings cannot be precisely dated. Instead we will utilize a topical method. Prominent and somewhat developed in this literature is the concept of fallen angels, whose fall was connected with and elaborated from Gen. 6:1-4 (1 Enoch 6–8). Another account has God sending angels or watchers to the earth to instruct mankind (Jubilees 4:15-22). The devil and his angels are said to have been cast out of heaven after they refused to worship Adam as Michael had urged them to do (Life of Adam and Eve 12–17). Accordingly God sent good angels to capture many of the rebel angels and to imprison them in the valleys of the earth for 70 generations until the final judgment (1 Enoch 10:4-17). Asmodaeus, an evil demon, killed the seven husbands of Sarah, and she had to be loosed from him (Tobit 3:8, 17). Demons were descended from the giants who ruled over humankind after their deaths (1 Enoch 15:8-9).[29] The devil out of revenge for his own expulsion tempted Eve (Life of Adam and Eve 12:1; 13:1-2; 16:1-4), using the serpent as his vessel (Apocalypse of Moses 16:5). "God made not death," but "by the envy of the devil death entered into the world" (Wisd. of Sol. 1:13; 2:24)—presumably an allusion to the seduction of Eve through the serpent. There is no clear conception until late in the period that Satan is the chief of all evil spirits and demons.[30] Those exercising leadership

---

27. Ibid., pp. 52-53.
28. William Lawrence Hendricks, "The Concept of Satan: A Biblical and Historical Approach and Its Relevance to the Christian Life" (Th.D. diss., Southwestern Baptist Theological Seminary, 1958), pp. 38-61.
29. But in 1 Enoch 19:1-2 demons are seen as preexisting the fall of Satan and evil spirits. Moreover, evil spirits try to lead human beings to offer sacrifices to demons as if they were gods. See Langton, *Essentials of Demonology*, p. 109.
30. Langton, *Essentials of Demonology*, p. 119.

over such beings included Semjaza (1 Enoch 6:3; 9:7; 10:11; 69:2), Azazel (1 Enoch 8:1-2; 9:6; 10:4-8; 13:1-2; Apocalypse of Abraham 13, 14, 20, 22, 23, 29, 31), Mastema (Jubilees 10:8, 11; 11:5, 11), Beliar (Jubilees 1:20; 15:33; Testaments of the Twelve Patriarchs),[31] and Satanail (2 Enoch 29:4-5). Satan also is seen to have rulership over evil spirits, including other Satans (Jubilees 10:11—over the one-tenth of the evil spirits not imprisoned; 1 Enoch 40:7; 53:3; 54:6; Martyrdom of Isaiah 2:2, 4; Assumption of Moses 10:1). Human beings are tempted through seven spirits, who are the personified lusts of human beings, but humans may either yield or resist (Testaments of the Twelve Patriarchs).[32] An evil impulse in humans is affirmed (2 [4] Esdras 4:30; 7:48). The fallen angels after long imprisonment will be destroyed at the last judgment (1 Enoch 19:1); seemingly this will also happen to the evil spirits (1 Enoch 16:1; 2 Enoch 7:1-5).

2. Rabbinic Literature

Langton has found two different accounts of the origin of Satan in rabbinic writings. One describes Satan's being created by God along with Eve on the sixth day of creation; this view closely connects Satan and the fall of humankind.[33] The other sees Sammael (i.e., Satan) as a fallen angel who is ruler over all other Satans.[34] Satan's fall is explained as caused by angelic jealousy and envy, for the angels had opposed the creation of human beings and had been outdone by Adam's successful naming of the animals.[35] Sammael and accompanying angels came to the earth and chose and took possession of the serpent as their instrument for tempting Eve.[36] Furthermore, the serpent's jealousy was activated by the knowledge as to how the angels were serving the human creatures.[37] Thus in the rabbinics the serpent and Satan are more closely related than in the Old Testament. Satan's threefold role as "accuser, seducer, and destroyer" is made manifest in comments on the trial of Abraham as to the offering of Isaac (Genesis 22).[38] The evil impulse in humans is seen as derived from creation and the occasion or opportunity for Satan's tempting,[39] but in one text Satan is identified with the impulse.[40] Satan serves as the angel of death,[41] and his own final destruction is anticipated.[42]

---

31. Test. of Levi 3:3; Test. of Dan 1:7; Test. of Benjamin 3:3.
32. Test. of Reuben 2:1–3:10; see also Test. of Judah 13:3; 16:1; Test. of Simeon 3:1; 4:7, 9; Test. of Dan 2:4.
33. *Bereshith Rabba* [Midrash on Gen.] 17.6.
34. *Ve'zot Ha' Brachah Rabba* [Midrash on Deut.] 11.10.
35. *Pirke de Rabbi Eliezer* 13-14.
36. *T.B. Baba Bathra* 16a; *Pirke de Rabbi Eliezer* 13.
37. *T.B. Sanhedrin* 59b.
38. *Ibid.* 89b; *Pirke de Rabbi Eliezer* 32.
39. *T.B. Berakoth* 61a; *T.B. Yoma* 69b.
40. *T.B. Baba Bathra* 16a.
41. *T.B. Aboda Zarah* 20b; *Ve'zot Ha' Brachah Rabba* 11.10.
42. *T.B. Sukkah* 52a; Langton, *Essentials of Demonology*, pp. 55-57.

3. Dead Sea Scrolls

In the literature from Qumran God is said to have assigned to created humans two spirits, one of truth and the other of perversion, one of light and the other of darkness, who seek opposite effects ("ways") in the lives of humans until the evil spirit will be finally destroyed.[43]

C. THE NEW TESTAMENT

1. Terms

The three terms most frequently used in the New Testament for the predominating evil spirit are *ho diabolos*, "the devil," meaning literally a slanderer or false accuser, used 37 times; *Satan* or *ho Satan*, "Satan," literally "the adversary," used 35 times; and *Beelzebul*, probably literally "the lord of flies," used seven times, all of which are in the Synoptic Gospels.[44] The other terms will be mentioned as the texts are discussed.

2. Synoptic Gospels

In the Synoptics Satan, or the devil, is considered to be the prince or chief of evil spirits in a kingdom of evil, not merely an evil spirit operating alone. He is first mentioned in connection with the wilderness temptations of Jesus (Mark 1:13 and par.), where he was in the role of tempter.

> It is generally admitted that the accounts of the temptation of Jesus preserved by the Synoptists must ultimately have been derived from Jesus Himself.[45]

William Robinson (1888-1963) regarded the wilderness usage as the most significant usage of the concept of Satan in the New Testament, contending that according to such texts Satan is unquestionably real and personal.[46] Satan, "the evil one," or the devil is mentioned in the parables of the soils and of the tares (Mark 4:15 and par.; Matt. 13:38-39 and par.), in Jesus' teaching about oaths (Matt. 5:37), and probably in the Lord's Prayer (Matt. 6:13). Satan/Beelzebul is said mistakenly to be the one casting out demons (Mark 3:22 and par.).

The Synoptics assume the existence of "demons" or "unclean spirits" but do not address the question of their origin. Demons bring physical maladies on human beings and not just morally bad effects. Langton saw Babylonian influence on the Synoptic accounts vis-à-vis physical maladies and seven spirits.[47] Jesus was clearly an exorcist of demons (Mark 1:21-27; 5:1-20; 9:14-29), and his disciples shared in that task (Mark 3:14-15; 6:7, 13, and par.; Luke 10:17, 20).

---

43. 1QS 3:13–4:26, as interpreted by William Sanford LaSor, *Amazing Dead Sea Scrolls and the Christian Faith* (Chicago: Moody Press, 1956), pp. 95-98.

44. Robinson, *The Devil and God*, p. 58.

45. Langton, *Essentials of Demonology*, p. 168.

46. *The Devil and God*, pp. 65-67.

47. *Essentials of Demonology*, pp. 147, 149-51.

Satan's influence on Peter's messianic understanding seems to be the import of Mark 8:33 and parallels. In response to the report of the 72 Jesus declared: " 'I saw Satan fall like lightning from heaven' " (Luke 10:18, RSV, TEV, NIV), and he healed a Jewish woman "whom Satan bound for eighteen years" (Luke 13:16, RSV). In the context of the last judgment Jesus referred to "the eternal fire prepared for the devil and his angels" (Matt. 25:41b, NIV). "Satan entered into Judas" Iscariot for his work of betrayal (Luke 22:3, RSV, JB, NEB), but Jesus prayed for Simon Peter to counter Satan's testing of him (Luke 22:31-32).

3. Gospel of John

The term "the devil" is used twice in the Fourth Gospel, when Jesus declared unbelieving Jews to have " 'the devil' " as their " 'father' " (8:44) and when the Evangelist reported the devil's having prompted Judas to betray Jesus (13:2). The single occurrence of "Satan" pertains to the Satanic entry of Judas when he took the bread at the Last Supper (13:27). Three times the phrase "the ruler of this world" or its shortened form appears: such a ruler "is coming" (14:30), "stands condemned" (16:11, NIV), and "will be cast out" (12:31).

4. Acts of the Apostles

The Acts contains four references to Satan or the devil. Peter interrogated Ananias about his Satan-led lying to the Holy Spirit (5:3) and, in addressing Cornelius and company, referred to Jesus' healing of those " 'oppressed by the devil' " (10:38, RSV). Paul, in speaking to Elymas the magician at Paphos, addressed him as " 'son of the devil' " (13:10), and, while addressing Herod Agrippa II, referred to the Gentiles as being turned " 'from the power of Satan to God' " (26:18).

5. Pauline Epistles

Paul made reference to "Satan" in a variety of contexts: apostolic travel (1 Thess. 2:18), sexual incontinence (1 Cor. 7:5), forgiveness among believers (2 Cor. 2:11), false apostles (2 Cor. 11:14), Paul's own "thorn in the flesh" (2 Cor. 12:7), God's victory over Satan (Rom. 16:20), excommunication (1 Cor. 5:5; 1 Tim. 1:19b, 20), the sins of younger widows (1 Tim. 5:15), and the "counterfeit miracles, signs and wonders" (NIV) that will accompany the coming of "the man of lawlessness" (2 Thess. 2:9). There are four references to "the devil," as the apostle deals with anger (Eph. 4:27), resistance to the devil's "schemes" (Eph. 6:11, NIV), lack of qualifications for bishops (1 Tim. 3:6), and correction of opponents (2 Tim. 2:26). Other terms used by the apostle include "the tempter" (1 Thess. 3:5), "the god of this world" (2 Cor. 4:4), "Belial" (2 Cor. 6:15), "the prince of the power of the air" (Eph. 2:2b), "the spirit that is now at work in the sons of disobedience" (Eph. 2:2c, RSV), and "the evil one" (Eph. 6:16). Paul identified idol feasts with the worship of "demons" (1 Cor. 10:14, 20-21) and referred to "principalities, powers, world-rulers of this present darkness, spiritual hosts of wickedness in the heavenly places" (Eph. 6:12, RSV).

6. General Epistles

The devil must be resisted by believers (Jas. 4:7b), for he "prowls around like a roaring lion, seeking some one to devour" (1 Pet. 5:8b, RSV). Jesus partook of human nature that through his death he might destroy the devil, who has a death-grip on human beings, and deliver from bondage all those have been lifelong slaves to the fear of death (Heb. 2:14-15). The angels who sinned were cast into Tartarus and bound in its "gloomy dungeons" (NIV), where they will remain until the last judgment (2 Pet. 2:4; Jude 6). Jude 9 employs the story of the archangel Michael's "disputing with the devil about the body of Moses" (NIV), which, it seems, had been told in the noncanonical Assumption of Moses.[48]

7. Johannine Epistles

Four times "the devil" is mentioned in 1 John, and five times "the evil one." The one who practices sin, does not practice righteousness, and does not love the Christian brethren belongs to "the children of the devil." It was the work of the devil, who had a long record of sinning, that the Son of God came to destroy (3:8, 10, 9). Cain the murderer was "of the evil one" (3:12), but Christians have "overcome the evil one" (2:13b, 14b) and he cannot harm them (5:18), even though the entire world is under the evil one's control (5:19).

8. Apocalypse

Four of the seven letters to the churches contain references to "Satan" or "the devil." The term "a synagogue of Satan" (2:9; 3:9) may have been a reference to intensive Jewish hostility toward Christians at Smyrna, and "Satan's throne" or dwelling place (2:13) was possibly an allusion to Pergamum as the eastern seat of Caesar-worship,[49] even as the forthcoming imprisonment of Christians is said to be the devil's doing (2:10). Presumably the prophetess Jezebel was claiming to teach "the deep things of the Satan" (2:24). The locusts[50] released by the trumpet sound of the fifth angel have as their king Abaddon (Hebrew) or Apollyon (Greek) (9:11), meaning "destruction" or "destroyer." Unrepentant humankind does not cease worshiping "demons" and idols (9:20); "the beast that comes up from the Abyss will attack the two witnesses," "overpower and kill them" (11:7, NIV); and "demonic spirits" coming from the dragon, the beast, and the

---

48. The *Assumption of Moses* survives only in fragments, which do not yield such a passage, but that Jude found and used such a passage was reported by Origen in *On First Principles* 3.2.1.
49. Langton, *Essentials of Demonology*, pp. 212-13.
50. For Langton the locusts themselves were demonic (ibid., p. 205).

false prophet help the earth's kings to prepare for battle (16:14). The "dragon" who seeks unsuccessfully to destroy the newborn male child of "the woman" is attacked and defeated in heavenly warfare by Michael and his angels and cast down to earth, only to renew his pursuit of the woman's child (ch. 12). He is also called "the deceiver of the whole inhabited earth" (12:9) and "the accuser of our brothers" (12:10b, NIV). Babylon "has become a dwelling place of demons" (18:2, RSV). Finally, Satan (= "the dragon" = the "ancient serpent" = "the devil") (12:9; 20:2) will be bound for a thousand years, loosed again briefly, defeated, and cast "into the lake of fire and brimstone" for eternal torment (20:1-10, RSV).

Now that we have completed our detailed examination of the Old Testament, intertestamental, and New Testament teachings, one question remains concerning all these materials: the question of sources. Did and, if so, to what extent did the Israelites, later Jews, and early Christians borrow their concepts of demons or evil spirits and of a chief of all such, Satan or the devil, from non-Hebrew sources? This is a difficult question for which it is unlikely that a clear, unambiguous answer can be obtained. Bernard J. Bamberger (1904-) was favorable to Canaanite origins.[51] Not a few modern scholars have stressed the heavy influence of Persian/Zoroastrian concepts on post-exilic Jews and on the New Testament.[52] Others such as Gustav Friedrich Oehler,[53] Heinrich Ewald,[54] Paul Heinisch (1878-1956),[55] William Lawrence Hendricks,[56] and Jeffrey Burton Russell (1934-)[57] have concluded that the concepts had essentially a Hebrew origin. Langton offered a composite answer. The concept of demons or evil spirits was held by Arab, Assyrian, Babylonian, and Greek peoples and need not be seen as distinctively Hebrew, but the concept of Satan, despite some parallel ideas among the Persians, seems to have been essentially Jewish with Yahwistic monotheism keeping in check dualistic tendencies.[58]

51. *Fallen Angels* (Philadelphia: Jewish Publication Society of America, 1952), pp. 7-13, 19, 21.

52. For example, Robinson, *The Devil and God*, pp. 52-53, 56-58; and Rivkah Schärf Kluger, *Satan in the Old Testament*, trans. Hildegard Nagel, Studies in Jungian Thought (Evanston, Ill.: Northwestern University Press, 1967), pp. 156-59, who limited the Persian influence to the late intertestamental writings and the New Testament.

53. *Theology of the Old Testament*, trans. George E. Day (New York: Funk and Wagnalls Company, 1883; Grand Rapids: Zondervan, n.d.), p. 450.

54. *Old and New Testament Theology*, trans. Thomas Goadby (Edinburgh: T. and T. Clark, 1888), pp. 72-79, who limited the Persian influence to the acceleration of the change already going on among the Jews (p. 77).

55. *Theology of the Old Testament*, trans. William G. Heidt, O.S.B. (Collegeville, Minn.: Order of St. Benedict, Inc., 1955), pp. 143, 144-45.

56. "The Concept of Satan: A Biblical and Historical Approach and Its Relevance to the Christian Life," pp. 21-23, 39-40, 63-65.

57. *The Devil: Perceptions of Evil from Antiquity to Primitive Christianity* (Ithaca, N.Y.: Cornell University Press, 1977), chs. 5-6. Russell has found little non-Hebrew influence on Israelite-Jewish concepts (pp. 217-20) but has found Hellenistic influence on the New Testament concepts (p. 221 and passim).

58. *Essentials of Demonology*, pp. 71, 220-21, 225.

II. THE HISTORY OF CHRISTIAN DOCTRINE

A. CHURCH FATHERS

The patristic authors more specifically than the New Testament attributed to the devil false teaching, or heresy.[59] According to Irenaeus the devil and his associates were spoiled and bound by the strong man, Jesus, who in recapitulation abolished death and perfected human beings after the image of God.[60] For Tertullian the "shows" (circus, theatre, wrestling, gladiatorial games) and cosmetics were instituted by or for the sake of the devil.[61] Unlike the other Fathers, Origen posited both the fall of rebellious eternal spirits prior to the creation of the material universe[62] and the final restoration of the devil.[63] Probably the most significant patristic teaching pertaining to Satan was the interpretation of Jesus' death and resurrection as the payment of a ransom to Satan for the release of humankind.[64]

B. DUALISTIC SECTS

Satan was usually quite prominent in the teachings of the dualistic movements that flourished between the ninth and the thirteenth centuries. These included the Paulicians and Thonraki in Armenia and Syria, the Bogomils and Patarenes in Bulgaria, Bosnia, and Hum, and the Cathars in Lombardy, Languedoc, and Provence. Most of these movements consisted of two branches: the strict dualists, who reckoned Satan to be of independent origin and not the creature of God; and the monarchians, who regarded Satan as the creature or elder Son of God, sometimes called Satanael, or "God's Satan."[65]

C. MARTIN LUTHER

Luther, "a thorough-going believer in the existence and activity of the Devil and demons,"[66] presented his "doctrine about the devil on the

---

59. Ignatius of Antioch, *Ephesians* 17, shorter recension; *Trallians* 10, longer recension; 11; *Philadelphians* 3, longer recension; 6; *Smyrneans* 7, longer recension; Tertullian, *Against Praxeas* 1.

60. *Against Heresies* 3.8.2; 3.18.6; 3.23.1; 5.21.2, 3; 5.22.1.

61. *Shows* 24; *Dress of Virgins* 14, 15, 20.

62. *First Principles* 1.5.5; 1.8.3.

63. Ibid. 3.6.5.

64. Clement of Alexandria, *Exhortation to Heathen* 9, 11; Origen, *Comm. on Matt.* 13.8-9; 16.8; *Against Celsus* 7.17; 8.54; Gregory of Nyssa, *Great Catech.* 23, 24. For more detailed treatment of the ante-Nicene doctrine of Satan, see the present author's "Satan," *The Encyclopedia of Early Christianity,* ed. Everett Ferguson (New York: Garland Publishing, Inc., 1990), pp. 833-35.

65. Steven Runciman, *The Medieval Manichee: A Study of the Christian Dualist Heresy* (Cambridge: University Press, 1947). Langton, *Satan, a Portrait,* pp. 65-84, has treated the doctrine of Satan in the writings of Anselm of Canterbury, Bernard of Clairvaux, Peter Lombard (c. 1105-c. 1160), Albert the Great (1193-1280), and Thomas Aquinas and in the literature of medieval monasticism and witchcraft. See also Jeffrey Burton Russell, *Lucifer: The Devil in the Middle Ages* (Ithaca, N.Y.: Cornell University Press, 1984).

66. Langton, *Satan, a Portrait,* p. 86.

authority of the Holy Scriptures and in continuity with ecclesiastical tradition."[67] Luther retained "most of the crude beliefs"[68] common to the Middle Ages and also drew on his personal experience with the devil in writing about the devil.[69] Luther, according to Paul Althaus, "takes the devil much more seriously than the Middle Ages";[70] in Reinhold Seeberg's assessment, "Luther added, so to speak, a hellish majesty to the devil."[71] The devil is the "great opponent of God and of Christ" who is in continuing conflict with God and who works in our sicknesses, our distresses, and our death. Human beings are either in the power of the devil or in God's power, and only the Holy Spirit can take them from the devil to God. Yet the devil for Luther is still "God's devil." Christians must exercise faith and use the Word of God against the devil.[72] Langton has held that Luther believed in magic, witchcraft, demon possession, and exorcism.[73] Gustav Aulén contended in detail that Luther revived the patristic emphasis on the saving work of Christ as victory over sin, the law, death, and the devil.[74] John Calvin's doctrine of Satan was confined to the biblical teaching and devoid of medieval piety and beliefs.[75]

D. John Milton

It was not a theologian but a poet, John Dryden (1631-1700), who first said that the "hero" of Milton's epic poem *Paradise Lost* was Satan,[76] and it was C. S. Lewis who declared that "Satan is the best drawn of Milton's characters."[77] How closely did Milton draw his Satan according to the Old Testament or the New Testament, and how much did he draw outside the biblical parameters? Scholars continue to deal with that issue. One recently argued that Milton's Satan had "absorbed" many of the qualities of the mythological Prometheus, including his "aspiration towards new and higher levels of existence" so that we are prone to admire Satan and "his vehement condemnation of civilization."[78] Another has contended that the "heavenly cycle" or "war in heaven" section of *Paradise Lost* (1-6, 9) was taken directly from Rev. 12:4, 7-9 and

67. Althaus, *The Theology of Martin Luther*, p. 163.

68. Langton, *Satan, a Portrait*, p. 87.

69. Althaus, *The Theology of Martin Luther*, p. 161.

70. Ibid., p. 162.

71. *Text-book of the History of Doctrines*, trans. Charles E. Hay, 2 vols. in 1 (Grand Rapids: Baker Book House, 1952), 2:246, n. 1.

72. Althaus, *The Theology of Martin Luther*, pp. 162-68.

73. *Satan, a Portrait*, pp. 87-88.

74. *Christus Victor: An Historical Study of the Three Main Types of the Idea of the Atonement*, trans. A. G. Hebert (New York: Macmillan, 1951), pp. 101-22.

75. Langton, *Satan, a Portrait*, p. 89.

76. Cited by R. J. Zwi Werblowsky, *Lucifer and Prometheus: A Study of Milton's Satan* (London: Routledge and Kegan Paul Ltd., 1952; New York: AMS Press, Inc., 1973), p. 3.

77. *A Preface to Paradise Lost* (London: Oxford University Press, 1942), p. 98.

78. Werblowsky, *Lucifer and Prometheus*, pp. xviii-xix.

that Milton took the Augustinian view of the binding of Satan for the duration of world history.[79]

E. F. D. E. SCHLEIERMACHER

Schleiermacher, the father of Liberal Protestant theology, stood at the fountainhead of modern doubt about and objection to the Christian doctrine of Satan and evil spirits. First, he raised questions about the how and why of Satan. How could Satan as a good angel have fallen? How could fallen Satan, if he retained his full natural powers and thus knew the futility of conflict with God, be evil at the same time? If, on the other hand, he lost some of his intelligence, why would he be so dangerous for human beings? Why did other angels follow Satan? Second, Jesus and the apostles did not expound any "new" doctrine or correct any existing doctrine about Satan. Indeed, the New Testament references to Satan were based on Jewish intertestamental writings, not on the Old Testament, and thus Jesus accommodated to such beliefs. The concept of Satan came not by divine revelation, is not connected with the way of salvation, and must not be made a condition of faith in Christ. The Jews actually fused three quite dissimilar ideas about Satan: servant of God in the court of heaven, fall of some of the angels, and the angel of death. Third, since questions about the devil are not essentially soteriological—there being no reference to Satan in Romans 1-8 or Jas. 1:13-14—the topic does not belong to Christian dogmatics but to cosmology and astronomy. Moreover, ideas about the devil may also have a legitimate place in poetry and hymnology. Fourth, Schleiermacher had some practical considerations. Demon possession is explicable as an effort to personalize the cause of our evil emotions. Human beings are prone to deny their guilt and to blame the devil, and belief in Satan will rob Christians of the joy of their inheritance in God's kingdom.[80]

F. DISPENSATIONALISM

At a time when many Protestants were indifferent toward or had completely rejected any belief in Satan, Dispensationalist theologians were giving emphasis to Satan and demons.[81]

G. LUNDENSIAN THEOLOGY

In Sweden the Lutheran theological movement associated with the University of Lund, which was characterized by a renewal of emphasis

---

79. Austin C. Dobbins, *Milton and the Book of Revelation: The Heavenly Cycle* (University, Ala.: University of Alabama Press, 1975), pp. iv-v, 124.

80. *The Christian Faith*, pp. 161-70, as summarized by Langton, *Satan, a Portrait*, pp. 96-99.

81. Lewis Sperry Chafer, *Satan: His Motive and Methods* (Chicago: Moody Press, 1919); Merrill F. Unger, *Biblical Demonology: A Study of the Spiritual Forces behind the Present World Unrest*; idem, *Demons in the World Today: A Study of Occultism in the Light of God's Word* (Wheaton, Ill.: Tyndale House Publishers, 1971); idem, *What Demons Can Do to Saints* (Chicago: Moody Press, 1977).

on divine love (*agapē*), in the work of Gustav Aulén asserted that the "classical view" of the saving work of Christ had been that of his victory over sin, death, and Satan and that it ought to be brought to the forefront of twentieth-century theology.[82]

III. CONTEMPORARY VALIDATION AND INTERPRETATION

Does a doctrine of Satan and evil spirits have a legitimate and proper place in Christian theology at the end of the twentieth century, and if so, what is that place and how can it be established in the face of continuing objections to and deviant understandings of the subject? It seems best to attempt to answer such a set of questions by setting forth the needs for well-orbed doctrine in the face of deviant understandings or unsatisfactory approaches to Satanic doctrine.

A. AVOIDANCE OF DEPERSONALIZATION

1. There is a need to avoid the depersonalization of Satan by reduction of the Satanic to the manifold lusts of humankind, as has been done by the San Francisco-based Church of Satan, founded by Anton Szandor LaVey (1930-85?) in 1966. The basic affirmations made in its *The Satanic Bible* refer to human lusts and humans' animal nature. Accordingly, Satanism "is a religion of the flesh, the mundane, the carnal—all of which are ruled by Satan."

> Most Satanists do not accept Satan as an anthropomorphic being with cloven hooves, a barbed tail, and horns. He merely represents a force of nature—the powers of darkness which have been named just that because no religion has taken these forces *out* of the darkness.[83]

Thus the Church of Satan has not taught a transhuman Satan. Rather, for this movement "Satan" is the embodiment of base human lusts and desires. The movement has affinities with nontheistic humanism.

2. There is also the need to avoid the complete depersonalization of Satan and evil spirits by the identification of these with "powerful [evil] social forces and structures,"[84] as Paul J. Tillich did in his *Systematic Theology*:

> This estranged world is ruled by structures of evil, symbolized as demonic powers. They rule individual souls, nations, and even nature. They produce anxiety in all its forms. It is the task of the Messiah to conquer them and to

---

82. *Christus Victor*, pp. 20-23, 172-76; Edgar M. Carlson, *The Reinterpretation of Luther* (Philadelphia: Westminster Press, 1948).

83. *The Satanic Bible* (Secaucus, N.J.: University Books, Inc., 1969), pp. 52, 62; see also Arthur Lyons, *The Second Coming: Satanism in America* (New York: Dodd, Mead, and Company, 1970), esp. ch. 8.

84. Erickson, *Christian Theology*, p. 446.

establish a new reality from which the demonic powers or the structures of destruction are excluded.[85]

It should by no means be denied that Satan and his forces work in, make use of, or gain control of social structures, for that seems to have been taught in the Apocalypse (Revelation 13), but Satan and evil spirits should not be completely identified *as* the structures and forces of human society.

B. AVOIDANCE OF NONCREATION BY GOD

1. There is, furthermore, the need to avoid the conclusion that Satan and his associates derived from nothingness or chaos and hence were not created by God, as Karl Barth seems to have taught. According to Barth, "nothingness" *(das Nichtige)* is a "stubborn" and "alien" "opposition and resistance to God's world dominion." God has set himself against nothingness, but nothingness is no "demonic" "monster." Nothingness "is to be known only at the heart of the Gospel, i.e., in Jesus Christ." Christ "shows Himself to be the total Victor." Nothingness "is neither God nor His creature," yet nothingness is real, for it is "not nothing." Nothing has the "ontic peculiarity" of being evil, but "nothingness has no perpetuity."[86] Although Barth does not specifically state such a conclusion, he seems strongly to infer that the devil was either derived from nothingness or is identical with nothingness. Indeed, Barth's doctrine of nothingness seems to compromise God's creatorship of all. It reopens the centuries-old danger of dualism that has "bedeviled" the doctrine of Satan.

2. There is the need to avoid not only the implied or covert dualism of Barth but also the clearly stated and defended dualism—or "triadism"?—of Edwin Lewis (1881-1959). In *The Creator and the Adversary*, Lewis, a Methodist theologian, insisted on the independent origin of the "Adversary." "If there is a Creator, there is certainly an Adversary." However the serpent of Genesis 3 is interpreted, "*it stands for evil,* which means that evil was in existence before Adam disobeyed."

> Any attempt to trace the demonic, as an existentive reality, to the will of God, is nothing but a tour de force. . . . In themselves considered, the divine and the demonic are absolute opposites.
>
> . . . .
>
> The ground of evil . . . is outside both the nature of God and the will of God, and is found in the Adversary. . . . In the beginning was the Adversary as well, and not only the Adversary but also a form of existence—later to be called 'the residue' or 'the residual constant'—which made it possible for the two to meet in conflict. Each of the three is itself and no other. Neither is to be explained by the other two. . . . God never began to be. The Adversary never began to be. The 'makings' of their battle-field never began to be. The only thing that began to be was the conflict itself. . . .[87]

85. 2:27.
86. *Church Dogmatics,* III/3, pp. 289, 290, 293, 311, 349, 353, 360.
87. (New York: Abingdon-Cokesbury Press, 1948), pp. 24, 125, 130, 133, and 140.

Lewis sacrificed both God's creatorship of all and God's certain sovereignty over all by extending the reality of Satan to the independent existence and self-contained agency of Satan. Although expressed in modern language in a dramatic setting, Lewis's theodicy should be seen as no more viable than ancient Zoroastrianism or Manicheeism.

C. RECOGNITION OF THE AUTHORITATIVE TESTIMONY OF JESUS

Present-day Christians need to come to proper conclusions as to the relation of belief in Satan and evil spirits to the teaching and activity of Jesus.

1. Some would, as Schleiermacher did, interpret Jesus' references to Satan or the devil in his teaching as a deliberate accommodation to prevailing Jewish beliefs on the part of Jesus. What this means is that Jesus did not really believe in the reality and activity of the devil and evil spirits but, knowing that many Jews did so believe, merely acquiesced in and gave lip service to such beliefs even if he could not affirm them. Langton, rejecting such a view, rightly saw in it "a very grave reflection" on Jesus' "character as a teacher."[88] Later in this study[89] we will devote attention to Jesus' reinterpretation of Jewish Messianism in teaching the self-giving and sufferings as well as the triumph of "the Son of Man." Does not such reinterpretation of Jewish Messianism in place of mere acquiescence show that Jesus was not an accommodationist in respect to his own understanding and teaching about his ministry and mission? Is it not reasonable, therefore, to expect of him reinterpretation rather than accommodation if he had not believed in the reality of Satan and evil spirits? A century ago James Petigru Boyce argued against such accommodation of Jesus on Satan by citing his hard sayings and his opposition to scribes, Pharisees, and Sadducees.[90]

2. Others would, as did Langton, interpret Jesus' teaching about Satan as part of the limitation of knowledge that inhered in his self-emptying to become human. According to this view, Jesus was unaware of any problems about the reality of Satan and evil spirits because he was a real human being set in a given historical context. Even as he declared that he did not know the time of his second coming (Mark 13:32 and par.), so also he likely did not know fully whether Satan and evil spirits really did exist and function, even as he likely did not have knowledge of modern astronomy. Langton concluded that

> we are not compelled to accept this teaching as ultimate truth merely because it formed part of the teaching of Jesus. For . . . in His incarnate condition Jesus was avowedly limited in knowledge. . . . [Thus] . . . Jesus accepted, without serious modification, the popular belief in Satan and the demons which was current in His time. Such an acceptance by Jesus does not prove that these popular beliefs correspond with reality.[91]

88. *Essentials of Demonology*, p. 223.
89. See below, Ch. 41, I, D, 5, c.
90. *Abstract of Systematic Theology*, p. 184.
91. *Essentials of Demonology*, pp. 223, 224.

Langton's embracing of the fallibility of Jesus' teaching in one important area opens the door to other possible fallible teachings and is not compatible with a high view of the authority inherent in the teaching of Jesus.

3. Yet others would and do accept the reality of the existence and work of Satan and evil spirits as taught by Jesus and the apostles. That very acceptance is basic to the fourth and final contemporary consideration.

D. EMPHASIS ON SATAN VIS-À-VIS THE CHRISTIAN LIFE

One of the pressing needs of the present is for Christians to correlate their formal beliefs and understandings about Satan with their actual living out of the Christian life. It should be recalled that the major thrust of the references in the New Testament epistles—Pauline, Johnnine, and general—is toward the Christian life. Some Christians may feel stymied or frustrated that they cannot explain more satisfactorily or fully the origin and transitions of Satan. Such, it should be remembered, was not a high priority in either the Old Testament or the New. Others may find themselves intrigued by the intricacies of some forms of eschatological doctrine so that they concentrate on what Satan is expected to do in the last days. Christians are responsible for resisting and overcoming Satan in their lives, their churches, and their societies in a way that they are not responsible for resolving every possible question about Satan's origin or his future activity. Lutheran theologians have been aggressive in reasserting the importance of Satan for contemporary Christianity. Gustav Aulén made a case—some would say that he overextended his case—for the centrality of the Christ as Victor motif for the doctrine of the saving work of Christ, and basic to that motif is the defeat of the devil by Christ through his death and resurrection. James Gus Kallas, Jr. (1928-), has sought to overcome the effects of Bultmannian demythologization[92] and to focus on Satan in the ministry of Jesus.[93] More assistance needs to be given to devout and not-so-devout believers in waging the warfare of the Christian life (Eph. 6:10-18) in the consciousness that Christ is the Victor and the Holy Spirit is the Paraclete.

We have treated the Christian doctrines of creation, providence, miracles, and suprahuman beings (angels, Satan, and evil spirits) in some detail. Now it is necessary to turn to the question posed in Psalm 8: What is mankind?

---

92. *The Satanward View: A Study in Pauline Theology* (Philadelphia: Westminster Press, 1966), esp. pp. 133-52.

93. *Jesus and the Power of Satan* (Philadelphia: Westminster Press, 1968). It is surprising to find Kallas in *God and Satan in the Apocalypse* (Minneapolis: Augsburg Publishing House, 1973), esp. p. 17, asserting that the Apocalypse "has little to say about Satan."

PART IV

Humankind and Sin

CHAPTER 30

Human Beings in the Image of God

The concept of human nature and destiny is, according to some, the crucial apologetic issue for Christianity today. In an age when atheism is militant and nontheistic religions are numerous it is often said that the starting point for Christian apologetics is the question of humankind.

> "Who am I and where did I come from? What makes me different from other creatures?" Philosophers, theologians, and scientists have mulled over these questions. The effort to explain human life has spawned religions, philosophies, legends, sagas, and scientific theories. In college classrooms, science laboratories, pulpits, endless books, and television lectures, the human being continues to try to account for himself.[1]

Hence it is essential that in the formulation of the Christian doctrines of humankind and sin we give some attention to competing conceptions of the essentially human.

In a well-orbed Christian doctrine of the human it is necessary to keep in balance the truths that human beings are creatures of God and that humans are sinners (against God, against fellow humans, and against themselves). One must reckon both with Ps. 8:5 (NIV), "You have made him a little lower than the heavenly beings and crowned him with glory and honor," and Rom. 3:23 (NIV), "for all have sinned and fall short of the glory of God." Blaise Pascal spoke of "the misery" or "wretchedness" and the "greatness" of humankind.[2] We will treat the Christian doctrine of the human, therefore, under two major divisions: human beings as creatures and human beings as sinners. First we will consider human beings as creatures under three perspectives, each of which is deeply rooted in the Old Testament: human beings in the image of God; the origin, antiquity, and unity of humankind; and human beings as man (male) and woman (female). We will also interpret human creaturehood through those biblical terms which are applied to human beings: "soul," "spirit," "flesh,"

---

1. Vernon O. Elmore, *Man as God's Creation*, Layman's Library of Christian Doctrine, vol. 6 (Nashville: Broadman Press, 1986), p. 24.

2. *Thoughts*, nos. 397, 409, 416, 430.

"body," "heart," etc. Subsequently we will examine the Christian doctrine of sin under the appropriate categories.

There is no more appropriate topic for the commencement of this study than the image of God in human beings, identified in classic Christian theology as the *imago Dei.* Any Christian theological undertaking that would take seriously the basic concepts of the Bible must deal with the term "the image of God," and any Christian theologian who takes seriously the history of Christian doctrine can ill afford to bypass or neglect this theme.

I. BIBLICAL TERMS AND TEXTS

The Christian who delves for the first time into the doctrine of the image of God in human beings may be surprised to discover that this theme is not to be found in all segments of biblical literature as a recurring theme. Rather, the specific texts are, with one exception, confined to the early chapters of Genesis and to the epistles of Paul.

A. OLD TESTAMENT

Two basic Hebrew nouns are used in the Old Testament for the divine image in human beings. Except for two passages in the Old Testament Apocrypha, which are canonical only in the Roman Catholic Bible, the occurrences of these terms in reference to the divine image in human beings are limited to Genesis.

1. The noun *ṣelem,* meaning "image" but also "shade" or "shadow," is used in Gen. 1:26a (RSV), "And God said, 'Let us make man in our *image,* after our likeness,' " and twice in Gen. 1:27 (RSV), "So God created man in his own *image,* in the *image* of God he created him; male and female he created them." Again the term is used in Gen. 9:6 (RSV): "Whoever sheds the blood of man, by man shall his blood be shed; for God made man in his own *image.*"[3] There are no further direct statements about the image of God in human beings in Genesis, in the Pentateuch, or in the rest of the Old Testament. Early Genesis neither states nor implies that human beings lost or failed to retain this image. According to Wisd. of Sol. 2:23, "For God created man for immortality, and made him the *image* of his own eternity," and in Ecclus. 17:3 we read: "He [the LORD] clothed them with strength like his own, and made them in his own *image.*"[4]

2. The noun *dᵉmût,* meaning "likeness" or "similitude," is used in Gen. 1:26a (RSV), " 'Let us make man in our image, after our *likeness,* ' "

---

3. *Ṣelem* was also used in Gen. 5:3, but in reference to Seth's being in the image of Adam.

4. Wisdom of Solomon survives only in Greek and was most likely written in Greek.

and in Gen. 5:1b (RSV, NIV), "When God created man, he made him in the *likeness* of God."[5]

Throughout most of the history of Christianity the relationship between ṣelem and dᵉmûṯ has been a topic for consideration, if not for dispute. Many exegetes and theologians have regarded the two terms as representing two very different realities, whereas many others have taken them to be synonyms. Among present-day Hebrew and Old Testament scholars, however, the great majority seems to hold to the synonymous view on the basis that the usage in Gen. 1:26 is an instance of synonymous Hebrew parallelism.[6]

B. NEW TESTAMENT

The Greek New Testament likewise uses two nouns for the image of God in humankind, although one of these occurs only once. Since these words do not appear in the same passage, it is difficult to determine to what extent they parallel the two Old Testament words.

1. The noun *eikōn*, meaning "image," appears four times in the Pauline letters in reference to the divine image in humankind. In 1 Cor. 11:7 (RSV, NIV) in the context of the veiling of Christian women Paul declared that the male human is not to cover his head "since he is the *image* and glory of God." Presumably Paul saw in the *imago Dei* an application to human males that did not apply to human females, even though such distinction was not made in Gen. 1:26-27. In 2 Cor. 3:18, when speaking of the ultimate glorification of believers, Paul affirmed that they "are being changed into his *image* from one degree of glory to another." According to Rom. 8:29 (RSV), "those whom he [God] foreknew he also predestinated to be conformed to the *image* of his Son, in order that he might be the first-born among many brethren." In Col. 3:10 (RSV) the same apostle, admonishing his readers to Christian living, contended that they had "put on the new nature ["new man" (KJV); "new self" (NIV)], which is being renewed in knowledge after the *image* of its creator." Although the pas-

---

5. Dᵉmûṯ was also used in Gen. 5:3, but in reference to Seth's being in the image of Adam.

6. For example, John Newton Thomas, " 'What Is Man?' The Biblical Doctrine of the Image of God," *Interpretation* 3 (April 1949): 154; Friedrich Horst, "Face to Face: The Biblical Doctrine of the Image of God," trans. John Bright, *Interpretation* 4 (July 1950): 259; N. W. Porteous, "Image of God," *The Interpreter's Dictionary of the Bible,* 4 vols. (New York: Abingdon Press, 1962), 2:682-83; Eichrodt, *Theology of the Old Testament,* 2:129; James I. Cook, "The Old Testament Concept of the Image of God," in idem, ed., *Grace upon Grace: Essays in Honor of Lester J. Kuyper* (Grand Rapids: Eerdmans, 1975), pp. 86-87; H. D. Preuss, *"dāmāh, dᵉmûṯ,"* *Theological Dictionary of the Old Testament,* ed. G. Johannes Botterweck and Helmer Ringgren, 5 vols. (Grand Rapids: Eerdmans, 1974-86), 3:259; Claus Westermann, *Genesis 1–11: A Commentary,* trans. John J. Scullion, S.J. (Minneapolis: Augsburg Publishing House, 1984), pp. 145-46; G. W. Bromiley, "Image of God," *The International Standard Bible Encyclopedia,* rev. ed., 4 vols. (Grand Rapids: Eerdmans, 1979-88), 2:803. The author is indebted to F. B. Huey, Jr., Ralph L. Smith, Boo Heflin, and D. David Garland.

sage does not use *eikōn*, Eph. 4:24 (RSV) declares that Christians have been taught to "put on the new nature, created after the likeness of God in true righteousness and holiness."[7]

2. The noun *homoiōsis*, meaning "likeness" or "similitude," is to be found only once, in Jas. 3:9 (RSV): "With it [the tongue] we bless the Lord and Father, and with it we curse men, who are made in the *likeness* of God."

Whereas 1 Cor. 11:7 and Jas. 3:9 seem to refer to the image as something that human beings (or male humans) have by virtue of creation, 2 Cor. 3:18, Rom. 8:29, and Col. 3:10 refer to the image as something into which or toward which Christians are being "changed," "conformed," or "renewed." This distinction and the further distinction between early Genesis and the second group of texts just cited help to clarify why the history of Christian doctrine has witnessed a variety of answers as to the precise nature of the image of God in humankind.

II. MAJOR INTERPRETATIONS: PAST AND PRESENT

It seems best to examine the various answers that have been given to the question, "What is the image of God in humankind?" by a unified approach that does not separate the historic answers from the contemporary ones.

A. HUMANKIND'S ERECT BODILY FORM OR STATURE

This view stems partly from the fact that the Hebrew word *ṣelem* can mean "figure, form, statue" as well as "image." Advocates of this view see the distinctiveness of the image to be humankind's upright physical posture in contrast to that of the quadruped animals. Such a view is capable of being defended as being quite consonant with the biological evolution of human beings. Hermann Gunkel in his commentary on Genesis held that Gen. 1:26-27 is to be understood in the light of Gen. 5:1-3; thus even as Seth had the stature and appearance of Adam his father, so humans have the stature and appearance[8] of God. Gunkel assumed that early Israelites thought of God as corporeal—corporeality being evidenced by anthropomorphisms. He was also quite open to the idea that Gen. 1:26 means that humans were also created after the image of the "'Elohim-beings," or angels.[9] Although some leading Mormon theologians (e.g., Joseph Fielding Smith, 1876-1972, and James Edward Talmadge, 1862-1933) do not mention the topic, there is some evidence that Mormons believe that the "image" of Gen. 1:26-27 and 5:3 presupposes

7. The word *eikōn* is also used in the New Testament to refer to Christ in relation to God the Father (esp. Colossians) and as the term for the statuary erected in honor of the first beast in Revelation 13.

8. *Gestalt und Aussehen.*

9. *Genesis*, 6th ed., rev. from 3d ed. by Paul Schorlemmer (Göttingen: Vandenhoeck und Ruprecht, 1964), pp. 111-13.

the physical or bodily nature of God the Father.[10] Charles Ryder Smith (1873-1956) acknowledged that the image "is the ground on which God gives man 'dominion' over his other creatures," but concluded that *ṣelem* and *dᵉmût* mean that God, angels, and human beings have "the same kind of 'form,'" that is, "'outline' or 'shape.'"[11] It is difficult to relate or apply this view to the New Testament texts pertaining to the image. Indeed, the erect or upright posture of human beings may be a symbol of the divine image, but the image itself would seem to be something more.

B. HUMAN DOMINION OR LORDSHIP OVER NATURE OR LOWER CREATION

This view of the image has been advocated on the basis of the dominion that is so integrally related to the image in Gen. 1:26-30 and so classically expressed in Ps. 8:5-8. This view has had numerous advocates, of whom the following are representative. The Polish Socinians in their *Racovian Catechism* (1609) rejected on the basis of Gen. 9:6 the view that the image could mean immortality and instead affirmed that it means "the authority of man, and his dominion over all inferior creatures, which result from the reason and judgement communicated to him."[12] Frederick Robert Tennant (1866-1957) held that, although the meaning of the *imago Dei* in the Genesis texts "is uncertain," in Ecclus. 17:1ff. the image "would appear to be identical with supremacy over the beasts and with rationality." Yet Wisd. of Sol. 2:23 identified the image with "immortality of the soul."[13] Gerhard von Rad concluded:

> Just as powerful earthly kings, to indicate their claim to dominion, erect an image of themselves in the provinces of their empire where they do not personally appear, so man is placed upon earth in God's image as God's sovereign emblem. He is really only God's representative, summoned to maintain and enforce God's claim to dominion over the earth.[14]

According to Sigmund Mowinckel (1884-1965),

> The 'godlikeness' of man in Ps. 8 consists above all in his sovereignty and power over all other beings, in his godlike 'honour and glory' compared to them.[15]

10. LeGrand Richards, *A Marvelous Work and a Wonder*, p. 16. Richards based this view of the image on Joseph Smith, Jr.'s alleged interview with the Father and the Son in 1820.
11. *The Bible Doctrine of Man* (London: Epworth Press, 1951), pp. 29-30.
12. *The Racovian Catechism* (London, 1818; reprint ed.; Lexington, Ky.: American Theological Library Association, 1962), sect. 2, ch. 1.
13. *The Sources of the Doctrines of the Fall and Original Sin* (Cambridge: University Press, 1903), p. 104, n. 1.
14. *Genesis: A Commentary*, trans. John H. Marks (Philadelphia: Westminster Press; London: SCM Press, 1961), p. 57.
15. *The Psalms in Israel's Worship*, trans. D. R. Ap-Thomas, 2 vols. (New York: Abingdon Press, 1962), 1:57.

For Charles Francis Digby Moule (1908-) the image means responsible dominion. Indeed,

> ·the Bible regards it as man's duty to use nature, not to abstain from using it; but that he must use it as a son of God and in obedience to God's will; and that his use or abuse of nature has far-reaching results in the whole structure of the world, inanimate as well as animate.[16]

On the basis of Gen. 1:26-27 Leonard Verduin (1897-) affirmed that "man is a creature meant for dominion-having and that as such he is in the image of his Maker." Such "dominion-having" is "closely akin to achieving sovereignty."[17] Frank Stagg, after considering that the image may be reckoned as humankind's personal, spiritual capacity, then concluded that dominion is the central idea.[18] Norman H. Snaith, commenting on Mowinckel's view, embraced dominion. The *imago Dei*

> refers only to man's domination of the world and everything that is in it. It says nothing about the nature of God, but everything concerning the function of man.[19]

Whereas this view of the image can claim strong support from Gen. 1:26-30 and from Ps. 8:5-8, although the words *ṣelem* and *dᵉmût* do not appear in the latter text, there are serious problems relative to the New Testament. None of the New Testament texts relative to the image directly connects the image with dominion.

Some have regarded dominion as the consequence of human beings' having been created in the image of God, not its content.[20] Karl Barth, who came to another conclusion about the basic meaning of the image, did refer to dominion as the "consequence" of the image.[21] William W. Stevens called dominion one of the chief "privileges of being in the image of God."[22]

C. HUMAN REASON, OR THE INTELLECTUAL FACULTY

This view locates the "image," though not the "likeness," in human reason, or the intellectual faculty. It predominated in the patristic and medieval periods and in the continuing Catholic tradition, as the study of David Cairns (1904-) has shown.[23] Moreover, it necessarily presupposed that "image" and "likeness" are to be markedly differentiated from

---

16. *Man and Nature in the New Testament: Some Reflections on Biblical Ecology* (London: Athlone Press, 1964; Philadelphia: Fortress Press, 1967), pp. 4-5, 16-21.

17. *Somewhat Less than God: The Biblical View of Man* (Grand Rapids: Eerdmans, 1970), pp. 27, 49.

18. *Polarities of Man's Existence in Biblical Perspective* (Philadelphia: Westminster Press, 1973), pp. 25-27.

19. "The Image of God," *Expository Times* 86 (October 1974): 24.

20. For evidence that some of the Church Fathers viewed dominion as an aspect or corollary of the image, see the present author's "Image of God," *The Encyclopedia of Early Christianity*, p. 453.

21. *Church Dogmatics*, III/1, pp. 187, 194.

22. *Doctrines of the Christian Religion*, p. 141.

23. *The Image of God in Man* (London: SCM Press, 1953), pp. 73-86, 110-20.

each other. Irenaeus likely fathered this distinction between the two terms.[24] It was common among the Church Fathers to locate the image of God in the human soul or spirit rather than in the body, but other writers, and sometimes also the very same writers, would locate the image in the reason or mind of human beings.[25] In this developing tradition as to the image/likeness, "image" came to mean the human endowment of reason and "likeness" the true or actual spiritual and moral likeness to God. Image was seen as natural, likeness as supernatural.[26] For Augustine of Hippo, who identified the image with the human soul[27] and with reason,[28] there are various "vestiges" of the Trinity in the minds of human beings.[29] Augustine also sought a middle ground between an unharmed image and a totally lost image.[30] John of Damascus interpreted the image as the "mind and free will" and the likeness as "virtue so far as possible."[31] This tradition was continued in Thomas Aquinas,[32] and the result was that the likeness was held to have been lost in the fall of humankind, but the image was not. Eastern Orthodoxy has even in the twentieth century maintained this position. "Image" is free will, reason, and the sense of moral responsibility and can never be lost. "Likeness" is the kinship of human beings to God or the "point of contact" between human beings and God; it can be destroyed by sin and must be acquired by human efforts.[33]

But, as previously noted, twentieth-century Hebrew exegetes are virtually unanimous in rejecting any genuine differentiation between ṣelem and dᵉmût in Gen. 1:26. Such a conclusion greatly weakens the case for the image as reason by removing any exegetical basis for the linguistic and terminological distinction on which the entire view rests.

A slight variation from this view of the image may be seen in James Orr's distinction between the primary and secondary senses of the image. Orr interpreted the image primarily in terms of powers: the personal, the "spiritual," the "self-conscious," the rational, being capable of "moral life," and being capable of "fellowship with God." His secondary meaning of the image was "the actual exhibition of that image in moral resemblance to God." In the primary sense the image "still remains, but in a broken and impaired condition." In the secondary sense the image has been by

24. Ibid., pp. 73-83.

25. See the present author's "Image of God," *The Encyclopedia of Early Christianity*, pp. 452-53.

26. Brunner, *The Christian Doctrine of Creation and Redemption*, p. 77.

27. *On the Trinity* 14.4; *On the City of God* 12.23; *On the Literal Meaning of Genesis* 10.2.

28. *On the Literal Meaning of Genesis* 3.20; 6.12; *Gospel of John* 3.4.

29. *On the Trinity*, bks. 8-10, 14. Prominent among these was the triadic memory, understanding, and will.

30. *On the Trinity* 14.4; *Retractations* 1.25.

31. *Exposition of the Orthodox Faith* 2.12.

32. Cairns, *The Image of God in Man*, pp. 114-20.

33. Timothy Ware, *The Orthodox Church* (Baltimore: Penguin Books, 1963), pp. 224-25.

virtue of the fall of humankind "largely destroyed."[34] The Reformation
heritage had made its mark on Orr's thinking.

D. HUMAN SPIRITUAL AND MORAL INNOCENCE, OR HUMANKIND'S ORIGINAL, PRELAPSARIAN RIGHTEOUSNESS

This view finds the image to be humankind's untested original
innocence or obedience or perfection prior to the fall of Adam and Eve
and their posterity. Martin Luther turned from the Scholastic interpretation of the image, built on Augustine and other Fathers, and embraced
this view. In his sermon on Gen. 1:26 in 1527, he connected the text with
1 Cor. 15:48-49 and Eph. 4:22-24 and distinguished between the "earthly"
image of Adam and the "heavenly" image of Christ. Human beings bear
Adam's image, having become like the devil, and need to bear the image
of Christ.[35] In his lecture on Gen. 1:26-27, delivered in 1535, Luther again
rejected the Scholastic view, according to which "similitude" could be
understood as faith, hope, and love. Such a view he saw as being dangerously unsafe by ascribing free will to sinful human beings. Instead Luther
taught that the image was lost through sin, and so was the likeness.
Intellect and will "have remained, but . . . very much impaired." The
image is to be restored by Christ through the gospel, and this restoration
is not to be finished before death.[36] John Calvin followed Luther's understanding of the image but modified it by a greater stress on a remnant or
vestige of the image after the fall. Deliberately rejecting five other views,[37]
Calvin opted for the perfection of unfallen Adam—"righteousness and
true holiness"—and located the image chiefly in the "mind and heart."[38]
Calvin could say that the image was destroyed[39] and obliterated by the
fall,[40] but he could also affirm that there were "remaining traces"[41] or
"some remnant"[42] of the image. But even the remnant was "vitiated and
maimed"[43] and "completely polluted."[44] The image is being "renewed
and restored" among Christians,[45] but such a transformation is indeed a
process.[46] Similarly C. F. Keil and Franz Delitzsch, after rejecting dominion and spiritual personality and after equating ṣelem and dᵉmût, concluded that ṣelem-dᵉmût is humankind's possessing "a creaturely copy of

34. *God's Image in Man and Its Defacement in the Light of Modern Denials* (2d ed.; London: Hodder and Stoughton; New York: Armstrong, 1906), pp. 56-59.
35. W.A., 24:48-51, as interpreted by Cairns, *The Image of God in Man*, p. 124.
36. *Lectures on Genesis 1–5*, in *Luther's Works*, 1:55-68, 337-38.
37. *Commentary on Genesis*, re 1:26; *Institutes of the Christian Religion*, 1559 ed., 1.15.3-4.
38. *Commentary on Genesis*, re 1:26.
39. Ibid.
40. *Institutes of the Christian Religion* 2.1.5.
41. Ibid. 2.2.17, trans. F. L. Battles.
42. *Commentary on Genesis*, re 9:6.
43. Ibid., re 1:26.
44. *Commentary on the Gospel of John*, re 3:6.
45. *Institutes of the Christian Religion* 3.7.6, trans. F. L. Battles.
46. *Commentary on 2 Corinthians*, re 3:18.

the holiness and blessedness of the divine life." This "was shattered by sin," and through Christ believers are being "transformed" again "into the image of God."[47]

The Pauline uses of *eikōn* in respect to transformation (2 Cor. 3:18), conforming to Christ (Rom. 8:29), and renewal (Col. 3:10) seem to be quite supportive of or conformable to this fourth view of the image. Gen. 9:6, however, seems to contradict it by its basing of the prohibition against murder on humankind's being in the image of God.

E. Capacities or Powers of Human Beings as Spiritual and Moral Creatures

This view locates the image in the cluster of capacities or powers that belong to human beings as creatures of God. This cluster is more extensive than reason, or the intellectual faculty. Although it may be traced to some extent to Augustine of Hippo, it has been essentially a modern view. Indeed, its indebtedness to the philosophy of personalism may be more important than scholars have yet acknowledged. Furthermore, its advocates seldom cite the biblical texts relative to the image or seek an exegetical base for their conclusions. W. T. Conner interpreted the image as humans' being "spiritual persons" with certain capacities or powers that constitute human beings as human beings and that belong to them despite their sin. He named five: (1) "intelligence," or the power to think, plan, recall to memory, and be self-conscious; (2) "freedom," that is, real, though limited, self-determination; (3) "rational affection," or the power, above instinct, to love; (4) the moral sense, or conscience, including an innate awareness of a distinction between right and wrong and an obligation to do the right and avoid the wrong; and (5) a spiritual affinity for God.[48] A. C. Knudson identified the image with endowments of knowledge, morality, and religious faith.[49] William W. Stevens considered the image to be humankind's existence as "a spiritual being, capable of fellowship with God, and capable of reflecting something of the character of God."[50] Eric C. Rust limited the image to one capacity, "human freedom, man's ability to respond truly in love."[51] Millard J. Erickson has advocated what he has called "the substantive or structural view" of the image, arguing that the image "refers to something man *is* rather than some-

---

47. *Commentary on the Old Testament,* vol. 1, *The Pentateuch,* 3 vols. in 1, trans. James Martin (Grand Rapids: Eerdmans, 1949), 1:63-64. Robert Lewis Dabney (1820-98), Southern Presbyterian, *Lectures in Systematic Theology* (1st publ. 1878; reprint ed.; Grand Rapids: Zondervan, 1972), pp. 293-94, and F. A. O. Pieper, Missouri Synod Lutheran, *Christian Dogmatics,* 1:515-26, followed Luther and Calvin.
48. *A System of Christian Doctrine,* pp. 303-5; *Revelation and God,* pp. 51-53.
49. *The Doctrine of Redemption,* pp. 86-89.
50. *Doctrines of the Christian Religion,* pp. 140-41.
51. "The Biblical Faith and Modern Science," *Review and Expositor* 71 (Spring 1974): 235.

thing he *has* or *does.*"[52] Erickson's view turns out to be a rather unspecific form of the cluster-of-capacities view.[53]

This view does have the advantage of assembling and correlating several characteristics of human persons that differentiate them from animals. But the view appears to be incompatible with the Pauline texts relative to the *imago Dei,* which uniformly presuppose that the image must be renewed or restored.

F. JUXTAPOSED CONFRONTATION OF MAN AND WOMAN, ESPECIALLY IN MARRIAGE, AS ANALOGOUS TO THE I/THOU NATURE OF GOD

This view, majoring on the fact that Gen. 1:27 and 5:1-2 closely associate image/likeness and maleness/femaleness, concludes that the image consists of the confrontation or juxtaposition of human beings as male and female, especially in and through marriage, as analogous to the I/Thou nature of the Triune God. Karl Barth in his *Church Dogmatics*[54] has been the principal exponent of this view, but he acknowledged that Wilhelm Vischer and Dietrich Bonhoeffer had anticipated and taught aspects of the view. Barth saw an analogy: God and humankind both include an "I" and a "Thou." Indeed, God created human beings so that God is the "original" or "prototype" and human beings are the "copy" or "imitation." But, for Barth, this analogy of relationship does not mean complete likeness, but rather "the correspondence of the unlike." Human bisexuality and the persons of the Trinity are not alike, but only analogous.[55]

This view clearly builds on the close association of image/likeness

52. *Christian Theology,* pp. 495-517, esp. 512-13.

53. Erickson's exposition of and argument for "the substantive or structural view" is not devoid of problems. (1) He has wrongly classified Luther and Calvin under the structural view (p. 501). (2) In treating Emil Brunner's view he has failed to report that Brunner's formal image is tied to the Old Testament usage (Genesis) and his material image to the New Testament usage (Paul) (pp. 502-4). (3) He does not take seriously enough the differences of approach on the image between Genesis and Paul, though he states on the one hand that the "image of God has not been lost as a result of sin" (p. 513) and on the other hand that the "New Testament makes clear that God will restore the damaged image, and perhaps even build upon and go beyond it (2 Cor. 3:18)" (p. 516). (4) If all human beings have the structural image, as Erickson holds (p. 513), do all humans have all the communicable attributes of God, as he seems to teach (p. 514)? (5) Why does not Erickson simply acknowledge some debt to the philosophy of personalism in the formulation of his view? (6) Why does Erickson have difficulty in listing or describing in detail "the powers of personality" that for him constitute the image (pp. 513, 514, 517)? He comments that "the text of Scripture itself never identifies what qualities within man might be the image" (p. 512). Could it be that the biblical writers never intended to offer such an interpretation of the image?

54. Erickson, *Christian Theology,* pp. 504-5, has delineated three stages in Barth's thought concerning the image: (1) a mother-fetus type of unity lost by the fall *(Epistle to the Romans);* (2) denial of any point of contact between human beings and God, or "any human capacity to receive the Word of God" (debate with Emil Brunner); and (3) the view being described here.

55. *Church Dogmatics,* III/1, pp. 194-97.

and maleness/femaleness in the Genesis texts. On the other hand, it is a novel interpretation in the long history of Christian doctrine.

G. Old Testament Sense of the Image (Responsible Creaturehood) and New Testament Sense of the Image (Spiritual and Moral Conformity to God)

This view differentiates the Old Testament (Genesis) sense of the image from the New Testament sense of the image (Paul), holding them to be complementary, not contradictory. Emil Brunner has been the chief exponent of this view. He referred to the Old Testament sense of the image as the "formal" image and to the New Testament sense of the image as the "material" image. The former, common to all humans and not lost by sin, means that human beings are responsible creatures before the Creator. The latter, presupposing a loss through sin, means restoration through Jesus Christ.[56] Dallas M. Roark accepted Brunner's basic distinction.[57] Rather than differentiate *ṣelem* and *dᵉmût*, as does the third view above, this view differentiates Genesis and Paul but only to correlate or combine them.

This view, like the sixth, has no long tradition in the history of Christian doctrine, but it does span the two testaments and gather up all the pertinent passages into one comprehensive view.[58]

H. Composites of Selected Views of the Image of God in Humankind

Some theologians have opted not for a single view of the image but for a composite of selected views, but normally they have done little toward the integration of the views placed in the composite. John Leadley Dagg (1794-1884) set forth a fourfold answer: "intelligence," "righteousness and the true holiness" (Col. 3:10; Eph. 4:24), "dominion . . . over all inferior creatures," and the "spirituality and immortality" of the human soul. Dagg was unspecific about the first, declared that the second was lost through the fall, taught that the third was altered by the fall in that thereafter other creatures rebelled against human beings, and concluded that the fourth remains.[59] Charles Hodge opted for a threefold

---

56. *Man in Revolt: A Christian Anthropology*, trans. Olive Wyon (New York: Charles Scribner's Sons, 1939), chs. 5–6; *The Christian Doctrine of Creation and Redemption*, pp. 55-61.
57. *The Christian Faith*, pp. 191-92.
58. Seven views of the image have been treated as "major" views. There are and have been other views; for example, Meister Eckhart's uncreated divine spark of the soul (S. M. Deutsch, "Eckhart," *New Schaff-Herzog Encyclopedia of Religious Knowledge*, 4:69-70); and the Italian Renaissance idea of "the secular triumphs of mankind and the great deeds of individuals" as expressive of the image and likeness, whether as "the capacity or drive of man to command and shape his world" (dominion) or as "the energy of his will and mind" (endowment). Charles Edward Trinkhaus, *In Our Image and Likeness: Humanity and Divinity in Italian Humanist Thought*, 2 vols. (Chicago: University of Chicago Press; London: Constable and Company Ltd., 1970), 1:xiii-xiv, xx-xxii.
59. *A Manual of Theology* (Charleston, S.C.: Southern Baptist Publication Society, 1857; reprint ed.; Harrisonburg, Va.: Gano Books, 1982), pp. 141-44.

composite: an "intellectual" nature, meaning "reason, conscience, and will"; moral perfection, or "original righteousness"; and "dominion over the creatures." The second was lost by the fall.[60] John Miley listed as components "the spiritual nature of man," endowments of intellect, emotions, and moral nature, personality ("the central truth"), and holiness.[61] A twofold composite was affirmed by A. H. Strong: "natural likeness to God, or personality" and "moral likeness to God, or holiness."[62] E. Y. Mullins had eight categories: "rational nature," conscience, "emotional nature," will, "self-determination," original sinlessness, dominion over nature, and immortality.[63] H. C. Thiessen chose three categories: "mental likeness," including reason, conscience, and will; "moral likeness," which seemed to include both the capacity for communion with God and original righteousness; and "social likeness," or the idea that God has a social nature and made human beings to have such.[64] H. Orton Wiley, after tracing the history of the doctrine, affirmed both "the natural or essential image" (i.e., "personality") and "the moral or incidental image," or the responsible use of the powers of the "essential image" (i.e., "holiness").[65]

A more extended and more integrated composite has been set forth by Anthony A. Hoekema in his recent monograph on the image. (1) Humankind in the image of God, as created, was "to *mirror* God" and to *represent* God. (2) The image has both "structural" ("broader") and "functional" ("narrower") meanings. (3) As sinners human beings have not "totally lost" the image, but it has been "perverted or distorted by the Fall." (4) Christ as the "true image of God" is "wholly directed to God," "wholly directed to the neighbor," and ruler over nature. (5) Humankind in the image of God has three interrelated relationships: "to be directed toward God," "to be directed toward one's fellowmen," and "to rule over nature," that is, both to "subdue" it (Gen. 1:28) and to "work" or serve and "take care of" or guard it (Gen. 2:15). (6) The renewed image means the enablement of the Christian to function again in all three relationships. (7) "Men and women together are the image of God." (8) The image "in its totality can only be seen in humankind as a whole." (9) Only with the perfected image will human renewal be completed.[66] One may ask whether Hoekema's "perverted or distorted" image has a biblical basis as well as a Reformation basis and what it really means to have the image "directed to the neighbor," but Hoekema seems to have made the composite approach a live option.

60. *Systematic Theology*, 2:96-103.
61. *Systematic Theology*, 2 vols. (New York: Eaton and Mains; Cincinnati: Jennings and Pye, 1892), 1:406-8.
62. *Systematic Theology*, pp. 514-23.
63. *The Christian Religion in Its Doctrinal Expression*, pp. 257-60.
64. *Introductory Lectures in Systematic Theology*, pp. 219-22.
65. *Christian Theology*, 2:30-39.
66. *Created in God's Image* (Grand Rapids: Eerdmans; Exeter, U.K.: Paternoster, 1986), ch. 5.

Protestant confessions of faith have generally not made precise statements or taken definitive positions concerning the image of God in humankind. Church councils and denominational bodies have tended not be decisive about this doctrine, possibly because they were not being constrained to be. Present-day Christians, therefore, are obliged to sift through a great body of opinion and evidence before being able to draw responsible conclusions, for the doctrine of the image is too important to be neglected or bypassed.

III. CONTEMPORARY NON-CHRISTIAN VIEWS OF HUMANKIND

The Christian doctrine of the *imago Dei*, as will be noted, has numerous implications as to the uniqueness, accountability, and worth of human beings. But this network of ideas is not shared or accepted by most of the contemporary non-Christian ideologies. Christians with their teaching about the human must interface with various contemporary views of human nature, origins, and destiny that have come to be expressed in biology-anthropology, politics-economics, psychology, philosophy, and other disciplines. Their differing emphases need to be examined, and the superior effectiveness of the Christian doctrine in supplying answers to the several dimensions of human life ought to be set forth in apologetic fashion.

Inasmuch as two theologians, both of whom have written during the 1980s, have explicated these non-Christian views of the human so fully, we will limit the present discussion to a mere identification of the topics treated by those authors, and the reader is referred to those books for the extended treatments. The authors are Dale Moody[67] and Millard J. Erickson.[68]

Moody	Erickson
Biological Man (Darwin, Bergson, T. H. Huxley, Julian Huxley, Teilhard de Chardin)	Man as an Animal
Political Man (Marx)[69]	Man as a Machine Man as an Economic Being
Psychological Man (Freud, Skinner)	Man as a Sexual Being (Freud)

67. *The Word of Truth*, pp. 253-70.

68. *Christian Theology*, pp. 462-70. See Leslie Forster Stevenson, *Seven Theories of Human Nature* (New York: Oxford University Press, 1974; 2d ed. 1987).

69. Moody treats also the political and social teachings of the Christian ethicist-theologian Reinhold Niebuhr.

Philosophical Man (Sartre, Heidegger)[70]	Man as a Pawn of the Universe (Bertrand Russell, Sartre, Camus)
Theological Man[71]	Man as a Free Being Man as a Social Being

IV. SOME IMPLICATIONS OF THE IMAGE OF GOD IN HUMAN BEINGS

A. HUMAN BEINGS AS RELIGIOUS BEINGS

Human beings are religious and engage in religious effort and practices, even if of a base, sensuous, and corrupt sort.[72] Mankind is conscious "of a higher Power to whom he is related and seeks to know how to adjust himself to this Power so as to secure his own peace and well-being."[73] The study of religions gives evidence that this religious consciousness is universal. The Christian doctrine of the image of God in humankind helps to explain why the human person "is religious by virtue of the fact that he is human."[74] One aspect or implication of the image is the innate capacity of humans to worship and yearn for God. "As the deer pants for streams of water, so my soul pants for you, O God" (Ps. 42:1, NIV). "Our heart is restless until it finds rest in you, O Lord."[75] Even those humans who deny the existence of a personal God tend to "personify Humanity, or Nature, or the Universe."[76] The human craving for an object of worship indicates that "man was made for the gospel, and the gospel was made for man."[77]

B. HUMAN BEINGS AS VALUABLE TO GOD

The Christian teaching is that, in spite of their sin, human beings are valuable in the sight of God. Jesus taught that human persons are of greater value than animals, religious institutions, and even the whole material universe (Matt. 12:12; Mark 2:27-28; Matt. 16:26). The entire redemptive purpose and plan of God, including the incarnation and death-resurrection of Jesus as the Son of God, is predicated on the veritable worthwhileness of God's redeeming human beings. Indeed, "there is no conflict between the worth of man as a moral and spiritual person and his

70. Moody deals also with the teachings of the Christian and existentialist thinker Søren Kierkegaard.
71. Moody treats here the Christian doctrine of humankind as found in the theologies of Wolfhart Pannenberg and Jürgen Moltmann.
72. See above, Ch. 4, V.
73. Conner, *Revelation and God*, pp. 57-58.
74. Ibid., p. 58.
75. Augustine of Hippo, *Confessions* 1.1.
76. Conner, *Revelation and God*, p. 53.
77. Conner, *Christian Doctrine* (Nashville: Broadman Press, 1937), p. 23.

unworthiness on account of his sin."[78] Careful distinction must be made between "man's being worth saving," which is to be affirmed, and "his being worthy of salvation," which is to be rejected. "Unless man is worth saving, God engaged in a foolish enterprise when he sent Christ to save sinners."[79]

During the twentieth century the Holocaust occurred, atomic bombs were invented and used and more lethal weapons have been amassed, more Christians have been put to death for their faith than in any preceding century, world population has soared to new heights, and abortion has become a major theological, moral, and civic issue. In view of these considerations it is especially important that the Christian doctrine of the value and worth of human life be believed, confessed, taught, and implemented.

C. HUMAN BEINGS AS NEVER PERMANENTLY SATISFIED WITH ANY OF THE REDUCTIONIST VIEWS OF HUMANKIND

Once human beings are seen as being "in the image of God and after his likeness," human beings find that the various reductionist views of human life are less convincing or less satisfying. These include: (1) Marxism's view of human beings as economic animals with class struggles, not God or human beings, as the basis for ethics; (2) Freud's view of humans as primarily and essentially the product of sexual drives and as dominated by aberrant sexual activity; (3) totalitarianism's view of human beings as the political tools of the omnicompetent civil state; (4) racism's view that racial/ethnic differences and conflicts are a very important aspect of human life and that superior and inferior races are to be differentiated; and (5) naturalism's view that a human being is "the outcome of accidental collocations of atoms."

Now that we have seen the importance of the Christian doctrine of the image of God in humankind it is possible to turn to other significant aspects of the Christian doctrine of humankind.

78. Conner, *Gospel Doctrines* (Nashville: Sunday School Board of the Southern Baptist Convention, 1925).

79. Conner, *The Work of the Holy Spirit* (Nashville: Broadman Press, 1949), p. 168.

CHAPTER 31

The Antiquity, the Origin, and the Unity of Humankind

How long has humanity created in the image of God lived on the earth? Do all human beings derive from a single human pair, or were there multiple origins? Is there a unity of humankind that transcends the racial or ethnic differences among human beings? These are questions that are of particular importance to Christians in the twentieth century. They are questions about which there are biblical materials, if not always direct biblical teachings. They are questions that have to be answered in the face of conclusions advanced by the sciences, especially anthropology and sociology. They are questions for which answers are needed for a full-orbed Christian doctrine of humankind.

I. THE ANTIQUITY OF HUMANKIND

A. BIBLICAL MATERIALS: TRADITIONAL APPROACH

Throughout most of the history of Christianity Christians assumed on the basis of their reading of Genesis that the length of human existence on the earth was rather limited. This conclusion normally resulted from efforts to calculate on the basis of the so-called genealogical passages in Genesis[1] the time of the creation of the first humans. Humphrey John Thewlis Johnson (1890-?), an English Catholic anthropologist, writing in 1923, summarized the view that had been common in the West until the beginning of the nineteenth century. Moses lived in the fifteenth century B.C. The universal flood of Noah's time had occurred less than a thousand years earlier. The creation of Adam and Eve had occurred little more than sixteen centuries earlier than the flood. Hence creation could be located about forty centuries before the birth of Jesus.[2] This is precisely what James Ussher had computed during the seventeenth century, namely, the

---

1. Gen. 5:1-32; 10:1-32; 11:10-32.
2. *Anthropology and the Fall* (New York: Benziger Brothers, 1923), pp. 3-4.

creation of all things, including the first humans, in 4004 B.C.[3] Calculations based on the Samaritan Pentateuch pushed the date back to 4243 B.C., and those based on the Septuagint back to 5328 B.C.[4]

B. Evidence from the Science of Anthropology

Beginning with the work of William Buckland (1784-1856) before the middle of the nineteenth century, those seeking animal fossils came to discover human fossil or skeletal remains. Charles Lyell (1797-1875) in his *The Antiquity of Man* (1863) pushed back further the age of human life on earth than had previous authors. For more than a century archaeologists, anthropologists, and others have participated in the discoveries and assessments of skulls, jaws, teeth, thighs, and arms that they have attributed to human beings and that they have dated by use of geological evidence and of fluorine. Notable among these were the Neanderthal man in Germany (1857ff.), the Cro-Magnon man in France (1868), the Java man (1891ff.), the Piltdown man in England (1912ff.), the Peking man (1921ff.), and more recent discoveries in southern and eastern Africa. Although interpretations of these human fossils have varied, they have been uniformly placed in one or more of the periods of the Stone Age, the end of which is normally dated prior to 4004 B.C.[5] Dale Moody has summarized anthropological dating as follows: Indian man in North America can be traced back 25,000 years, and so can Cro-Magnon man with his use of stone and bone tools and of art; Neanderthal man, whose burial practices are indicative of religion, can be traced back to from 40,000 to 100,000 years; and Java man, with his primitive use of fire and of language, can be traced to about 400,000 years ago.[6] Others hold that human language cannot be traced back more than 30,000 or 40,000 years.[7]

C. Reassessment of the Biblical Materials

As early as 1890 William Henry Green (1825-1900) of Princeton Theological Seminary, in the words of Bernard L. Ramm,[8] "demonstrated for certainty to Biblical scholars that the genealogies of Genesis were not strict father-son relationships."[9] Even Augustine of Hippo had said that the writer of Genesis 4 "was under no obligation to mention the names of all who may have been alive at the time, but only of those whom the scope of his work required him to mention."[10] Ramm concluded in 1954 that the

3. "Ussher, James," *The New Schaff-Herzog Encyclopedia of Religious Knowledge,* 12:114-15; J. A. Emerton, "Ussher, James," *Encyclopedia Britannica,* 1969 ed., 22:813.
4. Johnson, *Anthropology and the Fall,* p. 30, n. 1.
5. H. J. T. Johnson, *The Bible and Early Man* (New York: Declan X. McMullen Company, Inc., 1948), pp. 33-61; Moody, *The Word of Truth,* pp. 205-10.
6. Moody, *The Word of Truth,* pp. 205-10.
7. Erickson, *Christian Theology,* pp. 484-86.
8. *The Christian View of Science and Scripture,* p. 313.
9. Green, "Primeval Chronology," *Bibliotheca Sacra* 47 (April 1890): 285-303.
10. *On the City of God* 15.8.

"precise age of man" is not derivable from "the genealogies of Genesis" or from any other part of the Bible.[11]

Yet Genesis 1–3 seems to be intimately connected with Genesis 4–11, and the connection between Genesis 3 and Genesis 4 is especially to be noted. Ramm has taken account of the fact that in Genesis 4–5 there are "lists of names, ages of people, towns, agriculture, metallurgy, and music," which data imply "the ability to write, to count, to build, to farm, to smelt, and to compose" on the part of Adam's "immediate descendants," and yet evidence of civilization can hardly push its origin beyond 8,000 B.C. or 16,000 B.C. Furthermore, the early chapters of Genesis have some basic ties with Babylonian civilization that can hardly be harmonized with the creation of human beings at 400,000 B.C. or earlier.[12] A date of 400,000 B.C. for the creation of human beings still seems to pose problems vis-à-vis Genesis 1–11.[13]

D. POSSIBLE SOLUTIONS[14]

1. Rejection of All Anthropological/Geological Evidence and Holding to the Recent Origin of Humankind

Some, especially Protestant Christians, would resolve the question of human antiquity by rejecting all the evidence from anthropology and geology drawn from human fossils and by positing the creation of human beings either in 4004 B.C. or some other time not earlier than 10,000 B.C. This proposal was advocated earlier in this century by the Seventh-day Adventist author George McCready Price (1870-1963),[15] and it has more

11. *The Christian View of Science and Scripture*, p. 314. See also Buswell, *A Systematic Theology of the Christian Religion*, 1:332-43, who asserted that "we have scriptural evidence that the Hebrew record in Genesis 11 is not complete" (Luke 3:36; Gen. 11:12-13), that Jacob was a peoplic name (Gen. 46:3-4), and that the genealogies of Gen. 5 and 11 have largely to do with "families or dynasties."

12. Ibid., p. 327.

13. Ramm commented: "The problems of anthropology are far more pressing to evangelical Christianity than those of geology or astronomy, and even a theologian like [Emil] Brunner who rejects the plenary inspiration of Scripture finds himself sweating over the problems which anthropology presents to Christian theology" (ibid., p. 305). See Brunner, *The Christian Doctrine of Creation and Redemption*, p. 79.

14. This section is a restatement and updating of Ramm, *The Christian View of Science and Scripture*, pp. 315-28.

15. *Outlines of Modern Christianity and Modern Science* (Oakland: Pacific Press Publishing Company, 1902); *Illogical Geology: The Weakest Point in the Evolution Theory* (Los Angeles: Modern Heretic Company, 1906); *God's Two Books; or, Plain Facts about Evolution, Geology, and the Bible* (Washington, D.C.: Review and Herald Publishing Association, 1911); *The Fundamentals of Geology and Their Bearings on the Doctrine of a Literal Creation* (Mountain View, Calif.: Pacific Press, 1913); *Back to the Bible, or, The New Protestantism* (Washington, D.C.: Review and Herald, 1916; rev. ed. 1920); *Q.E.D., or, New Light on the Doctrine of Creation* (New York: Fleming H. Revell Company, 1917); "Geology," in Robert Marshall Brown, ed., *Geography and Geology* (Philadelphia: American Educational Institute, Inc., 1920); "Nature Study," in Price, ed., *Nature Study and Astronomy* (Philadelphia: ibid., 1921); *The New Geology* (Mountain View, Calif.: Pacific Press, 1923; 2d ed. 1926); *Science and Religion in a Nutshell* (Washington, D.C.: Review and Herald, 1923); *The Phantom of Organic Evolution* (New York: Revell, 1924); (with Joseph McCabe), *Is Evolution True? Verbatim Report of Debate between George*

recently been vigorously advocated by the Creation-Science movement under the leadership of Henry M. Morris.[16] It constitutes no "solution" for scientific anthropologists, who thereby are asked to disclaim all their findings.

2. Advocacy of Pre-Adamism

This is the hypothesis that one can properly differentiate fossil people (as "subhuman," "prehuman," or "pre-Adamite") and biblical humans (or the humans of Genesis 1–11). According to this view fossil people, or prehumans, died out before the creation of Adam, and thus the two, fossil people and biblical humans, did not coinhabit the earth. "Adam was a de novo creation possessing spiritual qualities these pre-Adamites lacked."[17] Although this view has been traced to the seventeenth century,[18] its principal advocacy has taken place since the late nineteenth century. Fabre d'Envieu,[19] Alexander Winchell (1824-91),[20] Reuben A. Torrey,[21] and Arthur Rendel Short (1880-1953)[22] espoused the view in the latter nineteenth or early twentieth centuries. Its most recent defender seems to have been an English anthropologist, Eustace Kenneth Victor Pearce, who has identified Adam of Eden (Genesis 2) with the new Stone

McCready Price . . . and Joseph McCabe . . . (London: Watts and Company, 1925; Girard, Kan.: Haldeman-Julius Company, c. 1928); The Predicament of Evolution (Nashville: Southern Publishing Association, 1925); Evolutionary Geology and the New Catastrophism (Mountain View, Calif.: Pacific Press, 1926); A History of Some Scientific Blunders (London: Oliphants Ltd.; New York: Revell, 1930); The Geological-Ages Hoax: A Plea for Logic in Theoretical Geology (New York: Revell, 1931); Modern Discoveries Which Help Us to Believe (New York: ibid., 1934); The Modern Flood Theory of Geology (New York: ibid., 1935); Some Scientific Stories and Allegories (Grand Rapids: Zondervan, 1936); Genesis Vindicated (Washington, D.C.: Review and Herald, 1941); How Did the World Begin? (New York: Revell, 1942); If You Were the Creator: A Reasonable Credo for Modern Man (Mountain View, Calif.: Pacific Press, 1942); Common-Sense Geology: A Simplified Study for the General Reader (Mountain View, Calif.: ibid., 1946); Feet of Clay: The Unscientific Nonsense of Historical Geology (Malverne, N.Y.: Christian Evidence League, 1949); The Story of the Fossils (Mountain View, Calif.: Pacific Press, 1954); and Problems and Methods in Geology (Malverne, N.Y.: Christian Evidence League, 1956).

16. See above, Ch. 25, II, C, 1 and 4.

17. Ramm, The Christian View of Science and Scripture, p. 316.

18. Joseph Pohle, God: The Author of Nature and the Supernatural, vol. 3, Dogmatic Theology, adapt. and ed. Arthur Preuss (St. Louis, London: B. Herder Book Company, 1946), p. 132, stated: "Pre-Adamism was reduced to a theological system by the French Calvinist Isaac Peyrère [Systema Theologicum ex Praeadamitarum Hypothesi, 1655], who later became a Catholic and abjured his error before Pope Alexander VII." See also Johnson, The Bible and Early Man, pp. 107-8.

19. Pohle, God, p. 135, n. 26, cited Fabre d'Envieu's Les origines de la terre et de l'homme (1878).

20. Adamites and Preadamites: or, A Popular Discussion concerning the Remote Representatives of the Human Species and Their Relation to the Biblical Adam (Syracuse, N.Y.: John T. Roberts, 1878); Preadamites: or a Demonstration of the Existence of Men before Adam (Chicago: S. C. Griggs and Company, 1880).

21. Difficulties and Alleged Errors and Contradictions in the Bible (New York: Fleming H. Revell Company, 1907), pp. 31-32, 36. Torrey tied pre-Adamism to the gap theory of Gen. 1:1-2 and was inclined to think that pre-Adamites lived "in Bible times."

22. Modern Discovery and the Bible (1st American ed., rev.; Chicago: Inter-Varsity Christian Fellowship, 1949), pp. 114-15; first published in Britain in 1942.

Age man, who was a farmer and breeder of animals, and the Adam of Genesis 1 with pre-Adamite man.[23] Described by Ramm as a "having our cake and eating it too" theory, pre-Adamism nevertheless has its problems. Three texts have been cited against Pre-Adamism: "and there was no man to work the ground" (Gen. 2:5d, NIV); "But for Adam no suitable helper was found" (Gen. 2:20b); and "she [Eve] would become the mother of all the living" (Gen. 3:20b). From an anthropological viewpoint, how is one to tell when pre-Adamites ceased and biblical humans began? In view of Torrey's claim that pre-Adamites sinned and were alive after the creation of biblical humans, one may ask whether the pre-Adamites had the opportunity of redemption.[24] Against Pearce's form of the theory is the fact that the image/likeness passage (Gen. 1:26-27) conveys the unique likeness of human beings to God the Creator more markedly than does Genesis 2.

3. *Regarding Early Genesis as Incapable of Being Associated with the Dating of Human Origins*

Two different forms of this perspective need to be identified.

a. Certain Roman Catholic scientists, especially E. C. Messenger and H. J. T. Johnson, who affirmed that the human soul came by special creation of God, interpreted Genesis 2 metaphorically, though not in such a way as to be *"non-historical,"* and concluded that Genesis 2 cannot be used to date human origins.[25]

b. Emil Brunner, taking Genesis 1–3 as mythical and nonhistorical, took God's creatorship as an inference from his lordship and posited human createdness on the basis of an existential encounter with God as Lord. Thus the question of the antiquity of humankind must be left entirely to the sciences.[26]

The more one finds a historical dimension to Genesis 1–3 the more unsatisfying will likely be these two attempted solutions.

4. *Direct Divine Creation of Adam and Eve at a Time Conformable with Anthropological Data*

Although Ramm did not specifically espouse this view, he did state:

> If the anthropologists are generally correct in their dating of man (and we believe they are), and if the Bible contains no specific date as to the origin of man, we are then free to try to work out a theory of the relationship between the two respecting both the inspiration of Scripture and the facts of science.[27]

There seems to be at present no agreed upon harmonization of early Genesis and anthropology. Because of the genuine difficulties, which have

23. *Who Was Adam?* (2d ed.; Exeter, U.K.: Paternoster Press, 1976), ch. 2.
24. Ramm, *The Christian View of Science and Scripture*, pp. 316-17.
25. Ibid., pp. 322-24.
26. Ibid., pp. 317-20.
27. Ibid., p. 314.

not been fully resolved, it is fitting to be cautious as to any final statement of the question.

E. Agreements between Geological and Anthropological Sciences and the Bible

It would be wrong to conclude from the lack of harmonization as to the precise time of the origin of human life on earth that there are no areas of agreement between anthropology and geology on the one hand and the Bible, as interpreted by twentieth-century Christians, on the other hand. Ramm cited three important areas of agreement: (1) "Both geology and Scripture teach that man is the latest major form to appear on the earth." (2) "Anthropology and Scripture agree that man is the highest form of life." (3) "Anthropology and the Bible both assert that man has much in common with the animals."[28]

II. THE ORIGIN OF HUMANKIND: MULTIPLE OR SINGLE?

A second issue concerning which Christian theology and anthropological science have interacted is that of the origin or origins of the human species. Is the Christian teaching that all human beings are the descendants of one couple, Adam and Eve, still valid, or must the theory of multiple human origins, called polygenism or polygeneticism, be accepted as valid?

A. Biblical Materials

1. Old Testament

Not only did the first creation account declare that God created human beings male and female (Gen. 1:27) but also it cited the divine mandate to the first humans to be fruitful and multiply (Gen. 1:28). Furthermore, prior to the record of the birth of their first child Genesis declared concerning Eve that "she would become the mother of all the living" (3:20b, NIV).

2. New Testament

In his sermon at Athens Paul affirmed: "'And he [God] made from one every nation of men to live on all the face of the earth . . .'" (Acts 17:26a, RSV). When Paul, in writing about the future resurrection, declared in an analogy that "in Adam all die" (1 Cor. 15:22), he most probably was thinking of all human beings as being Adam's descendants as well as sharing in his death. In his extended treatment of the differences between the activity of Adam and the work of Jesus Christ (Rom. 5:12-21), Paul alluded in the Greek two times to "one man" or "the one man" (vv. 12, 19), four times to "the one" (vv. 15, 16, 17), and once to the "one trespass" (v. 18). Whereas Paul's primary reference was likely the singular

28. Ibid., pp. 328-29.

personhood of Adam vis-à-vis the singular personhood of Jesus, it seems
unthinkable that Paul could have thought of any human being as un-
derived from Adam.

B. Anthropological Polygenism

During the nineteenth and twentieth centuries some scientific anthropologists have espoused polygenism, or polygeneticism, which is the
view that instead of the origination of the human race or humankind from
a single stock a multiple origin of humankind via independent evolution
is to be affirmed. Accordingly there would have been several or many
independent originations of human beings not necessarily at the same
time. Ramm cited Reginald Ruggles Gates (1882-) as a representative
exponent of polygenism.[29]

C. Theological Rejection of Polygenism

1. Roman Catholic Church

Pope Pius XII (1876-1958) in his encyclical *Humani Generis* (1950)
disallowed any Catholic acceptance of polygenism:

> No Catholic can hold that after Adam there existed on this earth true men
> who did not take their origin through natural generation from him as from
> the first parent of all, or that Adam is merely a symbol for a number of first
> parents. For it is unintelligible how such an opinion can be squared with
> what the sources of revealed truth and the documents of the Magisterium
> of the Church teach on original sin, which proceeds from sin actually
> committed by an individual Adam, and which, passed on to all by way of
> generation, is in everyone as his own.[30]

2. Protestantism

Protestants, for whom there is no centralized teaching authority,
have not dealt with the challenge of polygenism by means of church or
denominational pronouncements but have left the matter with individual
theologians and apologists. Ramm, assuming that a concept of the imputation of Adam's sin to all human beings is essential to Protestantism,
regarded the challenge of polygenism as a serious one.

> The sin of Adam imputed to humanity depends on the unity of humanity,
> not on the antiquity of humanity. Theology is more concerned with the proof
> that man is one, rather than the near or far antiquity of man. Polygeneticism
> is far more damaging to theology than any teaching of the vast antiquity of
> man.[31]

---

29. *The Christian View of Science and Scripture*, p. 306, citing Gates, *Human Ancestry from
a Genetical Point of View* (Cambridge, Mass.: Harvard University Press, 1948).
    30. Pope Pius XII, *The Encyclical "Humani Generis,"* trans. A. C. Cotter, S.J. (2d ed.;
Weston, Mass.: Weston College Press, 1952), para. 38, p. 43. Pius XII's statement does not
seem to rule out forms of pre-Adamism.
    31. *The Christian View of Science and Scripture*, p. 308.

Ramm proceeded to set forth four evidences for the unitary origin of humankind from the sciences of anatomy, physiology, psychology, and reproduction and used these in his case against polygeneticism. From anatomy comes the evidence that "the human body is the same form from pygmies to the giant Wattusies and from the fairest Scandinavian to the darkest negroid." From physiology comes the fact that variations in breathing and in pulse rates are very slight among human beings. From psychology comes the data that "the powers of perception, the patterns of reaction, and the function of the central nervous system are similar" in all human beings. From reproduction comes the paramount fact of "racial interfertility."[32] Ramm also argued for the improbability of polygeneticism:

> The calculus of probability is such that the chances of several sub-human ancestors evolving the same human races so that they are interfertile are so small as to make the entire phenomenon miraculous.[33]

D. THEOLOGICAL ACCEPTANCE OF POLYGENISM

Some Christian theologians have accepted polygenism, integrating it with their interpretation of Genesis. Dale Moody has contended that the mark placed on Cain (Gen. 4:15), the law of blood revenge (Gen. 4:15), the need for identifying Cain's wife as someone other than his sister, Cain's building of the city of Enoch (Gen. 4:17), and the 8,000- to 10,000-year age of certain excavated cities, Jericho being the oldest, necessitate the existence of other human beings contemporaneous with Adam, Eve, Cain, and Abel. Furthermore, Moody has differentiated collective Adam (Gen. 1:1–2:4a, P source), representative Adam (Gen. 2:4b–3:24, JE source), and individual Adam (Genesis 4, J source).[34] Whereas some advocates of pre-Adamism hold that the pre-Adamites or hominids died out before the Adam of Genesis 2 lived, Moody and polygeneticists hold to the contemporaneity of many stocks of *Homo sapiens* from pluralistic evolutionary origins.

E. ANTHROPOLOGY'S SHIFT AWAY FROM POLYGENISM

Pearce, writing in 1976, reported on the basis of works by anthropologists W. le Gros Clark, Raymond Firth, R. J. Harrison, L. C. Dunn, and Th. Dobzhansky that "the variety of races who live on earth now, are all descended from one stock, namely, the more recent *Homo sapiens*."[35] But even in 1923 H. J. T. Johnson, having noted that the peak of the controversy between monogenists and polygenists had occurred during the 1860s and 1870s, was reporting that "the old controversy . . . has now

32. Ibid., pp. 307-8.
33. Ibid., p. 306.
34. *The Word of Truth*, pp. 200-202.
35. *Who Was Adam?*, p. 14.

largely died down, the palm of victory appearing to rest with" the monogenists.[36]

III. THE UNITY OF HUMANKIND

The third issue pertaining to human beings created in the image of God is that of the fundamental unity of humankind in view of racial or ethnic differences among humans and of the phenomenon usually called "racism." On this issue Christian theology interacts with ethnology and sociology.

A. BIBLICAL MATERIALS

Already in this chapter reference has been made to the generational tables of Gen. 5:1-32, 10:1-32, and 11:10-32 and to the "of one" statement by Paul the apostle (Acts 17:26a). To these must now be added the account of the confusion of languages and scattering of peoples from the Tower of Babel (Gen. 11:1-9).

B. DIFFERING RACES OF HUMANKIND

It has been widely held during the modern era that humankind may be divided into basic races or ethnic families such as the Caucasian, Mongoloid, and Negroid, and that these races may be differentiated by basic physical characteristics, if indeed not also by other characteristics. Of special interest to Christians and to Jews are the questions as to whether the Bible contains any teaching that bears directly on the origin and nature of racial diversity and, whether or not, how racial diversity is to be related to basic human unity.

Some Christian theologians and historians have concluded that neither early Genesis nor any other part of the Bible provides specific data concerning racial differences among human beings. John William Dawson regarded Genesis 10 as a historical account of migrations from Sumer of the Chaldeans to places in western Asia, eastern Europe, and northern Africa that takes no account of later migrations and deals with no physical characteristics of different races, though it implies resemblances in language despite Gen. 11:1- 9.[37] According to Theophilus Goldridge Pinches (1856-1934), Genesis 10 was limited to what could be "obtained from merchants, travelers, envoys, and ambassadors" and did not intend to embrace all humankind.[38] For H. J. T. Johnson, the Caucasian, the Negroid, and the Mongolian races had "nothing to do with the Semitic,

---

36. *Anthropology and the Fall*, pp. 35-36.
37. *The Meeting-Place of Geology and History* (New York: Fleming H. Revell Company, 1894), pp. 186-88.
38. "Table of Nations," *The International Standard Bible Encylopedia*, 1939 ed., 5:2898-2900.

Japhetic and Hamitic . . . ones in Genesis 10."[39] Bernard Ramm concluded that the Bible presents no clear, unambiguous account as to the origin of races or of racial diversity among human beings. He rejected any "effort to derive the races of the entire world from Noah's sons or the Table of Nations." "It is a pious fiction to believe that Noah had a black son, a brown son, and a white son." Genesis 10 "gives no hint to any Negroid or Mongoloid peoples," and hence Noah's descendants "were all Caucasian as far as can be determined."[40]

On the other hand, Arthur C. Custance (1910-) has more recently revived and elaborated a theory that is built on the principle that early Genesis does specifically teach about the origin of racial diversity among human beings. Accordingly, Genesis 10 is said to be "a completely authentic statement of how the present world population originated and spread after the Flood in the three families headed respectively by Shem, Ham, and Japheth." Custance has also insisted that to each of these "families" of humankind was given a special responsibility for humankind, namely, "the spiritual" to the Shemites, "the physical" or technological to the Hamites, and "the intellectual" to the Japhethites, and that this division of responsibility is both recognized in the Bible and confirmed by later history. This means also that, for Custance, "all the so-called colored races—the 'yellow,' 'red,' 'brown,' and 'black'—the Mongoloid and the Negroid" were derived from Ham.[41]

Most probably Christian authors will continue to set forth differing views of the relation of early Genesis to racial differences, and the same is very likely to be true of the various scientific explanations of racial or ethnic differences.[42] However curious we may be about the issue and however much we may wish to find some widely agreed upon conclusions, it should be recognized that the phenomenon that is called "racism" poses more pressing problems for Christians and for churches today than the origin of the races.

C. RACISM'S DENIAL OR OBSCURING OF THE UNITY OF HUMANKIND

Although some contemporary conflicts between human groups are basically economic, linguistic, or religious rather than racial, racism has posed special problems, partly because it has rested on ideologies of superior and inferior races, and has threatened seriously the fundamental unity of humankind that derives from the doctrine of the creation of human beings. Racism expresses itself in diverse forms, but the most

---

39. *The Bible and Early Man,* pp. 120, 122.

40. *The Christian View of Science and Scripture,* pp. 337, 336.

41. *Noah's Three Sons: Human History in Three Dimensions,* vol. 1, The Doorway Papers (Grand Rapids: Zondervan, 1975), pp. 12-14.

42. See, for example, the genetic explanation of racism in William C. Boyd, *Genetics and the Races of Man: An Introduction to Modern Physical Anthropology* (Boston: Little, Brown and Company, 1950), esp. ch. 7.

potent and serious form in the history of the West has been white-black
racism. The fact that the ideology basic to much white-black racism has
been rejected by millions of people today does not eliminate the need for
understanding the arguments for racism that have been set forth in the
past, including those which invoked biblical authority in their behalf.
Human slavery of black people and later segregation of white and black
races were defended on the basis of certain specific arguments, which may
be summarized as follows:

1. Negroes or blacks do not have human souls. Josiah Priest
defended this view in 1852.[43] Augustine Verot (1804-76), the Roman
Catholic bishop of Savannah, Georgia, told the bishops of Vatican Council I (1869-70) that it was "more important to declare that black people
have souls—there were those in his part of the world who denied it—than
to struggle with recondite German philosophical theories about the
makeup of the human composite."[44]

2. Negroes or blacks constitute "another species of man," for Adam
is thought to have been "the father of only the white race."[45]

3. Negroes or blacks are reckoned to be "two-footed beasts" who
went into Noah's ark as animals, not as humans.[46]

That these first three arguments can rest on no biblical base and are
indeed false should be evident, and hence specific refutation is not necessary. But with the next three arguments, which have been associated with
specific biblical texts, refutation will be in order.

4. Negroes or blacks are under the curse of Cain. The mark placed
on Cain (Gen. 4:13-15) is taken to mean that Cain was a slave and turned
black.[47] Such an interpretation ignores the protective purpose for the mark
that is mentioned in the text, assumes without evidence that Cain became
a slave, and assumes without evidence that Cain became a black person.

5. Negroes or blacks are under the curse of Ham (Gen. 9:20-27).
Erickson has summarized this argument on the basis of its defense in 1861:

> ... Ham was born black; hence his descendants are the black race. A curse
> was placed upon Ham because of his wickedness; the curse involved the
> servitude of Ham's son Canaan to the descendants of Shem and Japheth.
> Thus all blacks are to be understood as under the curse of God, and slavery
> is justified because God intended it.[48]

43. *Bible Defense of Slavery: Origin, Fortunes and History of the Negro Race* (5th ed.;
Glasgow, Ky.: W. S. Brown, 1852), p. 33, as cited by Erickson, *Christian Theology*, p. 542.

44. James J. Hennesey, S.J., *American Catholics: A History of the Roman Catholic Community in the United States* (New York: Oxford University Press, 1981), p. 170.

45. W. S. Jenkins, *Pro-Slavery Thought in the Old South* (Chapel Hill: University of North
Carolina Press, 1935), p. 272, as cited by Erickson, *Christian Theology*, p. 543.

46. Ariel (Buckner H. Payne), *The Negro: What Is His Ethnological Status?* (2d ed.;
Cincinnati, 1867), pp. 45-46, as cited by Erickson, *Christian Theology*, p. 543.

47. Jenkins, *Pro-Slavery Thought in the Old South*, p. 119, as cited by Erickson, *Christian
Theology*, p. 543.

48. *Christian Theology*, pp. 542-43, based on Thornton Stringfellow, *Slavery: Its Origin,
Nature, and History Considered in the Light of Bible Teaching, Moral Justice, and Political Wisdom*

Charles Everett Tilson (1923-) in 1958 enumerated five faulty assumptions in the pro-slavery, segregationist interpretation of Gen. 9:20-27. First, it wrongly assumed "that God pronounced the curse," when it was pronounced by the drunken Noah (vv. 24-27). Second, it dubiously assumed "that the curse be biologically transferable," when Ezek. 18:20 would seem to speak to the contrary. Third, it faultily concluded that Ham was "the original victim of the curse," even though Ham's name does not appear in v. 25 and Canaan, whose name does appear, was "one of Ham's four children." Fourth, it questionably assumed "that the children of the original victim of the curse be slaves," when in fact "Canaan's descendants dominated the whole land of Palestine until long after the death of Moses, and Jerusalem, which took its name from Canaan's son Jebus, remained in Canaanite hands until David led Israel in its capture" 17 centuries after Noah. Fifth, it unjustifiably assumed "that the original victim of the curse be a member of the Negroid race." Tilson cited W. F. Albright as authority for the conclusion that all peoples associated with the Old Testament setting were Caucasian with the exception of the Cushites, or Ethiopians.[49]

6. Negroes or blacks should be segregated because the confusion of tongues (Gen. 11:1-9) was an act of God's providence designed "to frustrate the mistaken efforts of godless men to assure the permanent integration of the peoples of the earth."[50] Tilson pointed out four faulty assumptions with such interpretation of the text. First, it wrongly assumed "that God inflicted the confusion of tongues on men as a penalty for their attempt at racial integration." The event at Babel was not an attempted integration of ethnic or racial divisions. It involved concentrated human vanity and pride (v. 4) and was really an "attempted integration of God and man." Second, it doubtfully assumed "that the existence of linguistic differences denotes progress among men." Third, it also dubiously assumed "that linguistic differences and racial differences are coextensive." Fourth, it questionably assumed that the principal divisions among human beings after the Fall were "along racial lines."[51]

Such exegesis of texts in early Genesis in behalf of racism stands as a monumental example of genuine eisegesis, or reading into the text one's presuppositions, biases, and prejudices instead of reading out of the text its intended meaning. Fortunately such interpretation no longer elicits many advocates. The Civil Rights movement in the United States during the 1960s brought an end to legal segregation of and discrimination against blacks; this nonviolent revolution had as its ideologue and leader

---

(New York: J. F. Trow, 1861), p. 35. See also John L. Dagg, *The Elements of Moral Science* (New York: Sheldon and Company, 1860), pp. 338ff.

49. *Segregation and the Bible* (New York: Abingdon Press), pp. 23-27.

50. G. T. Gillespie, *A Christian View on Segregation* (Winona, Miss.: Association of Citizens' Councils, 1954), p. 9, as cited by Tilson, *Segregation and the Bible*, p. 27.

51. Tilson, *Segregation and the Bible*, pp. 27-28.

a Baptist minister, Martin Luther King, Jr. (1929-1968).[52] The African-American Muslims, however, in their early history embodied antiwhite black racism,[53] and during the 1980s resurgent white supremist racism in the United States has been allied with British Israel teaching.[54] In South Africa the system of *apartheid* still remains, and the Dutch Reformed church bodies in that nation did not until the latter 1980s declare it morally wrong and biblically indefensible.

D. Unity of Humankind by Virtue of Creation

Whatever explanation we may offer for the differentiation of humankind into "races," we ought not to obscure or deny the basic biblical emphasis on the unity or oneness of the whole of humankind under God. The oneness of the Creator is matched in biblical thought by the oneness of the human creatures. All who have been made in the image of God have more in common than they have in distinction from one another.

Furthermore, the alienation of persons within differing races from those in other races and the consequent oppression and conflict belong to the doctrine of sin. The reconciliation of such persons and such groups belongs to the doctrine of reconciliation through Jesus Christ. The fellowship of such persons and groups in and through Jesus Christ as Lord belongs to the doctrine of the church. Here the doctrine of creation forms the base and the limit of the discussion.

We have probed three issues pertaining to the Christian doctrine of humankind: the antiquity of humankind on the earth, whether greater or lesser; the origin of human beings, whether plural or singular; and the unity of humankind despite the diversity of racial characteristics and the impact of racism. Now we turn to the nature of human beings as male and female.

52. Kenneth L. Smith and Ira G. Zepp, Jr., *Search for the Beloved Community: The Thinking of Martin Luther King, Jr.* (Valley Forge, Pa.: Judson Press, 1974), esp. pp. 119-40; Ervin Smith, *The Ethics of Martin Luther King, Jr.*, vol. 2, Studies in American Religion (Lewiston, N.Y.: Edwin Mellen Press, 1981), esp. pp. 121-26; John J. Anstro, *Martin Luther King, Jr.: The Making of a Mind* (Maryknoll, N.Y.: Orbis Books, 1982), esp. pp. 106-9, 187-97, 240-50.

53. Robert L. Uzzel, "The Nation of Islam: Belief and Practice in Light of the American Constitutional Principle of Religious Liberty" (M.A. thesis, Baylor University, 1976).

54. J. Gordon Melton, *Encyclopedic Handbook of Cults in America*, Garland Reference Library of Social Science, vol. 213 (New York: Garland Publishing Inc., 1986), pp. 53-61.

CHAPTER 32

Man and Woman

American Protestant theologians during the nineteenth and the first half of the twentieth centuries almost without exception did not include in their systematic theologies any section concerning man and woman, presumably because the topic was not deemed to be germane to or essential for systematic theology. A noteworthy exception to this pattern was Francis Pieper, the Missouri Synod Lutheran, who refuted the view that women do not possess the image and strongly defended the subordination of women to men "even before the Fall," arguing that Americans must accept the biblical teaching on subordination as universally applicable and not as merely part of the Bible's Oriental culture.[1]

Karl Barth[2] and Emil Brunner[3] did give serious attention to the subject of man and woman in their systematic theologies, especially in the context of the image of God in human beings, and their treatments may have stimulated other theologians to include the topic in their systems. Two Baptist theologians writing during the 1980s, Dale Moody[4] and Millard J. Erickson,[5] have treated the topic, and the same is true of other writing theologians.[6]

In the study of the *imago Dei* above,[7] we made mention of the juxtaposition of male and female and the image of God in Gen. 1:27. Now we must consider the topic of maleness and femaleness itself. If admittedly such a topic belongs to Christian ethics, one may ask whether it also belongs to Christian theology. If maleness and femaleness are God-derived and God-ordained, then an affirmative answer is in order.

---

1. *Christian Dogmatics*, 1:523-26.
2. *Church Dogmatics*, III/1, pp. 288-329; III/2, trans. Harold Knight, G. W. Bromiley, J. K. S. Reid, and R. H. Fuller (Edinburgh: T. and T. Clark, 1960), pp. 285-324.
3. *The Christian Doctrine of Creation and Redemption*, pp. 63-65.
4. *The Word of Truth*, pp. 212-25.
5. *Christian Theology*, pp. 545-49.
6. Richard Rice, *The Reign of God*, pp. 105-9; J. Rodney Williams, *Renewal Theology*, pp. 203-6.
7. See above, Ch. 30, I, A, 1.

I. BIBLICAL PASSAGES

A. Old Testament

In the first creation account God is said to have created human beings as male and female (Gen. 1:27). According to the second creation account, the man's need for a "helper" was genuine, God formed woman (ʾiššâ) from a rib of man (ʾîš), and the intended pattern was set forth: "Therefore a man leaves his father and his mother and cleaves to his wife, and they become one flesh" (Gen. 2:18, 20b-24, esp. 24, RSV). "Adam lay with his wife Eve, and she became pregnant and gave birth to Cain. She said, 'With the help of the LORD I have brought forth a man'" (Gen. 4:1, NIV). The creation of "man" as "male and female" and in "the likeness of God" was reiterated in Gen. 5:1-2. The seventh commandment in the Jewish and Protestant sequence was: "You shall not commit adultery" (Exod. 20:14, RSV; par. Deut. 5:18). The Mosaic allowance of a "bill of divorce" was described in Deut. 24:1-4 (RSV):

> When a man takes a wife and marries her, if then she finds no favor in his eyes because he has found some indecency in her, and he writes her a bill of divorce and puts it in her hand and sends her out of his house, and she departs out of his house, and if she goes and becomes another man's wife, and the latter husband dislikes her and writes her a bill of divorce and puts it in her hand and sends her out of his house, or if the latter husband dies, who took her to be his wife, then her former husband, who sent her away, may not take her again to be his wife, after she has been defiled; for that is an abomination before the LORD. . . .

The good wife and mother was described and celebrated in Prov. 31:10-31, esp. vv. 10-12, 28-31 (RSV):

> A good wife who can find?
> She is far more precious than jewels.
> The heart of her husband trusts in her,
> and he will have no lack of gain.
> She does him good, and not harm,
> all the days of her life. . . .
> Her children rise up and call her blessed;
> her husband also, and he praises her:
> "Many women have done excellently,
> but you surpass them all."
> Charm is deceitful, and beauty is vain,
> but a woman who fears the LORD is to be praised.
> Give her of the fruit of her hands,
> and let her works praise her in the gates.

B. New Testament

When certain Pharisees queried Jesus as to whether it was " 'lawful to divorce one's wife for any cause,'" he replied: "Have you not read that

he who made them from the beginning made them male and female...?"
After quoting Gen. 2:24, Jesus commented: "So they are no longer two but
one [flesh]. What God has joined together, let no man put asunder" (Matt.
19:3-6, RSV).

The Pharisees put another question to him:

> "Why then," they asked, "did Moses command that a man give his wife a
> certificate of divorce and send her away?" Jesus replied, "Moses permitted
> you to divorce your wives because your hearts were hard. But it was not
> this way from the beginning. I tell you that anyone who divorces his wife,
> except for marital unfaithfulness,[8] and marries another woman commits
> adultery."

Jesus' disciples concluded from this teaching that " 'it is better not to
marry.' "

> Jesus replied, "Not everyone can accept this word, but only those to whom
> it has been given. For some are eunuchs because they were born that way;
> others were made that way by men; and others have renounced marriage
> because of the kingdom of heaven. The one who can accept this should
> accept it." (Matt. 19:7-12, NIV)

According to Paul, the unity of believers in Christ transcends the
diversity of maleness and femaleness (Gal. 3:28). The same apostle advised the Corinthian Christians:

> It is good for a man not to marry. But since there is so much immorality,
> each man should have his own wife, and each woman her own husband.
> The husband should fulfill his marital duty to his wife, and likewise the wife
> to her husband. In the same way, the husband's body does not belong to
> him alone but also to his wife. Do not deprive each other except by mutual
> consent and for a time, so that you may devote yourselves to prayer. Then
> come together again so that Satan will not tempt you because of your lack
> of self-control. I say this as a concession, not as a command. (1 Cor. 7:1b-6)

It is good for the unmarried and for widows to remain unmarried, but
they should marry if they do not have self-control (1 Cor. 7:8-9). The
separating wife should either remain unmarried or be reconciled to her
husband, and he should not divorce her (1 Cor. 7:10-11). A believer should
stay married to an unbelieving spouse if the spouse should be willing, but
if the unbelieving spouse should leave, the believer "is not bound" (1 Cor.
7:12-16, NIV). Paul encouraged virgins to remain single because of the
shortness of time and because those who are single can be more un-
dividedly devoted to "the Lord's affairs" (1 Cor. 7:25-35, NIV). Marriage
is acceptable, but the single life may be even a better choice (1 Cor. 7:36-
38). Even so widows are free to marry believing men (1 Cor. 7:39-40). Paul
based his instruction that believing women, but not men, should be veiled
when they pray or prophesy in public on the principle that the man is
"head" of the woman and "woman is the glory of man," woman being

---

8. Mark 10:11 does not contain such a phrase.

made "from" man and "for" man (1 Cor. 11:2-16, RSV). Having rebuked
sexual immorality among believers (Eph. 5:3-7), Paul admonished wives
to be submissive to their husbands as their "head," even as the church
submits to Christ, and husbands to have self-giving love for their wives,
even "as Christ loved the church and gave himself up for her" (Eph.
5:22-33, NIV). A similar admonition is given in Col. 3:18-19, and in Tit.
2:4-5 young women are instructed to love their husbands and children
and to be submissive to their husbands. A comparable wife-husband
instruction is given in 1 Pet. 3:1-7, except that it calls on wives not to major
on outward adornments and to live in such a manner that their unbelieving husbands may come to believe in Christ.

II. THEOLOGICAL INTERPRETATION

The issues raised and the insights gained concerning man and woman
throughout the history of the Christian church can be combined with the
contemporary issues and teachings in a single coordinated treatment.

A. MALENESS/FEMALENESS AND THE IMAGE OF GOD

The differentiation and relationship of man and woman, particularly as husband and wife, even as Karl Barth himself acknowledged, is
not to be equated fully with the *imago Dei*. Barth regarded the I-thou
relationship, rather than bisexuality, as that which constitutes the *imago
Dei*.[9] The man/woman differentiation/relationship with its sex polarity
is not the totality of human distinctiveness, though it is indeed part of it.[10]
We have already concluded that the juxtaposition of "male and female"
and "image" and "likeness" in Gen. 1:27 suggests the meaningful association of the two motifs.[11] The female was clearly created in the image of
God, as was the male (Gen. 1:27; 5:1-2).

The true and desired relationship between husband and wife points
to the reality of "existence in community," or fellowship, in contrast to the
reality of utter individualism. In order to be able to love, " 'man' has to be
created as a *pair* of human beings."[12] Creation as male and female is the
natural basis for potentially the truest I-thou relation among human
beings. But, to be sure, genuine *agapē* is expressible apart from the
marriage relationship and without the admixture of *erōs*. Dale Moody has
written of "the primacy of the social over the sexual."[13]

---

9. *Church Dogmatics*, III/1, pp. 195-97.
10. Brunner, *The Christian Doctrine of Creation and Redemption*, p. 63.
11. See above, Ch. 30, II, F.
12. Brunner, *The Christian Doctrine of Creation and Redemption*, p. 64.
13. *The Word of Truth*, pp. 214, 217.

B. REFUTATION OF ANDROGYNY

The existence of human beings as male and female, beginning with creation itself, stands in opposition to androgyny, or the alleged bisexual or nonsexual character of the earliest human beings.

The concept of androgyny stems from Plato's myth of Androgyny, the word itself being derived from *andros*, "male," and *gynē*, "female." Plato[14] "described a monster with four arms and four legs" who created "anxiety in Zeus, who split Androgyny into two halves with a bolt from the blue and a threat to quarter him." Then there was "a longing (*erōs*, sexual love) that tried to unite the two halves as man frantically looked for his 'better half.'"[15] Something akin to androgyny was accepted by certain of the Greek Church Fathers, especially Gregory of Nyssa, who held to "a double creation of our nature, one to express the divine similarity, the other to distinguish the sexes,"[16] whereas the Latin Fathers did not embrace such. Paul King Jewett has explained this difference of attitude toward androgyny on the basis that the Greek Fathers interpreted sin as sensuality rather than pride and made sexual lust to be the chief example of sensuality.[17] In the medieval West it seems that androgyny was taught by Duns Scotus,[18] and in the seventeenth century Jacob Boehme (1575-1624) taught it.[19] On the American frontier George Rapp (1757-1847), the founder of communities at Harmony, Indiana, and Economy, Pennsylvania, held to the view that Adam was created as an androgynous being and that the separation of Adam and Eve was the "true fall" of humanity.[20] Modern Eastern Orthodox writers have taught androgyny. Vladimir S. Solovyev (1853-1900) is thought to have inclined to androgyny, but such is difficult to find in his writings.[21] Nicolai Berdyaev accepted androgyny, including the idea that the two sexes resulted from the fall of humankind.

> Man is not only a sexual but a bisexual being, combining the masculine and the feminine principle in himself in different proportions and often in fierce conflict. A man in whom the feminine principle was completely absent

14. *Symposium* 189a-193d.

15. Moody, *The Word of Truth*, p. 215.

16. Ernest V. McClear, S.J., "The Fall of Man and Original Sin in the Theology of Gregory of Nyssa," *Theological Studies* 9 (1948):179-81, based on Gregory of Nyssa, *On the Making of Man* 16-18, 22.

17. *Man as Male and Female: A Study in Sexual Relationships from a Theological Point of View* (Grand Rapids: Eerdmans, 1975), pp. 25-26.

18. Niebuhr, *The Nature and Destiny of Man*, 1:184.

19. Franz Hartmann, *Jacob Boehme: Life and Doctrines* (Blauvelt, N.Y.: Rudolf Steiner Publications, 1977; 1st publ. in 1891), pp. 153-63; John Joseph Stoudt, *Jacob Boehme: His Life and Thought* (New York: Seabury Press, 1968; 1st publ. in 1957), pp. 259-70; David Walsh, *The Mysticism of Innerworldly Fulfillment*, University of Florida Monographs, Humanities, no. 53 (Gainesville: University of Florida Press, 1983), pp. 20, 28-29, 35, 74, 94-96.

20. Melton, *Biographical Dictionary of American Cult and Sect Leaders*, pp. 230-31.

21. See especially *The Meaning of Love*, trans. Jane Marshall (London: Geoffrey Bles, 1946).

would be an abstract being, completely severed from the cosmic element. A woman in whom the masculine principle was completely absent would not be a personality. The masculine principle is essentially personal and anthropological. The feminine principle is essentially communal and cosmic. It is only the union of these two principles that constitutes a complete human being. . . . While man remains a sexual being he cannot live in peace and harmony. . . . Original sin is connected in the first instance with division into two sexes and the Fall of the androgyn, i.e. of man as a complete being.[22]

Androgyny as a teaching is Platonic in origin, not biblical, and cannot be harmonized with Gen. 1:26-27 and 5:1-2. According to Genesis maleness and femaleness stem from creation, not from the fall. However human beings misuse and abuse their sexuality and that of others, sexual differentiation must not be reckoned as sin.

C. MONOGAMY AND PARENTHOOD

In the Old and the New Testaments monogamous marriage, with the exclusion of polygamous occurrences in the Old Testament,[23] which subsequently became the norm in Islam, was reckoned to be the divinely ordained pattern for marriage and the rightful matrix for the begetting and rearing of children.

Even anthropological scientists now are declaring that primitive peoples practiced monogamy rather than promiscuity, as certain earlier anthropologists had held.[24]

The actualization of the ideal of monogamy has become increasingly difficult in Western societies, wherein divorce, cohabitation apart from marriage, and homosexual practice abound. Consequently there are serious difficulties in the parental upbringing of children.

Increasing world population and what is reckoned as overpopulation in certain very populous nations have led to measures to limit the begetting of children.[25] The same pattern of limitation has been chosen by married persons for whom overpopulation is not the primary factor. Various forms of contraception have been developed and utilized to prevent conception as the result of sexual intercourse. The Roman Catholic Church has officially banned all such methods except the so-called natural method of abstinence during ovulation.[26] Even Catholics, however, are not choosing to reject all other methods.

---

22. *The Destiny of Man,* trans. Natalie Duddington (4th ed.; London: Geoffrey Bles, 1954), pp. 61-62, 64.

23. For example, Abraham, Jacob, David, and Solomon.

24. Pearce, *Who Was Adam?*, pp. 75-77.

25. For example, the effort in the People's Republic of China to limit each married couple to one child.

26. Pope Paul VI, *Humanae Vitae,* 25 July 1968, *Acta Apostolicae Sedis,* 60:481-503.

D. SINGLE STATE AS VALID BUT NOT ABOVE OR BELOW MARRIAGE

Virginity as an expression of the single state was approved by the apostle Paul (1 Cor. 7:25-35), especially in view of eschatological suffering. The single state needs to be recognized and respected today, and churches need to minister effectively to the needs of single persons.

The Catholic tradition, especially its Roman Catholic aspect, early came to embrace and insist on the exaltation of virginity above marriage. Jerome and his sympathizers were the vanguard in the exaltation of virginity. Unfortunately the fourth-century protest of Helvidius, Jerome's contemporary who rejected the new doctrine of the perpetual virginity of Mary, and the protest of Jovinian, another contemporary of Jerome, that virginity should not be elevated above marriage were not heeded by Latin Christianity as a whole.[27] Celibacy, or one's inability to contract marriage, came to be required of all the clergy in the West after the eleventh century. Today, despite an increasing shortage of (male) priests and an increasing willingness of women to assume roles in ministry, the requirement of a male celibate clergy remains, and neither married deacons nor women in religious orders can celebrate mass.[28] It is difficult to press the eschatologically oriented counsel of Paul (1 Corinthians 7) into a universal mandate for all ordained ministers of the gospel. Moreover, Paul's question in 1 Cor. 9:5 (RSV), "Do we [Barnabas and Paul] not have the right to be accompanied by a wife, as the other apostles and brothers of the Lord and Cephas?" anticipated an affirmative answer and stands against any required celibacy for ministry. Church history gives evidence that required clerical celibacy has not always been accompanied by virginity. Any continued defense of a mandatory celibate clergy must be based on pragmatic or prudential considerations rather than biblical theology.

The Church of Jesus Christ of Latter-day Saints, on the other hand, by its doctrine of celestial marriage, or sealing for eternity, has exalted marriage above the single state to the denigration of the latter. A woman cannot hope to attain to the highest of the three Mormon heavenly states and have "eternal increase" without being sealed to a man. Celestial marriage, therefore, serves as a quasi-sacrament with salvific results for women; without it neither men nor women can become "gods," but only "angels."[29]

The single state should not be exalted above marriage so that

---

27. Moody, *The Word of Truth,* p. 221.

28. Pope Paul VI, *Sacerdotalis caelibatus,* 24 June 1967, *Acta Apostolicae Sedis,* 59:657-97; and John-Baptist Villiger, *The Celibacy of the Priest in the Course of the Church History,* trans. Leo Alfred Schwander (Johannesburg: Premier Typographers Ltd., 1983?), made available by James D. Niedergeses, the Roman Catholic bishop of Nashville.

29. *Doctrine and Covenants* (1925 ed.), 132:15-22; Roy W. Doxey, *Prophecies and Prophetic Promises from the Doctrine and Covenants* (Salt Lake City: Deseret Book Company, 1970), pp. 165-74; LeGrand Richards, *A Marvelous Work and a Wonder,* pp. 193-202.

marriage is seen as an inferior state, and marriage should not be exalted above the single state so that the latter is reckoned as an inferior state. Human beings should be free to make voluntary and responsible decisions as to their entry into and continuance in these states.

E. CONJUGAL LOVE

The realization of conjugal love by a husband and a wife, as well as the propagation and upbringing of children, is a major and legitimate purpose of monogamous marriage. It enhances the seriousness of adultery, it helps to explain why both polygamy/polyandry and homosexual practice are contrary to the divine intention for human beings, and it is distorted and perverted by pornography.

Roman Catholic moral theology prior to Vatican Council II stressed almost exclusively the begetting and rearing of children as *the primary*, if not the sole, purpose of marriage. *The Pastoral Constitution on the Church in the Modern World,* adopted by Vatican Council II, elevated to a plane of equality with such a purpose the realization of conjugal love.[30]

Conjugal love in its truest sense is an expression of genuine affection between and mutual commitment of responsible persons who have given themselves to each other in the bond of marriage. Adultery—and indeed much sexual activity outside marriage—may be seen as an unwarranted distortion of the affection and denial of the commitment and may also prove to be, at least partly, the use of man or woman as a "thing" for self-gratification.[31]

The Mormon doctrine of celestial marriage, or sealing for eternity, may seem to non-Mormons in the light of Mormon history to have been in its earliest expression an extension of the teaching and practice of polygamy and in its later expression a substitute for the practice of polygamy, which practice was officially discouraged by church leaders under pressure from the United States government in 1890.[32]

Conjugal love cannot be rightly sundered from the God-ordained function of procreation (" 'be fruitful and multiply,' " Gen. 1:28b). Homosexual practice constitutes a fundamental sundering, whereby the possibility of procreation is excluded. Such practice reflects the fallenness

---

30. Pt. 2, ch. 1, para. 49, in Flannery, gen. ed., *Vatican Council II: The Conciliar and Post-Conciliar Documents,* pp. 952-53.

31. See an abridgment of the early Protestant treatise, Henry Bullinger, *The Christen State of Matrimonye* (1539), in James Leo Garrett, Jr., ed., *Calvin and the Reformed Tradition,* Broadman Christian Classics (Nashville: Broadman Press, 1980), pp. 92-121.

32. William J. Whalen, *The Latter-day Saints in the Modern World: An Account of Contemporary Mormonism* (New York: John Day Company, 1963), pp. 118-38; Gordon R. Lewis, *The Bible, the Christian, and the Latter-day Saints* (n.p.p.: Presbyterian and Reformed Publishing Company, 1966), pp. 9-10; Harry L. Ropp, *The Mormon Papers: Are the Mormon Scriptures Reliable?* (Downers Grove, Ill.: InterVarsity Press, 1977), p. 66. Non-Mormon authors writing about the Mormon faith have often cited the contrast between the disapproval of the polygamies of David and Solomon in the *Book of Mormon* (Jacob 1:15; 2:24) and the approval of David's polygamy in *Doctrine and Covenants* 132:38-39.

of human beings and of the sinful social order, not the design and intention of the Creator. The growing problem as to how to respond to homosexuals and homosexual practice has become a divisive issue in churches and denominations, especially the mainline Protestant denominations.[33] John R. W. Stott has summarized the biblical prohibitions against homosexual practice as follows: (1) The stories of Sodom (Gen. 19:1-13) and of Gibeah (Judges 19) regard it as forbidden. (2) There are Levitical prohibitions (Lev. 18:22; 20:13). (3) Homosexual practice as contrary to nature is listed among the sins of the Gentile world (Rom. 1:26-27). (4) The inclusion of "male prostitutes" *(malakoi)* and "homosexual offenders" *(arsenokoitai)* among the sins that will prevent the inheritance of the kingdom of God (1 Cor. 6:9-10) and that are against both law and gospel (1 Tim. 1:9-11) would seem to be conclusive.[34.]

Conjugal love is grossly distorted and perverted in the commercialized pornography that has proliferated in Western societies during recent years. By its glorification of perverted sexual activity such pornography threatens as well the monogamous family, and especially the Christian family. Eroticism in its bizarre extremes is presented as the summum bonum of human life, thereby blinding the consumers to the nature of *agapē*, which in the Christian understanding must always be preeminent over *erōs*.[35]

F. Worth and Status of Women

Although both the Old and the New Testaments are set in the context of patriarchal societies with strong emphasis on male dominance, the Bible affords no little evidence of the significance of women in salvation history. In the Old Testament Miriam, Deborah, and Esther had leadership roles. Jesus' attitude toward women may be seen in reference to the adulterous Samaritan woman, the woman with a hemorrhage, the Syro-Phoenician woman, Mary and Martha, and Mary Magdalene. The response of women to Jesus may be seen in Mary, Elizabeth, and Anna. Paul recognized such women as Phoebe and Priscilla as leaders.[36]

---

33. Don Williams, *The Bond That Breaks: Will Homosexuality Split the Church?* (Los Angeles: BIM, Inc., 1978). Williams insisted that the study of homosexuality should begin with the Bible, not with biology, psychology, and sociology, that the biblical study should commence with Gen. 1–3, not with the passages specifically mentioning homosexual activity, and that the gospel offers forgiveness and power for change to homosexuals.

34. *Homosexual Partnerships? Why Same-Sex Relationships Are Not a Christian Option* (Downers Grove, Ill.: InterVarsity Press, 1987), pp. 6-13.

35. John W. Drakeford and Jack Hamm, *Pornography: The Sexual Mirage* (Nashville: Thomas Nelson Inc., 1973); Andrea Dworkin, *Pornography: Men Possessing Women* (New York: G. P. Putnam's Sons, 1979); John H. Court, *Pornography: A Christian Critique* (Downers Grove, Ill.: InterVarsity Press; Exeter, U.K.: Paternoster Press, 1980); Tom Minnery, ed., *Pornography: A Human Tragedy* (Wheaton, Ill.: Christianity Today, Inc., 1986).

36. Erickson, *Christian Theology*, pp. 547-49. Note especially the role of women in the ministry of Jesus and in the primitive church according to Luke-Acts (Moody, *The Word of Truth*, pp. 218, 225).

Across the centuries Christianity has served to elevate, even if slowly, the recognized worth and status of womanhood in contrast to woman's quite inferior and almost servile role in many primitive and non-Christian societies.[37] This long-term elevation of womanly worth and status is an extension, if at times altogether unconsciously, of the "neither male nor female" of Gal. 3:28. This elevation has gone even beyond those limitations on Christian womanhood that are reflected in the Pauline epistles (e.g., 1 Cor. 14:33-36 and 1 Tim. 2:11-15).

Despite worldwide trends toward the recognition of the worth and personhood of women and toward the attainment by women of greater civic and economic opportunities, there is also in Western societies a serious criminal trend toward greater abuse of and brutality toward women.

The present-day Women's Liberation movement, so far as it draws from Judaism and Christianity and from the principles of political democracy, may serve the good purpose of seeking and obtaining much-deserved civic equality and nondiscriminatory economic opportunity for women and protection from personal abuse. But, insofar as it draws on naturalistic, humanistic, antimonogamous, antifamilial, antimaternal, de-feminizing, and lesbian presuppositions, it may serve the evil and anti-Christian purpose of downgrading the particularities of womanhood and woman's complementarity vis-à-vis man and of undermining the strength of the monogamous family at a most crucial time in social and religious history.

The status of the woman as wife in marriage has become a controversial issue toward the end of the twentieth century among Evangelical Protestants. The crucial issue has been the subordination of wives to husbands as mandated by Paul, and divisions have arisen as to the obligation of Christian wives to be subordinate today or as to the degree of subordination. First, the traditional approach to this issue has been to emphasize and insist on subordination of wives to husbands by stressing the meaning of the verb *hypotassein*, "to place under," "to be subject to," "to submit to," or "to keep one's place," used six times by Paul and once by Peter. Female or wifely subordination in such a traditional view has tended to be based on the assumed inferiority of the woman, rooted in man's having been created first according to Genesis 2, in Eve's being tempted by the serpent and tempting Adam, or in some other consideration. The traditional view seldom gives attention to the implications of Gen. 1:26-27 for the marriage relationship. It majors on a hierarchy of being: God, Christ, husband, and wife. Second, Paul King Jewett has rejected the hierarchical and subordinationist view on the grounds that

37. One wonders whether the anthropological claims for primitive matriarchal societies have been pressed beyond the evidence; for example, the late Stone Age village near Xi'an in the People's Republic of China.

Paul used rabbinic hermeneutics for understanding Genesis 2, that female subordination *"breaks the analogy of faith"* (Genesis 1, Jesus' attitude toward and relations to women, and Gal. 3:28), and that Christians must now do for the Pauline wifely subordination texts what in the recent past they did with the Pauline slave-master texts, namely, reinterpret them in view of the abolition of slavery.[38] Third, Karl Barth taught that both male and female are in the image of God and affirmed that women are both structurally and functionally different from men but sought to retain an aspect of wifely subordination on the basis that such subordination, being unique, is primarily to the Lord Jesus and only secondarily to the husband and is without any notion of female inferiority.[39] The third view, though not without its difficulties, seems to point toward a resolution of the contemporary issue.

G. Noneternality of Marriage

The existence of humankind in the relation of husbands and wives is seemingly not intended to be for eternity. Jesus taught: "For in the resurrection they neither marry nor are given in marriage, but are like angels in heaven" (Matt. 22:30, RSV). One should be careful to conclude that it is marriage, not sexuality, that is to disappear in eternity.[40] Even Augustine of Hippo taught that women would rise in the resurrection as women, not as men, and that their femininity would evoke the praise of God rather than masculine lust. He argued that "They shall not be given in marriage" is applicable only to females and that "Neither shall they marry" is applicable only to males.[41] A contrary position is to be found in the Latter-day Saints' doctrine of celestial marriage, or sealing for eternity.[42]

In this chapter we have made an effort to relate man and woman to the image of God, to the theory of androgyny, to monogamy and parenthood, to virginity and singleness, to conjugal love, to the worth and status of women, and to the heavenly state. We have not dealt with the important contemporary configuration of issues and concerns about divorce and remarriage but have left it to its proper and detailed treatment by Christian ethicists. We will treat the important contemporary issue as to the role of women in the church and its ministry and mission in Chapter 75.

38. *Man as Male and Female,* pp. 129-49.
39. *Church Dogmatics,* III/2, pp. 309-16. Jewett, *Man as Male and Female,* pp. 82-86, has offered a critique of Barth's interpretation.
40. Jewett, *Man as Male and Female,* pp. 40-43.
41. *On the City of God* 22.17.
42. See above, II, D.

CHAPTER 33

Constituents of the Human: Human Beings as Soul, Spirit, Flesh, Body, Heart, Mind, and the Like

A few authors have named the study of the theological significance of biblical terms such as soul, spirit, flesh, body, heart, and the like "biblical psychology."[1] Such a name, however, is too exclusively related by derivation to one of these terms, namely, soul, to serve adequately as the general name. Although there seems to be little agreement concerning an alternative, it may suffice to refer to these biblical terms and their diverse meanings as "constituents of the human."

At the outset one needs to realize that from the perspective of the Old Testament and the New Testament writings there is no undisputed, official list of such terms, even though some terms may be reckoned as major terms and other terms as minor terms merely on the basis of frequency or paucity of usages in the biblical writings. Indeed, it may be an open question as to whether the ancient Hebrews and the later Christians used these terms to connote separate elements or parts in human beings or used them as separate vantage points from which to view human beings in their entirety. Furthermore, twentieth-century Christians should be mindful of the philosophical and cultural influences that have affected the usage and meaning of these terms during the history of Christianity. Hence our study must begin with a careful examination of the biblical terms and their usages.

I. BIBLICAL TERMS FOR HUMAN BEINGS AND THEIR USAGES

The purpose of the present study will be to identify the biblical terms, to determine their specific and varied meanings as used in the two testa-

---

1. Franz Delitzsch, *A System of Biblical Psychology*, trans. Robert Ernest Wallis (Edinburgh: T. and T. Clark, 1899; reprint ed.; Grand Rapids: Baker Book House, 1966).

430

ments, and to draw certain general conclusions about these biblical terms prior to any more general theorizing about how they ought to be used in the present. In this undertaking we will make extensive use of the research of Myrtle Edith Wood (1921-).[2]

A. THE OLD TESTAMENT

1. The Term Nepeš, *Meaning "Breath" or "Soul" or "Life"*

Four distinct usages of this Old Testament term can be identified. First, probably the most basic meaning was that of personal and physical life that is terminated in death. "And as her [Rachel's] *soul* was departing (for she died), she called his name Benoni, but his father called his name Benjamin" (Gen. 35:18, RSV). "But if there is serious injury, you are to take *life* for *life*" (Exod. 21:23a, NIV). "And the LORD said to Satan, 'Behold, he is in your power; only spare his *life*' " (Job 2:6, RSV).

Second, *nepeš* had psychical usages expressive of feelings, emotion, desire, and appetite. The brothers of Joseph confessed, " 'In truth we are guilty concerning our brother, in that we saw the distress of his *soul* . . .' " (Gen. 42:21, RSV). Of the Servant of Yahweh it was said: "After the suffering of his *soul*, he will see the light of life and be satisfied" (Isa. 53:11a, NIV).

Third, *nepeš* could refer to a living person or to living persons in totality. According to Gen. 2:7, RSV, "the LORD God formed man of dust from the ground, and breathed into his nostrils the breath of life; and man became a living *being*." "And Abram took . . . the *persons* that they had gotten in Haran; and they set forth to go to the land of Canaan" (Gen. 12:5, RSV). Surely Abram did not take their incorporeal souls and leave their bodies in Haran! "And the king of Sodom said to Abram, 'Give me the *persons*, but take the goods for yourself' " (Gen. 14:21, RSV).

Fourth, *nepeš* at times could be a circumlocution or a substitute for a personal pronoun. Jacob instructed Esau: "And make me savoury meat, such as I love, and bring it to me, that I may eat; that my *soul* may bless thee before I die" (Gen. 27:4, KJV). "If a *person* sins because he does not speak up when he hears a public charge to testify . . . , he will be held responsible" (Lev. 5:1, NIV). "If one *person* sins unwittingly, he shall offer a female goat a year old for a sin offering" (Num. 15:27, RSV). Job asked: " 'Was not my *soul* grieved for the poor?' " (30:25b, RSV). In this usage *nepeš* was virtually a synonym for "self" or "I" or "anyone who."

In these Old Testament texts one does not find the later philosophical sense of "soul" as an animating principle or as a noncorporeal nature that will survive the body, that is, after death. Rather its usages are focused on personal, physical life now.

2. "The Usage of the Psychological Terms Psuche, Soma, Sarx, and Pneuma in the New Testament, as Based on Their Old Testament Equivalents" (Th.D. diss., Southwestern Baptist Theological Seminary, 1953).

2. *The Term* Rû(a)ḥ, *Meaning "Wind" or "Spirit"*

In the Old Testament this word was applied to God, to nature, and to human beings, and here the concern is for the third of these. First, *rû(a)ḥ* was used frequently in a psychical sense to refer to human attitudes or dispositions. Pharaoh's "*spirit* was troubled," and hence he "called for all the magicians of Egypt and all its wise men" (Gen. 41:8a, RSV). Num. 5:14 (RSV) refers to "the *spirit* of jealousy" that comes on a husband who suspects his wife of adultery. When the queen of Sheba had seen "all the wisdom" and the wealth of Solomon, "there was no more *spirit* in her" (1 Kings 10:5, RSV), that is, she was amazed. According to Proverbs, "he that is hasty of *spirit* exalteth folly" (KJV), and "he who rules his *spirit* [is better] than he who takes a city" (RSV) (14:29b; 16:32b). "The sacrifice acceptable to God is a broken *spirit*" (Ps. 51:17a, RSV), and God dwells "with him who is of a contrite and humble *spirit*" (Isa. 57:15b, RSV).

Second, *rû(a)ḥ* at times meant the directing energy or will in human beings. In the building of the tabernacle "they came, every one whose heart stirred him, and every one whose *spirit* moved him, and brought the LORD's offering" (Exod. 35:21a, RSV). The sovereign Yahweh declared: " 'Woe to the foolish prophets who follow their own *spirit* and have seen nothing' " (Ezek. 13:3, RSV, NIV).

Third, the word *rû(a)ḥ,* when it was used as a parallel to the Hebrew term for "heart," often served as an equivalent to the modern term "mind." The LORD desired that Israelites "not be like their fathers, . . . a generation whose heart was not steadfast, whose *spirit* was not faithful to God" (Ps. 78:8, RSV). "Cast away from you all the transgressions which you have committed against me, and get yourselves a new heart and a new *spirit*" (Ezek. 18:31, RSV).

Fourth, *rû(a)ḥ* was used for life-breath or vitality, and in such usages it was a synonym for *nepeš*. When Samson drank water, "his *spirit* returned, and he revived" (Judg. 15:19b, RSV). Of idols the psalmist declared: "nor is there any *breath* in their mouths" (135:17d, RSV). Concerning the valley of dry bones Yahweh promised: " 'I will cause *breath* to enter you, and you shall live' " (Ezek. 37:5). According to Gen. 6:7 animals also possess *rû(a)ḥ,* or "the breath of life."

3. *The Term* Bāśār, *Normally Translated "Flesh" but Literally the Muscular Portions of the Body*

First, *bāśār* could be used for one's spouse or for marriage or for consanguinity. Adam spoke of Eve as " 'flesh of my flesh' " (Gen. 2:23a), and human marriage was designed that a man should "be united to his wife, and they . . . become one flesh" (Gen. 2:24b, NIV). The brothers of Joseph decided to sell him to the Ishmaelites rather than kill him, " 'for he is our brother, our own *flesh*' " (Gen. 37:27, RSV). According to Hebrew legislation an Israelite who had become the slave of an alien could be redeemed by his "uncle or a cousin or any *blood relative* [KJV, "nigh of kin"] in his clan" (Lev. 25:49a, NIV).

Second, *bāśār*, like *nepeš*, was sometimes used in lieu of a personal pronoun. The psalmist declared: "my *flesh* faints for thee, as in a dry and weary land where no water is" (63:1b, RSV), and "my heart and *flesh* sing for joy to the living God" (84:2b, RSV).

Third, *bāśār* was used to connote living, created beings in contrast to God the Creator. The corruption of "all flesh" in Gen. 6:12b and the Noahic covenant with "all *flesh*" (Gen. 8:17) included only human beings, whereas the death of "all flesh" by flood (Gen. 7:21) included animals as well. The voice calling for the preparation of the Lord's way announced that his glory would be revealed and that "all *flesh* shall see it together" (Isa. 40:5, RSV).

In the Old Testament *bāśār* is never suggestive of inherent evil. Rather it conveys the ideas of weakness, frailty, and perishableness (Isa. 40:6-8).

4. No General Term for Body

The Old Testament has no general or comprehensive term for "body." The word *g^ešēm* is sometimes translated "bodies," but its use is largely confined to Daniel (3:27-28; 4:30; 5:21; 7:11). Other words may be more accurately rendered "back" or "carcass."

5. The Term Lēb or Lēbāb, Meaning "Heart"

The Hebrew *lēb* meant the center of a person's thought and will, not the center of emotions or feelings. This meaning can be seen in the words, "the imagination of the thoughts of his *heart*" (Gen. 6:5; RSV; see also 8:21), in the declaration, " 'I will harden his [Pharaoh's] *heart*' " (Exod. 4:21, RSV; see also 7:3), and in the statement, "The fool has said in his *heart*" (Ps. 14:1; 53:1).

But *lēb* was also used to mean a human disposition, as may be seen in the following texts: "whosoever [is] of a willing *heart*" (Exod. 35:5b, RSV); "Give . . . thy servant an understanding *heart*" (1 Kings 3:9); "God gave Solomon . . . largeness of *heart*" (1 Kings 4:29); "the rest also of Israel [were] of one *heart*' " (1 Chr. 12:38), and "A new *heart* also will I give you" (Ezek. 36:26a).

6. The Term K^elāyôt, Meaning "Kidneys"

The Old Testament uses *k^elāyôt* to refer to the seat of consciousness in human beings. The KJV preserved a literal translation, whereas most modern versions employ a modern equivalent: "for the righteous God trieth the hearts and *reins*" (Ps. 7:9, KJV); "Examine me, O LORD, and prove me; try my *reins* and my heart" (Ps. 26:2); "Thus my heart was grieved, and I was pricked in my *reins*" (Ps. 73:21). *K^elāyôt* could even be used in lieu of the personal pronoun: "Yea, my *reins* rejoice, when thy lips speak right things" (Prov. 23:16).

7. *The Term* Mē'îm, *Meaning "Bowels"*

Occasionally the Old Testament employs *mē'îm* for the seat of compassion or mercy. Again one finds that the KJV is quite literal and that modern versions have sought contemporary terms: of Ephraim it was said: "therefore my *bowels* are troubled for him" (Jer. 31:20c, KJV); "Behold, O LORD; for I am in distress: my *bowels* are troubled; mine heart is turned within me; for I have grievously rebelled . . ." (Lam. 1:20a; see also 2:11a).

Certain conclusions can be drawn concerning the Old Testament terms for human beings and their usages. *Nepeš* and *rû(a)ḥ,* although both used at times to connote vitality, were not fully synonymous. A person was not a *rû(a)ḥ* so much as he possessed *rû(a)ḥ. Rû(a)ḥ* was the life-force of God that makes a person alive. Both *nepeš* and *bāśār* were used of human beings in a holistic sense, the former from an individual or personal perspective and the latter from the standpoint of humankind's creaturely finitude. They were correlatives, not antitheses. The Hebrews, strictly speaking, did not view human beings as composed of two distinct parts or three distinct parts. Neither *nepeš* nor *rû(a)ḥ* was used to refer to immaterial or noncorporeal existence after death.

B. The Old Testament Apocrypha and Pseudepigrapha

All the books in this literature reflect the terms and concepts found in the canonical Old Testament with three exceptions:

1. Wisdom of Solomon (first century B.C.), in which the immortality of human "souls" was assumed (3:1-9; 4:7-11; 5:15-16), and possibly the preexistence of human souls was taught (8:19-20);

2. 2 (Slavonic) Enoch (first century A.D.), which taught the (Platonic) preexistence of souls (23:5); and

3. 4 Maccabees (first century A.D.), in which the Hebrew patriarchs were said to "live unto God" (7:19), the seven Jewish brothers put to death under Antiochus Epiphanes were said to have a "soul" that could not be killed (10:4), "immortality" (14:5), "eternal life" (15:3), and "immortal life" (16:13) and to "live unto God" (16:25), the mother of the seven was said to have the "hope" of "endurance" (17:4), and Antiochus himself to be punished after death (12:19, 13:15).[3]

C. The New Testament

1. *The Term* Psychē, *Meaning "Soul" or "Life"*

This term had uses similar to those of *nepeš* in the Old Testament. First, it was used to refer to human life or vitality up to death. Jesus asked, following the healing of a man with a withered hand, " 'Is it lawful on the

---

3. No effort is made here to include changing concepts of Sheol or of the resurrection, which are eschatological topics, in the intertestamental writings.

Sabbath . . . to save *life* or to kill?' " (Mark 3:4, RSV). He admonished: " 'do not be anxious about your *life*' " (Matt. 6:25a), and in the parable of the rich fool the word from God was: " 'Fool, this night your *soul* is required of you' " (Luke 12:20a). Of Barnabas and Paul the Jerusalem church wrote that they " 'have risked their *lives* for the sake of our Lord Jesus Christ' " (Acts 15:26).

Second, *psychē* could refer to living persons in their totality. On the Day of Pentecost there were added to the church in Jerusalem "about three thousand *souls*" (Acts 2:41b, RSV). "Let every *person*," Paul wrote, "be subject to the governing authorities" (Rom. 13:1a). In Noah's ark "eight *persons*" were "saved through water" (1 Pet. 3:20b).

Third, *psychē* sometimes meant life in its totality. According to Jesus, " 'a man's *life* does not consist in the abundance of his possessions' " (Luke 12:15, RSV). The early company of believers "were of one heart and *soul*" (Acts 4:32), and Paul desired to hear that the Philippian Christians "stand firm in one spirit with one *mind* striving side by side for the faith of the gospel" (Phil. 1:27b).

Fourth, *psychē*, like *nepeš* and *bāśār*, sometimes meant the self in lieu of the personal pronoun. In the Magnificat Mary declared: "My *soul* magnifies the Lord" (Luke 1:46, RSV). Matthew quoted an Isaianic passage about Yahweh's servant in which Yahweh referred to " 'my beloved with whom my *soul* is well pleased' " (12:18b), and in Gethsemane Jesus said to Peter, James, and John: " 'My *soul* is very sorrowful, even to death' " (Matt. 26:38a).

Fifth, at times *psychē* was connected with salvation in such a way as to suggest life, or one's total being. The "implanted word" "is able to save your *souls*" (Jas. 1:21b, RSV), and "the outcome of your faith" is that "you obtain the salvation of your *souls*" (1 Pet. 1:9).

Sixth, in a usage that goes beyond the Old Testament, *psychē* could refer to continued or restored life after death, this being in the teachings of Jesus. " 'And do not fear those who kill the body but cannot kill the *soul*; rather fear him who can destroy both *soul* and body in hell' " (Matt. 10:28, RSV). " 'He who finds his *life* will lose it, and he who loses his life for my sake will find it' " (Matt. 10:39). " 'For whoever would save his *life* will lose it, and whoever loses his life for my sake will find it' " (Matt. 16:25).

2. *The Term* Pneuma, *Meaning "Spirit" and Also "Wind" or "Breath"*

In the New Testament *pneuma* was used of God, of suprahuman beings, and of human beings; it is the third of these that is the present focus. First, *pneuma* could mean vitality or life-breath, especially when yielded in death. Jesus prayed: " 'Father, into thy hands I commit my *spirit!*' And having said this he breathed his last" (Luke 23:46, RSV). Similarly, Stephen requested, " 'Lord Jesus, receive my *spirit*' " (Acts 7:59b).

Second, *pneuma* could refer to human dispositions or attitudes. Paul's "*spirit* was provoked within him" upon seeing the idolatry of Athens (Acts 17:16, RSV), and according to Peter, Christian wives are to be adorned "with the imperishable jewel of a gentle and quiet *spirit*" (1 Pet. 3:4b).

Third, *pneuma*, like *psychē*, occasionally was the Hebrew substitute for the personal pronoun: " 'my *spirit* rejoices in God my Savior' " (Luke 1:47, RSV).

Fourth, *pneuma* could refer to mind or mental and emotional energy. "Jesus, perceiving in his *spirit* that they thus questioned within themselves, said ..." (Mark 2:8a, RSV), and "he sighed deeply in his *spirit*, and said, " 'Why does this generation seek a sign?' " (Mark 8:12a).

3. The Term Sarx, Meaning "Flesh"

Comparable to the Hebrew *bāśār*, *sarx* had various uses in the New Testament. First, it referred to humanity in contrast to God. This contrast heightens the significance of the incarnation ("And the Word became *flesh*," John 1:14a) and of the new birth ("That which is born of the *flesh* is *flesh*," John 3:6a, RSV). The incarnate Son was given "power over all *flesh*" (John 17:2a), and God promised to " 'pour out' " his Spirit " 'upon all *flesh*' " (Acts 2:17; see Joel 2:28). According to Paul, "no *human being* will be justified in his [God's] sight by works of the law" (Rom. 3:20a).

Second, when joined together with "blood," *sarx* referred to that which was essentially human. According to Jesus, " '*flesh* and blood has not revealed this to you' " (Matt. 16:17b, RSV). For Paul "*flesh* and blood cannot inherit the kingdom of God" but only those who will have "put on immortality" (1 Cor. 15:50, 53), and in the Christian warfare we are "not contending against *flesh* and blood" (Eph. 6:12a).

Third, *sarx* was at times used to refer to the material of the human body. Jesus taught: " 'the bread which I shall give for the life of the world is my *flesh*' " (John 6:51c, RSV). Indeed, human beings can enter the heavenly "sanctuary" "by the new and living way which he opened for us through the curtain, that is, through his *flesh*" (Heb. 10:20). Paul's allusion to a "thorn" given to him "in the *flesh*" (2 Cor. 12:7) is usually given a physical interpretation.

Fourth, *sarx* could refer to the way of sin as opposed to the way of God. "To set the mind on the *flesh* is death. ... For the mind that is set on the *flesh* is hostile to God ... and those who are in the *flesh* cannot please God" (Rom. 8:6-8, RSV).

4. The Term Sōma, Meaning "Body"

Lacking any full parallel in the Old Testament, *sōma* had diverse usages in the New Testament. First, *sōma* could be used to refer to a human corpse. Joseph of Arimathea asked Pilate "for the *body* of Jesus" and "took the *body*, and wrapped it. . . , and laid it in his own new tomb" (Matt. 27:58-60a, RSV). Peter, "then turning to the *body* [of Tabitha or Dorcas] ... said, 'Tabitha, rise' " (Acts 9:40b).

Second, *sōma* at times meant a human person at or near death. Believers "have been sanctified through the offering of the *body* of Jesus Christ once for all" (Heb. 10:10, RSV), and Paul hypothesized, "if I deliver my *body* to be burned" (1 Cor. 13:3b).

Third, *sōma* sometimes referred to the physical nature of human beings in the present. " 'Your eye is the lamp of your *body*; when your eye is sound, your whole *body* is full of light; but when it is not sound, your *body* is full of darkness' " (Luke 11:34, RSV). "For the wife does not rule over her own *body*, but the husband does; likewise, the husband does not rule over his *body*, but the wife does" (1 Cor. 7:4).

Fourth, occasionally *sōma* meant the physical involvement of human beings in sin: "Therefore, God gave them up in the lusts of their hearts to impurity, to the dishonoring of their *bodies* among themselves" (Rom. 1:24, RSV).

Fifth, *sōma* could refer in the teaching of Jesus to human beings after death: " 'it is better that you lose one of your members than that your whole *body* be thrown into hell' " (Matt. 5:29b, RSV), and " 'rather fear him who can destroy both soul and *body* in hell' " (Matt. 10:28b).

5. *The Term* Kardia, *Meaning "Heart"*

Kardia seems to refer to the seat of thought and will or decision-making in humans, not to the seat of emotions. Jesus taught that " 'the pure in *heart* . . . shall see God' " (Matt. 5:8, RSV) and that " 'where your treasure is, there will your *heart* be also' " (Matt. 6:21). The commandment to love God included loving him " 'with all your *heart*' " (Matt. 22:37). In the Pauline delineation of sin among Gentiles it was said that "their foolish *heart* was darkened" (Rom. 1:21b, KJV). On hearing Peter's sermon on the Day of Pentecost his hearers "were cut to the *heart*, and said to Peter and the rest of the apostles, 'Brethren, what shall we do?' " (Acts 2:37, RSV). Moreover, "man believes with his *heart* and so is justified, and he confesses with his lips and so is saved" (Rom. 10:10).

6. *The Term* Splanchna, *Meaning "Bowels"*

Parallel to the Old Testament usage is the Pauline use of *splanchna* as the seat of compassion or mercy; therefore the KJV rendered the term literally in contrast to the modern preference for paraphrase. To the Philippians Paul wrote: "For God is my record, how greatly I long after you all in the *bowels* of Jesus Christ" (1:8, KJV; see also 2:1). He admonished the Colossians: "Put on then, as God's chosen ones, holy and beloved, *bowels* of mercy" (3:12). In sending Onesimus back to Philemon, Paul wrote: "thou therefore receive him, that is, my own *bowels*" (v. 12).

7. The Term Nephros, Meaning "Kidneys"

Once in the New Testament *nephros* is used of humans: in the letter to the church at Thyatira God is said to be the one who "searcheth the *reins* and hearts" (Rev. 2:23b, KJV).

8. The Term Nous, Meaning "Mind"

Nous was almost exclusively a Pauline term and seems to have connoted the will as much or more than the intellect. On the one hand Paul wrote of serving "the law of God with my *mind*" (Rom. 7:25b, RSV; also v. 23), and on the other hand of being "captive to the law of sin" (Rom. 7:23b) and serving "the law of sin" "with my flesh" (Rom. 7:25c). Believers are to "be transformed by the renewal of your *mind*" (Rom. 12:2b), "renewed in the spirit of your *minds*" (Eph. 4:23), "united in the same *mind*" (1 Cor. 1:10c), and "convinced in his own *mind*" about divisive questions (Rom. 14:5b). See also Rev. 17:9a. All these uses of *nous* are positive in nature. Paul also used *nous* negatively. He referred to "a base *mind*" (Rom. 1:28b, RSV), "the futility of their [Gentile] *minds*" (Eph. 4:17b), those who are "depraved in *mind*" (1 Tim. 6:5a), and "*minds*" that "are corrupted" (Tit. 1:15c; see also 2 Tim. 3:8c).

9. The Term Dianoia, Meaning "Mind"

Dianoia, conveying the idea of mind or intellect, could be used positively or negatively. Loving God according to the second, new commandment included loving him "with all your *mind*" (Mark 12:30c, RSV, and par.). In quoting from Jer. 31:33, Heb. 8:10b and 10:16b state: " 'I will put my laws into their *minds*' " and " 'I will . . . write them on their *minds*.' " Believers are to "gird up their *minds*" (1 Pet. 1:13a), and apostolic letters are supposed to "have aroused" the "sincere *mind*" of the recipients "by way of reminder" (2 Pet. 3:1). In a negative vein Paul referred to those who had followed "the [evil] desires of body and *mind*" (Eph. 2:3b) and "once were estranged and hostile in *mind*, doing evil deeds" (Col. 1:21).

10. The Term Noēma, Meaning "Mind" or "Thought"

Paul used *noēma* both negatively and positively. Characteristic of Jews who read Moses with veiled face was the fact that "their *minds* were hardened" (2 Cor. 3:14a, RSV). Indeed, "the god of this world has blinded the *minds* of the unbelievers" (2 Cor. 4:4a), and even believers may find that their "*thoughts* will be led astray from a sincere and pure devotion to Christ" (2 Cor. 11:3b). But "the peace of God . . . will keep" believers' "hearts and *minds* in Christ Jesus" (Phil. 4:7).[4]

Certain conclusions can now be drawn concerning the New Testament terms for human beings and their usages. The terms *psychē, pneuma,*

---

4. The term "conscience" will be treated as an aspect of the consciousness of sin. See below, Ch. 37, II, A, 1.

and *sarx* were employed in ways quite similar to the Old Testament usage of *nepeš, rû(a)ḥ,* and *bāśār,* but there were distinctive uses such as *psychē* in reference to continued or restored life after death and *sarx* in the sense of the way of sin. *Sōma* as a general term with diverse uses had no Old Testament parallel. *Kardia, splanchna,* and *nephros* were used in ways quite consonant with the Old Testament use of parallel terms. The use of *nous, dianoia,* and *noēma,* however, represented a distinctive New Testament pattern, and such usage has been commonly ascribed to Greek or Hellenistic influence.

The study of the various uses of the terms that biblical writers applied to human beings has showed that these terms are somewhat nontechnical, that the uses of a single biblical word can be diverse, and that there are meanings common to more than one word. The Hebrew-oriented biblical writers referred to human beings by using numerous words. Those words were not intended, it seems, to compartmentalize humans into intricate subdivisions, and thus later Christians desiring to prove that there are two parts or three parts to human existence tend to ignore some of the biblical usages or to bend the biblical texts to their own theories. The Hebrew mind was more given to thinking of human life in holistic ways, and thus the various terms applied to human beings were more like different windows through which humans could be viewed than like pieces of a pie that has been cut.

In moving from the ancient world of the Bible to the late twentieth century in respect to the constituents of the human it is necessary to take into account the major influences on and expressions of human existence during the history of Christianity.

II. POSTBIBLICAL USAGE OF BIBLICAL TERMS FOR HUMAN BEINGS

The Christian doctrine of humankind was from the patristic age heavily influenced by Greek or Hellenistic thought. The entire Western Christian theological tradition has continued to reflect that influence, although the Eastern Christian tradition, especially in its Greek and Russian forms, has been even more completely influenced by the Hellenistic thought-world. Such influence has shaped the way in which Christians have understood the biblical terms for human beings as well as shaping the way in which Western Christians have theologized about those aspects of the human which are considered to be essential to human existence. Some of the leading questions and concepts in the Western Christian understanding of the human can best be understood within the framework of that Hellenistic influence.

A. SPECIFIC RESULTS OF THE CONTINUING HELLENISTIC INFLUENCE
   ON THE CHRISTIAN DOCTRINE OF THE CONSTITUENTS OF THE
   HUMAN

The Hellenistic influence on the Christian understanding of human
beings was marked by a strong soul-body dualism and by the substitution
of *nous* (mind) for *psychē* (soul).

1. The Lingering Concept of the Body as Evil

Beginning in the patristic age the view that the human body is
inherently or essentially evil began to permeate Christian thought, even
though the view was more Hellenistic and Gnostic than Christian. Inferred from this view of the body was the corollary that the body needs
to be suppressed or punished for the well-being of the human soul or
spirit. This corollary in turn was embraced by monastic and ascetic
movements within Christian history. Paul's statements about "the flesh"
as the way of sin were read as meaning the human body per se. Somewhat
like tritheism, which has lingered on the fringes of Christianity as a
recurring danger, the concept of the body as evil has lingered on so as to
lure a few to become its advocates.

2. The Soul as Chiefly a Metaphysical Entity with the Consequent
Question as to Its Origin

Another instance of Hellenistic influence has been the tendency of
Christian theologians and philosophers to regard the soul as a metaphysical entity, being of greater value than the body, and almost never in the
Old Testament senses of the life-breath or vitality within humans or the
very selfhood of human beings.

Consequently, the distinct origin of each human soul came to be
regarded as a major theological question, and theories as to the origin came
to be set forth and defended. There have been three major theories as to the
origin of human souls, and their respective advocates seem not to have
succeeded in their efforts to locate, quote, and utilize specific biblical texts
to support their theories.[5] Let us now examine the three theories.

a. Preexistence of Souls

Origen of Alexandria/Caesarea taught the eternal preexistence of a
company of spirits or souls waiting to become incarnate as angels, demons, or human beings.[6] After Origen's death his view was severely
questioned, and nearly three centuries after his death it was condemned
by imperial and conciliar authority.[7] The preexistence theory has not

5. Berkouwer, *Man: The Image of God*, pp. 295-99.
6. *On First Principles* 2.9.1, 6.
7. Emperor Justinian wrote "Fifteen Anathemas against Origen," art. 1 of which dealt
with preexistence of souls, and these presumably were adopted by the Synod of Constanti-

gained any considerable following during later Christian history, although a German theologian, Julius Müller (1801-78) did embrace it, not because he thought it was taught in the Bible but in order the better to explain human inborn sinfulness.[8]

b. Direct Divine Creationism

This is the theory that God directly creates each human soul at conception or early in the development of the fetus. It has had numerous exponents throughout the history of Christianity.

In the second century Irenaeus wrote: "But, as each one of us receives his body through the skillful working of God, so does he possess his soul."[9] At the turn of the fourth century Lactantius declared:

Therefore the manner of the production of souls belongs entirely to God alone. . . . [Indeed] souls are not given by parents, but by one and the same God and Father of all, who alone has the law and method of their birth.[10]

Pelagius also taught direct divine creation of souls.[11] Thomas Aquinas in the thirteenth century taught that human rational souls are not produced by the angels or by paternal semen but are created "immediately" by God. Each soul "begins to exist when the body does," and such daily creating by God is not inconsistent with God's rest (Gen. 2:2).[12]

Charles Hodge declared in 1873:

The common doctrine of the Church, and especially of the Reformed theologians, has ever been that the soul of the child is not generated or derived from the parents, but that it is created by the immediate agency of God.[13]

James P. Boyce, quoting favorably Hodge's arguments in detail, contended that the most weighty argument against the derivation of souls from parents was the recognition "that the idea of propagation of souls involves their materiality."[14] Henry C. Sheldon favored direct creationism but allowed that a yet unrealized combination of direct creationism and derivation from parents would be better.[15] In 1950 Pope Pius XII noted that "Catholic faith obliges us to hold that the human soul is immediately created by God."[16]

---

nople (543), according to Charles Joseph Hefele, *A History of the Councils of the Church*, trans. William R. Clark, 5 vols. (Edinburgh: T. and T. Clark, 1883, 1894-96), 4:221-28, esp. 225.

8. *The Christian Doctrine of Sin*, trans. William Urwick, 2 vols. (Edinburgh: T. and T. Clark, 1868) 2:358-68.

9. *Against Heresies* 2.33.5 (ANF, 1:410-11).

10. *On the Workmanship of God* 19 (ANF, 7:298-99).

11. *Libellus fidei* 9 (Migne, PL, 45:1718).

12. *Summa Theologica* I.90.3; *Summa contra Gentiles* II.87.1-8; 88-89; 83; 84.6.

13. *Systematic Theology*, 2:70.

14. *Abstract of Systematic Theology* (1887 ed.), pp. 200-212.

15. *System of Christian Doctrine*, pp. 284-87.

16. *The Encyclical "Humani Generis,"* para. 37, p. 41.

c. Traducianism, or Generationism

Traducianism, a term derived from the Latin verb *traducere*, "to lead across," is the theory that the soul as well as the body of each human being is produced by natural generation, or the process of reproduction, so that one's soul derives from one's parents. It also has had numerous exponents throughout the history of Christianity.

Early in the third century Tertullian wrote:

> How, then, is a living being conceived? Is the substance of both body and soul formed together at one and the same time? Or does one of them precede the other in natural formation? We indeed maintain that both are conceived, and formed, and perfectly simultaneously, as well as born together; and that not a moment's interval occurs in their conception, so that a prior place can be assigned to either.... For although we shall allow that there are two kinds of seed—that of the body and that of the soul—we still declare that they are inseparable, and therefore contemporaneous and simultaneous in origin.[17]

According to Gregory of Nyssa, writing in the latter fourth century, "the seminal cause of our constitution is neither a soul without body, nor a body without soul, but that, from animate and living bodies, it is generated at the first as a living and animate being, and that our humanity takes it and cherishes it like a nursling with the resources she herself possesses...."[18]

During the seventeenth century John Milton taught traducianism, holding that direct creationism would mean that God would be much too busy with "a servile task" of creating souls and contending that the doctrine of original sin is supportive of the traducian view.[19] Augustus H. Strong argued for traducianism on four grounds: (a) it best accords with the Bible, especially the once-for-all divine inbreathing (Gen. 2:7) and God's cessation from the work of creation (Gen. 2:2); (b) it is consistent with "vegetable and animal life"; (c) it accords with the "observed transmission . . . of mental and spiritual" as well as "physical" "characteristics in families and races"; and (d) it "admits a divine concurrence throughout the whole development of the human species."[20] According to E. Y. Mullins, traducianism best accounts for "the universal tendency to sin," "the transmission of traits of character from parent to child," and "the unity of the [human] race."[21] H. C. Thiessen found traducianism to be in accord with Scripture, with theology, and with a substantial view of human nature.[22]

Not all Christian theologians have embraced or espoused one of these major theories. Augustine of Hippo was unable to decide finally

---

17. *A Treatise on the Soul* 27 (ANF, 3:207-8).
18. *On the Making of Man* 29 (NPNF, 2d ser., 5:426).
19. *Christian Doctrine*, bk. 1, ch. 1 (*Complete Prose Works of John Milton*, 6:319).
20. *Systematic Theology*, pp. 488-97, esp. 494-96.
21. *The Christian Religion in Its Doctrinal Expression*, pp. 263, 262.
22. *Lectures in Systematic Theology* pp. 233-37.

between direct creationism and traducianism. His Neo-Platonism would
have tended to draw him to the former, and his doctrine of original sin as
Adamic guilt would have tended to pull him to the latter. He even asked
for Jerome's help in resolving his dilemma.[23] G. C. Berkouwer has called
the creationist-traducianist debate "an unfruitful controversy" and an
"apparently hopeless controversy" because both views build on the soul
as a metaphysical substance "separate from the body."[24] Dale Moody has
called for a "dynamic traducianism that unites creation and procreation
in process," but his only clue as to how that goal can be attained is his
insistence that Berkouwer adopt "creative evolution."[25] After centuries of
debate and advocacy of these theories, the question has seldom been
raised as to whether the presuppositions of the debate are valid.

3. The Innate or Inherent Immortality of Each Human Soul

The third instance of Hellenistic influence on the Christian doctrine
of the constituents of the human is the concept that each human soul is
innately or inherently immortal. This concept has had many advocates
and, especially in the modern period, some opponents.

a. Advocacy of the Innate Immortality of Each Soul

Preceded by the teaching of Ambrose and Jerome,[26] Augustine of
Hippo expounded this theme in one of his early philosophical treatises.[27]
The Fifth Lateran Council (1512-17), in opposition to Pietro Pomponazzi
(1462-1525) and the humanistic Neo-Platonists of the fifteenth century,
condemned their view that "the rational soul in all men is numerically one
unique principle, and that only this general soul is immortal."[28] The
council, therefore, was indirectly teaching the individuality and immortality of human souls. John Calvin assumed the immortality of the individual soul and rejected the concept of a world soul.[29] Calvin seems to
have been influential in bringing about the widespread Protestant acceptance of the innate immortality of the soul. Hence it has been common
practice for Protestant and Catholic theologians to assume or to teach
explicitly the innate immortality of the soul of each human being.

b. Rejection of the Innate Immortality of Each Soul

Rejection has taken two major forms during the nineteenth and
twentieth centuries.

---

23. *Letter 166: To Jerome* (ACW, 30:6-31).
24. *Man: The Image of God*, pp. 279-309, esp. 292, 307; Moody, *The Word of Truth*, pp. 182-83.
25. *The Word of Truth*, p. 183.
26. Kelly, *Early Christian Doctrines*, p. 345.
27. *The Immortality of the Soul* (387).
28. Ludwig Ott, *Fundamentals of Catholic Dogma*, p. 98.
29. *Institutes of the Christian Religion* (1559 ed.), 1.5.5.

1) Rejection by Seventh-day Adventists and Jehovah's Witnesses and their advocacy of conditional immortality

Both these movements, holding that God only is immortal and hence humans cannot be innately immortal, have proceeded to the conclusion that all wicked human beings will be utterly or completely annihilated at death and that immortality will be bestowed by God on the righteous at the second coming of Jesus.[30]

The official Seventh-day Adventist teaching has been expressed in the ninth article of the "Fundamental Beliefs of Seventh-day Adventists":

> 9. That God "only hath immortality" (1 Tim. 6:16). Mortal man possesses a nature inherently sinful and dying. Eternal life is the gift of God through faith in Christ (Rom. 6:23). "He that hath the Son hath life" (1 John 5:12). Immortality is bestowed upon the righteous at the second coming of Christ, when the righteous dead are raised from the grave and the living righteous translated to meet the Lord. . . .[31]

The teaching of Jehovah's Witnesses has been expressed in an authoritative source: On the basis of 1 Tim. 1:17 and 6:16 it is concluded that "Jehovah God alone is the one that has always been immortal and really possesses immortality." Christians are supposed to seek immortality (Rom. 2:7; 1 Cor. 15:53-54). "Later Christ Jesus [who, according to Jehovah's Witnesses, is not the eternal Son of God] received immortality as a reward for his faithful course of action, and it is also given, as a reward, to those who are of the true church or 'body of Christ.'" Thus immortality "is a reward for faithfulness" and "does not come automatically at birth." Gen. 2:17 is clearly the death sentence passed on all the descendants of Adam, and the devil "originated the doctrine of the inherent immortality of the soul" (Gen. 3:4).[32]

One should note carefully that the rejection of innate immortality of human souls by these two movements is coupled with the teaching of the annihilation of all wicked or unbelieving humans at death, with the result that they cease to exist. "Eternal life" is equated with continued existence, and the biblical evidence for the consciousness of the wicked after death ignored.

2) Rejection by biblical theologians during the middle third of the twentieth century and by certain systematic theologians

These theologians concluded that, since the biblical writings regard the immortality of human beings—or the gift of "eternal life"—as given by God, the immortality of human beings ought not to be considered as

---

30. Anthony A. Hoekema, *The Four Major Cults: Christian Science, Jehovah's Witnesses, Mormonism, Seventh-day Adventism* (Grand Rapids: Eerdmans, 1963), pp. 136, 294-95.

31. *Seventh-day Adventist Encyclopedia* (rev. ed.; Washington, D.C.: Review and Herald Publishing Association, 1976), p. 396.

32. *"Let God Be True"* (Brooklyn, N.Y.: Watch Tower Bible and Tract Society, 1946), pp. 63-67.

innate or inherent, as Greek thought had done. Earlier Henry Wheeler Robinson (1872-1945) had written: "The Hebrew idea of personality is an animated body and not an incarnated soul."[33] Emil Brunner asserted that

> the doctrine of the immortality of the soul as a *substance,* is of Platonist, and not of Biblical origin. It is a result of the view that the human spirit is essentially 'divine.' . . . The essential destiny of man is not substantial immortality, but eternal life.[34]

Oscar Cullmann stated that Jesus, facing the cross, "cannot obtain his victory by simply living on as an immortal soul, thus fundamentally not dying." Rather, Jesus "can conquer death only by actually dying." Cullmann also commented that Paul on his missionary journeys "surely met people who were unable to believe in this preaching of the resurrection *for the very reason* that they believed in the immortality of the soul."[35] According to Derwyn Randulph Grier Owen (1914-), the Greek New Testament word for "eternal," *aiōnios,* means " 'having to do with the age to come.' " *Aiōnios* life is "an eschatological concept, developed from the Hebrew tradition, and not a metaphysical concept, borrowed from the Greek." Moreover, human beings' "personal unity can be called, as a whole, either *sōma* (body) or *psychē* (soul) or *sarx* (flesh) or *pneuma* (Spirit), depending on the point of view from which man is being considered."[36] Dale Moody, being sympathetic to the protest by biblical theologians, has declared that

> the historical theologies of the churches, both Catholic and Protestant, have followed a view of the soul that is supported neither by the Scriptures nor by science. Yet the dogmatism that is unable to admit error will continue to rant against the belief that the soul is the self. . . .[37]

The biblical and systematic theologians objecting to the concept of the innate immortality of human souls because it is seen as an alien Hellenistic idea have made their case against innate immortality more persuasively than they have explained what their own views of the states of righteous and wicked after death are. It has not been unmistakably clear as to how their views differ from the annihilationism of the Seventh-day Adventists and the Jehovah's Witnesses.

---

33. "Hebrew Psychology," in A. S. Peake, ed., *The People and the Book: Essays on the Old Testament* (Oxford: Oxford University Press, 1925), p. 362.

34. *The Christian Doctrine of Creation and Redemption,* p. 69.

35. *Immortality of the Soul or Resurrection of the Dead? The Witness of the New Testament* (New York: Macmillan, 1958), pp. 25, 59.

36. *Body and Soul: A Study on the Christian View of Man* (Philadelphia: Westminster Press, 1956), pp. 186, 187, 196.

37. *The Word of Truth,* p. 186.

B. Views about the Essential or Constituent Elements in Human Beings as Created

One other major topic needs to be addressed, namely, those theories or views concerning whether human existence should so be understood that constituent elements as distinct parts of human life can be identified. Although these theories are not unrelated to the Hellenistic influence on Christian doctrine, they can be treated in a broader context. We will now proceed to describe three major theories.

1. Trichotomy

Trichotomy is the theory that human beings consist of three distinct parts, namely, body, soul, and spirit. The word "trichotomy" is derived from two Greek words, *tricha*, meaning "three parts," and *temnein*, meaning "to cut."

Two New Testament passages are usually cited as proof-texts in support of this theory: Paul's statement, "May your whole *spirit, soul* and *body* be kept blameless at the coming of our Lord Jesus Christ" (1 Thess. 5:23, NIV), and the declaration, "For the word of God is living and active, sharper than any two-edged sword, piercing to the division of *soul* and *spirit*, of joints and marrow, and discerning the thoughts and intentions of the heart" (Heb. 4:12, RSV). Advocates of trichotomy may utilize as secondary support or at least as a parallel theme Paul's differentiation of "the natural man" (*psychikos. . .anthrōpos*), "the carnal [ones]" (*sarkikoi*), and "the spiritual man" (*ho pneumatikos*) in 1 Cor. 2:14, 3:3, and 2:15 (KJV, RSV).

Trichotomists often describe "spirit" as that which especially has come from or is like unto God and "soul" as the principle of life in human beings, or the animating principle.

First advocated by Greek Christian writers such as Origen,[38] Apollinaris of Laodicea (c. 310-c. 390),[39] and Didymus the Blind (c. 313-c. 398),[40] trichotomy came to be expressed by the fifth-century Semi-Pelagians in terms of "spirit" as being exempted from the total impact of Adamic sin.[41] Balthasar Hubmaier (1481-1528), a Catholic priest turned Anabaptist pastor, similarly differentiated "the will of the flesh," "the will of the soul," and "the will of the spirit," the last of which did not participate in the fall of humankind.[42] Henry Alford (1810-71) sharply differentiated the *psychē* as "the lower portion of man's invisible part, which he has in common

---

38. *On First Principles* 3.4; *Commentary on Matthew* 13.2.

39. *Apodeixis*, as cited by Quasten, *Patrology*, 3:379. But Kelly, *Early Christian Doctrines*, p. 292, is doubtful that Apollinaris was a trichotomist.

40. *De Spiritu Sancto* 55, in Migne, *PG*, 39:1080.

41. Delitzsch, *Biblical Psychology*, p. 106.

42. *On Free Will* (1527), in George H. Williams and Angel M. Mergal, eds., *Spiritual and Anabaptist Writers*, vol. 25, LCC (Philadelphia: Westminster Press, 1957), pp. 116, 117, 120.

with the brute," from the *pneuma*, "the higher portion, receptive of the Spirit of God."[43]

2. *Dichotomy*

Dichotomy is the theory that human beings consist of two distinct parts, namely, body and soul or spirit. The word "dichotomy" is derived from two Greek words, *dicha*, meaning "in two" or "asunder," and *temnein*, meaning "to cut."

More biblical texts have been cited in favor of dichotomy than in favor of trichotomy. The *locus classicus* is Gen. 2:7 (RSV): "then the LORD God formed man of *dust* from the ground, and breathed into his nostrils the breath of life; and man became a living *being* [or, *soul*]." Among the Old Testament passages that have been cited in support have been the following: Isa. 10:18b, c, "the LORD will destroy both *soul* and *body*"; Eccl. 12:7, "and the *dust* returns to the earth as it was, and the *spirit* returns to God who gave it"; and Job 32:8 and 33:4, in which *"spirit"* and *"breath"* are taken to be in synonymous parallelism. Among the New Testament passages cited have been the following: Luke 1:46-47, in which "my *soul*" and "my *spirit*" are understood to be in synonymous parallelism; Matt. 10:28b, "rather fear him who can destroy both *soul* and *body* in hell"; 1 Cor. 5:3, 5, "For though absent in *body* I am present in *spirit* . . . [and] you are to deliver this man to Satan for the destruction of the *flesh*, that his *spirit* may be saved in the day of the Lord Jesus"; 1 Cor. 7:34, the unmarried woman is "anxious" about "how to be holy in *body* and *spirit*"; 2 Cor. 7:1b, "let us cleanse ourselves from every defilement of *body* and *spirit*"; Rom. 8:10, "although your *bodies* are dead because of sin, your *spirits* are alive because of righteousness"; Eph. 2:3b, "following the desires of *body* and *mind*"; Col. 2:5a, "For though I am absent in *body*, yet I am with you in spirit"; Jas. 2:26, "For as the *body* apart from the *spirit* is dead, so faith apart from works is dead"; and 3 John 2, "Beloved, I pray that all may go well with you and that you may be in *health;* I know that it is well with your *soul.*" These texts have been interpreted so as to point to the conclusion that the New Testament teaches that "soul" and "spirit" and "mind" are synonyms and were used interchangeably.

Dichotomists have usually regarded the question as to the origin of souls as very important. Some have tended to follow Greek or classical thought in magnifying the soul at the expense of the body.

Charles Hodge argued for dichotomy, calling it "realistic dualism," and branded trichotomy as "anti-Scriptural."[44] John Miley held that a "dichotomous view of man is clearly given in the Scriptures" and that a thorough biblical distinction between "soul" and "spirit" is un-

43. *The Greek Testament*, 4 vols. (London: Rivingtons; Cambridge: Deighton, Bell, and Company, 1865-71), 4:84-85 (re Heb. 4:12).
44. *Systematic Theology*, 2:42-51.

tenable.[45] William Newton Clarke advocated dichotomy on the basis both of Scripture and "common-sense."[46] Henry C. Sheldon opted for dichotomy, not because the Bible formally teaches it but on "rational grounds," but he wanted no dichotomy that disparages the body and leads to asceticism.[47] For A. H. Strong dichotomy is "confirmed by Scripture," *pneuma* being a "Godward" term and *psychē* being an "earthward" term.[48] Francis A. O. Pieper[49] taught dichotomy, and E. Y. Mullins,[50] Louis Berkhof,[51] and H. C. Thiessen[52] did so largely on biblical grounds. L. Harold DeWolf, refuting philosophical monism, found support for dichotomy in the Bible, Christian tradition, and "the common moral and intellectual experience of mankind."[53] Millard Erickson has noted that recent expressions of the dichotomous theory have held that the Old Testament had a unitary view of human beings and the New Testament expressed a body-soul dualism.[54]

3. Holism, or Monism

Holism is the view, hardly unified and explicit enough to be called a theory, that holds that human beings are biblically and theologically one as beings and hence only secondarily should be construed as having elements. It has gained acceptance during the twentieth century, especially as the result of the biblical theology movement.

Against trichotomy and dichotomy advocates of holism cite as evidence that there were not just two or three constituent elements of human beings the fourfold usage of Jesus in Mark 12:30 (RSV): "you shall love the Lord your God with all your heart [*kardias*], and with all your soul [*psychēs*], and with all your mind [*dianoias*], and with all your strength [*ischyos*]." In the parallels, Luke 10:27 uses the same four terms and Matt. 22:37 refers only to "heart," "soul," and "mind." Exponents of holism stress those biblical usages of "soul" in which the term conveys the idea of human selfhood. They also press the idea that traditional Christian thinking (dichotomy, trichotomy) has been deeply influenced by classical Greek thought.

Emil Brunner, noting that the debate between dichotomy and trichotomy had been often pursued, observed:

45. *Systematic Theology,* 2 vols. (New York: Eaton and Mains; Cincinnati: Jennings and Pye, 1892, 1894), 1:397-403.
46. *An Outline of Christian Theology* (New York: Charles Scribner's Sons, 1906), pp. 182-88.
47. *System of Christian Doctrine,* pp. 272-76.
48. *Systematic Theology,* pp. 483-88.
49. *Christian Dogmatics,* 1:477.
50. *The Christian Religion in Its Doctrinal Expression,* pp. 256-57.
51. *Systematic Theology,* pp. 191-96.
52. *Introductory Lectures in Systematic Theology,* pp. 225-28.
53. *A Theology of the Living Church* (1960 rev. ed.), pp. 15-53.
54. *Christian Theology,* p. 522. Erickson cited Louis Berkhof, *Systematic Theology,* pp. 192-95.

> The question of dichotomy or trichotomy is therefore an idle one. So far as the human soul as such—in contrast to the animal—is understood from the very outset as disposed for the acts of the spirit, outside the body there is only one element: the soul. . . . In so far, however, as the spiritual act as such is distinguished from the psychical—that is, so far as the specifically human element is concerned—of course even in the Bible a threefold nature is recognized: the body, the soul, which man has along with all that lives, and the spiritual or personal element, the reason and the 'heart.'[55]

Brunner also declared:

> The Christian faith is dualistic in the sense that it teaches the inevitable 'two-ness' of mind and body. The mind is not to be understood as a modification of, or emanation from, the body, nor does the body emanate from the mind.[56]

Brunner concluded:

> If . . . we start from the Biblical idea of personality, then the question: *dichotomy versus trichotomy* becomes pointless. The same human being who has been created by God has physical, psychical and spiritual functions, which as such are absolutely distinguishable, but which cannot be distinguished metaphysically. There is no *anima immortalis,* but only a personality, destined by God for eternity, a person who is body-soul-spirit, who dies as a whole, and is raised as a whole.[57]

John A. T. Robinson, holding that Paul's two most important terms for human beings, *sarx* and *sōma,* were derived from a common Hebrew background, insisted that Paul's teaching about humankind must be interpreted in the light of his Hebraic view of humankind's unity. Hence *sarx* and *sōma* are not to be differentiated sharply, but both are to be understood as referring to the whole person. Robinson was confident that the Greeks asked questions that Hebrews did not ask, namely, about *"form* and *matter," "the one* and the *many,"* and *"body* and *soul."*[58] James Barr criticized Robinson's treatment of Pauline anthropology, especially concerning too radical a distinction between Greek and Hebrew thought.[59] Erickson has developed a view that he has identified as "contingent monism" or "conditional unity," according to which the pneumopsychosomatic unity of human beings is broken at death and during the intermediate or pre-resurrection state.[60] This view serves the good purpose of seeking to deal positively with that factor which poses

55. *Man in Revolt: A Christian Anthropology,* trans. Olive Wyon (Philadelphia: Westminster Press, 1947), pp. 363-64.

56. Ibid., pp. 373-74.

57. Ibid., p. 363, n. 1.

58. *The Body: A Study in Pauline Theology,* Studies in Biblical Theology, no. 5 (London: SCM Press, 1952), pp. 11-33.

59. *The Semantics of Biblical Language* (London: Oxford University Press, 1961), pp. 34-38.

60. *Christian Theology,* pp. 536-39. Erickson has provided an extensive reply to naturalistic, linguistic-philosophical, and behaviorist views denying the human soul and has reinforced the Christian doctrine of an intermediate state. Concerning the intermediate state see below, Ch. 82.

problems for trichotomy, dichotomy, and holism, namely, the intermediate state.

If indeed human beings are fundamentally one and not fundamentally divided into constituent parts or elements, how then is this oneness
to be understood? Three recent answers should be noted. First, Karl Barth
held that the unity of a person's soul and body is effectuated by the
immortal Holy Spirit of God, not through the human spirit.[61] Arnold
Bruce Come (1918-) taught that the unity of soul and body is effectuated
through the human spirit, the spirit being the person's self in the image
of God.[62] Dale Moody affirmed that the unity of body and spirit is
effectuated through the human soul—the "living soul" of Gen. 2:7, all of
such souls having been created by the Holy Spirit.[63]

Asian Christian theology, especially the Chinese variety, may be
able to approach the question of the constituents of the human with
cultural tools not readily available to Western Christians. The correlation
of *yin* and *yang* in Chinese thought, according to Jung Young Lee, offers
an available option, but not an absolute alternative, to the Western pattern
of "either/or" thinking with its "excluded middle." The relation of body
and spirit is one of four Christian doctrinal themes that, according to Lee,
can be illuminated by *yin-yang* thinking.[64]

The study of the so-called constituents of the human, especially when
focused on the Bible, can have numerous implications for or applications
to ministry in the church today. Three of these will be noted by way of
illustration. First, when the witness of Christians to nonbelievers is called
"soul- winning," that term must not be understood as the rescue of the
immaterial part of the person from his present physical life or the saving
of only a part of the human being. "Soul-winning" must be life-winning
and involves the saving of all of human nature and existence. Second, a
unitary emphasis in the Christian doctrine of humankind helps to explain
the integral role of Jesus' healing ministry. The Greek verb *sōzein* could
mean "to make whole" as well as "to save." Even if we should hold that
Jesus' healing ministry had the primary purpose of testimony to the advent
of the kingdom of God, the fact remains that he did not ignore the sufferings
and deformities of human beings' physical lives. Third, the Christian hope
is not properly expressed in terms of the immortality of the soul per se but
needs to embrace and center in the resurrection of the body, indeed the
"spiritual body." Christian redemption encompasses the whole person.

61. *Church Dogmatics*, III/2, pp. 325-426.
62. *Human Spirit and Holy Spirit* (Philadelphia: Westminster Press, 1959), pp. 59, 75,
32, 86.
63. *The Word of Truth*, pp. 180-82.
64. "The Yin-Yang Way of Thinking," in Douglas J. Elwood, ed., *What Asian Christians
Are Thinking: A Theological Source Book* (2d ed.; Quezon City, Philippines: New Day Publishers, 1978), pp. 59-67. See also Lee's book, *The I: A Christian Concept of Man* (New York:
Philosophical Library, 1971).

CHAPTER 34

The Nature of Sin

Having studied the "greatness" of human beings as created in the image of God the Creator, of one stock despite racial and ethnic differences, created as male and female for togetherness under God, and describable in terms of soul, spirit, flesh, body, heart, mind, and the like, we must now address the "misery" of humankind, which is caused by human sin. The discussion of the Christian doctrine of humans as sinners will include the nature of sin, the origin of sin, the humanity-wide aspects of sin, the consciousness of sin, and the consequences of sin. We should, however, treat four introductory themes before we examine the major topics.

I. INTRODUCTORY THEMES

A. DISAPPEARANCE OF THE TERM "SIN"

Karl Augustus Menninger (1893-), the Kansas psychiatrist, in his book *Whatever Became of Sin?*, wrote of "the disappearance of sin" from and "the twilight of sin" in the vocabulary and thought of twentieth-century human beings in Western societies. He noted that wrongdoing has been identified as "crime," as "symptom" of illness, and as "collective irresponsibility" (e.g., concerning war, slavery, actions of corporations, and the environment). Menninger called on pastors, teachers, physicians, lawyers and judges, the police, the media, and statesmen to work for the recovery of sin as moral guilt.[1]

B. SIN AS A RELIGIOUS CONCEPT

James Orr, Walter T. Conner, Gustav Aulén, and other theologians of the twentieth century have insisted that sin is fundamentally and essentially a religious conception. The same deed may be a crime (against the state) or an immorality (against society), but sin is properly to be understood as ultimately against God.[2] According to Aulén, "Sin is a

---

1. (New York: Hawthorn Books, Inc., 1973), esp. chs. 3, 5–7, 10.
2. Conner, *The Gospel of Redemption*, pp. 1-2.

concept which cannot be used except in a religious sense,"[3] and for Orr, strictly speaking, we wrong fellow humans and we sin against God.[4] David the psalmist, although he had surely wronged both Uriah and Bathsheba, wrote: "Against thee, thee only have I sinned, and done that which is evil in thy sight" (Ps. 51:4a, RSV). Bertrand Russell (1872-1970), British mathematician and unbeliever, after attempting a nontheological approach to sin, concluded: "But although the *sense* of sin is easy to recognize and define, the *concept* of 'sin' is obscure, especially if we attempt to interpret it in nontheological terms."[5] Sin presupposes the existence of God as a personal being, as the Holy One. Apart from a personal God, sin would have little meaning, for the elements of personal offense and disrupted relations vis-à-vis the personal God would be removed. Sin presupposes that in God's nature and will there is an objective frame of reference definitive of sin.

C. SIN OR IGNORANCE AS THE CHIEF HUMAN PROBLEM?

Many in the modern era have opted for the notion that ignorance, not sin, is the fundamental human problem. This view is rooted in the teaching of Socrates that if one knows the right he will do the right. This view was shaped by the Enlightenment view of progress, according to which the attainment of full information would lead to human goodness. The view must meet the challenge of the rapidly exploding volume of information available today. How could any human being possibly know all of this? If he could, how would he live, and what would his relationships with other human beings be?[6] The Christian doctrine of humankind has emphasized the human inability to do and fulfill the right and true, thus pointing beyond lack of information or even lack of knowledge on a deeper level to human beings' opting rebelliously and wrongfully.

D. AWARENESS OF SIN

Although clearly teaching that all human beings are capable of being conscious of sin, Christian theology has sometimes affirmed that the meaning of sin is made known more fully in and through the Christian revelation of God. This is partly due to the gospel's exposure of the disposition of humans to hide or conceal their sin, which hiding thus blurs

---

3. *The Faith of the Christian Church*, p. 259.

4. *God's Image in Man*, p. 213.

5. *Human Society in Ethics and Politics* (New York: Mentor Books, 1962), p. 73. One may question the sincerity or the capability (or both) of Russell in such a definitional quest after noting his later statement (p. 80): "I conclude also that 'sin,' except in the sense of conduct toward which the agent, or the community, feels an emotion of disapproval, is a mistaken concept, calculated to promote needless cruelty and vindictiveness when it is others that are thought to sin, and a morbid self-abasement when it is ourselves whom we condemn." But his conclusion is nevertheless significant.

6. Calvin Linton, "Man's Difficulty—Ignorance or Evil?" *Christianity Today*, 12 March 1965, pp. 18-20; reprinted in Millard J. Erickson, ed., *Man's Need and God's Gift: Readings in Christian Theology* (Grand Rapids: Baker Book House, 1976), pp. 125-30.

their perception of sin itself until exposed to and by the light of the gospel. But it is also due to the more serious rejection of the self-giving, loving, redeeming action of God in Jesus Christ.[7]

I. INADEQUATE VIEWS AS TO THE NATURE AND ORIGIN OF HUMAN SIN

Before examining the acceptable answers to the question as to the nature of sin, we should take note of two unacceptable views that have often claimed to have support in the Bible and in the Christian tradition.[8]

A. THE VIEW THAT SIN IS DUE TO HUMANKIND'S ESSENTIAL FINITUDE OR CREATURELY WEAKNESS (PHILOSOPHICAL NATURALISM)

1. This view may be grounded in an overemphasis on the Old Testament concept of humans as "flesh" (esp. Isa. 40:5-8) to the neglect of the Old Testament doctrine of sin. The Old Testament does describe humans as "flesh" in the sense of their creaturely weakness and mortality. The principal terms in the Old Testament for sin, however, are other than *bāśār* (flesh). Consequently this view removes the element of willfulness from sin. Accordingly, humans sin because they are creatures and are inherently weak. The biblical emphasis is rather that humans sin in spite of the fact that they are created in the image of God.

2. This view was taught by Theodore Parker, who held that sin is related to humankind's moral and spiritual progress as falling is related to a child's learning to walk. Thus sin as moral blundering helps humans to learn how to live morally and spiritually.[9] On the contrary, both Scripture and human experience bear witness that human beings learn to sin by sinning.[10] Although Reinhold Niebuhr wrote much concerning human finitude, he did point out that sin is not to be attributed to finiteness but rather to human beings' refusal to admit their dependence on God and their efforts to hide this dependence from themselves. Thus

> the whole Biblical interpretation of life and history rests upon the assumption that the created world, the world of finite, dependent and contingent existence, is not evil by reason of its finiteness. . . . It is not his finiteness, dependence, and weakness but his anxiety about it which tempts him to sin.[11]

7. Conner, *The Gospel of Redemption*, pp. 14-16.
8. Ibid., pp. 7-10; Thiessen, *Introductory Lectures in Systematic Theology*, pp. 252-53; Wiley, *Christian Theology*, 2:67-70; Purkiser, ed., *Exploring Our Christian Faith*, pp. 224-31.
9. Theodore Parker, *Theism, Atheism and the Popular Theology*, ed. Charles W. Wendte (Boston: American Unitarian Association, n.d.), pp. 372-73; Walter T. Conner, "Theodore Parker's Theological System" (fellowship thesis, Rochester Theological Seminary, 1909), pp. 18-19.
10. Conner, *The Gospel of Redemption*, p. 9.
11. *The Nature and Destiny of Man*, 1:178-79.

3. Therefore, while it is true that humankind as finite and creaturely is subject to temptation and does sin, neither creatureliness nor finiteness in itself is the root cause of sin. It is *not* that humans are creatures and therefore sinners. Rather, it is that humans are creatures *but* also sinners.

B. THE VIEW THAT SIN IS DUE TO BODILY APPETITES OR INSTINCTS, OR ULTIMATELY TO HUMAN BEINGS' POSSESSION OF BODIES (PHILOSOPHICAL IDEALISM)

1. This view has often been based on a misunderstanding of the biblical term "flesh," especially Paul's use of the term and particularly in Romans 7–8. Paul referred to formerly living "in the flesh" as a way of life (7:5, RSV) and also to the present "flesh," or sinful nature (7:18; 8:5a). He alluded to a conflict or warfare between the "law of the mind" and "the law of sin" and acknowledged that he served the former with his "mind" and the latter with his "flesh" (7:23, 25b). To set one's mind on the "flesh" would mean death, hostility to God, and being non-pleasing to God (8:6-8). The opposite of this is to set one's mind on the Spirit of God (8:5b, 6a, 9). Paul also in this context referred to the fact that "sinful passions" were at work and sin was indwelling his "members" *(melesin)* (7:5, 23). But Paul never identified "flesh" and "members." It is obvious that Paul's use of "flesh" goes far beyond the use of the term in Isaiah 40. Yet Paul's distinction between "mind" and "flesh" and between "flesh" and "Spirit" should not be identified with a body-soul dualism. "Flesh" in Romans 7–8 is a religio-ethical distinction rather than the physical aspect of a physical/metaphysical distinction. These chapters do not provide Paul's concept of the origin of sin or of the cause of sin but rather present "the flesh" as the dominating sinful tendency in human beings.[12]

2. Paul's concept of "flesh" in Romans 7–8 must be interpreted in relation to his teachings elsewhere. In Gal. 5:19-23 the "works of the flesh" include what we today call sins of the mind as well as sins expressed through the body. That Paul had a high regard for the human body may be seen in his call to the Roman Christians to present their "bodies" as "a living sacrifice" to God (12:1, RSV), in his teaching the Corinthians that "your body is a temple of the Holy Spirit within you" and hence they should "glorify God" in their bodies (1 Cor. 6:19-20), and in his admonition, "let us cleanse ourselves from every defilement of body and spirit" (2 Cor. 7:1). Paul's close association of "the flesh" and "the members" in Romans 7 may indeed have been indicative of the fact that some sins are expressed through the human body, but Paul did not identify the human body as the source of sin.[13]

3. Romans 7–8 should also be related to the teachings of Jesus,

12. George Barker Stevens, *The Theology of the New Testament*, International Theological Library (New York: Charles Scribner's Sons, 1899), pp. 338-48.
13. Revere Franklin Weidner, *Biblical Theology of the New Testament*, 2 vols. (New York: Fleming H. Revell Company, 1891), 2:84-85; Willibald Beyschlag, *New Testament Theology*, trans. Neil Buchanan, 2 vols. (Edinburgh: T. and T. Clark, 1896), 2:27-48; W. T. Conner, *The*

especially to the fact of his greater condemnation of—to use a modern term—"the sins of the mind," namely, pride and hypocrisy, than of the so-called "sins of the body."

4. This view has been derived from or augmented from certain non-Christian sources, even though it has been embraced by Christians. These sources include Greek idealism, with its concepts of the superiority of mind over body or matter; Gnosticism, with its premise that matter is inherently evil; asceticism, with its mortification of the body so that the soul may prosper; and Manichaeism, with its probable residual influence on Augustine of Hippo's doctrine of original sin.

5. This view has been modified during the modern era under the impact of evolutionary thought. Accordingly, sin is said to be due to the remains or relic of the brute in humans or to the animal instinct in human beings. Hence sin is seen as a phase of human development, release from which is anticipated in future evolutionary development. Thus soul-body dualism gives way to an animal/human sequence.

6. We ought not, therefore, to conclude that the principal cause of sin is humans' being physical, for human beings consent to even the most sensual sins. The answer concerning the nature of sin and its origin must be found elsewhere.

II. DEFINITIONS OF SIN THAT SEEK TO EMBODY THE ESSENCE OR CORE OF THE CHRISTIAN DOCTRINE OF SIN

It would be possible and indeed valid to investigate concepts of sin as these are expressed in the different types of literature in the Old Testament and in the New Testament, following strictly the method of biblical theology.[14] But because so many of these concepts are found in several of

---

Faith of the New Testament (Nashville: Broadman Press, 1940), pp. 282-83; Bultmann, *Theology of the New Testament*, 1:232-46; Frank Stagg, *New Testament Theology* (Nashville: Broadman Press, 1962), pp. 24-28; Donald Guthrie, *New Testament Theology* (Leicester, U.K.; Downers Grove, Ill.: InterVarsity Press, 1981), pp. 171-75.

14. A very few Old Testament theologians have treated the doctrine of sin according to the major types of Old Testament literature: Oehler, *Theology of the Old Testament*, pp. 158-66, 455-59; and von Rad, *Old Testament Theology*, 1:154-60, 263-66; 2:64, 74, 180, 224, 229, 405-6. The majority of Old Testament theologians, however, have dealt with the doctrine on the basis of the entire Old Testament: Hermann Schultz, *Old Testament Theology*, trans. J. A. Paterson, 2 vols. (Edinburgh: T. and T. Clark, 1892), 2:281-313; Charles Piepenbring, *Theology of the Old Testament*, trans. H. G. Mitchell (New York: Thomas Y. Crowell and Company, 1893), pp. 185-201; Davidson, *The Theology of the Old Testament*, pp. 203-35; Knudson, *The Religious Teaching of the Old Testament*, pp. 239-65; Snaith, *The Distinctive Ideas of the Old Testament*, pp. 51-78; Otto J. Baab, *The Theology of the Old Testament* (New York: Abingdon-Cokesbury Press, 1949), pp. 84-113; Paul Heinisch, *Theology of the Old Testament*, trans. William Heidt (Collegeville, Minn.: Liturgical Press, 1950), pp. 197-206, 229-42; Paul von Imschoot, *Théologie de l'Ancien Testament*, 2 vols., Bibliothèque de Theologie, ser. 3, vol. 2 (Tournai, Belgium: Desclée and Company, 1956), 2:278-302; Ludwig Köhler, *Old Testament Theology*, trans. A. S. Todd (Philadelphia: Westminster Press, 1957), pp. 166-81; Jacob, *Theology of the Old Testament*, pp. 281-88; Vriezen, *An Outline of Old Testament Theology*, pp. 209-12; J. Barton Payne, *The Theology of the Older Testament* (Grand Rapids: Zondervan, 1962), pp. 194-221; and Eichrodt, *Theology of the Old Testament*, 1:374-81; 2:380-495.

the types of biblical writings, it seems more useful to examine the topics themselves, noting how and where they are set forth in the Bible. We will now identify seven different definitions, of which five are clearly set forth in the Bible.

A. SIN AS VIOLATION OR DISOBEDIENCE OF THE DIVINE COMMANDMENT, OR THE LAW OF GOD

1. The most commonly used biblical words for sin, the Hebrew verb *ḥāṭā'*, and the Greek verb *hamartanein,* both meaning "to miss the mark," implied a deviation from an objective standard. Wheeler Robinson said that *ḥāṭā'* meant to miss "some goal or path."[15] Whereas to the modern person these Hebrew and Greek verbs may indeed suggest a mistake rather than willful, conscious sin, in biblical usage the terms pointed to "a voluntary and culpable mistake."[16]

2. The Greek New Testament used the noun *parabasis*, derived from the verb *parabainein,* meaning "to go past, pass over, overstep, transgress, or violate," for the transgression of the Mosaic law (Gal. 3:19; Rom. 2:23; 4:15; Heb. 9:15) and for the transgressions of Adam (Rom. 5:14) and of Eve (1 Tim 2:14).

3. The New Testament, especially Paul, used the noun *paraptōma,* meaning "falling beside, deviation, or lapse," and derived from the verb *parapiptein,* meaning "to fall beside, deviate from the right path, or turn aside," as a term for sin. The verb was used in the Septuagint to translate the Hebrew verb *'āḇar,* meaning "to cross over or pass by." *Paraptōma* is translated in the RSV as "trespass" or "trespasses" in Matt. 6:14-15; Mark 11:25; Gal. 6:1; 2 Cor. 5:19; Rom. 4:25; 5:15-18, 20; 11:11-12; Eph. 1:7; 2:1, 5; and Col. 2:13 and as "sins" in Jas. 5:16. The word has been connected with treachery.[17]

New Testament theologians who have treated sin according to the method of biblical theology by types of literature include: Weidner, *Biblical Theology of the New Testament,* 1:210-11; 2:70-83, 104-5, 246-47; Beyschlag, *New Testament Theology,* 1:90-93, 228-30, 346-47, 372-74; 2:49-63, 104-7, 299-301, 437-39, 462-63; Stevens, *The Theology of the New Testament,* pp. 92-103, 187-98, 282-84, 297, 313-16, 349-61, 550-56; David Foster Estes, *An Outline of New Testament Theology* (Philadelphia: Judson Press, 1900), pp. 96-114; Conner, *The Faith of the New Testament,* pp. 117-23, 277-94, 425-42; Bultmann, *Theology of the New Testament,* 1:232-59; 2:21-32; Charles Caldwell Ryrie, *Biblical Theology of the New Testament* (Chicago: Moody Press, 1959), pp. 47-48, 57-59, 180-84, 293-94, 333-36; Ralph E. Knudsen, *Theology in the New Testament: A Basis for Christian Faith* (Valley Forge, Pa.: Judson Press, 1964), pp. 241-56; Karl Hermann Schelkle, *Theology of the New Testament,* trans. William A. Jurgens, 4 vols. (Collegeville, Minn.: Liturgical Press, 1971-78), 1:107, 114-26, 148-52, 156-57; Hans Conzelmann, *An Outline of the Theology of the New Testament,* trans. John Bowden (London: SCM Press, 1969), pp. 192-98, 226-35, 352-56; Kümmel, *The Theology of the New Testament,* pp. 146-47, 178-85, 288-91; George E. Ladd, *A Theology of the New Testament* (Grand Rapids: Eerdmans, 1974), pp. 226-27, 228-29, 398-99, 403-4, 405, 472-74, 613-15; Guthrie, *New Testament Theology,* pp. 187-218; Leon Morris, *New Testament Theology* (Grand Rapids: Zondervan, 1986), pp. 56-59, 64-66, 178-80, 277-81, 308-9.

15. *The Christian Doctrine of Man,* p. 43.
16. Erickson, *Christian Theology,* p. 568.
17. Ibid., p. 574.

4. The New Testament used the noun *anomia*, meaning "lawless-ness," in Matt. 7:23; 13:41; 23:28; 24:12; 2 Thess. 2:1-12; and 1 John 3:4. It used the noun *adikia*, meaning "unrighteousness," in 2 Thess. 2:10, 12; Rom. 1:18, 29; 2:8; 3:5; 6:13; Heb. 8:12; 2 Pet. 2:13, 15; and 1 John 1:9; 5:17. *Anomia* "always" referred "to a breaking of the law of God in the broader sense," "never . . . to a breaking of the law in the narrow sense of the Mosaic regulations."[18]

5. Often during the postbiblical history of Christianity the moral law has been interpreted in abstract fashion and apart from the personal nature and will of God. Consequently sin tended to be reduced to the "breaking of rules" and such thinking to bring about the danger of "moralism."[19] If sin should be defined too exclusively and too rigidly as disobedience of divine law, then the overt act of the sin of commission can be so stressed as to neglect the sin of omission or the sinful heart. The definition of sin as violation of divine law can be adequate only when the moral law is properly understood as the expression of the nature and will of God himself.

B. SIN AS BREAKING THE COVENANT WITH GOD, OR COVENANT UNFAITHFULNESS

1. Inasmuch as the concept of the covenant was very important in the thought of the Old Testament, it is not surprising that sin should be defined or expressed in the Old Testament as covenant-breaking. The most com-monly used Hebrew verb for breaking the covenant was *pārar*, meaning "to break off." It was used in the Pentateuch (Lev. 26:15-16; Deut. 17:2; 31:20) and in the major prophets (Isa. 24:5; 33:8; Jer. 31:32; 33:20; Ezek. 16:59; 17:19; 44:7). For example, the divine forecast before entry into Canaan was: " 'these people will soon prostitute themselves to the foreign gods of the land they are entering. They will forsake me and *break* the *covenant* I made with them' " (Deut. 31:16b, NIV). Yahweh's word through Jeremiah was: " 'Both the house of Israel and the house of Judah have *broken* the *covenant* I made with their forefathers' " (11:10c, NIV). The other Hebrew verb used to convey the idea of transgressing the covenant was *'ābar*, "to pass over." It is found in Josh. 7:11a, Judg. 2:20, 2 Kings 18:12, Hos. 8:1, and Jer. 34:18a. Hosea could report Yahweh's verdict: " 'But like Adam they have *trans-gressed* the *covenant*' " (6:7a, NASV). Walther Eichrodt traced the parallel occurrence in Israelite history of two strands of teaching about the covenant: one that assured that the covenant would continue and the other that it would be abrogated. Of Jeremiah's day he commented: "Just as it is God's condescending grace that is thrown into striking relief by the covenant-making at the time of the Exodus from Egypt, so it is ingratitude that sums up the breaking of that covenant by the people."[20]

18. Ibid., p. 570.
19. E. La B. Cherbonnier, *Hardness of Heart: A Contemporary Interpretation of the Doctrine of Sin* (Garden City, N.Y.: Doubleday and Company, Inc., 1955), pp. 61-67.
20. *Theology of the Old Testament*, 1:457-67, 58-61, esp. 59.

2. In the New Testament the concept of sin as covenant unfaithfulness, which is much less prominent than in the Old Testament, is seemingly conveyed by the word *asynthetous* in Rom. 1:31, which word the KJV
translated as "covenant breakers," Weymouth, RSV, and NIV as "faith-
less," and the NASV as "untrustworthy." The translation "covenant
breakers" seems to be accurate inasmuch as the word comes from *synti-
thēmi*, "to join together, or covenant," and has the alpha privative.

C. SIN AS WILLFUL, PRIDEFUL REBELLION AGAINST GOD, OR TURNING FROM GOD

1. The Old Testament term *pešaʿ*, which often has been translated
"transgression," may more accurately be rendered "rebellion." Norman H. Snaith held that *pešaʿ*, supplied the religious meaning of sin in
contrast to ethical violation and called this religious meaning "theo-
fugal."[21] The Old Testament used other Hebrew words to connote rebellion.[22]

2. The Bible, especially the Pentateuch, records three notable
Israelite rebellions between the Exodus from Egypt and the entry into
Canaan. First, there was the rebellion at Rephidim, called Massa
("proof" or "testing") or Meribah ("contention" or "rebellion"), where
there was a lack of water and there was murmuring or fault-finding
against Moses (Exod. 17:1-7; Deut. 33:8; Ps. 95:7b-11; Heb. 3:7–4:11). In
the Hebrews passage *apostēnai* (3:12) means "to fall away," and the word
"provocation" *(parapikrasmos)* (3:8, 15) is derived from the verb *parapi-
krainein*, meaning "to provoke, exasperate, or rouse to indignation" and
used in 3:16. The passage also twice (3:15; 4:7) quotes from Ps. 95:8 the
warning, "do not harden your hearts." Second, there was the rebellion
at Mount Sinai, which involved the making of the golden calf (Exod.
32:1-35; Deut. 9:6-21). Reference is made to "a stiff-necked people"
(Exod. 32:9, RSV), "a great sin" (Exod. 32:21, 30), and "a stubborn
people" (Deut. 9:6, 13) who "provoked the LORD" (Deut. 9:7) and "have
been rebellious against the LORD" (Deut. 9:7). The sin of rebellion was
there joined with the sin of idolatry. Third, there was the rebellion at
Kadesh-barnea, involving the reports of the spies to Canaan and a
proposed return to Egypt (Num. 13:1–14:38; 32:8-13; Deut. 1:26-40).
There were also the lesser rebellions at Taberah (Num. 11:1-3) and at
Kibroth-hattaavah (Num. 11:31-34).

3. The New Testament employed terms indicative of rebellious
disobedience. The noun *apeitheia*, meaning "disobedience," was used in
Eph. 2:2c and 5:6c, and its cognates, the adjective in Tit. 1:6c and 3:3a and
the verb in 1 Pet. 2:8b and 3:20a. The verb *apostēnai*, "to fall away," was
used in the parable of the soils (Luke 8:13) and, as cited, in Heb. 3:12. The

21. *The Distinctive Ideas of the Old Testament*, pp. 60, 63-64.
22. Erickson, *Christian Theology*, p. 572.

noun *apostasia*, meaning "falling away, apostasy, or defection," was used eschatologically in 2 Thess. 2:3.

4. Augustine of Hippo, commenting on Psalm 19, declared that pride began with the "apostasy from God."[23] John Calvin, following Augustine, wrote:

> Hence infidelity was at the root of the revolt. From infidelity, again, sprang ambition and pride, together with ingratitude. . . . In fine, infidelity opened the door to ambition, and ambition was the parent of rebellion, man casting off the fear of God, and giving free vent to his lust.[24]

D. SIN AS IDOLATRY, OR THE WORSHIP OF THE CREATURE OR THE CREATED—WHETHER OTHER CREATURES OR HUMAN BEINGS THEMSELVES — INSTEAD OF THE CREATOR

1. The Old Testament frequently alluded to idolatry both as sin and as utter folly. The tower of Babel was to be constructed with the motive: "'let us make a name for ourselves'" (Gen. 11:4c, RSV). The first commandment of the Decalogue prohibited the worship of "'other gods'" (Exod. 20:3; Deut. 5:7). Idols made and worshiped by human beings are utterly lifeless (Ps. 115:4-8; Isa. 40:18-20).

2. Paul's most focused and emphatic statement about idolatry was descriptive of the Gentile world (Rom. 1:22-25, RSV):

> Claiming to be wise, they became fools, and exchanged the glory of the immortal God for images resembling mortal man or birds or animals or reptiles. Therefore God gave them up . . . because they exchanged the truth about God for a lie and worshiped and served the creature rather than the Creator, who is blessed forever!

The noun *asebeia*, meaning "ungodliness" or "irreverence," and derived from the verb *sebein*, meaning "to worship," was, together with its verbal and adjectival cognates, used of the lack of true worship in Romans, 2 Peter, and Jude.[25]

3. Numerous Christian theologians have identified sin as idolatry. According to Martin Luther, "That to which your heart clings and entrusts itself is, I say, really your God."[26] John Calvin discussed the veneration of images as idolatry in an anti-Roman Catholic context and in contrast to the worship of the true Triune God.[27] Reinhold Niebuhr declared: "The most classical definition of sin in the New Testament, that of St. Paul [is as follows:]. . . . The sin of man is that he seeks to make himself God."[28] Humankind's rejection of general revelation, according to Emil Brunner,

---

23. *Expositions on the Book of Psalms*, Psalm 19, para. 14 (NPNF, 1st ser., 8:56)

24. *Institutes of the Christian Religion* (1559 ed.), trans. Henry Beveridge, 2.1.4.

25. Erickson, *Christian Theology*, p. 569.

26. *Large Catechism* 1.1, in *The Book of Concord: The Confessions of the Evangelical Lutheran Church*, trans. and ed. Theodore G. Tappert (Philadelphia: Fortress Press, 1959), p. 365.

27. *Institutes of the Christian Religion* (1559 ed.) 1.11-13.

28. *The Nature and Destiny of Man*, 1:150.

"becomes the source of the vanity of idolatry."[29] Edmond La Beaume Cherbonnier (1918-) stated:

> According to the Bible, sin is properly defined as misplaced allegiance or, to use its technical word for it, idolatry.
>
> . . . .
>
> For sin is simply another word for allegiance to a false god. It is interchangeable with the word 'idolatry.' Hence Christian theology often equates it with unbelief, not in the sense of 'incredulity,' but of trust in the wrong god.[30]

Cherbonnier elaborated on the theme that hardness of heart is the "hallmark of idolatry."[31] For John Macquarrie sin as idolatry had an ontological base.

> The basic sin is indeed idolatry, the effort to found life . . . and give it meaning in terms of finite entities alone, to the exclusion of Being. We call this forgetting of Being 'idolatry,' because the beings have supplanted Being, the creatures have taken over God's place. . . . Like faith, it [idolatry] is an attitude of commitment, and indeed . . . is a kind of perversion of faith. . . . But this temptation for man to idolize himself and become his own God has reached overwhelming proportions in the current technological age. . . .[32]

Millard Erickson has opted for idolatry, rather than sensuousness or selfishness or pride, as "the essence of sin."[33]

E. SIN AS UNBELIEF, OR NOT BELIEVING OR TRUSTING IN THE TRUE GOD

1. The Old Testament does not contain a well-developed concept of "believing not" or "trusting not" in Yahweh God, but there are some usages of the Hebrew verb 'āman, meaning "to believe" or "to remain steadfast," with the negative (Num. 20:12; Deut. 1:32; 9:23; 2 Kings 17:14; Ps. 78:22, 32).

2. In the New Testament unbelief, or believing not, commonly meant the deliberate rejection of the revelation of God in Jesus and hence of Jesus himself. Believing not is a major theme in the Gospel of John. Indeed, "he who does not believe is condemned already, because he has not believed in the name of the only Son of God" (3:18b, RSV). Sometimes the not believing was directed to Jesus' works or miracles (10:25a, 26; 10:38a; 12:37, 39); at other times the not believing was directed to Jesus himself (8:45, 46b; 16:9). Unbelief was also described as blindness (9:39).

3. Unbelief was also presented in the New Testament in its intensive form: blasphemy against the Holy Spirit (Matt. 12:22-32); "an evil, unbelieving heart" (Heb. 3:12, RSV); deliberate sinning after receiving the knowledge of the truth (Heb. 10:26-29), and the "sin that leads to death"

---

29. *Revelation and Reason*, p. 65.
30. *Hardness of Heart*, pp. 13, 42.
31. Ibid., pp. 45-58.
32. *Principles of Christian Theology*, pp. 238-39.
33. *Christian Theology*, pp. 577-80.

(1 John 5:16c, NIV). "To many in the modern world," Alan Richardson wrote, "the statement that unbelief is sin seems a hard saying, but it is the consistent biblical point of view."[34]

4. Unbelief is not the rejection of postbiblical dogmatic formulations about the person of Jesus as the incarnate Son of God but of Jesus himself as God's Son and Word, the Revealer and Redeemer. It implies an exposure to the light and truth of God in Jesus Christ, and it involves a deliberate rejection of that light and truth. Piet J. A. M. Schoonenberg, S.J. (1911-), has interpreted human sin as the continuity of resistance to the Holy Spirit that was climaxed by the crucifixion of Jesus.[35] Dallas M. Roark has opted for the terms "unbelieving-disobedience" or "disobeying-in unbelief."[36]

Now we shall consider two modern definitions of sin that are not so directly related to specific biblical terms or passages.

F. SIN AS SELFISHNESS

Certain modern Protestant theologians, particularly in the United States and Great Britain, have given a high priority to the definition of sin as human selfishness. Alvah Hovey (1820-1903) reckoned "preference of self to God" as accounting "for nearly and perhaps all sin."[37] According to James Orr, sin "is the exaltation of self against God: the setting up of self-will against God's will: at bottom Egoism."[38] A. H. Strong affirmed that "the essential principle of sin" is "selfishness." "By selfishness we mean not simply the exaggerated self-love which constitutes the antithesis of benevolence but that choice of self as the supreme end which constitutes the antithesis of supreme love to God."[39] Such a definition of sin in terms of selfishness makes selfishness to be very comparable to idolatry. The definition of sin as selfishness was especially important among the adherents of the Social Gospel. Walter Rauschenbusch, while referring to "three forms of sin—sensuousness, selfishness, and godlessness"—as being "ascending and expanding stages, in which we sin against our higher self, against the good of men, and against the universal good," proceeded to declare: "Sin is essentially selfishness. That definition is more in harmony with the social gospel than with any individualistic type of religion."[40]

Some forms of the definition of sin as selfishness have tended to make sin too anthropocentric. Selfishness can suffice as a definition of sin

---

34. *An Introduction to the Theology of the New Testament* (New York: Harper and Row, 1958), p. 31.

35. *Man and Sin: A Theological View*, trans. Joseph Donceel, S.J. (Notre Dame, Ind.: University of Notre Dame Press, 1965), pp. 23-24.

36. *The Christian Faith*, pp. 214-15.

37. *Manual of Christian Theology* (2d ed.; New York: Silver, Burdett and Company, c. 1900), pp. 160-62.

38. *God's Image in Man*, p. 217.

39. *Systematic Theology*, pp. 567-73, esp. 567.

40. *A Theology for the Social Gospel*, pp. 47, 50.

only if conceived of as the assertion of self-will in opposition to the divine will as well as contrary to the well-being of one's neighbor.

G. Sin as Sloth, or Apathy

Harvey Gallagher Cox (1929-), an American Baptist theologian and Harvard professor, criticizing the prevalence of the concept of sin as prideful rebellion—the human being "as the fist-shaking contemptuous insurrectionary"—on the ground that it is more Greek and bourgeois than biblical, has opted for "sloth" as the key contemporary term for sin. "Sloth" is a translation of the Latin word *acedia*, which was derived from the Greek noun *akēdos*, which was composed of *a*, "not," and *kēdos*, "care." Hence the basic meaning is said to be not caring, or apathy. The Church Fathers listed "sloth" along with pride, covetousness, lust, anger, gluttony, and envy as one of the seven deadly or capital sins.[41] According to Cox, sloth

> means the determined or lackadaisical refusal to live up to one's essential humanity[,] . . . the torpid unwillingness to revel in the delights or to share in the responsibilities of being 'fully human.'[42]

Sloth is humankind's abdication of responsibility, of the human *"gubernatio mundi."*

> We need to make a whole new start in reformulating a biblical doctrine of sin which makes sense of a modern world, with its dutifully compliant Eichmanns and its lawbreaking Martin Luther Kings, and is at the same time closer to the Bible than the one we have now. . . .[43]

Cox's doctrine of sin as sloth is an important addition to our understanding of sin, although, of course, the idea of sloth as sinful is very old. It is more an expression of the sin of omission than of the sin of commission. But it is hardly adequate as the primary insight regarding sin and surely not as a total or exclusive definition of sin.

The foregoing examination of concepts as essential or central to the nature of sin has embraced disobedience/violation of divine commandment/law, covenant-breaking or covenant-unfaithfulness, willful or prideful rebellion, idolatry or the worship of the creature, unbelief, selfishness, and sloth or apathy. The list is not exhaustive or inclusive. The contemporary Christian is not compelled to opt for only one of these, or even two or three. Although some definitions may be reckoned to be more basic or central than others, all can claim some significance for the explication of sin.

41. Billy Graham, *The 7 Deadly Sins* (Grand Rapids: Zondervan, 1955); Karl A. Olson, *Seven Sins and Seven Virtues* (New York: Harper and Bros., 1962); Donald Capps, *Deadly Sins and Saving Virtues* (Philadelphia: Fortress Press, 1987); H. Stephen Shoemaker, *The Jekyll and Hyde Syndrome: A New Encounter with the Seven Deadly Sins and Seven Lively Virtues* (Nashville: Broadman Press, 1987).
42. *God's Revolution and Man's Responsibility* (Valley Forge, Pa.: Judson Press, 1965), pp. 41-43. According to Cox, "God has placed the tiller of history in man's hand, but man has gone to his hammock and let the winds and tides sweep his ship along" (p. 39).
43. Ibid., pp. 48, 42.

III. QUESTIONS ABOUT THE NATURE AND MEANING OF SIN

A. IS SIN NATURAL OR UNNATURAL?

The issue to which this question is addressed involves the proper correlation of human creaturehood, human sinfulness, and the universality of sin among human beings. Sin is not "natural" in the sense that God made human beings sinners. Rather, God pronounced the entire creation "good." Sin must be explained in terms of the willful or volitional actions of human creatures. In this sense sin is "contra-natural," for it is contrary to God's order and design of creation. Certain post-Reformation Lutheran theologians, notably Matthias Flacius (1520-75), came dangerously close to embracing the view that sin is in every sense natural.[44] Cherbonnier has concluded that "sin [is] misconceived as intrinsic to human nature."[45] On the other hand, sin is "natural" in the sense that the prevalence or universality of sin among humans makes the sinful to seem to be the order of nature. It was seemingly in this sense that Paul reflected on the past lives of Christians: "so we were by nature children of wrath, like the rest of mankind" (Eph. 2:3b, RSV). Calvin seems to have addressed our question from its two standpoints when he wrote that "man is corrupted by a natural viciousness, but not by one which proceeded from nature."[46]

B. IS SIN ALWAYS FULLY DELIBERATE, VOLUNTARY, AND CONSCIOUS?

There has been a Christian viewpoint, especially explicit and strong in the Wesleyan tradition, that has insisted on the absolute necessity of voluntariness and knowledge of divine law in respect to sin. John Wesley once declared:

> Nothing is sin, strictly speaking, but a voluntary transgression of a known law of God. Therefore, every voluntary breach of the law of love is sin; and nothing else, if we speak properly.[47]

The same voluntariness was reiterated by the British theologian Frederick Robert Tennant, who defined sin as "an activity of the will, expressed in thought, word or deed, contrary to the individual's conscience, to his notion of what is good or right, his knowledge of the moral law or the will of God."[48]

But recently this invariable voluntarism has been questioned in the Wesleyan tradition itself. Some would see the questioning as the result of the treatment of the unconscious in the novels of Fyodor Dostoevsky and

---

44. G. Kawerau, "Flacius, Matthias," *The New Schaff-Herzog Encyclopedia of Religious Knowledge*, 4:322-23.
45. *Hardness of Heart*, pp. 68-84.
46. *Institutes of the Christian Religion* (1559 ed.), trans. Henry Beveridge, 2.1.11.
47. "Letter CCCCXIX, June 16, 1772," *Works*, 14 vols. (London: Wesleyan Conference Office, 1872), 12:394.
48. *The Origin and Propagation of Sin* (Cambridge: University Press, 1902), p. 160.

the probing of the unconscious by Freudian psychology. Frederic Greeves (1903-), an English Methodist, has argued for the existence of some ignorance in respect to sin.[49] Did not the Old Testament law differentiate between the "unwitting" (RSV) sin, or sin of inadvertence (Lev. 4:2, 22, 27; 5:18; Num. 15:22-29), and the sin "with a high hand" (Num. 15:30, RSV), with sacrifices availing only for the former? Did not Augustine of Hippo distinguish between "errors" that are not always sins but are evils and sins in the proper sense?[50] Robert Newton Flew (1886-1962), another English Methodist, differing with both Wesley and Tennant, has held: "Our worst sins are often those of which we are unconscious."[51] Greeves has observed that "the problem of human *ignorance* is not the same problem as that of human *impotence;* our ignorance of what is 'right' is the concern that weighs most heavily on our present-day thought, whereas it was man's inability to do the will of God which most deeply concerned the New Testament writers and most of the great teachers of the Church." He concluded: "It is, then, in this conscious or unconscious rejection of God as God that sinning consists."[52] Reinhold Niebuhr also declared: "Sin is thus both unconscious and conscious."[53]

One caution, however, needs to be observed with respect to the recent espousal of unconscious sin. One needs to ask and perhaps to keep on asking the question: How is the sin of ignorance to be related to human accountability before God?

C. OUGHT WE TO SPEAK OF "SIN" OR OF "SINS"?

Actually both of these terms are proper and appropriate. Biblically, theologically, and ethically one can speak both of "sin" and of "sins." On the one hand, "sin" (singular) is an attitude or state. The rabbis had their doctrine of *yēṣer hā-rāʻ* or "evil imagination," especially in the Mishnah and perhaps also in Ecclesiasticus. Their doctrine was probably derived from Gen. 6:5 and 8:21.[54] Jesus in his teaching stressed the motive rather than merely the overt act of sinning. Particularly can this be observed in the Sermon on the Mount in the "you have said. . . , but I say unto you" utterances:

Matt. 5:21-22	Murder	→ Anger
Matt. 5:27-28	Adultery	→ Lust
Matt. 5:33-34	False Vows	→ No Oaths
Matt. 5:38-39	Retaliation	→ Nonresistance
Matt. 5:43-44	Love of Neighbor	→ Love of Enemies

49. *The Meaning of Sin* (London: Epworth Press, 1956).

50. *Enchiridion* 22.

51. *The Idea of Perfection in Christian Theology: An Historical Study of the Christian Ideal for the Present Life* (London: Oxford University Press, 1934), p. 333.

52. *The Meaning of Sin*, pp. 28, 132.

53. *The Nature and Destiny of Man*, 1:265.

54. George Foot Moore, *Judaism in the First Centuries of the Christian Era, the Age of the Tannaim*, 3 vols. (Cambridge, Mass.: Harvard University Press, 1927-30), 1:479-96; Sydney Cave, *The Christian Estimate of Man* (London: Gerald Duckworth and Company, Ltd., 1944), p. 16, n. 1.

Jesus taught that the nature of the tree determines the nature of the fruit (Matt. 7:17) and stressed inner defilement rather than the ceremonial defilement of the Pharisees (Mark 7:15). In Jesus' teaching "[t]he moral quality of the deed lies in the quality of the motive."[55] The Gospel of John stressed the singularity of sin or the sinful state in 1:29b (RSV): "Behold the Lamb of God, who takes away the *sin* of the world."

On the other hand, "sins" (plural) are deeds or acts or omissions, both in the sense of occurrences and of habit. The Old Testament emphasized and identified sins as acts or deeds, and the New Testament retained this pattern while intensifying the idea of sin (singular). The New Testament contains various passages that constitute catalogues or listings of particular sins; especially noteworthy are Rom. 1:29-31, which contains a list of 21 sins, and Gal. 5:19-21, which cites 15 "deeds of the flesh." Frederick Clifton Grant has provided an alphabetical list of 115 sins mentioned in the New Testament, "not counting duplications."[56]

Therefore, both "sin" and "sins" are essential to the biblical understanding of sin. Sinful motives issue in sinful actions. Sinful actions or deeds or omissions establish the pattern or habit that is the sinful state.

D. Ought "Sins" to Be Classified?

Late Judaism, just prior to the time of Jesus, made "an increasing attempt to differentiate between different *kinds* of sins."[57] Roman Catholic dogmatics and moral theology have for centuries made a distinction between "mortal sins" and "venial sins."[58] But even in such a system the actual identification or classification of particular sins depends on the knowledge and willfulness of the sinner. Efforts to effectuate a strict or rigid classification of sins are most likely to be misleading or fruitless and hence are unwise.[59]

We have probed certain inadequate views as to the nature of sin, studied seven different definitions of sin's nature, and briefly answered four questions concerning sin. But our best efforts to describe and define the nature of sin do not remove the mystery that inheres in sin itself.

55. Conner, *The Gospel of Redemption*, p. 27.
56. *An Introduction to New Testament Thought* (New York: Abingdon Press, 1950), pp. 176-77.
57. Greeves, *The Meaning of Sin*, p. 97.
58. E. J. Mahoney, "Sin and Repentance," in Smith, ed., *The Teaching of the Catholic Church*, pp. 925-29, 945-52.
59. For a Protestant view that favors such classifications, see Pieper, *Christian Dogmatics*, 1:564-77.

CHAPTER 35

The Original State and the Fall
of Humankind

Having considered the nature and meaning of sin, we now turn to the question of its origin, that is, "Whence came it?" The term "origin of sin" is not to be taken as synonymous with the term "original sin." The latter is a technical theological term, first used by Augustine of Hippo, which means original guilt and deals with the relation of the sin of Adam and Eve to the sin of all humankind. We will treat "original sin" in the next chapter.[1] The term "origin of sin" in the present context means the actual beginning of sin among humans or in God's entire creation.

James Stuart Stewart (1896-) suggested that the Apostle Paul gave a threefold answer to the question of the origin of sin: (1) that sin originated in human choice, or from "the flesh" (Rom. 7:25; 8:3); (2) that sin derived from the sinful choice of the first humans, Adam [and Eve] (Rom. 5:12-21); and (3) that sin originated with the rebellion of supramundane beings (Eph. 2:2; 6:12).[2] On the assumption that Stewart is correct in interpreting Paul, one may ask whether these are three quite independent answers, as Stewart thought, or are three phases of one comprehensive answer. Furthermore, one may ask whether Paul thereby spoke for all the Scriptures in offering such answers.

Previously we studied the doctrine of Satan[3] and explored the Pauline concept of "flesh."[4] It is now necessary to deal more directly with the sinful choices of Adam and Eve. The Bible presents sin, for the most part at least, as the willful decision of human beings. Even the universality of sin taught in the Bible does not take away willfulness and individual responsibility. Yet sin's dominance throughout humankind allows a focusing of attention on the sin of the progenitors of humanity. According to Genesis 3, Adam and Eve were led to sin not only by willful choice but

---

1. See below, Ch. 36.
2. *A Man in Christ: The Vital Elements of St. Paul's Religion* (London: Hodder and Stoughton; New York: Harper, 1935), p. 106.
3. See above, Ch. 29.
4. See above, Ch. 34, I, B, 1 and 2.

466

by the temptation of the serpent, which Christian theology by virtue of the New Testament Apocalypse has identified with Satan, or the devil.

What was human existence like before the advent of sin? How was human existence different after the advent of sin? These are the theological topics known as the original state and fall of humankind. After a citation of the pertinent biblical passages, we will center our attention on two aspects of the subject: historicity and nature.

I. BIBLICAL PASSAGES

Before one seeks to locate the various biblical passages that refer specifically to the original state and fall of human beings, one could easily assume that the texts are numerous, but such is not the case. There are only a few of these passages. The most important one is obviously the pertinent portions of Genesis 1–3.

> And God saw everything that he had made, and behold it was very good.... So when the woman saw that the tree was good for food, and that it was a delight to the eyes, and that the tree was to be desired to make one wise, she took of its fruit and ate; and she also gave some to her husband, and he ate.... therefore the LORD God sent him forth from the garden of Eden, to till the ground from which he was taken. (1:31a; 3:6, 23, RSV)

Ezek. 28:11-19, which was previously considered in respect to the doctrine of Satan,[5] belongs, whatever one's conclusion as to the identity of the one being described, to the list of texts, for it speaks of perfection (v. 11a), Eden (v. 12), blamelessness until "iniquity" came (v. 15), and a casting forth "from the mountain of God" (v. 16b, RSV). In 1 Cor. 15:21-22 Paul indirectly alluded to the first sin by twice referring to the death that came through Adam. In 2 Cor. 11:3 (RSV) his use of Eve's succumbing to temptation was that of an analogy to reinforce the fact that Christians were being "led astray from a sincere and pure devotion to Christ." In Rom. 5:12a, 15b, 16b, 17a, 18a, and 19a (RSV) one finds six references to the sin of Adam:

> Therefore as sin came into the world through one man.... For if many died through one man's trespass.... For the judgment following one trespass brought condemnation.... If, because of one man's trespass, death reigned through that one man.... Then as one man's trespass led to condemnation for all men.... For as by one man's disobedience many were made sinners....

First Tim. 2:14 (RSV) is a statement designed to enforce the admonition that women should not teach men in church: "and Adam was not deceived, but the woman was deceived and became a transgressor."

---

5. See above, Ch. 29, I, A, 2, c.

II. REALITY AND HISTORICITY OF AN ORIGINAL (SINLESS) STATE AND A FALL OF HUMANKIND

This topic has been one of the major controversial issues in twentieth-century Christian theology, especially Protestant theology. Concerning such a state and fall there have been three principal positions.

A. LIBERAL PROTESTANTISM'S DENIAL OF BOTH THE REALITY AND THE HISTORICITY OF AN ORIGINAL STATE AND FALL OF HUMANKIND

Theological liberalism of various types at the end of the nineteenth century and the beginning of the twentieth tended to conclude that evolutionary science had made untenable not only a historical Eden and a historical fall but also any real fall of humankind in any sense. F. R. Tennant, the author of three major monographs[6] on the doctrine of sin early in the twentieth century, may be seen as a major or representative spokesman for Liberal Protestantism's reinterpretation of the fall of humankind and the doctrine of sin in response to evolutionary science. Tennant posed the question:

> Instead of resorting to a hypothetical previous existence or extra-temporal self-decision, can we find the ground of the possibility and occasion for sin in our natural constitution regarded as the perfectly normal result of a process of development through which the race has passed previously to the acquisition of full moral personality; and can we assign the rise of evil itself simply to the difficulty of the task which has to be encountered by every individual person alike, the task of enforcing his inherited organic nature to obey a moral law which he has only gradually been enabled to discern?[7]

Mary Frances Thelen (1911-) provided a summary[8] of Tennant's threefold critique of the traditional doctrine of the fall, which critique was actually of the doctrine of "original sin."[9] Preliminary to Tennant's threefold critique he criticized the doctrine of original sin on the ground that such is "not sin at all, since a bias toward sin which is inherited, or which is in any way prior to the volitional activity of the individual, is something for which he cannot be held responsible or pronounced guilty."[10] Tennant's first criticism of any historical fall was that such a teaching had been invalidated or falsified by modern science. Only late in their evolution did

6. *The Origin and Propagation of Sin; The Sources of the Doctrines of the Fall and Original Sin* (Cambridge: University Press, 1903); and *The Concept of Sin* (Cambridge: University Press, 1912).

7. *The Origin and Propagation of Sin*, p. 81.

8. *Man as Sinner in Contemporary American Realistic Theology* (New York: King's Crown Press, 1946), pp. 14-22.

9. Specific treatment of this topic will be given below, Ch. 36, II, C, 1 and III, B. It is sufficient at this point to note that Tennant understood the term broadly so as to include both the views by which the sin of Adam and Eve itself is imputed to all human beings and the views by which only depravity or a bias to sin is imputed to Adam's posterity.

10. Thelen, *Man as Sinner in Contemporary American Realistic Theology*, p. 14.

human beings come to have conscience, and only then could they sin. Sin, therefore, is "a kind of spiritual 'lag' or a biological survival," "the survival or misuse of habits and tendencies" from his animal past.[11] Second, Tennant denied any such " 'corruption of the will' or 'bias toward sin,' as the doctrine of the Fall seeks to explain." Indeed, the "universality of actual sin" can be explained well by "the difficulty of sinlessness." Furthermore, "a bias toward good" is just as logical as "a bias toward evil," and "any bias toward evil," to be effective, would have to await humankind's relatively late acquisition of volition. Third, humanity-wide "solidarity in wrongdoing, although real, is sufficiently accounted for by a recognition of the phenomena of physical inheritance and social inheritance of the *material* of sin, without requiring direct inheritance of a taint of the will." Tennant sought to reconcile Augustine of Hippo and Pelagius so as to conclude that "whereas inheritance affects our outlook in innumerable ways, . . . it does not control the will itself. The will is free."[12] Tennant offered an essentially ethical rather than religious definition of sin, stressing the moral law and accountability. For him the universality of sin was "not an *a priori* deduction but an empirical generalization which is only approximately true," for there have been exceptions: children dying before becoming capable of moral behavior, Jesus, and others who have been without sin.[13]

James Orr summarized Liberal Protestantism's view by stating: "The myth of the *fall* of man is replaced by the scientific theory of the *ascent* of man."[14]

B. NEOORTHODOX PROTESTANTISM'S DENIAL OF THE HISTORICITY OF AN ORIGINAL SINLESS STATE AND FALL OF HUMANKIND AND AFFIRMATION OF THE INDIVIDUAL, EXISTENTIAL FALL OF EVERY HUMAN BEING

Neoorthodox theologians accepted the verdict that evolutionary science and Genesis 1–3 are utterly incompatible and irreconcilable, and hence a twentieth-century Christian must opt for one or the other.

1. Emil Brunner contended that "Adam in Paradise" cannot be reconciled with a post-Copernican view of time and space; it is surprising that he did not contend that it could not be reconciled with a post-Darwinian approach to human origins. Accordingly, Adam in Paradise, a concept that for Brunner had been shaped by Augustine of Hippo, was "historically connected with the history of the people of Israel" and was chronologically contemporary with the six days of creation. According to Brunner, one must accept such Adamic doctrine and reject evolutionary science, one must make an effort at synthesis, or one must abandon the historicity of

---

11. Ibid., pp. 14-15.
12. Ibid., pp. 15-17.
13. Ibid., pp. 17, 20, 21.
14. *God's Image in Man*, p. 14.

Adam and retain evolutionary science. Brunner opted for the third alternative.[15] The earlier view of Brunner had been that of a meta-historical fall of preexistent Adam.[16] Later he came to reject that view as being Platonic, Gnostic, and Origenistic and as leading ultimately to the abandonment of the biblical concept of creation.[17] Instead, Brunner affirmed the individual fall of every human being, the "man in contradiction."

2. Reinhold Niebuhr also rejected the historicity of Eden and of the fall as being the error of "literalism." According to Niebuhr, "the self in the moment of transcending itself" obtains "the consciousness and memory of original perfection." "Perfection before the Fall is . . . perfection before the act. . . . The self may act even when the action is not overt."[18] Such was Niebuhr's version of the existential fall.

3. John S. Whale expressed the Neoorthodox position in a clear statement that has been widely read and quoted:

> The idea of a Fall from an original state of perfection is really a limiting conception, a theological *Grenzbegriff*. It is not a scientific statement about the dawn of history. The Fall is symbolism, necessary to the intellect, but inconceivable by the imagination. It involves no scientific description of absolute beginnings. Eden is on no map, and Adam's fall fits no historical calendar. Moses is not nearer to the Fall than we are, because he lived three thousand years before our time. The Fall refers not to some datable aboriginal calamity in the historic past of humanity, but to a dimension of human experience which is always present—namely, that we who have been created for fellowship with God repudiate it continually; and that the whole of mankind does this along with us. Everyman is his own 'Adam,' and all men are solidarily 'Adam.' Thus Paradise before the Fall, the *status perfectionis*, is not a period of history, but our 'memory' of a divinely intended quality of life, given to us along with our consciousness of guilt.[19]

Neoorthodoxy, influenced by evolutionary science as had been Liberal Protestantism, sought instead to retain the fallenness of humanity, but by abandoning an original sinless state and the distinctive sinning of Adam and Eve and by positing that in sinning humans remember what God intended them to be.

15. *The Christian Doctrine of Creation and Redemption*, pp. 48-50.
16. *Man in Revolt: A Christian Anthropology*, trans. Olive Wyon (New York: Charles Scribner's Sons, 1939), p. 142.
17. *The Christian Doctrine of Creation and Redemption*, pp. 101-2; see also Cairns, *The Image of God in Man*, ch. 12, esp. p. 154.
18. *The Nature and Destiny of Man*, 1:293-94. Niebuhr further contended that the rejection of an original sinless state and historical fall of humankind
> clarifies and corrects both Catholic and Protestant thought. Against Protestant thought it becomes possible to maintain that the image of God is preserved in spite of man's sin. In distinction from Catholic thought it is possible to eliminate the unwarranted distinction between a completely lost original justice and an uncorrupted natural justice. (ibid., 1:292)

See below, Ch. 36, III, B, 2, d.
19. *Christian Doctrine*, pp. 51-52. The framers of the Dutch Roman Catholic catechism sought to combine the historical-primeval and the existential-contemporary dimensions of the fall. *A New Catechism: Catholic Faith for Adults*, pp. 263-64.

C. TRADITIONAL OR CONSERVATIVE CHRISTIANITY'S AFFIRMATION
OF THE HISTORICITY AND REALITY OF THE ORIGINAL STATE AND
FALL OF HUMANKIND AS BIBLICAL AND PRESENTLY TENABLE

1. *Augustinian Teaching*

Augustine of Hippo, whose teaching on Adam has greatly influenced later Christian thought, had no inclination to question or to reject the historicity of the fall of Adam and Eve and assumed that such was an acceptable truth.

2. *Eastern Orthodoxy*

The Eastern Orthodox churches have experienced no major denials of a historical fall of humankind, but neither have they magnified the doctrine of the fall to the extent Western Christianity has.

3. *Official Roman Catholic Position in the Twentieth Century*

According to a decision of the Pontifical Biblical Commission in 1909, "the literal historical sense" of the fall is not to be denied.[20] Hence one reads as the authoritative *(de fide)* teaching of the Roman Catholic Church: "Our First Parents in Paradise sinned grievously through transgression of the Divine probationary commandment."[21] The twentieth-century affirmation of the dogma is based on the decree of the Council of Trent concerning original sin: "If anyone does not confess that the first man, Adam, when he transgressed the commandment of God in paradise, immediately lost the holiness and justice in which he had been constituted, and through the offense of that prevarication incurred the wrath and indignation of God, . . . let him be anathema."[22]

4. *Conservative Protestant Teaching*

a. Charles Hodge

Hodge taught that Gen. 2:15-17; 3:1-6 as an "account of the probation and fall of man is neither an allegory nor a myth, but a true history." He argued for this conclusion from (a) the superiority of the Genesis account to the mythological accounts of other nations, (b) its forming "an integral part of the book Genesis" and (c) of biblical history, (d) its recorded facts being assumed by the rest of the Old Testament and by the New Testament, and (e) its recorded facts underlying "the whole doctrinal system revealed in the the the Scriptures."[23]

---

20. Ott, *Fundamentals of Catholic Dogma*, p. 106.
21. Ibid.
22. *Canons and Decrees of the Council of Trent*, trans. H. J. Schroeder, 17 June 1546, p. 21.
23. *Systematic Theology*, 2:123-24.

b. A. H. Strong

Strong asserted that "it is important for us to know that sin is not an inevitable accompaniment of human nature, but that it had a historical beginning." According to Strong, "our view of inspiration would permit us to regard that account as inspired, even if it were mythical or allegorical." But its *general character* [is] *not mythical, but historical.*" Strong's supportive arguments resemble those of Hodge.[24]

c. James Orr

Orr argued for the necessity of the fall of humankind even if it had not been narrated in Genesis.

> At no point in Scripture history does man appear as standing in right or normal relations with God. His condition is invariably pictured as, naturally, one of rebellion against God, and of great and deepening corruption.

> If a fall were not narrated in the opening chapters of Genesis, we should still have to postulate something of the kind to account for the Bible's own representations of the state of man.[25]

d. Herman Bavinck

The Dutch theologian wrote:

> There is no other explanation possible of Gen. 3 than that it is the narration of a fall, which consists in the transgression of an explicit command of God, thus bearing a moral significance, and therefore followed by repentance, shame, fear and punishment. . . .
> It is indeed remarkable how very seldom the OT refers to this history of the Fall. . . .
> Nevertheless, the Fall is the silent hypothesis of the whole Bib. [Biblical] doctrine of sin and redemption; it does not rest only on a few vague passages, but forms an indispensable element in the revelation of salvation. The whole contemplation of man and humanity, of Nature and history, of ethical and physical evil, of redemption and the way in which to obtain it, is connected in Scripture with a Fall, such as Gen. 3 relates to us.

> [Indeed] science can never reach to the oldest origins and the ultimate destinies of humanity, and historical and critical inquiry will never be able to prove either the veracity or the unveracity of this history.[26]

e. Elliott Controversy among Southern Baptists

In the Southern Baptist Convention the Elliott Controversy during 1962-63 concerning *The Message of Genesis*[27] by Ralph Harrison Elliott (1925-) dealt with the differences between a primarily symbolical method

24. *Systematic Theology*, pp. 582-83.
25. *God's Image in Man*, pp. 199, 201.
26. "The Fall," *International Standard Bible Encyclopedia* (1915), 2:1092.
27. (Nashville: Broadman Press, 1961; St. Louis: Bethany Press, 1963).

of interpreting Genesis 1–11 (Elliott and others) and a primarily historical method of interpreting Genesis 1–11 (opponents of Elliott).[28]

5. *Restatement of the Reality and Historicity of the Original State and Fall of Humankind*

a. An interpretation of Genesis 1–3 so as to allow the possibility of considerable *time* between the creation of the universe and the creation of human beings serves to relieve the objection that "Adam" had to be "contemporaneous" with all the creative process.

b. A recognition that Genesis 1–3 is not a historiographical narrative of precisely the same nature as the Gospel accounts of the crucifixion of Jesus prevents our speaking of Genesis 1–3 as historical accounts in the sense of modern "scientific" history or in the sense of interpreted eyewitness accounts of other events recorded in the Bible.

c. Yet if and when every element of historicity in humankind's "fall" should be denied, the concept of the original state preceding the fall is also robbed of any temporal reality or significance except as the hypothetical presupposition of the sin of every human being, that is, the existential fall.

d. So long as sin is not regarded as absolutely necessary to human existence (or, not ordained by creation), sin must have had an origin in humanity or human history. *Somebody must have been first* (the origin of humanity in an original pair, and the occurrence of sin among these), *or else many began a kind of simultaneous sinning* (origination of humankind through many emergent beings, and the widespread beginnings of sin in more or less simultaneous fashion). The unlikelihood of the multiple origins of humankind has already been treated.[29]

e. A contemporary doctrine of the historical fall need not be thoroughly Augustinian but may be built on Paul and Irenaeus instead of Paul and Augustine.[30]

f. The purely existential view of the fall of humankind is subject to the same weaknesses as various gnosticizing approaches to Christian doctrine. Shall it be a metahistorical fall (in pre-history), or an existential fall (in personal history)? Can the concept of the existential fall escape the danger of atomizing the solidarity of sin? Does it tend to remove the meaning of the fall as a lapse from something to something else very different?

g. Therefore, the teaching of an original or prelapsarian state and a "historical" fall is still a viable option for Christian doctrine.

28. See the present author in James Leo Garrett, Jr., E. Glenn Hinson, and James E. Tull, *Are Southern Baptists "Evangelicals"?* (Macon, Ga.: Mercer University Press, 1983), pp. 111-15.
29. See above, Ch. 31, II, B, C, D, and E.
30. Cave, *The Christian Estimate of Man*, p. 219.

III. NATURE OF THE ORIGINAL STATE AND FALL OF HUMANKIND

The biblical texts relative to the original state and fall provide very few details pertaining to human existence before the advent of sin and only some more specificity as to the fall. Christian theologians have through the centuries drawn out implications, made inferences, and engaged in speculation on these two themes. The result has been that there are several theological patterns or schools concerning the original state and fall. We will now survey these patterns, omitting for the present the impact of the fall on the posterity of the first humans.[31]

A. AUGUSTINIAN PATTERN

Augustine of Hippo, especially in his later years, gave considerable attention to prelapsarian Adam. He taught that (1) Adam, after the begetting of sons, would eventually have been changed into a "spiritual being"; (2) Adam would have enjoyed immortality if he had continued to obey God; (3) Adam enjoyed "perfect health and a mind untroubled by passion"; and (4) Adam possessed "the gift of free will." But the most distinctive of Augustine's teachings pertained to the intellectual endowment of Adam. Impressed with Adam's ability to name the animals and rejecting the view that unfallen Adam was "of low intellectual attainments though of high moral character," (5) he held that Adam had "an intellect which far exceeded that of the most brilliant genius among his descendants."[32] Recalling the words of the children's nursery rhyme, one can easily think of Augustine's doctrine of unfallen Adam as a "Humpty Dumpty" view.[33] The fall brought separation or alienation from God, shame and guilt, expulsion from Eden, suffering and pain, the loss of *libertas* (the right use of free will), and death.[34]

B. PELAGIAN PATTERN

For Pelagius and his associates unfallen Adam had no definite nature or disposition such as later theologians would describe as "original righteousness." He had only the capacity and freedom to become something. He was created mortal, and hence after his sin death was not in the

---

31. To be treated below, Ch. 36.
32. Gerald Bonner, *St. Augustine of Hippo: Life and Controversies,* Library of History of Doctrine (Philadelphia: Westminster Press, 1963), pp. 366-67. See Augustine, *On the Merits and Remission of Sins* 1.2.2; *Enchiridion* 104; *On the Literal Meaning of Genesis* 6.25.36; *On the City of God* 14.26; *Contra secundam Juliani responsionem imperfectum opus* 5.1.
33. "Humpty Dumpty sat on a wall,
Humpty Dumpty had a great fall;
All the king's horses and all the king's men
Couldn't put Humpty Dumpty together again."
34. *On the Merits and Remission of Sin* 1.2.4; *On Marriage and Concupiscence* 2.14 (5); *Against Two Letters of the Pelagians* 1.5; *On the City of God* 13.1; *On Rebuke and Grace* 33 (12); *Contra secundam Juliani responsionem imperfectum opus* 6.17, 22, 23, 25, 26, 27, 30.

nature of punishment. By the fall he did not lose his freedom of will or the rightful use of it, and he did not come to have a sinful nature. Sin was to be viewed atomically, not organically. Adam did bequeath to his posterity a bad example, and his posterity did not enjoy the full use of reason that he had had in the beginning.[34]

C. EASTERN ORTHODOX PATTERN

According to twentieth-century Eastern Orthodoxy, "Adam began in a state of innocence and simplicity." Building on Irenaeus rather than Augustine, Eastern Orthodoxy holds that "God set Adam on the right path, but Adam had in front of him a long road to traverse in order to reach his final goal." Originally endowed with the image of God, the human person "was called to acquire the likeness by his own efforts (assisted of course by the grace of God)." The fall itself consisted of human "disobedience of the will of God." It resulted in separation from God, self-disintegration, disease, and death. By the fall the free will, or the power of choice between good and evil, was not lost, but its scope was restricted.[35]

D. TRIDENTINE ROMAN CATHOLIC PATTERN

Beginning with the Council of Trent, when it was dogmatically formulated, and continuing on until Vatican Council II, Roman Catholic dogmatics taught a view of the original state and fall of humankind that stressed its more than natural features. Accordingly, Adam and Eve were after creation endowed with "sanctifying grace" and with four accompanying "gifts," which together constituted the *donum superadditum* (additional gift). These four gifts, called "preternatural gifts," were immortality, or the exemption from death; impassibility, or freedom from suffering; knowledge, which was infused by God and not acquired by Adam and Eve; and integrity, or wholeness, meaning the total absence of "concupiscence." The first human sin, identified as a "mortal sin," brought to Adam and Eve and their posterity the loss of sanctifying grace and the four accompanying gifts. Consequently, they came to be subject to death, suffering, loss of knowledge, and concupiscence. In the fall, however, the free will of human beings was retained. Sometimes other results of the fall are specified such as subjection to Satan, deterioration in body and soul, and eternal damnation.[36]

---

34. Wiggers, *An Historical Presentation of Augustinism and Pelagianism*, pp. 137-40.
35. Ware, *The Orthodox Church*, pp. 224-30.
36. Joseph Pohle, *God: The Author of Nature and the Supernatural*, vol. 3, Dogmatic Theology, trans. and ed. Arthur Preus (St. Louis: B. Herder Book Company, 1946), pp. 190-218; B. V. Miller, "The Fall of Man and Original Sin," in Smith, ed., *The Teaching of the Catholic Church*, pp. 320-59. Pohle acknowledged that the doctrine of the endowment of Adam and Eve with "sanctifying grace" was built on the Church Fathers and not on Scripture (pp. 197-200).

E. REFORMED AND LUTHERAN PATTERN

These Protestant traditions have specifically rejected the Tridentine pattern with its concept of the *donum superadditum* on the ground that it makes the fall of humans more difficult, not less difficult, to explain, for God in some measure becomes responsible for the malfunctioning of the original grace and gifts. Instead, Adam is said to have had "original righteousness"—a term that Trent also had used, but for Protestants meaning not only freedom from sin but rightness with God, spouse, and nature. "Original righteousness" was said to have been natural, not supernatural (Hodge). Adam and Eve had both freedom and responsibility. Their state could be described as "innocence and childlike intercourse with God" (Oehler), as that of being "positively good" and upright in body and soul (Pieper), or as "maturity and perfection" (Hodge). Adam was not a "brute" (Pieper), and there was no "development from savagery" (Strong). Neither were the first humans subject to "a necessary and universal law of progress" (Strong). They enjoyed "perfect health" and "immortality" and exercised their God-ordained dominion over other creatures (Pieper).[38] Resulting from the first sin were alienation, guilt, suffering, and death.

F. WESLEYAN PATTERN

Theologians in the Wesleyan heritage have taught that prelapsarian Adam had "primitive holiness." They have seen their position as a *via media* between Augustine and Pelagius, both of whom had ignored "holiness as a subjective state" (Wiley). They have made a sharp differentiation between "subjective" holiness, or a spontaneous tendency to obey the good coupled with a holiness of nature wherein one is not "meritorious and rewardable" (Miley), and an "ethical holiness," or a character such as results from "free moral action in obedience to the divine will" (Miley) and such as makes one "meritorious or rewardable." Adam had only the "subjective" holiness, not the "ethical holiness." He also had the "presence and agency of the Holy Spirit" (Wiley). Adam experienced "probation" and temptation before the fall and suffered, together with his posterity, moral depravity and death as results of the fall (Miley).[39]

G. POST-VATICAN COUNCIL II SYMBOLIC ROMAN CATHOLIC PATTERN

The recent Dutch catechism interpreted the "narratives" of Genesis 1–11 as "symbols in which the kernel of all human history is described, including that which is yet to come." Identifying Adam with humankind,

---

38. Hodge, *Systematic Theology*, 2:92-96, 99-106; Pieper, *Christian Dogmatics*, 1:516-18, 520-22; Strong, *Systematic Theology*, pp. 514-32; Oehler, *Theology of the Old Testament*, 1:156-57.
    39. Miley, *Systematic Theology*, 1:409-45; Wiley, *Christian Theology*, 2:39-65; see also Sheldon, *System of Christian Doctrine*, p. 304.

the catechism taught that "the primeval history recounts a Fall four times over: the eating of the forbidden fruit, the murder of a brother, the corruption of Noah's contemporaries and the building of the tower of Babel."[40]

It is much easier to criticize aspects of the seven patterns than it is to offer a pattern or synthesis of patterns that seems to be more authentic or viable. Augustine, it would seem, went too far, surely beyond the Bible, in positing that Adam was the greatest intellectual genius in human history. Pelagius did not go far enough in affirming either a prelapsarian nature or a sinful nature. One can question Eastern Orthodoxy's handling of image/likeness and freedom of the will. The Tridentine pattern seems to impose supernatural/preternatural elements that make the free choice of Adam and Eve more difficult to explain. The Reformed-Lutheran pattern may ascribe to Adam (and Eve) more "maturity" than is warranted, but the Wesleyan pattern still must explain how with a spontaneous tendency to obey the good and the presence and work of the Holy Spirit Adam and Eve still sinned. The symbolic pattern with its fourfold depiction of the fall needs to explain more adequately when the first humans were sinless and when sin occurred.

One other matter deserves attention. Most of the expositors[41] of the doctrine of the original state and fall have written of Adam's prelapsarian state, Adam's fall, and the results of Adam's sin. There has been a noticeable silence as to Eve's participation in the prelapsarian state, the fall, and its consequences. One may attempt to explain this by pointing to the fact that Paul mentioned only Adam in Rom. 5:12-21, but there are 2 Cor. 11:3 and 1 Tim. 2:14. Feminists may seek to explain the silence in terms of male chauvinism, which in this context means preoccupation with males when interpreting the Bible and doing the work of theology. But this silence is indefensible from the biblical perspective. If there was a prelapsarian Adam, there surely was a prelapsarian Eve. If there was an Adamic fall, there was indeed an Evenic fall. If certain results issued from Adam's sin, the same could be said of Eve's. If there is Adamic depravity, there is assuredly Evenic depravity. This is one aspect of the equality of male and female derived from the Scriptures that even contemporary theologians, male and female, have been slow to affirm.

---

40. *A New Catechism: Catholic Faith for Adults,* pp. 261-62. See also Herbert Haag, *Is Original Sin in Scripture?*, trans. Dorothy Thompson (New York: Sheed and Ward, 1969).

41. Pohle, *God: The Author of Nature and the Supernatural,* pp. 200-218, did refer to "our first parents" when expounding the four preternatural gifts. Miller, "The Fall of Man and Original Sin," did at times refer to "Adam and Eve" (pp. 320, 323, 325).

CHAPTER 36

Sin, Adam and Eve, and Humanity

In addition to probing the nature of sin and the origin of sin among human beings, we must address the humanity-wide aspects of sin. Are all human beings sinners? Does sin affect human society, and, if so, how? Do all human beings have a sinful bias, bent, or nature out of which come specific sins? Can sin be properly called "inevitable"? How ought the relation of the sin of Adam and Eve to our sin and the opposite be understood? These questions call for answers. In this chapter we will first search for biblical materials pertaining to these questions and then examine views and theories framed during the postbiblical history of Christianity.

I. UNIVERSALITY OF SIN

The doctrine of the universality of sin means that all human beings, with the exception of Jesus Christ, have been and are sinners. Roman Catholic dogmatics makes one additional exception: by the dogma of the immaculate conception of Mary (1854) she is said to have been "preserved free" from the moment of her own conception by her parents from what is called "original sin."[1]

A. EVIDENCES FOR THE UNIVERSALITY OF SIN

1. *Biblical Teachings*

a. Passages Teaching or Declaring Such Universality

The Old Testament contains far more texts about the universality of sin than about the fall of the first humans, and the New Testament continues the emphasis on universality.

1) *Old Testament*

Of Noah's generation it was said: "The LORD saw that the wickedness of man was great in the earth, and that every imagination of the thoughts of his heart was only evil continually" (Gen. 6:5, RSV). Simi-

---

1. "The Decree of Pope Pius IX on the Immaculate Conception of the Blessed Virgin Mary," in Schaff, *The Creeds of Christendom*, 2:211-12.

larly, that same "imagination of man's heart" was said to have been "evil from his youth" (Gen. 8:21). Such texts imply, if they do not teach, the universality of sin. In Solomon's prayer at the dedication of the temple, parenthetical allusion to universality was made while asking divine compassion on the people if and when taken into captivity (1 Kings 8:46a). The fullest of the Servant Songs declared: "All we like sheep have gone astray; we have turned every one to his own way" (Isa. 53:6a, b). In a prayer for restoration from captivity we read: "we all became like a man who is unclean and all our righteous deeds like a filthy rag; we have all withered like leaves and our iniquities sweep us away like the wind" (Isa. 64:6, NEB). " 'Can the Ethiopian change his skin or the leopard his spots? Then also you can do good who are accustomed to do evil' " (Jer. 13:23, RSV). Job asked: " 'Who can bring a clean thing out of an unclean? There is not one'" (14:4), and Eliphaz asked, " 'What is man, that he can be clean? Or he that is born of woman, that he can be righteous?'" (Job 15:14). In Proverbs one reads: "Who can say, 'I have made my heart clean; I am pure from my sin'?" (20:9). The Preacher declared: "Surely there is not a righteous man on earth who does good and never sins" (Eccl. 7:20). Israel's hymnbook contains the same teaching. "They have all gone astray, they are all alike corrupt; there is none that does good, no, not one" (Ps. 14:3). Ps. 36:1-4 details the way of the wicked, and Ps. 53:1-3 is even more specific:

> The fool says in his heart, "There is no God." They are corrupt, doing abominable iniquity; there is none that does good. God looks down from heaven upon the sons of men to see if there are any that are wise, that seek after God. They have all fallen away; they are all alike depraved; there is none that does good, no, not one.

"If thou, O LORD, shouldst mark iniquities, Lord, who could stand?" (Ps. 130:3), for "no man living is righteous before thee" (Ps. 143:2).

2) New Testament

In announcing the Father's gift of the Holy Spirit, Jesus assumed human evil in his "how much more" approach: " 'If you then, who are evil, know how to give good gifts to your children, how much more will the heavenly Father give the Holy Spirit to those who ask him!' " (Luke 11:13, RSV). Quoting Ps. 14:1-2 in the midst of his statement, Paul declared to the Romans (3:9, 22b-23):

> What then? Are we Jews any better off? No, not at all; for I have already charged that all men, both Jews and Greeks, are under the power of sin. . . . For there is no distinction; since all have sinned and fall short of the glory of God.

All of humankind, according to Paul, are "by nature children of wrath" (Eph. 2:3b). For John the message was the same. "If we say we have no sin," he wrote to Christians, "we deceive ourselves, and the truth is not in us" (1 John 1:8, 10). Indeed, "the whole world is in the power of the evil one" (1 John 5:19b).

b. Other Biblical Evidence

(1) The New Testament contains calls for all humans to repent of sin (Acts 17:30; 2 Pet. 3:9), presents the new birth as needed by all humans (John 3:5), and presents the universality of human death as presupposing the universality of sin (Rom. 5:12).

(2) Even the heroes of the Bible are presented as sinners: "Noah, Abraham, Moses, David," Peter, James and John, and Paul.[2]

2. *Extrabiblical Evidence*

a. Consciousness of Guilt

The widespread sense of shame and failure and consciousness of guilt that one finds in human life and experience is an indirect testimony to some objective reason for such, namely, that all human beings sin.

b. Sacrifice

The widespread, almost universal, occurrence of sacrifices in the history of religion, including sacrifices for sin, is further evidence that all human beings do sin and hence need to make reparations for or obtain forgiveness of sin.

B. THE MEANING OF THE UNIVERSALITY OF SIN

In what follows we will briefly explain two aspects of the meaning of the truth that all human beings are sinners, namely, the personal and the social, the individual and the corporate.

1. *Universality of Personal Sinning*

On the basis of the biblical passages cited above and the corroboration of human experience Christians affirm that every human being, except Jesus Christ, who has attained to moral responsibility has actually sinned. Without negating the empirical dimension, we should mean by such an affirmation more than a kind of mathematical reporting that all observed human beings give evidence of having sinned. Such an affirmation can be made before any such count of earth's billions can be completed. "Even Pelagians and Socinians are [i.e., were] ready to admit that sin is universal."[3]

2. *Social Interaction and Solidarity of Sin*

To affirm that "all have sinned, and come short of the glory of God" (Rom. 3:23, KJV) is to mean more than the worldwide aggregation of the

2. Erickson, *Christian Theology*, p. 624.
3. Berkhof, *Systematic Theology*, p. 239.

sinning of individual human beings. Indeed, it means that all human social relationships, societal institutions and structures, and indeed the whole human (and one may venture to say "cosmic") order have been affected by and reflect the reality of sin. In the Gospel of John the term "world" was sometimes used in this sense (7:7; 15:18-19; 17:6, 14, 16, 25). In Europe and North America Christians in the modern era have been made more aware of the social dimensions of sin by virtue of the Social Gospel movement.

II. UNIVERSALITY OF DEPRAVITY

Those Christian thinkers who understand "depravity" as being essentially and in itself "sin" would treat depravity as a type of sin and hence under the heading of sin, but those who understand "depravity" as tending or leading to sin but not sin per se would treat depravity under a category other than that of sin proper.

A. ETYMOLOGY

The English word "depravity" is derived from the Latin preposition *de*, meaning "thoroughly," and the adjective *pravus*, meaning "crooked."

B. BIBLICAL TEXTS CITED

The biblical passages most often cited as pertaining to the theological concept of depravity are probably the following. First, the psalmist declares: "Behold, I was brought forth in iniquity, and in sin did my mother conceive me" (51:5, RSV). The same text reads in the NIV: "Surely I was sinful at birth, sinful from the time my mother conceived me." The text should not be taken as a warrant for concluding that procreation or childbirth is inherently evil. Such an idea was acceptable to the Manichaeans, but it does not conform to the Hebraic way of thinking. Rather, the text indicates that sinfulness is very deeply rooted in human life and pervasive throughout the human story, generation after generation. Second, there is Jeremiah's report of Yahweh's word: " 'The heart is deceitful above all things, and desperately corrupt' " (" 'sick,' " NASV) (17:9, RSV). Third, Rom. 7:18a (NIV) declares: "I know that nothing good lives in me, that is, in my sinful nature." Finally, Eph. 2:3 is likewise cited in reference to depravity.

C. DEFINING "DEPRAVITY"

There is widespread agreement among Christian thinkers that every human being possesses a depraved or corrupted or fallen nature and that out of that depraved nature arises or occurs sin, or what some call "actual sin." But Christian theologians are not fully agreed as to the precise definition that ought to be given to the term "depravity."

1. Depravity as Hereditary Corruption

John Calvin defined "original sin" as "a hereditary corruption and depravity of our nature, extending to all parts of the soul, which first makes us obnoxious to the wrath of God, and then produces in us works which in Scripture are termed works of the flesh." Calvin made it clear that, for him, "original sin" was much more than the lack of original righteousness or than concupiscence, as Thomas Aquinas had held. For Calvin, therefore, depravity was the "hereditary corruption" of a person's total being.[4]

2. Depravity as the Inevitability of Sinning

Walter T. Conner held that "depravity" means that it is "not only possible that he [a human being] may sin because of the power of choice, but certain (though not necessary) that he will sin on account of his moral weakness and inherent tendency toward evil." In such a definition "moral weakness" should not be equated with creaturely weakness or finitude. Conner used "certain" while disclaiming "necessary." For him, therefore, depravity was virtually the inevitability of human sinning.[5]

Not only have there been different definitions of depravity but also there have been differences at the point of whether depravity is really sin per se or only a tendency or nature that leads to sin. The explication of these differences can best be undertaken when discussing the various theories as to the relation of the sin of Adam and Eve to our sin.[6]

D. WHAT OF "TOTAL DEPRAVITY"?

Protestant theologians have been prone to affirm the "total depravity" of humankind, using the term in a somewhat specialized sense. Some wrong notions have sometimes been associated with or attributed to "total depravity." The term should not, therefore, be taken to mean that all human beings are presently as corrupt as possible or to mean that all human beings are equally sinful in every respect.[7]

In addition to the meanings associated with the term "depravity" in general, the term "total depravity" has generally conveyed two basic meanings:

1. Totality of Human Personhood in Sin

Total depravity means that every aspect of a person's being is affected by sin.[8] It means that there is "corruption at the very center of

4. *Institutes of the Christian Religion* 2.1.8, trans. Henry Beveridge; see Thomas Aquinas, *Summa Theologica*, I-II, q. 82, art. 3.
5. *The Gospel of Redemption*, p. 22.
6. See below, III, B.
7. Conner, *The Gospel of Redemption*, p. 24; Berkhof, *Systematic Theology*, p. 246; E. G. Robinson, *Christian Theology* (Rochester, N.Y.: E. R. Andrews, 1894), p. 163.
8. Conner, *The Gospel of Redemption*, p. 24.

man's being" and "infection in every part of man's being."[9] This corruption "extends to every part of man's nature, to all the faculties and powers of both soul and body."[10]

2. Humankind's Total Inability

Total depravity also means that "man is totally unable to deliver himself from the power of sin"[11] and totally unable "to please God or come to him unless moved by [God's] grace."[12]

Other meanings have been associated with "total depravity." Louis Berkhof found it to mean that in human beings "there is no spiritual good" in the sense of "good in relation to God,"[13] and for Conner it meant that humans, "without the redeeming power of God's grace, . . . will forever sink deeper and deeper into sin."[14] Indeed, depravity provides a more realistic assessment of the human situation than unwarranted optimism.

> The congenital weakness of human nature is the submerged rock on which the complacent claims of an optimistic humanism are shipwrecked.[15]

E. DEPRAVITY AND CREATION

In affirming the depravity, or the total depravity, of human beings, the Christian must never lose sight of the truth that humans are still creatures of almighty God. Matthias Flacius, whose thought has been introduced earlier,[16] held that "no distinction should be made, even in the mind, between man's nature itself after the Fall and original sin, and that the two cannot be differentiated in the mind."[17] We should understand his term "original sin" in terms of depravity but recognize clearly that depraved human beings originated in the creative work of God, being created in God's image, and will ultimately be accountable to God in the last judgment. Meanwhile they, being depraved, may be transformed in their natures by the redeeming and regenerating work of God in Jesus Christ.

III. THE SIN OF ADAM AND EVE AND OUR SIN

If all human beings, except Jesus Christ, have sinned and do sin, if all human beings have a depraved or corrupted nature, if sin is more than

9. Bloesch, *Essentials of Evangelical Theology,* 1:90.
10. Berkhof, *Systematic Theology,* p. 247.
11. Conner, *The Gospel of Redemption,* p. 24.
12. Bloesch, *Essentials of Evangelical Theology,* 1:90.
13. *Systematic Theology,* p. 247.
14. Conner, *The Gospel of Redemption,* p. 25.
15. Whale, *Christian Doctrine,* pp. 40-41. Even John Locke (1632-1704) held to depravity, according to W. M. Spellman, *John Locke and the Problem of Depravity* (Oxford: Oxford University Press, 1988), esp. pp. 1-7, 203-14.
16. See above, Ch. 34, III, A.
17. *Formula of Concord,* Epitome 1, antithesis 9; Solid Declaration, ch. 1, in *The Book of Concord: The Confessions of the Evangelical Lutheran Church,* trans. and ed. Theodore G. Tappert (Philadelphia: Muhlenberg Press, 1959), pp. 468, 508-19.

the individual acts of isolated individual human beings, and if human sin did commence with the sin of Adam and Eve, then the question must be asked: How is the sin of Adam and Eve related to the depravity and sinning of the rest of humankind, and vice versa? This question was of major importance, it seems, for Paul the apostle, if not for other biblical writers. Some Christian theologians have placed this question under the rubric of the imputation of guilt, whereas for others it has been connected with the transmission of depravity or with the sinning of individual human beings. In dealing with this question anew, we would do well to remember that the Old Testament made a place for the corporate and for the individual: "visiting the iniquity of the fathers upon the children to the third and fourth generation of those who hate me" (Exod. 20:5c, RSV), and "the soul that sins dies" (Ezek. 18:4c). We must try to determine Paul's meaning and the meaning that can be affirmed as Christian truth today.

A. *Textus Classicus:* Rom. 5:12-21

One biblical text related to the topic under consideration stands out in the splendor of its uniqueness, Rom. 5:12-21, the RSV text of which reads:

> 12 Therefore as sin came into the world through one man and death through sin, and so death spread to all men because all men sinned—13 sin indeed was in the world before the law was given, but sin is not counted where there is no law. 14 Yet death reigned from Adam to Moses, even over those whose sins were not like the transgression of Adam, who was a type of the one who was to come.
>
> 15 But the free gift is not like the trespass. For if many died through one man's trespass, much more have the grace of God and the free gift in the grace of that one man Jesus Christ abounded for many. 16 And the free gift is not like the effect of that one man's sin. For the judgment following one trespass brought condemnation, but the free gift following many trespasses brings justification. 17 If, because of one man's trespass, death reigned through that one man, much more will those who receive the abundance of grace and the free gift of righteousness reign in life through the one man Jesus Christ.
>
> 18 Then as one man's trespass led to condemnation for all men, so one man's act of righteousness leads to acquittal and life for all men. 19 Law came in to increase the trespass; but where sin increased, grace abounded all the more, 21 so that, as sin reigned in death, grace also might reign through righteousness to eternal life through Jesus Christ our Lord.

The passage, it should be noted at the outset, provides a panoramic contrast between the effects wrought through two men, Adam and Jesus Christ. This contrast may be summarized as follows:

The man Adam → Sin → Condemnation → Death
The man Jesus Christ → Grace → Justification → Life

The passage contains four nouns for sin: *hamartia,* "missing the mark" (vv. 12 [twice], 13 [twice], 20, 21); *parabasis,* "going over, disregarding, transgression" (v. 14); *paraptōma*, "falling beside, deviation, trespass" (vv. 15 [twice], 16, 17, 18, 20); and *parakoēs*, "hearing amiss, unwillingness to hear, disobedience" (v. 19).

How ought Rom. 5:12-21 to be viewed in relation to the entire Epistle to the Romans and to Paul's entire doctrine of sin? Exegetes and theologians have differed in their answers. Anders Nygren, denying that Rom. 5:12-21 was in any sense "a parenthesis or a digression in the apostle's thought," concluded:

> Rather do we here come to the high point of the epistle. This is the point where all the lines of his thinking converge, both those of the preceding chapters and those of the chapters that follow.[18]

John Murray (1898-) quoted Nygren's statement approvingly.[19] On the other hand, W. T. Conner viewed the passage in a different light, especially as to its importance for the issues of guilt and condemnation. His argument was fourfold. First, the passage "has been given too prominent a place in Paul's doctrine of sin." Second, in the passage "Paul is not discussing primarily the question of sin and condemnation" but rather "the sweep of Christ's redemptive work." Third, theologians should "go to Romans 1:18-3:21 to get Paul's doctrine of sin and guilt rather than to Romans 5:12-21." Fourth, "if we interpret Rom. 5:12-21 in such a way as to make Paul responsible for a view that is inconsistent with his view in Romans 1:18 to 3:20, we had better revise our interpretation of 5:12-21."[20] Dale Moody observed that in Romans "the universality of individual sins is stated first as an empirical fact, with reference to the sin of the First Adam coming later as a corollary to the redemption that is in Jesus Christ, the Last Adam."[21] How one regards the passage in relation to the entire epistle, therefore, may be not only reflective of but also determinative of one's view of sin as taught in the passage.

The key or crucial phrase in the entire passage with respect to the doctrine of sin is found in v. 12b: "for that all have sinned" (KJV) *(eph' hō pantes hēmarton)*. These words have been variously translated in modern English versions of the New Testament:

"because all men sinned" (RSV, Goodspeed)
"because all sinned" (NASV, NIV)
"inasmuch as all men have sinned" (NEB)
"because everyone has sinned" (JB)
"in that all sinned" (Berkeley)
"because all had sinned" (Montgomery)

18. *Commentary on Romans*, trans. Carl C. Rasmussen (Philadelphia: Muhlenberg Press, 1949), p. 209.
19. *The Imputation of Adam's Sin* (Grand Rapids: Eerdmans, 1959), p. 6.
20. *The Faith of the New Testament*, pp. 286-89.
21. *The Word of Truth*, p. 280.

Augustine of Hippo, who utilized the Old Latin versions of the New Testament that prevailed prior to Jerome's Vulgate, mistakenly read the Greek *eph' hō*, "because," as equivalent to the Latin *in quo*, "in whom," and thus misinterpreted the phrase to mean "in whom all have sinned." This mistranslation served as biblical "support" for Augustine's doctrine of *peccatum originale*, or "original sin."

A very basic question needs to be raised concerning v. 12b, the answers to which are not unrelated to the history of the exegesis of this phrase. The question is this: How do all human beings sin? The possible answers are numerous, and they have usually been phrased so as not to mention Eve. Did they sin by being united with or at least potentially in Adam as their progenitor? Did they sin through Adam as their covenantal representative? Do they sin by inheriting Adam's fallen nature and then becoming guilty of Adam's sin? Do they sin because of an inexplicable defect or fault in their own wills? Do they sin by yielding to the pressures of societal evil and committing sin, both individual and corporate? Do they sin by willful sins growing out of a fallen nature inherited from Adam? Do they sin by following the bad example of Adam in sinning? To conclude that one of these possible answers is undoubtedly the intent of Paul in v. 12b is unlikely on the basis of exegesis of the text alone.

The Apostle Paul in this text is like a painter who is painting with a broad brush, not with a fine brush for the details. Although in Rom. 5:12-21 Paul seems not to imply that all human beings will actually and effectually be redeemed through Jesus Christ, he does not in the passage itself indicate precisely how the individual human being appropriates for himself the redemption available through Christ. Likewise, it seems, Paul does not settle indisputably for his day and for all time to come the question as to how the sin of individual human beings is related to and hence ought properly to be understood vis-à-vis the sin of Adam and Eve. From the fifth century A.D. onward there have been numerous efforts to explain or theorize about this relationship, and it is to these theories that we now turn.

B. THEORIES AS TO THE RELATION OF THE SIN OF ADAM AND EVE TO OUR SIN

The principal historic theories may most usefully be classified according to whether or not they teach the imputation of any guilt for the sin of Adam and Eve to all other members of the human race. Imputation, therefore, becomes the principle of classification.

1. *Theories Teaching the Imputation of Guilt*

a. Theory of Realism, or of the Oneness of Human Nature in Adam

According to this theory, common human nature as one existed in prelapsarian Adam so that when he sinned, not only he but also this common human nature that was one in him sinned. Every human born into the world is an individualization of this common human nature and is thus guilty and punishable for the sin that was committed by the common human nature in Adam. This theory, which rests on Platonic philosophy, has been attributed to Augustine of Hippo. Indeed, some passages in Augustine's writings suggest this theory. Especially is this true of his saying that "all sinned, since all were that one man"[22] and a more extended statement in *On the City of God*.[23] But John Murray has made a rather persuasive argument, somewhat against A. H. Strong, to the effect that Augustine, when studied in context, will be seen to be giving primary emphasis, contra Pelagius, to the theme that by "propagation" and not by "imitation" has the one sin of Adam resulted in the condemnation of all humankind. Hence Augustine was not completely given to the realistic theory but majored even more on the idea that Adam's defilement or depravity was transmitted by natural generation.[24] It was in this setting that Augustine could suggest that the pleasurable exercise of the sex drive that occurs in copulation is the medium for its transmission.[25]

W. G. T. Shedd seems to have been a more consistent and singular advocate of the realistic view.[26] A. H. Strong also embraced the theory, teaching that all humans "existed, not individually, but seminally" in Adam as head.[27] Millard Erickson has stated that he has "espoused" realism, or the theory of "natural headship," and following Strong and not heeding Murray's correction, he has attributed this view singularly to Augustine. But, perhaps because he is a Baptist, Erickson, realizing that such thinking has often led to or been coupled with infant baptism, exempted infants and young children from the imputation and also noted that Christ's grace was not imputed alike to believers and nonbelievers. He then, in conclusion, abandoned realism and instead opted for what we will later identify as the Placean theory of the imputation of depravity.[28]

b. Covenantal or Federal or Representative Theory

According to this theory God appointed Adam as the representative of the entire human race. God made a so-called "covenant of works"[29] with Adam and all humanity. Thus, on the condition of his obedience, human beings would have eternal life, and on the condition of his disobedience, Adam and all humanity would be subject to corruption and death. After and because of Adam's sin God has imputed to all humans the guilt

22. *On the Merits and Remission of Sins* 1.10.11.
23. 13.14.
24. *The Imputation of Adam's Sin*, pp. 29-32.
25. Bonner, *St. Augustine of Hippo: Life and Controversies*, pp. 374-78.
26. *Dogmatic Theology*, 2:29-32, 41-44, 181-92; Murray, *The Imputation of Adam's Sin*, pp. 24-25, 32-33.
27. *Systematic Theology*, pp. 619-37; Murray, *The Imputation of Adam's Sin*, pp. 25-27.
28. *Christian Theology*, pp. 636-39.
29. See above, Ch. 7, I, A, n. 1.

of Adam's sin. Adam's descendants are born with a depraved nature, which always leads to sin and is sinful. The depravity, however, is the effect of the imputation and not its cause. Thus, like realism, the federal theory is a theory of the immediate imputation of Adamic guilt to all human beings.[30]

John Cocceius was an early exponent of this theory, and Francis Turretin was an important factor in the shift from the realism of the older Calvinism to the federalism of the later Calvinism.[31] The Westminster Confession of Faith embraced both realism[32] and federalism,[33] but the Larger Catechism was more committed to federalism.[34] Charles Hodge explicated the covenant of works without dependence on any specific biblical texts and then defended federalism as the proper theory of imputation, holding that Adam was "not only the natural, but also the federal head of his posterity" and asserting that Rom. 5:12-21 formally teaches federalism.[35] James P. Boyce followed Hodge, arguing that "the federal relationship becomes necessary in connection with salvation through Christ." The extensive body of biblical texts cited by Boyce shows that Yahweh dealt with Israel corporately, that Israelite leaders exercised a representative role, or that there was representation in the sacrificial system but does not address the question of Adam's sin per se.[36] Murray defended federalism on the basis that Rom. 5:12-21 implies a need for parallels between Christ and Adam.[37] Federalists accept and utilize the concept of humankind's seminal unity in Adam but do not accept the numerical oneness of unborn humanity in Adam.[38] Critics of federalism and the covenant of works have asked for evidence of specific biblical teaching.

c. Theory of Mediate Imputation through Depravity

Josua de la Place, or Placeus (1596-1665? 1655?), of Saumur, France, advocated the theory that depravity is the medium through which the imputation of Adam's guilt to all human beings takes place. All humans are born with depravity, and it is not only the source of sin but also sin itself.[39] La Place was at first understood to be teaching that there was no

30. Strong, *Systematic Theology*, pp. 612-13.

31. Shedd, *Dogmatic Theology*, 2:36.

32. Ch. 6, sect. 3: "They [Adam and Eve] being the root *(radix)* of all mankind, the guilt of this sin was imputed . . . to all their posterity. . . ."

33. Ch. 7, sects. 2, 3: "The first covenant . . . was a covenant of works, wherein life was promised to Adam, and in him to his posterity, upon condition of perfect and personal obedience." "Man by his fall having made himself incapable of life by that covenant, the Lord was pleased to make a second. . . ."

34. *Larger Catechism*, q. 22; *Shorter Catechism*, q. 16.

35. *Systematic Theology*, 2:117-22, 192-205.

36. *Abstract of Systematic Theology*, pp. 252-58.

37. *The Imputation of Adam's Sin*, pp. 38-41.

38. Ibid., pp. 26-27.

39. Strong, *Systematic Theology*, p. 617.

imputation of the guilt of Adam's first sin to humankind. The condemnation by the Reformed Synod of Charenton (1644-45) seemingly was based on a misunderstanding of La Place's teaching. In reply he maintained that he did not deny imputation and did not restrict original sin to hereditary corruption. Rather he insisted that the imputation "was *mediate*, not *immediate*," it being "mediated through the inheritance from him [Adam] of a corrupt nature."[40]

Murray, contrary to Charles Hodge and William Cunningham (1805-61) and supporting B. B. Warfield, has concluded that Jonathan Edwards did not teach a form of mediate imputation but that later New England theologians (Samuel Hopkins [1721-1803], Nathanael Emmons [1745-1840], Timothy Dwight [1752-1817], and Nathaniel William Taylor [1786-1858]), progressively diminished to the point of denying any doctrine of imputation.[41] American theologians who did accept the Placean theory included Henry Boynton Smith (1815-77).[42]

2. Theories Not Teaching the Imputation of Guilt

a. Theory of a Bad Example

This view was first advanced by Pelagius and then held in later centuries by Socinians and Unitarians. Adam by sinning injured himself, but the effect of sin on his posterity was basically that of a bad example. His sin was not imputed to his posterity and did not corrupt or pollute human nature. Every newborn human being is innocent and fully able to obey God, as Adam had been at his creation. God imputes to human beings only those sins which they have "personally and consciously" committed. By persistent sinning each human can acquire the "habit of sinning." Physical death is natural, not punitive.[43]

b. Theory of Social as well as Biological Transmission of Moral Evil

Walter Rauschenbusch stressed the social dimension of sin without losing its character as revolt against God. Holding to organic evolution, he "rejected the historicity of Adam." While retaining the biological transmission of moral evil, examples of which would be idiocy, feeble-mindedness, neuroses, and perverse desires, Rauschenbusch placed greater emphasis on its social transmission. The latter he related to his concepts of the "Kingdom of evil" and of "collective guilt" for social sins. With no place for a historical Adam and with no concern for historic

---

40. Murray, *The Imputation of Adam's Sin*, pp. 42-46.

41. Ibid., pp. 47-64.

42. *System of Christian Theology*, ed. William S. Karr (3d ed.; New York: A. C. Armstrong, 1888), pp. 304-8, as cited by Murray, *The Imputation of Adam's Sin*, p. 47, n. 66; pp. 169, 284, 285, 314-23, as cited by Strong, *Systematic Theology*, p. 617.

43. Wiggers, *An Historical Presentation of Augustinism and Pelagianism*, pp. 83-88; Strong, *Systematic Theology*, p. 597.

theories of imputation of guilt, he in effect limited imputation to actual sins, individual and collective.[44]

c. Theory of "Voluntarily Appropriated Depravity"

As a result of Adam's sin, this theory holds, all human beings lack original righteousness or primitive holiness and, apart from divine help, are unable to obey God. This inability is physical and intellectual, but does not include the will. The Holy Spirit is at work to enable the human will to resist depravity and to obey God, if the human will will cooperate with the Spirit. Adam's guilt is not imputed to humankind, and neither is human depravity until each human voluntarily and consciously appropriates it by sinning. Physical and spiritual death are not the penalty for Adam's sin but for the sin of all humans.[45]

Some have attempted to trace this view to certain Greek Fathers and to the Semi-Pelagians.[46] It has been held of late within the Wesleyan tradition; John Miley[47] and H. Orton Wiley[48] have expounded it.

d. Theory of an "Inevitable" Defect or Bias in the Human Will

Reinhold Niebuhr, the representative exponent of this view, denied the historicity of Adam and held to the existential fall of every human being. For him original sin is a defect or bias in the human will that precedes and presupposes the act of sinning and for which human beings are responsible. This defect in the will is "inevitable" but not "necessary," and the same may be said of each existential fall. For Niebuhr, God imputes to human beings both their actual sins and the biased or defective will that is responsible for them.[49]

e. Theory of Uncondemnable Depravity

This theory holds that human depravity always leads to sin but is not sin per se, and hence human beings are not condemned for their depravity but for the sins to which depravity has led. It can be traced to the theology of the Zurich Reformer, Ulrich Zwingli, who defined sin in a twofold way: as "that disease which we contract from the author of our race, in consequence of which we are given over to love of ourselves" and as "that which is contrary to the Law." He concluded that "sin that is transgression is born of sin that is disease."[50] More specifically Zwingli defined "original sin" as "disease" (morbus) and combined disease "with

44. *A Theology for the Social Gospel*, pp. 38-44, 57-68; Smith, *Changing Conceptions of Original Sin*, pp. 198-206.
45. Strong, *Systematic Theology*, pp. 601-2.
46. Ibid., p. 601; Wiley, *Christian Theology*, 2:122-23.
47. *Systematic Theology*, 1:508-9, 521-33.
48. *Christian Theology*, 2:96-100, 107-9, 118-40.
49. *The Nature and Destiny of Man*, 1:256-80.
50. *Commentary on True and False Religion* (1525), ch. 10, ed. Samuel Macaulay Jackson and Clarence Nevin Heller (Durham, N.C.: Labyrinth Press, 1981), pp. 138, 139, 140.

a defect *(vitium)*, and that a lasting one, as when stammering, blindness, or gout is hereditary in a family." Original sin is thus a "disease" but not "sin," "because sin implies guilt, and guilt comes from a transgression or trespass." Zwingli did hold that original sin "damns" "so far as its force and nature are concerned," but he exempted the children of Christians and held that the remedy of the blood of Christ was sufficient to overcome it.[51]

The New England Congregational theologians Hopkins, Emmons, Dwight, and Taylor espoused this theory. They agreed that human beings are not guilty of Adam's sin and that depravity is not imputed to all humans. Depravity does exist but is acquired. The connection between Adam's sin and ours is a "divine constitution," which turns out to be a synonym for the inevitability of sinning. Taylor called depravity a "predominant" "sinful elective preference." According to the New England school, human beings are only accountable and condemnable for their own sins, by the committing of which they join Adam's rebellion.[52]

Charles Grandison Finney (1792-1875) also identified with this view. Differentiating between "physical depravity," or disease, and "moral depravity" and yet holding that humankind has both, Finney defined moral depravity as "selfishness," and "self-interest, self-gratification, or self-indulgence as an end." He refuted the view of those who were insisting that moral depravity is sin itself.[53]

The theories that teach that to all human beings have been imputed the sin and guilt of Adam (and one should add, of Eve) (realistic, federal, Placean) face in some circles the problems attendant on a historical original state and fall of humankind. In more inclusive circles these theories face the objection as to the justice of human beings, yet unborn, being reckoned guilty of the sin of ancient progenitors. Ezekiel's doctrine of individual accountability for sin continues to be cited against these theories. Others have contended that imputational theories ignore or fail to square with Rom. 1:18–3:20. John Murray has made as strong a case for imputation of Adamic guilt on the basis of Rom. 5:12-21 as any, but even his exegesis does not establish a "covenant of works."

The theories of a nonimputational nature that focus on depravity rather than on the sin of Adam and Eve (Wesleyan, Zwinglian–New England) ask the basic question: Is each human being guilty for a depraved nature as well as for specific voluntary sins? The answers differ only slightly: not until willfully appropriated by sinning (Wesleyan); no, not really (New England, with Zwingli slightly differing). One finds in the Bible much emphasis on humans' being guilty of hardening their heart,

51. *Original Sin* (1526), in *On Providence and Other Essays,* ed. for Samuel Macaulay Jackson by William John Hinke (Durham, N.C.: Labyrinth Press, 1983), pp. 3, 4, 5, 15.
52. Murray, *The Imputation of Adam's Sin,* pp. 48-52.
53. *Lectures on Systematic Theology,* ed. J. H. Fairchild (New York: George H. Doran Company, 1878), lects. 22-24.

of being stiff-necked, of rebelling against God, of forsaking the covenant, of having an evil heart, and so on. Some of these expressions can be taken as suggestive of a sinful nature, but not necessarily of an inherited and/or condemnable sinful nature.

The Pelagian theory tends to look at human sinfulness in an atomistic fashion so that the impact of sin on other human beings is minimized. The Adamic blot on the human escutcheon can be too easily dismissed or relegated to lesser significance. Modern awareness of the social dimensions of human sinfulness hardly fits into a strict Pelagian model.

The theories of social transmission (Rauschenbusch) and of existential sinning (Niebuhr) may serve to complement one another. The former does not rule out altogether biological transmission, and the latter, when understood in the light of Niebuhr's total teaching, has social consequences. Today the interaction of sin throughout all humankind may be a more relevant way of expressing the corporate aspects of sin than that characterizing many of the earlier theories. Twentieth-century human beings have been made more aware of "man's inhumanity to man," partly because of changes in communication. In the century of the Holocaust, the advent of nuclear weaponry, the rise of organized crime, and the coming of international terrorism, we have become more aware than some of our forefathers of the social consequences of sin. No one can live today apart from the effects of fellow humans on him or her and his or her effects on fellow humans. John Donne (1572-1631) was certain: "No man is an island, entire of itself,"[54] and George Washington Truett (1867-1944) repeatedly affirmed that "we all are bound up in the bundle of life."[55] Moral evil has ever-widening effects like ripples on a lake. It is not difficult in today's socio-cultural situation to acknowledge the pervasive interaction of moral evil among all human beings. It may be more difficult to reach agreement as to the specific responsibility of individual human beings for sin that has such detrimental effects on the many.

Even so, we must recognize that sin and society had their beginnings in humanity's ancient past, and thus the truth of the universal pervasiveness and interaction of sin can never be fully severed from the question of sin's origin. Our human solidarity in sin is with our ancient parents Adam and Eve, as well as with a multitude of contemporary Adams and Eves.

Certain questions, which serve both to summarize and to point to a conclusion, can now be asked.

Do we have a sinful nature? Pelagius has said, No; all others have said, Yes.

54. *Devotions* 17.
55. "The Conquest of Fear," in *"Follow Thou Me"* (New York: Harper and Bros., 1932), p. 105, where Truett made the statement in the context of needed brotherly interdependence, and "It Pays to Do Right" (Fort Worth: Radio and Television Commission, Southern Baptist Convention, 194?), where Truett used these words in the context of the universality of sin. Per Stephen Danzey and Bette and Wendell Haynes.

Can I be held accountable and punishable for deeds growing out of a nature (or context) that I have inherited? The Wesleyans have said, Yes, by willful sinning through an undepraved, Spirit-wooed will. Zwingli has said, Yes, for they grew out of the nature. New Englanders have said, Yes, I am accountable, but the sinful nature has been acquired. Rauschenbusch has said, Yes, when committed by individuals and by groups.

Am I responsible for a "nature" that I have inherited or received? Placeus has said, Yes, for that nature is the medium through which I was made guilty of the sin of Adam and Eve. Niebuhr has said, I am accountable for my biased or defective will, but I cannot trace it to an ancient ancestor. All other nonimputationists have said, No.

Am I guilty of the sin of Adam and Eve in addition to being guilty for sins that I have consciously, voluntarily, or at least personally committed? Realists have said, Yes, by being in the common human nature that was one with Adam when he sinned and before the individuation of other humans. Federalists have said, Yes, by being joined through a "covenant of works" with Adam. Placeus has said, Yes, inasmuch as that guilt is mediated to me through my depravity.

To affirm the universality of sin is easy and to affirm the universality of depravity is not difficult, but to settle on the relationship of the sin of Adam and Eve to our sin is indeed difficult, as the number of the theories would seem to suggest. Whatever conclusion be adopted, it should make a place for a sinful nature as well as sinful deeds, should see sin both individually and socially, and should present the consequences of progenitorial sin in such a way that we humans today can be aware of all that for which we are responsible.

CHAPTER 37

Temptation; Consciousness of Sin

Before we consider the consciousness of sin, it will be helpful to give attention to the nature and meaning of temptation. They are closely related topics, but they also need to be differentiated properly.

I. TEMPTATION

Temptation means the occasion, the incitement, or the inducement to human sin.

A. BIBLICAL TERMS AND TEACHINGS

1. Old Testament

Behind and beyond word usage that specifically meant incitement to sin was the wider and more common Old Testament conception of testing or trying, which was not directly related to any inducement to moral evil. The Hebrew verbs *nāsāh* and *bāḥan*, both of which can mean "to try, prove, or tempt," were normally used to refer to testing or trying in a general sense. Sometimes they were used of God's testing of humans, and at other times they were used of humans' testing of God. *Nāsāh* was used of God's testing of human beings in Gen. 22:1; Exod. 16:4; 20:20; Deut. 13:3; Judg. 2:22; and Ps. 26:2. *Bāḥan* was used of God's testing of humans in Jer. 20:12a; Prov. 17:3; Ps. 7:9b; 11:5a; 66:10; 81:7c; 139:23; and Job 17:18; 23:10b. *Nāsāh* was used of human, chiefly Israelite, testing of Yahweh in Exod. 17:2b, 7; Num. 14:22b; Deut. 6:16; Isa. 7:12; and Ps. 78:18; 95:9; 106:14. *Bāḥan* was used of human testing of God in Ps. 95:9 and Mal. 3:10, 15.

The Hebrew verb *nāśa'*, meaning "to lift up, or beguile," was used in the sense of temptation to sin in Gen. 3:13 (RSV): "The serpent *beguiled* me, and I ate." The account of the temptation of Adam and Eve (Genesis 3) specifies a threefold approach of the tempter in the temptation of Eve and a threefold appeal of the forbidden fruit to Eve. First, the tempter said, "Did God say, 'You shall not eat of any tree of the garden'?" (v. 1), thereby extending or exaggerating the divine prohibition. Second, the tempter said, " 'You will not die' " (v. 4) (see 2:17). Third, he declared, " 'For God

494

knows that when you eat of it your eyes will be opened, and you will be like God, knowing good and evil' " (v. 5). The three appeals to Eve respecting the fruit of the tree of the knowledge of good and evil were: "good for food" (appetite); "a delight to the eyes" (aesthetics); and "to make one wise" (wisdom) (v. 6a). Moreover, "she took of its fruit and ate; and she also gave some to her husband, and he ate" (v. 6b).

2. New Testament

The family of words used in the New Testament to mean induce-ment to sin was also used more generally to convey the idea of testing. The verb *peirazein*,[1] meaning "to try, prove, or tempt," was used several times in the Synoptic Gospels to refer to Jesus in the sense of testing (Luke 11:16; Mark 8:11 and par.; 10:2 and par.; 12:15 and par.; Matt. 22:35; John 8:6; Acts 5:9; 15:10; and Heb. 3:9; 11:37). In the sense of temptation to sin this verb was used in Mark 1:13a and par.; 1 Thess. 3:5; Gal. 6:1; 1 Cor. 7:5; 10:13b; Heb. 2:18 (twice); 4:15; and Jas. 1:13-14 (four times). The noun *peirasmos*,[2] meaning "trial, proof, or temptation," was used of testings or trials in Luke 22:28; Acts 20:19; Gal. 4:14; Heb. 3:8; Jas. 1:2, 12; 1 Pet. 1:6; 2 Pet. 2:9; and Rev. 3:10. It was used of temptation to sin in Luke 4:13; Matt. 6:13 (par. Luke 11:4); Luke 8:13b; 22:40b, 46 and par.; 1 Cor. 10:13a, c (twice); and 1 Tim. 6:9a.

In the New Testament, Satan's tempting and God's testing are clearly differentiated, as may be seen in the wilderness temptations of Jesus (Matt. 4:1-11 and par.) and in filial discipline (Heb. 12:5-11). Temp-tation is the occasion for sin or the incitement to sin, but not the cause of sin. Temptation is attributed to lust (Jas. 1:14) and to the devil (Matt. 4:1; 1 Thess. 3:5). In the full-orbed sense of temptation to evil, God neither tempts humans nor is tempted (Jas. 1:13).

B. RECENT PROTESTANT THEOLOGY

1. Nineteenth- and Twentieth-Century Conservative Protestant Theologians

These theologians have tended to write more about temptation than other theologians and have focused their writing on the temptation of Adam and Eve, not on the temptation of human beings generally or of present-day Christians. Some (Charles Hodge,[3] A. H. Strong,[4] Louis Berkhof,[5] L. S. Chafer[6]) have strongly asserted that Genesis 3 is not to be taken as "myth" or as "allegory" but as literal history. Some (Charles

1. The compound verb *ekpeirazein* was used in Matt. 4:7 and par., Luke 10:25, and 1 Cor. 10:9 of testing.
2. The participle *ho peirazōn*, "the tempter," was used in Matt. 4:3 and 1 Thess. 3:5.
3. *Systematic Theology*, 2:123-24.
4. *Systematic Theology*, pp. 582-83.
5. *Systematic Theology* (1941 ed.), p. 223.
6. *Systematic Theology*, 2:204-5.

Hodge,[7] R. R. Byrum,[8] Louis Berkhof,[9] J. C. Wenger[10]) have interpreted
the serpent as a literal animal used as the instrument of Satan, whereas
others (W. G. T. Shedd,[11] L. S. Chafer,[12] J. Oliver Buswell,[13] J. Rodman
Williams[14]) have referred to the tempting by Satan with little regard for
the serpent or by making an absolute identification of the serpent with
Satan.

There was a tendency among these theologians to present a symbolic
as well as a literal interpretation of "the tree of life" and of "the tree of the
knowledge of good and evil." Geerhardus Vos[15] and J. C. Wenger looked
upon the latter tree as "the maturity tree."

> It could not have meant the temptation tree because God tempts no one to
> evil. Undoubtedly full moral maturity would have been reached not only
> by falling into sin but also by obedience. . . . God created man holy in the
> sense that he was sinless and yet he was merely innocent, not positively holy.
> It was the intention of God to bring man to full maturity and to confirm him
> in holiness by providing for him an experience which would enable him to
> confirm his holiness by a free choice of obedience to God.[16]

The appeals to Eve of the forbidden fruit were viewed as "morally
indifferent" "influences" (Archibald Alexander Hodge[17]) and as "normal
desires" (W. T. Conner[18]). The religio-ethical issue at stake was obedience
to the specific command of God. L. S. Chafer wrote:

> There was no inherent wrong in the eating of fruit. The first sin did not
> consist in a dietetic error. It was not a question of nourishing or injurious
> food. The tree and its fruit became the ground of testing with respect to the
> creature's obedience to his Creator and an issue as extensive and real as life
> itself.[19]

The appeals to Eve were connected with 1 John 2:16 (J. C. Wenger,[20]
J. Oliver Buswell[21]).

The tempter's first word (Gen. 3:1) was interpreted as implying
God's "arbitrarily withholding the means of their [Adam's and Eve's]
gratification"[22] and as expressive of doubt as to the good intention of God

7. *Systematic Theology*, 2:127.
8. *Christian Theology*, p. 320.
9. *Systematic Theology* (1941 ed.), p. 224.
10. *Introduction to Theology*, p. 88.
11. *Dogmatic Theology*, 2:154-56, 161.
12. *Systematic Theology*, 2:203.
13. *A Systematic Theology of the Christian Religion*, 1:264-65.
14. *Renewal Theology*, p. 224.
15. *Biblical Theology: Old and New Testaments* (Grand Rapids: Eerdmans, 1948), pp. 41-43.
16. Wenger, *Introduction to Theology*, p. 88.
17. *Outlines of Theology* (enl. ed.; New York: A. C. Armstrong and Son, 1891), p. 323.
18. *The Gospel of Redemption*, pp. 5-6.
19. *Systematic Theology*, 2:211.
20. *Introduction to Theology*, p. 89.
21. *A Systematic Theology of the Christian Religion*, 1:283.
22. Strong, *Systematic Theology*, p. 584.

by "infringement of human liberty and rights."[23] The second word (Gen. 3:4) was seen as the denial of "the veracity of God"[24] and as unbelief.[25] The third word of the tempter (Gen. 3:5) was taken as a charge against God "of jealousy and fraud in keeping his creatures in a position of ignorance and dependence"[26] and as the tempter's promise that the tree had "magical powers to confer a knowledge of good and evil."[27]

2. Christian Existentialist Theologians

Søren Kierkegaard in a psycho-theological study placed "anxiety" in the role of the context of sin that temptation had traditionally occupied. Although he gave attention to Genesis 3, Kierkegaard's focus was on the "hereditary sin" and "sin" of contemporary humans. Anxiety was identified with "innocence," differentiated from fear, related especially to the human spirit, said to be more prevalent among women than among men, and defined as "entangled freedom." It was seen as "the presupposition of hereditary sin," the explanation of the continuance of hereditary sin, the consequence of sin for the individual, and even the ally of saving faith.[28] For the purpose of the present consideration of temptation, Kierkegaard's most relevant statement may be the following:

> Anxiety is the psychological state that precedes sin. It approaches sin as closely as possible, as anxiously as possible, but without explaining sin, which breaks forth only in the qualitative leap.[29]

Quoting favorably the preceding statement by Kierkegaard, Reinhold Niebuhr likewise emphasized "anxiety," which he reckoned also as the "basis of all human creativity."

> Anxiety is the inevitable concomitant of the paradox of freedom and finiteness in which man is involved. Anxiety is the internal precondition of sin. . . . Anxiety is the internal description of the state of temptation. It must not be identified with sin because there is always the ideal possibility that faith would purge anxiety of the tendency toward sinful self-assertion. . . . It must be distinguished from sin partly because it is its precondition and not its actuality, and partly because it is the basis of all human creativity as well as the precondition of sin.
>
> . . . .
>
> Anxiety, as a permanent concomitant of freedom, is thus both the source of creativity and a temptation to sin.[30]

23. Berkhof, *Systematic Theology* (1941 ed.), p. 223.
24. Strong, *Systematic Theology*, p. 584.
25. Berkhof, *Systematic Theology* (1941 ed.), p. 223.
26. Strong, *Systematic Theology*, p. 584.
27. Wenger, *Introduction to Theology*, p. 88, based on Vos, *Biblical Theology*, p. 43.
28. *The Concept of Anxiety: A Simple Psychologically Orienting Deliberation on the Dogmatic Issue of Hereditary Sin*, ed. and trans. Reidar Thomte (Princeton, N.J.: Princeton University Press, 1980), esp. pp. 41, 42, 44, 47, 49, 25, 52, 81, 11, and 155. The same treatise by Kierkegaard had been published under the English title *The Concept of Dread*, trans. Walter Lowrie (Princeton, N.J.: Princeton University Press, 1946).
29. Ibid., p. 92.
30. *The Nature and Destiny of Man*, 1:194-95, 195, 197-98.

C. THE CHRISTIAN LIFE

Temptation is by no means to be confined to the pre-Christian experience of Christians and the experience of nonbelievers. It does not necessarily decrease as one continues in and grows in Christian character and service but may indeed increase. Temptation addresses not only those walking on the fringes of Christian discipleship but also those who claim to be ministering in Christ's name. It comes not only to those in hierarchically governed churches but also to those in congregationally governed churches. The available incitement to sex, money, fame, or power or to a combination of these so that, if yielded to, one's ministry would be destroyed is enough to make one cry out for the promised "way to escape" (1 Cor. 10:13).

II. CONSCIOUSNESS OF SIN

Previously,[31] in taking note of the emphasis made in the Wesleyan tradition on sin as fully conscious, voluntary, and deliberate, we have allowed for the possibility of some limitations to such voluntarism or to the knowledge of the full range of the reality of sin. Nevertheless, our major stress needs to continue to be on humans' being truly conscious of their sin. As a result, we need to examine three aspects of the consciousness of sin. What are the *means* whereby human beings become conscious of sin? At what *time* do human beings first experience such consciousness of sin? What is the intended *climax* and *consequence* of such consciousness of sin?

A. MEANS OF THE CONSCIOUSNESS OF SIN

1. Conscience

"Conscience" as a Greek noun was used by Paul in Rom. 2:15 (RSV): "while their conscience (*syneidēseōs*) also bears witness (*symmartyrousēs*) and their conflicting thoughts accuse (*katēgorountōn*) or perhaps excuse them." But *syneidēsis*, which was derived from *syn*, meaning "with," and *oida*, meaning "to know," and hence from *synoida*, a perfect tense with a present sense meaning "to share in knowledge," was not frequently used in the New Testament. In Rom. 2:15 it was coordinated with "the requirements of the law . . . written on their hearts" (NIV). C. A. Pierce has refuted the theory of the Stoic origin of the term and has called the term "the catchword of Corinth." *Syneidēsis* is found only three times in the Septuagint (Eccl. 10:20; Ecclus. 42:18; Wisd. 17:11).[32] This fact strengthens the assumption that there was no clear Semitic background to the New Testament usage of the term. According to Paul, human beings, whose

---

31. See above, Ch. 34, III, B.
32. *Conscience in the New Testament*, Studies in Biblical Theology, vol. 15 (London: SCM Press, 1955), pp. 13-20, 60-65, 56-59. Pierce lists 32 uses of *syneidēsis* in the New Testament (p. 62).

consciences give testimony to "the work of the law written on their hearts" (KJV), are subject to accusation as well as excuse. The excusing is not a proof-text for the saving effect of general revelation[33] but rather indicates the double-sided nature of conscience applied in specific moral decisions.

The Christian understanding of conscience, rooted in Paul, differs from both the Socratic and the Kantian approaches to the good or the moral law. Socrates was confident that if humans knew the good they would do the good. Kant gave an essentially moral, rather than religious, emphasis to the categorical imperative, was confident that humans could, at least in life after death, fulfill the moral law, and yet accepted some form of radical evil. In neither Socrates nor Kant was the accusing conscience significant.

Should "conscience" be identified with "moral consciousness"? The answer can be affirmative if both terms refer to something basic to the make-up of human beings and not merely to particular moral decisions or judgments by human beings. "Conscience," therefore, should be differentiated from "moral judgments" or "moral decisions," for the latter are the content of conscience and the product of religio-environmental conditioning as well as of the conscience and the choice of human beings. One would expect Reinhold Niebuhr to have warned at this point: "The particular content of the voice of conscience is of course conditioned by all the relativities of history . . . and conscience may be, in its very content, a vehicle of sin."[34] To complicate the matter of clarifying terms, one may note that Thomas Aquinas called the internal capacity to discern right from wrong "synderesis" and named the ability to distinguish right from wrong in particular situations "conscientia."[35]

Paul seems to have assumed that the exercise of conscience is a universal human experience. About this universality Niebuhr commented: "The significance of the Biblical interpretation of conscience lies precisely in this, that a universal human experience—the sense of being commanded, placed under obligation and judged—is interpreted as a relation between God and man in which it is God who makes demands and judgments upon man."[36]

But how inclusive are the functions of conscience? According to W. T. Conner, there are three aspects of conscience: "an awareness that there is a distinction between right and wrong"; a sense of obligation "to do the right and avoid the wrong"; and some awareness as to what specifically is right and what is wrong.[37] These are the principle of conscience, the obligation of conscience, and the content of conscience. But, among modern philosophers, there has been no little dissent to such

33. See above, Ch. 3, II, C, 2, a.
34. *The Nature and Destiny of Man*, 1:291.
35. *Summa Theologica*, I, q. 79, arts. 12, 13.
36. *The Nature and Destiny of Man*, 1:138.
37. *The Gospel of Redemption*, p. 13.

a view of conscience. Paul Tillich pointed out that, whereas Martin Luther had grounded the "transmoral conscience" in justification by faith, Friedrich Nietzsche sought to destroy the autonomy of the "'moral conscience'" in that "the bad conscience is a sickness," and Martin Heidegger made the "good, *transmoral* conscience" to consist of "*the acceptance of the bad, moral conscience.*"[38]

Does conscience in reality lead human beings to a consciousness of sin? Luther, Niebuhr has emphasized, insisted

> that the law, and man's uneasy conscience, are the first point of contact between God and man. This conscience is the righteousness of the sinner (*justitia peccatoris*). Man's own heart accuses him (*cor accusator*). Without faith this accusation leads to despair and with faith it may lead to repentance.[39]

Emil Brunner insisted:

> A man who had no conscience could not be addressed as a sinner.... And yet, apart from the Christian revelation, man does not know the real meaning and content of this law [written on the hearts].[40]

One may say with Luther that conscience needs to be coupled with law or say with Brunner that conscience needs to be coupled with the gospel, but in either case conscience serves to bring human beings to the consciousness of sin.

2. Law

A second means whereby human beings may come to the consciousness of sin is that which in Hebrew was called *tôrāh* and in Greek *nomos*.

a. Definitions and Usages

"Law" has been defined theologically by Brunner as "the impersonal, concrete, and fixed expression of" the will of God in place of "the fatherly, personal will,"[41] and by Conner as "the embodiment of the moral requirements of God in published ordinances."[42] The term "law" has been and is used in various ways and with differing meanings so that these need carefully to be differentiated, as Brunner has done. Seven such usages may be delineated:

1) God's direction of human life—the root meaning of *tôrāh*, including penal, ceremonial, and moral aspects

38. *The Protestant Era,* trans. James Luther Adams (Chicago: University of Chicago Press, 1948), pp. 145-49.
39. *The Nature and Destiny of Man,* 1:290. Niebuhr cited M. A. H. Stomps, *Die Anthropologie Martin Luthers: Eine philosophische Untersuchung* (Frankfurt am Main: Vittorio Klostermann, 1935), pp. 111-14, and Stomps had cited especially Luther's *Commentary on Romans,* 2.43, 70, 71, and *W.A.,* 3:24, 29, 31, 35, 153, 322, 602; 18:763; 37:59.
40. *The Christian Doctrine of Creation and Redemption,* p. 227.
41. Ibid., p. 120.
42. *The Gospel of Redemption,* p. 13.

2) The entire covenant relation of Israel with Yahweh
3) The Pentateuch, or first five books of the Old Testament
4) The Decalogue, or Ten Commandments (Exod. 20:1-17; Deut. 5:6-21)
5) The Old Covenant in contrast to the New Covenant
6) The law in contrast to promise or gospel (Paul, Luther)
7) The law as "tutor" or "guardian" (Gal. 3:23, 25) to lead to Jesus Christ[43]

Usages 4) and 6), those involving the Decalogue and the contrast with promise or gospel, are more directly associated with the consciousness of sin than the other uses.

b. Revelatory or Accusative Function

Although in Christian theology several legitimate functions of the "law" have been recognized, such as the prohibitory, the revelatory, and the didactic, it is the revelatory[44] or accusatory[45] function of the law that is most important for the consciousness of sin. Paul the apostle took the revelatory or accusatory function of the law to the point wherein the law was virtually an incitement to sin, or temptation. We will not attempt here to settle the exegetical question as to whether Romans 7 portrayed Saul the Pharisee or Paul the Christian. Rather we will note three stages in Paul's encounter with the law:

1) Once alive apart from or without the law (v. 9a)

This was true in the sense that the awareness of God's demand had been less apparent or vivid. For "if it had not been for the law, I should not have known sin" (v. 7b, RSV).

2) Becoming aware of the death-bringing law and of one's own failure by virtue of sinning to fulfill or obey the law—"I died" (v. 9b)

[T]he very commandment which promised life proved to be death to me. For sin, finding opportunity in the commandment, deceived me and by it killed me. (vv. 10-11)

3) Deliverance through Jesus Christ (vv. 24-25)

Sin, intensified by the law, can only be overcome through Jesus Christ.

In a positive vein the law "promised life" (v. 10), "is holy and just and good" (v. 12), and "is spiritual" (v. 14). Yet, negatively, the law "had

---

43. *The Christian Doctrine of Creation and Redemption,* pp. 214-30; *Revelation and Reason,* p. 332.
44. See Rom. 7:7-14.
45. See Rom. 2:12-16 as the *usus elenchticus legis,* the "conscience" being the "law . . . written on their hearts" (RSV).

both taken away their [people's] ignorance and become itself an incitement to sin."[46]

One should conclude, therefore, that under the gospel of Christ, or the gospel of grace, the law has a revelatory or convictive function. This function is not limited to those who were Jews and then became Christians. The magisterial Reformers of the sixteenth century stressed the proclamation of the law so as to evoke conviction of sin and repentance. Although the life situation sermon common to the twentieth-century pulpit has had little or no place for such, we ought not to regard the proclamation of the law in its revelatory or accusatory function as a thing of the past.

3. Gospel, Centered in the Cross of Jesus Christ

The deepest revelation of the nature and awfulness of sin is not in the conscience of human beings or through the law of God but in the message centered in the death of Jesus Christ as the Son of God. His cross was not only a revelation of God's love for sinful humankind but also an unmasking of the very nature and awfulness of sin: the rejection of Jesus' interiorizing of the law, the refusal of God's greatest gift to humanity, the violent putting to death by creaturely humans of the Creator's Son, and the spurning of that very self-giving love (agapē) by which God chose to redeem humankind. "It is a strong paradox that part of the 'good news' is the revelation of the true meaning of sin."[47]

Walter Rauschenbusch identified and stressed certain social or "public" sins that led to the crucifixion of Jesus: "religious bigotry," "graft and political power," "corruption of justice," "mob spirit and mob action," "militarism," and "class contempt."[48] In the strange workings of God's providence it was in the darkness of Calvary that sin was most fully brought to light and exposed. Indeed, "The light of God's grace does two things for the sinful heart: it reveals its darkness and it increases that darkness in the case of those who reject the light of grace."[49]

In summary, conscience is or can be the internal manifestation of the reality of sin in contrast with God's commands. The law is or can be the external manifestation of the reality of sin in contrast with God's commands. The gospel of the cross is or can be the manifestation of the reality of sin in contrast with God's supreme and gracious gift, his Son, to humankind.

B. TIME OF THE CONSCIOUSNESS OF SIN

The question as to the time (or times) when human beings first come to the consciousness of sin leads to the theological topic that Baptists and

---

46. Greeves, *The Meaning of Sin,* p. 117.
47. Ibid., p. 123.
48. *A Theology for the Social Gospel,* pp. 248-58.
49. Conner, *The Gospel of Redemption,* p. 15.

other adherents to believer's baptism only have called "the age of account-ability," or "the age of discretion." Such an age has been normally under-stood or defined as the time when one may attain to a true and responsible consciousness of sin. As we will explain more fully later, recent discus-sions have tended to shift the focus from "the age of accountability" to "the age of respondability." But first, we need to look at the older term and its usage.

Subsequent discussion[50] will make clear that the New Testament contains no details as to any baptism of children or infants. In the present context it must also be acknowledged that the New Testament is silent as to the spiritual state or condition of infants or young children before God. Specific New Testament teaching about "the age of accountability," exegeti-cally derived, is virtually nonexistent. This means that the history of Chris-tian doctrine provides most of the considerations and materials on this topic.

Certain Christian confessional traditions, notably the Roman Catholic prior to Vatican Council II, have taught theologically that the guilt for the sin of Adam and Eve has been imputed to all humankind, and such imputation is understood to mean that all babies are born having the guilt of "original sin," which we understand to mean Adamic and Evenic guilt. Thus Christian baptism, including infant baptisms, is said to be both necessary and efficacious for the remission of "original sin."[51]

Theologians in the heritage of believer's baptism have taken another approach. Surprisingly, early English Baptist theologians such as John Gill and Andrew Fuller (1754-1815) left no discussion of this topic, and John Leadley Dagg and James Petigru Boyce, the earliest writing theologians among Southern Baptists, did not seemingly address the subject of sin, salvation, and the young child. Theologians who have treated the subject have generally defended the safety of infants, especially of those dying in infancy or early childhood and prior to attainment to the age of account-ability.

Such theological defense has tended to be based on one of the following three considerations: (1) the idea that sin in the full sense of responsible and accountable sin does not occur in or is not committed by the infant/young child prior to this "age of accountability"; (2) the idea that the saving or redemptive work of Jesus Christ applies to and is efficacious for such young children; or (3) a combination of these two.

1. Infants/Young Children Not Committing Sin and Not Able to Repent and Believe prior to the "Age of Accountability"

This view assumes a doctrine of sin very similar to that of the Zwinglian–New England position previously discussed.[52] Depravity is

50. See below, Ch. 74, I.
51. Pohle, *God: The Author of Nature and the Supernatural*, pp. 253-59.
52. See above, Ch. 36, III, B, 2, e.

taken to be "sinful," because it always leads, in later life, to sin per se, but depravity is not sin and does not entail guilt. Hence infants and very young children are depraved but have not yet sinned. E. Y. Mullins, an exponent of this position, wrote that

> there is comparatively little direct teaching in the Scriptures as to the salvation of infants dying in infancy. And yet there is abundant indirect evidence. . . . Christ's union with the human race made his atoning work efficacious in some measure for all mankind . . . (1 Cor. 15:22). This does not teach universalism, but it suggests that there is a similarity between the racial effects of the act of Adam and that of Christ. Christ "died for all" (2 Cor. 5:15). . . . Men are not condemned therefore for hereditary or original sin. They are condemned only for their own sins. They are called to repentance and faith by the gospel. It is their own action of rejection which is the basis of their condemnation. Infants dying in infancy cannot repent, or believe, or perform works of any kind, good or bad. We do not know how the grace of God operates in them. But we are fully assured that Christ provided for them, and that they are created anew in him and saved.[53]

Mullins thus joined the concept that condemnable sin does not occur prior to the age of accountability with the concept that infants and very young children cannot repent and believe. Lingering in the background of his thought is the idea that the redemptive work of Christ may cover or apply to those young ones who die at an early age.

2. *The Redemptive Work of God in Jesus Christ Applicable to and Efficacious for Infants and Young Children Who Die during Infancy or Early Childhood*

This view was set forth by Menno Simons (1496-1561), the Dutch Anabaptist; by A. H. Strong, a Northern Baptist; and by William W. Stevens, a Southern Baptist. Menno Simons wrote in 1539:

> Little ones must wait according to God's Word until they can understand the holy Gospel of grace and sincerely confess it; and then, and then only is it time, no matter how young or how old, for them to receive Christian baptism as the infallible Word of our beloved Lord Jesus Christ has taught and commanded all true believers in His holy Gospel. Matt. 28:19; Mark 16:16. If they die before coming to years of discretion, that is, in childhood, before they have come to years of understanding and before they have faith, then they die under the promise of God, and that by no other means than the generous promise of grace through Christ Jesus. Luke 18:16. And if they come to years of discretion and have faith, then they should be baptized. But if they do not accept or believe the Word when they shall have arrived at the years of discretion, no matter whether they are baptized or not, they will be damned, as Christ himself teaches. Mark 16:16.[54]

53. *The Christian Religion in Its Doctrinal Expression*, pp. 301-2.
54. *Christian Baptism*, in *The Complete Works of Menno Simons*, trans. Leonard Verduin and ed. John C. Wenger (Scottdale, Pa.: Herald Press, 1956), p. 241.

Hence for Menno Simons infants or young children who die early die "under the promise of God" and "by . . . the generous promise of grace through Christ Jesus."

As noted previously,[55] Strong was an exponent of the realistic theory of the imputation of the guilt of the sin of Adam and Eve to all humankind. His discussion of the state of young children was not directly related to the doctrine of imputation, and one can wonder whether the two can be harmonized. Infants, being "in a state of sin, need to be regenerated" through Jesus Christ. In comparison with personal transgressors, however, they are relatively innocent, being submissive and trustful. These infants, being "the objects of a special divine compassion and care," if dying in infancy or early childhood, "receive salvation through Christ," though seemingly apart from "personal faith." Their regeneration by the Holy Spirit will probably occur "in connection with the infant soul's first view of Christ in the other world."[56] Strong, therefore, though never explaining how all humans are guilty of the sin of the first humans and how at the same time infants and young children are relatively innocent, held that dying infants or young children will be eschatologically regenerated through Christ in the Spirit and be reckoned among the company of the saved.

Stevens, citing Matt. 18:3-4, 10, 14 and Matt. 19:13-14, taught that infants who die before the age of accountability are redeemed by Christ, but *not* in limbo.[57]

According to this second approach infants are to be saved through Christ. Presumably this means being saved or redeemed in some sense from sin. But what is the sin from which these dying young ones are to be delivered? The exponents of the second approach have not answered this question clearly.

3. Infants/Young Children Not Committing Sin before the Age of Accountability and God's Redeeming Those Who Die Early from Their Evil Potentiality

W. T. Conner expounded this combination view. He explained the young child's not being a sinner and hence not guilty until the age of accountability in much the same way as those who took the first approach. Then he declared:

> In view of these considerations we believe that we are justified in holding that the child dying in infancy is saved. In other words, where there has been conscious and positive identification of oneself with evil, there must be also, under the grace of God, conscious and positive repudiation of evil and identification of oneself with right before there can be deliverance from evil. Up to the point of positive identification of oneself with right or wrong, there

55. See above, Ch. 36, III, B, 1, a.
56. *Systematic Theology*, pp. 660-64.
57. *Doctrines of the Christian Religion*, pp. 162-63.

is only the potentiality of moral life. In the case of the child, that potentiality is evil except for the positive influence of the grace of God in redeeming from this evil potentiality or the life of transgression that grows out of it. So far as the bent of the child's nature and the social influences of the world order are concerned, these are toward evil. To save the child from this evil inheritance requires the grace of God, which transcends nature and the world order.[58]

Conner joined the concept that the infant/young child does not sin accountably with resultant personal guilt until the age of accountability to the concept that the grace of God redeems the infant/young child who dies early from the actualization of his/her potential for evil or sin.

Is the age of accountability, that is, the age of the commission and consciousness of sin, the same as the age wherein valid conversion to Jesus Christ may take place? Today, for those in the heritage of believer's baptism the focus has tended to shift from the age of accountability and the safety of the dying child to the question as to what is the earliest age at which genuine and valid repentance, faith, and conversion can be expected to occur. William Lawrence Hendricks defined the age of accountability as "a time or period of life when one is aware enough of God to respond to him." He then expanded that definition to mean the time "when the individual is aware of the message and meaning of Christian gospel," when he/she is able "to grasp and accept the basic truths of the gospel," and when "one is brought to a decision for or against Christ by the Spirit."[59] Hendricks also called on Baptists and others in the heritage of believer's baptism to "place more emphasis on a serious view of accountability than on the concept of age." "It is a mistake to set an arbitrary age for conversion. It is likewise a mistake to ignore the capacity of given age levels."[60] Obviously, the question as to when the young child does become a sinner has yielded more and more to the question as to when the child can be validly converted to Christ. The latter question inevitably leads to the question as to the earliest age at which children should be received for baptism and church membership.[61] The latter questions belong to the doctrines of salvation and of the church.

The question of the age of accountability may have been downgraded in importance by the decreasing incidence of infant and early childhood mortality in the developed nations and by the contemporary religious, moral, and political preoccupation with the widespread occurrence and legality of abortion. But it should not be assumed that the older religious question as to the safety of the infant/young child is unrelated to abortion. Moreover, the parents of infants and young children who have died and the pastors and ministers to children who regularly are

58. *The Gospel of Redemption,* pp. 34-35.
59. "The Age of Accountability," in Clifford Ingle, ed., *Children and Conversion* (Nashville: Broadman Press, 1970), pp. 84, 87, 92, 97.
60. Ibid., p. 95.
61. Gideon G. Yoder, *The Nature and Evangelism of Children* (Scottdale, Pa.: Herald Press, 1959).

confronted with the "age of 'respondability' " are not so likely to relegate the concerns associated with the age of accountability to the status of unimportance.

C. INTENDED CLIMAX AND CONSEQUENCE OF THE CONSCIOUSNESS OF SIN

The intended outcome of the consciousness of sin can be stated in terms of two aspects, which are, of course, closely related.

1. Recognition of the Willful, Disobedient, Prideful, and Responsible Nature of Sin

Perhaps no more graphic and telling interpretation of sin as pride has been written in the modern era than that by Reinhold Niebuhr. He followed Augustine of Hippo and John Calvin in defining sin as pride rather than follow "early Greek theology, or medieval or modern liberal thought," all of which were influenced by the classical view of humankind in defining sin as sensuality. Niebuhr identified and described three or rather four types of pride:

a. "[P]ride of Power"

Niebuhr cited two forms of this pride, one that is "particularly characteristic of individuals and groups whose position in society is, or seems to be, secure" (see Babylon in Isa. 23:1-5), and the other that which is "prompted by the sense of insecurity." Niebuhr found that "[g]reed as a form of the will-to-power has been a particularly flagrant sin in the modern era," indeed "the besetting sin of a bourgeois culture."[62]

b. "[I]ntellectual Pride"

This is the failure to recognize that "[a]ll human knowledge is . . . finite knowledge." It is forgetting one's involvement "in a temporary process" and imagining oneself to be "in complete transcendence over history."[63]

c. "[M]oral Pride"

This type of pride "is revealed in all 'self-righteous' judgments in which the other is condemned because he fails to conform to the highly arbitrary standards of the self." It "is the pretension of finite man that his highly conditioned virtue is the final righteousness and that his very relative moral standards are absolute." Niebuhr cited Rom. 10:2-3. "Moral pride thus makes virtue the very vehicle of sin, a fact which explains why the New Testament is so critical of the righteous in comparison with 'publicans and sinners.' "[64]

---

62. *The Nature and Destiny of Man*, 1:198, 201-3.
63. Ibid., pp. 207, 208.
64. Ibid., p. 212.

d. "[S]piritual Pride"

"The ultimate sin is the religious sin of making the self-deification implied in moral pride explicit." Niebuhr cited as examples the Indian caste system, the Roman Catholic identification of the church with the kingdom of God, and the Protestant misuse of the priesthood of all believers so that it becomes "an individual self-deification." "There is no final guarantee against the spiritual pride of man."[65] Sins by religious leaders constitute one of the most heinous forms of sin in any era.

A true consciousness of sin, therefore, is intended to make clear the true nature of sin. It is also intended to lead sinful human beings to renounce and turn from sin.

2. *Consciousness of Sin That Involves the Conviction of Sin unto Repentance through the Holy Spirit*

It is God's purpose that the consciousness of sin become fully the conviction of sin. Jesus promised that the Holy Spirit would be the one to effectuate that conviction:

> And when he comes, he will convince the world of sin and of righteousness and of judgment; of sin, because they do not believe in me; of righteousness, because I go to the Father, and you will see me no more; of judgment, because the ruler of this world is judged. (John 16:8-11, RSV)

The conviction of sin issues in true repentance. Although we will undertake the study of repentance later,[66] it should be noted here that repentance in the New Testament is not synonymous with regret or sorrow but includes a turning from sin. Paul in 2 Cor. 7:8-11 (Charles B. Williams) differentiated sorrow (*lypē*, noun), regret (*metamelomai*, verb), and repentance (*metanoia*, noun):

> For, although I did cause you sorrow (*elypēsa*) by that letter, I do not now regret (*metamelomai*) it; although I did regret (*metamelomēn*) it then. I see that the letter caused you sorrow (*elypēsen*) only for a time. I am glad of it now, not because you had such sorrow (*elypēthēte*), but because your sorrow led you (*elypēthēte*) to repentance (*metanoian*), for you took your sorrow (*elypēthēte*) in accordance with (the will of) God, so that you should not suffer any loss at all from me. For the sorrow (*lypē*) that comes in accordance with (the will of) God results in repentance (*metanoian*) that leads to salvation and leaves no regrets (*ametamelēton*); but the sorrow (*lypē*) the world produces results in death. For see what this very sorrow suffered (*lypēthēnai*) in accordance with (the will of) God has done for you! How earnest it has made you, how concerned to clear yourselves, how indignant, how alarmed, how much it made you long to see me, how loyal to me, how determined to punish the offender!

65. Ibid., pp. 213-15.
66. See below, Ch. 58.

True conviction of sin wrought by the Holy Spirit and leading to repentance necessarily involves the sinner's making his own the divine condemnation of his sin.

> There is a practically universal sense in the hearts of men that something is wrong in their lives. Sometimes it is quite hazy and indefinite. To become evangelical conviction for sin, it must become something more definite and keen than a general sense of wrongness. That something definite comes under gospel influences by the power of the Spirit. But the Spirit does not bring this conviction to man apart from his own moral consciousness or conscience, but by quickening man's conscience. It is not gospel conviction for sin until the condemnation passed on the unbeliever by the gospel becomes the sinner's own self-condemnation. God's condemnation of the sinner must become the sinner's condemnation of self.[67]

Temptation is the occasion, the incitement, or the inducement to sin, but not sin itself. Human beings are or can be made conscious of sin through conscience, the law, and the gospel of the cross. This consciousness of sin is first possible, it seems, when a child attains to the age of accountability, and it is intended to lead to the recognition of sin as sin, indeed the conviction of sin by the Spirit that leads to repentance and faith in Jesus Christ.

---

67. Conner, *The Work of the Holy Spirit* (Nashville: Broadman Press, 1949), pp. 174-75.

CHAPTER 38

Consequences of Sin

The final topic for consideration under the Christian doctrine of sin is the consequences of sin. Without denying the punitive dimension of these consequences, we have chosen to use language that would emphasize the assured results of sin. The consequences, it seems, can best be identified and interpreted under three basic categories: sinners and God, sinners and their fellow human beings, and sinners and themselves.[1]

I. SINNERS AND GOD

A. ALIENATION, OR ENMITY

1. Biblical Teachings

According to Gen. 3:8 (NASV) Adam and Eve "hid themselves from the presence of the LORD God among the trees of the garden," and according to 3:23a (NIV), "the LORD God banished him [Adam] from the Garden of Eden." In Jesus' parable of the prodigal son "the younger son," having obtained in advance his portion of the inheritance, "gathered everything together and went on a journey into a distant country" (Luke 15:13, NASV). More specifically, Paul declared that "while we were enemies, we were reconciled to God through the death of His Son" (Rom. 5:10a). Furthermore, "the mind set on the flesh is hostile toward God" (Rom. 8:7a), and "those who are in the flesh cannot please God" (Rom. 8:8). In Eph. 4:18b Paul used an expression to describe the former state of Gentiles who had become Christians: "alienated" (RSV) or "excluded from the life of God" (NASV).

2. Theological Interpretation

a. Alienation/enmity is an active, and not merely a passive, hostility that produces separation from God.

1. Strong, *Systematic Theology*, pp. 637-60, treating the consequences from the perspective of the sin of Adam and Eve, specified depravity, guilt, and penalty (death). Conner, *The Gospel of Redemption*, pp. 36-49, employed the three categories being used here and added suffering and death. Erickson, *Christian Theology*, pp. 601-19, used the three categories being used here.

b. Alienation/enmity involves the rejection of the knowledge of the true God. The Gentiles, "though they knew God, . . . did not honor Him as God, or give thanks" (Rom. 1:21b, NASV). Formerly they were "without God in the world" (Eph. 2:12d). They had been "without God," not in the sense of having received no revelation of God whatsoever, for such would contradict Rom. 1:18-32, but in the sense of not having appropriated savingly the true knowledge of the Triune God.

c. Alienation/enmity brings about the corruption, but not the abandonment, of religion. The Gentiles "exchanged the glory of the incorruptible God for an image in the form of corruptible man and of birds and four-footed animals and crawling creatures" (Rom. 1:23) and "exchanged the truth of God for a lie, and worshiped and served the creature rather than the Creator" (Rom. 1:25). Modern philosophies that are pantheistic or humanistic in nature call for the expression of reverence toward Nature or for the elevation of Man.

d. Paul Tillich used "estrangement" as the key term for the nature of sin,[2] yet he did not strictly identify sin and estrangement.[3] Estrangement, according to Tillich, expresses itself in unbelief, hubris (pride), and concupiscence.[4]

B. Unfreedom, or Bondage

1. Biblical Teachings

This theme is found both in the teaching of Jesus as given in the Gospel of John and in Paul's Epistle to the Romans.

> Jesus answered them, "Truly, truly, I say to you, every one who commits sin is a slave to sin. The slave does not continue in the house for ever; the son continues for ever. So if the Son makes you free, you will be free indeed." (John 8:34-36, RSV)

The context is the teaching of Jesus respecting liberation through the truth that is found in his "word" (v. 31) and the claim of the Jews never to have been "in bondage to any one" (v. 33). These Jews seem to have forgotten the Babylonian captivity and the Seleucid rule thrown off by the Maccabees! Jesus affirmed that bondage or servitude as an effect of sin makes necessary liberation by the Son of God.

Paul interrogated the Roman Christians:

> Do you not know that if you yield yourselves to any one as obedient slaves, you are slaves of the one whom you obey, either of sin, which leads to death, or of obedience, which leads to righteousness? But thanks be to God, that you who were once slaves of sin have become obedient from the heart to the standard of teaching to which you were committed, and, having been set free from sin, have become slaves of righteousness. (6:16-18, RSV)

2. *Systematic Theology*, 2:44-59.
3. Ibid., 2:46.
4. Ibid., 2:47-55.

Paul used the analogy of servitude in reference to sin's effects and declared that Christians had been "set free" by or in Christ. Strictly speaking, Romans 7 has to do with inability rather than bondage or servitude, but the inability itself is an expression of what Paul has previously called servitude.

2. Historic Formulations

The bondage, or unfreedom, of human beings as sinners has received much attention by Christian theologians throughout the history of Christianity, especially when joined with the question of the freedom or bondage of the human will. Contemporary formulation of the bondage of sin should be based on the knowledge of the principal answers proposed in the past; therefore, we will now undertake a survey of these answers.

a. Fifth Century

1) Pelagius

Pelagius stressed as a central theme the "unconditional free will and responsibility" of human beings. He set forth three aspects of human action: "the power (posse), the will (velle), and the realization (esse)." The power "comes exclusively from God, but the other two belong to us; hence, according as we act, we merit praise or blame." The will of human beings, according to Pelagius, has no "intrinsic bias in favour of wrongdoing as a result of the Fall." Adam's sin brought death and "a habit of disobedience," but there is no transmitted or congenital fault in humankind. Likewise, there is no "special pressure on man's will to choose the good," the term "grace" having other meanings for Pelagius.[5]

2) Augustine of Hippo

Contrary to Pelagius, Augustine taught that in the fall humans lost their liberty (libertas), that is, their rightful use of their free will to fulfill God's purpose or will. But Augustine did not teach that fallen human beings had lost their free will (liberum arbitrium), that is, free choice.

> His language occasionally appears to suggest this, but his normal doctrine is that, while we retain our free will intact, the sole use to which in our unregenerate state we put it is to do wrong. In this sense he can speak of "a cruel necessity of sinning" resting upon the human race. By this he means, not that our wills are in the grip of any physical or metaphysical determinism, but rather that, our choice remaining free, we spontaneously, as a matter of psychological fact, opt for perverse courses.[6]

5. Kelly, *Early Christian Doctrines*, pp. 357-59, based on Pelagius, *Ad Demet.* 2 (*PL*, 30:16-17), and Augustine, *On the Grace of Christ and Original Sin* 1.5; 1.2; 1.8; 1.36; *Opus imperfectum contra Iulianum* 6.8; 6.21.
6. Kelly, *Early Christian Doctrines*, pp. 365-66, based on Augustine, *Enchiridion* 30; *Epistle 145* 2; *Against the Two Letters of Pelagius* 1.5; 3.24; *Sermon 156* 12; *On the Gospel of John* 5.1; *On the Perfection of the Righteousness of Man* 9; *Opus imperfectum contra Iulianum* 1.106; 5.61.

Augustine taught four distinct "stages" in human history ("prior to the Law," "under the Law," "under grace," and "in peace"), with each of which "concupiscence" has a different relationship.[7] Moreover, in the prelapsarian state Adam was *able not to sin,* whereas in heavenly glory the redeemed will *not . . . be able to sin.*[8] Augustine's doctrine of grace must be related to the issue of freedom. Teaching that "God's omnipotent will, operating on our wills by grace, is irresistible," he yet allowed that "it rests with the recipient's will to accept or reject" that grace.[9]

b. Medieval Era: Peter Lombard

Lombard's position has been summarized as follows: "[M]an is free, not in the sense that he has an equal choice between good and evil, but in the sense that he does evil voluntarily and not by constraint."[10]

c. Reformation

1) Martin Luther and Desiderius Erasmus

Erasmus published in 1524 *On the Freedom of the Will: A Diatribe or Discourse,* in which he defined free will as "a power of the human will by which a man can apply himself to the things which lead to eternal salvation, or turn away from them."[11] In reply and refutation Luther issued in 1525 *On the Bondage of the Will.* Luther insisted that Erasmus's crediting humankind "with a will that is free in the things of God is too much." "A lost freedom . . . is no freedom at all."[12] He made much of God's hardening the heart of Pharaoh. Luther argued for the bondage of the will from the universality of guilt among human beings (Romans 1), from the universal dominion of sin (Romans 3), from the nonceremonial nature of works that justify, from the role of the law in revealing sin, from the nature of salvation by faith in Christ and Christ alone, from the faultiness of the doctrine of merits, and from the inability of human beings to believe the gospel apart from divine initiative.[13]

2) John Calvin

Calvin held that by virtue of Adam's fall humankind had lost free will, that is, "a free choice of good and evil."[14] Contrary to the philoso-

7. *Propositions from the Epistle to the Romans* 13-18, trans. Paula Fredriksen Landes.
8. *On Rebuke and Grace* 33.
9. Kelly, *Early Christian Doctrines,* p. 368.
10. Niebuhr, *The Nature and Destiny of Man,* 1:259, based on Calvin, *Institutes of the Christian Religion* (1559 ed.) 2.2.7.
11. Trans. E. Gordon Rupp and A. N. Marlow, in *Luther and Erasmus: Free Will and Salvation,* vol. 17, Library of Christian Classics (Philadelphia: Westminster Press, 1969), pp. 33-97, esp. 47.
12. Trans. J. I. Packer and O. R. Johnston (Westwood, N.J.: Fleming H. Revell Company, 1957), pp. 137, 148.
13. Ibid., pp. 195-203, 273-318.
14. *Institutes of the Christian Religion* 1.15.8.

phers, the Church Fathers except for Augustine, and the Scholastics, he expounded the doctrine of the bondage of the will.[15] Human beings *necessarily* come under the bondage of sin but not by "compulsion"; rather they come voluntarily. Humans are not deprived of their wills but of the soundness of their wills. By conversion to Christ the human will is turned from evil to good, and thus the unsoundness of the will is remedied.[16]

d. Post-Reformation Era

1) James Arminius (1560-1609)

Clearly dividing the human story into three stages, *"primitive inno-cence," "subsequent corruption,"* and *"renewed righteousness,"* Arminius held that in the second of these stages "man is not capable, of and by himself, either to think, to will, or to do that which is really good."[17] His "free will" "towards the true good is not only wounded, maimed, infirm, bent, and weakened; but it is also imprisoned, destroyed, and lost." Fallen human beings have "no powers whatever except such as are excited by Divine grace."[18]

2) Jonathan Edwards

In his massive refutation of mid-eighteenth-century Arminianism with its focus on the alleged freedom or nondetermination of the human will, Edwards differentiated "natural necessity" from "moral neces-sity," holding the latter to be the necessity arising from "moral causes" such as "inclination or motives" that affect "volitions and actions." He likewise differentiated "natural inability" and "moral inability," the latter consisting of a lack of "inclination" or "sufficient motives" or the strength of contrary inclinations or motives. Edwards further differ-entiated a *"particular and occasional* moral inability" from a *"general and habitual* moral inability." The fundamental deficiency is not merely in ability but in will. The liberty of moral agency does not consist in self-determining power, for there is "a *universal, determining providence."* Every event is ordered by God either by design or by permission. Thus human total depravity is explicable through moral necessity that does not excuse sin.[19]

15. Ibid. 3.2.
16. Ibid. 2.3.5-6.
17. *A Declaration of the Sentiments* 3, in *The Writings of James Arminius*, 3 vols., vol. 1, trans. James Nichols (Grand Rapids: Baker Book House, 1956), p. 252.
18. *Disputations on Some of the Principal Subjects of the Christian Religion* 11.7, in ibid., p. 526.
19. *A Careful and Strict Enquiry into the Modern Prevailing Notions of That Freedom of Will, Which Is Supposed to Be Essential to Moral Agency, Virtue and Vice, Reward and Punishment, Praise and Blame*, pt. 1, sect. 4, and concl., ed. Paul Ramsey, in *The Works of Jonathan Edwards*, 7 vols., gen. ed. Perry Miller (New Haven: Yale University Press; London: Oxford University Press, 1957-85), 1:156-62, 431-33.

e. Twentieth Century

1) Emil Brunner

Brunner emphasized the importance of unfreedom, the danger of its misinterpretation, and its true meaning.

> The decisive point for the understanding of man is the understanding of freedom. . . . Those who do not understand freedom, do not understand man. Those who do not understand the 'unfreedom' of man do not understand sin.
>
> . . . .
>
> We must . . . be on our guard against the error of combining the *servum arbitrium* with any kind of determinist metaphysic. . . .[20]

This would mean safeguarding unfreedom from its unwarranted identification with any form of determinist metaphysic—whether Stoic, Manichaean, predestinationist, or modern behaviorist. According to Brunner,

> By the very fact of sinning he [the human being] has become the slave of sin. . . . Sin is therefore responsible action, which alone closes the door to freedom—not to all freedom, but to the freedom of being no longer a sinner but a human being who is well- pleasing to God.[21]

2) Reinhold Niebuhr

Niebuhr declared: "Man is most free in the discovery that he is not free."[22]

3) George MacDonald (1824-1905)

According to MacDonald, "A man is in bondage to whatever he cannot part with that is less than himself."[23]

Such a line of Christian thinkers, apart from Pelagius and Erasmus, has given testimony to the bondage or unfreedom of sin. Authors such as Augustine and Edwards have helped to explain how we can properly speak of the "bondage" or "servitude" or "unfreedom" of sin in human beings who willfully and, for the most part at least, consciously sin.

C. WRATH

We have previously[24] discussed the wrath of God as the divine displeasure concerning and resistance to human sin. Wrath is both an attribute of God and a response of God to human sin. It is directed both to the sin that is a rejection of general or universal revelation (Rom. 1:18) and to the sin that is a rejection of the particular, historical revelation that is in Jesus Christ (John 3:36). But it is also true that human beings as sinners

---

20. *The Christian Doctrine of Creation and Redemption*, pp. 121, 122.
21. Ibid., pp. 106-7.
22. *The Nature and Destiny of Man*, 1:276.
23. *Unspoken Sermons*, 2d ser., "The Way," quoted by C. S. Lewis, *George MacDonald: An Anthology* (Garden City, N.Y.: Doubleday and Company, 1962), p. 53.
24. See above, Ch. 16, V, C.

encounter, face, and stand under the wrath of God, and this is one of the results of sinning.

D. GUILT

1. Terminology and Meaning

The English word "guilt," which is an Anglo-Saxon derivative, was used by the KJV to translate one term in each of the testaments. The Hebrew verb 'āšam and its cognates were used in Gen. 26:10; 42:21; Lev. 4:3, 13, 22, 27; 5:2, 3, 4, 5, 17, 19; 6:4; Num. 5:6; Judg. 21:22; Hos. 5:15; Isa. 24:6; Jer. 2:3; 50:7; Ezek. 22:4; Prov. 30:10; Ps. 34:21, 22; 1 Chr. 21:3; 2 Chr. 24:18; 28:13; and Ezra 10:19. In the New Testament enochos, meaning "held in, subject to" and hence "guilty of" or "liable to," was used in Mark 3:29; Matt. 5:21-22; Mark 14:64 and par.; 1 Cor. 11:27; and Jas. 2:10.[25]

The English term means blameworthiness, ill-deservedness, or condemnability before God. It means that human beings are rightly subject to the wrath and judgment of God. Millard Erickson has defined guilt as "the objective state of having violated God's intention for man and thus being liable to punishment."[26] W. W. Stevens's definition of guilt as "the self-condemnation of man based on God's disapproval of his sin"[27] is more properly addressed to the consciousness of guilt.

2. Consciousness

Over against and along with the objective fact of human guilt before God is the subjective realization of that guilt, which is often described as the consciousness of guilt. The existence of the consciousness is evidenced even by the concept of a "guilt complex" and by human effort to rationalize or justify sin. Yet the fact that humans deny, hide, obscure, pass the blame for, and rationalize their sin and the fact that sin blinds sinners to sin mean that the consciousness of sin is not a totally accurate or infallible index to guilt itself.[28]

3. Inequality or Degrees

Is it proper to speak of the inequality of guilt among human beings with the inference that there may be degrees of guilt before God, or must we think of the equality of human beings in guilt? Some Protestant theologians have denied or deemphasized degrees of human guilt. Gustav Aulén asserted that "from a religious point of view there can be no degrees of guilt," though there can be from a "moral" point of view.[29] Other Protestant

25. Erickson, *Christian Theology*, pp. 576-77.
26. Ibid., p. 605.
27. *Doctrines of the Christian Religion*, p. 157.
28. Conner, *The Gospel of Redemption*, pp. 19-20.
29. *The Faith of the Christian Church*, pp. 280, 287-88.

theologians have affirmed and taught degrees of guilt. A. H. Strong thought that degrees of guilt were taught in the Bible but decried casuistry of an unbiblical nature. He contrasted depravity and personal transgression, "sins of ignorance" and "sins of knowledge," "sins of infirmity" and "sins of presumption," pardonable sin and the sin against the Holy Spirit.[30] W. T. Conner also found degrees of guilt to be a biblical teaching. He stressed "light and privilege" and "the measure of wilfulness."[31]

What, then, is the biblical basis for degrees of guilt? First, there is the Pentateuchal distinction between sins of inadvertence and the sin of presumption, the former being provided for through the sacrifices and the latter placing the sinner outside the covenantal relationship.[32] Second, the cities (Chorazin, Bethsaida, Capernaum) in which Jesus taught and ministered were said to be under heavier condemnation than Tyre and Sidon and than Sodom and Gomorrah (Matt. 11:20-24 and par.). Third, the parable of the faithful and wise steward (Luke 12:41-48) describes two servants who differed in their knowledge of their master's will and hence received different punishments. Fourth, Heb. 10:26-31 alludes to deliberate sin leading to "worse punishment."

E. JUDGMENT

Divine judgment is another of the consequences of human sin. This is true of both temporal judgments and the final or last judgment. But the detailed treatment of this theme can be better undertaken as a facet of the doctrine of the last things.[33]

F. DEATH

1. Biblical Passages

Several biblical texts embody the concept that death is the penal consequence of sin. In the Old Testament one finds Gen. 2:17b (RSV), " 'for in the day that you eat of it you shall die,' " and Ezek. 18:4c, "the soul that sins shall die." That death came from Adam's sin is the import of Paul's "For as by a man came death" (1 Cor. 15:21), and that all humans share in that death seems to be the meaning of "For as in Adam all die" (1 Cor. 15:22). More punitive imagery can be seen in "The sting of death is sin" (1 Cor. 15:56a). The coming of death through sin is again stated in Rom. 5:12, and the reign of death is introduced in Rom. 5:17a. The "end" of the "things of which you are now ashamed" is "death" (Rom. 6:21), and "the wages of sin is death" (Rom. 6:23). Indeed, "[t]o set the mind on the flesh is death" (Rom. 8:6a), and "desire when it has conceived gives birth to sin; and sin when it is full-grown brings forth death" (Jas. 1:15).

30. *Systematic Theology*, pp. 648-52.
31. *The Gospel of Redemption*, pp. 21-22.
32. See above, Ch. 34, III, B.
33. See below, Ch. 87.

2. Theological Interpretation

Both Roman Catholic theology and Protestant theology have rejected the view that death as the penalty for sin means the annihilation of the human being, body and soul, at the moment of death, as taught by Seventh-day Adventists and Jehovah's Witnesses,[34] and the view that the penal consequence of sin is physical death only.[35] Basic to this theological topic is the fact that Christian theologians have differentiated three meanings of death: physical death, or the cessation of life in the body; spiritual death, or the separation of a human being from the life of God; and eternal death, or the final, eternal separation of a human being from the life of God. Louis Berkhof has contended that this threefold distinction is not to be found in the Bible.[36] Nevertheless, Protestant theologians have developed numerous views as to the specific way in which death is the penal consequence of sin.

Some theologians have concluded that physical death, spiritual death, and eternal death—all three—are the penal consequence of sin. James P. Boyce,[37] John C. Wenger,[38] and Millard J. Erickson[39] have arrived at that conclusion. Others have taught that the penal consequence of sin vis-à-vis death was solely spiritual death. John L. Dagg[40] took this position, and Dale Moody[41] has contended for it after refuting idealistic and naturalistic theories about death and reviewing the New Testament texts, though it is likely that Moody did not intend to exclude eternal death. Still others have held that spiritual death is the primary but not the exclusive mortal penalty for sin. Ezekiel G. Robinson contended for it, citing 1 Cor. 15:45-49 and Rom. 5:12ff. and geological findings about animal death before the appearance of humans on the earth and affirming that humans were "constitutionally mortal" with provision for their "immortality."[42] H. Orton Wiley espoused the same view, teaching that spiritual death "is due to the withdrawal of the Holy Spirit as the bond of union between the soul and God."[43] Louis Berkhof seems to have favored this view.[44] Yet other theologians have affirmed that both physi-

---

34. See above, Ch. 33, II, A, 3, b, 1).

35. Wiley, *Christian Theology*, 2:91, mistakenly attributed this view to the Pelagians.

36. *Systematic Theology*, pp. 258-59. John 8:51 and 11:26 are two of the few, perhaps even the only two texts that can be assigned to eternal death only. David Alan Sapp, "An Introduction to Adam Christology in Paul: A History of Interpretation, the Jewish Background, and an Exegesis of Romans 5:12-21" (Ph.D. diss., Southwestern Baptist Theological Seminary, 1990), pp. 196-200, has found six different meanings of "death" in the Pauline epistles alone.

37. *Abstract of Systematic Theology*, pp. 239-47.

38. *Introduction to Theology*, pp. 93-94.

39. *Christian Theology*, pp. 611-15.

40. *A Manual of Theology*, pp. 148-50. According to Wiggers, *An Historical Presentation of Augustinism and Pelagianism*, pp. 301, 308, Pelagius (Augustine, *On the Merits and Forgiveness of Sins* 1.2-4) and Julian of Eclanum (Augustine, *Opus imperfectum contra Iulianum* 6.10) both taught that Gen. 2:17 refers only to spiritual death.

41. *The Word of Truth*, pp. 293-99.

42. *Christian Theology*, pp. 129-32.

43. *Christian Theology*, 2:91-95.

44. *Systematic Theology*, pp. 258-59.

cal death and spiritual death are the penal consequences of sin and the fulfillment of Gen. 2:17b. A. H. Strong, while taking this position, also insisted that "seeds of death" had been "implanted" in the original humans and that these seeds developed when Adam and Eve sinned.[45] E. Y. Mullins advocated this view, refuting the view that death would have been necessary to prevent human overpopulation and suggesting that there would have been other means such as translation for human exit from this world.[46] W. T. Conner espoused this view, though it is likely that he was not excluding eternal death.[47] Anthony A. Hoekema, refuting Karl Barth's view that death is "an aspect of God's good creation," concluded that both physical death and spiritual death are consequences of sin.[48] Other Protestant theologians, not addressing so specifically the threefold usage of "death," have stressed that death is the instrument of divine judgment.[49]

II. SINNERS AND THEIR FELLOW HUMAN BEINGS

Although sin should be reckoned as being supremely an offense against or a failure before God, sin also has its consequences for the relationships which human beings have with their fellow human beings. Human society under the influence of sin is a veritable network of evil, which, according to the Gospel of John, is describable as "the world."[50] The traditional triad of opposition to the Christian as he or she seeks to live the Christian life has been "the world, the flesh,[51] and the devil.[52]" The "new man" in Christ must live in confrontation with "the world," but it also true that the "old man" has so sinned as to be "the world" in the special Johannine sense. Millard Erickson, in treating the social consequences of sin, discussed not only "the world" but also "the powers" and the biblical concept of corporate personality.[53] In the present discussion two themes, hatred, or the opposite of love, and injustice, or the opposite of righteousness, will be the key concepts.

A. HATRED

Hatred is the opposite of God's intended purpose for human relations, namely, love, and the counterpart to the selfish egocentricity of human beings. At the dawn of biblical history stands the account of Cain's

45. *Systematic Theology*, pp. 590-93, 656-60.
46. *The Christian Religion in Its Doctrinal Expression*, pp. 297-99.
47. *The Gospel of Redemption*, pp. 48-49.
48. Hoekema, *The Bible and the Future* (rev. ed.; Grand Rapids: Eerdmans, 1982), pp. 79-85; Barth, *Church Dogmatics*, III/2, pp. 596-98, 632.
49. Aulén, *The Faith of the Christian Church*, p. 229; Milne, *Know the Truth*, p. 267.
50. See above, Ch. 36, I, B, 2.
51. See above, Ch. 34, I, B, 1.
52. See above, Ch. 29.
53. *Christian Theology*, pp. 643-55.

murder of Abel (Gen. 4:1-16). The account points to the truth that all human relations and institutions are under the sway of sin.

Hatred in the family, often driven by selfishness or jealousy, tends to break or dissolve a marriage or divide a family. Hatred in the race or clan, which is not merely due to ignorance, produces deep, tragic rifts between groups of humans, such as the biblical antagonism between Jews and Gentiles (Eph. 2:14-16)[54] and modern forms of group alienation and antagonism (blacks and whites, Arabs and Jews). Hatred between economic classes or groups, such as between management and labor or between "have" nations and "have not" nations, can lead to bloodshed and brutality. Hatred between citizens of different nations, accentuated by the massive self-interest of the modern nation-state, leads to oppression, violence, war, and the fear and danger of total human annihilation.

B. INJUSTICE

Not only in restricted interpersonal relations, that is, between two individuals or within the circle of the family or in a small local community, but even more in the larger structures and institutions of society sin's effects are existent and evident. "Man's inhumanity to man" is expressed in various ways, none more significant than injustice, which includes not just lack of opportunity in the economic and political realms but exploitation and oppression. Seeing more clearly the societal consequences of sin is one of the abiding contributions of the Social Gospel movement.

In fact, the evil that adheres to and abides in the social order may be more ingrained and less subject to redemption than the evil in individual lives. This was the thesis of Reinhold Niebuhr's *Moral Man and Immoral Society*.[55] The Social Gospel movement erred in its too facile "solution by reformation" of social evils, but the purely individualistic approach to the effects of sin also errs. According to Niebuhr, political democracy is "possible" because of the human "capacity for justice" but "necessary" because of the human "inclination to injustice" to fellow humans.[56] With his realistic view of human and societal injustice, Niebuhr taught that the true expression of love of neighbor in the economic and political order is found in the quest for justice.[57]

Millard Erickson has identified and described three "strategies for

54. Not only does sin seriously affect human groups as well as individuals but the reconciling work of Jesus Christ is efficacious for human groups as well as for individual human beings.

55. *Moral Man and Immoral Society: A Study in Ethics and Politics* (New York, London: Charles Scribner's Sons, 1932), esp. pp. xi-xxv.

56. *The Children of Light and the Children of Darkness* (New York: Charles Scribner's Sons, 1944), p. xi.

57. *Christianity and Power Politics* (New York: Charles Scribner's Sons, 1940), pp. 25-27; *Christian Realism and Political Problems* (New York: Charles Scribner's Sons, 1953), pp. 166-68.

overcoming social sin" that are being employed toward the end of the twentieth century.[58] First, there is the reliance on *regeneration* of individual persons as the principal means for transforming society, with evangelism as the principal method. The idea is that only changed human beings can remake a sinful society and that altered social structures peopled by unregenerate humans will become equally corrupt or unjust as the previous ones. This method may be accompanied by Christian helping ministries and by publicly funded social welfare, but not by major efforts for economic or political change. It is practiced widely by Evangelical Protestants today.[59]

Second, there is the strategy of attempting to *reform* the structures of society by nonviolent means. While not necessarily denying the need for Christian conversion, the adherents of this strategy put their emphasis on societal change through election of different political officeholders, through new legislation, through better law enforcement, through strikes and economic boycotts, and the like. The nonviolent resistance movements led by Mohandas K. Gandhi and by Martin Luther King, Jr., should be seen as forms of the method of reform. This strategy is being employed by mainline Protestants and numerous Roman Catholics.

Third, there is the strategy of *revolution,* or the violent overthrow of governments and/or economic systems, which are seen as hopelessly unjust and corrupt, and the replacement of these governments and/or economic systems with new regimes and systems that allegedly will make possible justice. Little or nothing is said by those espousing this strategy concerning personal sin or the need for spiritual and moral rebirth. Much is said about the beneficent results that are anticipated from the new regimes and systems. This strategy has been advocated by various Latin American theologians of liberation.[60]

Erickson advocated a "combination" of the first and second strategies.[61]

58. *Christian Theology,* pp. 655-58.

59. Carl F. H. Henry, *Aspects of Christian Social Ethics* (Grand Rapids: Eerdmans, 1964), pp. 15-30. Henry delineated four strategies: revolution, reform, revaluation, and regeneration. On such social issues as abortion, Evangelicals are today employing the reform method and not just that of regeneration.

60. For a statement by one of the movement's "foremost participant-critics in Latin America," see José Míguez-Boníno, *Doing Theology in a Revolutionary Situation* (Philadelphia: Fortress Press, 1975), pp. ix, 106- 31. See also "Medellin [Second General Conference of Latin American Bishops, 1968] Document on Peace," paras. 15-19, in Deane William Ferm, ed., *Third World Liberation Theologies: A Reader* (Maryknoll, N.Y.: Orbis Books, 1986), pp. 7-9; Sacred Congregation for the Doctrine of the Faith, *Instruction on Certain Aspects of the "Theology of Liberation,"* sect. 8, in Juan Luis Segundo, S.J., *Theology and the Church: A Response to Cardinal Ratzinger and a Warning to the Whole Church,* trans. John W. Diercksmeier (Minneapolis: Winston Press, 1985), pp. 179- 80; and Segundo, op. cit., pp. 107-38.

61. *Christian Theology,* p. 658.

III. SINNERS AND THEMSELVES

Sin deeply affects sinners themselves as well as their relationships with God and with fellow humans. We will focus on three aspects of these reflexive effects.

A. SELF-CENTEREDNESS, OR EGOCENTRICITY

According to Gustav Aulén, sin is "negatively unbelief and positively egocentricity."[62] Frederic Greeves has contended that "egocentricity" is "more appropriate" as a "description of the basic sin" than "pride."[63] The self-centeredness of sin means that the human personality abides alone. Jesus said: "Unless a grain of wheat falls into earth and dies, it remains alone *(monos menei)*; but if it dies, it bears much fruit" (John 12:24, RSV). Sin is, therefore, abiding alone; it is "monomenic."

Consequently, the first demand of Christian discipleship is the denial or renunciation of self, indeed of the self-centeredness of sin. "If any one would come after me, let him deny himself and take up his cross and follow me" (Matt. 16:24). In the words of George MacDonald, "You will be dead so long as you refuse to die."[64]

William Whiting (Bill) Borden (1887-1913), the young missionary preparing to work among Muslims in China who died en route in Cairo of cerebral meningitis, had written in his notebook while a freshman at Yale University:

> In every man's heart there is a throne and a cross. If Christ is on the throne, self is on the cross; and if self, even a little bit, is on the throne, Jesus is on the cross in that man's heart.[65]

B. SELF-DISINTEGRATION

Sin destroys the wholeness of human beings by breaking down or damaging their capacities and powers.

1. Folly, or Delusion

Paul, when describing unredeemed Gentiles, said that they were "futile" or "vain in their reasonings and their senseless heart was darkened" (Rom. 1:21), and "professing to be wise, they became fools" (Rom. 1:22). He referred to their being "in the vanity [or, futility] of their minds" (Eph. 4:17c), to their "being darkened in their understanding" (Eph. 4:18a, RSV) and to their "ignorance" (Eph. 4:18b, RSV). Sin promises its delights, satisfactions, and "liberation," but these are temporary and ultimately debilitating. Sin is unable to fulfill its promises on a long-term basis. Instead of wisdom it brings folly, and instead of life its "wages" are "death" (Rom. 6:23).

---

62. *The Faith of the Christian Church,* p. 260.
63. *The Meaning of Sin,* p. 133.
64. *Lilith,* ch. 31, quoted by Lewis, *George MacDonald: An Anthology,* p. 151.
65. Mrs. Howard Taylor, *Borden of Yale '09* (Philadelphia: China Inland Mission, 1926), p. 122.

Evangelical theology at its best has acknowledged that human reason has been adversely affected by sin. Donald G. Bloesch has affirmed:

> Man in sin is not guided by the light of clear intelligence but gropes in the darkness of fear and resentment. . . . The structure of man's reason is not impaired, but the way in which he reasons is surely distorted by sin.[66]

Reinhold Niebuhr had earlier written that, in contrast to the anticipated prideful self-confidence of reason, "the human reason remains a servant of the passions of nature within him and a victim of the caprices of nature about him."[67]

2. Hardness, or Callousness

Paul described unregenerate humans, whether Gentiles or Jews, as having become "callous" (RSV) or "past feeling" (KJV) (Eph. 4:19a) and, building on the Old Testament concept, alluded to their "hardness of heart" (Eph. 4:18c, RSV). The disintegration of sin may be seen today in the multiplication of frustrations and in the depersonalization of human life and relations.

C. SELF-DEFEAT

In one sense sin is its own punishment. Sin issues not in triumph for humankind but rather in defeat, not in fulfillment but in failure. Those who seek wealth or material prosperity as their *summum bonum* lose at death their quest, for "a man's life consists not in the abundance of his possessions" (Luke 12:15, RSV). Likewise, those who seek the power of domination over other human beings, the satisfaction of unbridled sexual lusts, the prideful attainments of the intellect, or the superiority of self-righteousness are destined to arrive at the same disastrous disappointment and defeat.

Many have heard the oft-quoted words of Augustine of Hippo, "for Thou hast formed us for Thyself, and our hearts are restless till they find rest in Thee."[68] Augustine also emphasized the truth that sin constitutes its own punishment.

> [B]y my own sin didst Thou justly punish me. For it is even as Thou hast appointed, that every inordinate affection should bring its own punishment.[69]

Sin has wrought hurtful and disastrous results for humans' relationship with God, for their relations to their fellow humans, and for themselves. Only God's own intervention could remedy humankind's plight. So God sent forth his only Son!

---

66. *Essentials of Evangelical Theology*, 1:102.
67. *Beyond Tragedy: Essays on the Christian Interpretation of History* (New York: Charles Scribner's Sons, 1937), pp. 101-2.
68. *Confessions* 1.1.1, NPNF, 1st ser., 1:45.
69. Ibid. 1.12.19, NPNF, 1st ser., 1:51.

PART V

The Person of Jesus Christ

CHAPTER 39

Jesus as a Human Being

We now enter upon one of the most important aspects of Christian theology, namely, the doctrines of the person of Jesus Christ and the work of Jesus Christ. Christian theology has customarily drawn a distinction between the "person" of Jesus Christ and the "work" of Jesus Christ. The former term has usually been applied to the answer to the question, "Who is Jesus Christ?" The latter term has ordinarily been used in reference to the question, "What has Jesus Christ done for us?" The doctrine of the person of Christ has been traditionally concerned with the deity and the humanity of Jesus and their interrelation. It may also include such related topics as Jesus' virginal conception, sinlessness, and miracles and the various titles applied to Jesus. The doctrine of the work of Christ, sometimes called in the English-speaking world the doctrine of the "atonement," has been primarily concerned to interpret the saving significance of the death of Jesus, coupled with his resurrection and related to his life.

The term "person of Christ" should be differentiated from the term "life of Christ." The life of Jesus Christ is the sequence of events that taken together constitute his earthly life and ministry. The person of Christ seeks to describe the nature of Jesus Christ as the God-man.

Christian theologians have differed among themselves as to the arrangement of the doctrines of the person of Christ and the work of Christ within a system of Christian theology. Some theologians have treated these two doctrines consecutively, placing the "person" before the "work." Among the theologians who have followed such an arrangement have been John L. Dagg,[1] James P. Boyce,[2] A. H. Strong,[3] William Newton Clarke,[4] Millard J. Erickson,[5] and Bruce Milne.[6] Other theologians have treated these two doctrines in different parts of their theological systems but still have treated the "person" prior to discussing the "work." E. G.

1. *A Manual of Theology*, pp. 179-233.
2. *Abstract of Systematic Theology*, pp. 272-340.
3. *Systematic Theology*, pp. 665-776.
4. *An Outline of Christian Theology*, pp. 260-368.
5. *Christian Theology*, pp. 659-841.
6. *Know the Truth*, pp. 125-75.

Robinson,[7] E. Y. Mullins,[8] W. T. Conner,[9] W. W. Stevens,[10] and Dallas Roark[11] are among those who have followed the second pattern. Still other theologians have treated these doctrines consecutively, placing the "work" before the "person." Among the theologians following that method have been Theodor Haering,[12] Emil Brunner,[13] and Dale Moody.[14] Sometimes called the "inductive method," this arrangement has sometimes appealed to the authority of Philip Melanchthon's statement, "This is to know Christ, to know his benefits."[15] The present study will follow the pattern of discussing "person" and "work" consecutively, with "person" being treated first, but without any radical separation of the two doctrines.

In treating the doctrine of the work of Christ, numerous theologians have utilized as an organizing pattern the "threefold office" (*munus triplex*) of Christ, namely, as Prophet, Priest, and King. The concept of the threefold office is traceable to Eusebius of Caesarea (c. 263–c. 339),[16] but the Protestant Reformers made its usage commonplace. Among the theologians who have employed the threefold office have been John Calvin,[17] John L. Dagg,[18] Charles Hodge,[19] James P. Boyce,[20] A. H. Strong,[21] Theodor Haering,[22] Emil Brunner,[23] Dale Moody,[24] Bruce Milne,[25] and Millard Erickson.[26] Although the present study does not use the threefold office as an organizing pattern, it does treat as titles and functions of Jesus prophethood, priesthood, and kingship.

Christian theologians have followed three major approaches to the doctrine of the person of Christ. First, there is the *Chalcedonian* model. First expressed in the Council of Chalcedon (451), this approach focuses

7. *Christian Theology*, pp. 196-229, 252-96.

8. *The Christian Religion in Its Doctrinal Expression*, pp. 167-202, 303-37.

9. *Revelation and God*, pp. 149-205; *The Gospel of Redemption*, pp. 75-136.

10. *Doctrines of the Christian Religion*, pp. 70-94, 164-99.

11. *The Christian Faith*, pp. 114-32, 147-73.

12. *The Christian Faith*, 2:578-711.

13. *The Christian Doctrine of Creation and Redemption*, pp. 271-378.

14. *The Word of Truth*, pp. 366-426.

15. See above, Ch. 13, n. 4.

16. *Ecclesiastical History* 1.3.8; *The Proof of the Gospel* 4.15.

17. *Institutes of the Christian Religion* (1559 ed.) 2.15. Calvin's order was Prophet, King, and Priest. See also Richard A. Muller, *Christ and the Decree: Christology and Predestination in Reformed Theology from Calvin to Perkins* (Grand Rapids: Baker Book House, 1988), pp. 31-33.

18. *A Manual of Theology*, pp. 207-29.

19. *Systematic Theology*, 2:459-79, 596-609.

20. *Abstract of Systematic Theology*, pp. 291-95.

21. *Systematic Theology*, pp. 710-76.

22. *The Christian Faith*, 2:603-67.

23. *The Christian Doctrine of Creation and Redemption*, pp. 271-307.

24. *The Word of Truth*, pp. 366-85. Moody referred to Prophet, Priest, and Potentate.

25. *Know the Truth*, pp. 151-62.

26. *Christian Theology*, pp. 762-69. Erickson referred to Revealer, Ruler, and Reconciler. Otto Weber, *Foundations of Dogmatics*, 2:174-76, contended that the doctrine of the threefold office prevents a "one-sided" emphasis, whether on Prophet, Priest, or King.

on Jesus' having "two natures" but within "one person." This approach was strongly influenced by the language and thought of Hellenistic philosophy, but it seemed to offer a *via media* between heretical extremes in Christology that had been set forth during the fourth and fifth centuries. During later centuries Eastern Orthodox, Roman Catholic, and Protestant traditions have looked approvingly at the Chalcedonian model. It is fundamentally a metaphysical and psychological approach to Christology.[27]

Second, there is the *kenotic* pattern. Arising in nineteenth-century German Lutheranism, this approach to Christology has provided an alternative to the Chalcedonian pattern for many Protestants. It centers in the sequence of preexistence, self-emptying, and re-ascent or glorification. Two stages, the downward self-emptying of the incarnation and the upward self-fulfillment of victory over temptation, resurrection, and ascension, constitute the main theme of Christology, not the two natures, human and divine. It is fundamentally a historical approach, not a metaphysical one.[28]

Third, there is the alternative of two *beginning point* patterns. The twentieth century has witnessed the emergence of a pair of Christological patterns that provide two options in Christology. One is the commencement of the doctrine of Jesus Christ with the preexistent Logos or Son and the movement toward the human, historical Jesus. The other is the commencement of the doctrine with the human, historical Jesus and movement toward the transcendent aspects of Christology. A notable example of the former was Emil Brunner's *The Mediator*,[29] whereas a representative of the latter was Wolfhart Pannenberg's *Jesus—God and Man*.[30] The former begins Christology "from above," and the latter "from below." Erickson has found that the Christology "from above" is related to faith and the Christology "from below" to reason, and that the Christology "from above" majors on the Gospel of John and the Pauline epistles while that "from below" majors on the Synoptic Gospels.[31] If the Christology "from above" is almost certain to reach the human, historical Jesus and make adequate provision for that aspect, there has been some doubt as to whether the Christology "from below" always results in adequate inclusion of the preexistence, deity, and lordship of Jesus. Reginald Horace

---

27. Robert Victor Sellers, *The Council of Chalcedon: A Historical and Doctrinal Survey* (London: S.P.C.K., 1953).

28. C. A. Beckwith, "Kenosis," *The New Schaff-Herzog Encyclopedia of Religious Knowledge*, 6:315-19.

29. *The Mediator: A Study of the Central Doctrine of the Christian Faith*, trans. Olive Wyon (Philadelphia: Westminster Press, 1947).

30. Trans. Lewis L. Wilkins and Duane A. Priebe (Philadelphia: Westminster Press, 1968).

31. *Christian Theology*, pp. 665-71. Erickson, pp. 671-75, has proposed an alternative to the "from above" and "from below" patterns beginning with the apostolic kerygma. But he has reported that Brunner began with the kerygma. Furthermore, there still remains the question as to which topics or rubrics are to be treated at the outset.

Fuller (1915-), who has utilized the pattern "from below," has sought to
lay to rest such doubts and fears.

> If we immerse ourselves first in the study of the Jesus phenomenon as such,
> we will find ourselves confronted in the first instance with a Christology
> from below. But as we penetrate further, we shall find ourselves being
> led—cautiously, perhaps, at the start—to an "above" way of thinking, for
> in this historical Jesus, in his words and works, we find ourselves confronted
> with the claim that here is the presence of God himself. Hence there is
> already an "above" element in the Jesus phenomenon itself. This "above"
> element, however, is in the first instance God himself, uniquely, definitively,
> and finally. It is not, to begin with, Jesus in his own being who is "from
> above." At its earliest stages, both before and, as we hope to show, later—
> after the Easter event—what we call Christology is at this time really a
> "theology of Jesus." That is to say, the God present in Jesus is God himself.
> It is not that Jesus in his own being is identical with the God who is present
> in him. Of course this is not a "low" Christology, even if the title "eschato-
> logical prophet" is used to characterize the Jesus thus conceived, for this is
> the unique, final, definitive—in short, eschatological—presence of God in
> a human being. Such a presence was never in a human being before, nor has
> it been since, nor—unless the eschatological quality of that experience of
> Jesus be completely negated—will there ever be until the end of time. But
> still, this is not to say that the God encountered in Jesus is Jesus himself.
> Some scholars today would be content with such a Christology. We have to
> admit its attractions, and to say that it is all right as far as it goes, for that is
> as far as the church had come by about the year 50 C.E. Only with the
> Johannine literature do we really reach an "above" christology that is related
> to the actual being of Jesus himself rather than to God in the human being
> Jesus. Therefore, we must always remember that in the early days the
> movement of christology was from "below" to "above."[32]

More is at stake between a Christology "from below" and a Christology "from above" than the point of beginning or the order of topics
being treated. The ultimate question is the outcome, the final or completed
Christology. In the chapters to follow, we will make an effort to show that
Christology can begin "from below," can incorporate all the transcendent
aspects of the person of Christ, and can result in full-orbed, balanced
doctrine.

At least three reasons can be given for commencing the doctrine of
the person of Jesus Christ with his humanity. First, this is the perspective
from which Jesus was first beheld and perceived—as the man, Jesus of
Nazareth. Second, Jesus' humanity is today, unlike some past eras, relatively noncontroversial among Christian scholars, although some may
downplay it. Third, human beings at the end of the twentieth century are
very interested in all things human, and Jesus' humanity may serve as an
apologetic bridge, even to humanists, secularists, and atheists.

---

32. Fuller, in Reginald H. Fuller and Pheme Perkins, *Who Is This Christ? Gospel
Christology and Contemporary Faith* (Philadelphia: Fortress Press, 1983), pp. 7-8. It is not
necessary to accept every aspect of Fuller's analysis, only his major thrust.

I. JESUS' HUMANITY ACCORDING TO THE NEW TESTAMENT

A. SYNOPTIC GOSPELS

The Synoptists assume that Jesus was a human being but "nowhere seek to prove" it. Such lack of attempted proof marks the entire New Testament. "The New Testament no more attempts to demonstrate the manhood of Jesus than the Old Testament to prove the being of God."[33] Instead the Synoptists give abundance of indirect witness to Jesus' humanity throughout their gospels. What Vincent Taylor wrote of Martin Luther could have been said of the Synoptists:

> Luther puts the reality of the Incarnation well when he says: "He ate, drank, slept, and waked; was weary, sad, joyous; wept, laughed; was hungry, thirsty, cold; sweated, talked, worked, prayed."[34]

What a twentieth-century theologian wrote of the New Testament applied especially to the Synoptists:

> Jesus was born, had family connections, lived in his home at Nazareth, was subject to his parents, rejoiced, was tempted, craved human sympathy, prayed, was obedient to God, had a body, mind, soul, suffered, died, and rose again.[35]

B. PAULINE EPISTLES

Paul's preoccupation with Jesus Christ as the risen, exalted Lord could easily lead modern interpreters to the erroneous conclusion that Paul had no interest in the historical Jesus or even did not reckon Jesus as being fully human. Paul is most likely to have assumed some acquaintance with the orally circulating Gospel materials then in the process of being gathered into the written Synoptic Gospels. He did mention Jesus' birth "of a woman" (Gal. 4:4, Berkeley, NEB, JB, NASV), his being descended from the line of David (Rom. 1:3), and his being from the Israelites (Rom. 9:4-5). He also alluded to Jesus' having instituted the Lord's Supper (1 Cor. 11:23-26) and made numerous references to his death and resurrection. Paul's comparison/contrast respecting Adam and Jesus Christ (1 Cor. 15:22, 45; Rom. 5:12-21) seems to have presupposed a humanity common to both. In his self-emptying statement, which some take to be hymnic,[36] the preexistent one is said to have taken the "form of a servant," to have been born "in the likeness of men," and to have been found "in human form" (Phil. 2:7-8, RSV). The "one mediator between God and men" is "the man Christ Jesus" (1 Tim. 2:5).

33. H. R. Mackintosh, *The Doctrine of the Person of Jesus Christ,* International Theological Library (New York: Charles Scribner's Sons, 1916), pp. 10, 383.
34. *Doctrine and Evangelism* (London: Epworth Press, 1953), pp. 35-36.
35. Conner, *Revelation and God,* p. 152.
36. Ralph P. Martin, *Carmen Christi: Philippians ii.5-11 in Recent Interpretation and in the Setting of Early Christian Worship* (Cambridge: University Press, 1967).

C. ACTS OF THE APOSTLES

Peter in his sermon on the Day of Pentecost referred to Jesus as " 'Jesus of Nazareth, a man attested to you by God . . .' " (2:22b, RSV). Paul in his sermon at Antioch of Pisidia declared that " 'through this one [*dia toutou*, a genitive masculine singular] forgiveness of sins is announced to you' " (13:38). In his sermon at Athens Paul announced that God " 'has fixed a day on which he will judge the world in righteousness by a man whom he has appointed' " (17:31).[37]

D. EPISTLE TO THE HEBREWS

This tractate emphasizes the humanity of Jesus, especially because his high priesthood in behalf of humankind depended on his full identification with human beings. "Since the children [given by God] have flesh and blood, he too shared in their humanity so that by his death he might destroy him who holds the power of death—that is, the devil" (2:14, NIV). His being tempted enabled Jesus as high priest "to sympathize with our weaknesses" (4:15a), and indeed "[e]very high priest is selected from among men" (5:1a), and so was Jesus Christ (5:5).

> During the days of Jesus' life on earth, he offered up prayers and petitions with loud cries and tears to the one who could save him from death, and he was heard because of his reverent submission. Although he was a son, he learned obedience from what he suffered. . . . (5:5-8)

E. JOHANNINE WRITINGS

As in the case of the Pauline epistles, the Gospel of John by virtue of its preoccupation with the deity of the Son of God and the Son's relationship with God the Father could be mistakenly thought to reflect no concern for the human Jesus. "The real fact is that manifestations of the humanity of Jesus are recorded with greater vividness in the Fourth Gospel than in any of the first three."[38] The eternal Word "became flesh and dwelt among us" (1:14a, RSV). Jesus attended with his mother a marriage feast (2:1-11), was weary at Jacob's well (4:6), depended on God the Father in performing miracles (5:19) and for his teaching (8:28), and wept at the grave of Lazarus (11:35). He shrank from the approaching cross (12:27), cared for his mother just prior to his death (19:26-27), thirsted while on the cross (19:28), and had the marks of the spear and nails after his resurrection (20:25).

The prologue to the First Epistle of John stated that "the Word of life" had been "heard," "seen," "looked at," and "touched" (1:1, NIV). Reference to "the blood of Jesus" (1:7) meant a genuine death, and the line of demarcation was to be drawn between everyone who "acknowledges

37. The term "the Son of man" in 7:56 is taken as a messianic designation, not as evidence for Jesus' humanity.
38. Mackintosh, *The Doctrine of the Person of Jesus Christ*, p. 99.

that Jesus has come in the flesh" as being from God and everyone who "does not acknowledge Jesus" as not being from God (4:2b, 3a).

II. JESUS' HUMANITY IN THE HISTORY OF CHRISTIAN DOCTRINE

A. DOCETISM

Docetism, which flourished from about A.D. 70 to about A.D. 170, was the first Christological heresy. Incorporating the fundamental Gnostic concept that the body, like all matter, is evil, this movement taught that Jesus only "seemed" or "appeared" to be a man. The term "Docetism" was derived from the Greek verb *dokein,* meaning "to think or suppose" and also "to seem or appear." According to this view, Jesus was God masquerading in human form. Such a view indeed reflects the strength of the doctrine of the deity of Jesus Christ during the time Docetism flourished. The First Epistle of John (esp. 1:1-3; 4:1-3) may have been written at least partly to refute and persuade from Docetism.[39]

B. OLD ROMAN SYMBOL (R), OR APOSTLES' CREED

In some of its second- and third-century forms, both Greek and Latin, the Old Roman Symbol contained the words "born from the Holy Spirit and the Virgin Mary," "crucified under Pontius Pilate," and "died." These words are found in the second or Christological portion of R. Recent creedal scholars have inclined to the conclusion that anti-Docetic, anti-Gnostic polemic was one of the major reasons for the inclusion of these words. Jesus' birth from Mary and his death were marks of being human, and the reference to Pilate may have been an effort at historical dating.[40]

C. DYNAMIC MONARCHIANISM AND MODALISTIC MONARCHIANISM, OR SABELLIANISM

Whereas Dynamic Monarchianism (Theodotus of Byzantium, Paul of Samosata), being defective with respect to the deity of Jesus, clearly acknowledged his full humanity, Modalistic Monarchianism (Noetus, Praxeas, Sabellius), being emphatic about the deity of the Son of God, obscured the full humanity of Jesus by reckoning Jesus as only a mode of the one God. Praxeas approached Docetism.

39. Harnack, *History of Dogma,* 1:194, 237-38, 258-59, 275-76; 2:276-83, 370; 3:16; 4:138-46; Kelly, *Early Christian Doctrines,* pp. 141, 147, 197-98, 463; Bethune-Baker, *An Introduction to the Early History of Christian Doctrine,* pp. 75, 79-80; G. Krüger, "Docetism," *The New Schaff-Herzog Encyclopedia of Religious Knowledge,* 3:460.
40. J. N. D. Kelly, *Early Christian Creeds,* pp. 144-52.

He recognized no human soul in Jesus, and the flesh which with him did duty for complete human nature can hardly have been more than a bare selfless vesture of the indwelling God.[41]

D. ARIUS AND ATHANASIUS

It is common knowledge that Arius and Athanasius were antagonists in the crisis that surfaced at the Council of Nicaea I (325). They differed significantly as to Jesus' relation to God the Father. Arius denied the eternal preexistence of the Word and his identity of essence or substance with the Father (or, the one God). On the other hand, Athanasius affirmed the eternal preexistence of the Word and his full identity of essence or substance with the Father. But, strange as it may seem, Arius and Athanasius shared a common view of Jesus' humanity, and the views of both were defective, at least by later standards, in this regard. Arius denied that Jesus had a human rational soul but acknowledged that he had a real human body. The Word took the place of a human soul. Athanasius spoke of the Word's "becoming man" but often only in the sense of "assuming flesh." For Athanasius the Word seemingly "fashioned a body for Himself in the Virgin's womb," and seemingly the Word had no human rational soul. According to J. N. D. Kelly, the Christology of Athanasius was a "Word-flesh" rather than a "Word-man" Christology.[42]

E. NICENE CREED (N) (325)

The creed that was adopted by the Council of Nicaea I was in its wording quite specific as to Jesus' humanity. The "Lord Jesus Christ" is described as the one "who for us men and for our salvation came down and was made flesh, was made man, suffered, and rose again the third day."[43] The fact that he "was made man" was included as well as "was made flesh" seems to suggest that the framers wished to be very specific about his humanity.

F. APOLLINARIS VERSUS THE CAPPADOCIAN FATHERS AND CONSTANTINOPLE I (381)

According to the traditional interpretation of the teaching of Apollinaris, he was a trichotomist who held that Christ had a human body and a human (animal) soul but not a human spirit (or, rational soul), the Word functioning in place of the human spirit. This was, therefore, a denial of the full humanity of Jesus. On the other hand, Kelly, for whom the question as to whether Apollinaris was a trichotomist cannot be definitely answered and hence is of secondary importance, has understood that he held to an extreme form of the Word-flesh Christology.[44] Undisputed is

41. Mackintosh, *The Doctrine of the Person of Jesus Christ*, p. 151.
42. Kelly, *Early Christian Doctrines*, pp. 284-89.
43. Kelly, *Early Christian Creeds*, p. 216.
44. *Early Christian Doctrines*, pp. 290-95.

Jesus as a Human Being

the fact that the formula of Apollinaris was: "one incarnate nature of the Word of God." For him, therefore, "Christ's flesh is not consubstantial with ours, since it is the very flesh of God."[45] The teaching of Apollinaris was rejected by the Cappadocian Fathers on the ground that it denied a genuine incarnation. Among the several arguments advanced by the Cappadocians against him[46] was that of Gregory of Nazianzus that "that which He has not assumed He has not healed; but that which is united to His Godhead is also saved, for the problem of sin is rooted in the human spirit."[47] The teaching of Apollinaris was condemned by the Council of Constantinople I (381).

G. SCHOOL OF ANTIOCH AND NESTORIUS

Theodore of Mopsuestia, who was greatly influential in shaping the Christology that came to be associated with Antioch, stressed the reality of Jesus' humanity and of his ethical life and taught two independent natures, divine and human, united in one personality by an ethical bond— the union being perfected at Jesus' ascension. Mackintosh has seen this as a "concord of will and purpose, not the oneness of a single personal life."[48] Previously Diodore of Tarsus (?–before 394) had taught a doctrine of the two sons, the Son of God and the son of David.[49] At Constantinople Nestorius (after 381–c. 451) became involved in controversy when he objected to the popular term *theotokos,* meaning "God-bearer" or "Mother of God." He was willing to accept the term *Christotokos,* or "Christ-bearer." He was trying to resist the ideas that the "Godhead itself was born of a woman" and that Jesus' humanity was "not real manhood" like ours. That for which Nestorius was condemned by the Council of Ephesus (431) and that which has been called the "heresy" of "Nestorianism" was the radical separation of the two natures of Jesus so that there were virtually two persons, two Christs. Modern scholarship, however, has become less certain that Nestorius was actually teaching that for which he was condemned.[50]

H. CYRIL AND THE SCHOOL OF ALEXANDRIA

The opponent of Nestorius, Cyril (?-444), the patriarch of Alexandria, was representative of the school of Alexandria. He taught that the Word "not only assumed but became flesh, and formed the personal subject in the God-man." He retained the formula of Apollinaris, "one incarnate nature of the Word of God," using it against Nestorius. Jesus

45. Mackintosh, *The Doctrine of the Person of Jesus Christ,* p. 199.
46. Kelly, *Early Christian Doctrines,* pp. 296-97.
47. *Epistle 101* (NPNF, 2d ser., 7:440).
48. *The Doctrine of the Person of Jesus Christ,* p. 203.
49. Kelly, *Early Christian Doctrines,* pp. 302-3.
50. J. F. Bethune-Baker, *Nestorius and His Teaching: A Fresh Examination of the Evidence* (Cambridge: University Press, 1908), esp. pp. 197-211.

Christ was "one out of two natures." These two natures were not "confused or mingled" but in "intimate cohesion," their hypostatic or natural union is a "permanent" state, and there can be "a certain interchange" of their properties. Some, such as Mackintosh, have concluded that, for Cyril, the full humanity that the Word assumed was impersonal—humanity, but not a human being. Thus, for Cyril, the human nature of Jesus Christ "is personal only in the Logos."[51] Others, such as Kelly, have been doubtful that Cyril's concept of the humanity of Christ was indeed impersonal. They understand Cyril's Christology as that of two stages, one prior to and the other after the incarnation, but the person of the Word remains the same. In the Apollinarian formula Cyril understood "nature" to mean "concrete individual." Also by "flesh" Cyril meant "human nature in its fulness, including a rational soul."[52] Through much politico-ecclesiastical intrigue Cyril's view prevailed at the Council of Ephesus, thanks to the bishop of Rome. In 433 Cyril accepted the Symbol of Union drafted by the Antiochene, Theodoret of Cyrus (c. 393–c. 466).

I. EUTYCHES, LEO, AND THE COUNCIL OF CHALCEDON

Eutyches (c. 378-454), a monk in Constantinople, was teaching "an extreme and virtually Docetic form of" the one-nature doctrine when for his teaching he was deposed by the local synod in Constantinople in 448. For him presumably "the Lord's humanity was totally absorbed by His deity," for he held to only one nature after the incarnation and denied that Christ's humanity was consubstantial with ours. Kelly's final verdict was that Eutyches was not a Docetist or an Apollinarian but "a confused and unskilled thinker."[53]

Eutyches was supported by Dioscorus, Cyril's successor in Alexandria, but opposed by Flavian of Constantinople and Leo of Rome. In 449 Leo sent a now famous Tome to Flavian, in which he stressed, among other things, that Christ's two natures "coexist in this one Person without mixture or confusion" and act separately but in concert. The council that Dioscorus helped to persuade the emperor to call and that he dominated refused to hear Leo's Tome, vindicated Eutyches, and set aside the Symbol of Union of 433. This council has been known by Leo's term, the "Robber Synod."[54]

The Council of Chalcedon (451), made possible by the death of one emperor and the accession of another and following Leo's deputies rather than Dioscorus, rejected the Christological errors of the preceding century and a half and affirmed "our Lord Jesus Christ, the same perfect in Godhead and also perfect in manhood, truly God and truly man, of a rational soul and body, co-essential with the Father according to the

51. *The Doctrine of the Person of Jesus Christ*, pp. 205-7.
52. *Early Christian Doctrines*, pp. 317-23.
53. Ibid., pp. 331-33.
54. Ibid., pp. 333-34, 337; Leo I, *Epistle 95* 2.

Godhead, and co-essential with us according to the Manhood . . . to be acknowledged in two natures. . . ."[55]

J. MONOPHYSITES, LEONTIUS, AND MONOTHELITES

After Chalcedon, Monophysites, or advocates of the one nature of the divine-human Christ, continued to press their view, and at the Council of Constantinople II (553) Chalcedonian Christology was reinterpreted in Monophysite terms, with "nature" and "person" being synonyms.

Leontius of Byzantium (c. 485-543) taught that the humanity of Christ neither was impersonal nor possessed "an independent personality or centre of conscious moral life," but instead, using as a formula *enhypostasia*, he held that the human nature had personality only in and through the divine Word. He also allowed for an exchange of attributes or qualities between the two natures.[56]

The question then arose as to whether Christ had one will or two wills, one energy or two energies. The Dyothelites, holding to two wills and two energies, ultimately prevailed over the Monothelites, who defended one will and one energy, at the Council of Constantinople III (680-81). Conciliar decisions about Christology had resulted in the seemingly contradictory affirmation of one nature in Christ (Constantinople II) and of two wills and energies (Constantinople III).

K. MEDIEVAL WEST

The Symbol of Chalcedon with its two-nature doctrine continued to be acknowledged formally, and monks such as Bernard of Clairvaux had a great attachment to the humanity of Jesus. But the Christology of an impersonal humanity of Christ was radically affirmed by Peter Lombard and retained by Thomas Aquinas, whose Christology Mackintosh has labeled as "Monophysite." Moreover, as the intercession of Mary and the saints was increasingly sought, Jesus became remote or was removed to the realm of deity alone.[57] The art of the period majored on such themes as the Madonna and the Child and the crucified Christ but depicted little of Jesus' public ministry.

L. LUTHER AND CALVIN

Sydney Cave concluded that, whereas Calvin taught the two-nature doctrine of Chalcedon with an Antiochene emphasis, giving special attention to Jesus' humanity, Luther, though also teaching that Jesus was human, leaned more definitely to the Alexandrian emphasis on the one divine-human Christ.[58] Paul Althaus, in interpreting Luther's Christology, has

---

55. Schaff, *The Creeds of Christendom*, 2:62.
56. Mackintosh, *The Doctrine of the Person of Jesus Christ*, pp. 217-18.
57. Ibid., pp. 226-29.
58. *The Doctrine of the Person of Jesus Christ* (New York: Charles Scribner's Sons, 1925), pp. 151-52.

stressed Luther's acceptance of the ancient dogmas, his teaching that Jesus "is true God" who brought salvation, his teaching of his humanity, and his teaching the two-nature doctrine, a kind of Christology "from below," and the Word's self-emptying. Only one element in Althaus's analysis offers support to Cave, namely, that Luther taught the "impersonality of the human nature of Christ."[59] Care must be taken lest too much of a Christological distinction be made between these two Reformers.

M. RADICAL REFORMERS

Certain of the Radical Reformers developed and defended a doctrine of the "celestial flesh" of Christ, which, to their opponents, seemed to be a resurgence of monophysite teaching. Clement Ziegler (?–c. 1533) differentiated a preexistent body of Christ from a fleshly body that he took from Mary. For others Christ owed even less to Mary. Caspar Schwenckfeld (1489-1561) held that Christ had two natures but the human nature was "uncreaturely" and hardly distinguishable from his divine nature, though it did come from the Virgin Mary. Melchior Hofmann (c. 1495–c. 1543) taught that the body of Jesus Christ was entirely from heaven and took nothing from Mary, like water flowing through a pipe. He became flesh but did not take flesh, and he had only one nature. According to Michael Servetus, the divine body that came from heaven was consubstantial with the Father. Menno Simons did allow that Jesus was nourished by Mary while in the womb, but there were not two natures and he was no earthly man.[60]

N. KENOTICISM

In nineteenth-century German Lutheranism a new Christological movement arose because Lutheran orthodoxy was seen as having failed to magnify the self-emptying of the Word or Son and having neglected the humanity of Jesus, and because there had been dissatisfaction with the Calvinist doctrine of two natures. The new school built its theory on Paul's use of *ekenōsen*, "he emptied himself" (Berkeley, RSV, JB, NASV), in Phil. 2:7a. Gottfried Thomasius (1802-75) of Erlangen taught that Jesus surrendered his relative attributes (omnipotence, omniscience, omnipresence) but retained his immanent attributes (holiness, truth, love, etc.). Wolfgang Friedrich Gess (1819-91) took the theory to its extreme by asserting that Jesus surrendered both kinds of attributes and that in the incarnation he " 'reduces Himself to the germ of a human soul,' " though subsequently as a human being he regained his identity with the Word.[61]

59. *The Theology of Martin Luther*, pp. 179-95. See also Richard A. Muller, *Christ and the Decree*, pp. 27-30, who has insisted that Calvin began his Christology with "the essentially Anselmic argument concerning the necessity of the mediator, the God-man," rather than with the Chalcedonian focus on the two natures in the one person.
60. Williams, *The Radical Reformation*, pp. 325-37, 394-96.
61. Mackintosh, *The Doctrine of the Person of Jesus Christ*, pp. 264-69.

Kenoticism did give emphasis to a self-giving in the incarnation that was designed to demonstrate the genuine humanity of the incarnate Word as well as to show the glories of his preexistent state. But, on the other hand, it has been criticized for contravening the immutability of God,[62] for teaching a "temporary theophany" instead of the incarnation,[63] and for denying a genuine simultaneous union of the divine and the human in Jesus.[64]

O. "JESUS OF HISTORY" SCHOOL AND LEFT-WING RITSCHLIANS

The "Jesus of history" school, by opting for a return to the so-called "historical Jesus" and by engaging in the writing of lives of Jesus, served to stress the humanity of Jesus, but often in a context in which Jesus was viewed as little more than an ethical teacher.[65] Left-wing Ritschlians carried this historical emphasis to an obscuring or a denial of the transcendent elements in Christology, that is, preexistence, ascension, the Trinity, and the like, while reckoning Jesus as having *the religious value of God.*"[66] Yet the "Jesus of history" movement did help to put to an end Docetism, at least of an avowed type.[67]

P. FORM CRITICISM

The Form Critics of the New Testament have accepted the humanity of Jesus but often have had little interest in its actual concrete manifestation, for they have been inclined to think that "the real historical Jesus is beyond recapture."[68]

Q. NEOORTHODOXY

Although Karl Barth did not avow any denial of the humanity of Jesus, he has been criticized for downplaying it.[69] According to Donald Macpherson Baillie (1887-1954), the Neoorthodox reaction against the "Jesus of history" movement led to a "theology of the Word of God" or "Logotheism" rather than to a "theology of the Word-made-flesh."[70] Yet Barth taught that the Logos assumed "fallen human nature," while also teaching that Jesus was sinless.[71] Barth had a doctrine of the "divine incognito" that surely had implications for Jesus' humanity, and Emil Brunner, according to Baillie, set no limits on "the completely human character of our Lord's experience."[72]

---

62. Ibid., p. 270.
63. Donald M. Baillie, *God Was in Christ: An Essay on Incarnation and Atonement* (New York: Charles Scribner's Sons, 1948), pp. 96-97.
64. Ibid., pp. 97-98.
65. Ibid., pp. 30-34, 39-53.
66. Mackintosh, *The Doctrine of the Person of Jesus Christ,* pp. 278-81.
67. Baillie, *God Was in Christ,* pp. 11-20.
68. Ibid., pp. 54-55.
69. Ibid., pp. 34-37.
70. Ibid., pp. 53-54.
71. Ibid., pp. 16-17.
72. Ibid., pp. 17-19.

R. Wolfhart Pannenberg

Pannenberg, beginning Christology "from below" with the human Jesus, asks initially about the union of the human Jesus with God. He finds this union to have been established by Jesus' resurrection, which retroactively applied to the whole of Jesus' existence. Thus he also has a Christology "from before."[73]

III. THEOLOGICAL INTERPRETATION OF JESUS' HUMANITY

In view of the numerous affirmations and denials of Jesus' humanity during the postbiblical history of Christianity and the many efforts to describe that humanity and to correlate it with his deity, one may be inclined to wonder whether all of this can be significant for Christians today and, if so, in what way. Indeed, Jesus' humanity needs to be clarified, so far as possible, and its importance for Christian beliefs and Christian living needs to be explained.

A. Characteristics of Jesus' Humanity

It is important to identify in one context the most prominent marks of Jesus' humanity, some of which have been mentioned earlier in this chapter.

1. Growth

Christian doctrine specifically affirms the reality of Jesus' growth. This teaching is based on Luke 2:40: "And the child grew and became strong, filled with wisdom; and the favor of God was upon him," and Luke 2:52: "And Jesus increased in wisdom and in stature, and in favor with God and man" (RSV). This growth was in the context of his family, the synagogue, and the Nazareth community.

2. Temptation

As a human being Jesus was really tempted. These temptations were not pretended or feigned; they were not designed merely as lessons for his disciples. They were not, one might say, like shadow-boxing. Especially noteworthy were his temptations in the wilderness (Matt. 4:1-11 and par.) and in the Garden of Gethsemane (Mark 14:32-42 and par.). On the one hand, Jesus is said to have been tempted "in every aspect" "as we are" (Heb. 4:15b, RSV); on the other, his temptations in the wilderness were peculiarly messianic. Jesus' temptations give evidence of intense struggle. Jesus resisted sin, overcoming all temptations, and was indeed sinless. "Although He was a Son, He learned obedience from the things which He suffered" (Heb. 5:8, NASV).

---

73. *Jesus—God and Man*, esp. pp. 33-37, 53-73; E. Frank Tupper, *The Theology of Wolfhart Pannenberg* (Philadelphia: Westminster Press, 1973), pp. 129-85.

The man who yields to a particular temptation has not felt its full power. He has given in while the temptation has yet something in reserve. Only the man who does not yield to a temptation, who, as regards that particular temptation, is sinless, knows the full extent of that temptation. Thus Jesus, the sinless One, is the only one who really knows the full extent of temptation's power, and He knows it precisely because he did not yield.[74]

3. Physical Exhaustion, Thirst, Hunger, Pain, and Suffering

Jesus is reported to have been physically weary (John 4:6), to have been thirsty (John 4:7; 19:28) and hungry (Luke 4:2; Matt. 21:18), and to have suffered pain and agony (Heb. 5:8; 1 Pet. 3:23b). Jesus is the continuing refutation of the concept of the impassibility of God. As noted earlier,[75] this concept has long persisted within Christian thought. If impassibility be true, then either Jesus did not really suffer or Jesus was not God. It is not adequate to claim that Jesus suffered only in his human nature, for that would imply a schizophrenic crucifixion.

4. Emotions

Jesus experienced a wide range of human emotions, though not remorse concerning or consciousness of personal sin. He knew joy (John 15:11), love for others (Mark 10:21), compassion (Matt. 9:36), amazement (Luke 7:9; Mark 6:6), indignation (Mark 10:14), anger (Mark 3:5), weeping (John 11:35), and sorrow (Matt. 26:37-38). He was troubled (Matt. 26:37; John 12:27), anguished (Luke 22:44), and lonely (Matt. 27:38).[76]

5. Limitations of Knowledge and Power

Jesus affirmed his own limitation of knowledge as to the time of his second coming (Mark 13:32) and manifested restraint in invoking divine power for his own benefit (Matt. 26:53, var. transls., "twelve legions of angels"). But such limitations did not, as Leon Morris has contended, constitute error on the part of Jesus.[77] Morris did not find completely adequate the distinction made by Edward John Bicknell (1882-1934) between Jesus' "discursive knowledge," which was limited, and his "intuitive knowledge," which was unlimited.[78]

6. Individuality

The Alexandrian school of Christology may have placed such an interpretation on Jesus' humanity as to teach or imply that Jesus had only an impersonal humanity. At its best such a teaching was an effort to

---

74. Leon Morris, *The Lord from Heaven: A Study of the New Testament Teaching on the Deity and Humanity of Jesus Christ* (London: Inter-Varsity Press, 1958), pp. 51-52.
75. See above, Ch. 19, V.
76. Morris, *The Lord from Heaven*, pp. 44-45.
77. Ibid., pp. 48-49.
78. Ibid., pp. 47-48; Bicknell, *A Theological Introduction to the Thirty-Nine Articles of the Church of England* (London: Longmans, Green and Company, 1933), pp. 88-89.

prevent an undue separation of Jesus' human nature from the divine Word or Son; at worst it denied that Jesus was a man. Rather, Mackintosh has declared: "Jesus, as man, was possessed of personal individuality. He was not only Man, he was *a* man."[79] But his individuality and his relationship with all humankind are not mutually exclusive. As a "real individual" he is "able to exert universal saving power" and "be the universal, focal member of our organic race."[80] "Though set within a specific race and age, He is none the less in the plenitude of His manhood the Man of every age, the Elder Brother of us all."[81]

7. Dependence on God the Father

Jesus prayed to the Father, expressed trust in the Father, and submitted to the will of the Father. Mackintosh has referred to "the perfectly human quality of our Lord's religious life."[82] It was this very dependence, as Jürgen Moltmann has forcefully asserted,[83] which was threatened in Gethsemane and on the cross by the Father's "appalling silence" and nonremoval of Jesus' "cup" of suffering and death and by Jesus' experience of Godforsakenness.

B. CONSEQUENCES OF JESUS' HUMANITY

Four important consequences of Jesus' being fully human, which have been derived from Mackintosh,[84] need now to be stated.

1. Reality of His Incarnation

Unless Jesus was fully human, there was no genuine incarnation of God with and in Jesus. Later[85] we will consider the various major defective understandings of the incarnation.

2. Jesus' Oneness with Us

By virtue of his becoming a human being, "flesh" being interpreted as full humanity and not as a bodily nature only, Jesus has and makes evident a common humanity shared with all human beings. The ancient creedal language, "consubstantial with us according to manhood," was designed to express this truth.

3. His Humanity as the Basis for His Saving Work

Here we will make no attempt to answer the question as to whether the Son of God would have become human if human beings had not

---

79. *The Doctrine of the Person of Jesus Christ*, p. 385.
80. Ibid., pp. 388-90, esp. 389.
81. Ibid., p. 392.
82. Ibid., p. 399.
83. *The Trinity and the Kingdom: The Doctrine of God*, trans. Margaret Kohl (San Francisco: Harper and Row, 1981), pp. 75-80.
84. *The Doctrine of the Person of Jesus Christ*, pp. 404-6, 400.
85. See below, Ch. 42.

sinned—a question to which most Western Christian thinkers have given a negative answer.[86] Rather, we are affirming that the actual incarnation of God in Jesus provided the divinely appointed *modus operandi* for the salvation or reconciliation of human beings to God.

4. Reality of a Perfect Example for Humankind

If human beings would know what God expects of them, let them look at Jesus. In affirming that Jesus is the "ideal or normal man," one should hasten to add "that manhood of this ideal type has existed but once in history." Indeed, since sin "dehumanizes" human beings, sin in Jesus would not have made him "more a man, but less."[87] According to Dale Moody, "Jesus was the only perfect man who ever lived out his life to the end in complete devotion to both God and others."[88]

The manhood of Jesus was both presupposed and specifically affirmed by the New Testament writers. It was both denied or obscured and clearly taught during later centuries. Both its characteristics and its consequences have been identified. Now we turn to the titles attributed in the New Testament to Jesus.

86. See below, Ch. 46, III, D.
87. Mackintosh, *The Doctrine of the Person of Jesus Christ*, pp. 400, 401.
88. *The Word of Truth*, p. 416.

CHAPTER 40

Jesus as Rabbi/Teacher, Prophet, and Messianic Son of David

The method of studying the person of Christ "from below" allows for a proper treatment of the major titles given to Jesus in the New Testament—a subject to which certain New Testament theologians during the twentieth century have given detailed scrutiny.[1] Although a study of such titles may yield more understanding of Jesus' functions than of his person, the titles should nevertheless be examined. First, we should consider "rabbi" or "teacher," "prophet," "son of David," and "Messiah."

I. JESUS AS RABBI/TEACHER

A. NEW TESTAMENT GOSPELS

According to the Gospels Jesus was addressed both as "Rabbi," an Aramaic word derived from the word *rab*, meaning "lord,"[2] and as "Teacher." Matthew (26:25), Mark (10:51; 11:21), and John (1:38, 49; 3:2, 26; 6:25; 20:16) record instances in which Jesus was called "Rabbi." In the Synoptic Gospels Jesus was more frequently addressed as "Teacher." To take only one Gospel, notice the 12 occurrences of the term "Teacher" in Mark: 4:38; 5:35; 9:17, 38; 10:17, 20, 35; 12:14, 19, 32; 13:1; 14:14. "Teacher" appears frequently in the Passion Week narratives in the Synoptics. The term was translated "Master" by the KJV, JB, and NEB, but the ASV, RSV, NASV, Berkeley, and other modern versions have more properly rendered it as "Teacher," especially since "master" no longer connotes "teacher" in the English language.

Two other words applied to Jesus in the Gospels more nearly approximate the term "Master" and may be so translated. One of these,

---

1. Oscar Cullmann, *The Christology of the New Testament*, trans. Shirley C. Guthrie and Charles A. M. Hall (Philadelphia: Westminster Press, 1959; rev. ed. 1963); Vincent Taylor, *The Names of Jesus* (London: Macmillan, 1953); Ferdinand Hahn, *The Titles of Jesus in Christology: Their History in Early Christianity*, trans. Harold Knight and George Ogg (London: Lutterworth Press, 1969).

2. Goppelt, *Theology of the New Testament*, 1:163, n. 2.

epistata, used only in Luke (5:5; 8:24, 45; 9:33, 49; 17:13), means "superintendent" or "overseer," being literally "one who stands over." The other term, *kathēgētēs*, which appears in Matt. 23:10, means "guide," or literally "one who goes before or leads."

That the Greek term *didaskalos* was generally regarded as synonymous with "Rabbi" may be seen in John 1:38 and 20:16 and by implication from Matt. 23:8. Instances in the Gospels in which Jesus was said to have "taught" outnumber those in which he is said to have "preached" by about four to one. At times the roles of teaching and preaching were correlated, especially by Matthew (9:35; 11:1).

That Jesus was no ordinary rabbi or scribe became evident to his hearers, who "were astonished at his teaching, for he taught them as one who had authority, and not as the scribes" (Mark 1:22, RSV, and par.). His teaching was said to be "new" (Mark 1:27). Even certain Pharisees and Herodians, trying to ensnare Jesus, declared that he truly taught "the way of God" (Mark 12:14). Leonhard Goppelt noted three distinctives in Jesus' role as teacher: his followers were called by him, whereas followers of a rabbi selected their rabbi; his followers, unlike rabbis, were not to become "teachers" or "guides" because Jesus was the "One . . . Leader" (Matt. 23:10, NASV); and "Teacher" did not become the commonly used title for Jesus among his disciples that "Teacher of Righteousness" did in the Qumran community.[3] In reply to criticism about his lacking rabbinical studies, Jesus insisted that his teaching was not his "but his who sent me" (John 7:16, RSV). The ultimate witness to the message and mission of Jesus was God the Father (Matt. 16:17; John 5:32; 8:18).

B. Modern Usage

1. The Enlightenment, Romanticism, and Deism

The eighteenth-century Enlightenment fathered the modern idea of Jesus' being primarily an ethical teacher. Such a view was not altogether distinguishable from Romanticism's idea of Jesus as a religious genius. According to these perspectives, the uniqueness of Jesus lay in the quality of his teaching rather than in the saving value of his death or in the identity of his person. It was thought that the teaching of Jesus could be, to a considerable extent, separated or extracted from orthodoxy's claims concerning the person of Jesus Christ and his atoning or saving death. Likewise, the distance or difference between Jesus and other human beings was only one of degree, not of kind.

The new and growing discipline of comparative religion seized on this concept of Jesus as ethical teacher as the basis for the comparison of Christianity with other major world religions. Such comparisons often had in view minimizing the uniqueness of Christianity by finding common strands in the ethics of Jesus, Buddha, Confucius, and others.

3. *Theology of the New Testament*, 1:164.

For the Deists Jesus became only one expositor of eternal, timeless, universal truths; at best he was a teacher of natural religion.[4]

2. Ritschlianism

For the Ritschlian school also Jesus was viewed as ethical teacher but much more in relation to his vocation as founder and proclaimer of the kingdom of God. Therein Jesus was more distinctive than in the Enlightenment or Deism, and yet the Ritschlians failed to affirm the more transcendent aspects of Christology.[5]

In view of modern efforts to identify the central role of Jesus as ethical teacher, religious genius, and/or expositor of timeless truths, Jesus' teaching role must be clearly related to other titles and functions, including the incarnate Word and the eternal Son of God.

II. JESUS AS PROPHET

A. BIBLICAL, INTERTESTAMENTAL, AND OTHER WRITINGS

1. Old Testament and Intertestamental Writings

The canonical Old Testament contains emphases both on the cessation of prophecy (Ps. 74:9) and on the restoration of prophecy. Instances of the latter include the promise of a future prophet like Moses (Deut. 18:15-22), the widespread prophesying to accompany the outpouring of God's Spirit (Joel 2:28-32), and the promise of the return of Elijah (Mal. 4:5). The Old Testament Apocrypha and Pseudepigrapha contain expressions of anticipation of a renewal of prophecy in Judaism. In Maccabean times the altar of burnt offerings was to be taken down and its stones carefully preserved "until a prophet should come and decide . . . concerning them" (1 Macc. 4:44), and Simon Maccabeus was to be "leader and high priest for ever, until a faithful prophet should come" (1 Macc. 14:41). According to Ecclus. 48:10, Elijah seems to have been poised ready to return for his restorative work. Sibylline Oracles 5:256-59, according to the experts, was a Christian interpolation.

2. New Testament

The term "prophet" was not used directly by Jesus according to the Gospels as a self-designation. He was, however, addressed as "prophet."

The New Testament Gospels identified John the Baptist as a prophet. Oscar Cullmann has understood this identification as a reference to the

4. See, for example, *Jefferson's Extracts from the Gospels: "The Philosophy of Jesus" and "The Life and Morals of Jesus,"* ed. Dickinson W. Adams, The Papers of Thomas Jefferson, 2d ser. (Princeton, N.J.: Princeton University Press, 1983).

5. Orr, *The Ritschlian Theology and the Evangelical Faith,* pp. 125-35; Mackintosh, *Types of Modern Theology,* pp. 153-67; David L. Mueller, *An Introduction to the Theology of Albrecht Ritschl* (Philadelphia: Westminster Press, 1969), pp. 57-59, 158, 169-70; James Richmond, *Ritschl: A Reappraisal; A Study in Systematic Theology* (Glasgow: William Collins Sons and Company, 1978), pp. 168-219.

eschatological prophet, or prophet of the last times. John was to prepare the way for the Lord (Luke 1:17, 76). God's word came to him (Luke 3:2). Jesus referred to John as "a prophet," as "more than a prophet," and as "Elijah who is to come" (Matt. 11:7-15). Cullmann has interpreted "the coming one" (Matt. 11:3) as the equivalent of eschatological prophet.[6] Jesus declared that "Elijah has already come" (Matt. 17:10-13), and the Evangelist recorded this as a reference to John the Baptist. Later disciples of John the Baptist[7] seem to have regarded him as "the Prophet" (= Messiah), or the forerunner of God. Such disciples may indeed have coalesced with the Mandaeans, who have survived until the twentieth century in Iraq[8] and in whose tradition Jesus was a "false Messiah" while John was "the Prophet." Such devotion to John the Baptist may help to explain why, in the Gospel of John, the Baptist denied being "the Messiah," "Elijah," and "the prophet" (1:20-21) and claimed to be only "the voice of one crying in the wilderness" (1:23). Such statements, together with the Baptist's deferring to Jesus (1:26-27, 30-31), may have been used by the Evangelist as a polemic against the developing sect of the Baptist.

In the Gospels Jesus was referred to three times as "a prophet." First, after the raising of the son of the widow of Nain the multitude declared, "'A great prophet has arisen among us'" (Luke 7:16, RSV). Second, Jesus used the term in his saying, "'A prophet is not without honor, except in his own country, and among his own kin, and in his own house'" (Mark 6:4). Third, after his final entry into Jerusalem, the chief priests and Pharisees, wanting to arrest him, yet "feared the multitudes, because they held him to be a prophet" (Matt. 21:46). Popular viewpoints as to Jesus included the possibility that he was "a prophet, like one of the prophets of old," if not John the Baptist raised from the dead or Elijah (Mark 6:14-15). The same options were posed at Caesarea Philippi (Mark 8:28). Twice in the Gospels Jesus was acclaimed by a group as "the prophet." After the feeding of the five thousand the people present declared, "'This is indeed the prophet who is to come into the world'" (John 6:14). On his final entry into Jerusalem the crowds announced, "'This is the prophet Jesus, from Nazareth in Galilee!'" (Matt. 21:11). Cullmann concluded that neither Jesus himself nor the Synoptists specifically identified Jesus as the eschatological prophet, and the same can be said for the Fourth Evangelist.[9]

In the Acts of the Apostles Peter (3:22) and Stephen (7:37) were reported to have quoted Deut. 18:15 and affirmed its fulfillment in Jesus Christ.

In the Pseudo-Clementine writings Christ was identified as "the true

---

6. *The Christology of the New Testament*, p. 36.
7. Pseudo-Clementine *Recognitions* 1:60.
8. K. Kessler, "Mandaeans," *The New Schaff-Herzog Encyclopedia of Religious Knowledge*, 7:146-51.
9. *The Christology of the New Testament*, p. 36.

Prophet" (*Recognitions* 1.44, 57, 69; 2.28, 32, 48; 3.41; 5.10; 8.59; 10.51; *Homilies* 3.20).

B. Postbiblical Usage

Gentile Christianity did not retain "Prophet" as a major title or means of identification for Jesus. Cullmann has analyzed the advantages and disadvantages of the term. Its advantages include its representing the proclamation of the eschatological kingdom of God rather than political activity and its capacity to be correlated with such other titles as "Messiah," "Word," "Son of God," and "Servant of the Lord." Its disadvantages include its inability to convey the centrality of the saving death of Jesus, the reality of his present heavenly intercession, or his preexistence.[10] The concept of a last and great prophet assumed a major place in Islam, and this very fact may have served to prevent any widespread reascendancy of prophetology as a phase of the Christian teaching concerning Jesus Christ.

From the Reformation onward Christian theology has had some place for Jesus as Prophet in the doctrine of the threefold office of Christ. John Calvin interpreted his prophetic office as that of teacher of the true wisdom.[11] John L. Dagg called Jesus "the great Prophet of the Church."[12] According to Charles Hodge, Christ exercised his prophetic office before his incarnation, during his ministry, and after his ascension.[13] Christ, declared A. H. Strong, fulfilled his prophetic office through teaching, predicting, and working miracles.[14] Dale Moody has placed far less emphasis on the concept of the eschatological prophet than has Cullmann. He treated the likenesses and dissimilarities between Moses and Jesus, the former prophets and Jesus, the latter prophets and Jesus, and John the Baptist and Jesus, and then expounded Jesus' use of parables, pronouncements of doom, proclamation of the kingdom, and the like.[15]

For all his identity with the prophetic tradition Jesus was always, as he said of John the Baptist, "more than a prophet" (Matt. 11:9 and par.). He was the Word "made flesh." The person of Jesus and the work of Jesus, whether revelatory or redemptive, must be understood together. As the messianic Son of God Jesus announced the drawing near of the kingdom of God, taught, and lived among or before his disciples. While he taught, his face was set toward Jerusalem and the cross. The passion narratives occupy major portions of the canonical Gospels. By redeeming us through his death and resurrection he has revealed God's nature and will. The categories of "Teacher" and "Prophet," therefore, must always be supple-

10. Ibid., pp. 43-49.
11. *Institutes of the Christian Religion* (1559 ed.) 2.15.
12. *A Manual of Theology*, p. 209.
13. *Systematic Theology*, 2:463.
14. *Systematic Theology*, p. 711.
15. *The Word of Truth*, pp. 366-71.

mented by and correlated with other aspects of the doctrines of the person and work of Jesus Christ.

III. JESUS AS SON OF DAVID

A. OLD TESTAMENT

The concept of the Son of David, according to Robert Harrell Culpepper (1924-), arose out of the displacement of charismatic leadership (judges, Saul, David) in Israel by dynastic leadership or kingship (Solomon and successors) and out of nostalgic retrospection to the age of David.[16] The initial and basic text was 2 Sam. 7:12-14a, 16 (RSV):

> When your [David's] days are fulfilled and you lie down with your fathers, I will raise up your offspring after you, who shall come forth from your body, and I will establish the throne of his kingdom for ever. I will be his father, and he shall be my son.... And your house and your kingdom shall be made sure for ever before me; your throne shall be established for ever.

Certain of the royal Psalms contain references to the Son of David.

> I will proclaim the decree of the Lord: He said to me, You are my Son; today I have become your Father.... Kiss the Son, lest he be angry and you be destroyed in your way.... (2:7, 12a, NIV)

Yahweh's "unfailing kindness" is shown "to David and his descendants forever" (18:50), the "royal son" is to be endowed with God's righteousness (72:1), Yahweh promises to establish David's line "forever" and to make his "throne firm through all generations" (89:4; see also vv. 29, 36-37), and Yahweh has sworn to David an irrevocable oath that one of his descendants would be on the throne, provided that David's sons "keep my covenant and the statutes I teach them" (132:11-12b). After captivity the covenant people would serve "David their king" (Jer. 30:9), who would be "one king" over a returned, reunited people (Ezek. 37:22, 24-25). Zechariah saw Zion's king, being "righteous and having salvation" and riding as a gentle person on a donkey (9:9).

B. OLD TESTAMENT PSEUDEPIGRAPHA

In the Psalms of Solomon, ch. 17 (esp. vv. 4, 21), one finds the depiction of the Son of David, identified as the Messiah, as a warring ruler, purging Jerusalem of godless nations, gathering a holy people, and ruling over other nations.[17]

C. NEW TESTAMENT GOSPELS

The term "Son of David," which was rooted in 2 Sam. 7:14 and had been used in the pre-Christian Psalms of Solomon 17:21, was used by

16. *Interpreting the Atonement* (Grand Rapids: Eerdmans, 1966), pp. 30-32.
17. R. B. Wright, "Psalms of Solomon: Introduction," in *The Old Testament Pseudepigrapha*, ed. James H. Charlesworth, 2 vols. (Garden City, N.Y.: Doubleday and Company, 1983, 1985), 2:642-46.

Matthew (1:1; 9:27; 12:23; 15:22; 20:30; 21:9, 15) more frequently than by Mark (10:47; 12:35, 37a) or by Luke (3:23, 31; 18:38-39; 20:41-44). In the genealogies of Matthew and Luke, coupled with Jesus' birth in Bethlehem, "the city of David" (Luke 2:4), and the virginal conception,[18] the term was used in the presentation of Jesus as of the lineage of David and as the "goal of Old Testament salvation history."[19] The term "Son of David" was especially used in connection with Jesus' healings: of two blind men; of a blind, mute, and demon-possessed man; of a demon-possessed daughter; of Bartimaeus (and one other?), and of the blind and lame at the temple. Three times in such texts it was joined with the petition, "Have mercy on me (us)." Leonhard Goppelt found the term in such contexts to be a "technical term for the King of salvation of the end time."[20] The most crucial of all texts for the understanding of the "Son of David" is Mark 12:35-37a and parallels. The inclusion of this passage in all three Synoptic Gospels is further attestation of its importance. Jesus asked:

> "How is it that the teachers of the law say that the Christ is the son of David? David himself, speaking by the Holy Spirit, declared:
>
> 'The LORD said to my Lord:
>   "Sit at my right hand
> until I put your enemies
>   under your feet."' [Ps. 110:1]
>
> David himself calls him 'Lord.' How then can he be his son?" (NIV)

The text has been a difficult one to interpret. At least five interpretations can be noted. First, Wilhelm Wrede held that Jesus was rejecting altogether the title "Son of David," and he cited in support the second-century Epistle of Barnabas 12:10-11.[21] Second, Joachim Jeremias understood David's "Son" to have had a present meaning and David's "Lord" a future meaning.[22] Third, Goppelt took the title as used in this passage, on the basis of the usage in Rom. 1:3, to be a mark of lowliness,[23] and Ferdinand Hahn understood it as referring to the earthly Jesus.[24] Fourth, Werner Georg Kümmel (1905-) thought that Jesus was rejecting the religio-political sense of the term while holding to his Davidic lineage.[25] Fifth, according to Oscar Cullmann, Jesus was arguing against the idea that the Messiah *must* be of Davidic lineage without necessarily denying the fact of such lineage, and

---

18. Hahn, *The Titles of Jesus in Christology*, pp. 258-65.
19. Goppelt, *Theology of the New Testament*, 1:168.
20. Ibid., 1:167.
21. "Jesus als Davidssohn," in *Vörtrage und Studien* (1907), pp. 166ff., as cited by Hahn, *The Titles of Jesus in Christology*, pp. 252; 271, n. 79.
22. *Theology of the New Testament*, p. 259.
23. *Theology of the New Testament*, 1:168.
24. *The Titles of Jesus in Christology*, p. 253.
25. *The Theology of the New Testament*, pp. 73-74.

hence a greater than David had come.[26] The fourth and fifth seem to be more persuasive.

D. PAULINE EPISTLES

In Rom. 1:3 the term "Son of David" was connected with Jesus' descent "according to the flesh" (RSV) or "human nature" (NIV). For Hahn this meant lowliness and an earthly mission in contrast to divine nature and exaltation (1:4).[27]

E. NEW TESTAMENT APOCALYPSE

In the letter to the church at Philadelphia Jesus was said to hold the "key of David" (3:7b). According to Hahn, this was the key "to the still future and therefore locked kingdom of the Messiah."[28] He was called "the Root of David" (5:5, NIV), which may be understood as "the young shoot or sprout of the root."[29] Likewise he was called "the Root and Offspring of David" (22:16b, NIV).

The term "Son of David" did not become a major or frequently employed term for Jesus Christ in postapostolic Christianity.

IV. JESUS AS MESSIAH

A. BIBLICAL AND INTERTESTAMENTAL WRITINGS

1. Etymology and Translation of Term

The Hebrew word *māšî(a)ḥ*, meaning "anointed one," was transliterated into Greek as *messias* and translated into Greek as *Christos*, a substantive derived from the Greek verb *chriein*, meaning "to anoint." The Latin translation is *Christus*, and hence we have the English "Christ."[30]

2. Old Testament

The predominant usage of *māšî(a)ḥ* in the Old Testament was in reference to leaders who had been anointed for their roles or tasks. Aaron and his sons were anointed as priests (Exod. 28:41; Lev. 6:22), Saul was anointed as king of Israel (1 Sam. 9:16; 24:6), as were David (1 Sam. 16:13; Ps. 89:3, 20; 132:10, 17) and Jehu (1 Kings 19:6), Elisha was anointed as prophet-successor to Elijah (1 Kings 19:6), and Cyrus, the non-Jew, was called "Yahweh's anointed" (Isa. 45:1).

Was *māšî(a)ḥ* ever applied in the Old Testament to a future coming one? Whereas popular Christian opinion may offer an overwhelming

---

26. *The Christology of the New Testament*, pp. 130-33.
27. *The Titles of Jesus in Christology*, p. 245.
28. Ibid., p. 245.
29. Ibid., p. 244.
30. Cullmann, *The Christology of the New Testament*, p. 112; Kümmel, *The Theology of the New Testament*, p. 68.

"yes," precise study of the Old Testament would conclude that it could have occurred in only one passage, Dan. 9:25a (RSV), wherein "an anointed one, a prince" was mentioned in connection with the "seventy weeks." Normally descriptions of the "ideal ruler" (Isa. 9:6-7; 11:1-10; Jer. 23:5-6; Ezek. 34:23-24) did not refer to him as "anointed one."[31]

3. Intertestamental Writings

Certain late Jewish apocalypses, as Cullmann has pointed out,[32] depicted the messianic king as one who would bring in a "provisional" kingdom rather than the "final" or "eternal" kingdom. These include 2 Esdras 7:28-29; 12:32 and 2 Baruch 29:3; 30:1; 39:7; 40:1; 70:9; and 72:2. A seemingly more traditional view of the Messiah can be seen in 1 Enoch 48:10 and 52:4 and in Psalms of Solomon 17:36 and 18:6, 8. Concerning an important development of the late intertestamental period Cullmann has observed that

> the Qumran texts (*Manual of Discipline* 9.11; *Serek ha'eda* 2.12ff.), the *Damascus Document* (12.23; 14.19; 19.10; 20.1), and the *Testaments of the Twelve Patriarchs* (Reub. 6.7ff.; Sim. 7.2, etc.) distinguish between a priestly and a political-royal Messiah, between a Messiah of Levi and one of Judah, between the "Messiah of Aaron" and the "Messiah of Israel." In each of these cases the priestly Messiah is superior to the royal one.[33]

At the time of Jesus, Judaism had numerous different ideas about the Messiah, not "a single fixed concept of the Messiah," but the theme of a political Messiah surely was dominant.[34]

4. New Testament

a. Synoptic Gospels

Here we do not propose to deal with the question as to whether or to what extent Jesus was conscious of being the Messiah or the Son of Man, for we will examine that question later.[35] Rather, the focus must be on the questions as to whether Jesus was identified as the "Messiah" and whether Jesus accepted such identification.

Mark contains three texts in which it is said that the title "Messiah" was ascribed or attributed to Jesus. The first is Mark 8:29 (NIV), in which Peter confessed, " 'You are the Christ,' " with Luke (9:20) rendering this, " 'The Christ of God,' " and Matthew (16:16), " 'You are the Christ, the Son of the living God.' " Goppelt thought that the term "Christ" here did not mean messianic king in the full sense but only the Promised One, or the Son of Man.[36] Kümmel, holding that the subsequent verses did not belong

---

31. Richardson, *An Introduction to the Theology of the New Testament*, p. 125.
32. *The Christology of the New Testament*, p. 116.
33. Ibid., p. 86.
34. Ibid., pp. 111-12.
35. See below, Ch. 41, I, D, 5.
36. *Theology of the New Testament*, 1:170.

to the original text, concluded that we cannot know what was Jesus' response to the confession.[37] Cullmann's conclusion was that, in view of his use of "Son of man" (8:31) and ascription of suffering to him, Jesus neither affirmed nor denied the ascription of messiahship.[38] Ethelbert Stauffer held that Jesus accepted the title.[39] In the second text narrating Jesus' trial before the Sanhedrin the focus is on the question by Caiaphas and the answer by Jesus (Mark 14:61b-62, NIV). Mark recorded the question as " 'Are you the Christ, the Son of the Blessed One?' " Matthew's wording is: " 'Tell us if you are the Christ, the Son of God' " (26:63d), and Luke's is: " 'If you are the Christ, . . . tell us' " (22:67a). Noteworthy is the fact that Jesus' answer relative to the Son of Man (Mark 14:62) seems to be a combination of Ps. 110:1 and Dan. 7:13. Kümmel concluded that Jesus gave an affirmative answer but did not use the title "Messiah" on his own initiative.[40] But Cullmann did not take Jesus' reply to be a clear affirmative answer. Emphasizing that, whereas Mark reported Jesus' initial reply as " 'I am' " and Matthew (v. 64a) reported it as " 'Yes, it is as you say,' " Cullmann took the Matthean form and Jesus' substitution of the term "Son of Man" to mean that Jesus was avoiding an answer to Caiaphas's "trick question" in such a way that he neither affirmed nor denied messiahship but shifted attention to the Son of Man.[41] The third text pertains to Jesus' trial before Pilate (Mark 15:2 and par.). Pilate's question has been understood as a Roman translation of the Hebrew "Messiah": " 'Are you the king of the Jews?' " This was tantamount to an inquiry as to whether Jesus was a subversive against Rome. Cullmann, taking Jesus' reply, " 'Yes, it is as you say,' " and correlating with it John 18:33-38, especially v. 33a, " 'My kingdom is not of this world,' " has again found Jesus to be evading a direct acceptance of the messianic title or its Roman equivalent.[42]

Only twice does the term "Christ" appear in the sayings of Jesus as recorded by the Synoptic Gospels. According to Mark 9:41 (RSV), " 'whoever gives you a cup of water to drink because you bear the name of Christ, will by no means lose his reward.' " This is an anarthrous use of the Greek *Christos*. Matt. 23:10, on the other hand, involves an articular use of *Christos*: " 'Neither be called masters, for you have one master, the Christ.' "[43]

37. *The Theology of the New Testament*, p. 69.
38. *The Christology of the New Testament*, p. 122.
39. *New Testament Theology*, trans. John Marsh (New York: Macmillan, 1955), p. 112.
40. *The Theology of the New Testament*, p. 72.
41. *The Christology of the New Testament*, pp. 117-20. Cullmann suggested that the probable Aramaic equivalent to *Sy eipas*, namely, *'āmartā*, is not indicative of a clear affirmation.
42. *The Christology of the New Testament*, p. 121.
43. Jeremias, *New Testament Theology: The Proclamation of Jesus*, p. 258. According to Stauffer, *New Testament Theology*, p. 113, the term "Christ" eventually "took into itself the greater part of the content of the idea of the Son of Man."

b. Gospel of John

Twice the term was transliterated as *Messias* (1:41; 4:25), but in each instance the translated *Christos* was added for clarification. Elsewhere in the Fourth Gospel only *Christos* was used. The stated purpose of this gospel is "that you may believe that Jesus is the Christ, the Son of God, and that believing you may have life in his name" (20:31, RSV). In the prologue "grace and truth" are said to have come "through Jesus Christ" (1:17). In only one passage, "and Jesus Christ whom thou hast sent" (17:3), is there a possibility that the term "Christ" can be reckoned as having been included in the sayings as traceable to Jesus himself, and this is debatable.

Most of the usages of "Christ" involve an ascription of messiahship or a denial of messiahship to Jesus by an individual or a group. John the Baptist insisted, " 'I am not the Christ' " (1:20, 25; 3:28). Andrew testified that he had "found the Messiah" (1:41). The woman at the well at Sychar expected that "Messiah would come" (4:25) and asked of her townspeople, " 'Can this be the Christ?' " (4:29). Mary of Bethany confessed her faith in Jesus as " 'the Christ' " (11:27). Some of the people of Jerusalem during the Feast of Tabernacles expressed doubt that Jesus was the Christ (7:26-27, 41b-42), while others were open to the possibility (7:31) or affirmed it (7:41a). Some attending the Feast of Dedication wanted a clear indication by Jesus of his being the Christ (10:24). During the passion week the crowd exclaimed about the perpetuity of the Christ in contrast to Jesus' being lifted up (12:34). The synagogue policy toward those who confessed Jesus as "Christ" was exclusion (9:22).

c. Pauline Epistles

In the letters of Paul the term *Christos* has become a personal name for Jesus and not primarily a title to be ascribed to him, although the use of "Christ Jesus" may reflect a residual use of the title.[44]

B. TWENTIETH CENTURY

Looking back over nearly two millennia of the history of Christianity, the contemporary Christian should not find it difficult to recognize the extensive and persistent influence of the term "Messiah." Not only did this term become, as Cullmann has asserted, "more or less the crystallization point of all New Testament Christological views,"[45] but also it has had a dominating role in our Christian vocabulary, as the terms "Christian," "Christology," and "Christianity" indicate.

The history-of-religion school and the Bultmannian school of theological studies have given considerable attention to the subject of the title "Messiah" in relation to Jesus, and the results have been largely negative.

44. Cullmann, *The Christology of the New Testament*, p. 112.
45. Ibid., p. 111.

Wilhelm Wrede, in his book *The Messianic Secret,*[46] held that Mark's Gospel taught that Jesus deliberately concealed his messiahship from the Jewish public and revealed it only to his disciples, who, however, misunderstood his teaching. This theory of secrecy and concealment, according to Wrede, was intended by Mark to explain why the then current Christian tradition was not messianic. The "bottom line" was that Jesus did not intend to be the Messiah and was not the Messiah, and hence messianic consciousness was to be rejected entirely. Wilhelm Bousset (1865-1920)[47] worked out a theory that the primitive church transferred from Jewish apocalypticism the concept of the Son of Man and applied it to Jesus. The Bultmannians, holding to Wrede's idea that the "messianic secret" was Mark's theory, deviated by holding that Jesus had been acclaimed Messiah prior to the writing of Mark's Gospel. They also concluded that Jesus neither used nor accepted titles.[48] In contrast one should take note of the more positive conclusions of Goppelt. Concerning Wrede's assemblage of four groups of passages in Mark, Goppelt has found the ones in which Jesus commanded that the demons be silent and in which he prohibited those healed from telling others about the healings to be irrelevant to the question of the messianic secret. Furthermore, those texts dealing with the secrets of the kingdom do not specifically mention messiahship. The fourth group, those mostly about the disciples' failure to understand, was little used by Matthew and Luke. In concluding that there are four "layers" of tradition about the messianic secret, Goppelt was yet able to reckon as historical the Petrine confession at Caesarea Philippi.[49]

Concerning the terms "Son of David" and "Messiah" it is important to draw the conclusion that their New Testament usage embraced two polarities, that of humiliation and suffering and that of exaltation, victory, and rulership. The former polarity was unique to Jesus and must be understood in view of the uses of "Son of man" and "Servant of the Lord." This motif of humiliation and suffering was missed by Albert Schweitzer and by his predecessor, Johannes Weiss (1863-1914), who set forth a totally futurist, apocalyptic interpretation of Jesus' preaching of the kingdom of God.[50] The latter polarity, inherited from the preceding popular Messianism as well as the intertestamental writings, was not eliminated by Jesus but tempered by his passion and recast in light of his resurrection and ascension.

46. Trans. J. O. G. Greig (Cambridge: James Clarke, 1971).

47. *Kyrios Christos: A History of the Belief in Christ from the Beginnings of Christianity to Irenaeus,* trans. John E. Steely (Nashville: Abingdon Press, 1970), pp. 33-34, 49-50.

48. Goppelt, *Theology of the New Testament,* 1:161-62. Günther Bornkamm was an exception on the ascription of titles.

49. Ibid., 1:172-77, 171.

50. Stephen C. Neill, *The Interpretation of the New Testament, 1861-1961* (London, New York: Oxford University Press, 1964), pp. 197-98.

CHAPTER 41

Jesus as Son of Man, Servant of the LORD, Sinless One, High Priest, and Savior

Continuing our study of the major titles ascribed to Jesus, we must now examine certain titles that were especially but not exclusively related to his sufferings and death. Four of the five subjects to be investigated in this chapter are titles that were applied to Jesus in the New Testament writings, and the other one is a state or condition that characterized Jesus.

I. JESUS AS SON OF MAN

The title "Son of Man," despite modern critical assertions to the contrary, was the principal self-designation used by Jesus. The term had been used in the Old Testament and in the intertestamental writings. Yet Christian theologians in the past have neglected this theme, and popular piety has wrongly interpreted it as nothing more than a synonym for the humanity of Jesus.

A. OLD TESTAMENT

The term that we identify as "Son of Man" was normally in Hebrew *ben-'āḏām*, whereas in Aramaic it was normally *bar 'ᵉnāš* or *bar 'ᵉnāšā'*. Whether the term meant not only an individual human being but also corporate humanity has been debated.[1]

There were three distinct usages of the term "Son of Man" in the Old Testament. First, it was used as a synonym for humankind in Ps. 8:4. That text clearly involved a collective or corporate usage. Second, it was used as a term of self-identification for the prophet Ezekiel (2:1 et al.). Third, it was used for a heavenly being to whom "authority" and "everlasting dominion" were given and who was identifiable with the "saints" of "the Most High" (Dan. 7:13, NIV). Most twentieth-century biblical theologians, with

---

1. Hahn, *The Titles of Jesus in Christology*, pp. 15-19.

the exception of John Young Campbell (1887-?), George Simpson Duncan (1884-1965), and Eduard Schweizer (1913-),[2] have agreed that the text in Daniel formed the principal background for Jesus' use of the term, and this position is supported by the quotations of Dan. 7:13 in the New Testament.[3]

B. OLD TESTAMENT PSEUDEPIGRAPHA

In 2 (or 4) Esdras 13:3 a man out of the sea appeared as an apocalyptic deliverer who was identified as the Messiah, and in 1 Enoch 46, 48–49, 52, 62, 69, and 71 "the Son of man," also identified as the Messiah, was presented as the first of God's creatures, who remains hidden until he will come to judge and rule the world. Oscar Cullmann has asserted that in both of these books "the Son of man" is both an individual being and an apocalyptic figure.[4] Reginald H. Fuller has found that in 1 Enoch "emerges the most complete picture of the Son of man in the Jewish tradition" and that therein "the Son of man . . . is a composite figure, in which motifs from the Davidic Messianology and from the Isaianic Servant of Yahweh have been combined with apocalyptic features."[5] This is indeed an important observation, but, as later discussion in this chapter should make clear, 1 Enoch does not contain the concept that the Son of Man suffers for others.

C. SOURCE OR SOURCES OF THE TERM

Ferdinand Hahn, in line with the Bultmannian school, has held "that the Son of man figure in Judaism is not to be explained apart from foreign influences."[6] But Joachim Jeremias has denied that the term can for certain be derived from Mesopotamian, Persian, Indian, or Gnostic sources and has left the way open for the likely explanation that "Son of Man" was essentially a Semitic term.[7]

D. SYNOPTIC GOSPELS

1. Prevalence of the Term

The Greek term *ho huios tou anthrōpou* is understood to have been a translation of the Aramaic *bar 'ᵉnāš* and was frequently employed in all four New Testament Gospels. According to Jeremias,

2. Campbell, *Three New Testament Studies* (Leiden: E. J. Brill, 1965), pp. 29-40 (first publ. in 1947); Duncan, *Jesus, Son of Man: Studies Contributory to a Modern Portrait* (New York: Macmillan, 1949), pp. 135-46; Schweizer, *Erniedrigung und Erhöhung bei Jesus und seinen Nachfolgern* (1962), pp. 34-35, as quoted by Goppelt, *Theology of the New Testament*, 1:182. Schweizer and Duncan sought to base Jesus' usage on that in Ezekiel.
3. Mark 13:26 and par.; 14:62 and par.; Rev. 14:14.
4. *The Christology of the New Testament*, pp. 140-41. Cullmann, pp. 141-50, also found in Philo, the Pseudo-Clementine writings, and certain of the rabbinic literature an "Adamic" pattern, wherein the "Son of Man" as a heavenly figure was associated or identified with the first human.
5. *The Foundations of New Testament Christology*, pp. 39, 40.
6. *The Titles of Jesus in Christology*, p. 20.
7. *New Testament Theology: The Proclamation of Jesus*, p. 266.

it is the unanimous testimony of all four gospels that Jesus spoke of himself as "Son of Man." The title *ho huios tou anthrōpou* occurs 82 times in the gospels, 69 in the synoptics, 13 in John. If we count the parallels only once, the synoptic instances are compressed to 38. . . .[8]

2. Meanings of the Term

a. In Reference to Humankind

In a few passages among the sayings of Jesus the term probably, though not certainly, was employed in line with its generic background so as to refer to humankind in the collective sense.[9] Such may be the case with Mark 2:27-28 (RSV), "so the Son of man is lord even of the sabbath," and with Matt. 12:32, "whoever says a word against the Son of man will be forgiven," especially since the Markan parallel to the latter reads "will be forgiven the sons of men" (3:28).

b. In Reference to Jesus

The predominant referent in the Synoptic uses of "Son of man" was Jesus himself, although some biblical scholars during the present century have greatly restricted the number of texts that they will allow to refer to him.

3. Origin or Origins of the "Son of Man" Sayings

A crucial and controversial issue in New Testament studies during the twentieth century has been the ascription of the Synoptic "Son of man" sayings, whether to the primitive church primarily or to Jesus primarily or some other answer. We will identify three principal positions.

a. All Present Tense Usages and Some Future Tense Usages of "Son of Man" Ascribed to the Primitive Church

Rudolf Bultmann contended that among the future Son of Man sayings some texts clearly differentiated Jesus and the Son of Man by referring to the Son of Man in the third person (e.g., Mark 8:38; Matt. 24:27, 37, 44), whereas in other texts the identification of the two was left undecided. On the other hand, the Son of Man sayings in the present tense, Bultmann acknowledged, did identify Jesus as the Son of Man. Bultmann, therefore, concluded that only those few texts making the differentiation are authentic sayings of Jesus and that those texts in which Jesus and the Son of Man are identified embody sayings that were produced by the primitive church.[10]

---

8. Ibid., p. 259. Edward Allison McDowell, Jr., *Son of Man and Suffering Servant: A Historical and Exegetical Study of Synoptic Narratives Revealing the Consciousness of Jesus concerning His Person and Mission* (Nashville: Broadman Press, 1944), p. 96, found 46 nonduplicated usages in the Synoptics.

9. Richardson, *An Introduction to the Theology of the New Testament*, p. 128, and Stauffer, *New Testament Theology*, p. 111, insisted that every usage in the Synoptics was intended to refer to Jesus.

10. *Theology of the New Testament*, 1:29-30.

b. All Future Tense Usages of "Son of Man" Ascribed to Jesus,
   and All Present Tense Usages Either Ascribed to the Primitive
   Church or Taken as Modifications of Authentic "I" Sayings

Reginald Fuller allowed for the authenticity (i.e., derivation from
Jesus) of all future tense Son of Man sayings. He specified that those
present tense sayings which can be seen as modifications of first-person
language can likewise be ascribed. The remainder of the present tense
sayings he ascribed to the primitive church. Moreover, Fuller insisted that
between the two sets of sayings there is "a subtle connection." Jesus "in
his earthly life was exercising proleptically the functions of the future,
eschatological Son of Man."[11]

c. Almost All "Son of Man" Sayings Ascribed to Jesus

This has been the conclusion of Richardson,[12] Kümmel,[13] Ladd,[14]
and Goppelt.[15] According to Richardson, "The difficulty about Jesus's
references to the coming Son of Man in the third person is an artificial one,
and the sense of his words is not at all obscure."[16] Furthermore, "Son of
Man" was "a term which could be made to carry the meaning which Jesus
wanted to pour into it."[17] This third position leads to the conclusion that
"Son of man" was indeed Jesus' most often used self-designation.

4. *Classification of the "Son of Man" Sayings*

Recent New Testament theologians outside the Bultmannian school
have moved to a virtual consensus concerning the propriety of a threefold
classification of the Synoptic "Son of man" sayings.[18] This classification
may be summarized as follows:

a. Present tense sayings that involve his "hidden majesty"
   (Stauffer) or present service on earth (Ladd)[19]
b. Sayings that speak of his sufferings, death, and resurrection[20]
c. Sayings that refer to his future exaltation, coming, and glory[21]

11. *The Foundations of New Testament Christology*, pp. 119-25, 142-51, 150.
12. *An Introduction to the Theology of the New Testament*, pp. 128, 135-36.
13. *The Theology of the New Testament*, pp. 76-90.
14. *A Theology of the New Testament*, p. 153.
15. *Theology of the New Testament*, 1:183-93.
16. *An Introduction to the Theology of the New Testament*, p. 135.
17. Ibid., p. 145.
18. Stauffer, *New Testament Theology*, pp. 109-10; Richardson, *An Introduction to the Theology of the New Testament*, pp. 132-34; Kümmel, *The Theology of the New Testament*, pp. 79-90; Ladd, *A Theology of the New Testament*, pp. 149-51; Goppelt, *Theology of the New Testament*, 1:183-93.
19. Mark 2:10 and par.; Luke 6:22; Matt. 16:13; Matt. 8:20 and par.; Matt. 11:19 and par.; Matt. 13:37; Luke 19:10; Mark 14:41 and par.
20. Matt. 12:40 and par.; Mark 8:31 and par.; Mark 9:9, 12, 31 and par.; Mark 10:33 and par.; Mark 10:45 and par.; Luke 17:24-25; Matt. 26:2; Mark 14:21, 41 and par.; Luke 22:48.
21. Matt. 10:23; 13:41; Mark 8:38 and par.; Mark 9:1 and par.; Matt. 19:28; Luke 17:22, 30; Luke 18:8; Matt. 24:27 and par.; Mark 13:26 and par.; Matt. 24:30, 37, 39 and par.; Matt. 24:44; Luke 17:30; Luke 21:36; Matt. 14:62 and par.; Matt. 25:31.

5. Jesus' Consciousness of Being "the Son of Man"

a. Bultmann and his school have rejected any possibility that Jesus had any consciousness of being "the Son of Man" or "the Messiah." Bultmann himself held that there was no evidence that Jesus thought that he was *"destined to be the future Messiah,"* that for the Synoptists *"Jesus' life and work . . . was not messianic,"* and that the existential faith of modern Christians is unrelated to the historical question as to whether Jesus had any messianic consciousness.[22] According to Günther Bornkamm, although Jesus' messianic identity may have been kept secret, as Wrede had contended vis-à-vis Mark, Jesus did not call himself "Son of Man" or take any other messianic title, and hence the question of messianic consciousness is irrelevant.[23]

b. Emil Brunner rejected as both unnecessary and ineffective the efforts to probe and identify the messianic consciousness of Jesus. The New Testament writers, he noted, had little interest in such, and one should not use the accounts of Jesus' baptism and transfiguration in such an effort. One soon reaches "the limit of scientific knowledge," and unbelievers are more prone to attempt such "a psychological construction."[24]

c. The validity of at least modest inquiry into the messianic consciousness of Jesus, undertaken not so much for psychological reconstruction as for exegetical completeness, has been recognized by Edward Allison McDowell, Jr. (1898-1975),[25] W. T. Conner,[26] W. G. Kümmel,[27] and Leonhard Goppelt.[28]

Any tracing of probable awareness by Jesus of the mission of the Son of Man or the Servant of the Lord usually begins with Jesus' baptism. Mark 1:11 (and par.) combines the Son-King motif (Ps. 2:7b) and the Servant of the Lord motif (Isa. 42:1b). His baptism has been interpreted as an act of identification with sinful human beings, the climax of which was to be the cross. The wilderness temptations are regarded by some scholars as specifically directed to Jesus' messianic mission. Each of the three can be identified with an institution in the life of Israel: the manna, the temple, and the Davidic kingdom (Matthean order). The temptation to turn stones into bread was an invitation to use supernatural power given for the messianic mission for the satisfaction of personal needs[29] or "to seize the controls of

22. *The Theology of the New Testament*, 1:30, 27, 26.

23. *Jesus of Nazareth*, trans. Irene and Fraser McLuskey with James M. Robinson (New York: Harper and Row, 1960), pp. 171-72, 177, 172. Culpepper, *Interpreting the Atonement*, p. 59, n. 47, found the ultimate issue connected with messianic consciousness to be the reliability of the Gospel of Mark.

24. *The Mediator*, pp. 361-63.

25. *Son of Man and Suffering Servant*, pp. 13-21.

26. *The Cross in the New Testament*, ed. Jesse J. Northcutt (Nashville: Broadman Press, 1954), pp. 2-3, 18-19.

27. *The Theology of the New Testament*, pp. 81, 85, 88-90.

28. *Theology of the New Testament*, 1:186, 187-93.

29. Conner, *The Cross in the New Testament*, pp. 9-10.

nature" from the Father.[30] Overcoming that temptation served to establish the primacy of faith as dependence. The temptation to jump from the pinnacle of the temple has been taken generally to have been a temptation to presume on God the Father rather than to exercise faith[31] or to expect "a suspension of natural law" in Jesus' behalf coupled with the escort of angels.[32] It may also have been peculiarly messianic in view of a prevailing rabbinic tradition, connected with Isa. 60:1, that "in the hour when King Messiah comes, He stands on the roof of the Temple, and proclaims to them, that the hour of their deliverance has come."[33] Consequently Jesus was being tempted to follow a traditional, temple-oriented messiahship.[34] The temptation to accept worldly kingdoms as offered by Satan was to be lured to embrace a political messianism and this-worldly kingdom, or "to become a beneficent conqueror," more political than military.[35] It may also be seen as a temptation to reject the arduous, painful way of suffering and death and to yield to or compromise with Satan.[36] Jeremias regarded all three temptations as being "concerned with one and the same temptation: *the emergence of Jesus as a political Messiah.*"[37]

In the synagogue at Nazareth Jesus declared the present fulfillment of the Isaianic utterance about the liberator who was "anointed" by "the Spirit of the Lord" (Luke 4:16-21). Jesus responded to the query from the disciples of John the Baptist concerning whether he was "the Coming One" by reference to his miracles and proclamation of the gospel to the poor (Matt. 11:2-6 and par.). Peter's confession at Caesarea Philippi is followed in the Synoptic Gospels by Jesus' teaching the disciples concerning the suffering, rejection, death, and resurrection of the Son of Man, by Peter's protestation, and by Jesus' rebuke of Peter (Mark 8:27–9:1 and par.). Jesus' final entry into Jerusalem displayed the sign of the nature of his messianism—his riding on a donkey in nonmilitary fashion (Zech. 9:9; Mark 11:1-10 and par.). While there are limits to the quest for the messianic consciousness of Jesus and overstatement is to be avoided, one surely finds evidence of a deepening awareness of what obedience to the Father and fulfillment of the Son's mission would mean.

E. PAULINE EPISTLES

Paul did not utilize the title in its familiar Greek form, *ho huios tou anthrōpou*. He did employ the concepts of original man, or Adam, and of

30. McDowell, *Son of Man and Suffering Servant*, p. 30.
31. Conner, *The Cross in the New Testament*, pp. 10-11.
32. McDowell, *Son of Man and Suffering Servant*, p. 31.
33. Yalkut Shimeoni, vol. 2, para. 359, p. 56d, lines 22ff., as cited by Alfred Edersheim, *The Life and Times of Jesus the Messiah*, 2 vols. (8th rev. ed.; New York: Longmans, Green and Company, 1896), 2:729.
34. McDowell, *Son of Man and Suffering Servant*, p. 34.
35. Ibid., pp. 37, 41.
36. Conner, *The Cross in the New Testament*, p. 12.
37. *New Testament Theology: The Proclamation of Jesus*, pp. 71-72.

the "last Adam," or second Adam, who is "from heaven." In 1 Cor. 15:45-49, especially verses 45 and 47, "the first man Adam" and "the last Adam," or "the second man," were contrasted. In Rom. 5:12-21 "Adam," identified as "one man" (vv. 12, 15, 16, 18, 19), was contrasted with "Jesus Christ" (vv. 15, 17, 21), identified as "the one man" (vv. 15, 17, 19).[38]

F. Acts of the Apostles

The term "Son of man" was applied by Stephen to Jesus (7:56). Cullmann has interpreted this usage as indicative of the role of Jesus as witness or advocate, not of the role of judge.[39]

G. Epistle to the Hebrews

The author in 2:5-9 quoted Ps. 8:4-6 and interpreted the "Son of man" as being Jesus Christ rather than humankind in the psalm. Everything will be ultimately subjected to Jesus (v. 8), whom God has "made . . . for a while lower than the angels" (v. 7a, RSV).

H. Gospel of John

The 12 usages of the term "Son of man" in this Gospel provide a salvation-history pattern. God's angels ascend and descend on the Son of Man (1:51), and the Son of Man descends from heaven (3:13). Jesus' disciples, in order to have life, must "eat the flesh of the Son of man and drink his blood" (6:53, RSV), for he gives "the food which endures to eternal life" (6:27). The identity of the Son of Man was posed as a question (12:34d). The Son of Man was to be "lifted up" (3:14; 8:28; 12:34c), the verb meaning, to be sure, crucifixion but perhaps also resurrection and ascension, and he was to be "glorified" (12:23; 13:31), the verb meaning, it seems, crucifixion, resurrection, and ascension. Indeed, the Son of Man was to ascend (6:62) and to execute final judgment (5:27).

I. Apocalypse of John

In 1:13 (RSV) the risen Jesus was referred to as "one like a son of man" in a context that connotes dominion, and in 14:14 the same words were applied to one seated on a cloud, "with a golden crown on his head, and a sharp sickle in his hand," ready for the harvest, which is judgment.

J. Church History

Throughout most of Christian history the term "Son of Man" was regarded as the counterpart or antonym of "Son of God" and hence as indicative of Jesus' genuine humanity. Surely this was the common pattern among the Church Fathers.[40] Usually the actual Synoptic texts that

---

38. Cullmann, *The Christology of the New Testament*, pp. 166-81.
39. Ibid., p. 183.
40. Ladd, *A Theology of the New Testament*, p. 146.

employ the term were neglected. Only in the twentieth century have the origin of the term in Jewish apocalyptic literature and its unique role as Jesus' favorite self-designation been so clarified as to provide another meaning. Even yet popular Christian usage has not been fully informed and corrected by the scholarly conclusion.

II. JESUS AS THE SERVANT OF THE LORD (OR, OF GOD)

Another significant biblical term applied to Jesus Christ is "the servant of the LORD" (Old Testament) or "the servant of God" (New Testament), also popularly known as "the suffering Servant."

A. OLD TESTAMENT: ISAIAH

1. Texts: "Servant of Yahweh" Songs

Four passages in Isaiah that used 'ebed, meaning "Servant," which many would take to be equivalent to 'Ebed Yahweh, meaning "Servant of the LORD," have been identified as the Servant of Yahweh songs. They are Isa. 42:1-4 (or 1-7); 49:1-7 (or 1-6); 50:4-11 (or 4-9); and 52:13–53:12. These passages were first clearly identified as the Servant songs by Bernhard Duhm (1847-1928) in 1875.[41] Isa. 42:1-4 treats of justice to the nations. Isa. 49:1-6 speaks of the gathering of Israel to Yahweh and Israel's being "a light to the nations." Isa. 50:4-9 refers to Yahweh's instruction of the Servant, the Servant's endurance of rejection, and Yahweh's vindication of the Servant. Isa. 52:13–53:12 presents the vicarious, sin-bearing suffering of the Servant.

2. Nature of the Sufferings of the Servant

According to Robert H. Culpepper, the sufferings of the Servant have five principal characteristics: "innocence," together with "silence" and "voluntariness"; "completeness"; accord with the divine will; vicarious-ness "in nature" and redemptiveness "in effect"; and victoriousness.[42]

3. Identity of the Suffering Servant

Modern Old Testament scholarship has been deeply involved in a debate on the question: Who is this "Servant of the LORD"? Is the Servant to be understood as a collective unit, or group, or corporate personality? Is the Servant rather to be understood as an individual person? In other terms, is the Servant Israel, a remnant of Israel, or a single person? The answers have been numerous and at times ambiguous; but neither are the answers necessarily to be taken as mutually exclusive.

---

41. *Die Theologie der Propheten als Grundlage für die innere Entwicklung-geschichte der israelitischen Religion dargestellt* (Bonn: A. Marcus, 1875), as cited by Culpepper, *Interpreting the Atonement*, pp. 33-34.

42. *Interpreting the Atonement*, pp. 36-38.

Some of the leading answers which have been proposed are that the Servant in the Songs is Israel, ideal Israel, the remnant, a mythological figure, the Messiah, or an historical figure such as Moses, Hezekiah, Jehoiachin, Jeremiah, Ezekiel, Cyrus, Zerubbabel, Deutero-Isaiah himself, or a combination of several of these.[43]

H. H. Rowley[44] and Culpepper[45] have seen a narrowing process within the Servant songs from Israel (49:3) to the remnant (49:5-6) and to an individual (52:13–53:12). Cullmann, agreeing, has also identified the work of the Servant as that of vicarious representation, the one taking the place of the many, and of reestablishment of Yahweh's covenant with his people.[46]

4. *Servant of the* LORD *and Messiah*

Within the Old Testament there seems to have been almost no correlation and indeed no identification of the two concepts, Messiah and Servant of the LORD, even though the term "my servant" was used in messianic contexts (Ezek. 34:23-24; 37:24-25; Zech. 3:8). The same can likely be said of the prevalent Jewish messianism of the New Testament era.[47] Joachim Jeremias sought to prove that pre-Christian rabbinic Judaism knew the concept of a suffering Messiah,[48] but Oscar Cullmann was unconvinced.[49] The exceptions to this pattern are to be found in the Old Testament Pseudepigrapha.

B. INTERTESTAMENTAL WRITINGS

1. *Old Testament Pseudepigrapha*

1 (Ethiopic) Enoch 48:4, 7 and 2 (or 4) Esdras 13:9 ascribed to the Messiah certain characteristics of the Servant of the LORD. But, as Cullmann has noted,[50] vicarious suffering was not ascribed to the Messiah. The suffering of the Messiah or end-time deliverer was neither voluntary nor vicarious. Rather, he was to suffer because that was to be his destiny.

2. *Qumran Literature*

According to the literature of Qumran, the "Teacher of Righteousness" does suffer, but whether he is to be put to death is not certain.

43. Ibid., p. 34.
44. *The Servant of the Lord and Other Essays on the Old Testament* (London: Lutterworth Press, 1952), pp. 39-41, 49-57.
45. *Interpreting the Atonement*, pp. 34-35.
46. *The Christology of the New Testament*, pp. 54-55.
47. Ibid., p. 56.
48. "*pais theou* in Later Judaism in the Period after the LXX," in *Theological Dictionary of the New Testament*, ed. Gerhard Friedrich and trans. Geoffrey W. Bromiley (Grand Rapids: Eerdmans, 1968), 5:686-87.
49. *The Christology of the New Testament*, p. 57.
50. Ibid., p. 56.

William Hugh Brownlee (1917-83) advanced the thesis that the Qumran community ascribed the functions of the Servant of the LORD to the community of Qumran itself and that the Teacher of Righteousness would actually carry out such functions.[51] But neither the community nor the Teacher was identical with the expected Messiah, whether the priestly one or the royal one. Hence Cullmann concluded that the Qumran writings still embodied prophetic suffering but not suffering in behalf of others.[52]

C. NEW TESTAMENT

The New Testament term for "servant of God" is *pais theou*, which both in late pre-Christian Judaism and in the New Testament era had two meanings, "child of God" and "servant of God."

1. *Synoptic Gospels*

a. Probable Quotations of or Allusions to the Servant Songs, Especially by Jesus Himself

As previously noted,[53] the words of the "voice from heaven" at the baptism of Jesus included a quotation from Isa. 42:1b, "in whom my soul delights" (RSV). The words "a ransom for many" (Mark 10:45, RSV), literally "a ransom instead of many," seem to convey the thought of the fourth Servant song (Isa. 52:13–53:12). The text, then, united the concepts of the Son of Man and the Servant of the Lord. Do the accounts of the Last Supper contain any allusion to Isaiah 53? This is possibly true of " 'This is my blood of the covenant, which is poured out for many' " (Mark 14:24, RSV). Luke 22:20 and 1 Cor. 11:24 used "for you [plural]," Mark used "for many," and Matthew used "concerning many" (26:28). Seemingly the only direct quotation in the Synoptics from the Servant songs was Luke 22:37 (RSV), " 'And he was reckoned with transgressors' " (Isa. 53:12d).

b. Passages concerning Jesus' Sufferings Not Directly Connected with the Servant Songs

The sufferings of Jesus were indicated by his saying that the "bridegroom" would be "taken away" (Mark 2:18-22), by his query of the disciples as to whether they could drink his "cup" and be baptized with his "baptism" (Mark 10:38 and par.), by his saying that "a prophet" cannot "perish away from Jerusalem" (Luke 13:33b, RSV), by his use of the "sign" of the prophet Jonah (Matt. 12:39b-40), by his parable of the evil tenants who kill even the heir of the owner of the vineyard (Mark 12:1-12), and by the anointing of Jesus' body by a woman of Bethany " 'beforehand for burying' " (Mark 14:3-9, esp. v. 8, RSV).

---

51. "The Servant of the Lord in the Qumran Scrolls, I," *Bulletin of the American Schools of Oriental Research*, no. 132, December 1953, pp. 8-15; II, no. 135, October 1954, pp. 33-38.
52. *The Christology of the New Testament*, pp. 57-58.
53. See above, I, D, 5, c.

c. Union of the Servant of the LORD and Son of Man Themes in Jesus

In opposition to the Bultmann school's postulate that the "Son of Man" teachings were for the most part the creation of the primitive church and to Jeremias's thesis that pre-Christian rabbinic Judaism had already interpreted the Messiah as one who would suffer, other twentieth-century scholars have attributed to Jesus the bringing together of the suffering Servant motif and the Son of Man–Messiah motifs.[54] This bringing together of the two was the outworking of his voluntary obedience to the Father.

2. *Acts of the Apostles*

In a sermon by Peter the God of the patriarchs was said to have "glorified his servant Jesus" (3:13a, RSV) and to have "raised up his servant" (3:26a). In the prayer of Jerusalem believers Jesus is referred to as God's "holy servant" (4:27, 30b). Acts 8:32-33 is a quotation of Isa. 53:7-8.

3. *Pauline Epistles*

Overt references to the Servant songs in Paul are few in number, but some of the concepts can be identified. Christ "died *for our sins* in accordance with the scriptures" (1 Cor. 15:3b, RSV). 2 Cor. 5:21 contains the basic idea of Isaiah 53. Christ "was put to death *for our trespasses* and raised for our justification" (Rom. 4:25). Jesus, "though he was in the form of God, . . . emptied himself, taking the form of a servant, being born in the likeness of men" (Phil. 2:7).

4. *Petrine Epistles*

The words " 'He committed no sin, and no deceit was found in his mouth' " (1 Pet. 2:22, NIV) are quoted from Isa. 53:9b, and "by his wounds you have been healed" (1 Pet. 2:24c) from Isa. 53:5d.

5. *The Gospel of John*

John the Baptist's acclaim of Jesus as "the Lamb of God" (John 1:29, 36) employed the Greek term *ho amnos tou theou*. The probable Aramaic expression for which this Greek was a translation, *talyā' dě'lāhā'*, can be translated either "Lamb of God" or "Servant of God." Cullmann regarded this term as a variant of *pais theou*.[55] Jesus as "the good shepherd" "lays

54. Reginald H. Fuller, *The Mission and Achievement of Jesus: An Examination of the Presuppositions of New Testament Theology*, Studies in Biblical Theology (Chicago: Alec R. Allenson, Inc., 1954), pp. 103-8; Conner, *The Cross in the New Testament*, pp. 4-8; Cullmann, *The Christology of the New Testament*, pp. 60-69; T. W. Manson, *The Servant-Messiah: A Study of the Public Ministry of Jesus* (Cambridge: University Press, 1961), pp. 25-35, 80-88; Goppelt, *Theology of the New Testament*, 1:190-93.

55. *The Christology of the New Testament*, pp. 71-72. Cullmann used the findings of C. F. Birney and Jeremias.

down his life for his sheep" (John 10:11, RSV). John 12:38b is a quotation of Isa. 53:1.

D. CHURCH HISTORY

Postapostolic Christianity did not retain "Servant of the LORD" as a major title for Jesus. The Servant motif was shifted from its early role as a title for Jesus to its later connection with the church's doctrine of the saving work of Jesus, especially his passion and crucifixion. For example, one may find the idea of the suffering Servant to an extent in John Calvin's doctrine of penal substitution, which is subsumed under Jesus' descent to Hades,[56] and that of the Lamb in the joyfully experienced wounds theology of the Moravian Brethren at Herrnhut.[57]

A twentieth-century denial of the centrality of the suffering servanthood of Jesus has come from certain European scholars[58] who have alleged that Jesus was a Zealot who employed and evoked violence and was crucified as an insurrectionist. A similar loss of the centrality of Jesus' suffering servanthood is possible within certain expressions of the contemporary theology of liberation. Some theologians of liberation have dealt with this issue forthrightly, avoiding the danger just mentioned. Segundo Galilea has said that Jesus did not join the Herodians, the Essenes, or the Zealots and was not a political, temporal Messiah, as may be seen from his wilderness temptations onward. But preaching the kingdom of God could "give rise to authentic liberation movements among human beings," for Jesus "sowed in the Roman system the lasting seeds of liberty and community."[59] Other theologians of liberation seem to downplay redemptive suffering. James Cone has declared that God

has chosen them [American blacks and other oppressed] not for redemptive suffering but for freedom. Black people are not elected to be Yahweh's suffering people.[60]

---

56. *Institutes of the Christian Religion* (1559 ed.) 2.16.8-12.

57. A. J. Lewis, *Zinzendorf the Ecumenical Pioneer: A Study in the Moravian Contribution to Christian Mission and Unity* (London: SCM Press, 1962), pp. 69-74.

58. Robert Eisler, *The Messiah Jesus and John the Baptist according to Flavius Josephus' Recently Rediscovered "Capture of Jerusalem" and the Other Jewish and Christian Sources*, trans. Alexander Haggerty Krappe (London: Methuen and Company; New York: Dial Press, 1931); esp. pp. 457-527; Samuel George Frederick Brandon, *The Fall of Jerusalem and the Christian Church: A Study of the Efforts of Jewish Overthrow of A.D. 70 on Christians* (London: S.P.C.K., 1951); idem, *Jesus and the Zealots: A Study of the Political Factor in Primitive Christianity* (New York: Charles Scribner's Sons, 1967).

59. *Following Jesus*, trans. Helen Phillips, M.M. (Maryknoll, N.Y.: Orbis Books, 1981), pp. 97-109, esp. 103, 106.

60. *A Black Theology of Liberation* (Philadelphia: Lippincott, 1970), p. 108.

III. JESUS AS SINLESS

A. NEW TESTAMENT

The New Testament contains both explicit teaching that Jesus did not sin and implicit or indirect witness to his sinlessness.

1. Explicit Teaching, Including Disputed Passages

a. Synoptic Gospels

Simon Peter "fell down at Jesus' knees, saying, 'Depart from me, for I am a sinful man, O Lord' " (Luke 5:8, RSV). On the way to the cross Jesus declared:

> For behold, the days are coming when they will say, "Blessed are the barren, and the wombs that never bore, and the breasts that never nursed." Then they will begin to say to the mountains, "Fall on us," and to the hills, "Cover us"! [Hos. 10:8]. For if they do these things in the green tree, what will happen in the dry? (Luke 23:29-31, NASV)

Perhaps in this enigmatic statement "the green tree" was suggestive of innocence or sinlessness, whereas "the dry" indicated the guilty of Jerusalem. The penitent thief being crucified with Jesus said: " 'And we indeed justly, for we are receiving what we deserve for our deeds; but this man has done nothing wrong' " (Luke 23:41, NASV). Did he mean innocence of any crime against the Roman government, or innocence of any sin?

b. Gospel of John

Peter confessed: " 'and we have believed, and have come to know, that you are the Holy One of God' " (6:69, RSV). Did Peter intend to say that Jesus was the divine One of God, or the sinless One of God? Jesus directly asked, " 'Which of you convicts me of sin?' " (8:46a, RSV). Leon Morris has noted that neither Jesus' enemies, who made many accusations against him, nor his friends and disciples ever truly attributed sin to him.[61] Jesus also declared: " 'I will not speak with you much longer, for the prince of this world is coming. He has no hold on me' " (14:30, NIV).

c. Pauline Epistles

Paul's classic statement is: "For our sake he made him to be sin who knew no sin, so that in him we might become the righteousness of God" (2 Cor. 5:21, RSV).

d. Epistle of James

Of the rich James wrote: "You have condemned, you have killed the righteous man; he does not resist you" (5:6, RSV).

---

61. *The Lord from Heaven*, p. 21.

e. Petrine Epistles

Attention has already[62] been given to 1 Pet. 2:22. Another statement (1 Pet. 3:18, RSV) is significant: "For Christ also died for sins once for all, the righteous for the unrighteous, that he might bring us to God."

f. Epistle to the Hebrews

"For we have not a high priest who is unable to sympathize with our weaknesses, but one who in every respect has been tempted as we are, yet without sinning" (4:15, RSV). Indeed, this high priest "has no need, like those high priests, to offer sacrifices daily, first for his own sins and then for those of the people" (7:27a).

g. Johannine Epistles

Two texts pertain to Jesus' sinlessness. "My little children, I am writing this to you so that you may not sin; but if any one does sin, we have an advocate with the Father, Jesus Christ the righteous" (1 John 2:1, RSV). "You know that he appeared to take away sins, and in him there is no sin" (1 John 3:5).

2. *Implicit Teaching*

a. Jesus taught that all human beings should confess their sins to God and pray for divine forgiveness (Matt. 6:12; Luke 11:4), and yet he did not apparently confess any sin of his own or ask for the Father's forgiveness. Couple with these facts his own clear-cut denunciations of hypocrisy.[63] Either Jesus needed not to confess sin and seek the forgiveness of his own sin *or* he was a hypocrite or moral imposter by his own standards!

b. Jesus' own actions in forgiving the sins of certain human beings (e.g., the paralytic in Mark 2:5 and the sinful woman in Luke 7:48) implied "a purity of nature equal to God's own, an unconsciousness of sin and a consciousness of holiness which we can describe as nothing less than divine." Furthermore, "the men whose sins He forgives hate sin as the unforgiven never do."[64]

c. Jesus' role as the perfect moral ideal or norm or example for humankind, as claimed both by Jesus and by the New Testament writers, presupposes his sinlessness. Jesus taught: "anyone who does not take his cross and follow me is not worthy of me" (Matt. 10:38, NIV). Discipleship involves drinking Jesus' cup and being baptized with his baptism of suffering (Mark 10:38). Paul admonished the Corinthian Christians: "Follow my example [literally, "be imitators of me"] as I follow the example of Christ" (1 Cor. 11:1, NIV). According to Peter, "Christ suffered for you,

62. See above, II, C, 4.
63. Andrew Martin Fairbairn, *The Philosophy of the Christian Religion* (5th ed.; London: Hodder and Stoughton, 1907), pp. 363-64.
64. Ibid., p. 364.

leaving you an example, that you should follow in his steps" (1 Pet. 2:21, NIV). According to John, "Whoever claims to live in him must walk as Jesus did" (1 John 2:6, NIV).

3. *Special Problem of an Alleged Proof-Text against Jesus' Sinlessness: Mark 10:18 and Parallels*

It has been said that Jesus' question to the rich young ruler, "Why do you call me good?" (NIV), is evidence that Jesus did not regard himself as without sin. In response it first should be noted that the word "me," not the word "good," is in the emphatic position in the sentence. Numerous indeed have been the interpretations during the modern era of Jesus' question and his utterance that immediately follows: "No one is good—except God alone." The saying has been taken to reflect the humility of Jesus.[65] It has been taken as a warning against making an ascription of goodness to be a matter of courtesy, for Jesus' goodness differed profoundly from Pharisaic goodness.[66] The rich young ruler has been seen to have had "a superficial view of the good," or a kind of legal goodness.[67] Moreover, Jesus was refusing to accept "conventional flattery."[68] Others have seen in the rich young ruler's use of "good teacher" the meaning of good man, but not God's man; hence he would have anticipated the later problem of Socinianism.[69]

How then ought the goodness of Jesus to be related to God the Father, who, according to Jesus, is "alone" "good"? Some have understood Jesus to be saying that goodness can only be comprehended in reference to God the Father[70] or that "all goodness has its source in God"[71] or that Jesus was pointing his inquirer to God's "absolute" goodness.[72] Others have seen Jesus' statement as reflecting "a universal doctrine of Judaism," namely, God's "perfect goodness."[73] Jesus' question could mean: Do you mean goodness "in the absolute sense as applied to God"?[74]

65. William Newton Clarke, "Commentary on the Gospel of Mark," *An American Commentary on the New Testament,* ed. Alvah Hovey (Philadelphia: American Baptist Publication Society, 1881), pp. 148-49.

66. A. B. Bruce, "The Synoptic Gospels," *The Expositor's Greek Testament,* 5 vols. (Grand Rapids: Eerdmans, n.d.), 1:248-49.

67. G. C. Berkouwer, *The Person of Christ,* trans. John Vriend (Grand Rapids: Eerdmans, 1954), p. 243.

68. Halford E. Luccock, "The Gospel according to St. Mark: Exposition," *The Interpreter's Bible,* 12 vols. (New York: Abingdon-Cokesbury Press, 1951), 7:802.

69. Henry Alford, *The Greek Testament,* 4 vols. (6th ed.; London: Rivingtons, 1868), 1:383-84.

70. Clarke, "Commentary on the Gospel of Mark," pp. 148-49.

71. Luccock, "The Gospel according to St. Mark: Exposition," 7:802.

72. H. B. Swete, *The Gospel according to St. Mark* (London: Macmillan and Company, 1909), p. 223.

73. Frederick C. Grant, "The Gospel according to St. Mark: Introduction and Exegesis," *The Interpreter's Bible,* 7:801.

74. A. T. Robertson, *Word Pictures in the New Testament,* 6 vols. (New York: Harper and Bros., 1930-33), 1:351.

By contrast Jesus' "own goodness" is "subject to growth and trial in the circumstances of the Incarnation."[75] With such possible explanations it is not necessary to reckon Mark 10:18 as evidence against the sinlessness of Jesus.[76]

B. THEOLOGICAL INTERPRETATION

1. Sinlessness and Twentieth-Century Denials

The sinlessness of Jesus is to be affirmed despite and in response to twentieth-century denials of that sinlessness. Nels F. S. Ferré held to the "unsinlessness" of Jesus, contending that "Jesus in the most natural and indirect instances seems to have been humbly conscious of sin before God." Ferré did not charge Jesus with "gross acts of misconduct" but rather with sin as "the acceptance of anxiety" (in relation to Heb. 5:7). Ferré pressed his argument by claiming that in order to save us from sin Jesus had to assume sin "within himself," by sharing our "alienation" and its result, "anxiety." He seemed to contradict Heb. 2:14-15 and 4:15 by his climactic claim: *"To remove Jesus from our sin categorically is to deny the Incarnation and to destroy its reality and power."*[77]

2. Sinlessness a Positive as Well as Negative Concept

As applied to Jesus, sinlessness is not only a negative but also a positive concept. It is more than the absence of sinning, more than un-tested innocence. It is positive Godlikeness or righteousness perfected through temptation, struggle, and suffering (Heb. 2:10; 5:8-9). Of Jesus it may be said: *Potuit non peccare* (He was able not to sin). Andrew Martin Fairbairn (1838-1912) held that the term "sinless," when applied to Jesus, "is stronger than innocence" in that his will has been "tried, but not overcome" and "is more comprehensive than holy, for the holy may, on the one hand, be men saved from sin, and, on the other, men who have attained beatitude; but the sinless has done no sin, and yet lives in deadliest conflict with it and in sorest trouble from it."[78]

3. Sinlessness, Virginal Conception, and Depravity

The sinlessness of Jesus does not need to be validated theologically, as some would seek to do,[79] on the twofold basis of the virginal conception of Jesus and Jesus' consequent avoidance of and noncontamination by Adamic corruption. Such an attempted validation rests, at least partly, on premodern ideas as to the sole derivation of major characteristics from one's father that are no longer accepted in biology. The sinlessness of Jesus

---

75. Vincent Taylor, *The Gospel according to St. Mark* (London: Macmillan, 1957), p. 427.
76. Mackintosh, *The Doctrine of the Person of Christ*, p. 37.
77. *Christ and the Christian* (New York: Harper, 1958), pp. 110-14.
78. *The Philosophy of the Christian Religion*, p. 376.
79. For example, Shedd, *Dogmatic Theology*, 2:304.

is indeed a religious or moral "miracle," not merely an automatic derivative from biological data. "No miracle of Christ," declared H. R. Mackintosh, "equals the miracle of His sinless life." His sinlessness is "unintel-
ligible save as it originated in, and was nourished by, a vital and organic
connection with the Father, who alone is holy with the holiness manifest
in Jesus." His difference from other humans "must lie in that element of
His being in virtue of which He is one with God."[80]

4. Sinfulness of Jesus: Impossible or Possible?

It is not necessary, in order to defend or protect the sinlessness of
Jesus, to affirm that Jesus could not have sinned. This position is represented by the Latin declaration: *Non potuit peccare* (He was not able to sin).
Louis Berkhof defended the impeccability of Jesus on the basis of "the
essential bond between the human and divine natures." In doing so he
altered the nature of Jesus' temptations, especially in the wilderness and
in Gethsemane, and reduced the significance of Jesus' will in his obedience
of the Father.[81] G. C. Berkouwer, refuting Hans Ludwig Windisch (1881-
1935) in his commentary on Hebrews and Heinrich Vogel (1902-) in his
book *Christologie,* who had rejected the impeccability of Jesus, and building rather on Abraham Kuyper and Herman Bavinck, who had accepted
it, defended impeccability on the basis of the personal union with the
Word, but in terms that are reminiscent of Apollinarianism.[82]

5. Sinlessness and Saving Work

The sinlessness of Jesus was clearly set forth by New Testament
writers as the basis for or as a qualification for his sacrificial or redemptive
work in behalf of human beings. The principal texts have been quoted
previously[83]: 2 Cor. 5:21; Heb. 7:26-27; and 1 Pet. 3:18. "The mystery of the
Son of man is precisely that his guilt-bearing and spotless holiness can go
together."[84]

IV. JESUS AS HIGH PRIEST

A. OLD TESTAMENT

1. Jewish High Priesthood

Priesthood was a characteristic feature of the religion of ancient
Israel. Encamped before Mount Sinai, the entire people of Israel was
described as "a kingdom of priests and a holy nation" (Exod. 19:6, RSV).
The special priesthood in Israel was of Aaron and his descendants (Exod.

---

80. *The Doctrine of the Person of Jesus Christ,* pp. 403, 404.
81. *Systematic Theology,* pp. 318-19.
82. *The Person of Christ,* pp. 251-67.
83. See above, III, A, 1, c, e, f.
84. Berkouwer, *The Person of Christ,* p. 250.

28:1-4). This Aaronic priesthood was assisted by the Levites (Num. 3:5-10). The annual ritual of atonement was the unique responsibility of Aaron (Leviticus 16), and special requirements were prescribed for "the priest who is chief among his brethren" (Lev. 21:10-15).

The high priesthood came to have political as well as religious significance during the postexilic period. By the time of Jesus the Sadducees had a virtual monopoly on the Jewish high priesthood. In view of the Sadducees' opposition to Jesus, it is remarkable indeed that the work of Jesus came to be described by his disciples in terms of high priesthood.

2. High Priest and Messiah-King

Was any connection ever made in the Old Testament between the high priesthood and the expectation of the Son of David, or Messiah? Two passages may be instructive in this regard. Gen. 14:17-20 records the blessing of Abram by Melchizedek and Abram's yielding of a tithe of military spoil to this one who was both king and priest. In Ps. 110:4 the king was addressed: " 'You are a priest for ever after the order of Melchizedek' " (RSV). Psalm 110 was interpreted as messianic by the Septuagint and by Jesus, according to Mark 12:35-37.[85]

B. INTERTESTAMENTAL WRITINGS

As previously noted,[86] the Manual of Discipline, the Damascus Document, and the Testaments of the Twelve Patriarchs all refer to a twofold messiahship, the one priestly and the other royal, with the priestly Messiah being superior to the kingly Messiah. At least some Jews, therefore, expected a priestly Messiah who would supplant the existing high priest.[87]

C. NEW TESTAMENT

1. Synoptic Gospels

When he appeared before Caiaphas the high priest, Jesus answered the question of Caiaphas as to whether he was "the Christ, the Son of the Blessed" by combining a reference to Ps. 110:1 with a reference to Dan. 7:13 (Mark 14:61-62). Cullmann has asked:

> Is it not significant that Jesus applies to himself a saying about the eternal High Priest precisely when he stands before the Jewish high priest and is questioned by him concerning his claim to be the Messiah? He says in effect that his messiahship is not that of an earthly Messiah . . . but that he is the heavenly Son of Man and the heavenly High Priest.[88]

---

85. Cullmann, *The Christology of the New Testament*, pp. 83-84.
86. See above, Ch. 40, IV, A, 3.
87. Cullmann, *The Christology of the New Testament*, p. 86.
88. Ibid., pp. 88-89.

2. Pauline Epistles

Paul did not apply the term "high priest" to Jesus. He did employ the term "mediator" (*mesitēs*)[89] in 1 Tim. 2:5a (RSV): "there is one mediator between God and man, the man Christ Jesus."

3. Epistle to the Hebrews

The high priesthood of Jesus is one of the principal themes of this epistle. The author used the term "high priest" ten times: 2:17; 3:1; 4:14, 15; 5:5, 10; 6:20; 7:26; 8:1; and 9:11.[90] Accordingly, Jesus the Son of God was appointed to the high priesthood "after the order of Melchizedek" by God the Father (5:4–6:10). Such priesthood was his "not according to legal requirement concerning bodily descent but by the power of an indestructible life" (7:16b). Jesus' priesthood is like that of Melchizedek in being nonsuccessional (7:3). The Melchizedekan priesthood was superior to the Levitic-Aaronic priesthood, for Levi "in the loins of his ancestor" Moses paid tithes to Melchizedek as his superior (7:4-10). Jesus shares in the superiority over the Levitic-Aaronic priesthood (7:15).

Jesus' high priesthood is superior to the Levitic-Aaronic priesthood in eight aspects. First, though sharing the temptations common to the Aaronic priests and indeed common to all human beings, Jesus was *without sin* (4:15; 5:3; 7:26, 27). Jesus shared with Jewish priests a sympathy for the weaknesses of human beings (4:15; 5:2). Second, Jesus was addressed with an oath (Ps. 110:4), and such an oath "makes Jesus the *surety* of a better covenant" (7:21-22). Third, the *continuity* of Jesus' priesthood so as not to be terminated by death is a mark of its superiority (7:23, 24, 28). Thus Jesus "always lives to make intercession[91] for those who draw near to God through him" (7:25). Fourth, Jesus has obtained a "much more excellent" *ministry* than that of the Aaronic priests (8:6). Fifth, Jesus ministers in a better *sanctuary*, one that "is set up not by man but by the Lord," a "heavenly sanctuary" (8:1, 2, 5; 9:1-8, 11). Sixth, Jesus' priesthood involves a new and better *covenant* than the old covenant with Israel (8:6-13). Seventh, Jesus by his own death offered a "once-for-all" *sacrifice* for sin in contrast with the daily, repeated sacrifices of Aaronic priests (7:27; 9:12, 25, 26; 10:10). Finally, the superiority of Jesus' priesthood is to be seen in that by his sacrifice the *consciences* of worshipers (believers) are cleansed and purified (9:9-14; 10:1-4, 19-22).

Two other important emphases were made in Hebrews respecting the priestly office of Jesus. One of these pointed to the past, while the other applies to the present. In addition to the once-for-all sacrifice of Jesus no

---

89. Frank Stagg, *New Testament Theology* (Nashville: Broadman Press, 1962), pp. 72-73, noting that "between" does not appear in the Greek of 1 Tim. 2:5, warned against making Jesus a " 'middle man.' " The term *mesitēs* was also used in Heb. 8:6; 9:15; 12:24.

90. Taylor, *The Names of Jesus*, p. 114.

91. *entygchanein*, "to hit upon, light upon one; hence, to converse, consult with, or make intercession for" (*hyper*).

other offering for sin is needed (10:18), and no other sacrifice for sin is efficacious if his great sacrifice be spurned (10:26). As risen high priest Jesus continues his intercessory work in behalf of humans (7:25), and thus Christians are to approach God with confidence in order to receive mercy and assisting grace (4:16).

4. *The Gospel and First Epistle of John*

The prayer of Jesus recorded in John 17 has since the sixteenth century been regarded by many as his "high-priestly prayer." The prayer was first so denominated, it seems, by David Chytraeus (?-1600), a Lutheran.[92] Jesus prayed for the Father's glorification of the Son (17:1-5), for the guarding and the unity of his disciples (17:6-19), and for the unity of those who would yet believe in him as a testimony to unbelieving humankind (17:20-26). In 1 John 2:1 Jesus is called "an advocate with the Father."

V. JESUS AS SAVIOR

A. OLD TESTAMENT

The biblical words "to save" and "salvation" are terms descriptive of deliverance and more general in meaning than the term "to redeem." The deliverances to which the Old Testament writers referred were chiefly from temporal danger, disease, and death, not from sin. God was called the God of salvation, especially in the Psalms (24:5; 27:1; 35:3; 62:2, 6; 65:5; 79:9) and Isaiah (12:2; 17:10; 62:11). In Isaiah 40–66 he is called "Savior" (43:3, 11; 45:15, 21; 60:16; 63:8). Other Old Testament passages referring to God as "saving" or to God's "salvation" include Deut. 32:15; 1 Sam. 10:19; Mic. 7:7; Jer. 14:8; and Hab. 3:18. Possibly only once in the Old Testament does the term "Savior" have distinct messianic significance, and in that passage, which pertains to an altar in Egypt, the term "Messiah" does not appear:

> It will be a sign and a witness to the LORD of hosts in the land of Egypt; when they cry to the LORD because of oppressors, he will send them a savior, and will defend and deliver them. (Isa. 19:20, RSV)

Human leaders such as Moses and the judges were also called "saviors" (Judg. 3:9, 15; 2 Kings 13:5; Neh. 9:27).

B. OLD TESTAMENT APOCRYPHA

The same kind of identification of God with salvation that one finds in the Old Testament is also to be found in the Old Testament Apocrypha: Baruch 4:22; Ecclus. 51:1; Judith 9:11; 1 Macc. 4:30; Wisd. of Sol. 16:7.

---

92. E. C. Hoskyns, *The Fourth Gospel*, ed. F. N. Davey (2d ed.; London: Faber and Faber Ltd., 1947), p. 494.

The Person of Jesus Christ

C. NEW TESTAMENT

Although the Hellenistic world referred to human heroes and rulers as "saviors"[93] and although the mystery religions used the term for gods who allegedly delivered human beings from death to immortality,[94] the application of the term *sōtēr* by New Testament writers to Jesus can be explained largely in terms of the Old Testament or Hebrew background. In Matt. 1:21 the name "Jesus" is one of the Hebrew forms of the title "Savior" that had been applied to God in the Old Testament. Cullmann has argued for the non-Palestinian origin of *sōtēr*, for otherwise to Jews Matt. 1:21 would read as "Jeshua Jeshua."[95]

In the New Testament "salvation" and "savior" are very closely related to sin and its effects so that the deliverance is primarily from sin. Even so the term *sōzein* in the Synoptic Gospels can mean physically "to heal" or "to make whole" (Mark 5:28, 34; Matt. 14:36; Luke 17:19).

The term "Savior" appeared only rarely in reference to Jesus in the Gospels (Luke 2:11; John 4:42) and in the Acts of the Apostles (5:31; 13:23). This has led Cullmann to conclude: "Neither by himself nor by others was Jesus ever called *Soter* during his lifetime."[96] The term "Savior" was used frequently only in Titus (1:4; 2:13; 3:6) and 2 Peter (1:11; 2:20; 3:2; 3:18), and there it was usually joined with the title "Lord." The term was also used in Eph. 5:23; Phil. 3:20; and 1 John 4:14.

The noun "salvation" and the verb "to save" were, of course, used more frequently throughout the New Testament. For example, Jesus saves lost human beings (Luke 19:10). His salvation avails for both Jews and Gentiles (Rom. 1:16-17; 10:13). Jesus provides the only effectual salvation for humankind (Acts 4:12).

D. MODERN CHRISTIANITY

Many nineteenth- and twentieth-century Christians, especially Evangelical Protestants, have made a larger place within their religious vocabulary for the term "Savior" as applied to Jesus than did the New Testament writers.

At the end of the twentieth century Jesus' role as Savior, especially as the only Savior of humankind, is being threatened by the inroads of a religious relativism that builds on the fact of worldwide religious diversity. In response, Russell F. Aldwinckle (1911-) has concluded:

> Our conclusion is that the claim for the unique saviorhood of Jesus is not inconsistent with a genuine openness in regard to the destiny of these, whether in the past or the present, who have not yet confessed him as Lord.

93. For example, Asklepios in *Eclogue* 4 by Vergil.
94. S. Angus, *The Mystery-Religions and Christianity: A Study in the Religious Background of Early Christianity* (New York: Charles Scribner's Sons, 1925), pp. 137-38; H. A. A. Kennedy, *St. Paul and the Mystery-Religions* (London: Hodder and Stoughton, 1913), pp. 215-20.
95. *The Christology of the New Testament*, pp. 244-45.
96. Ibid., p. 241.

We cannot anticipate the final judgment of God because we lack the complete knowledge of the future which would make such a judgment possible.... This, however, is no reason why Christians should not continue to say, 'By none other name shall men be saved.' This is not a claim to self-righteousness or perfection achieved in our own strength. It is a humble confession of the grace of God manifested in Jesus Christ beyond all our merit and deserving.[97]

In summary, the New Testament, drawing on the language and concepts of the Old Testament and sometimes also the intertestamental writings, referred to Jesus by means of the titles "Son of Man," "Servant of God," "High Priest," and "Savior" and taught that he was without sin. To varying degrees this language has been retained by Christians during later centuries.

97. *Jesus—A Savior or the Savior? Religious Pluralism in Christian Perspective* (Macon, Ga.: Mercer University Press, 1982), p. 214.

CHAPTER 42

Jesus: Only Son of God, Virginally Conceived

As we continue our investigation of the major titles ascribed to Jesus, it is now proper that we give attention to the title "the Son of God" and that we interpret the deity of Jesus, even as previously we interpreted Jesus' humanity.[1] In addition, we will treat the virginal conception of Jesus, more popularly known as the virgin birth of Jesus.

I. JESUS AS THE ONLY SON OF GOD

A. BIBLICAL TEACHINGS

1. Old Testament

Whereas the Old Testament at times described the relation of the people of Israel to God as sonship (Exod. 4:22; Hos. 11:1) and elsewhere seemingly used "sons of God" to refer to angels (Gen. 6:2; Job 1:6; 38:7), it also referred to a royal son who would be uniquely related to God (2 Sam. 7:14; Ps. 2:7).[2]

2. Intertestamental Writings

Sparse indeed are the texts in intertestamental writings that specify "the Son of God," but Hahn has concluded that "the motif of divine sonship . . . in the sense of appointment to office and assignment of dominion, practically belongs to royal messianism within the sphere of Palestinian late Judaism."[3]

---

1. See above, Ch. 39.
2. Taylor, *The Names of Jesus*, p. 52.
3. *The Titles of Jesus in Christology*, p. 284.

3. New Testament

a. Synoptic Gospels

The term "the Son of God" was seemingly not a self- designation by Jesus.[4] Mark's Gospel was written about "Jesus Christ, the Son of God" (1:1). Luke (1:32, 35), in his account of Jesus' being conceived by the Holy Spirit and born of Mary the virgin, quoted angelic utterances to Mary that used the words "the Son of the Most High" and "the Son of God." The voice from heaven at Jesus' baptism referred to him as "my beloved Son" (Mark 1:11, RSV). In the wilderness temptations the devil acclaimed him as "the Son of God," for the "if" in Matt. 4:6 can be translated "since." The words "my beloved Son" were also used at the transfiguration (Mark 9:7). A very clear statement of the Father-Son relationship, though not using the term "the Son of God," is to be found in Matt. 11:27.[5] Simon Peter in his Caesarean confession identified Jesus as "the Son of the living God" (Matt. 16:16), but according to the Matthean order Peter had already confessed after Jesus' walking on the water, " 'Truly you are the Son of God' " (Matt. 14:33). The parable of the vineyard (Mark 12:1-12) set the unique divine sonship of Jesus in contrast to the mere humanity of the Hebrew prophets. According to the Synoptics, Jesus did not seem to have the same hesitation about being addressed as "the Son of God" as he had about being called "Messiah."[6] Caiaphas asked Jesus: " 'Are you the Christ, the Son of the Blessed One?' " (Mark 14:61b, NIV). The Roman centurion who witnessed the crucifixion declared, " 'Truly this man was the Son of God!' " (Mark 15:39). Only Matthew (28:19b) records the dominical command for baptism " 'in the name of the Father and of the Son and of the Holy Spirit.' " All three Synoptic Gospels clearly identify Jesus as the Son of God.

Rudolf Bultmann set forth a dubious theory that a Hellenistic, non-Jewish idea of a divine man was borrowed from Hellenism and applied by Hellenistic Christians and the Synoptists to Jesus.[7] Oscar Cullmann held that the sonship ascribed to Jesus within the Synoptics meant the Son's complete obedience to the Father and hence a unity of will between Jesus and God the Father.[8] But what of any divine presence or divine nature in respect to Jesus? Cullmann must be correct in seeking to avoid reading later Trinitarian and Christological controversies and formulations back into the Synoptic Gospels. But one may ask whether Cullmann worked from an anti-ontological bias on this issue. Even in the Synoptics was not the sonship more than moral oneness or a unity of the will?

4. Goppelt, *Theology of the New Testament*, 1:109.
5. Taylor, *The Names of Jesus*, pp. 60-65, has defended the authenticity of Matt. 11:27 (= Luke 10:22) and of Mark 13:32.
6. Cullmann, *The Christology of the New Testament*, p. 282.
7. *Theology of the New Testament*, 1:130.
8. *The Christology of the New Testament*, p. 282.

b. Acts of the Apostles

Saul after his conversion proclaimed in the Damascus synagogues Jesus as "the Son of God" (Acts 9:20). In his sermon in Antioch of Pisidia he quoted a sonship text (Ps. 2:7; Acts 13:33).

c. Pauline Epistles

Paul used the term "Son" in reference to Jesus 16 times, 11 of which involved "his Son," four "the Son of God," and one "the Son." "He used it relatively less frequently than the authors of the Epistle to the Hebrews and the Gospel of John."[9] Goppelt found that "six of Paul's usages certainly belonged to formulas and expressions that had been passed on to him" and nine "were the apostle's own formulations."[10]

The Son of God was sent by the Father (Gal. 4:4; Rom. 8:3). He is "the image of the invisible God" and the object of the Father's love (Col. 1:13, 15). Jesus was preached as the Son of God (2 Cor. 1:19); indeed, the gospel pertains to God's Son (Rom. 1:3, 9). Paul could say that God "was pleased to reveal his Son in me" (Gal. 1:16) and that faith is directed to the Son of God (Gal. 2:20). God did not spare his Son the death of the cross (Rom. 8:32), and human beings "were reconciled to God by the death of his Son" (Rom. 5:10). Jesus was "designated Son of God in power . . . by his resurrection from the dead" (Rom. 1:4). "God has sent the Spirit of his Son into our hearts" (Gal. 4:6), and believers share "the fellowship of his Son" (1 Cor. 1:9). They are "to be conformed to the image of his [God's] Son" (Rom. 8:29), and "the knowledge of the Son of God" is the goal of Christian maturity (Eph. 4:13). The Son will ultimately be subjected to God the Father (1 Cor. 15:28), and Christians "wait for his [God's] Son from heaven" (1 Thess. 1:10).

Bultmann posited the theory that Hellenistic Christians borrowed from a Gnostic redeemer myth the concept of a divine son so that Jesus could be said by Paul to be preexistent, the agent of creation, and the one who descended and ascended.[11] Other scholars have concluded that the redeemer myth cannot be proved to have existed in pre-Christian times,[12] and Martin Hengel has found that Paul's use of the "Son of God," indicative of *"the close bond between Jesus Christ and God, that is, of his function as the mediator of salvation"* between humankind and God, was rooted in Jewish "terminology" and "thought-patterns."[13]

---

9. Goppelt, *Theology of the New Testament,* 2:72.

10. Ibid.

11. *Theology of the New Testament,* 1:295, 298-99; 2:6, 12-14, 66-67.

12. Robert McLachlan Wilson, *Gnosis and the New Testament* (Philadelphia: Fortress Press, 1968), pp. 27-28, 57-58; Leonhard Goppelt, *Apostolic and Post-Apostolic Times,* trans. Robert A. Guelich (New York: Harper and Row, 1970), pp. 97-98.

13. *The Son of God: The Origin of Christology and the History of Jewish-Hellenistic Religion,* trans. John Bowden (Philadelphia: Fortress Press, 1976), pp. 10, 57.

d. The Epistle to the Hebrews

This epistle presented God's Son as superior to angels (1:4-14) and to Moses (3:1-6) and as the bearer of a unique and comprehensive revelation of God (1:1-3). It also regarded Jesus the Son as the high priest (4:14) who "learned obedience through what he suffered" (5:8).

e. The Gospel and First Epistle of John[14]

The Gospel of John emphasized God's sending or giving of his Son (3:16, 17; 5:37, 38), and the same theme appeared in 1 John (4:9, 10, 14). "I and the Father are one" (John 10:30). Believing on the Son of God is one way of describing how persons become Christians (3:18, 36; 6:40; 1 John 3:23; 5:10, 13). Indeed, John's Gospel was "written that you may believe that Jesus is the Christ, the Son of God, and that believing you may have life in his name" (20:31). John 5:19-29 dealt at length with the relationship of the Father and the Son. The assertion of Jesus' divine sonship called forth hostile opposition from the Jews (10:36; 19:7), and confession of this sonship was one of the marks of a true Christian (1 John 2:22-25; 4:15).

In the Gospel and First Epistle of John the divine sonship of Jesus meant not merely the obedience of his will to that of God the Father; it clearly involved participation in the nature of God.

According to Martin Hengel,[15] the theological significance of the New Testament usage of "the Son of God" is fivefold: the once-for-all, "unsurpassable" expression of God's love in Jesus his Son; our salvation as dependent on God's sending Jesus; the Old Testament as fulfilled in the Messiah-Son; God's identification with Jesus' death and resurrection; and belief in God's revelation in his Son as the basis for freedom of the children of God.

Not only the term "Son of God" but also the terms "Word of God" and "Lord," as used in the New Testament, convey the concept of the deity of Jesus Christ. Other ascriptions of deity include the "fullness" texts (Col. 1:19; 2:9).

B. HISTORY OF CHRISTIAN DOCTRINE

Although recognition of Jesus as the God-man is basic to Christianity, various groups throughout the centuries of the Christian era have denied or emasculated the deity of Jesus Christ. In view of the somewhat detailed treatment of the history of doctrine under Jesus' humanity,[16] the present inquiry will be limited to the major denials of Jesus' deity.

---

14. Numerous Johannine passages relative to the Son have been treated under God as Father; see above, Ch. 20, II, C.

15. *The Son of God: The Origin of Christology and the History of Jewish-Hellenistic Religion,* p. 93.

16. See above, Ch. 39, II.

582 The Person of Jesus Christ

The Person of Jesus Christ

1. Patristic Age

The Ebionites, a second-century Jewish sect, regarded Jesus as a pious Jew whom God selected to serve as Messiah. The Dynamic Monarchians of the second and third centuries looked on Jesus as a human being especially endowed at his baptism with the "power" of God, but not partaking of the very nature of God.[17]

Arius and his followers during the fourth century contended that Jesus was an exalted creature of God—in fact, the first of God's creatures—but was not God. He was in effect a demigod, that is, more than human but less than God. "There was when he was not," Arius insisted. Jesus was preexistent but not eternally preexistent.[18]

2. Reformation Era

After his conviction and condemnation in Geneva in 1553 on charges of Anabaptism and anti-Trinitarianism, Michael Servetus, uttering his last words before being burned at the stake, prayed: "O Jesus, Son of the eternal God, have pity on me!" George Huntston Williams (1914-) has observed: "In his extremity he was explicit in his belief, still refusing to ascribe eternity to the person of Jesus Christ the Son."[19]

In sixteenth- and early seventeenth-century Poland, the Socinians denied that Jesus possessed a divine nature, while holding to his virginal conception, sinlessness, resurrection, dominion as resembling or equal to God's, and being indwelt by the Holy Spirit.[20] Francis David of Transylvania and Simon Budny (c. 1533–after 1584) of Lithuania and their followers denied that it was proper to worship or adore Jesus.[21]

3. Modern Era

During the post-Reformation and modern eras various people and movements have tried to retain a semblance of Christianity while denying explicitly or implicitly the deity of Jesus. We cannot trace these in detail here; instead we will cite two examples. Anglo-American Unitarianism has espoused either an Arian view of Jesus or a purely human view, both being denials of his essential deity.[22] The contemporary American move-

17. Bethune-Baker, *An Introduction to the Early History of Christian Doctrine*, pp. 98-102; Kelly, *Early Christian Doctrines*, pp. 115-19.

18. Henry Melvill Gwatkin, *Studies of Arianism* (2d ed.; Cambridge: Deighton Bell and Company, 1900), pp. 20-28; idem, *The Arian Controversy* (London: Longmans, Green, and Company, 1914), pp. 6-8; Robert C. Gregg and Dennis E. Groh, *Early Arianism: A View of Salvation* (Philadelphia: Fortress Press, 1981), pp. 1-42, 77-129.

19. *The Radical Reformation*, p. 614.

20. *The Racovian Catechism*, sect. 4.

21. Williams, *The Radical Reformation*, pp. 727-32, 738-40, 761-62.

22. Charles C. Forman, " 'Elected Now by Time': The Unitarian Controversy, 1805-1835," in Conrad Wright, ed., *A Stream of Light: A Sesquicentennial History of American Unitarianism* (Boston: Unitarian Universalist Association, 1975), pp. 3-26; James Drummond, *Studies in Christian Doctrine* (London: Philip Green, 1908), pp. 301-12.

ment known as the Way International, founded by Victor Paul Wierwille (1916-85), denies that Jesus is "God" or "God the Son" but acknowledges that he is "the Son of God" in a very subordinationist sense, involving a unity of wills but not of natures between Jesus and God.[23]

The deity of Jesus is also denied either explicitly or implicitly by the various non-Christian world religions such as Judaism, Islam, Hinduism, and Buddhism, but that topic lies beyond the boundaries of the present exposition.

C. SYSTEMATIC FORMULATION

1. The deity of Jesus Christ means that no mere portion or segment of deity rests or abides in Jesus but rather that the "fullness" of deity dwells in him (Col. 1:19; 2:9).

2. The deity of Jesus Christ means that his divine nature is the same as, and not unlike or merely like, that of God the Father. This issue was controverted during the fourth-century Arian controversy.

3. The deity of Jesus Christ means that he as the only Son of God provides an authentic revelation or disclosure of God the Father. "He who has seen me has seen the Father" (John 14:9, RSV).

4. The deity of Jesus Christ means that his sonship is eternal and not temporally constricted (John 1:1; 8:58). His divine nature was not something awarded to or bestowed on one who began as only human. Origen tried to convey this truth through his concept of the eternal generation of the Son of God.

5. The deity of Jesus Christ means that his sufferings at the hands of evil people were in the plan of God the sufferings of God in behalf of humankind. "God was in Christ reconciling the world to himself" (2 Cor. 5:19, NEB, Berkeley).

6. The deity of Jesus Christ means that his offer/pronouncement of the forgiveness of sins is not the blasphemy of an imposter but truly the gift of the God of grace.

7. The deity of Jesus Christ means that he is the only, the eternal, and the unique Son of God (John 1:18; Heb. 1:3), different from those human beings who are through him adopted as "children of God" (Gal. 4:4-7; Rom. 8:15-17).

8. The deity of Jesus Christ means that the Son of God has taken humanity in the one person of Jesus, that Jesus is truly the God-man, and, therefore, that it is proper and appropriate for believing human beings to worship him.[24]

9. The deity of Jesus Christ means that Jesus' promise of ultimate triumph has the guarantee and security of God (1 Cor. 15:24-26).

23. Wierwille, *Jesus Christ Is Not God* (New Knoxville, Ohio: American Christian Press, 1975), pp. 27-55.
24. Erickson, *Christian Theology,* pp. 703-4.

Although denied within by heretics and denied without by the adherents of non-Christian religions, the deity of Jesus the Son of God is still central to Christian truth and to the Christian movement. The Christian revelation/redemption stands or falls with the truth that Jesus is truly God.

II. JESUS AS VIRGINALLY CONCEIVED

Although the term commonly used for this event during the modern era, both among Protestants and among Roman Catholics, has been "virgin birth," we choose rather, for reasons to be explained presently,[25] to use the more precise term "virginal conception."

A. NEW TESTAMENT TEXTS

The New Testament accounts of the virginal conception of Jesus are two: Matt. 1:18-25 and Luke 1:26-38. According to these accounts Jesus was born of Mary without a human father, being begotten by the Holy Spirit. Noteworthy in these passages are the following items: the words "before they came together" (Matt. 1:18c, NIV); the angelic explanation, " 'what is conceived in her is from the Holy Spirit' " (Matt. 1:20c); the words "no union with her until she gave birth to a son" (Matt. 1:25a); Mary's question, " 'How will this be . . . since I am a virgin?' " (Luke 1:34); and the angelic answer, " 'The Holy Spirit will come upon you, and the power of the Most High will overshadow you' " (Luke 1:35b). Thomas David Boslooper (1923-) has commented: "The story of Jesus' birth from Mary stands in pristine simplicity in the midst of a constellation of narratives that preface Matthew and Luke."[26] It now becomes necessary to inquire as to how the various methods of biblical criticism have dealt with these passages.

1. Textual Criticism

a. Textual criticism does not yield any significant evidence of important textual variants within Matt. 1:18-25 and Luke 1:26-38. Agnes Smith Lewis (1843?-1926) discovered in 1892 the Sinaitic Syriac text of Matthew, in which 1:16 reads: "Jacob begat Joseph; Joseph, to whom was betrothed Mary, the Virgin, begat Jesus, who is called Christ." Mrs. Lewis interpreted this text as referring to the " 'social status' " of Jesus.[27] F. Pierce Ramsay held that "begat" meant "became the legal father of," basing this interpretation partly on what was said of Jehoiachin (Jer. 22:30; 1 Chr. 3:17).[28]

25. See below, II, D, 4. Raymond Edward Brown, S.S., *The Virginal Conception and Bodily Resurrection of Jesus* (New York: Paulist Press, 1973), p. 27, has defined "the virginal conception" as "the belief that Jesus was conceived in the womb of a virgin without the intervention of a human father, i.e., without male seed."

26. *The Virgin Birth* (Philadelphia: Westminster Press, 1962), p. 19.

27. Ibid., pp. 214-16.

28. *The Virgin Birth: A Study of the Argument, for and against* (New York: Fleming H. Revell Company, 1926), p. 51.

b. Is it possible that these entire passages were absent from early manuscripts or early versions of the Gospels of Matthew and/or Luke? James Orr asked at the beginning of the present century:

> Is there a single unmutilated MS. of the Gospels—older or younger—from which these chapters in Matthew and Luke are absent? *Not one.* Are these sections absent from any of the [ancient] Versions? So far as our evidence goes—No.[29]

According to Epiphanius (c. 315-403), the account of the virginal conception did not appear in the Gospel of the Ebionites, for Matthew 1–2 was seemingly omitted from that Gospel.[30] We know that the Ebionites rejected the virginal conception of Jesus as a teaching. Nor did the Lucan account appear in the shortened Gospel of Luke set forth by Marcion, who posited the advent of Jesus in a Christophany at Capernaum. Marcion's Luke omitted many other passages to be found in canonical Luke.[31] The Gospel of the Hebrews, however, seemingly referred to the coming from heaven of Michael, called Mary, to whom was entrusted the care of the Christ.[32] Boslooper has concluded: "Textual criticism has established the integrity of the virgin birth pericope in the present canonical setting."[33]

2. *Literary Criticism*

a. Among the variations between the two accounts is the fact that "Matthew does not mention the former residence of Joseph and Mary at Nazareth, and speaks as if, after Christ's birth, they went to Nazareth for the first time [cf. Matt. 2:23]." Such variations warrant the belief that these are independent accounts that "in reality remarkably corroborate and supplement each other."[34]

b. James Orr itemized 12 elements that are common to both the Matthean and Lucan accounts:

1) Jesus was born in the last days of Herod—Matt. 2:1, 13; Luke 1:5.
2) He was conceived by the Holy Ghost—Matt. 1:18, 20; Luke 1:35.
3) His mother was a Virgin—Matt. 1:18, 20, 23; Luke 1:27, 34.
4) She was betrothed to Joseph—Matt. 1:18; Luke 1:27; 2:5.
5) Joseph was of the house and lineage of David—Matt. 1:16, 20; Luke 1:27; 2:4.
6) Jesus was born at Bethlehem—Matt. 2:1; Luke 2:4, 6.

---

29. *The Virgin Birth of Christ* (New York: Charles Scribner's Sons, 1907), p. 40.

30. *Haereses* 30.13.2-6, cited by Edgar Hennecke and Wilhelm Schneemelcher, eds., *New Testament Apocrypha*, trans. A. J. B. Higgins et al., ed. R. McL. Wilson, 2 vols. (London: Lutterworth Press; Philadelphia: Westminster Press, 1963, 1966), 1:156-57.

31. Blackman, *Marcion and His Influence*, pp. 45-47.

32. Excerpt from discourse ascribed to Cyril of Jerusalem, quoted by Hennecke and Schneemelcher, eds., *New Testament Apocrypha*, 1:163.

33. *The Virgin Birth*, p. 218.

34. Orr, *The Virgin Birth of Christ*, p. 34.

7) By divine direction He was called Jesus—Matt. 1:21; Luke 1:31.

8) He was declared to be a Saviour—Matt. 1:21; Luke 2:11.

9) Joseph knew beforehand of Mary's condition and its cause—Matt. 1:18-20; Luke 2:5.

10) Nevertheless he took Mary to wife, and assumed full paternal responsibilities for her child—was from the first *in loco parentis* to Jesus—Matt. 1:20, 24, 25; Luke 2:5ff.

11) The Annunciation and birth were attended by revelations and visions—Matt. 1:20, etc.; Luke 1:27, 28, etc.

12) After the birth of Jesus, Joseph and Mary dwelt in Nazareth—Matt. 2:23; Luke 2:39.[35]

Literary criticism does not pose any major problems for the historicity of the virginal conception of Jesus, except when presuppositions contrary to historicity have been assumed.

3. Form Criticism

Martin Dibelius classified the virginal conception accounts as "legends," a legend being "the story of a saintly man in whose works and faith interest is taken," rather than as "myths," a myth being "a many-sided interaction between mythological but not human persons." Luke 1:34-35 was not an addition to the legend. The passages were both "an addition to Christian preaching" and "a later excrescence to a growing Christology."[36] Harris Lachlan MacNeill (1871-?), however, classified the virginal conception passages as "*mythos* in the classical sense of the word, denoting historical material in which, or around which, fancy and imagination have to some degree woven legendary material." But he insisted "that their mythical character does not exclude them entirely from the realm of history." Luke 1–2 "is the precipitate of the life and faith of a religious community rather than the expression of an individual," and the community was likely Jewish messianic rather than "distinctively . . . Christian."[37] Paul Sevier Minear (1906-) described the early church's shaping of the virginal conception passages under three categories: *Sitz im Leben* ("life situation"); *Sitz im Glauben* ("faith situation"); and *Sitz im Loben* ("worship situation").[38] Where, under form criticism, is the line to be drawn between the authentic and historical on the one hand and the

35. Ibid., pp. 36-37.

36. Boslooper, *The Virgin Birth*, pp. 207-10, based on Dibelius, *From Tradition to Gospel*, trans. Bertram Lee Woolf (New York: Charles Scribner's Sons, 1935); idem, *Jungfrauensohn und Krippenkind: Untersuchungen zur Geburtsgeschichte Jesu im Lukas-Evangelium* (Heidelberg: C. Winter, 1932); idem, *Jesus*, trans. Charles B. Hedrick and Frederick C. Grant (Philadelphia: Westminster Press, 1949).

37. Boslooper, *The Virgin Birth*, pp. 210-12, based on MacNeill, "The *Sitz im Leben* of Luke 1:5–2:20," *Journal of Biblical Literature* 65 (June 1946): 123-30.

38. Boslooper, *The Virgin Birth*, pp. 212-14, based on Minear, "The Interpreter and the Birth Narratives," in *Symbolae Biblicae Upsalienses, Supplementhäften Till Svensk Exegetisk Årsbok*, 13 (1950).

legendary and mythical on the other? In a more positive vein Boslooper
has concluded: "Form criticism has determined the original textual independence of the narrative of Jesus' miraculous conception from the surrounding infancy narratives." Joining to this statement the results of
textual criticism, he stated that the two "taken together imply that one
hand was responsible for the finished product."[39]

Raymond Edward Brown, S.S. (1928-), has seen the virginal conception as "one of the few points on which they [Matt. and Luke] agree" and
has used this factor to argue that the tradition of virginal conception
"antedated both accounts."[40]

4. Redaction Criticism

Adolf Harnack and Firmin Nicolardot at the beginning of the present
century posited the theory that Luke 1:34-35 "may be explained as the point
of juncture between originally individual traditions, i.e., the narrative as a
means of forming a bridge between two originally separate traditions."[41]

Some twentieth-century critics have contended that the account of
the virginal conception of Jesus in Luke's Gospel was not part of the
original Gospel of Luke. This contention was not based on evidence from
textual criticism. Vincent Taylor, for example, concluded that Luke 1:34-35
"is an interpolation made by Luke himself on his own material."[42]

Textual criticism has afforded no substantial evidence that Matt.
1:18-25 and Luke 1:26-38 were not included in the original text of Matthew
and Luke. Literary criticism, when employed without alien presuppositions, presents no major problem to these accounts. The treatments of
these accounts by form critics and by redaction critics are highly conjec-
tural in nature, and their conclusions cannot be proved even as they may
not be finally disproved.

B. HISTORY OF CHRISTIAN DOCTRINE

Theological scholarship has yet to produce a comprehensive history
of the doctrine of the virginal conception of Jesus Christ. Hans von
Campenhausen has studied the patristic phase,[43] and Thomas D.
Boslooper has probed numerous aspects of the patristic, post-Reformation, and modern periods.[44]

39. Boslooper, The Virgin Birth, p. 218.

40. The Virginal Conception and Bodily Resurrection of Jesus, p. 53.

41. Boslooper, The Virgin Birth, p. 218, based on Harnack, The Date of the Acts and of the
Synoptic Gospels, trans. J. R. Wilkinson, New Testament Studies, vol. 3 (New York: G. P.
Putnam's Sons, 1911), pp. 153-56; and Nicolardot, Les procédes de rédaction des trois premiers
évangélistes (Paris: Fischbacher, 1908), pp. 169-70.

42. Boslooper, The Virgin Birth, p. 216, based on Taylor, The Historical Evidence for the
Virgin Birth (Oxford: Clarendon Press, 1920), pp. 32-34.

43. The Virgin Birth in the Theology of the Ancient Church, trans. Frank Clarke, Studies
in Historical Theology, no. 2 (London: SCM Press, 1964).

44. The Virgin Birth, pp. 27-132.

1. Patristic Age

Boslooper has commented concerning the second and third centuries:

> From Ignatius through Origen, the virgin birth was at the crux of the church's controversy with the non-Christian world. With the Jews, the Christians struggled over the relationship of the virgin birth to the Old Testament. With the Gentiles, the Christians carried on a discussion of the relationship of the virgin birth to apparent parallels in other religious traditions.[45]

For most of the Church Fathers the virginal conception of Jesus was associated with his humanity rather than with his deity. According to Campenhausen, Ignatius of Antioch (c. 35–c. 107) treated the theme in a doctrinal setting, Justin Martyr treated it in an apologetic setting, and Irenaeus treated it in both doctrinal and apologetic settings.[46] Tertullian said: "Whoever wishes to see Jesus the Son of David must believe in Him through the Virgin's birth."[47]

2. Medieval Period

In the medieval West the doctrine, augmented by the elevation of virginity above marriage, "served as the first step in the ladder that carried the church to heights of speculative Marian theology." A doctrine of Mary "and a body of extracanonical literature to support it developed simultaneously."[48]

3. Reformation and Post-Reformation Eras

Boslooper has taken the virginal conception as "one of the principal wedges" that separated supernaturalists and naturalists within Protestantism.[49] But, it would seem, the naturalist rejection of the virginal conception made little headway until the time of the Enlightenment, when rejection of miracle meant inevitably the rejection of the virginal conception.

4. Modern Era

The differing answers given by naturalists and supernaturalists predominated in Protestantism during the nineteenth and twentieth centuries. The Enlightenment's rejection came to a climax in Heinrich Eberhard Gottlob Paulus (1761-1851), who identified the Holy Spirit with Mary's imagination and held that a fanatical man Gabriel, not an angel, impregnated Mary. Immanuel Kant, G. W. F. Hegel, F. D. E. Schleier-

---

45. Ibid., p. 19.
46. *The Virgin Birth in the Theology of the Ancient Church,* pp. 29-46.
47. *Against Marcion* 4.36.
48. Boslooper, *The Virgin Birth,* p. 19.
49. Ibid.

macher, and Albrecht Ritschl, rejecting the historicity of the virginal conception, sought to shift the emphasis to the meaning of the story. David Friedrich Strauss (1808-74) reckoned the conception/birth narratives as "myth" and hence as nonhistorical and used the Matthean and Lucan genealogies against historicity on the ground that they originally were designed to undergird the idea that Jesus was "a naturally begotten man."[50] Protestant expositions and defenses of the virginal conception have been made by Hermann Olshausen (1796-1839), Johann Peter Lange (1802-82), Bernhard Weiss (1827-1918), E. de Pressensé (1824-91), A. M. Fairbairn, James Orr, John Gresham Machen, and Archibald Thomas Robertson (1863-1934).[51]

C. MAJOR OBJECTIONS

We will now give specific consideration to ten major objections to the doctrine of the virginal conception of Jesus Christ.

1. Silence of Other New Testament Writers

It has often been noted that the virginal conception was not mentioned by New Testament authors other than Matthew and Luke,[52] and it has been asserted that this theme did not form part of the apostolic kerygma, or preaching.[53] Concerning the latter assertion it may be said that it is possible that some of the early disciples of Jesus did not know of the manner of his birth. It is also possible that there would have been some natural reticence to discuss this event during the lifetime of Mary. Absence from the kerygma is no proof of the nonhistoricity of certain aspects of Jesus' life and ministry; take, for example, his baptism and his transfiguration, neither of which was part of the kerygma as derivable from the Acts of the Apostles. Concerning the former factor we may say that the so-called silence of Mark, John, Paul, and others is not a conclusive argument. Matthew recorded that the people of Nazareth asked, " 'Is not this the carpenter's son?' " (13:55a, RSV), whereas Mark recorded the saying as follows: " 'Is not this the carpenter, the son of Mary...?' " (6:3a). The virginal conception may have suggested the language of John 1:12-13 concerning the rebirth of believers.[54] Rom. 1:3-4 can be taken to mean that Jesus was of two origins, and not merely that he had two natures. Richard Joseph Cooke (1853-1931) contended that the Jerusalem church knew of

50. Ibid., pp. 87-99, esp. 97.

51. Ibid., pp. 113-32. According to Brown, *The Virginal Conception and Bodily Resurrection of Jesus*, pp. 22-27, the Roman Catholic Church was marked by "a unanimity in regarding the historicity of the virginal conception as unquestionable" prior to Vatican Council II, but since that council, especially in the Netherlands but also elsewhere, doubts as to historicity have increased.

52. Emil Brunner, *The Mediator*, pp. 323-24.

53. Brunner, *The Christian Doctrine of Creation and Redemption*, p. 354.

54. See Wilbert Francis Howard, *Christianity according to St. John* (London: Duckworth, 1943), pp. 66-67, for a textual variant known to Augustine of Hippo.

the virginal conception during the period after Pentecost, with Mary as
the probably source, that Paul during his visits to that church and by close
association with Luke also knew of it, and that his silence can likely be
explained either by the fact that the virginal conception was not germane
to the themes of his epistles or by his prudence in dealing with Gentile
converts who were steeped in pagan stories of heroes born of gods and
human mothers.[55] The argument from silence was also answered by
William Evans, who cited the nonreference to God in the book of Esther.[56]

2. Outgrowth of Hellenistic Jewish Interpretation of Isa. 7:14

Adolf Harnack set forth the thesis that the Matthean and Lucan
accounts, not pointing to an actual event, are to be explained as developments from the interpretation of Isa. 7:14 that was held among the Hellenistic Jews of Palestine.[57] This thesis faces the problem of the meaning
of the Hebrew noun ʿalmāh, usually translated "young woman," and its
translation in the Septuagint by the Greek parthenos, usually translated
"virgin." Furthermore, according to Alfred Edersheim,[58] the Jews of the
synagogue did not consider Isa. 7:14 to be a messianic text. Isa. 7:14 could
hardly become the basis for an account of the virginal conception of Jesus
if this conception did not have a basis in fact. On the contrary, the
knowledge of the actual virginal conception may have led Christians to
give to Isa. 7:14 an interpretation prophetic of the virginal conception.
Moreover, Johannes Weiss cited the Ebionite idea that Jesus was begotten
at his baptism in fulfillment of Ps. 2:7.[59]

3. Rejection by Second-Century Groups and Teachers

Argued by some as an objection against the authenticity of the
virginal conception of Jesus has been the fact that this conception was
rejected by the Ebionites, by some of the second-century Gnostics such as
Cerinthus, and by Marcion. Against such an argument stand the Apostles'
Creed and numerous Church Fathers such as Ignatius of Antioch, Justin
Martyr, Irenaeus, and Tertullian. Furthermore, as Emil Brunner has
noted,[60] Arius and other heretics of the patristic age accepted the virginal
conception of Jesus, and yet adherence to that doctrine did not guarantee
the full orthodoxy of these men.

55. *Did Paul Know of the Virgin Birth? An Historical Study* (New York: Macmillan, 1926).
56. *Why I Believe in the Virgin Birth of Jesus Christ* (Los Angeles: Biola Book Room, 1924),
p. 21.
57. *New Testament Studies*, vol. 3, *The Date of the Acts and of the Synoptic Gospels*, pp.
145-49.
58. *The Life and Times of Jesus the Messiah*, 1:157 (cont. of n. 3).
59. *The History of Primitive Christianity*, compl. Rudolf Knopf, transl. by four, ed.
Frederick C. Grant, 2 vols. (New York: Wilson-Erickson, Inc., 1937), 2:736-37.
60. *The Christian Doctrine of Creation and Redemption*, pp. 354-55.

4. *Derivation from Parallel Pagan Stories of Heroes or Gods Born without a Human Father*

Some have contended that the accounts in Matthew and Luke were the result of borrowing from so-called parallel pagan stories as to how various heroes or gods were born without a human father. Two questions are involved in such an explanation. Is there an exact parallel? Are the early Christians likely to have done such borrowing? The vile character of Greek and Roman mythology and the nonhistorical nature of the myths work against this theory. Efforts have been made to find parallels in Buddhist, Krishna, Zoroastrian, Mithraic, Egyptian, and Graeco-Roman religions.[61] In none of these cases do we have a true parallel to the virginal conception of Jesus. The so-called parallels "consistently involve a type of *hieros gamos* where a divine male, in human or other form, impregnates a woman, either through normal sexual intercourse or through some substitute form of penetration."[62] The Christian story differs not only by virtue of the unique "personality" and "teaching" of Jesus but also in that his conception and birth were "without anthropomorphism, sensuality, or suggestions of moral irregularity."[63] Boslooper has strongly stressed that the Christian doctrine of the virginal conception bears witness to the validity of monogamous marriage.[64] Furthermore, with the strong Jewish attitudes of exclusion and rejection of Gentiles and their ways it is unthinkable that devout Jewish Christians would have borrowed a pagan myth and incorporated it into their affirmations concerning the Jewish Messiah.

5. *Postbiblical Invention to Support Growing Mariology*

William Grayson Birch (190?-) has argued that the virginal conception of Jesus cannot be found in the canonical Scriptures, that it originated as a belief during later centuries to give support to the developing Mariology, which Birch brands as "idolatry," and was thus added to the Christian creeds, and that it should be rejected today and removed from the creeds and confessions of faith.[65] This thesis ignores all the evidence provided by textual and literary criticism. Furthermore, its argument may apply to the Roman Catholic dogma of the perpetual virginity of Mary, but not to the virginal conception of Jesus.

6. *Replacement for the Original Teaching That Jesus Had "Dual Paternity," That Is, from God and from Joseph*

William E. Phipps (1930-) has recently advanced the theory that Jesus' paternity was originally thought to have been a "dual paternity,"

---

61. Boslooper, *The Virgin Birth*, pp. 135-86.
62. Brown, *The Virginal Conception and Bodily Resurrection of Jesus*, p. 62.
63. Boslooper, *The Virgin Birth*, pp. 228, 185.
64. Ibid., pp. 186, 234-36.
65. *Mary and the Virgin Birth Error* (Berne, Ind.: Publishers Printing House, Inc., 1966), esp. p. 168.

meaning that both Joseph and God were in some sense his father. He has traced "dual paternity" to Old Testament passages that attribute births both to Yahweh and human fathers: Cain (Gen. 4:1); Isaac (Gen. 21:1-2); Reuben (Gen. 29:31-32); Joseph (Gen. 30:22-24); and Obed (Ruth 4:13). According to Phipps, during the second century the virginal conception was substituted for the earlier account of dual paternity. Luke 1:34 and 3:23 stand in the way of Phipps's theory, and thus he must pronounce them interpolations; likewise, the Matthean account was said to have been expanded.[66] The Matthean and Lucan accounts clearly describe something that involved no dual paternity; only by subjective suppositions about interpolations and an alleged earlier "dual paternity" explanation can their clear teaching be overturned.

7. Unscientific Violation of Natural Law

Especially during the nineteenth and twentieth centuries it has been argued that the account of the virginal conception of Jesus alleges something to have occurred that would have been a violation of natural law and ordinary life processes. It would have violated the repetition that is required for the scientific method. What is held, then, by naturalists to be utterly unscientific must be rejected as not having occurred. L. Harold DeWolf, who was not a defender of the doctrine of the virginal conception of Jesus, stated that on the question as to whether Jesus was born of a virgin "the issue for a theist turns not on the limit of God's power but on the historical evidence."[67] Furthermore, there is the fact of animal parthenogenesis, and even Origen saw in it an analogy to the virginal conception. Today there is possible asexual reproduction as a facet of experimental embryology.[68]

8. Contradiction to the Incarnation of the Preexistent Son of God

Wolfhart Pannenberg has concluded that the "legend" of the virginal conception "stands in an irreconcilable contradiction to the Christology of the incarnation of the preexistent Son of God found in Paul and John." Accordingly Paul and John taught that the preexistent Son of God had already "bound himself to the man Jesus." Pannenberg argued further: "Sonship cannot at the same time consist in preexistence and still have its origin only in the divine procreation of Jesus in Mary."[69] Brown has found Pannenberg's position to rest on the contemporary critical assumption that Christology in the New Testament "developed backwards" from the belief in the second coming to Jesus' resurrection and

---

66. *Paul against Supernaturalism: The Growth of the Miraculous in Christianity* (New York: Philosophical Library, 1987), pp. 45-71.

67. *A Theology of the Living Church*, p. 231.

68. Brown, *The Virginal Conception and Bodily Resurrection of Jesus*, p. 29, n. 35; Origen, *Against Celsus* 1.37.

69. *Jesus—God and Man*, p. 143.

from that to his public ministry. For Brown an answer to Pannenberg can be found in the fact that "the later Church did reconcile" preexistence and virginal conception "by establishing a sequence whereby the pre-existent Word or Son took flesh in the womb of the Virgin Mary and became man."[70]

9. Untruth Because Jesus Was Conceived by a Human Father outside Marriage

Radical feminist theologians have espoused the idea that Jesus' conception was illegitimate, thus reviving an idea that can be traced at least to Celsus in the second century. Mary Daly has rejected the Catholic dogmas related to Jesus and Mary, contending that therein Mary was utterly passive, unlike the female activism in parthenogenesis. Accordingly Mary "is portrayed/betrayed as Total Rape Victim—a pale derivative symbol disguising the conquered Goddess." Miss Daly then suggested that this was "a mind/spirit rape" that made unnecessary physical rape.[71] Jane Schaberg (1938-) has accepted the tradition that Jesus was illegitimate as valid. Mary is not to be viewed as a goddess but as "a woman in need of a Goddess, . . . a woman we look at, not up at." She "represents the oppressed who have been liberated."

> Mary is a woman who has access to the sacred outside the patriarchal family and its control. The illegitimate conception turns out to be grace not disgrace, order within disorder.[72]

One should take note of the fact that these Catholic feminists have rejected Mariological dogmas and not solely the virginal conception of Jesus. They wish to utilize the reinterpreted Mary in their theology of liberation. Concerning the virginal conception one must choose between the line of critics stemming from Celsus and the testimony of Matthew, Luke, and numerous Church Fathers.

10. Docetic Idea

During the twentieth century certain Protestant theologians have argued that the doctrine of the virginal conception of Jesus is a docetic idea. According to Emil Brunner, Jesus, in order to be fully human, must have been born in the same way in which every other human being is born.[73] For Nels F. S. Ferré the virginal conception "may exclude a full doctrine of the Incarnation" and, if misused, can "destroy the central affirmation of the Incarnation."[74] But did not Jesus live (without sin) in a way different

---

70. *The Virginal Conception and Bodily Resurrection of Jesus*, pp. 43-45.
71. *Gyn/ecology: The Metaethics of Radical Feminism* (Boston: Beacon Press, 1978), pp. 83-85.
72. *The Illegitimacy of Jesus: A Feminist Theological Interpretation of the Infancy Narratives* (San Francisco: Harper and Row, 1987), esp. pp. 195-99.
73. *The Christian Doctrine of Creation and Redemption*, p. 355.
74. *Christ and the Christian* (New York: Harper and Bros., 1958), pp. 100, 216.

from that by which other human beings lived? Furthermore, did he not die (for the sins of humankind) in a somewhat different way from the manner and significance of the death of other human beings, and yet was he not fully human in his dying? Then why not also in his conception?

D. SYSTEMATIC FORMULATION

1. Virginal Conception and Incarnation

The virginal conception stands in an auxiliary or modal position in relation to the incarnation of the Word or Son of God. It is the divinely ordered method of the incarnation of God in Jesus Christ, or "an essential, historical indication of the Incarnation."[75] It is possible, of course, that God could have chosen and effectuated another method, but it is difficult to conjecture a more appropriate method for the incarnation. To be the Redeemer of humankind, Jesus must identify himself with human beings and at the same time transcend the human race. Thus he was fittingly begotten of the Holy Spirit and born of a woman.[76] Douglas Allen Edwards, C.R. (1893-1953), declared that had it not been for the tradition of the virginal conception, "it is extremely improbable that the doctrine of the Incarnation would have ever gained a permanent lodgement in the human mind."[77] The contention that the two are absolutely necessary for each other can be traced to Tertullian,[78] and W. T. Conner predicted that "ultimately the ideas of the Incarnation and the Virgin Birth will stand or fall together."[79] According to Carl F. H. Henry, the virginal conception shows that "the work of Incarnation and Reconciliation involves a definite intervening act on the part of God himself." Indeed, a "new creation" was possible even in the "old order." "By the exclusion of the male it is made quite clear that what is to be done is something which man of himself cannot do. . . ."[80] For Otto Alfred Wilhelm Piper (1891-1982), "it is only through the Virgin Birth as a decisive act of holy history that we are enabled to understand the way in which God brings about the consummation of his redemptive plan, that is, through the non-recurrent event of the ministry of Jesus rather than through a series of incarnations as, for example, in Buddhism."[81]

2. Virginal Conception and Two Natures of Jesus Christ

On the one hand, the early Church Fathers regarded the virginal conception of Jesus as an evidence of his true and full humanity, and thus

---

75. Carl F. H. Henry, "Our Lord's Virgin Birth," *Christianity Today* 4 (7 December 1959): 20.

76. Conner, *Revelation and God*, p. 159.

77. *The Virgin Birth in History and Faith*, p. 25.

78. *Against Marcion* 4.10.

79. *Revelation and God*, p. 159.

80. "Our Lord's Virgin Birth," p. 20.

81. "The Virgin Birth: The Meaning of the Gospel Accounts," *Interpretation* 18 (April 1964): 148.

it served to answer the teachings of Ebionitism, Docetism, Marcionitism, and Gnosticism.[82] On the other hand, in twentieth-century Protestantism, especially in the United States and under the impact of the Modernist-Fundamentalist controversy, the virginal conception has been interpreted as an evidence for or an important fact in the deity of Jesus.[83]

3. Virginal Conception and Sinlessness of Jesus

Christian theologians have commonly affirmed that the virginal conception was God's method of transcending original sin or human depravity in the person and life of Jesus.[84] James Orr declared that "commonly in practice belief in the miraculous birth and belief in the sinlessness of Jesus stand or fall together."[85] A problem develops, however, if and when an absolute cause/effect relationship be ascribed to the virginal conception and the sinlessness of Jesus. Previously we have assessed this danger.[86] Furthermore, "the science of genetics has found that hereditary traits come from the mother as well as the father."[87] The rejection of the virginal conception by such twentieth-century theologians as Emil Brunner, Nels Ferré, and Paul Tillich was partly due to their assuming that a certain linkage between virginal conception and sinlessness was evidently essential to the virginal conception.[88]

4. "Virginal Conception" rather than "Virgin Birth"

Dale Moody was correct in 1953 when he pointed out that "virgin birth" is a misnomer for Protestant theologians, inasmuch as the miracle lay in the manner of the conception and not in the manner of the birth.[89] Only Roman Catholic theologians with their dogma of the perpetual virginity of Mary, according to which Mary was said to be a virgin before, during, and after parturition,[90] have any reason to use or to stress the term "virgin birth." Despite the likelihood that some persons will confuse the term "virginal conception of Jesus" with the Roman Catholic dogma of the immaculate conception of Mary, the former term deserves to be employed consistently and with clarity.

82. Orr, *The Virgin Birth of Christ*, pp. 136-50, 185-86; Campenhausen, *The Virgin Birth in the Theology of the Ancient Church*, pp. 21-24.

83. J. G. Machen, *The Virgin Birth of Christ* (New York: Harper and Bros., 1930), pp. 387-91.

84. For example, Conner, *Revelation and God*, pp. 158-59.

85. *The Virgin Birth of Christ*, p. 192.

86. See above, Ch. 41, III, B, 3.

87. Edward John Carnell, "The Virgin Birth of Christ," *Christianity Today* 4 (7 December 1959): 9.

88. Boslooper, *The Virgin Birth*, p. 20, based on Brunner, *The Mediator*, pp. 322-27; Ferré, *The Sun and the Umbrella* (New York: Harper and Bros., 1953), pp. 28-29; and Tillich, *Systematic Theology*, 2:126-27, 149.

89. "On the Virgin Birth of Jesus Christ," *Review and Expositor* 50 (October 1953): 453-62.

90. Ott, *Fundamentals of Catholic Dogma*, pp. 203-7.

5. *Virginal Conception and Roman Catholic Dogmas*

The virginal conception of Jesus is the doctrine that Jesus' conception involved the participation of the Holy Spirit and Mary without participation of a male human being. In the words of the Old Roman Symbol, Jesus was the one *"qui natus est de Spiritu sancto et Maria virgine."*[91] On the other hand, the immaculate conception of Mary is the Roman Catholic dogma that Mary the mother of Jesus in the event of her own conception by her parents was from the moment of that conception singularly exempted from original sin. This dogma was defined by Pope Pius IX, without benefit of council, in his *Ineffabilis Deus* in 1854. Furthermore, the perpetual virginity of Mary is the much older Roman Catholic dogma that Mary during and after the birth of Jesus continued to be a virgin and had no other children. The New Testament references to the "brothers" of Jesus are explained either as children of Joseph by a former marriage or as cousins of Jesus. This teaching was rejected by Tertullian, Jovinian, and Helvidius, but defended by Ambrose, Jerome, and Augustine of Hippo. The Council of Constantinople II (553) gave to Mary the title "perpetual virgin" (*aeiparthenos*).

6. *Virginal Conception: Mythical or Historical?*

On the issue as to whether the virginal conception ought to be reckoned as mythical or as historical, Orr, Machen, Piper, and Douglas Edwards have stood for historicity and against numerous nineteenth- and twentieth- century critics and theologians, including Boslooper. Both Roman Catholics and Protestants have been criticized by Boslooper, the latter for "insisting upon 'the literal historicity'" of the narratives of the virginal conception, for such an insistence removes "Jesus' origin from the context of history." For Boslooper the advocates of historicity "are simply admitting that they think mythically."[92] But Boslooper never faces the ultimate question: Was Jesus miraculously conceived of the virgin Mary without a human father? Did it happen? Boslooper seems to make the virginal conception a mythical teaching device by which certain Christian truths may be conveyed to "the primitive mentality" of the first century.[93] In so doing he has dehistoricized the virginal conception of Jesus.

7. *Virginal Conception and Christian Faith*

The question has frequently been raised, especially by the strongest advocates of the doctrine of the virginal conception of Jesus, as to whether one can be a Christian without definite knowledge and conscious acceptance of the virginal conception as an aspect of Christian truth. In reply one may contend that a person may well become a Christian without having at the time of conversion any specific or clear understanding about or conscious acceptance of the doctrine of the virginal conception. To insist on the absolute necessity of such for conversion to Jesus Christ would be to cast grave doubt on many childhood or adolescent conversions. On the other hand, when a Christian becomes informed about basic Christian beliefs, he/she must confront the historic teaching of the virginal conception and make some decision as to its acceptance or rejection and its interpretation. It is difficult to understand why in the light of the evidence one would want to reject the doctrine. But we do well to leave matters related to final judgment to the Judge of all humankind.

Acceptance or rejection of the historicity and doctrine of the virginal conception of Jesus during the modern period has tended to be correlated with basic distinctions between the predominantly supernatural or transcendent school and the predominantly natural or immanental school of theology and Christology. Brown has rightly observed that "a denial of the virginal conception has more often favored an adoptionist Christology rather than a pre-existent Christology."[94] Contrary to this general observation, however, some have held to the incarnation while rejecting the virginal conception; among these have been Heinrich August Wilhelm Meyer[95] (1800-73) and Emil Brunner.[96]

In this chapter we have carefully examined biblical, church-historical, apologetic, and doctrinal considerations in affirming and clarifying the virginal conception of Jesus Christ.

---

94. *The Virginal Conception and Bodily Resurrection of Jesus*, p. 43, n. 58.
95. *Critical and Exegetical Commentary on the New Testament*, 20 vols., trans. and ed. William P. Dickson, Frederick Crombie, et al. (Edinburgh: T. and T. Clark, 1877-84), 1:65-67.
96. *The Mediator*, pp. 322-27.

CHAPTER 43

Jesus: Eternally Preexistent
and Incarnate Word

This chapter will constitute an examination of the concept and title of "Word of God" as applied to Jesus Christ, the related concept of the eternal preexistence of the Word (or the Son), and the related concept of the incarnation of the Word of God. Previously[1] we identified and cited pertinent passages for three uses of the term "word of God" in the New Testament (evangelical, Christological, and scriptural). We will now interpret the second of these in greater detail and in the context of the person of Jesus Christ.

I. JESUS AS THE WORD OF GOD

A. OLD TESTAMENT

Unique in the ancient world was the declaration within the Old Testament that the one God spoke and everything else was created. God's speaking is a repetitive feature in the first creation account (Gen. 1:3, 6, 9, 11, 14, 20, 24, 26, 29). "By the word of the LORD the heavens were made" (Ps. 33:6a, RSV). The word of God was issued as a command (Ps. 147:15) and expected to be fruitful or productive (Isa. 55:10-11). God's word was sent forth for deliverance from death (Ps. 107:20). Was "the Word" (*dābār*) of God or of Yahweh hypostatized by the Old Testament writers? Richardson held that originally *dābār* was not hypostatized.[2] According to Cullmann it was near to personification in Isa. 55:10-11.[3] Ladd concluded that both *dābār* and "wisdom" were "semi-hypostatized" in the Old Testament.[4] Was the *dābār* of God the principal source for the Johannine concept of the Word of God? Thomas Walter Manson (1893-1958) con-

---

1. See above, Ch. 11, I.
2. *An Introduction to the Theology of the New Testament*, p. 160.
3. *The Christology of the New Testament*, p. 255.
4. *A Theology of the New Testament*, p. 240.

tended strongly for this,[5] but Ladd cautioned that Manson may have "overstated the case."[6]

B. INTERTESTAMENTAL WRITINGS

The personified Word was evident in Wisd. of Sol. 18:15: "Thine all-powerful word leaped from heaven down from the royal throne, a stern warrior into the midst of the doomed land."

Philo elaborated a distinct concept of the Word, or Logos. Donald Guthrie (1916-) noted five characteristics of Philo's doctrine. The Word, for Philo, "has no distinct personality."[7] The preexistence of the Word is uncertain and unclear. The Word is not conjoined with "light" and "life." There is "no suggestion that the *logos* could become incarnate." The Word "definitely had a mediatorial function to bridge the gap between the transcendent God and the world."[8] According to Ladd, the word was both "the original pattern of the world and the power that fashions it."[9]

C. HELLENISTIC THOUGHT

For Heraclitus the *logos* was the "eternal principle of order in the universe" in the midst of constant change.[10] In Stoicism *logos* was "the cosmic law which rules the universe and at the same time is present in the human intellect."[11] Likewise it was the basis for humankind's rational moral life, indeed an "all-pervading fire or fiery vapor."[12] Platonism conceived of the *logos* impersonally with no thought of involvement with humanity or in history.[13] In the Hermetic literature the *logos* was "the active expression of the mind of God."[14] In Gnosticism the *logos* was one of numerous emanations who was sent "not to redeem the world but to free the souls of light from entanglement in the dark, material world."[15] C. H. Dodd favored the view that Hellenistic thought was the principal background for the Johannine concept of the Word.[16]

---

5. *Studies in the Gospels and Epistles,* ed. Matthew Black (Manchester: University Press, 1962), p. 118.

6. *A Theology of the New Testament,* p. 238.

7. Cullmann, *The Christology of the New Testament,* p. 252, allowed for the possibility of both personal and impersonal strands in Philo.

8. *New Testament Theology* (Leicester, U.K.; Downers Grove, Ill.: Inter-Varsity Press, 1981), pp. 322-23.

9. Ladd, *A Theology of the New Testament,* p. 239.

10. Ibid., p. 238.

11. Cullmann, *The Christology of the New Testament,* p. 251.

12. Ladd, *A Theology of the New Testament,* pp. 251-52.

13. Cullmann, *The Christology of the New Testament,* pp. 251-52.

14. Ladd, *A Theology of the New Testament,* pp. 239-40.

15. Goppelt, *A Theology of the New Testament,* 2:298.

16. *The Interpretation of the Fourth Gospel* (Cambridge: University Press, 1953), pp. 263-82.

D. NEW TESTAMENT

In the New Testament "Jesus is not represented as referring to himself as the Logos."[17] John was "the only NT writer to describe Christ as the Word of God."[18] "In the beginning was the Word, and the Word was with God, and the Word was God. . . . And the Word became flesh and dwelt among us, full of grace and truth" (John 1:1, 14a, RSV). John wrote with "startling originality,"[19] for there was no parallel in the Hellenistic world,[20] especially in the conjunction of preexistence and incarnation.[21] He may have chosen "Word" for apologetic reasons.[22] He seems to have taken for granted that his readers would understand the term.[23] Israel's prophets had been bearers of "the word of the Lord," but they themselves were not the Word. Jesus not only spoke God's word; he was the Word of God, and that incarnate. W. G. Kümmel has taken the "Word of life" in 1 John 1:1 to refer to "divine and human discourse,"[24] but Guthrie[25] and others have understood it as referring to Jesus Christ. In Rev. 19:13 "the Word of God" is in the role of conqueror and ruler. Richardson found that in the Johannine writings the Word, along with wisdom, "is the controlling theological conception."[26]

E. PATRISTIC AGE

The doctrine of Christ as the Word of God flowered during the patristic age, especially among the Greek Fathers, for whom it was an important link with Hellenistic culture.

F. MODERN ERA

Jesus as the Word of God has often played a minor role in popular Christian affirmations about Jesus, being used less frequently than certain other titles, but in well-orbed Christological formulations it has continued to have a significant place.

II. JESUS AS ETERNALLY PREEXISTENT

Here it will be necessary to treat together the two themes, the preexistence of Jesus Christ and the eternality or eternity of Jesus Christ; even though these can be differentiated, they can best be discussed together.

---

17. Ladd, *A Theology of the New Testament*, p. 238.
18. Richardson, *An Introduction to the Theology of the New Testament*, p. 159.
19. Ibid., p. 162.
20. Guthrie, *New Testament Theology*, p. 328.
21. Ladd, *A Theology of the New Testament*, p. 241.
22. Richardson, *An Introduction to the Theology of the New Testament*, p. 161.
23. Kümmel, *The Theology of the New Testament*, p. 280.
24. Ibid., p. 278.
25. *New Testament Theology*, p. 329.
26. *An Introduction to the Theology of the New Testament*, p. 165.

A. New Testament

1. Synoptic Gospels

Did Jesus understand and hence in his teaching presuppose his own preexistence? Ethelbert Stauffer suggested that Jesus did. Stauffer argued on the basis of Matthew's quotation of Ps. 78:2b, " 'I will utter things hidden since the creation of the world' " (13:35, NIV), being fulfilled through Jesus' parables and Jesus' reference to " 'the kingdom prepared for you since the creation of the world' " (Matt. 25:34d).[27] H. R. Mackintosh, alluding to Matt. 11:25-27, stated that Jesus "spoke expressly of His pre-temporal life," but Mackintosh acknowledged that Jesus' consciousness of preexistence was an emerging awareness.[28]

2. Pauline Epistles

Paul clearly taught the preexistence of Jesus but not specifically his eternal preexistence. Kümmel was of the opinion that all of Paul's references to preexistence were incidental except Col. 1:15-17a.[29] In 1 Cor. 8:6 Paul alluded to Christ's role in creation, and in 1 Cor. 10:4 to his having been contemporaneous with Moses. His statement about the impoverishment of "our Lord Jesus Christ" (2 Cor. 8:9) necessarily presupposed a prior state of riches. In Phil. 2:6-8 the self-emptying of "Christ Jesus" was joined with his divine nature and "equality with God" that preceded the self-emptying. In Col. 1:15-17a the apostle presented Christ both as the agent of creation and as the sustainer of the created order.

3. The Epistle to the Hebrews

The Epistle to the Hebrews affirmed the agency of God's Son both in creation (1:2c) and in sustenance (1:3b). In 5:6, a quotation of Ps. 110:4b, it declared the coeternality of sonship and high priesthood.[30]

4. The Gospel and First Epistle of John

"The eternal Sonship of Christ," wrote Emil Brunner, "only becomes the main theme of the Christian message in the Gospel of John."[31] The opening words of this gospel are: "In the beginning was the Word" (1:1a).

> It is hardly open to doubt that the apostle here means to assert the absolute eternity of the Logos. . . . Christ is, then, pre-mundane. . . . All things came into existence through his agency [1:3], but he was in the beginning.[32]

Jesus affirmed that he lived prior to Abraham (8:58) and prayed to the Father for the restoration of "the glory I had with you before the world

27. *New Testament Theology*, p. 52.
28. *The Doctrine of the Person of Jesus Christ*, pp. 446, 29, 106.
29. *The Theology of the New Testament*, p. 170.
30. Wiley, *Christian Theology*, 2:173.
31. *The Christian Doctrine of Creation and Redemption*, p. 340.
32. Stevens, *The Theology of the New Testament*, p. 581.

began" (17:5, NIV). Interpreting "the Word of life" (1 John 1:1c) as referring to Jesus Christ, we must note that some interpreters[33] take "from the beginning" (1:1a) to mean Jesus' baptism and the calling of his first disciples or the beginning of the proclamation of the gospel of Christ, whereas others[34] understand it as a reference to eternity or pre-creation.

B. History of Christian Doctrine

1. Patristic Age[35]

Did not the primitive church struggle with Adoptionism as a solution to the question of the identity of Jesus? Some[36] find the Adoptionist conclusion in the pages of the New Testament, while others[37] find it surfacing only in the second century A.D. To declare that Jesus was a human being who at some point in time was given an adoptive sonship by the one God and with it a semidivine status is to deny the eternal preexistence of Jesus. Hence the rejection of Adoptionism was necessary if Jesus' eternal preexistence was to be affirmed.

Sabellianism did not deny the eternal preexistence of the Son but ignored the differences between the Father and the Son. It failed properly to interpret: "and the Word was with God, and the Word was God" (John 1:1b, c).

Arianism was a major challenge to the eternality and the divine nature of Jesus Christ, though not to preexistence. It demonstrated that preexistence per se is not a guarantee of eternity or deity.

2. Modern Era

During the latter nineteenth century several rejections of or alternatives to the eternal personal preexistence of Jesus Christ were formulated in German Protestantism. Albrecht Ritschl, turning away from transcendence to perceived religious values, seemed not to allow for such personal preexistence as would be essential to the Son's self-giving

33. For example, for the former, Raymond E. Brown, S.S., *The Epistles of John*, The Anchor Bible, vol. 30 (Garden City, N.Y.: Doubleday and Company, 1982), pp. 155-58; for the latter, J. L. Houlden, *A Commentary on the Johannine Epistles*, Harper's New Testament Commentaries (New York: Harper and Row, 1973), pp. 49-50; R. Alan Culpepper, *1 John, 2 John, 3 John*, Knox Preaching Guides (Atlanta: John Knox Press, 1985).

34. For example, Brooke Foss Westcott, *The Epistles of John* (3d ed.; Cambridge: Macmillan, 1892), p. 5; Alfred Plummer, *The Epistles of John* (Grand Rapids: Baker Book House, 1980; 1st publ. in 1886), pp. 14-15; W. T. Conner, *The Epistles of John: Their Meaning and Message* (New York: Fleming H. Revell Company, 1929), p. 18; Curtis Vaughan, *1, 2, 3 John*, Bible Study Commentary (Grand Rapids: Zondervan, 1970), p. 20.

35. Brunner, *The Christian Doctrine of Creation and Redemption*, pp. 343-49.

36. James D. G. Dunn, *Christology in the Making: A New Testament Inquiry into the Origins of the Doctrine of the Incarnation* (Philadelphia: Westminster Press, 1980), pp. 33-46.

37. Harnack, *History of Dogma*, 1:191-99; 3:20-32, 50, and Aloys Grillmeier, S.J., *Christ in Christian Tradition: From the Apostolic Age to Chalcedon (451)*, trans. J. S. Bowden (New York: Sheed and Ward, 1965), pp. 63-64, 92, 182, 217, trace it to Hermas and to the Dynamic Monarchians.

love.[38] Hans Hinrich Wendt (1853-1928) was afraid that the personal preexistence of Jesus would inevitably lead to tritheism, but such criticism fails to take into account the problems associated with the term "person."[39] Adolf Harnack traced the idea to the concept of the preexistence of the Messiah in Jewish apocalypses and reckoned the apostolic use of the concept to be syncretistic, but other scholars were finding evidence only for pre-Christian belief in "the pre-existence of the Messiah's *name*."[40] Paul Lobstein (1850-1922) reinterpreted eternal preexistence to mean that the Son preexisted only in the Father's mind as chosen or elected by the Father.[41] Otto Pfleiderer (1839-1908) allowed for preexistence but only that of a " 'spiritual' man."[42] Otto Kirn (1857-1911) made preexistence an important religious symbol on the boundary of our knowledge, but even symbols point to real meanings.[43]

C. SYSTEMATIC FORMULATION

1. The eternal preexistence of Jesus as the Son of God is a necessary corollary of his deity. It has "formed the seed-plot of all Christological and Trinitarian reflection."[44] Those who in Christian history have denied his deity have usually denied his preexistence; Arius, as noted, did make a place for created, but not eternal, preexistence.

2. The eternal preexistence of the Son of God makes possible an incarnational self-emptying of the Son. Any doctrine of *kenosis* must proceed from the preexistence as well as from the deity of the Son of God.

3. The eternal preexistence of the Son of God is not merely a topic for abstract speculation, but it relates to divine salvation. It is designed to answer the question: Is the Redeemer eternal and divine? It poses the negatively designed query: Is God's love in Christ truly "triumphant" if Christ be not eternal?[45]

---

38. Mackintosh, *The Doctrine of the Person of Jesus Christ*, pp. 450-51, based on Ritschl, *The Christian Doctrine of Justification and Reconciliation: The Positive Development of the Doctrine*, trans. H. R. Mackintosh and A. B. Macaulay (Clifton, N.J.: Reference Book Publishers, 1966), p. 471.

39. Mackintosh, *The Doctrine of the Person of Jesus Christ*, pp. 452-53, based on Wendt, *System der christlichen Lehre* (Göttingen: Vandenhoeck und Ruprecht, 1907), pp. 368ff.

40. Mackintosh, *The Doctrine of the Person of Jesus Christ*, pp. 449-50, based on Harnack, *History of Dogma*, 1:100-107.

41. Mackintosh, *The Doctrine of the Person of Jesus Christ*, pp. 454-56, based on Lobstein, *La notion de la preexistence du Fils de Dieu; Fragment de christologie experimentale* (Paris: Librarie Fischbacher, 1883).

42. Wiley, *Christian Theology*, 2:171-72, probably based on Pfleiderer, *The Early Christian Conception of Christ: Its Significance and Value in the History of Religion* (New York: G. P. Putnam's Sons; London: Williams and Norgate, 1905), pp. 16-24.

43. Mackintosh, *The Doctrine of the Person of Jesus Christ*, pp. 456-57, based on Kirn, *Grundriss der evangelischen Dogmatik* (3d rev. ed.; Leipzig: A. Deichert, 1910), p. 107.

44. Mackintosh, *The Doctrine of the Person of Jesus Christ*, p. 459.

45. Ibid., p. 460.

4. The eternal preexistence of the Son of God makes possible an immanental Trinity and not merely an economic Trinity.[46]

5. There are limits to our understanding of the eternal preexistence of Jesus as the Son of God. "We cannot know the pre-temporal as we do the earthly life of Christ, or even as we do (in a real sense) His life of exalted glory."[47]

Theodor Haering wrote:

The love of God which was effective for us in Christ as the Son, is so truly the love of God, the effective Revelation which he makes of His own nature, that it is eternally bestowed on Him, the Bringer of this eternal love, not only in the sense of ideal pre-existence, not only on Him as the correlative in the world's history of the eternal love of God, but also, apart from His earthly existence, as the love of the Father to the Son in the mystery of the eternal life of God, and therefore, as no other word is available for us, in a state of real pre-existence.[48]

III. JESUS AS THE INCARNATE WORD OF GOD

A. NEW TESTAMENT TEXTS

1. Pauline Epistles

In the fullness of time "God sent forth his Son, born of woman" (Gal. 4:4, RSV). Christ Jesus "emptied himself, taking the form of a servant, being born in the likeness of men" (Phil. 2:7).

2. The Gospel and First Epistle of John

"And the Word became flesh and dwelt among us" (John 1:14a). Here "flesh" is not a synonym for the human body but for the fullness of humanity. The "Word of life," "which we have heard, which we have seen with our eyes, which we have looked at and our hands have touched . . . appeared" (1 John 1:1-2a, NIV).

B. HISTORY OF CHRISTIAN DOCTRINE

1. Patristic Age

Some heretical or faulty answers, especially stemming from the patristic age, can help to clarify what the incarnation of the Word is not, as Donald M. Baillie aptly noted.[49]

46. See above, Ch. 23, III, A.
47. Mackintosh, *The Doctrine of the Person of Jesus Christ,* p. 461.
48. *The Christian Faith,* 2:704.
49. *God Was in Christ,* pp. 79-84.

a. Polytheism

The incarnation does not mean that Jesus was added to the pantheon of gods.[50]

b. Pagan Mythology

The incarnation does not mean "that God changed into a Man."[51] Jesus is not to be understood as having lived first in a divine stage and then as having metamorphosed into a human stage. Rather, in the incarnation of the eternal and divine Word the God-man does not cease to be God.

c. Adoptionism

The incarnation "does not mean that Jesus began by being a man, and grew into divinity, [or] became divine." Baillie noted that "the adjective 'divine' hardly occurs in the New Testament," its writers preferring to state that "Jesus is God."[52] Did Jesus then teach and perform miracles as a mere man? Did he die as ordinary man?

d. Arianism

The incarnation does not mean "that Jesus was some kind of intermediate being, neither God nor man in the full sense, but something between." The "mediator" of 1 Tim. 2:5 "was not something between God and Man: He was God *and* Man."[53]

e. Apollinarianism

The incarnation does not mean that "the eternal Son of God" inhabited "a human body for thirty years on earth" but had no human mind or spirit. This is drawing too hard and fast a line between his deity and his humanity.[54] J. N. D. Kelly correctly concluded that a full-orbed Christology was a Word-man Christology and not merely a Word-flesh Christology.[55]

2. *Modern Period*

a. Dorner's Theory of Gradual Incarnation

Isaak August Dorner (1809-84) and others held to a theory of the gradual incarnation of Jesus Christ as the God-man. By this was meant a gradual or progressive union of deity and humanity that was not complete until Jesus' resurrection. This union was "accomplished by a gradual

50. Ibid., p. 80.
51. Ibid., p. 82. Shedd, *Dogmatic Theology*, 2:266, contended that incarnation "must be distinguished from transmutation, or transubstantiation."
52. Baillie, *God Was in Christ*, pp. 81-82.
53. Ibid., p. 80.
54. Ibid., pp. 80-81.
55. *Early Christian Doctrines*, pp. 281, 310.

606 The Person of Jesus Christ

communication of the fulness of the divine Logos to the man Christ Jesus" through the instrumentality of "the human consciousness of Jesus."[56]

The gradual theory is based on the concept of evolutionary development. It runs counter to Luke 1:35 and Phil. 2:7. It mistakes "an incomplete consciousness of the union for an incomplete union." It is close to the so-called Nestorian concept of the "double personality" of Jesus Christ.[57]

b. Kenotic Theories of the Son's Self-Emptying

Previously[58] we described the kenotic theories of Gottfried Thomasius and Friedrich Gess and noted certain criticisms of kenoticism, especially that it teaches a "temporary theophany" rather than a full incarnation and that it denies the simultaneous union of the human and the divine in Jesus.

In addition we should be aware that certain British theologians early in the twentieth century set forth kenotic views that differed from the earlier German expressions. Peter Taylor Forsyth posited a "kenosis," or "self-emptying," and a "plerosis," or "self-fulfilment." He denied an abandonment of certain attributes and referred to a retraction of attributes from actuality to potentiality.[59] Mackintosh agreed about the attributes and referred to "self-limitation," "self-abnegation," and "self-abasement." He contended that four factors demand some kind of kenoticism. First, Christ is the present divine object of faith and worship for Christians. Second, his deity is eternal and personal. Third, his life on earth was fully human, being characterized by limited power and knowledge, growth, temptation, and dependence on the Father. Fourth, Christ did not have "two wills" or "two consciousnesses." Hence a genuine surrender of "glory" and "prerogatives" "must have preceded the advent of God in Christ."[60]

c. British Anglican Debate of the Latter 1970s

In a volume edited by John Hick, *The Myth of God Incarnate*, Hick, Maurice F. Wiles, Dennis Eric Nineham (1921-), Leslie Houlden, and others set forth the views that the incarnation is logically contradictory, that the doctrine came not from Jesus but from his disciples and from fourth- and fifth-century Christianity, that the theme of incarnation can be found in other religions, and that incarnation should be surrendered

---

56. Strong, *Systematic Theology*, pp. 688-89; Dorner, *History of the Development of the Doctrine of the Person of Christ*, trans. W. L. Alexander and D. W. Simon, 5 vols. (Edinburgh: T. and T. Clark, 1872-82), 3:248-60; idem, *A System of Christian Doctrine*, trans. Alfred Cave and J. S. Banks, 4 vols. (Edinburgh: T. and T. Clark, 1883-88), 3:300-339.

57. Strong, *Systematic Theology*, pp. 689-90.

58. See above, Ch. 39, II, N.

59. *The Person and Place of Jesus Christ* (London: Hodder and Stoughton, 1909), pp. 291-357.

60. *The Doctrine of the Person of Jesus Christ*, pp. 476-79, 463, 466, 467, 469-70.

in favor of a general concept of divine immanence.[61] *The Truth of God Incarnate*, edited by Michael Green and contributed to by Anglican Evangelicals such as Green, Stephen Charles Neill (1900-1984), and Brian Leslie Hebblethwaite (1939-), and by Basil Christopher Butler (1902-86), a Roman Catholic, was published as a refutative reply. Green asserted that in the New Testament claims to transcendence were made concerning Jesus and the titles applied to him implied such, that the so-called Hellenistic parallels to the incarnation were either post-Christian or not truly parallel and that so-called Jewish parallels are untenable in the light of Jewish monotheism, that early Christians were led to the deity and incarnation of Jesus by his teaching, life, claims, fulfillment of prophecy, death, and resurrection, and that there are numerous faults in the "historical skepticism" that has of late been applied to Jesus.[62] Neill pointed out that history is "unique," "unpredictable," "unrepeatable," "unalterable," and "irreversible."[63] For Hebblethwaite the incarnation and the Trinity are the "two central doctrines which set out the *unique* features of the Christian faith in God." That the incarnation was God's chosen method of revelation means that "God in Christ takes upon *himself* responsibility for all the world's ills" and means that we have the divine presence on the human side of the divine-human divide.[64] According to Butler, the New Testament writers took the story of Jesus to be true and did not, as the Greeks, seek to demythologize or allegorize it, and Chalcedon means two things: "Christianity has its source and center in a historical figure, Jesus of Nazareth," and Jesus is fully human and yet God but "not schizophrenic."[65] The debate was continued through another volume, with a widening number of contributors from both sides.[66] Klaas Runia (1926-) has presented an eightfold critique of *The Myth of God Incarnate*.[67]

C. SYSTEMATIC FORMULATION

1. *Mystery*

We do well to acknowledge that we cannot, even with our best theological minds, fully fathom or explicate the incarnation. Its meaning exceeds our human capacities of perception and indeed that which has been revealed through the inspired Scriptures.

61. (London: SCM Press, 1977).
62. Green, "Jesus in the New Testament" and "Jesus and Historical Skepticism," in Green, ed. (Sevenoaks, Kent, U.K.: Hodder and Stoughton; Grand Rapids: Eerdmans, 1977), pp. 18-33, 36-57, 107-39.
63. "Jesus and History," in Green, ed., *The Truth of God Incarnate*, pp. 72-73.
64. "Jesus, God Incarnate," in ibid., pp. 101-3.
65. "Jesus and Later Orthodoxy," in ibid., pp. 92-94, 96-99.
66. Michael Goulder, ed., *Incarnation and Myth: The Debate Continued* (London: SCM Press; Grand Rapids: Eerdmans, 1979).
67. *The Present-day Christological Debate*, Issues in Contemporary Theology (Leicester, Downers Grove, Ill.: Inter-Varsity Press, 1984), pp. 81-85.

2. Paradox

The quest for the meaning of the incarnation is aided by the application to it of paradox. According to Ian Ramsey, paradox deals with that which is "not only spatio-temporal, but more than spatio-temporal as well," and "Christian paradox . . . arises when an attempt is made to use the historical to talk about what is historical and more."[68] Never has the hyphen been used with greater significance than in the term "the God-man." Christian theology has "the perennial task" to "think out the meaning of the Christian conviction that God was incarnate in Jesus, that Jesus is God and Man. God *and* Man: that conjunction 'and' is the crux."[69]

3. Tenability

Despite recent and earlier denials, the incarnation of the Word of God can be affirmed with integrity, based on strong support from the New Testament and from the patristic age.

4. Centrality

The incarnation is not a marginal or peripheral Christian teaching that is negotiable with its insistent modern rejectors. It belongs rather to the very center of the historic and essential Christian affirmations.

> Christ, by highest heav'n adored;
> Christ, the everlasting Lord!
> Late in time behold Him come,
> Offspring of the Virgin's womb:
> Veiled in flesh the Godhead see;
> Hail th' incarnate Deity,
> Pleased as man with men to dwell,
> Jesus, our Emmanuel.[70]

68. *Christian Empiricism*, ed. Jerry H. Gill (London: Sheldon Press, 1974), p. 107.
69. Baillie, *God Was in Christ*, p. 83.
70. Charles Wesley.

CHAPTER 44

Jesus as Lord and King

The last of the titles applied to Jesus in the New Testament that we will examine in the present study is "Lord," together with the less frequently employed "Prince" and "King." We will make an effort to assess the extent to which these terms convey deity, royalty, and/or rulership.

I. JESUS AS LORD

A. LORDSHIP IN NON-HEBRAIC USAGE DURING THE FIRST CENTURY A.D.

The Greek noun *kyrios*, usually meaning "lord" and comparable to the Latin *Caesar*, was sometimes used to refer to human kings or rulers; for example, Ptolemy XIII of Egypt, Herod the Great, and Herod Agrippa I and II. Sometimes it was used to refer to the deities of the mystery religions; *kyrios* was used of Osiris, Serapis, and Hermes, and *kyria* was used of Isis, Artemis or Diana, and Cybele.[1]

The Romans employed *kyrios* and the Latin *dominus*, meaning "lord," in reference to their emperor, although there is dispute as to whether this usage clearly denoted deity.[2] Emperors so denominated included Caligula, Claudius, Nero, and Domitian.[3]

B. LORDSHIP IN JEWISH USAGE: SIXTH CENTURY B.C. TO FIRST CENTURY A.D.

After their Babylonian captivity the Jews were accustomed to make a verbal substitution when reading and pronouncing the covenant name of God in Hebrew, the name "Yahweh." Out of reverence for the divine name they uttered "LORD" (*ʾadōnāy*) when reading in the Hebrew Bible the word *Yahweh*.[4] Among Greek-speaking Jews the term uttered was the

1. Taylor, *The Names of Jesus*, p. 39.
2. Karl Heim, *Jesus the Lord: The Sovereign Authority of Jesus and God's Revelation in Christ*, trans. D. H. van Daalen (Edinburgh: Oliver and Boyd, 1959; Philadelphia: Muhlenberg Press, 1961), p. 54.
3. Taylor, *The Names of Jesus*, p. 39.
4. See Gustaf Dalman, *The Words of Jesus: Considered in the Light of Post-Biblical Jewish*

Greek term *ho kyrios* (the Lord).[5] To these Jews, therefore, lordship was equivalent to deity, for only Yahweh was properly to be called *kyrios*. Against such background and usage Jews of the day of Jesus heard the affirmation, "Jesus is Lord."

Gustav Adolf Deissmann (1866-1937) concluded: "It may be said with certainty that at the time when Christianity originated 'Lord' was a divine predicate intelligible to the whole Eastern world."[6]

C. LORDSHIP ACCORDING TO THE NEW TESTAMENT

1. Origin of the Term

The question as to the source or sources from which the early Christians drew the term "Lord" has been a matter of scholarly debate during the twentieth century. Wilhelm Bousset set forth the view that the term was derived from the Hellenistic mystery religions through the Christian church of Antioch of Syria.[7] Ferdinand Hahn[8] declared:

> If Wilhelm Bousset and Rudolf Bultmann[9] championed exclusively the Hellenistic character of the Kyrios predicate of Jesus, Werner Foerster[10] on the other hand defended the thesis of a Palestinian origin which in its main outlines had been sketched out by Gustav Dalman[11] and which more recently has again been taken up by Oscar Cullmann[12] and Eduard Schweizer.[13]

Alfred Edward John Rawlinson (1884-1960) asserted that the Aramaic term *māranā' ṭā'* in 1 Cor. 16:22 is "the Achilles' heel of the theory of Bousset,"[14] Vincent Taylor concluded that "we do not need to take a step outside Palestine to account for the confession 'Jesus is Lord,'"[15] and Charles F. D. Moule offered a detailed refutation of the view, common

Writings and the Aramaic Language, trans. D. M. Kay (Edinburgh: T. and T. Clark, 1902), pp. 179-83.

5. Goppelt, *New Testament Theology*, 2:83-84.

6. *Light from the Ancient East: The New Testament Illustrated by Recently Discovered Texts of the Graeco-Roman World*, trans. Lionel R. M. Strachan (rev. ed.; New York: Harper, 1922), p. 350.

7. *Kyrios Christos: A History of the Belief in Christ from the Beginnings of Christianity to Irenaeus*, trans. John E. Steely (Nashville: Abingdon Press, 1970), pp. 138-48.

8. *The Titles of Jesus in Christology*, p. 68.

9. *Theology of the New Testament*, 1:51-52, 124-26.

10. *Herr Ist Jesus: Herkunft und Bedeutung des urchristlichen Kyrios-Bekenntnisses* (Gütersloh: C. Bertelsmann, 1924); idem, "kyrios et al.," in Kittel, ed., *Theological Dictionary of the New Testament*, 3:1094.

11. *The Words of Jesus*, pp. 326-31.

12. *The Christology of the New Testament*, pp. 195-220.

13. "Discipleship and Belief in Jesus as Lord from Jesus to the Hellenistic Church," *New Testament Studies* 2 (1955-56): 87-99; *Erniedrigung und Erhöhung bei Jesus und seinem Nachfolgern* (Zurich: Zwingli-Verlag, 1955), pp. 93ff.

14. *The New Testament Doctrine of the Christ* (New York: Longmans, Green and Company, 1926), p. 235.

15. *The Names of Jesus*, p. 51.

since Bousset, that the Palestinian church only "invoked" Jesus as "Master" whereas under the influence of mystery religions Jesus was "acclaimed" as "Lord."[16] More recently Leonhard Goppelt has espoused a threefold synthesis: the Aramaic-speaking Christian use of *māranā'*, meaning "our Lord," the use of *ho kyrios* in reference to Isis, Serapis, and Artemis, and the reading of *ho kyrios* instead of the Tetragrammaton (YHWH) in the Septuagint.[17]

Whatever conclusion is drawn as to origin or origins, the frequent usage of "Lord" in reference to Jesus in the New Testament is beyond dispute. Whereas "Lord" is used 139 times in the New Testament of God the Father, it is used 489 times of Jesus.[18] The latter usage occurred in all books except Titus, and 1, 2, and 3 John.[19]

2. *Synoptic Gospels*

Not every reference to Jesus as "Lord" in the Synoptic Gospels carries with it the connotation of the deity of Jesus. In fact, when Jesus was called "Lord"—usually the vocative *kyrie*—by others prior to his resurrection, the meaning was usually something less than deity. The Roman centurion (Matt. 8:6, 8 and par.) and the Syrophoenician woman (Mark 7:28 and par.) probably addressed Jesus as "Lord" in the sense of "sir." At times Jesus' disciples seem to have addressed him as "Lord" in the sense of rabbi or teacher (Matt. 8:21 and par.) or to have referred to him in the sense of "Master" when speaking to others (Mark 11:3 and par.). After Peter's Caesarean confession "Lord" may have been applied to Jesus in the sense of messianic king (Luke 12:41; 13:23; Matt. 18:21).

In his own teaching, however, Jesus likely applied the term "Lord" to himself so as to indicate his deity. Present-day scholars are not agreed as to which passages are so to be classified, but probably Matt. 24:42 and especially Mark 12:35-37 and parallels should be so interpreted.[20] The latter text argues that David's Lord, that is, the messianic Lord, is superior to David the king.

3. *Acts of the Apostles*

The early chapters of the Acts abound in references to Jesus as "Lord." He is the exalted messianic ruler (2:36), the risen one (4:33), the leader of the community of the resurrection (1:24-25; 9:31), the sustainer of the martyred Stephen (7:55, 59), the sovereign over Jew and Gentile (10:36), and the "judge of the living and the dead" (10:42). Frederick Fyvie Bruce (1910-) has argued that the speeches in the Acts are faithful sum-

16. *The Origin of Christology* (Cambridge: University Press, 1977), pp. 36-44.
17. *New Testament Theology*, 2:81-86.
18. John M. Sykes, "The Lordship of Jesus," *Review and Expositor* 49 (January 1952): 27.
19. Stagg, *New Testament Theology*, p. 64.
20. Taylor, *The Names of Jesus*, pp. 42, 50.

maries of speeches actually delivered and not speeches contrived by
Luke.[21] On that basis the use of the term "Lord" in reference to Jesus in
the Jerusalem church can be seen as evidence against the theory of the
Hellenistic origin of "Lord" for Christian usage. According to John Madison Sykes, Jr. (1917-), in early Acts Jesus' identification as "Lord" "fulfilled all that the term 'Lord' implied when it was used for God in the Old
Testament, with the exception of the idea of his being Creator."[22]

4. Pauline Epistles

The Pauline letters abound in occurrences of "Lord" in reference to
Jesus. Preexistence and participation in creation are included in the functions of Jesus as "Lord." Against the polytheisms of Graeco-Roman religion he affirmed "one God, the Father" and "one Lord, Jesus Christ,
through whom are all things and through whom we exist" (1 Cor. 8:6,
RSV). Indeed, "no one speaking by the Spirit of God ever says 'Jesus be
cursed!' and no one can say 'Jesus is Lord' except by the Holy Spirit"
(1 Cor. 12:3). The Aramaic expression, "Our Lord, come!" (1 Cor. 16:22),
also translatable as "Our Lord comes," may point to his second coming
or to his presence in Christian worship or to both. As Lord he was
"designated Son of God in power according to the Spirit of holiness by his
resurrection from the dead" (Rom. 1:4). Probably the earliest Christian
confessional formula was "Jesus is Lord," as may be learned from Rom.
10:9 and Phil. 2:11. The audible confession "Jesus is Lord" corresponds to
and accompanies the inner persuasion that "God raised him from the
dead" (Rom. 10:9), and the universal confession of Jesus as "Lord" will
glorify the Father (Phil. 2:11).

5. General Epistles

In the Petrine epistles reference is frequently made to "the" or "our
Lord Jesus Christ" (1 Pet. 1:3; 2 Pet. 1:8, 11, 14, 16; 2:20; 3:18). The same is
true of the Epistle of Jude (vv. 4, 17, 21, 25). In Heb. 2:3 (NIV) "the Lord"
first announced the salvation that had been "confirmed to us by those who
heard him," and allusion is made to "our Lord Jesus, that great Shepherd
of the sheep" (Heb. 13:20).

6. Gospel of John

Excluding two passages wherein there are variant textual readings
(4:1; 6:23), we note that Jesus was addressed during his public ministry by
several as "Lord": Peter (6:68; 13:6, 9; 13:37); the man blind from birth
(9:38); Mary, Martha, and the disciples at the raising of Lazarus (11:3, 12,
21, 27, 32, 34, 39); John (13:25); Thomas (14:5); Philip (14:8), and Judas
(14:22). The term seems to have been equivalent to Messiah or possibly

21. *The Speeches in the Acts of the Apostles* (London: Tyndale Press, 1942), p. 27.
22. "The Lordship of Jesus," p. 30.

the Son of God. Jesus himself alluded to the use of the term by his disciples (13:13). "Lord" was employed more frequently in the postresurrection chapters (20–21). Mary Magdalene (20:2, 13, 18), the disciples except for Thomas (20:25), and John (21:7) made indirect allusions to Jesus as "Lord." So did the Evangelist (20:20; 21:12). Thomas confessed Jesus directly as " 'My Lord and my God' " (20:28), and Peter thrice avowed his love of the "Lord" (21:15-17).

7. Revelation

Although the predominant usage of "Lord" in the Revelation was in reference to God the Father, Jesus was called "Lord Jesus" (22:20-21), "Lord of lords and King of kings" (17:14), and "King of kings and Lord of lords" (19:16).

8. The Entire New Testament

Dale Moody has differentiated a "functional" meaning of Jesus as "Lord" in the Synoptic Gospels and the Acts from an expanded "ontic" meaning of Jesus as "Lord" in Paul, the Epistle to the Hebrews, and the Johannine writings. Only the latter "includes pre-existence and the participation of Jesus in the eternal Being of God."[23] This distinction ought not to be pressed to the conclusion that the Jerusalem church had no interest whatever in the identity or nature of Jesus himself.

Cullmann has emphasized that the lordship of Jesus in the New Testament and in the second-century Christian writings included his lordship over the world as well as his lordship over the church, or believers. His lordship over the world includes all creatures, all "unseen powers," human governments, and the universe as a whole. Both lordships will cease when the Son of God surrenders his authority to the Father (1 Cor. 15:24). The two lordships resemble two concentric circles, with the lordship over the church on the inside as the center. Nonbelievers are not conscious of Christ's lordship over the world.[24] Cullmann has not specifically related the two lordships to the Christian doctrines of sin and salvation. Christ's lordship over the world must be interpreted in the light of the disobedience that is sin, and the two lordships must allow for the radical discontinuity between faith and unbelief.

Ethelbert Stauffer concluded:

> But of all the christological titles the richest is that of 'Lord.' Its history is a compendium and at the same time a *repetitorium* of NT christology. For in a few years it passes through the main stages of the development of christological titles, and so takes us once more along the road from the pedagogic and monarchic to the divine honouring of Jesus Christ.[25]

23. *The Word of Truth*, pp. 383-85.
24. *The Christology of the New Testament*, pp. 223-32.
25. *New Testament Theology*, p. 114. Cullmann, *The Christology of the New Testament*, p. 236, n. 2, agreed; Stagg, *New Testament Theology*, p. 64, disagreed.

D. "Prince" according to the New Testament

The noun *archēgos,* used of Jesus in Acts 3:15 and 5:31 and Heb. 2:10 and 12:2, by its etymology suggests that the word relates to "the beginning." Hence it has been translated "Author" in Acts 3:15 (RSV, NIV). Crucifiers killed "the Author of life." The term also may connote firstness or priority. Hence Moffatt renders it in all passages by "pioneer," meaning first in time or pathbreaker. Others have translated it in both passages in Acts as "Prince" (KJV, NASV), and still others as "Leader" (RSV, NEB), meaning first in importance or authority. In Acts 5:31 the term, joined with "Savior," is used in reference to the ascension and heavenly session of Jesus. In Heb. 2:10 Jesus is the "leader" (Phillips, JB, NEB) or "author" (NIV) or "pioneer" (RSV) "of our salvation," and in Heb. 12:2 that and "perfecter of our faith" (RSV, NIV). Both Vincent Taylor[26] and Leon Morris[27] favor a combination of meanings.

E. Systematic Formulation

The confession/doctrine that "Jesus is Lord" can have at least three basic meanings for contemporary Christians.

1. Deity

Within the Jewish heritage the lordship of Jesus was first of all a declaration of his deity. To Jesus was ascribed the very term that postexilic Jews had reverently and uniquely applied to the one God of the covenant. Jesus' lordship was apprehended in the light of his resurrection. The "God of peace" "brought again from the dead our Lord Jesus, the great shepherd of the sheep" (Heb. 13:20, RSV). Jesus is the risen, living Lord whose exalted status at the right hand of the Father is to be acknowledged by his disciples and whose divine presence with them and in them is realized through the Holy Spirit. "Lord," as applied to Jesus, therefore, is, respecting deity, tantamount to "the Son of God." The Christian affirmation of Jesus as divine Lord must today be made amid and over against denials and competing claims from non-Christian world religions, heretical Western quasi-Christian cults, and atheism, humanism, and allied movements.

2. Dominion

The lordship of Jesus is also an indication of his dominion, or rulership. Lordship and kingship, both of which were ascribed to Jesus, are correlative concepts. Attention has been given to Cullmann's insistence that Jesus' lordship is over the world as well as over the church. Living under the dominion or sovereignty of Jesus the Lord was normative for the early Christians. To make this dominion an optional feature of the Christian life, as some Evangelical Christians have tended to do in the recent past, is

26. *The Names of Jesus,* p. 91.
27. *The Lord from Heaven,* pp. 59-60.

a distortion of Christian teaching. To reckon that receiving Jesus as Savior is absolutely necessary for becoming a Christian but that to reckon Jesus as Lord of one's life is optional for Christians is indeed an error and cannot be established from the New Testament.[28] Indeed, the term "Lord" predominated in early Acts and in several of Paul's epistles, whereas "Savior" predominated only in the Pastoral Epistles and in 2 Peter. Skeptical unbelievers wait to see Jesus' lordship as dominion, as distinct from captivity to contemporary culture, demonstrated in the lives of present-day Christians. Living out the lordship of Jesus in Western societies is much more difficult than confessing his lordship.

3. Direction

The lordship of Jesus involves his actual direction of the lives of his disciples through their obedient surrender to Jesus and increasing conformity to him. In his teaching Jesus called for an obedient hearing of his words (Matt. 7:24-27), for self-renunciation in discipleship (Mark 8:34), and for an allegiance to himself that transcended possessions (Luke 18:22) and family allegiances (Luke 9:59-62; 14:16). The early Christians did not so much elevate Jesus the teacher to lordship as they reinterpreted his teaching in view of their postresurrection apprehension of his lordship. Karl Heim, writing after the experience of Nazism in Germany, which he described as "a satanic temptation on the largest scale," emphasized that Jesus' lordship must be singular or unshared and must be that of our contemporary. Moreover, Jesus is universal Leader because his leadership deals with ultimate things and requires surrender.[29] Donald M. Baillie was quite critical of Heim's application of *Führerschaft* ("Leadership") to Jesus, seemingly because it had been corrupted by usage in reference to modern political totalitarianism,[30] but Dale Moody was commendatory.[31] Today those who profess his lordship stand under the imperative of obedience to his commands and conformity to his very nature. This obligation persists even though contemporary Christians do not agree fully as to the manner in which this obedience ought to be expressed vis-à-vis specific issues in the political and social order. Jesus is Lord and Master.

II. JESUS AS KING

We have suggested previously the royal implications deriving from the usage of the terms "Son of David," "Son of Man," and "Son of God," [32]

---

28. John A. Mackay, *God's Order: The Ephesian Letter and This Present Time* (New York: Macmillan, 1957), pp. 110-11.
29. *Jesus the Lord*, pp. 51-63, esp. 58, 51-53, 59-60.
30. *God Was in Christ*, pp. 98-105.
31. *The Word of Truth*, p. 385.
32. See above, Ch. 40, III, A; Ch. 41, I, B; Ch. 42, I, A, 1 and 2.

but they have been more fully delineated by Dale Moody.[33] In addition to such terms, however, the noun *basileus,* meaning "king," was ascribed to Jesus in the New Testament. The present discussion will focus on that title as ascribed to Jesus and to the nature of his kingship. We will treat the concept of "the kingdom of God" subsequently[34] under the doctrine of the last things.

A. OLD TESTAMENT

Vincent Taylor has asserted that the New Testament usage of "king" in reference to Jesus was derived from two Old Testament texts.[35] In the messianic Psalm 2 (v. 7) we read: " 'I will tell of the decree of the LORD: He said to me, "You are my son, today I have begotten you . . ."' " (RSV). According to the prophet Zechariah, "Rejoice greatly, O daughter of Zion! Shout aloud, O daughter of Jerusalem! Lo, your king comes to you; triumphant and victorious is he, humble and riding on an ass, on a colt the foal of an ass" (9:9).

B. NEW TESTAMENT

1. *The Four Gospels*

a. The Title "King"

1) *The title "King of the Jews"*

This expression occurs 16 times in the four Gospels. Matthew employed it in the question of the wise men concerning the newborn Jesus (2:2). All other usages pertain to Jesus' trial before Pilate and his crucifixion. Pilate used this language when he queried Jesus concerning his identity (Mark 15:2 and par.). It was used by Pilate when he spoke to the crowd about the possible release of Jesus (Mark 15:9 and par.). Pilate used the words "your King" in presenting Jesus to the crowd at Gabbatha (John 19:14-15). The Roman soldiers mocked Jesus as "the King of the Jews" (Mark 15:18 and par.). The superscription placed above Jesus' cross contained the words " 'The King of the Jews' " (Mark 15:26 and par.), and the chief priests protested against such wording (John 19:21).

2) *The title "King of Israel"*

This expression was used four times in the Gospels. Nathanael early in the public ministry applied this title to Jesus (John 1:49). It was used in the Johannine account of Jesus' final entry into Jerusalem (12:13). It appeared in the account of the mocking of Jesus by the chief priests and scribes (Mark 15:32 and par.).

33. *The Word of Truth,* pp. 379-83.
34. See below, Ch. 85.
35. *The Names of Jesus,* p. 75.

Cullmann, who regarded *basileus* as a "variant" of *kyrios*, commented on the passages previously cited as follows:

> Most of these passages refer to the Roman accusation of Jesus. The inscription on the cross gives as the reason for his sentence the charge that he aspired to kingship. The expression is thus used here in the political sense of the Zealots, whereas the first Christians attributed to it a non-political meaning related to the *Kyrios* title. . . . [Indeed] the title King emphasizes more strongly Jesus' lordship over his Church, since the Church takes the place of Israel and he fulfils the kingship of Israel. The title *Kyrios* on the other hand emphasizes more strongly Jesus' lordship over the whole world, over all the visible and invisible creation.
>
> Despite the subtle distinction one may make in principle between the application of the two titles to Jesus, they are interchangeable. . . . *Kyrios* is thus equivalent to *Basileus* in all the passages which especially emphasize opposition to the claims of the Roman emperor.[36]

b. Jesus' Understanding of the Nature of His Kingship

The Gospel of John provides evidence that Jesus had to differentiate his own understanding of his kingship from popular notions about kingship. After the feeding of the five thousand, John 6:15 (RSV) records: "Perceiving then that they were about to come and take him by force to make him king, Jesus withdrew again to the hills by himself." To Pilate Jesus declared: " 'My kingship[37] is not of this world; if my kingship were of this world, my servants would fight, that I might not be handed over to the Jews; but my kingship is not from the world' " (John 18:36, RSV).

The risen Lord claimed to have been given "all authority (*exousia*) in heaven and on earth" (Matt. 28:18b). But, according to the Gospels, Jesus never applied to himself the term "king."

2. The Acts, the Epistles, and the Apocalypse

a. Scope of Jesus' Kingship

In Thessalonica Jesus was understood to be a "king" who was Caesar's rival (Acts 17:7). The term "king," therefore, was "politically dangerous." Taylor explained Paul's nonusage of the term "king" and its not appearing in 1 Peter as related to the attitude of those authors toward the Roman Empire.[38] But the impact of Ps. 110:1 on New Testament writers was great. Paul was confident that Christ "must reign until he ha[d] put all his enemies under his feet," including the enemy of "death" (1 Cor. 15:25-26, NIV). Ps. 110:1 was to be applied to God's "Son," but not to angels (Heb. 1:13). In the Apocalypse (1:5; 17:14; 19:16) Jesus was more boldly presented as the king who rules over all human or earthly kings. In his heavenly session Christ has "angels, authorities and powers in submission to him" (1 Pet. 3:22c, NIV).

---

36. *The Christology of the New Testament*, p. 221.
37. The Greek is *basileia*; it is translated "kingdom" by KJV, Berkeley, JB, and NASV.
38. *The Names of Jesus*, p. 77.

b. Time of Jesus' Kingship

The question as to when Jesus began to exercise his kingship is one that cannot be divorced from the question of the advent of the kingdom of God. It will be sufficient here to take note of the fact that the Scofield Reference Bible in its comment on Luke 17:21[39] allowed for the outward presence of Jesus as the king and his disciples, though not the outward form of the kingdom, during Jesus' public ministry. Peter in his sermon on the Day of Pentecost, after quoting Ps. 16:8-11, found the fulfillment of God's oath that David's descendant be enthroned to have been in the resurrection of Jesus (Acts 2:30-31). Furthermore, Peter saw the ascension of Jesus as the fulfillment of the sitting at God's right hand and ruling over enemies that was described in Ps. 110:1 (Acts 2:34). The "right hand" was the first place of authority under an emperor or king, and God's "right hand" meant the place or station of authority next to that of God. Jesus was said to have been exalted to (Acts 5:31a), to have become seated at (Eph. 1:20b; Col. 3:1b; Heb. 1:3e), to be at (1 Pet. 3:22b), and to be standing at (Acts 7:55-56) "the right hand of God." Moody has correctly pointed out that all three New Testament passages that quote Ps. 2:7 "without change" and thus deal with the begetting of the Son of God have as their contexts the "coronation" of Jesus, not his conception or birth.[40] But Heb. 10:13 suggests that during Jesus' heavenly session his rule over enemies is not yet complete, and from 1 Cor. 15:24-28 we can conclude that his rule will in some sense be altered, if not ended, when he "hands over the kingdom to God the Father" (v. 24, NIV).

C. HISTORY OF CHRISTIAN DOCTRINE

From John Calvin's time to the latter twentieth century Christian theologians who have utilized the threefold office in setting forth the person and work of Jesus Christ have explicated, at least to some degree, his kingly or royal office.

Before, during, and after World War II Continental European Protestant theology gave a major new emphasis to the kingship of Christ. W. A. Visser 't Hooft, contending that the kingly office had usually been underemphasized, described how the German church struggle with its Confessing Church and its Barmen Declaration (1934) and the similar struggles in Norway and the Netherlands had led to a keen new awareness of Christ's kingship over the world as well as over the church. Christ's kingship, which is both present and future and which has its prophetic and priestly aspects, means "Christocracy" but not "ecclesiocracy."[41]

In democratic societies that have no human royalty Christians may

39. 1917 ed.
40. *The Word of Truth*, p. 381.
41. *The Kingship of Christ: An Interpretation of Recent European Theology* (New York, London: Harper and Bros., 1948), pp. 15-64, 82-88, 129-34.

be somewhat reluctant or less emphatic about Christ's present kingship. Those who major on the futurity of God's kingdom often exclude from their theology Christ's present, though not future, kingship. Those who too readily equate the church and the kingdom of God tend to obscure, if not deny, the future dimensions of Christ's kingship.

Inasmuch as we have now completed the examination of the major titles ascribed to Jesus, it is possible to attempt a brief assessment of the overall treatment of these titles. Cullmann sought to explicate the Christology of the New Testament by disregarding the later Christological formulations of the patristic age.[42] In interpreting the various titles he stressed the functions ascribed to Jesus rather than the nature or being ascribed to him. For this functional emphasis Cullmann was criticized, first by Europeans who wrote soon after Cullmann's book was issued[43] and later by Millard Erickson.[44] Cullmann was surely correct in not reading back anachronistically into the New Testament passages meanings formulated in later centuries. But was he correct in downplaying the concept of Jesus' nature or being and its relation to the Father's nature or being? Were John, the author of Hebrews, and Paul without an interest in the person of Jesus? Modern functionalists are not without presuppositions, such as salvation history. Hahn's treatment was too heavily influenced by the history-of-religion school, and Taylor sought to be comprehensive in scope rather than thorough on each title. Even with such critical assessments we can acknowledge that we can know more fully the meanings of these titles than was true a century ago.

The present study began with an examination of Jesus' humanity. It proceeded through a somewhat detailed study of various titles applied to Jesus. In connection with "Son of God" and "Word of God" it presented the deity of Jesus Christ. Now one task remains, namely, to examine the nature of the unity of the person of Jesus Christ.

---

42. *The Christology of the New Testament*, p. 3.
43. Ibid., pp. 329-31.
44. *Christian Theology*, pp. 698-703.

CHAPTER 45

The Unity of the Person
of Jesus Christ

Previously we considered Jesus as a human being (humanity),[1] Jesus as the Son of God (deity),[2] and Jesus as the enfleshment or humanization of the eternally preexistent Word of God (incarnation).[3] One other consideration is essential to a full-orbed treatment of the person of Jesus Christ, namely, that of the unity of the person of Jesus Christ. What is the nature and significance of such a theme?

I. NEW TESTAMENT

In the New Testament writings one does not find a specific discussion of the unity of the person of Jesus Christ. One does find texts that imply or point to this unity or the unity of his two natures and important considerations from silence.

The divine and human natures of Jesus are alluded to in contexts wherein Jesus Christ is also thought of as one person: Gal. 4:4; Rom. 1:1-4; 9:5; Phil. 2:6-8; John 1:14; and 1 John 1:1-3; 4:2-3.

In the New Testament one finds "no interchange of 'I' and 'thou' between the human and the divine natures, such as we find between the persons of the Trinity (John 17:23)." Furthermore, "Christ never uses the plural number in referring to himself, unless it be in John 3:11—'we speak that we do know,'—and even here 'we' is more probably used as inclusive of the disciples."[4]

II. HISTORY OF CHRISTIAN DOCTRINE

Two major denials of the unity of the two natures in the one person of Jesus Christ emerged during the patristic age and were ultimately rejected

1. See above, Ch. 39.
2. See above, Ch. 42, I.
3. See above, Ch. 43.
4. Strong, *Systematic Theology*, p. 684.

by Catholic Christianity. At least four distinct models or conceptual modes for the expression of the unity of Christ's person were set forth during the same era of the Church Fathers.

A. Two Denials

1. Nestorianism

Modern patristic scholars continue to debate the issue as to whether Nestorius, onetime patriarch of Constantinople, actually taught the doctrine that has been labeled "Nestorianism," primarily because of the discovery in 1895 of his *The Bazaar of Heracleides*,[5] a treatise composed by Nestorius about A.D. 450.[6] But we must continue to identify "Nestorianism" as the extreme differentiation and separation of the divine and the human natures in Jesus Christ that results virtually in two persons and downplays the unity of Jesus Christ. Thus there could be no exchange of attributes between the natures, as, for example, respecting suffering. This is the view that was condemned by the Council of Ephesus (A.D. 431) and that later Christianity has rejected as unorthodox or heretical. Insofar as Jesus' divine and human natures are interpreted as equivalent to two persons or centers of personal life, the essential unity of Jesus Christ is denied.[7] Charles Gore (1853-1932) charged that the "Christ of Nestorius was . . . simply a deified man, not God incarnate."[8] Rather like "the Siamese twins, Chang and Eng, man and God are joined together."[9]

2. Eutychianism

This term derived from the teaching of a fifth-century cleric in Constantinople, Eutyches, allegedly "the founder of an extreme and virtually Docetic form of monophysitism," that is, the "teaching that the Lord's humanity was totally absorbed by His divinity." The teaching of Eutyches can also be reckoned as the fusion of the divine and the human natures of Jesus Christ "into a *tertium quid*."[10] Consequently, after the incarnation there was only one nature in Jesus. Eutyches's teaching was condemned by a synod in Constantinople in 448 and by the Council of Chalcedon (451). Insofar as Jesus' divine and human natures are thought to be absorbed the one by the other or to be fused, the unity of Jesus can be preserved, but his respective natures in the incarnation are lost or denied.

5. Trans. and ed. G. R. Driver and Leonard Hodgson (Oxford: Clarendon Press, 1925; reprint ed.; New York: AMS Press, 1978).

6. Kelly, *Early Christian Doctrines*, pp. 310-17; J. F. Bethune-Baker, *Nestorius and His Teaching: A Fresh Examination of the Evidence* (Cambridge: University Press, 1908; reprint ed.; New York: Kraus Reprint Company, 1969).

7. Charles Hodge, *Systematic Theology*, 3:401; Strong, *Systematic Theology*, p. 671.

8. *The Incarnation of the Son of God* (London: John Murray, 1891), p. 94.

9. Strong, *Systematic Theology*, p. 671.

10. Kelly, *Early Christian Doctrines*, pp. 331, 333. But Kelly has found Eutyches himself to have been neither "Docetist" nor "Apollinarian."

B. FOUR MODELS, OR CONCEPTUAL MODES

1. *Tabernacling* (skēncsis) *or indwelling* (enoikēsis)

One of the linguistic modes for expressing the union of the divine and the human in Jesus Christ both in the New Testament and among the Church Fathers was the pair of nouns, *skēnōsis,* meaning "tabernacling," and *enoikēsis,* meaning "indwelling." According to John 1:14, the eternal and divine Word "became flesh and dwelt *(eskēnōsen)* among us." Theodore of Mopsuestia, representative of Antiochene Christology and referring both to the one who assumed (God) and the one who was assumed (man), identified the union as an "indwelling" *(enoikēsis),* taught that the Godhead permanently indwells the "temple" or "shrine" of his humanity, and declared that the union is "by favour or grace" *(kath' eudokian).*[11] Modern Anglican theologians such as Lionel Spencer Thornton (1884-1961)[12] and William Norman Pittenger[13] have sympathetically identified with the theme of indwelling, even though Thornton emphasized more fully the transcendence of the Word.[14] Pittenger declared:

> The *most complete,* the *fullest,* the *most organic and integrated union* of Godhead and manhood which is conceivable is precisely one in which by gracious indwelling of God in man and by manhood's free response in surrender and love, there is established a relationship which is neither accidental nor incidental, on the one hand, nor mechanical and physical, on the other; but a full, free, gracious unity of the two in Jesus Christ. . . .[15]

2. *Conjunction or Connection* (synapheia[16])

Also employed by the Antiochene theologians was the term *synapheia,* meaning a "conjunction" or "connection" of the two natures of Jesus Christ. Gregory of Nyssa had used the term of the two natures together with the term "fusion" *(symphuian)* so as to validate the exchange of attributes.[17] Theodore of Mopsuestia employed the term when affirming the Holy Spirit as "the medium of this conjunction."[18] Nestorius preferred the term *synapheia* to the term *henōsis,* though he employed the latter, for the former, declared J. N. D. Kelly, "seemed" to Nestorius "to

---

11. *Catechetical Homilies* 8.5; 16.2; 8.7; *De incarnatione 7,* as cited by Kelly, *Early Christian Doctrines,* p. 305.

12. *The Incarnate Lord* (London: Longmans, Green and Company, 1928), esp. pp. 163-64, 232, 278.

13. *The Word Incarnate: A Study of the Doctrine of the Person of Christ,* Library of Constructive Theology (Welwyn, Hertfordshire, U.K.: James Nisbet and Company, Ltd., 1959).

14. Ibid., pp. 107-9.

15. Ibid., p. 188.

16. This noun is derived from the verb *aptō,* middle, "to fasten, bind to, join," and the noun *aphē,* "grip" or "junction."

17. *Against Eunomius* 5.5, as cited by Kelly, *Early Christian Doctrines,* p. 299.

18. *Comm. in Ioh.* 16.15; 17.11 (J. M. Vosté, *CSCO,* vol. 116, pp. 212, 226), as cited by Kelly, *Early Christian Doctrines,* p. 308. Kelly sees Theodore's usage as veering toward adoptionism.

avoid all suspicion of a confusion or mixing of the natures."[19] But for the Alexandrians *synapheia* could suggest the mere joining of two "natures" that were tantamount to two "persons" or "concrete individual[s]."[20]

3. *Natural* (physikē) *or Personal* (kath' hypostasin) *Union* (henōsis)

The Alexandrian school preferred to speak of a "natural" or "personal" "union" of the Logos and humanity. Apollinaris referred to "a unity of nature" *(henōsis physikē)* between the Word and the body of the Word.[21] For Cyril of Alexandria the union was "natural" *(physikē or kata physin)* or "hypostatic" *(kath' hypostasin)*, so that "the concrete being of the Word, being truly united to human nature, without any change or confusion, is understood to be, and is, one Christ."[22] This same Cyril appropriated from Apollinaris the oft-quoted formula: "one incarnate nature of the Word of God" *(mia physis tou theou logou sesarkōmenē)*.[23] In the second and third of Cyril's twelve anathemas against Nestorius the hypostatic or natural union was affirmed, and in the third a mere "association" or "conjunction" *(synapheia)* of "hypostases" after the incarnation was rejected.[24] The Symbol of Union (A.D. 433) used the term *henōsis*, not *synapheia*, but described it as "a union without confusion."[25] Some such qualification is needed if *henōsis* is not to signify the abolition of a human nature in Jesus Christ.

4. *Chalcedon's Four Adverbs*

By the use of four adverbs—rendered as prepositional phrases in English, consisting of two pairs of two each, the Symbol of Chalcedon (A.D. 451)[26] sought to safeguard both the two natures and the one person of Jesus Christ. The adverbs designed to safeguard the two natures and applied to those natures were *asynchytōs*,[27] "without confusion," and *atreptōs*,[28] "without change." The adverbs designed to safeguard the one person and applied to the two natures were *adiairetōs*,[29] "without division," and *achōristōs*,[30] "without separation." The first two adverbs were intended to withstand Eutychianism, the latter two to withstand Nestori-

19. *Early Christian Doctrines*, pp. 314-15, based on *The Bazaar of Heracleides*, pp. 262, 81, 275, 299, 202.
20. Kelly, *Early Christian Doctrines*, p. 318.
21. Apollinaris, Fragments 129, 148 (Lietzmann, *Apollinaris von Laodicea und seine Schule* [1904], pp. 29, 247, as cited by Kelly, *Early Christian Doctrines*, p. 293).
22. *Apol. contra* [Diod. et] *Theod.* (Migne, *PG*, 76.401), cited by Kelly, *Early Christian Doctrines*, p. 320.
23. Kelly, *Early Christian Doctrines*, pp. 293, 319.
24. Ep. 17, cited by Kelly, *Early Christian Doctrines*, p. 324.
25. Quoted by Kelly, *Early Christian Doctrines*, p. 329.
26. In *Documents of the Christian Church*, ed. Henry Bettenson (2d ed.; London: Oxford University Press, 1963), p. 73.
27. Derived from the verb *syncheō*, "to commingle, confound, demolish."
28. Derived from the adjective *treptikos*, "causing change in," and the verb *trepō*, "to turn around."
29. Derived from the verb *diaireō*, "to divide, cleave."
30. Derived from the verb *chōrizō*, "to separate, part."

anism. Chalcedon's quest for balance and rejection of extremes helps to explain the centuries-long impact of its Symbol.

III. SYSTEMATIC FORMULATION

A. The unity of the person of Jesus Christ means that there is no "double personality"[31] or independent functioning of separate natures[32] in him. Indeed, the Word took "into union with himself, not an individual man with already developed personality, but human nature which ... had no separate existence before its union with the divine."[33] There cannot be, therefore, two wills or two energies in Jesus Christ.[34]

B. The unity of the person of Jesus Christ means that there has been no fusion of the divine and the human natures or absorption of one of the natures into the other nature. Monophysitism, or the doctrine that Jesus Christ had as the incarnate Son of God only one nature, has consistently placed in jeopardy the genuine humanity of Jesus.[35]

C. The unity of the person of Jesus Christ means that the incarnation did not bring about a reality that is neither divine nor human but instead is a third or different reality. Jesus is "a very complex person" but not "an amalgam of human and divine qualities merged into some sort of *tertium quid*."[36]

D. The unity of the person of Jesus Christ means that the God-man was not existent until the incarnation but continues after the exaltation. To be rejected is any notion that Jesus had a preexistent human soul. "The trinitarian personality of the Son of God did not begin at the incarnation, but the *theanthropic* personality of Jesus Christ did."[37] To be accepted is the truth that in his ascended and exalted state Jesus continues to be the God-man. The priestly office of the fully human Jesus is to continue (Heb. 2:14; 7:24). "Unlike the avatars of the East, the incarnation was a permanent assumption of human nature by the second person of the Trinity. In the ascension of Christ, glorified humanity has attained the throne of the universe."[38]

---

31. Strong, *Systematic Theology*, pp. 694-95.

32. Erickson, *Christian Theology*, pp. 735-36.

33. Strong, *Systematic Theology*, p. 694.

34. Such was affirmed by the Council of Constantinople III (680-81). Karl Joseph Hefele, *A History of the Christian Councils*, 5 vols., trans. and ed. William R. Clark et al. (2d ed.; Edinburgh: T. and T. Clark, 1894-96), 5:149-78; Leo Donald Davis, S.J., *The First Seven Ecumenical Councils (325-787): Their History and Theology*, Theology and Life Series, vol. 21 (Wilmington, Del.: Michael Glazier, Inc., 1987), pp. 258-89, esp. 282-84.

35. Brunner, *The Christian Doctrine of Creation and Redemption*, p. 361, affirmed that "Monophysitism is right in stressing the truth that Jesus, in the wholeness of His Person, is revelation."

36. Erickson, *Christian Theology*, p. 738.

37. Shedd, *Dogmatic Theology*, 2:269.

38. Strong, *Systematic Theology*, p. 698. Shedd, *Dogmatic Theology*, 2:322, asserted that after this exaltation Jesus retained "all *essential* properties of humanity," but not all "*accidental* properties" such as hunger and suffering.

E. The unity of the person of Jesus Christ means that in assuming human nature the eternal Word did not abandon his divine nature. The nineteenth-century German expressions of Kenotic Christology that majored on the surrender of divine attributes threatened the loss of the divine nature.[39]

F. The unity of the person of Jesus Christ means that Christians, in reflecting on this theme, should proceed from the actual birth, life, ministry, death, resurrection, and ascension of Jesus, not from abstract considerations of deity and humanity,[40] and should reverently acknowledge the unfathomable, nonanalogical mystery of his person.[41]

Although the New Testament only implies or points to the unity of the person of Jesus Christ, Christian theology in the patristic and subsequent eras has explicated the doctrine and witnessed to its essentiality and centrality.

---

39. Erickson, *Christian Theology*, pp. 734-35.
40. Ibid., p. 736.
41. Strong, *Systematic Theology*, p. 693; Brunner, *The Christian Doctrine of Creation and Redemption*, pp. 358-59.

Index of Subjects

Index of Authors

Index of Biblical References